CONTENTS

Titles may be modified and shortened

Contents

Facing Unpleasant Facts 1937–1939

Eric Arthur Blair – better known as George Orwell – was born on 25 June 1903 in Bengal. He was educated at Eton and then served with the Indian Imperial Police in Burma. He lived in Paris for two years, and then returned to England where he worked as a private tutor, schoolteacher and bookshop assistant. He fought on the Republican side in the Spanish Civil War and was wounded in the throat. During the Second World War he served as Talks Producer for the Indian Service of the BBC and then joined *Tribune* as its literary editor. He died in London in January 1950.

Dr. Peter Davison is Professor of English and Media at De Montfort University, Leicester. He has written and edited fifteen books as well as the Facsimile Edition of the Manuscript of *Nineteen Eighty-Four* and the twenty volumes of Orwell's *Complete Works*. From 1992 to 1994 he was President of the Bibliographical Society, whose journal he edited for twelve years. From 1961 Ian Angus was Deputy Librarian and Keeper of the Orwell Archive at University College, London, and from 1975 Librarian of King's College, London. With Sonia Orwell he co-edited the *Collected Essays, Journalism and Letters of George Orwell* (4 vols., 1986). Since early retirement in 1982 he has divided his time equally between assisting in the editing of the complete edition and growing olives in Italy.
Sheila Davison was a teacher until she retired, for some time teaching the deaf. She checked and proofread all twenty volumes of the complete edition and assisted with the research and indexing.

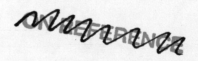

Down and Out in Paris and London
Burmese Days
A Clergyman's Daughter
Keep the Aspidistra Flying
The Road to Wigan Pier
Homage to Catalonia
Coming Up for Air
Animal Farm
Nineteen Eighty-Four
A Kind of Compulsion (1903–36)
Facing Unpleasant Facts (1937–39)
A Patriot After All (1940–41)
All Propaganda is Lies (1941–42)
Keeping Our Little Corner Clean (1942–43)
Two Wasted Years (1943)
I Have Tried to Tell the Truth (1943–44)
I Belong to the Left (1945)
Smothered Under Journalism (1946)
It is What I Think (1947–48)
Our Job is to Make Life Worth Living (1949–50)

Also by Peter Davison

Books: *Songs of the British Music Hall: A Critical Study; Popular Appeal in English Drama to 1850; Contemporary Drama and the Popular Dramatic Tradition; Hamlet: Text and Performance; Henry V: Masterguide; Othello: The Critical Debate; Orwell: A Literary Life*

Editions: Anonymous: *The Fair Maid of the Exchange* (with Arthur Brown); Shakespeare: *Richard II;* Shakespeare: *The Merchant of Venice;* Shakespeare: *1 Henry IV;* Shakespeare: *2 Henry IV;* Shakespeare: *The First Quarto of King Richard III;* Marston: *The Dutch Courtesan; Facsimile of the Manuscript of Nineteen Eighty-Four; Sheridan: A Casebook; The Book Encompassed: Studies in Twentieth-Century Bibliography*

Series: *Theatrum Redivivum* 17 Volumes (with James Binns); *Literary Taste, Culture, and Mass Communication* 14 Volumes (with Edward Shils and Rolf Meyersohn)

Academic Journals: *ALTA: University of Birmingham Review*, 1966–70; *The Library: Transactions of the Bibliographical Society*, 1971–82

Publication of *The Complete Works of George Orwell* is a unique
bibliographic event as well as a major step in Orwell
scholarship. Meticulous textual research by
Dr Peter Davison has revealed that all the current editions
of Orwell have been mutilated to a greater or lesser extent.
This authoritative edition incorporates in Volumes 10-20
all Orwell's known essays, poems, plays, letters, journalism,
broadcasts, and diaries, and also letters by his wife, Eileen,
and members of his family. In addition there are very many of
the letters in newspapers and magazines of readers' reactions
to Orwell's articles and reviews. Where the hands of others
have intervened, Orwell's original intentions have been restored.

Facing Unpleasant Facts

Facts

1937-1939

GEORGE ORWELL

Edited by Peter Davison
Assisted by Ian Angus and Sheila Davison

SECKER & WARBURG

LONDON

Revised and updated edition published by Secker & Warburg 2000

2 4 6 8 10 9 7 5 3 1

First published in Great Britain in 1998 by
Secker & Warburg
Random House, 20 Vauxhall Bridge Road,
London SW1V 2SA

Random House Australia (Pty) Limited
20 Alfred Street, Milsons Point, Sydney,
New South Wales 2061, Australia

Random House New Zealand Limited
18 Poland Road, Glenfield,
Auckland 10, New Zealand

Random House South Africa (Pty) Limited
Endulini, 5A Jubilee Road, Parktown 2193, South Africa

The Random House Group Limited Reg. No. 954009

A CIP catalogue record for this book
is available from the British Library

ISBN 0 436 20538 6

Papers used by The Random House Group Limited are natural,
recyclable products made from wood grown in sustainable forests;
the manufacturing processes conform to the environmental
regulations of the country of origin

Typeset in Monophoto Bemno
by Deltatype Limited, Birkenhead, Merseyside
Printed and bound in Great Britain by
Mackays of Chatham PLC

Contents

Contents

INTRODUCTION to VOLUME XI

1937 TO 1939: Facing Unpleasant Facts

By 1937 Orwell had published four books (two of which he was later to reject) and had established himself as a book reviewer. His talents were coming to be recognised but the sales of his books and the kind of reviewing he did brought him little money. Nevertheless, in 1936 he had married Eileen O'Shaughnessy and they had settled in a small cottage and village store in Hertfordshire. There he wrote of his experiences investigating the effects of the Depression in the North of England and he delivered the manuscript, *The Road to Wigan Pier*, a day or two before Christmas Day, 1936. This was published on 8 March 1937, when Orwell was serving in the front line in Spain, fighting for the Republicans in the Civil War. His account of what he saw and experienced in Spain was published, with difficulty, as *Homage to Catalonia* on 25 April 1938. A third book, the novel, *Coming Up for Air*, written in Marrakech, was published on 12 June 1939. These three years were, therefore, productive but, as this volume shows, taxing and frustrating. Orwell was seriously ill in 1938 and had to be admitted to a sanatorium in Kent; he found the difficulty, indeed, the impossibility, of getting the truth published intensely exasperating, and, despite the large sales of *The Road to Wigan Pier*, he was always short of money. However, the experiences of Wigan and Spain were to inspire his endeavours for the rest of his short life, and the lasting worth of the three books published in these years shows that his experiences have continued to be shared by many thousands of people throughout the world. The first two directly, and the third indirectly, reveal what Orwell suspected from childhood, that he had 'a facility with words and a power of facing unpleasant facts' ('Why I Write', 1946, XVIII, *3007*).

Ironically, perhaps the most 'unpleasant' document in this volume is one that Orwell never saw but which typifies the worst aspect of his experience in Spain: the deposition indicting the Orwells before the Tribunal for Espionage and High Treason in Valencia as 'rabid Trotskyists' and for being members of the Independent Labour Party (*374A*). The background and implications of this document are fully analysed (pp. 30–37). Grounds for accusing Orwell arose, in part, from the seizure of his papers and diary from Eileen's hotel bedroom (see his letter to Charles Doran, 2 August 1937, *386*, p. 64). It is possible that these documents are included in the dossier on Orwell which is known to exist in the NKVD files in Moscow. Unfortunately, access to this archive stopped before a search could be made (see p. 36). What the deposition demonstrates is the reign of terror at the time the POUM was being suppressed. Eileen, wrote Sir Richard Rees, who was working in the POUM office in April 1937, 'was the first person in whom I had witnessed the effects of living under a political terror' (*George Orwell: Fugitive from the*

Camp of Victory (1961) 147). The letters and articles in the earlier part of this volume amply demonstrate Orwell's reactions, in particular his correspondence (previously unpublished) with George Kopp (and see the *Independent News* account of Kopp's release following Eileen's letter to Jack Common, 5 March 1939, p. 339), H. N. Brailsford (see especially two letters to Brailsford in Volume XX, Appendix 14, *413A* and *414B*), Amy Charlesworth, and Charles Doran. These give some indication of what led to Orwell's stance against violent revolution and to the writing of *Animal Farm* and *Nineteen Eighty-Four* and they explain just why he wrote so angrily to Nancy Cunard in August 1937 regarding *Authors Take Sides on the Spanish War* (*386A*).

The Volume opens with Jennie Lee's revealing account of Orwell's arrival (with boots) in Barcelona. There is Orwell's correspondence with Yvonne Davet, whom he never met, but with whom he corresponded before and after the war regarding the translation of his books and articles into French. Although it was not published until five years after his death, Madam Davet had translated *Homage to Catalonia* in 1938–39 and Orwell commented on her translation and provided explicatory notes. When Orwell wrote in French, English translations are provided. Full details are given of the invitation to Orwell to join the Lucknow newspaper, the *Pioneer*, and some letters throw a new light on Orwell's personal relationships, especially his attempt to make surreptitious assignations with Lydia Jackson (see headnote to *534A*, and *542A,B*, and *545A* and its afternote).

An intriguing feature of this volume is a score of letters written by Eileen and one to her from Orwell's sister, Marjorie. Writing to Marjorie after the Munich Agreement, Eileen confessed, 'It's very odd to feel that Chamberlain is our only hope . . . certainly the man has courage' (p. 206).

In addition to many letters previously unpublished and reviews not before reprinted, the volume includes Orwell's 'Diary of Events Leading Up to the War' (abstracts from newspapers little and well known, the most quoted being the *Daily Telegraph*); his Domestic Diary, 9 August 1938 to 31 December 1939; the Morocco Diary; his abstracts from the *Daily Worker* and *News Chronicle* reports on the Spanish Civil War, used in writing *Homage to Catalonia*; and his Marrakech Notebook. Orwell sometimes illustrated his diaries and the illustrations are all included. There is a personal, place, and title index.

ACKNOWLEDGEMENTS and PROVENANCES

specific to Volume XI

The editor wishes to express his gratitude to the following institutions and libraries, their trustees, curators, and staffs for their co-operation and valuable help, for making copies of Orwell material available, and for allowing it to be reproduced: Henry W. and Albert A. Berg Collection, New York Public Library, Astor, Lenox, and Tilden Foundations; British Library, Department of Manuscripts (for the Orwell papers, Add. Mss 49384 and 73083); and India Office Library and Records; University Libraries, State University of New York at Buffalo; Eton College Library; Lilly Library, Indiana University, Bloomington, Indiana; Liverpool City Libraries; British Library of Political and Economic Science, London School of Economics and Political Science; John Rylands University Library of Manchester; Jack Common papers, University of Newcastle upon Tyne Library; Harry Ransom Humanities Research Center, University of Texas at Austin; McFarlin Library, University of Tulsa; and the Library of University College London for material in the Orwell Archive.

Gratitude must be expressed to Victor Gollancz Ltd for having made available its material relating to Orwell, with particular thanks to Livia Gollancz for her help and valuable information.

Thanks are due to Bertha Doran, Rosemary Davidson and Judith Williams for having made available the Orwell letters in their possession. I am deeply indebted to those whose Orwell letters are available because they donated them or presented copies of them to the Orwell Archive: Amy Charlesworth, Henry Dakin, Humphrey Dakin, Yvonne Davet, Geoffrey Gorer, Frank Jellinek, Olga Parker, Sir Richard Rees and John Sceats. Thanks must be given to Bernard Crick and Michael Shelden through whom many Orwell letters published in these volumes were made available to the Orwell Archive.

I am grateful to the *Guardian* for permission to publish Orwell's letter to the editor of the *Manchester Guardian* and the editor's reply. Thanks are also due to West Kent Medical Authority, Preston Hall, Aylesford for permission to publish Orwell's letter to Dr J. B. McDougall and to quote from Orwell's medical records.

I would like to thank the following for permission to reproduce material which first appeared in their pages: the *Guardian*, *The Listener* (by courtesy of the BBC and the Independent Television Association Ltd) and *The New Statesman*.

I would like to thank the following for granting me permission to use material whose copyright they own: Pat Ashley to reprint Maurice Ashley's reply to Orwell in *The Times Literary Supplement*; University of Sussex

Library to quote from a letter by Geoffrey Gorer; Rosemary Davidson to quote from *A Russian's England*, by Elisaveta Fen (Lydia Jackson); Michel Kopp, Mary Kopp Wheeler and other members of the family to publish letters by their father, Georges Kopp; Charles Osborne to quote from letters by John Lehmann; and Jean Faulks to quote from letters by Ethel Mannin.

I am grateful to four institutions for supplying the following material: Centre d'Estudis Històrics Internationals, Universitat de Barcelona for 'The Report to Tribunal for Espionage and High Treason, Valencia'; Internationaal Instituut voor Sociale Geschiedenis, Amsterdam and the William R. Perkins Library, Duke University, Durham, North Carolina for copies of *S.I.A. Bulletin*; and the Working Class Movement Library, Salford for copies of *Socialist Correspondence*.

Special thanks are due to Gill Furlong and her assistants in the Orwell Archive and to Barry Bloomfield, A. J. Farrington and Andrew Griffin of the British Library, India Office Library and Records.

For their help and valuable information I am indebted to the following: Bill Alexander, Tony Atienza (Archivist, Marx Memorial Library), Sam Bornstein, Janet Carleton, Stafford Cottman, Richard D. Davies (Archivist, Leeds Russian Archive), Bert Govaerts, Karen Hatherley, William Hetherington (Archivist, Peace Pledge Union), Alan Hollinghurst (*The Times Literary Supplement*), James Joll, Alain Kahan (Working Class Movement Library, Salford), Miklos Kun, Douglas Moyle, Jordi Planes (Secretary General, Centre d'Estudis Històrics Internacionals, Barcelona), Hugh Thomas, P. J. Thwaites and James D. Young.

My thanks are due to Michael Davison, Janet Percival and Ian Willison for their translations.

A number of individual acknowledgements are made in foot and headnotes to those who have provided information in books or verbally that I have quoted or referred to.

The editor and publishers have made every effort to trace copyright holders of the material published in this volume, but in some cases this has not proved possible. The publishers therefore wish to apologise to the authors or copyright holders of any material which has been reproduced without permission and due acknowledgement.

PROVENANCES

The locations of letters and documents printed in this volume are indicated against their item numbers in the list given below. Where there are letters or documents at an item which come from more than one source, this is indicated, e.g. 484 Lilly, OA, Tulsa.

However, letters and documents which are not listed below should be taken as being available for consultation in the Orwell Archive, University College London, either as originals or in the form of copies. Sonia Orwell gave all the Orwell papers then in her possession to the Orwell Archive at its foundation in 1960. Many friends, relations and associates of Orwell have given their Orwell letters or copies of them to the Orwell Archive. There were in Orwell's pamphlet collection that Sonia Orwell gave to the British Museum in 1950 some Orwell papers (now in the British Library. Departments of Manuscripts, Add. Mss. 49384 and 73083) and copies of these, at her request, were given by the Director and Principal Librarian of the British Museum to the Orwell Archive in 1965. For simplicity's sake, the British Library Orwell papers are not indicated as such in the location list, but are regarded as being available for consultation in the form of copies in the Orwell Archive.

KEY TO LOCATIONS

Berg — Henry W. and Albert A. Berg Collection, The New York Public Library, Astor, Lenox and Tilden Foundations

Buffalo — The Poetry/Rare Books Collection, University Libraries, State University of New York at Buffalo

Davidson — Rosemary Davidson

Drumchapel — Waverley Secondary School, Drumchapel, Glasgow

Eton — Eton College Library

IOL — British Library, India Office Library

Lilly — Lilly Library, Indiana University, Bloomington, Indiana

Liverpool — Autograph Letters Collection, Liverpool City Libraries

LSE — ILP Papers, British Library of Political and Economic Science, London School of Economics and Political Science

Madrid — Archivo Histórico Nacional de España, Madrid

Manchester — The Guardian Archives, The John Rylands University Library of Manchester

Newcastle — Jack Common Papers, University of Newcastle upon Tyne Library

OA — Orwell Archive, University College London Library

Texas — Harry Ransom Humanities Research Center, University of Texas at Austin

Tulsa — McFarlin Library, University of Tulsa

VG — Victor Gollancz Ltd

Williams — Judith Williams

356 Lilly	375A LSE	391 Lilly
358 Lilly	376 Texas	395 Berg
359 Liverpool	377 Lilly	398 Manchester
361 Lilly	380 Lilly	405 Berg
365 Lilly	381 Texas	412 Lilly
368 VG	386 Drumchapel	418 Texas
370 Berg	386A Williams	419 Texas
374A Madrid	388 Berg	423 Berg
375 Lilly	390 VG	425 Lilly

Acknowledgements and Provenances

426 IOL
427 Berg
432 Newcastle
433 Berg
434 Texas
435 Texas
437 Berg
443 Berg
444 Lilly
447 Lilly
448 Buffalo
450 Lilly
454 Texas
458 Lilly
459 Lilly
640 Lilly
461 Berg
464 Buffalo
465 Berg
467 Berg

468 Berg
475 Eton
476 Berg
484 Lilly, OA, Tulsa
486 Berg
489 Berg
491 Lilly
495 Lilly
496 Berg
501 Berg
505 Drumchapel
506 Lilly
510 Berg
514 Lilly
516 Berg
517 Eton
521 Texas
525 Newcastle
533 Newcastle
534A Davidson

535 Newcastle
537 Lilly
539 Newcastle
542 Lilly
542A Davidson
542B Davidson
543 Lilly
544 Berg
545 Berg
545A Davidson
546 Lilly
548 Lilly
551 Berg
555 Lilly
557 Lilly
561 Lilly
572 Lilly
573 Lilly
581 Lilly

Editorial Note

THE CONTENTS are, in the main, arranged in chronological order of Orwell's writing. Letters arising from his articles or reviews are usually grouped immediately after that item and Orwell's replies to those letters follow thereon. If there is a long delay between when it is known an article or essay was completed and its publication, it is printed at the date of completion. If items are printed much earlier in the chronological sequence than their date of publication, a cross-reference is given at the date of publication. All entries, whether written by Orwell or anyone else, including lengthy notes and cross-references, are given an item number. Because the printing of the edition has taken place over seven years, some letters came to light after the initial editing and the numbering of items had been completed. These items (or those that had in consequence to be repositioned) are given a letter after the number: e.g., 335A. Some items included after printing and page-proofing had been completed are given in a final appendix to Volume XX and two (received by the editor in mid January 1997) in the Introduction to Volume XV. Numbers preceding item titles are in roman; when referred to in notes they are italicised.

The provenance of items is given in the preliminaries to each volume. Every item that requires explanation about its source or date, or about textual problems it may pose, is provided with such an explanation. Some articles and broadcasts exist in more than one version. The basis upon which they have been edited is explained and lists of variant readings provided. No Procrustean bed has been devised into which such items must be constrained; individual circumstances have been taken into account and editorial practice explained.

Although this is not what is called a 'diplomatic edition'—that is, one that represents the original precisely even in all its deformities to the point of reproducing a letter set upside down—the fundamental approach in presenting these texts has been to interfere with them as little as possible consistent with the removal of deformities and typographic errors. Orwell took great pains over the writing of his books: the facsimile edition of *Nineteen Eighty-Four*[1] shows that, but in order to meet the demands of broadcasting and publication schedules he often wrote fast and under great pressure. The speed with which he sometimes wrote meant that what he produced was not always what he would have wished to have published had he had time to revise. And, of course, as with any printing, errors can be introduced by those setting the type. It would be easy in places to surmise what Orwell would have done but I have only made changes where there would otherwise have been confusion. Obvious spelling mistakes, which could well be the compositor's or typist's (and the typist might be Orwell), have been corrected silently, but if there is any doubt, a footnote has drawn attention to the problem.

In brief, therefore, I have tried to present what Orwell wrote in his manuscripts and typescripts, not what I thought he should have written; and what he was represented as having written and not what I think should have been typed or printed on his behalf. This is not a 'warts and all' approach because gross errors are amended, significant changes noted, and textual complexities are discussed in preliminary notes. The aim is to bring Orwell, not the editor's version of Orwell, to the fore. Although textual issues are given due weight, an attempt has been made to produce an attractive, readable text.

The setting of this edition has been directly from xeroxes of original letters (if typed), typed copies of manuscript (prepared by one or other of the editors), surviving scripts for broadcasts, and xeroxes of essays, articles, and reviews as originally published (unless a headnote states otherwise). For *The Collected Essays, Journalism and Letters of George Orwell* a 1968 house style was adopted but for this edition, no attempt has been made to impose a late twentieth-century house style on the very different styles used by journals and editors of fifty to eighty years ago. Texts are therefore reproduced in the style given them in the journals from which they are reprinted. To 'correct' might well cause even more confusion as to what was and was not Orwell's: see below regarding paragraphing. Nevertheless, although it is not possible *to know*, one may sometimes hazard a guess at what underlies a printed text. Thus, I believe that most often when 'address' and 'aggression' are printed, Orwell typed or wrote 'adress' (especially until about the outbreak of World War II) and 'agression.' Although American spellings (such as 'Labor') have been retained in articles published in the United States, on very rare occasions, if I could be certain that a form of a word had been printed that Orwell would not have used—such as the American 'accommodations'—I have changed it to the form he would have used: 'accommodation'. Some variations, especially of proper names, have been accepted even if they look incongruous; so, 'Chiang Kai-Shek' as part of a book title but 'Chiang Kai-shek' throughout the text that follows.

Hyphenation presents tricky problems, especially when the first part of a word appears at the end of a line. Examples can be found in the originals of, for example, 'the middle-class,' 'the middle class', and 'the middleclass.' What should one do when a line ends with 'middle-'? Is it 'fore-deck' or 'foredeck'? If 'fore-' appears at the end of a line of the copy being reproduced, should the word be hyphenated or not? *OED* 1991 still hyphenates; Chambers in 1972 spelt it as one word. Where it would help (and it does not include every problem word), the ninth edition of F. Howard Collins, *Authors' & Printers' Dictionary*, Oxford University Press, 1946 (an edition appropriate to the mature Orwell) has been drawn upon. But Collins does not include fore-deck/foredeck. On a number of occasions Orwell's letters, or the text itself, is either obscure or wrong. In order to avoid the irritating repetition of *sic*, a small degree sign has been placed above the line at the doubtful point (°). It is hoped that this will be clear but inconspicuous. It is not usually repeated to mark a repetition of that characteristic in the same item. Orwell was sparing in his use of the question-mark in his letters; his practice has in the main been followed.

Paragraphing presents intractable problems. Orwell tended to write in long-paragraphs. Indeed, it is possible to show from the use of many short paragraphs that News Review scripts so written are not by Orwell. The key example is News Review, 30, 11 July 1942 (*1267*), for which there is also external evidence that this is not by Orwell. This has twenty-one paragraphs as compared to eight in the script for the following week. It so happens that we know that Orwell was not at the BBC for two weeks before the 11 July nor on that day: he was on holiday, fishing at Callow End, Worcestershire (and on that day caught a single dace). But though paragraph length is helpful in such instances in identifying Orwell's work, that is not always so. It is of no use when considering his articles published in Paris in 1928–29 nor those he wrote for the *Manchester Evening News*. These tend to have extremely short paragraphs—sometimes paragraphs of only a line or two, splitting the sense illogically. A good example is the series of reviews published on 2 November 1944 (*2572*) where a two-line paragraph about Trollope's *The Small House at Allington* should clearly be part of the preceding four-line paragraph, both relating the books discussed to Barchester; see also *2463*, *n. 2* and *2608*, *n. 4*. There is no question but that this is the work of sub-editors. It would often be possible to make a reasonable stab at paragraphing more intelligently, but, as with verbal clarification, the result might be the more confusing as to what really was Orwell's work and what this editor's. It has been thought better to leave the house-styles as they are, even if it is plain that it is not Orwell's style, rather than pass off changes as if the edited concoction represented Orwell's work.

Usually it is fairly certain that titles of essays are Orwell's but it is not always possible to know whether titles of articles are his. Reviews were also frequently given titles. Orwell's own typescript for his review of Harold Laski's *Faith, Reason and Civilisation* (*2309*), which survived because rejected by the *Manchester Evening News*, has neither heading (other than the name of the author and title of the book being reviewed), nor sub-headings. That would seem to be his style. In nearly every case titles of reviews and groups of letters, and cross-heads inserted by sub-editors, have been cut out. Occasionally such a title is kept if it is an aid to clarity but it is never placed within quotation marks. Other than for his BBC broadcasts (where Orwell's authorship is clear unless stated otherwise), titles are placed within single quotation marks if it is fairly certain that they are Orwell's.

Telegrams and cables are printed in small capitals. Quite often articles and reviews have passages in capitals. These look unsightly and, in the main, they have been reduced to small capitals. The exceptions are where the typography makes a point, as in the sound of an explosion: BOOM! Orwell sometimes abbreviated words. He always wrote an ampersand for 'and' and there are various abbreviated forms for such words as 'about'. It is not always plain just what letters make up abbreviations (and this sometimes applies to his signatures) and these have regularly been spelt out with the exception of the ampersand for 'and'. This serves as a reminder that the original is handwritten. Orwell often shortened some words and abbreviations in his own way, e.g., Gov.t, Sup.ts (Superintendents), NB. and N.W (each with a single stop), and ie.; these forms have been retained. In order that the diaries should readily be apparent for what they are, they have been set in sloped roman (rather than italic, long passages of which can be tiring to the eye), with roman for textual variations. Square and half square brackets are used to differentiate sources for the diaries (see, for example, the headnote to War-Time Diary II, *1025*) and for what was written and actually broadcast (see, for example, Orwell's adaptation of Ignazio Silone's *The Fox*, *2270*). Particular usages are explained in headnotes to broadcasts etc., and before the first entries of diaries and notebooks.

Orwell usually dated his letters but there are exceptions and sometimes he (and Eileen) give only the day of the week. Where a date has to be guessed it is placed within square brackets and a justification for the dating is given. If Orwell simply signs a letter, the name he used is given without comment. If he signs over a typed version of his name, or initials a copy of a letter, what he signed or initialled is given over the typed version. There has been some slight regularisation of his initialling of letters. If he omitted the final stop after 'E. A. B', no stop is added (and, as here, editorial punctuation *follows* the final quotation mark instead of being inside it). Sometimes Orwell placed the stops midway up the letters: 'E·A·B'; this has been regularised to 'E. A. B'.

Wherever changes are made in a text that can be deemed to be even slightly significant the alteration is either placed within square brackets (for example, an obviously missing word) or the alteration is footnoted. Attention should be drawn to one particular category of change. Orwell had a remarkably good memory. He quoted not only poetry but prose from memory. Mulk Raj Anand has said that, at the BBC, Orwell could, and would, quote lengthy passages from the Book of Common Prayer.[2] As so often with people with this gift, the quotation is not always exact. If what Orwell argues depends precisely upon what he is quoting, the quotation is not corrected if it is inaccurate but a footnote gives the correct reading. If his argument does not depend upon the words actually quoted, the quotation is corrected and a footnote records that.

So far as possible, I have endeavoured to footnote everything that might puzzle a reader at the risk of annoying some readers by seeming to annotate too readily and too frequently what is known to them. I have, therefore, tried to identify all references to people, events, books, and institutions. However, I have not been so presumptuous as to attempt to rewrite the history of this century and, in the main, have relied upon a small number of easily accessible histories. Thus, for the Spanish Civil War I have referred in the main to *The Spanish Civil War* by Hugh Thomas; and for the Second World War, to Winston Churchill's and Liddell Hart's histories. The former has useful and conveniently available documents, and the latter was by a historian with whom Orwell corresponded. They were both his contemporaries and he reviewed the work of both men. These have been checked for factual information from more recent sources, one by Continental historians deliberately chosen as an aid to objectivity in an edition that will have world-wide circulation. It is assumed that readers with a particular interest in World War II will draw on their own knowledge and sources and the annotation is relatively light in providing such background information. Similarly, biographical details are, paradoxically, relatively modest for people as well known as T. S. Eliot and E. M. Forster, but far fuller for those who are significant to Orwell but less well known and about whom information is harder to track down, for example, George(s) Kopp, Joseph Czapski, and Victor Serge. It is tricky judging how often biographical and explicatory information should be reproduced. I have assumed most people will not want more than one volume at a time before them and so have repeated myself (often in shortened form with cross-references to fuller notes) more, perhaps, than is strictly necessary. Whilst I would claim that I have made every attempt not to mislead, it is important that historical and biographical information be checked if a detail is significant to a scholar's argument. History, as Orwell was quick to show, is not a matter of simple, indisputable fact. In annotating I have tried not to be contentious nor to direct the reader unfairly, but annotation cannot be wholly impartial.[3]

Each opening is dated. These dates, though drawn from the printed matter, are not necessarily those of the text reproduced on the page on which a date appears. The dates, known or calculated of letters, articles, broadcasts, diaries, etc., will correspond with the running-head date, but, for example, when correspondence (which may have run on for several weeks) springs from an article and follows directly on that article, the date of the article is continued *within square brackets*. Sometimes an item is printed out of chronological order (the reason for which is always given) and the running-head date will again be set within square brackets. Wherever practicable, the running-head date is that of the first item of the opening; if an opening has no date, the last date of a preceding opening is carried forward. Articles published in journals dated by month are considered for the purpose to be published on the first of the month. Inevitably some dates are more specific than is wholly justified, e.g., that for 'British Cookery' (2954). However, it is hoped that if readers always treat dates within square brackets with circumspection, the dates will give a clear indication of 'where they are' in Orwell's life.

Great efforts have been made to ensure the accuracy of these volumes. The three editors and Roberta Leighton (in New York) have read and re-read them a total of six times but it is obvious that errors will, as it used to be put so charmingly in the sixteenth century, have 'escaped in the printing.' I offer one plea for understanding. Much of the copy-preparation and proof-reading has been of type set during and after the war when newsprint was in short supply and mere literary articles would be set in microscopic-sized type. Many of the BBC scripts were blown up from microfilm and extremely difficult to puzzle out. When one proof-reads against xeroxes of dim printing on creased paper, the possibilities for error are increased and the eyes so run with tears that vision is impaired. We hope we have corrected most errors, but we know we shall not have caught them all.

P.D.

A slightly fuller version of this note is printed in the preliminaries to Volume X.

1. *George Orwell, Nineteen Eighty-Four: The Facsimile of the Extant Manuscript*, edited by Peter Davison, London, New York, and Weston Mass., 1984.
2. Information from W. J. West, 22 July 1994.
3. The problems of presenting acceptable history even for the professional historian are well outlined by Norman Davies in *Europe: A History*, Oxford University Press, Oxford and New York, 1996, 2–7. I am obviously attempting nothing so grand, yet even 'simple' historical explication is not always quite so simple.

REFERENCES

References to Orwell's books are to the editions in Vols I to IX of the *Complete Works* (edited P. Davison, published by Secker & Warburg, 1986–87). The pagination is almost always identical with that in the Penguin Twentieth-Century Classics edition, 1989–90. The volumes are numbered in chronological order and references are by volume number (in roman), page, and, if necessary (after a diagonal) line, so: II.37/5 means line five of page 37 of *Burmese Days*. Secker editions have Textual Notes and apparatus. Penguin editions have A Note on the Text; these are not identical with the Secker Textual Notes and Penguin editions do not list variants. There is a 32-page introduction to the Secker *Down and Out in Paris and London*. Items in Volumes X to XX are numbered individually; they (and their notes) are referred to by italicised numerals, e.g. *2736* and *2736 n. 3*.

REFERENCE WORKS: These are the principal reference works frequently consulted:

The Oxford English Dictionary, second edition (Compact Version, Oxford 1991): (OED).

The Dictionary of National Biography (Oxford 1885–1900, with supplements and *The Twentieth-Century*, 1901–): (DNB).

Dictionary of American Biography (New York, 1946, with supplements).

Dictionnaire biographique du mouvement ouvrier français, publié sous la direction de Jean Maitron, 4ᵉ ptie 1914–1939: De la Première à la Seconde Guerre mondiale (t. 16–43, Paris, Les Éditions Ouvrières, 1981–93).

Who's Who; Who Was Who; Who's Who in the Theatre; Who Was Who in Literature 1906–1934 (2 vols., Detroit, 1979); *Who Was Who Among English and European Authors 1931–1949* (3 vols., Detroit 1978); *Contemporary Authors* and its *Cumulative Index* (Detroit, 1993); *Who's Who In Filmland*, edited and compiled by Langford Reed and Hetty Spiers (1928); Roy Busby, *British Music Hall: An Illustrated Who's Who from 1850 to the Present Day* (London and New Hampshire, USA, 1976).

The Feminist Companion to Literature in English, edited by Virginia Blain, Patricia Clements, and Isobel Grundy, Batsford 1990.

The New Cambridge Bibliography of English Literature, edited by George Watson and Ian Willison, 4 vols., Cambridge, 1974–79.

Martin Seymour-Smith, *Guide to Modern World Literature*, 3rd revised edition, Macmillan 1985.

The War Papers, co-ordinating editor, Richard Widdows, 75 Parts, Marshall Cavendish, 1976–78.

The following are referred to by abbreviations:

CEJL: *The Collected Essays, Journalism and Letters of George Orwell*, ed. Sonia Orwell

References

and Ian Angus, 4 volumes, Secker & Warburg 1968; Penguin Books, 1970; references are by volume and page number of the more conveniently available Penguin edition.

Crick: Bernard Crick, *George Orwell: A Life*, 1980; 3rd edition, Penguin Books, Harmondsworth, 1992 edition. References are to the 1992 edition.

Eric & Us: Jacintha Buddicom, *Eric and Us: A Remembrance of George Orwell*, Leslie Frewin, 1974.

Lewis: Peter Lewis, *George Orwell: The Road to 1984*, Heinemann, 1981.

Liddell Hart: B. H. Liddell Hart, *History of the Second World War*, Cassell, 1970; 8th Printing, Pan, 1983.

Orwell Remembered: Audrey Coppard and Bernard Crick, eds., *Orwell Remembered*, Ariel Books, BBC, 1984.

Remembering Orwell: Stephen Wadhams, *Remembering Orwell*, Penguin Books Canada, Markham, Ontario; Penguin Books, Harmondsworth, 1984.

Shelden: Michael Shelden, *Orwell: The Authorised Biography*, Heinemann, London; Harper Collins, New York; 1991. The American pagination differs from that of the English edition; both are given in references, the English first.

Stansky and Abrahams I: Peter Stansky and William Abrahams, *The Unknown Orwell*, Constable 1972; edition referred to here, Granada, St Albans, 1981.

Stansky and Abrahams II: Peter Stansky and William Abrahams, *The Transformation*, Constable 1979; edition referred to here, Granada, St Albans, 1981.

Thomas: Hugh Thomas, *The Spanish Civil War*, 3rd edition; Hamish Hamilton and Penguin Books, Harmondsworth, 1977.

Thompson: John Thompson, *Orwell's London*, Fourth Estate 1984.

West: *Broadcasts*: W. J. West, *Orwell: The War Broadcasts*, Duckworth/BBC 1985.

West: *Commentaries*: W. J. West, *Orwell: The War Commentaries*, Duckworth/BBC, 1985.

Willison: I. R. Willison, 'George Orwell: Some Materials for a Bibliography,' Librarianship Diploma Thesis, University College London, 1953. A copy is held by the Orwell Archive, UCL.

2194 Days of War: *2194 Days of War*, compiled by Cesare Salmaggi and Alfredo Pallavisini, translated by Hugh Young, Arnoldo Mondadori, Milan 1977; rev. edn Galley Press, Leicester 1988.

A Bibliography of works, books, memoirs and essays found helpful in preparing Volumes X to XX of *The Complete Works of George Orwell* will be found in the preliminaries to Volume X.

CHRONOLOGY

In the main, Orwell's publications except books are not listed

25 June 1903 Eric Arthur Blair born in Motihari, Bengal, India.

Christmas 1936 Leaves to fight for the Republicans in Spanish Civil War.

January–June 1937 Serves in Independent Labour Party contingent with the POUM militia on the Aragón front.

8 March 1937 *The Road to Wigan Pier* published by Gollancz in trade and Left Book Club editions. Published by Harcourt, Brace, New York, 1958.

c. 28 April–10 May 1937 On leave in Barcelona during Communist attempt to suppress revolutionary parties (including the POUM).

20 May 1937 Wounded in the throat by a Fascist sniper at Huesca.

23 June 1937 Escapes with Eileen from Spain into France (at Banyuls).

1–7 July 1937 Arrives back at Wallington; starts to write *Homage to Catalonia* shortly thereafter.

July 1937 *New Statesman & Nation* refuses to publish Orwell's article on the POUM or his review of Borkenau's *The Spanish Cockpit*.

13 July 1937 Deposition presented to Tribunal for Espionage & High Treason, Valencia, charging the Orwells with 'rabid Trotskyism' and being agents of the POUM.

5 August 1937 Addresses ILP Conferences on his experiences in Spain.

28 December 1937 Invited to join *The Pioneer*, Lucknow.

Mid Jan 1938 Completes *Homage to Catalonia*.

8 Mar 1938 Falls ill with tubercular lesion in one lung; gives up idea of working as leader writer for *The Pioneer*.

15 March–1 Sept 1938 Patient at Preston Hall, a sanatorium at Aylesford, Kent.

25 April 1938 *Homage to Catalonia*, having been refused by Gollancz, is published by Secker & Warburg. Published by Harcourt, Brace, New York, 1952; as *Omaggio alla Catalonia*, Milan, December 1948.

June 1938 Joins the Independent Labour Party.

Writes pamphlet, 'Socialism and War'; submitted to Hogarth Press; in November abandons attempts to have it published. The pamphlet has not survived.

2 Sept 1938–26 Mar 1939 In French Morocco (mainly at Marrakech); writes *Coming Up for Air*.

11 April 1939 Returns to Wallington.

Late May–mid Dec 1939 Writes *Inside the Whale*.

12 June 1939 *Coming Up for Air* published by Gollancz. Published by Harcourt, Brace, New York, January 1950.

28 June 1939 His father, Richard Blair, dies with Orwell at his bedside.

24–31 Aug 1939 Stays with L. H. Myers in Hampshire.

3 Sept 1939 War breaks out. Shortly after, Orwell leaves Independent Labour Party because of its opposition to the war.

---

21 January 1950 Orwell dies of pulmonary tuberculosis, aged 46.

THE COMPLETE WORKS OF
GEORGE ORWELL · ELEVEN

FACING UNPLEASANT FACTS

1937

355A. Jennie Lee on Orwell's Arrival in Barcelona

Orwell had hoped to leave England for Spain about 23 December 1936 (see *340*) after seeing Gollancz on the 21st about the publication of *The Road to Wigan Pier* (see *341*). He arrived in Barcelona about 26 December 1936 (Crick, 315). Some months after Orwell died, Jennie Lee (Labour MP for Cannock)[1] wrote on 23 June 1950 to Miss Margaret M. Goalby of Presteigne, Radnorshire, who had asked her about Orwell. This is part of that letter.

In the first year of the Spanish Civil War I was sitting with friends in a hotel in Barcelona when a tall thin man with a ravished complexion came over to the table. He asked me if I was Jennie Lee, and if so, could I tell him where to join up. He said he was an author: had got an advance on a book from Gollancz,[2] and had arrived ready to drive a car or do anything else, preferably to fight in the front line. I was suspicious and asked what credentials he had brought from England. Apparently he had none. He had seen no-one, simply paid his own way out. He won me over by pointing to the boots over his shoulder. He knew he could not get boots big enough for he was over six feet. This was George Orwell and his boots arriving to fight in Spain.

I came to know him as a deeply kind man and a creative writer. . . . He was a satirist who did not conform to any orthodox political or social pattern. . . . The only thing I can be quite certain of is, that up to his last day George was a man of utter integrity; deeply kind, and ready to sacrifice his last worldly possessions – he never had much – in the cause of democratic socialism. Part of his malaise was that he was not only a socialist but profoundly liberal. He hated regimentation wherever he found it, even in the socialist ranks.

1. Jennie Lee (1904–1988; Baroness Lee of Asheridge, 1970). Born to a Scottish miner, James Lee, who was chairman of his local ILP branch, she became the first Minister for the Arts and served in the Labour governments, 1964–70. She made a profound impression as Minister for the Arts. She married Aneurin Bevan in 1934. See also *2622 headnote*. For Orwell's Profile of Bevan, see *2765*.
2. This advance was for *The Road to Wigan Pier*.

356. Eileen Blair to Miss Perriam

17 January 1937   Typewritten

The Stores, Wallington,
Near Baldock, Herts.

Dear Miss Perriam,[1]

Thank you very much for your letter. My husband said that Gollancz had warned him that the book would have to be rushed through and that it might be impossible to let the proofs out of the office at all, but the final arrangement was that I was to have the proofs even if they could only be spared for twenty-four hours. Perhaps even that wasn't possible—anyway I suppose this means that no alterations have been necessary in the text to conform with any laws and conventions, which is satisfactory, and we must just hope that the proof-correctors have not made too many "emendations."

The word my husband particularly wants changed is in Chapter I, the last paragraph but one.[2] In the manuscript the sentence is: "For the first time in my life, in a bare patch beside the line, I saw rooks copulating." According to my husband, Gollancz and he altered *copulating* to *courting*, but he wishes the phrase to read " . . . I saw rooks *treading*", because he has seen rooks courting hundreds of times. Of course if by any chance Gollancz changed his mind and left *copulating*, that would be better still, but I expect there is no hope of that. If you can get this alteration made, I shall be most grateful again; I'm so sorry the misunderstanding arose, because I'm afraid it is an irritating nuisance for you.

I have had a postcard from Eric from Sientamo,[3] a village where they halted for food, a few miles from the front. He says the peasants are carrying on as though nothing had happened although the buildings have been almost smashed to pieces by bombs and shell-fire.

Yours sincerely,
Eileen Blair.

1. Secretary to Leonard Moore, Orwell's literary agent.
2. See *The Road to Wigan Pier*, *CW*, V, 228, and Textual Note 16/16.
3. Siétamo. Orwell refers to his arrival there in *Homage to Catalonia*, *CW*, VI, 14. See also Shelden, 273–79; U.S.: 248–53.

357. Draft Contract with Victor Gollancz Ltd

[Undated; early January 1937?]

Among Orwell's papers is a roughly typed draft of a contract by which 'EB grants to G exclusive right to publish in English next 3 "new and original full-length novels" after Keep the A.' The note form of this statement and the errors and overtypings in the draft indicate that it was probably prepared rapidly. It is neither signed nor annotated. It must have been prepared after the publication of *Keep the Aspidistra Flying* (20 April 1936) and some time before Eileen's letter of

31 January 1937, with which she returned the signed contract; see *358*. Just after Orwell left for Spain, Gollancz wrote to Orwell's literary agent, Leonard Moore, raising the need for a new agreement; see *341*. This suggests early January 1937 for this draft. In his letter to Moore of 25 April 1939 (see *546*), Orwell wrote, 'I didn't see our last contract, which you may remember was drawn up while I was in Spain, but I understood from my wife that Gollancz undertook to publish my next three works of fiction.' This confirms that the contract was completed after Orwell went to Spain, in December 1936, and before Eileen left to join him, in February 1937. It is almost certain that Eileen signed the contract on her husband's behalf, Orwell having authorised Christy & Moore on 11 December 1936 to accept her decisions as his own on all literary matters; see *338*.

1. EB grants to G exclusive right to publish in English next 3 "new and original full-length novels" after Keep the A.
2. G. undertakes to publish each within 6 months of delivery of ms.
3. *Royalties*:
   In the United Kingdom— 10% on first 1000, 12½% on next 1000, 15% on next 3000 and 20% thereafter;
   In Colonies   – 4d. per copy sold;
   Cheap editions   – 10% if published at 2/- – 3/6; 7½% if published under 2/-.
   Book Societies   – if 2000 or more are sold to a Book Society at a discount of 50% or more of the published price, a royalty of 10%.
   Advance on publication– £100 or two-thirds of royalties earned on last novel during first 6 months after publication, whichever is greater. Maximum advance £250. Royalties from sales to Book Societies not counted in assessing next advance.
4. G. decides size of edition, format, date of publication, questions of advertising and free copies etc. as usual.
5. After one year G. may publish cheap edition. If after 2 years he has not done so and shall fail to do so within six months of notification from EB, then the right to issue cheaper editions shall revert to EB.
6. EB won't be libellous or criminally plagiaristic (as usual).
7. If at any time G. thinks the sale has practically ceased, G. shall give EB the option of purchasing at cost price the plates and unsold stock (if any). If EB does not make the purchase within 2 months G shall be at liberty to dispose of surplus stock as remainders and EB will not be entitled to royalties on such sales unless the stock is sold above cost when he will get 10%.
8. If G. allows a novel to go out of print or off the market and if within 3 months after receiving a written notice from EB to do so G has not published an edition of 500 copies, all rights in such novel shall revert to the author.
9. 6 free copies for EB and right to buy others at two-thirds of published price.

10. Accounts of sales to be made up to 25th March and 29th September in each year and sent to EB within 3 months of "such making up of account and the amount due to the Author shall be payable within one month of such rendering of account".

11. If G. breaks his contract or goes bankrupt all rights revert to EB who can buy remaining copies at cost price and "moulds and plates at an equitable valuation".

12. Although this agreement refers to three novels it does so separately and not collectively.

13. EB lets Christy and Moore take the money.

358. Eileen Blair to Leonard Moore

31 January 1937   Handwritten

The Stores, Wallington,
Near Baldock, Herts.

Dear Mr Moore,

I enclose the signed agreement.[1] I am afraid there was a little delay before your letter was forwarded to me[2]—I got it yesterday—but when I read the agreement I was delighted, as I know my husband will be when he hears the details. I had not fully realised before how satisfactory it was; in your office the other day I was being rather single-minded.

There is quite good news in[3] Spain, though it comes very erratically. Eric has been created a 'cabo', which is I think a kind of corporal[4] & which distresses him because he has to get up early to turn out the guard, but he also has a dug-out in which he can make tea. There is apparently no 'proper' fighting as neither side has efficient artillery or even rifles.[5] He says he thinks the government forces ought to attack but are not going to. I hope no crisis will arise needing his decision as letters take from 7 to 10[6] days to get here.

With many thanks,
Yours sincerely,
Eileen Blair.

1. See draft agreement, 357.
2. The agreement may have been sent to Eileen's brother's house in Greenwich.
3. 'in' is uncertain; it is represented by no more than a short, slightly wavy, horizontal line.
4. Orwell refers to his promotion in *Homage to Catalonia, CW,* VI, 25.
5. Orwell records that rifles were issued on their third morning in Alcubierre, *Homage to Catalonia, CW,* VI, 16.
6. '10' is possibly '16.' Eileen seems to be more concerned that a battle could affect the publication of her husband's work than that it might endanger his life. Her objectivity, surely deceptive, might be considered in the light of that attributed to Orwell at the end of his life.

359. To James Hanley

[c. 10 February 1937][1]   Handwritten

Juventud Communist Iberica,
Monte Oscurio°
Alcubierre, Huesca
Commandante Kopp.[2]

Dear Mr Hanley,[3]

Many thanks for your letter. I dare say my wife has already acknowledged it, as it reached me open & she is dealing with my correspondence while I am away. I'm sorry I cannot write much of a letter—I am not in very comfortable circumstances here—but anyway it was kind of you to write & I am glad you found the book[4] interesting. It is due out about March 10th I believe, but I shall probably still be in the line here when it comes out, so shan't know how it gets on. Gollancz thought parts of it might give offence in certain quarters but that it was worth risking.

Yours sincerely
Eric Blair ("George Orwell")

1. This postcard is franked 'Valencia 13.11.37.'
2. George(s) Kopp (1902–1951), Russian by birth, Belgian by nationality, was Orwell's commander in Spain. He was a civil engineer but also something of an imposter. After World War II he farmed in Scotland and in 1944 married Doreen Hunton, Eileen's sister-in- law, Gwen O'Shaugnessy's half-sister. He died in Marseilles. Although Orwell and Kopp remained friends, their relationship cooled in the late 1940s. Doreen Kopp wrote to Ian Angus, 29 April 1967, that when Orwell joined her husband's company, 'he was very intrigued to find one Englishman who described himself as a "grocer". He was anxious to meet an English grocer wishing to fight in Spain! It was of course very typical of George as he always wanted to be taken for a working man.' For a fuller account of Kopp, see *535, n. 1.*
3. James Hanley (1901–1985) was the author of upwards of fifty books, eighteen by this time. The first was *Drift* (1930). His second book, *Boy*, was published in expurgated and unexpurgated editions in 1931. In 1935 the first volume of The Furys Chronicle appeared, and in 1937 *Broken Water: An Autobiographical Excursion*, reviewed by Orwell in *Time and Tide*; see *406*. His *Grey Children: A Study in Humbug and Misery* was concerned with unemployment among miners in South Wales, and was reviewed by Orwell in *Time and Tide*; see *409*.
4. *The Road to Wigan Pier*, published on 8 March 1937.

360. *The Spanish Revolution: Bulletin of the Workers' Party of Marxist Unification*[1] (POUM[2])

3 February 1937

British Author With the Militia

At the beginning of January, we received a visit in Barcelona from Eric Blair, the well-known British author, whose work is so much appreciated in all English-speaking left circles of thought. Comrade Blair came to Barcelona, and said he wanted to be of some use to the workers' cause. In view of his literary abilities and intellectual attainments, it appeared that the most useful work he could do in Barcelona would be that of a propaganda journalist in constant communication with socialist organs of opinion in Britain. He said: 'I have decided that I can be of most use to the workers as a fighter at the front.' He spent exactly seven days in Barcelona, and he is now fighting with the Spanish comrades of the P.O.U.M. on the Aragon front.

In a postcard which he sent us, he says: 'When I have persuaded them to teach me something about the machine-gun, I hope to be drafted to the front line trenches.'

1. *The Spanish Revolution* was published fortnightly from 10 Rambla de los Estudios, Barcelona, and presented the POUM's case in the propaganda war being waged within the government forces. It was available in London (from the Independent Labour Party and the Marxist League) and in New York, Chicago, and Toronto. This issue also had a longer article, 'Fighting Men from Britain,' and one summarising 'The Stalinist Position,' 'The P.O.U.M.'s Position,' and 'The Anarchist Position' under the heading 'If they are not Socialist, nor Communist, nor Marxist, What Are They?' In addition to explaining why ILP men were fighting under the POUM banner, this and later articles reveal a tone strikingly similar to the propaganda fed people at home during World War I. Training, it was explained, lasted fifteen days, 'and by that time they should be ready for service at the front.' The food was said to be good but it would 'take the lads a week to get used to the drinking of wine at practically every meal.' Each man was given a packet of cigarettes a day 'and the pay received is remarkably good, namely 10 pesetas.' Pay came as a surprise, 'as all of our lads had volunteered to fight and had never considered the possibility of such a regular sum.' Its frequency is not mentioned. A peseta was worth about fourpence; see *363, n. 5*. Orwell kept copies of *The Spanish Revolution* among his papers until his death.

2. POUM, Partido Obrero de Unificación Marxista (Workers' Party of Marxist Unification) was described by Orwell in *Homage to Catalonia* as 'one of those dissident Communist parties which have appeared in many countries in the last few years as a result of the opposition to "Stalinism"; i.e. to the change, real or apparent, in Communist policy. It was made up partly of ex-Communists and partly of an earlier party, the Workers' and Peasants' Bloc. Numerically it was a small party, with not much influence outside Catalonia, and chiefly important because it contained an unusually high proportion of politically conscious members. . . . It did not represent any block of trade unions.' He gives the membership as 10,000 in July 1936; 70,000 in December 1936; and 40,000 in June 1937, but warns that the figures are from POUM sources, and 'a hostile estimate would probably divide them by four'; see *CW*, VI, 202–03.

361. Eileen Blair to Leonard Moore

11 February 1937   Typewritten

24 Croom's Hill,
Greenwich, S.E. 10.

Dear Mr. Moore,

Thank you very much for your letter. I do, of course, agree with you that Mr. Gollancz should make the separate edition of Part I of *Wigan Pier* and I very much hope he will do so.

The news that the book is definitely chosen for the Left Book Club is splendid, and I am glad to have it now because there is a possibility that I may go to Spain next week—in any case I am hoping to go the week after next, and I am now in town making the necessary arrangements. I will call at your office before I go, in case there is something I should have done and have not done, but there are several matters I can deal with now.

I have arranged with my husband's bank that they will credit him with cheques made out to him and sent direct to them. Would you therefore send any cheques you may have for him to The Manager, Barclay's Bank, Baldock, Herts.? I thought it wise to do this, although I fear it may be more trouble to you, because the mails to Spain are so unreliable. The bank has arranged for me a credit in Barcelona so that I can draw money there as we may need it.

My address in Barcelona will be Hotel Continental, Boulevard de las Ramblas, Barcelona, and from there I ought to be in fairly good touch with my husband.

The only other question to be dealt with, so far as I know, concerns complimentary copies of the book. My husband suggests that I should ask you to send them for him, and I therefore attach a list of the people he wishes to have copies. I do not know whether we shall be given any of the Left Book Club edition, but if so they could be sent to my brother, Laurence O'Shaughnessy, at this address, with his own complimentary copy. I intended of course to do all this myself before going away, but my husband thinks he may get some leave at the end of this month and wants me to be in Barcelona as soon as possible.[1]

With many thanks,
Yours sincerely,
Eileen Blair.

THE ROAD TO WIGAN PIER

Please send one copy (10/6 edition) to each of the following:

Sir Richard Rees, 9 Chesham Place, W. (*Please forward*)

Henry Miller, esq., 18, Villa Seurat, Paris XIV.

Mrs. Sinclair Fierz, 1B, Oakwood Road, Golders Green, N.W.

Mrs. Dennis Collings, c/o Mrs. P. Jaques, Four Ways, Reydon, Near Southwold. (*Please forward*)

Geoffrey Gorer, esq., The Elms, Fitzroy Park, N.W.6.

Mrs. Adam,[2] The Stores, Wallington, Near Baldock, Herts.

Mr. & Mrs. R. W. Blair, Montagu House, Southwold, Suffolk.

Laurence O'Shaughnessy, esq., F.R.C.S., 24 Croom's Hill, Greenwich, S.E.10.

●

And two copies (10/6 edition) to Mrs. Eric Blair, Hotel Contintal,° Boulevard de las Ramblas, Barcelona, Spain.

Free copies of the Left Book Club edition, if any, to be sent to Mr. Laurence O'Shaughnessy.[3]

---

1. As annotated in Moore's office, the third paragraph has been marked with two parallel lines and the second sentence is underlined; the third paragraph has a bold cross marked beside it and 'Note,' the address being underlined; the last paragraph has two parallel lines by it and 'No?' written beside the suggestion that Left Book Club copies might be supplied; this has been crossed out and '2 copies' added.

2. Nellie Limouzin, Orwell's aunt; see *174, n. 1* and *189, n. 1.*
3. All the instructions have been ticked except that for the Left Book Club copies. From the annotations, it would appear that the six copies for the first five addresses were sent on 7 March 1937 and that two Left Book Club copies were sent to O'Shaughnessy five days later. O'Shaughnessy's consulting-room telephone number, Langham 3475, and his home number, Greenwich 0890, are written beside his name and address. Croom's Hill is spelt with and without an apostrophe by Eileen and Orwell (as it is in different London atlases); the writer's form is followed here.

362. Publication of *The Road to Wigan Pier*

The Road to Wigan Pier was published by Victor Gollancz Ltd on 8 March 1937, less than twelve weeks after Orwell had delivered the typescript to his agent. It was not proofread by either Orwell or Eileen. It appeared as a Left Book Club selection and a cloth-bound trade edition. Part I, also with thirty-two pages of plates, was published as a Left Book Club supplementary volume, 'for propaganda distribution,' in May 1937.

Publication details of *The Road to Wigan Pier* are quite complicated, but can be summarised: Left Book Club edition: 44,039; trade edition: 2,150; Part I: 890; lost in air-raid: 150—a total of 47,229 copies.

Type was distributed on 14 June 1939, and the volume was not reprinted in Orwell's lifetime. It was published by Harcourt, Brace and Company in New York in 1958 in an edition that reproduced the illustrations from the Left Book Club edition plates. In 1959 it was included in Secker & Warburg's Uniform Edition,[1] and was first published by Penguin Books in 1962. Except for the first English and U.S. editions, no editions reproduced the plates until the Complete Works edition of 1986; they were introduced into Penguin's Twentieth-Century Classics series in 1989. In addition to reviews in the 'public' press (see Stansky and Abrahams, II, 162, 192, 195), Harold Laski reviewed *The Road to Wigan Pier* in the Left Book Club's own periodical, *The Left News*, March 1937.

On 31 May 1937 the Moscow journal *International Literature* wrote to Orwell requesting a contribution and a copy of *The Road to Wigan Pier*. As Crick records, Orwell sent the book, promised a contribution, but explained that he was recovering from a wound sustained whilst serving with the POUM. The journal replied on 25 August 1937. He was right, it said, 'to be frank with us' and 'right to inform us of your service in the militia of the POUM.' Their magazine had 'nothing to do with POUM-members; this organization, as the long experience of the Spanish people's struggle against insurgents and fascist interventions has shown, is part of Franco's 'fifth column' which is acting in the rear [of] the heroic army of Republican Spain' (Crick, 345–46). See also Shelden, 271–73; U.S.: 247–48.

1. Secker & Warburg initiated a Uniform Edition of Orwell's works with the publication of a second edition of *Coming Up for Air* in May 1948.

363. Eileen Blair to her mother
      22 March 1937   Handwritten

Seccion Inglesa
10 Rambla de los Estudios
Barcelona.[1]

Dearest Mummy,

I enclose a 'letter' I began to write to you in the trenches! It ends abruptly—
I think I've lost a sheet—& is practically illegible but you may as well have a
letter written from a real fighting line, & you'll read enough to get the
essential news. I *thoroughly* enjoyed being at the front. If the doctor had
been a good doctor I should have moved heaven & earth to stay (indeed
before seeing the doctor I had already pushed heaven & earth a little) as a
nurse—the line is still so quiet that he could well have trained me in
preparation for the activity that must come. But the doctor is quite
ignorant & incredibly dirty. They have a tiny hospital at Monflorite in
which he dresses the villagers' cut fingers etc. & does emergency work on
any war wounds that do occur. Used dressings are thrown out of the
window unless the window happens to be shut when they rebound onto
the floor—& the doctor's hands have never been known to be washed. So I
decided he must have a previously trained assistant (I have one in view—a
man). Eric did go to him but he says there is nothing the matter except
'cold, over-fatigue, etc.' This of course is quite true. However, the
weather is better now & of course the leave is overdue, but another section
on the Huesca front made an attack the other day which had rather serious
results & leave is stopped there for the moment. Bob Edwards[2] who
commands the I.L.P. contingent has to be away for a couple of weeks &
Eric is commanding in his absence, which will be quite fun in a way. My
visit to the front ended in a suitable way because Kopp decided I must have
'a few more hours' & arranged a car to leave Monflorite at 3:15 a.m. We
went to bed at 10 or so & at 3 Kopp came & shouted & I got up & George[3] (I
can't remember which half of the family I write to) went to sleep again I
hope. In this way he got 2 nights proper rest & seems much better. The
whole visit's unreality was accentuated by the fact that there were *no* lights,
not a candle or a torch; one got up & went to bed in black dark, & on the last
night I emerged in black dark & waded knee deep in mud in & out of
strange buildings until I saw the faint glow from the Comité Militar where
Kopp was waiting with his car.

On Tuesday we had the only bombardment of Barcelona since I came. It
was quite interesting. Spanish people are normally incredibly noisy &
pushing but in a° emergency they appear to go *quiet*. Not that there was
any real emergency but the bombs fell closer to the middle of the town
than usual & did make enough noise to excite people fairly reasonably.
There were very few casualties.

I'm enjoying Barcelona again—I wanted a change. You might send this
letter on to Eric & Gwen, whom I thank for *tea*. Three lbs of it has just

come & will be much appreciated. The contingent is just running out, Bob Edwards tells me. The other message for Eric is that as usual I am writing this in the last moments before someone leaves for France & also as usual my cheque book is not here, but he will have the cheque for £10 within 2 weeks anyway & meanwhile I should be very grateful if he gave Fenner Brockway[4] the pesetas (In case anything funny happened to the last letter, I asked him to buy £10 worth of pesetas & give them to Fenner Brockway to be brought out by hand. Living is very cheap here, but I spend a lot on the I.L.P. contingent as none of them have had any pay & they all need things. Also I've lent John[5] 500 ps. because he ran out. I guard my five English pounds, which I could exchange at a fairly decent rate, because I must have something to use when we—whoever we may be—cross the frontier again.)

I hope everyone is well—& I hope for a letter soon to say so. Gwen wrote a long letter which was exciting—even I fall into the universal habit of yearning over England. Perhaps the same thing happens in the colonies. When a waiter lit my cigarette the other day I said he had a nice lighter & he said 'Si, si, es bien, es *Ingles*!' Then he handed it to me, obviously thinking I should like to caress it a little. It was a Dunhill—bought in Barcelona I expect as a matter of fact because there are plenty of Dunhill & other lighters but a shortage of spirit for them. Kopp, Eric's commander, longed for Lea & Perrins° Worcester Sauce. I discovered this by accident & found some in Barcelona—they have Crosse & Blackwell's pickles too but the good English marmalade is finished although the prices of these things are fantastic.

After seeing George[6] I am pretty confident that we shall be home before the winter—& possibly much sooner of course. You might write another letter to the aunt[7] some time. I have *never* heard from her & neither has Eric,[8] which worries me rather. I think she may be very sad about living in Wallington. By the way, George[9] is positively urgent about the gas-stove—he wanted me to write & order it at once, but I still think it would be better to wait until just before our return, particularly as I have not yet heard from Moore about the advance on the book.[10] Which reminds me that the reviews are better than I anticipated, as the interesting ones haven't come through yet.

I had a bath last night—a great excitement. And I've had 3 superb dinners in succession. I don't know whether I shall miss this café life. I have coffee about three times a day & drinks oftener, & although theoretically I eat in a rather grim pension at least six times a week I get headed off into one of about four places where the food is really quite good by any standards though limited of course. Every night I mean to go home early & write letters or something & every night I get home the next morning. The cafés are open till 1.30 & one starts one's after-dinner coffee about 10. But the sherry is *undrinkable*—& I meant to bring home some little casks of it!

Give Maud[11] my love & tell her I'll write some time. And give anyone else my love but I shan't be writing to them. (This letter is to the 3 O'Shaughnesseys,[12] who are thus 'you' not 'they'.) It is a dull letter again I think. I shall do this life better justice in conversation—or I hope so.

Much love
Eileen

1. Offices of the POUM journal, *The Spanish Revolution*. See *360*.
2. Robert Edwards (1906–), unsuccessful Independent Labour Party parliamentary candidate in 1935, was a Labour and Co-operative M.P. from 1955 to 1987. In January 1937 he was Captain of the ILP contingent in Spain, linked to the POUM. He left Spain at the end of March to attend the ILP conference at Glasgow, but was unable to return because of the government ban on British nationals' participating in the Spanish civil war. In 1926 and 1934 he led delegations to the Soviet Union; was General Secretary of the Chemical Workers' Union, 1947–71; National Officer, Transport and General Workers' Union, 1971–76; and member of the European Parliament, 1977–79. See *Orwell Remembered*, 146–48, and especially Shelden, 264–65; U.S.: 289–90, which convincingly demolishes Edwards's accusation that Orwell went to Spain solely to find material for a book.
3. Eileen started to write 'Eric' but overwrote 'George.' Her brother, Dr. Laurence Frederick O'Shaughnessy, a distinguished thoracic surgeon (see *632, n. 1*), was called Eric (a shortening of his second name). His wife, Gwen, was also a doctor.
4. Fenner Brockway (1888–1988; Lord Brockway, 1964) was General Secretary of the ILP, 1928, 1933–39, and its representative in Spain for a time. A devoted worker for many causes, particularly peace, he resigned from the ILP in 1946 and rejoined the Labour Party, which he represented in Parliament, 1950–64. See *3294, n. 1*. For Orwell's review of his *Workers' Front*, see *428*.
5. John McNair (1887–1968), a Tynesider, was an indefatigable worker for the cause of socialism all his life. He left school at twelve, and ran into trouble with employers because of his left-wing sympathies. In order to find work, he went to France and stayed for twenty-five years, becoming a leather merchant, founding a French football club with eight teams, and lecturing on English poets at the Sorbonne. He returned to England in 1936, rejoined the ILP, and was its General Secretary, 1939–55. The first British worker to go to Spain, where he remained from August 1936 to June 1937, he was the representative in Barcelona of the ILP. A constant contributor to *The New Leader*, the weekly organ of the ILP (later *The Socialist Leader*), he wrote the official biography of James Maxton, the leader of the ILP, *The Beloved Rebel* (1955). In a footnote to *Homage to Catalonia*, CW, VI, 151, Orwell gives the purchasing value of the peseta as 'about fourpence' (pre-metric currency); 500 pesetas would be about £8 6s 8d or $41.00.
6. Eileen again began writing 'Eric,' over which she wrote 'George.'
7. Almost certainly Orwell's aunt Nellie Limouzin, then living at The Stores, Wallington, the Orwells' cottage.
8. Eileen must here mean her husband.
9. Before writing 'George,' Eileen wrote 'Eric,' but crossed it out.
10. *The Road to Wigan Pier*.
11. Possibly an aunt of Eileen's whose second name was Maud.
12. Eileen's mother, her brother, 'Eric,' and his wife, Gwen.

364. To Eileen Blair

[5? April 1937]   Handwritten; undated

[Hospital, Monflorite]

Dearest,
You really are a wonderful wife. When I saw the cigars my heart melted away. They will solve all tobacco problems for a long time to come. McNair tells me you are all right for money, as you can borrow & then repay when

B.E.[1] brings some pesetas, but don't go beggaring yourself, & above all don't go short of food, tobacco etc. I hate to hear of your having a cold & feeling run down. Don't let them overwork you either, & don't worry about me, as I am much better & expect to go back to the lines tomorrow or the day after. Mercifully the poisoning in my hand didn't spread, & it is now almost well, tho' of course the wound is still open. I can use it fairly well & intend to have a shave today, for the first time in about 5 days. The weather is much better, real spring most of the time, & the look of the earth makes me think of our garden at home & wonder whether the wallflowers are coming out & whether old Hatchett is sowing the potatoes. Yes, Pollitt's review[2] was pretty bad, tho' of course good as publicity. I suppose he must have heard I was serving in the Poum militia. I don't pay much attention to the *Sunday Times* reviews[3] as G[4] advertises so much there that they daren't down his books, but the *Observer* was an improvement on last time. I told McNair that when I came on leave I would do the *New Leader* an article, as they wanted one, but it will be such a come-down after B.E's that I don't expect they'll print it. I'm afraid it is not much use expecting leave before about the 20th April. This is rather annoying in my own case as it comes about through my having exchanged from one unit to another—a lot of the men I came to the front with are now going on leave. If they suggested that I should go on leave earlier I don't think I would say no, but they are not likely to & I am not going to press them. There are also some indications—I don't know how much one can rely on these—that they expect an action hereabouts, & I am not going on leave just before that comes off if I can help it. Everyone has been very good to me while I have been in hospital, visiting me every day etc. I think now that the weather is getting better I can stick out another month without getting ill, & then what a rest we will have, & go fishing too if it is in any way possible.

As I write this Michael, Parker & Buttonshaw[5] have just come in, & you should have seen their faces when they saw the margarine. As to the photos, of course there are lots of people who want copies, & I have written the numbers wanted on the backs, & perhaps you can get reproductions. I suppose it doesn't cost too much—I shouldn't like to disappoint the Spanish machine-gunners etc. Of course some of the photos were a mess. The one which has Buttonshaw looking very blurred in the foreground is a photo of a shell-burst, which you can see rather faintly on the left, just beyond the house.

I shall have to stop in a moment, as I am not certain when McNair is going back & I want to have this letter ready for him. Thanks ever so much for sending the things, dear, & do keep well & happy. I told McNair I would have a talk with him about the situation when I came on leave, & you might at some opportune moment say something to him about my wanting to go to Madrid etc. Goodbye, love. I'll write again soon.

With all my love
Eric

1. Bob Edwards; see *363, n. 2.*
2. Harry Pollitt (1890–1960), a Lancashire boiler-maker and founder-member of the

Communist Party of Great Britain in 1920, became its general secretary in 1929. With Rajani Palme Dutt, (see *519, n. 45*), he led the party until his death. He was, however, removed from leadership in the autumn of 1939 until Germany's invasion of Russia in July 1941 for his temporary advocacy of a war of democracy against fascism. His review of *The Road to Wigan Pier* appeared in the *Daily Worker*, 17 March 1937.

3. *The Road to Wigan Pier* was reviewed by Edward Shanks in the *Sunday Times* and by Hugh Massingham in *The Observer*, 14 March 1937.
4. Victor Gollancz.
5. Michael Wilton (English), also given as Milton, Buck Parker (South African), and Buttonshaw (American) were members of Orwell's unit. Douglas Moyle, another member, told Ian Angus, 18 February 1970, that Buttonshaw was very sympathetic to the European left and regarded Orwell as 'the typical Englishman—tall, carried himself well, well educated and well spoken.'

365. Eileen Blair to Leonard Moore

12 April 1937   Typewritten

Seccion Inglesa,
10, Rambla de los Estudios,
Barcelona.

Dear Mr. Moore,

I hope you received my message of thanks for sending out the two copies of Wigan Pier when it was first published. Now I wish to thank you for the four further copies, two of the 10/6 edition and two of the L.B.C. edition, which came on Saturday. The press cuttings are coming through very well too, and on the whole are very satisfactory. Everyone I hear from is most impressed by the book—I wonder what you thought of it.

I saw my husband a month ago at the front, where, as this is a revolutionary war, I was allowed to stay in the front line dug-outs all day. The Fascists threw in a small bombardment and quite a lot of machine-gun fire, which was then comparatively rare on the Huesca front, so it was quite an interesting visit—indeed I never enjoyed anything more. Eric was then fairly well, though very tired; since then he has had a rest two miles behind the line as he got a poisoned arm,[1] but I think he is now back in the line and the front has been active for the last week. He is keeping quite a good diary[2] and I have great hopes for the book. Unfortunately the activity on his part of the front has interfered with his leave, which is now long overdue, but I hope he will be down here in a week or two.

I should be very grateful if you could let us know whether Gollancz paid the second advance on publication, as he said he was prepared to do. We are still solvent, but when Eric comes on leave we must discuss our future arrangements which will partly depend on the advance. As a matter of fact, there may be a letter now on the way from the bank. The mails are so slow and so irregular that it is very difficult to manage any sort of business.[3]

With many thanks,
Yours sincerely,
Eileen Blair.

1. See *Homage to Catalonia, CW*, VI, 52.
2. Orwell's diary was taken from Eileen's hotel room in Barcelona by the police (see *CW*, VI, 164). It is possibly now in the NKVD Archive in Moscow with the dossier on him compiled by the NKVD; see XI, 36.
3. This letter was date-stamped in Moore's office on 19 April and answered on 21 April 1937.

366. Night Attack on the Aragon Front

The New Leader, 30 April 1937

This article was headed by the statement 'The whole of this story is in the words of the men who took part in it. It consists entirely of extracts from letters to John McNair from Bob Smillie, Eric Blair, Albert Gross and Paddy Donovan.' It was illustrated by photographs of Bob Edwards, C. Justessen, Frank Frankford, Urias Jones, Stafford Cottman, Bob Smillie, Hugh McNeill, Reg Hiddlestone, and Philip Hunter. A tribute from George Kopp, Commander of the 3rd Regiment, Division Lenin, POUM (see *359, n. 2*) was also printed, and is given here. Orwell describes this attack in chapter VI of *Homage to Catalonia*. Douglas Moyle (see *408, n. 1*), a friend of Orwell's in Spain and on their return, told Ian Angus that Orwell was 'quite cross with how the ILP handled the story,' which the participants read when copies of *The New Leader* arrived in Spain. He was displeased at the way 'they blew it up into a sort of 1914–18 battle.' Moyle continued: 'George never felt quite the same about the ILP after that & did not encourage them to use him for propaganda purposes when he came back to England' (letter of 9 April 1965).

FORWARD!

It was a dirty night. Rain was coming down in sheets and a perfect gale was blowing outside, making us glad that our dugouts in our new advanced positions were finished. Our Captain Ben poked his head in.

"Fifteen volunteers wanted for a little job to-night," he called. In a few minutes we were ready.

At 1.45 a.m. it was pitch dark and drizzling. "Coats off." "Bombs handy." "From now on no talking and no noise." The orders passed down from one to another. We moved out into no man's land.

Our objective was a Fascist parapet which dominated our lines. The plan was that we were to creep up, cut the wire, all throw our bombs at an agreed signal, and then rush the parapet. Meanwhile the shock troops were to assault another position in the rear of ours to prevent a counter-attack from that side. Our part of the job worked more or less according to plan.

*

We moved forward in single file through pools of water into ditches which soaked us up to the thighs, through fields, cutting barbed wire as we went. Visibility was almost nil. We got within about thirty yards of the enemy, and could hear two sentries chatting together quietly. Then with a red spear of flame, a sentry's rifle went off. Jorge rose up and flung the first bomb. "Bombs!" Over they went. Hell started. On our left a machine gun opened on us, rifles spattered a stream of bullets over our head. A few yards in front a bomb burst with a roar and a sheet of flame and sparks like a gigantic firework display. More bombs exploded around us. We began to wriggle back a bit. Thomas called out, "I'm hit." Thompson, too, said, "I've caught one." "Go back," we said, but he refused.

A Spanish comrade rose and rushed forward. "Por ellos—Arriba!" (For the others—charge!) "Charge!" shouted Blair. "Over to the right and in!" called Paddy Donovan. "Are we downhearted?" cried the French Captain Benjamin.

In front of the parapet was Eric Blair's tall figure coolly strolling forward through the storm of fire. He leapt at the parapet, then stumbled. Hell, had they got him? No, he was over, closely followed by Gross, of Hammersmith, Frankfort, of Hackney, and Bob Smillie, with the others right after them.

The trench had been hastily evacuated. The last of the retreating Fascists, clothed only in a blanket, was thirty yards away. Blair gave chase, but the man knew the ground and got away. In a corner of the trench was one dead man; in a dugout was another body.

*

We looked around quickly, less than a dozen of us. We had got them out. Now to hold the position. There was already the beginning of a counter-attack in our rear. Guns were jammed with the mud we had been through. Only six or seven rifles were working; with them we began returning enemy fire on one side, while on the other, where there was an unprotected gap, we took sandbags from the parapet to build a small breastwork behind which three or four men could lie down and fire. We had used up most of our bombs. We had captured a quantity of Fascist bombs, but they were of a different make from ours, and we were not certain how to use them.

"Visca P.O.U.M!" we yelled, trying to gather reinforcements, and to give the impression we were a thousand instead of ten.

"They're coming back!" Over went a bomb. The explosion was followed by fearful screams, and the line of fire moved back fifty yards.

"Reinforcements!" Four Germans of the shock battalion had arrived, but the others were lost in the pitch dark.

"Ammunition, a box full," cried one of us.

"Hang it, that last shot took my hat off," yelled Mike Wilton.

*

A hundred yards away a machine gun opened fire and scattered the dust from sandbags into our eyes and mouths. Thompson, in spite of a painful arm wound, had insisted on carrying sacks to build the new parapet. "Now load my rifle," he said. "It's my left hand that's wounded and I can still fire."

O'Hara, among the first to reach the parapet, left it again to bandage up two other comrades who were lying out under fire. With great bravery and coolness he achieved this difficult task.

"Give me a Mauser," said Tanky. "My Worcester's jammed."

"Anybody else need bandaging?" yells O'Hara.

"Here's a telescope," said Moyle.

So an hour compressed itself into a few fleeting impressions.

Soon it became evident that the parapet on our left had not been taken. From three sides we were assailed by a hurricane of machine-gun and rifle fire; mortar and artillery had started, and we knew we were in for a tough time. The Fascists were closing in. It was obvious that we should have to clear out soon. Benjamin gave the order to retire. Reluctantly we retreated through the heavy fire to our own lines, taking as booty 2,000 rounds of ammunition and some bombs.

When we got in, Jorge, Hiddlestone and Coles were missing. They did not appear until about an hour later. Jorge was hit through the shoulder, Hiddlestone's arm was badly shattered, and Coles had stayed to help Hiddlestone in.

Our boys of the good old I.L.P. did their job and damn well. "Well done, English boys," said the Spanish Captain Jorge. To-night we are going out to get a box of bombs we had to leave in no man's land.

Tribute from George Kopp

We have had a very hot time here these last days, and have advanced some thousand yards. The enemy counter-attacked, but did not succeed in regaining an inch of the lost ground. On the night of the 13th we made a somewhat audacious raid on the enemy's positions of the Ermita Salas in order to relieve pressure on the Alcaso Front.

Thanks largely to the courage and discipline of the English comrades who were in charge of assaulting the principal enemy parapet, our action forced some twenty lorries carrying a thousand enemy troops to be sent urgently from the Alcaso Front, and our anarchist comrades there were thus able to make a further advance as well as to consolidate positions already taken.

The whole-page display was completed by an appeal for money, particularly to buy medical supplies, attributed to Buck Parker, a member of the ILP contingent who was in a hospital in Barcelona, having been wounded some days before the attack described.

367. Eileen Blair to Dr. Laurence ('Eric') O'Shaughnessy

1 May 1937   Handwritten

10 Rambla de los Estudios,
Barcelona.

Dear Eric,

You have a hard life. I mean to write to Mother with the news, but there are some business matters. Now I think of these, they're inextricably connected with the news so Mother must share this letter.

George is here on leave. He arrived completely ragged, almost barefoot, a little lousy, dark brown, & looking really very well. For the previous 12 hours he had been in trains consuming anis, muscatel out of anis bottles, sardines & chocolate. In Barcelona food is plentiful at the moment but there is nothing plain. So it is not surprising that he ceased to be well. Now after two days in bed he is really cured but still persuadable so having a 'quiet day'. This is the day to have on May 1st. They were asked to report at the barracks, but he isn't well enough & has already applied for his discharge papers so he hasn't gone. The rest of the contingent never thought of going. When the discharge is through he will probably join the International Brigade. Of course we—perhaps particularly I—are politically suspect but we told all the truth to the I.B. man here & he was so shattered that he was practically offering me executive jobs by the end of half an hour, & I gather that they will take George. Of course I must leave Barcelona but I should do that in any case as to stay would be pointless. Madrid is probably closed to me, so it means Valencia for the moment with Madrid & Albacete in view but at long distance. To join the I.B. with George's history is strange but it is what he thought he was doing in the first place & it's the only way of getting to Madrid. So there it is. Out of this arises a further money crisis because when I leave Barcelona I shall leave all my affiliations—& my address & even my credit at the bank; & it will take a little time to get connected again perhaps. Meanwhile we spend immense sums of money for Spain on new equipment etc. I did write to you about getting money through banks—i.e. your bank buys pesetas[1] with your pounds & instructs a bank in Barcelona to pay me the number of pesetas you bought. If this can be done will you do it (about another 2000 pesetas[2] I should think), & will you ask the bank to cable. Probably I shall be here for a couple of weeks but I'm not *sure* where I shall go next & I want if possible to have some money in hand before leaving. If the bank business can't be done I frankly don't know what can – i.e. I must use the credit at 60 to the £. before leaving here & find some method of getting money through my new friends, whoever they may be (I have met the Times correspondent at Valencia).

The other business is the cottage. I gather & hear from Mrs Blair that the aunt is not only tiring but tired, & I have written to her suggesting evacuation with all the arrangements under headings. You take over in a manner of speaking. If she shows you the letter it may alarm you, but twenty minutes will settle most of the problems. There are several things to be paid, but they're all matters of shillings & the shop may have—should have—a few pounds in hand. The shop will be closed. I've said you can buy any perishables. It is not of course suggested that you should *pay* for these, except in the aunt's eyes, but she will never give anything away so you might dump doubtful stuff in the car & dispose of it anyhow you like. If Mother is at Greenwich she might perhaps go over *after* the aunt is out & see that there is nothing to attract *mice*.[3] There is a chance that Arthur Clinton,[4] who was wounded, may go & recuperate in the cottage. He is perhaps the nicest man in the world & I hope he may be able to use it. He'll

21

return to England unfit, ineligible for dole & penniless. If he wants the cottage he'll ask you about it of course.

We shall owe you money. We *have* money in our sense of the word, but I haven't much fancy for sending cheques if they get lost in the post.

I must take this to the office now—one of the contingent is going home tomorrow & will take it. I have in progress an immense letter to mother, started two or three weeks ago, which will arrive in due course. I am very well.

About the L.C.C. pay I fully agree that there must be no *sessional* payment—it is a vicious system.[5]

My love to Gwen. By the way, I gather from the correspondence that she isn't coming. If this is wrong & she is coming of course I'll wait in Barcelona.

Yours
Eileen.

For the bank's information my name is Eileen Maud Blair & my passport number 174234

I really am sorry for you—but what can I do?

1. A line has been drawn in the margin by 'bank; & it will take a little time . . . your bank buys pesetas,' presumably by Eileen's brother. In January 1937 the U.S. dollar stood at 4.91 to the pound.
2. Exchange rates were suspended during the civil war. In January 1936 there were 36 pesetas to the pound, and in January 1940, 39 pesetas. Eileen writes, below, of using 'credit at 60 to the £.' At 60, 2,000 pesetas would cost just over £33; at 36, £55.11s. Presumably Eileen hoped for more than 60.
3. The words 'letter it may alarm you . . . to attract *mice*' have been bracketed in the margin, presumably by Eileen's brother. Two groups of indecipherable letters possibly mean 'all done.'
4. A member of the ILP contingent. He was with Orwell in the Sanatorium Maurín; see *Homage to Catalonia, CW*, VI, 153.
5. Eileen was objecting to payment by the London County Council of a fee for each session worked instead of at an annual rate. If one was booked for a session but not required, time had been set aside for no financial recompense.

368. To Victor Gollancz

9 May 1937   Handwritten

Hotel Continental   Barcelona

Dear Mr Gollancz,

I didn't get an opportunity earlier to write & thank you for the introduction you wrote to "Wigan Pier," in fact I didn't even see the book, or rather the L.B.C. edition of it, till about 10 days ago when I came on leave, & since then I have been rather occupied. I spent my first week of leave in being slightly ill, then there was 3 or 4 days of street-fighting in which we were all more or less involved, in fact it was practically impossible to keep out of it. I liked the introduction very much, though of course I could have answered some of the criticisms you made. It was the kind of discussion of what one is really talking about that one always wants & never seems to get from the professional reviewers. I have had a lot of reviews sent on to me, some of them very hostile but I should think mostly good from a publicity point of view. Also great numbers of letters from readers.

I shall be going back to the front probably in a few days & barring accidents I expect to be there till about August. After that I think I shall come home, as it will be about time I started on another book. I greatly hope I come out of this alive if only to write a book about it. It is not easy here to get hold of any facts outside the circle of one's own experience, but with that limitation I have seen a great deal that is of immense interest to me. Owing partly to an accident I joined the P.O.U.M. militia instead of the International Brigade,[1] which was a pity in one way because it meant that I have never seen the Madrid front; on the other hand it has brought me into contact with Spaniards rather than Englishmen & especially with genuine revolutionaries. I hope I shall get a chance to write the truth about what I have seen. The stuff appearing in the English papers is largely the most appalling lies—more I can't say, owing to the censorship. If I can get back in August I hope to have a book ready for you about the beginning of next year.

Yours sincerely,
Eric A. Blair

1. The International Brigade was composed of foreign volunteers, mostly Communist, and played an important part in the defence of Madrid. Its headquarters was at Albacete; see 367 and 374A.

369. Orwell's Wound

Orwell was shot through the throat by a sniper on 20 May 1937. He discusses the incident in *Homage to Catalonia, CW*, VI, 137–39. Eileen sent a telegram from Barcelona at noon on 24 May 1937 to Orwell's parents in Southwold. This read: 'Eric slightly wounded   progress excellent   sends love   no need for anxiety   Eileen.' This reached Southwold just after 2:00 P.M. Orwell's commandant, George Kopp, wrote a report on his condition on 31 May and 1 June 1937. When this report was lost (see Eileen's letter to her brother, *373*), Kopp wrote another, for Dr. Laurence O'Shaughnessy, Orwell's brother-in-law, dated 'Barcelona, the 10th. of June 1937' (see below). It differs slightly from the version given in *Orwell Remembered*, 158–61. Kopp illustrated his report with a drawing of the bullet's path through Orwell's throat; Bert Govaerts, who uncovered details of Kopp's life (see *359, n. 2*), suggests that this shows his training in engineering drawing. Kopp's report is in the British Library, Mss Add. 49384, and is reproduced by kind permission of the Trustees.

Eric was wounded the 20th of May at 5 a.m. The bullet entered the neck just under the larynx, slightly at the left side of it's° vertical axis and went out at the dorsal right side of the neck's base. It was a normal 7 mm bore,

23

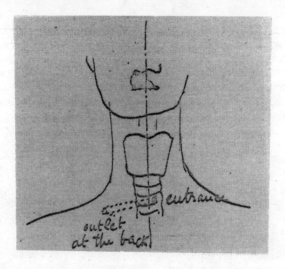

copper-plated spanish° Mauser bullet, shot from a distance of some 175 yards. At this range, it still had a velocity of some 600 feet per second and a cauterising temperature. Under the impact, Eric fell on his back. The hemorrhaging was insignificant. After dressing at a first aid post some half a mile from the actual line, he was transferred to Barbastro and then to the Hospital of Lerida, where I saw him with Eileen some 50 hours after him° having been wounded.

Eric's general state was some sort of excellent; the temperature (taken in the left arm-pit) had never reached 37°C. Eric complained about his right arm aching from the shoulder down to the tip of the middle finger along a humero-cubital line and about a pain, according to himself severe but not unbearable, in the left side somwhere° between the ultimate rib and the spleen. His voice was hoarse and feeble, but covering all the practical purposes of conversational speech. Breathing absolutely regular. Sense of humour untouched.

At the Hospital in Lerida, Eric only received an external treatment of his wound. After a couple of days, the dressing of the entrance wound could be dispensed with. He remained at this Hospital, under care of Dr. Farré, up to the 27th when he was transferred to Tarragona.

Dr. Farré told me on the 22[d] of May that no essential organ had been touched by some sort of unexplainable luck; he admitted that the pain in the arm might be produced by abrasion of one of the arm's main nerves and that the pain in the left side was probably due to hitting the ground when falling from his tremendous height. He told me that there was nothing to fear about the basic wound.

We had Eric ordered to be evacuated from Tarragona to Barcelona and went to fetch him the 29th of May; we found him with a semi-complete aphorisia[1] and a slight fever. The pain in the left side had disappeared in due course. The one in the arm (supposed of nervous origin) subsisted unchanged. The doctor at Tarragona's Hospital had told Eric on that very morning that his larynx was "broken" and that he would never recover a normal voice. In fact, Eric was able to utter any articulate sound but feebly and with the characteristic, grinding, noise of the brakes of a model T, very antiquated, Ford; his speech was inaudible outside a range of two yards.

Eric reached the sanatorium Maurin in Barcelona on the 29th at 10 p.m., having travelled 60 miles in a saloon-car without any special accommodation. His temperature reached at 11 p.m. 37.8°C (in left arm-pit); he received an aspirin and went immediately to bed, without any meal.

On Sunday, 30th, his voice had improved considerably, his temperature was normal in the morning and his apetite° restored. He was able to walk about the place and it's° park without any exhaustion. I saw him from 11 a.m. to 6p.m. and found his voice and spirits continuously improving during this period. Eileen was with her husband all the time and states his comportment was absolutely peace-timely.

Today, 30th.[2] Eric travelled by tram and tube, on his own initiative, down to the Centre of Barcelona, where I met him at 11.45 a.m. He explained his escapade by the want of cocktails and decent lunch, which were duly produced by Eileen's tender care (with help of a barman and several waiters).

Eric's temperature had remained normal, the pain in the left side had not reappeared and the pain in the right arm was rather reduced. His voice, according to himself, had improved since yesterday, but Eileen and I don't share this impression, without thinking it was worse. I explain this apparent contradiction by the fact that to reach his present quality of speech costs him less effort than yesterday.

I arranged to have Eric thoroughly examined to-morrow morning by Professor Grau of Barcelona's University and for a subsequent treatment either by some professor, either[3] by another prominent specialist of this town.

I propose to add to this "bulletin" Professor's° Grau opinion with the narrative of the manipulations he will perform on my friend's throat.

Professor Grau examined Eric to day, 1st of June, at 9.30 a.m. at the "Hospital General de Cataluña". His diagnostic is:
"incomplete semi-paralysis of the larynx due to abrasion of the right-side larynx dilating[4] nerve."

He confirmed Dr. Farré's statement that no essential organ had been touched; the bullet went right through, between the trachea and the carotid.

Professor Grau said that electrotherapy was the only thing to be recommended just now and some sort of promise to restore Eric's voice in a long, indefinite, but reasonable time.

He took Eric to Dr. Barraquer, specialist[5] in electric treatments of nervous disturbances and began by having a private talk of some 12 minutes with his colleague. It is unknown if they spoke of Eric's wound or of some other topic. When Eric, Eileen and myself were ushered in Dr. Barraquer's study, Professor Grau explained the case just as if he had never spoken of it before and wanted his friend to investigate any possible nervous lesions outside of the purely laryngic zone out of which he some sort of hated to walk.[6]

Dr. Barraquer's additional diagnostic was:

"abrasions of the first right-side spinal rachidean nerve,"

which accounts for the pain in the arm. Dr. Barraquer also advocated electrotherapy for both of the nervous lesions and it was agreed upon Eric coming twice a week (on Wed. and Fri.) to have an electrical treatment and once a week (on Fridays) to let Professor Grau look into his throat and hear him saying 'aaaaaah' whilst his tongue is maintained stretched out at full length by the Professor.

Both of the doctors concerned with the case are decent, efficient and fully civilised people, with a lot of similar cases having passed before them since war begun; the machinery and installations of the General Catalonian Hospital is complete and modern; most of the nurses are brunettes.

Of course, the doctors have not given any definite opinion upon the duration of the treatment and I felt I could not possibly put any questions about it before they can prove by some sittings the effect of electrotherapy on Eric's nerves. I think that in any case, it would be advisable to let the treatment go at least two weeks and then ask the medical people 'what about having it continued in England?'

I advocate you writing to Dr. Barraquer (who speaks a fairly good english[o]) a 'colleague's letter' in the reply to which you may be told something more than we, mere mortals, are admitted to hear. Then you would be able to form a reasonable opinion about the case and send Eileen definite instructions which, I am sure she will follow without any reluctance, so high is her admiration for your professional capacities.

With the hope I shall some day have the opportunity of sharing this feeling not only from faith but on experimental evidence, I remain

Yours sincerely
Georges Kopp

Dr. Barraquer's adress:[o]
Dr. Barraquer
Hospital General de Cataluña
Barcelona.

1. Kopp meant 'aphasia.'
2. Presumably 31 May.
3. Kopp meant 'or.'

4. Kopp wrote 'dilatating.'
5. Kopp wrote 'specialised.'
6. Kopp presumably intended 'talk.'

370. To Mr. Thompson

8 June 1937   Handwritten

Sanatori Maurin[1]   Sarria   Barcelona

Dear Mr Thompson,[2]

Please forgive me for only now answering your letter dated 12.3.37. I have been in Spain since the beginning of the year, most of that time at the front, &

my letters have only got to me at long intervals. I got yours about a fortnight ago, I think. You kindly said that you intended reviewing my last book[3] & I thought that if it was not too late I would write & warn you that from your point of view I am on the wrong side of the fence, as I have been fighting for what you call "the Caballero[4] clique of capitalists." However I have got a Fascist bullet in me now, if that is any consolation to you, & shall probably have to come home shortly. I just thought I would tell you lest you should think I am a sympathiser with your viewpoint, which on the whole I am not. But thanks very much for writing.

Yours sincerely
George Orwell

1. Sanatorium Maurín was run by the POUM. In *Homage to Catalonia*, *CW*, VI, 152, Orwell describes it as being near Tibidabo, 'the queer-shaped mountain that rises abruptly behind Barcelona.' Sarria (not 'Sania' as sometimes recorded) is the name of an old township in the Barcelona area.
2. Unidentified.
3. *The Road to Wigan Pier*.
4. Francisco Largo Caballero (1869–1946), a left-wing Socialist and Prime Minister and Minister of War in the Popular Front government of Socialists, Communists, Anarchists, and some liberal Republicans from 4 September 1936 to 17 May 1937. He is described by Thomas as 'a good trade-union organizer without vision' whose 'political errors of judgement . . . were at the heart of the problems of the republic in the months before the conflict' (933). The Germans imprisoned him in a concentration camp for four years; he died in Paris, not long after his release, in 1946.

371. To Cyril Connolly

8 June 1937   Handwritten

Sanatori Maurin   Sania   Barcelona

Dear Cyril,
I wonder if you will be in town during the next few weeks. If you will & would like to meet, you might drop a line to that effect to
at. 24 Crooms Hill
Greenwich S.E. 10.
If I can get my discharge papers I ought to be home in about a fortnight. I have been nastily wounded, not really a very bad wound, a bullet through the throat which of course ought to have killed me but has merely given me nervous pains in the right arm & robbed me of most of my voice. The doctors here don't seem certain whether I shall get my voice back or not. Personally I believe I shall, as some days it is much better than others, but in any case I want to get home & be properly treated. I was just reading one of your articles on Spain in a February New Statesman. It is a credit to the New Statesman that it is the only paper, apart from a few obscure ones such as the New Leader, where any but the Communist viewpoint has ever got through. Liston Oak's article[1] recently on the Barcelona troubles was very good & well balanced. I was all through that business & know what lies most of the stuff in

the papers was. Thanks also for recently telling the public that I should probably write a book on Spain, as I shall, of course, once this bloody arm is right. I have seen wonderful things & at last really believe in Socialism, which I never did before. On the whole, though I am sorry not to have seen Madrid, I am glad to have been on a comparatively little-known front among Anarchists & Poum people instead of in the International Brigade, as I should have been if I had come here with C.P. credentials instead of I.L.P. ones. A pity you didn't come up to our position & see me when you were in Aragon. I would have enjoyed giving you tea in a dugout.

Yours
Eric Blair

1. 'Behind Barcelona's Barricades,' by Liston M. Oak, *The New Statesman & Nation*, 15 May 1937.

371A. Reprint of Section of *The Road to Wigan Pier*

A short section from *The Road to Wigan Pier* was reprinted in the *News Chronicle*, 10 June 1937, as the fourth in a five-day series 'giving the work of young writers already famous among critics, less well-known by the public.' The section chosen was from 'Before I had been down a mine' (*CW*, V, 21, line 33) to 'when he comes back to the pit, suffers badly for the first few days' (25, lines 15–16).

Part of the first three lines of p. 138, 'one sniff . . . evil despotism' are quoted in a preliminary biographical note. In the passage reprinted, Orwell expresses surprise at the number of mice in the mine galleries. On 16 June, the *News Chronicle* published a letter from Ifor R. Middletone explaining that mice got into the pit ponies' fodder on the surface and so found their way below ground where they bred. By coincidence, another letter that day refers to a Tenants' League set up in the East End of London under the chairmanship of the Rev Gilbert Shaw to present views of tenants to a government committee considering the renewal of the Rent Acts. Shaw had helped provide illustrations for *The Road to Wigan Pier*; see *CW*, I, xxxiv, and, for his name in Victor Gollancz's handwriting, the illustration on p. xxxiii and X, 530.

372. To Frederick Bardford

10 June 1937

Orwell wrote to Frederick Bardford from the Sanatorium Maurín, Barcelona, explaining that he had been wounded, that letters reached him at rare intervals and answering them was difficult. (Summary from Kingston Galleries, Somerville, Mass., Catalogue 32, item 164.) It has not proved possible to trace this letter.

373. Eileen Blair to Dr. Laurence ('Eric') O'Shaughnessy

[*c.* 10 June 1937][1]   Handwritten; undated

Dear Eric,
Ten days ago George Kopp wrote you an account of the medical investigations & reports on Eric, & I wrote letters to you & Mrs Blair & the aunt. As we wanted you all to get the correspondence quickly we gave them to a man who was crossing into France, to be sent Air Mail from there. Today we hear that he lost the whole packet. So everyone will be feeling bitterly neglected, including me as I had expected a reassuring cable. I've written at least three letters & four postcards each to the three addresses since, but I don't know which have arrived or when. You might ask mother to telephone Mrs Blair & write [to the][2] aunt—or better telephone yourself & give a medical opinion.

Eric is I think much better, though he cannot be brought to admit any improvement. His voice certainly improves very *slowly*, but he uses his arm much more freely though it is still very painful at times. He eats as much as anyone else & can walk about & do any ordinary thing quite effectively for a short time. He is *violently* depressed, which I think encouraging. I have now agreed to spend two or three days on the Mediteranean° (in France) on the way home—probably at Port-Vendre.°[3] In any case we shall probably have to wait somewhere for money. The discharge is not through but I think we can leave next week, wire you for money when we arrive at Port Vendre or other resting place, go on to Paris & spend there two nights & the day between, & then get the morning train to England. I do not altogether like this protracted travel, but no urgent complication seems possible now, & he has an overwhelming desire to follow this programme—anyway it has overwhelmed me.

Give my love to everyone. I now realise I haven't explained that the enclosed letter from G.K. is a copy of the one that was lost.

Thank you very much for the liniment & the things for Lois, which I collected today.

Eileen.

Did you get £20 from Fenner Brockway?

1. See headnote to 'Orwell's Wound'; *369*.
2. 'to the' is represented by two (or three) indecipherable letters.
3. They spent three days at Banyuls-sur-Mer, about ten kilometres north of the Spanish border and some five south of Port-Vendres. It was 'the first station up the line' into France, a 'quiet fishing-town,' as Orwell wrote in *Homage to Catalonia*, *CW*, VI, 184. They continued their journey via Paris, where 'the Exhibition was in full swing, though we managed to avoid visiting it' (186).

374. B. C. Rake to Orwell
21 June 1937   PP/EB/MB

B.C. Rake, who had served in the police in Burma, retired to Norfolk on a half-pension and read some of Orwell's work, including *Burmese Days*. He had written to Orwell through Victor Gollancz Ltd, and Orwell had replied. On 21 June Rake thanked Orwell for his reply and asked if he would care to stay with him at his home, Fishley Place, Acle. Though he could not afford to entertain him in style, it was quiet, and Orwell could work, if he wished, or take a short holiday.

374A. Escape from Spain, 23 June 1937

On 23 June 1937, Eileen and Orwell, with John McNair and Stafford Cottman, provided with documents from the British consulate, boarded the morning train from Barcelona to Paris. Sitting in the restaurant car as if they were tourists, they safely crossed into France. The Orwells stayed for a few days at the little port of Banyuls-sur-Mer before returning to England. Sir Richard Rees later wrote that the strain of her experience in Barcelona showed clearly on Eileen's face and in her behaviour: 'In Eileen Blair I had seen for the first time the symptoms of a human being living under a political Terror.'[1] The nature of this Terror is exemplified by a list of statements referring to Eileen and her husband to the Tribunal for Espionage and High Treason, Valencia, three weeks after they had escaped. This is, according to Victor Alba, a part of the *legajo*, or official judiciary record of the trial against POUM (letter to the editor, 27 February 1999). The implications of this document (which was unknown to Orwell) explain why Orwell turned so adamantly against Communism. It shows how he and his comrades were betrayed by those supposedly fighting with them against Fascism. The Spanish document is reproduced with its errors uncorrected; errors in spelling names have not been reproduced in translation. I am very grateful to Robert A. McNeil, for providing an accurate copy of this document, and for improving the translation previously printed.

Report to Tribunal for Espionage and High Treason, Valencia

BARCELONA 13 de Julio de 1937.

ENRIC° BLAIR y su mujer EILEEN BLAIR.

Resulta de su correspondencia que son trotzquistas pronunciados.

Son de la I.R.P.° de Inglaterra.

ENRIC° BLAIR establa del comitè de la ILP que funcionaba en el divisiòn, Lenin al frente de la Granja (HUESCA).

Enclase con I.L.P. Inglaterra (Correspondencia D. MOYLE y JOHN MACNAIR).

En el material de CHARLES DORAN se encuentra una carta dirigida a ERIC B/ de JOHN MACNAIR, pidiendole de escribir noticias a la ILP.- Se tiene que considerarlos como agentes de enlace de la ILP del POUM. Vivian en el hotel Falcon, apoyados por la Ejecutiva Comitè del POUM. Credeencial° de la Ejecutiva Comité POUM firmado por JORGE KOPP (por su caracter da lugar a suponer que es una credencial sirviendo durante los sucesos de mayo en favor de EILEEN B.

ERIC B. ha tomado parte de los sucesos de MAYO.
Enlace con ALBACETE por medio de DAVID WICKES.
Enlace con MOSCOU.-
Eilenº B. estaba en el frente de Huesca el 13–3–37, (fecha inscrita en una fotografia) Tiene una credencial extendida en BARCELONA el 17–3–37. Su marido tiene un permiso de salir del frente para ir a Barcelona extendido el 14–3–37.

Translation by Robert A. McNeil

Barcelona 13 July, 1937

ERIC BLAIR and his wife EILEEN BLAIR.

It is clear from their correspondence that they are confirmed Trotskyists. They belong to the IRP [sic] of England.
ERIC BLAIR was on the ILP Committee functioning in the Lenin Division on the Granja front (HUESCA).
Liaison wih the ILP of England (correspondence of D. MOYLE and JOHN MACNAIR)
Among the effects of CHARLES DORAN is found a letter addressed to ERIC B. from JOHN MACNAIR, asking him to write reports for the ILP.-
They must be considered as liaison officers of the ILP with POUM.
They were living in the Hotel Falcon, supported by the POUM Executive Committee.
Credential from the POUM Executive Committee signed by JORGE KOPP (from its character it seems to be a credential in favour of EILEEN B. valid for the events of May. [No closing bracket]
ERIC B. took part in the events of MAY.
Liaison with ALBACETE by means of DAVID WICKES.
Liaison with MOSCOW.-
Eileen B. was on the Huesca front on 13-3-37 (date inscribed on a photograph). She has a credential issued in BARCELONA on 17-3-37. Her husband has a permit to leave the front to go to Barcelona, issued on 14-3-37.

This document in the Archivo Histórico Nacional de España, Madrid, was sent to the editor by Karen Hatherley; it is reproduced by kind permission of the Centre d'Estudis Històrics Internationals (CEHI), Barcelona; the editor is grateful to its Secretary General, Sr Jordi Planes, for his assistance. The document, with some variants, is included by Victor Alba in his El Processo del P.O.U.M. (Madrid, 1989). I am grateful to Stephen Schwartz for comments on the first edition. The trial of the leaders of the POUM and of Orwell (in his absence) took place in Barcelona in October and November 1938 (see 497). Robert McNeil also found a document in Barcelona (not in Alba), similar to the Orwell document, concerning Charles Doran (see 386 and 505). Doran is also described as 'trotzkista pronunciado'. Among names in the Doran document is Karl Radek (see 3649, n. 3, XX/139), whom it is stated Doran defended. Doran also possessed a newspaper cutting about Lt Norman Baillie Stewart ('the prisoner in the Tower'), who had been accused of selling secrets to German agents.

The Events of May 1937 in Barcelona have been the subject of much dispute. Not surprisingly, Communists blamed the Anarchists and Trotskyists (the CNT and the POUM), and the POUM and the CNT blamed the Communists.

A vicious little book by Georges Soria, *Trotskyism in the Service of Franco: Facts and Documents on the Activities of the P.O.U.M.* (London edition, published by Lawrence & Wishart, undated; New York, 1938), was timed to 'appear before the trial of Trotskyist leaders has taken place' and accuses the POUM of being 'one of the most important instruments which the Spanish rebels use in their struggle against the legitimate Spanish Government.' The POUM was, Soria stated, 'the direct instrument of Fascism in Spain' (6,5,44). Amongst the 'evidence' assembled is F. A. Frankfort's account of collaboration between the POUM and the Fascist forces on the Huesca front. This had first been published in the *Daily Worker*, 14 September 1937, and angrily refuted by Orwell and his colleagues (see *399*). Soria does not refer to this refutation. Soria's book is representative of the Communist misinformation which appeared widely in the press at the time and which Orwell addresses in Appendix II of *Homage to Catalonia*. In short, the Communists' allies in the fight against Franco (Orwell being one) were accused of being undercover Fascists and deliberately fomenting an uprising in Barcelona.

Despite his well-founded suspicions, Orwell, in *Homage to Catalonia*, could not bring himself to believe that anyone had deliberately planned the May events: 'the fighting was only preconcerted in the sense that everyone expected it. There were no signs of any very definite plan on either side . . . was it perhaps a Communist *coup d'état*. . . ? . . . I do not believe it was'; and, he says, no additional troops were brought into Barcelona nor had food been laid up by either side (219, 223). However, it now seems that Orwell was deceived. As far back as October 1936—before Orwell had even set out for Spain—Alexander Orlov, head of the NKVA in Spain, assured his Headquarters that 'the Trotskyist organization POUM can easily be liquidated'.[2] Such 'liquidation' would be at the hands of their Communist 'allies' starting in May 1937. José Diaz, Secretary General of the Spanish Communist Party, denounced the POUM as 'agents of fascism, who . . . carry out their major mission as agents of our enemies in our own country.'[3] In *Communist International*, January 1937, Francisco Antón (later Political Commissar for General Miaja, who commanded the combined 5 and 18 Army Corps at the battle of Brunete), wrote: 'One of the necessary conditions for the victory of our people must be the destruction, with an iron hand, of the Trotskyite traitors. . . . The Trotskyites are just as dangerous as the armies of fascism'; and in a special Spanish edition of *Inprecor*, 17 May 1938, he contributed an article with the revealing title 'Trotskyists in Spain—Open Agents of Fascism.'[4] There is little doubt that the Events of May were deliberately fomented at the instigation of the Soviets, thus enabling Alexander Orlov, NKVD chief in Spain, to order the arrest of all the POUM's leaders on 14 June 1937.[5] David T. Cattell states that 'in their oppression of the *POUM*, the Communists made full use of the GPU [NKVD]. . . . All members of the *POUM* were subject to arrest, secret trials, and even execution with no chance to defend themselves.'[6]

Orwell, as he freely admits in *Homage to Catalonia*, was ill-informed to the point of näiveté about the political situation in Spain and he reported only what he witnessed—a virtue but also a limitation. This document shows that his fears for his safety and that of his wife and comrades were well founded. As late as 1984 Bill Alexander, a political commissar and commander of the British Battalion of the XVth International Brigade, underplayed their danger, writing that Orwell and others 'decided they might be arrested and left Spain.'[7] David Corkhill and Stuart Rawnsley, in 1981, expressed themselves more forcibly:

Orwell 'joined the rest of the ILPers in beating a hasty retreat to the safety of the French frontier.'⁸ It is now plain that had they not done so they would surely have been imprisoned, if not actually executed, and Orwell's health being what it was, he might well have suffered Bob Smillie's fate.

This document reports on what was found when searching Eileen's room at the Continental Hotel as described in *Homage to Catalonia* (164). (It is ironic that Communists complain of inaccuracies in *Homage to Catalonia*; it was they who stole his diaries: perhaps one day they will turn up in NKVD or Ministry of Foreign Affairs files in Moscow.) Charles Doran's effects were also rifled. On the basis of what they took away, this report was drawn up. Its general import has been suspected for a long time, but its specific details show the involvement of Moscow (doubtless the NKVD, through the Russian Consul-General's office in Barcelona) and the International Brigade itself. (The Russian Consul-General, Vladimir Antonov-Ovsëenko (1884–1937), referred to by Orwell in *Homage to Catalonia* (234), had led the attack on the Winter Palace in 1917 and had been a supporter of Trotsky, but he later allied himself to Stalin. He was recalled in June 1937 to take up the post of People's Commissar for Justice. However, and presumably unknown to him, he had been condemned to ten years' imprisonment at one of a series of purge trials in Moscow on 8 February 1937; he was shot soon after his return.)⁹

Albacete was the International Brigade base. The Archivist of the Marx Memorial Library, Tony Atienza (assisted by Bill Alexander), identified David L. Wickes as a clerk who then lived in the Forest Hill–Lower Sydenham area of London; in December 1936 he volunteered for the International Brigade through the Secretary of the Luton Socialist League. He was turned down on the grounds that he had no military experience. He volunteered again in June 1937, this time for an ambulance unit. He was supported by F. L. Kerran, a car worker and Labour Party Parliamentary candidate for Luton in 1935 (since 1924 he had stood unsuccessfully three times at Stoke Newington and Hull), and by Fenner Brockway and John McNair, ILP stalwarts, the latter being named in the document reproduced above. He was accepted, but when he arrived in Spain it was decided he was not suitable for ambulance work. Because he had a working knowledge of French, German, and Spanish, he was appointed, despite his ILP recommendation, to Brigade Headquarters in Albacete. Alexander recalled that he seemed to have no strong political affiliations. He is not mentioned in either Bill Rust's *Britons in Spain* (1939) or Alexander's *British Volunteers for Liberty: Spain, 1936–1939* (1982).¹⁰

The section of Brigade Headquarters to which the document of charges against Orwell and his wife would have been sent, was undoubtedly either the Political Commissariat or the political police, the SIM (Servicio Investigación Militar). The Political Commissariat 'maintained its absolute dominance over the internal affairs of the Brigades through a variety of means including control over the Brigade press, censorship, control of appointments to military and political posts, and, ultimately, the Brigade police apparatus, which carried with it the power to imprison and execute without recourse to or review by higher authority'; the Commissariat had a network of political commissars at brigade, battalion, and company level, every military commander worked in conjunction with a commissar; and the Brigade ran a school at Albacete for its political commissars.'¹¹ The Comintern exercised control over the International Brigades through the Political Commissariat and assigned personnel (usually trained in Moscow) to oversee its activities.¹² The Political Commissariat had at its 'direct disposition' the political police, the SIM, which ran its own prison at Albacete, where it held, questioned, tortured, and executed those whom it suspected of being dissidents, in the manner of its 'parent organisation, the Soviet NKVD,' both SIM and NKVD being closely interconnected.[13]

British commissars listed by Rust include: Ralph Fox, Walter Tapsell (circulation manager of the Daily Worker), George Aitken, D. F. Springhall, William Paynter, Bert Williams, Bob Elliott, Jack Roberts, Eric Whalley, Tom Oldershaw, Arthur Nicholl, Hugh Slater (who later edited Polemic, to which Orwell contributed several important articles; see 3562, n. 8), Johnny Power, and Harry Dobson.[14] Alexander lists in addition: Peter Kerrigan, John Mahon, Bill Rust (of the Political Bureau of the Communist Party of Great Britain and the Daily Worker correspondent), George Brown, Alec Torrance, Bill Rowe, Bob Cooney, and Morris Miller; he also lists two American commissars at Brigade, Steve Nelson and Dave Doran.[15] There were thus at least twenty-two British political commissars, a ratio to the total enlistment of over one in ten. Rust explains that, following practice in France in 1789 and Russia in 1917, a political commissar was appointed alongside every commander of the Republican Army in order 'to weld conflicting ideologies together for a common purpose'; he and the commander jointly signed all reports and orders; and, in Rust's words, the commissar was 'the collaborator of the commander, the political adviser and friend of the men,' though he does not mention to what degree friendship extended to the executions that were rife in some brigades (though infrequent in the British Battalion). Furthermore, the commissars fought alongside the men.[16] Casualties among the brigades were extremely high.[17] Alexander lists 526 killed of some 2,050 British brigaders—more than 25% of those who had enlisted; eight of the 22 British commissars named fell, 36%. (Rust and Alexander ignore those who died fighting with the POUM.) The British commissars at battalion level, and usually at company level, were Communist Party members 'with a record of activity in Britain.'[18]

The rank and file of the British Battalion were in no way responsible for the fate of the POUM. Indeed, when they learned of the way their former comrades had been treated, their morale declined. 'Volunteers returned home disgruntled. The liquidation of the POUM created a deservedly bad impression,' says Thomas.[19] One such was Leslie Preger. He had visited the Soviet Union in 1934 and did two tours of duty with the International Brigade. However, on returning home he 'drifted away' from the Communist Party 'especially because of their attitude to the P.O.U.M.ists and anarchists.'[20] Even after their return to England, some of those who had fought with the POUM were hounded by members of the Communist Party; see Orwell's letters to Charles Doran, 2 August 1937 (386), and Miss Charlesworth, 30 August 1937 (393), on the POUM and the Communists.[21]

It is difficult to assess what the British political commissars knew of the fate of the POUM and to what extent they were party to it. They were too far away from Barcelona, and too busily engaged in fighting on their own front, to be involved in a direct way against those who had fought with the POUM, but it is hard to imagine that they did not know that accusations of the kind made by the French Communist Georges Soria and those published in the Daily Worker (for example, Frankfort's story) were false. Nothing more tarnishes the record of those who directed the fight against Fascism in Spain than the scale of executions of brigaders regarded as dissidents. This caught up many, many more than those who could justly be accused of spying; it was certainly aggravated by the paranoiac suspicions of the NKVD; and it was operated by the Political Commissariat and carried out with the approval of some, at least, of the political commissars, including those from the British Battalion. André Marty, a leading member of the French Communist Party and Deputy in the French Parliament, 'placed in direct control of the International Brigades by the Comintern,' admitted executing some 500 brigaders, thoroughly justifying his soubriquet, Le Boucher d'Albacete.[22] Something of Marty's reputation had evidently reached the Huesca front, where Orwell was serving with the POUM, for when Bob Edwards, Captain of the ILP contingent, tried to persuade Orwell not to leave his colleagues to join the International Brigade, he warned him of the 'virtually dictatorial control wielded in the Brigades by André Marty and the NKVD representatives.' As George Woodcock commented, 'It is unlikely that [Orwell] would long have survived the attentions of Marty's political commissars if he had joined the International Brigades.'[23] Fred Copeman, who commanded the British Battalion for several months, but who later left the Communist Party, describes how the brigade directed that two British brigaders be summarily executed, *pour encourager les autres*, after their unit broke when they unexpectedly came under fire from Italian tanks. The firing squad was made up of volunteers from the British Battalion.[24] He also records that certain British political commissars supported the Political Commissariat in demanding the death penalty for indiscipline.[25] Thus, although the motivation for much of the Terror that assailed the International Brigades (the effects of which Sir Richard Rees saw in Eileen Blair) may be traced back to the NKVD, it can hardly have escaped the notice of British political commissars.[26] Nevertheless, memoirs of those who served in Spain but later left the Party are almost as reticent on this subject as are Rust and Alexander. Charlotte Haldane does hint at the 'obscure circumstances' of Walter Tapsell's death and she records that when she tried to discover how her friend and colleague Arnold Reid (onetime editor of the U.S. Party's journal *New Masses*) had died, she was told by William Rust that he had been 'sold down the river by his own Party' rather than 'killed in action.'[27] Both men, though loyal Communists, had expressed independent opinions. Tapsell had, indeed, been held at Brigade Headquarters on an earlier occasion and only rescued by Copeman, who had instructed the British machine-gun company to come to their aid should the need arise.[28] Of one thing there can be no doubt: genuine Terror haunted Albacete and Barcelona in and after May 1937.

Orwell may have been no political theoretician, especially in 1937; and he certainly did not have the facts available to him that have now surfaced; but, intuitively, he assessed the position accurately. The vision of a socialist society that he experienced on first arriving in Barcelona was not destroyed by Franco; it was betrayed by his Communist allies. As described by him in *Homage to Catalonia*, this has all the inevitability of tragedy. That 'peculiar evil feeling in the air—an atmosphere of suspicion, fear, uncertainty, and veiled hatred' that he found on his final visit to Barcelona[29] was precisely that of the miasma of evil and terror dramatised in his favourite Shakespeare play, *Macbeth*. The effect of that experience marked all else he wrote and did until the day he died.

Two problems remain unsolved. What happened to David L. Wickes? What must he have felt when he read of the charges of espionage and treason arising solely from association with the ILP, especially since he had been recommended by one of the ILP leaders named in the document? Neither the Archive of the British Battalion at the Marx Memorial Library nor Alexander's memory can throw light on what happened to him after this document was received in

Albacete. No D. L. Wickes appeared in 1993 in the 104 volumes of the British telephone directory. He may have died, emigrated, or simply be 'ex-directory.' Did he fail to escape the attentions of the SIM and the Political Commissariat? His name does not appear in Burnett Bolloten's monumental history, *The Spanish Civil War* (1991).

The second problem is based on uncertain ground. In 1995 the editor was told by chance and in confidence when working on a matter that had nothing to do with Orwell, that a former British member of the SIM had stated that whilst engaged in censoring letters in Spain for the SIM he had read a number of Orwell's letters. These, he said, were written in different colours and it was believed that Orwell was surreptitiously sending information to England that laid him open to the charge of espionage. He said no letters survived. The deposition reproduced above mentions the Orwells' correspondence. What whoever laid the charge seemed to find objectionable was that Orwell and Eileen were 'rabid Trotskyists' and that Orwell was writing about ILP matters. The charge of 'trotskyism' could mean almost anything and the accusation that refers to the ILP is no more than guilt by association with an organisation that could only be regarded as reprehensible by the Communists. Orwell refers in a letter to Charles Doran (*386*) that all his *documents* were seized from Eileen's hotel room. These are believed to include his Spanish war diary and it is possible this ended up in the NKVD files in Moscow (though there is no reference to Orwell or Blair in *The KGB's Literary Archive* by Vitaly Shentalinsky, translated by John Crowfoot, 1995). In March 1996, Miklos Kun, grandson of the Hungarian Communist leader, Bela Kun, purged by Stalin about 1939 (see *446, 10.7.39* and *562, 7.8.39*), told the editor that there was a dossier on Orwell in the NKVD archives in Moscow. Unfortunately access was denied before this could be examined.

Orwell sometimes used differently-coloured pencils and inks when writing to differentiate parts of his texts; see, for example, his Payments Book, *2831*. He could, quite innocently, have been driven to that in the front line if writing materials were in short supply. My informant (not himself the former SIM agent) was specific that letters, not diaries, had been censored. If this story is true, and that whilst at the front Orwell was sending back military information (not merely his political opinions and ILP information), it is remarkable that Orwell was not arrested before he left for leave in Barcelona, when he was in Barcelona during the May Events, or on his return to the front. The deposition was drawn up three weeks after Orwell and Eileen left Spain; when he was being sought, just before he escaped to France, he was being sought as a member of the POUM (and perhaps because of his association with the ILP). It has not been possible to check this story, but it is at least probable that what the SIM found objectionable was no more than the 'trotskyite' opinions and the ILP information referred to in the deposition 'coloured' by the pencils in which the notes were written.

1. Shelden, 301–02; U.S.: 274–76, quoting Rees, *For Love or Money* (1960), 153. For Burnett Bolloten's application of the word 'terror,' see his *The Spanish Civil War* (1991), 570–71.
2. Christopher Andrew and Vasili Mitrokhin, *The Mitrokhin Archive* (1999), p. 95, quoting John Costello and Oleg Tsarev, *Deadly Illusions* (1993), p. 281. See Thomas, 442, 523ff., 702–6.
3. Thomas, 649. See also Smith and Mosher, who quote José Diaz declaring on 9 May 1937, shortly after the outbreak of the troubles in Barcelona. 'Our principal enemies are the Fascists. However, these include not only the Fascists themselves, but also Trotskyists. . . . If the government knows this, why doesn't it treat them like the Fascists and exterminate them pitilessly' (132). This government was that of Largo Caballero, the fall of which after the Events of May was 'so swift as to be hardly believable' (Thomas, 673). David T. Cattell notes

that one reason the Communists withdrew their support from Caballero was that 'he refused to carry the attacks on the Anarchists and the *POUM*ists to the extent desired by the Communists . . . he was not willing to resort to terror against them and to the annihilation of the *POUM* altogether' (*Communism and the Spanish Civil War* 1955, 132).

4. See R. Dan Richardson, *Comintern Army: The International Brigades and the Spanish Civil War* (1982), 140 and relevant note 13 (209–10).
5. Thomas, 702–04.
6. Cattell, 137.
7. 'George Orwell and Spain,' *Inside the Myth* (1984), 94.
8. *The Road to Spain* (1981), xii.
9. See Thomas, 702–03, and Robert Conquest, *Inside Stalin's Secret Police: NKVD Politics, 1936–39* (1985), 60.
10. In conversation with Atienza and Alexander, 10 December 1992.
11. Richardson, chap. 8, particularly 119 and 126.
12. Richardson, 94–95. See also Burnett Bolloten, *The Spanish Civil War*, 274–77, 373–75 for an account of the work of the 'corps of commissars.'
13. Richardson, 161–62, 164.
14. *Britons in Spain: The History of the British Battalion of the XVth International Brigade* (1939), 27, 32, 50, 56, 83, 87, 95, 118, 124, 155, 159.
15. *British Volunteers for Liberty: Spain 1936–39* (1982), 74, 121, 130, 149, 158–59, 210. Doran had men executed for political dissidence (Richardson, 129).
16. Rust, 31–32.
17. Of 59,380 foreigners in the brigades, 9,934 died (16.7%) and 7,686 (12.9%) were badly wounded; see Paul Preston, *The Spanish Civil War 1936–39* (1986), 160. Casualty rates, according to Clive Fleay, were: among the French, about 30%; the Americans, 35%; the Germans and Austrians, 40%. Only the Italians suffered much lighter casualties—and they were the only unit not to be commanded by Communists.
18. Alexander, 38.
19. Thomas, 780.
20. *The Road to Spain*, 33.
21. Richardson gives some account of the hounding of those in other countries who had deserted the cause, 171–72.
22. Richardson, 51, 175.
23. George Woodcock, *Orwell's Message: '1984' and the Present* (1984), 71.
24. *Reason in Revolt* (1948), 147–48. It is unclear whether those executed appear in the lists of 'Volunteers for Liberty' who gave their lives.
25. *Reason in Revolt*, 136–40, Copeman, commander at that time, and Aitken, the Political Commissar, opposed such severe measures, fearing they would incite a mutiny among the British (Richardson, 99–101).
26. See Richardson, chap. 10, 'Dissidence, Desertion, and the Terror,' 159–76.
27. Charlotte Haldane, *Truth Will Out* (1949), 127, 137. See also Richardson, 172.
28. *Reason in Revolt*, 136–37.
29. *Homage to Catalonia*, 148.

375. To Leonard Moore

8 July 1937   Typewritten

The two letters referred to in the first line of this letter were from Victor Gollancz, dated 5 July, and from Fredric Warburg,[1] Director, with Roger Senhouse,[2] of Martin Secker & Warburg,[3] of 6 July. Gollancz was responding to a report given him by Norman Collins of a conversation with Orwell on Saturday, 3 July. Although he could not be sure until he had seen the typescript of what was to be *Homage to Catalonia*, he thought it probable that he would not wish to publish the book. Although not a Communist, he said, he felt he should never publish anything 'which could harm the fight against fascism.' He saw the irony of rejecting an account by someone who had been on the spot whilst he sat quietly in his office, and he made plain that he thought Orwell as keenly anti-fascist as anyone; but he had to decide in the light of the information he had. He concluded by saying he hoped Orwell would continue to regard Gollancz as his main publisher, *Homage to Catalonia* being but an exception to the usual arrangement, and he reminded Orwell that they had an agreement to publish his next three novels (see 357). It was as friendly a rejection as one could hope for.

As one door closed with that letter, another opened with Warburg's letter. He told Orwell that John Aplin and Reginald Reynolds, both of the ILP (see 375A), had suggested that 'a book from you would not only be of great interest but of considerable political importance,' and he asked Orwell to discuss this possibility with him.

It is probable that this letter to Moore and that to John Lehmann on the same date were typed by Eileen. The mode of setting out the address, the use of full stops in it, and the placing of the addressee's name at the margin are not typical of Orwell, but are precisely like Eileen's practice in her letters of 17 January and 11 February 1937 (though these styles are not here reproduced). The signature on the letter to Moore is firm, that on the letter to Lehmann is distinctly shaky. The telephone number, Greenwich 0896, was typed on the letter to Moore. It and the address at Greenwich are those of Eileen's brother, Dr. Laurence O'Shaughnessy.

24, Croom's Hill, Greenwich, S.E. 10.

Dear Mr. Moore,
I enclose herewith two letters, one from Gollancz and the other from Seckers'.° I saw Collins and from what he said and from Gollancz's letter I think it very unlikely that he would touch a book of that description. Meanwhile, Seckers' wrote to me on their own initiative and I went to see them. Of course I told them that I was completely in your hands as to business arrangements and could not promise anything, but I saw no harm in discussing with them the probable scope of my book about Spain. They seem very anxious to get hold of it, although I told them that I should have to go back to Gollancz for subsequent books, and they hinted that they were willing to make a good offer. Perhaps you might look into this. One advantage of taking the book to Seckers' is that, although they are rather obscure publishers, they cater for a public that would welcome a book of that kind. I don't know whether you have any means of discovering how James's[4] 'World Revolution' sold, but the people who read that book would be the kind likely to read a book on Spain written from the non-Communist standpoint.

I haven't been too well and have got a sort of blood poisoning in my right hand, a recurrence of something I had at the front. I am staying in London until it is ready for the doctor to deal with it, but with luck I hope to go down to the cottage about Monday.[5]

Yours sincerely,
Eric A. Blair

1. Fredric Warburg (1898–1980), Orwell's second publisher, began his career with George Routledge & Sons in 1922 on coming down from Oxford, 'fit for practically nothing or,

perhaps more accurately, for nothing practical' (*An Occupation for Gentlemen*, 77–83). He joined Martin Secker in 1936 to form Martin Secker & Warburg, so ensuring that this distinguished publishing house did not go out of business. When Gollancz turned down *Homage to Catalonia*, he took it, and when, later, Gollancz and several other publishers declined to publish *Animal Farm*, he brought it out. From then on, Secker & Warburg published all Orwell's books in England. Warburg devotes considerable attention to Orwell in his autobiographies, *An Occupation for Gentlemen* (1959) and *All Authors are Equal* (1973), the title of which is derived from Orwell, who is one of its dedicatees. See also *Orwell Remembered*, 193–99.

2. Roger Senhouse (c. 1900–1965) was educated at Eton (where in his last year he overlapped with Orwell) and Oxford. He joined Martin Secker Ltd in 1936 and remained as a director until he retired in November 1962. He is vividly described by Warburg in *An Occupation for Gentlemen*, 159–65, and, perhaps more graphically, in *All Authors are Equal*, 2–3: ' . . . he seemed larger than life. . . . His rages . . . were uninhibitedly magnificent. . . . Physically brave as a lion, he was something of a moral coward. He had a real appreciation of literature, coupled with a fabulous memory. He was a connoisseur of modern paintings and of rare books. . . . He was one of the best copy editors and proof readers I have ever known. . . . He might truly be described as one of the last of the distinguished line of English eccentrics.'

3. Martin Secker had founded the publishing house that bore his name in 1910, some twenty-five years before Warburg and Senhouse joined him and, in effect, took it over. Among the authors he had published were Compton Mackenzie, Frank Swinnerton, Francis Brett Young, Hugh Walpole, Norman Douglas, James Elroy Flecker, and D. H. Lawrence. He published translations of Thomas Mann's *Buddenbrooks*, Franz Kafka's *The Castle*, and Lion Feuchtwanger's *Jew Süss*. 'The firm was a literary sensation but never succeeded in consolidating itself financially' (*An Occupation for Gentlemen*, 151–52). Secker retired in 1938.

4. C. L. R. James; referred to by Orwell in his review of other books in *Time and Tide*, 9 October 1937; see *401*.

5. Annotated in Moore's office: 'Offer to Crichton-Stuart. Duckworth if Warburg fails.' Patrick Crichton-Stuart, of Gerald Duckworth & Co, wrote to Orwell on 7 July saying that he had lunched with Mrs. Jackson (Elizaveta Fen) and learned he was writing a book on his experiences in Spain. He said he would 'like to handle the MS. here. . . . A candid confession of your experiences, surprises, and disillusionment, would have a very marked effect on the jaded public.' He invited Orwell to meet him when he came to London.

375A. Minutes of the I.L.P. N[ational] A[dministrative]. C[ouncil]

Although not signed by Fenner Brockway until 13 November 1937, these minutes indicate what lay behind Aplin's and Reynolds's approach to Warburg on behalf of the ILP.

Minutes 29   Books on I.L.P. Lines

The Party has been at a great disadvantage owing to the absence of books stating our political philosophy and policy. The "Left Book Club" is a powerful instrument for the C.P. in this respect. I[1] have spent hours on this problem, but the difficulties of finance and organisation are immense. The best we have been able to do so far is to encourage Messrs. Secker and Warburg to publish a number of books. In addition to those already issued the following, among others, are in hand:—

"Power and the State"	by C.A. Smith
"Barcelona Tragedy"	by George Orwell
"Women and the Revolution"	by Ethel Mannin[2]
"From Lenin to Stalin"	by Victor Serge
"Workers' Front"	by Fenner Brockway[3]

The Socialist Bookshop is negotiating with Mr. Warburg for the publication of a "Socialist Library" edition of such books at 2s.6. This ought to have the full backing of the Party. An essential accompaniment of the renaissance of the Party is the publication of books putting our case. It is significant of the emergence and importance of our distinctive philosophy, analysis, and policy that recognition should be given to it in the publishing world. The Publications Committee of the Party should continually consider the possibility of books to be suggested to the publishers.

1. Fenner Brockway; General Secretary of the I.L.P.; see *363, n. 4*.
2. See *575*.
3. Smith's book does not appear to have been published; the others were issued by Secker & Warburg—Orwell's as *Homage to Catalonia*. The title 'Barcelona Tragedy' is not otherwise recorded. Ethel Mannin's *Women and the Revolution* appeared in 1938, as did Brockway's *Workers' Front*. Victor Serge's book had appeared in French, as *De Lénine à Staline*, as a special number of *La Crapouillot*, in Paris in January 1937. It was 67 folio pages. The Secker & Warburg edition, translated by Ralph Manheim, was 254 octavo pages. The same translation was also published in New York, but in 112 pages, by Pioneer Publishers, probably in 1937.

376. To John Lehmann

8 July 1937   Typewritten

The Stores, Wallington, Near Baldock, Herts.

Dear Lehmann,[1]
Thank you for your letter. I would have been very glad to contribute something to *New Writing* No. 4, but of course I have not set pen to paper for months past. No doubt later on I shall have something that might be suitable, and I will send it along in case you can use it for No. 5. I was so glad on getting back to find that *New Writing* is still going.

No, my wound was not very bad. It caused me to lose my voice for a while, but it is coming back and ought to be normal quite soon.[2]

Yours sincerely,
George Orwell

1. John Lehmann (see *312, n. 1*) had written to Orwell on 5 July to ask him if he was writing anything on Spain that would be suitable for *New Writing*, his literary magazine committed to anti-Fascism. ('Shooting an Elephant' had appeared in Number 2.) On 9 July, Lehmann wrote to say he was counting on Orwell for issue five. Orwell did not contribute again to *New Writing* until 'Marrakech' appeared in New Series 3, Christmas 1939.
2. This letter was probably typed by Eileen. Though dated the same as the preceding letter, from Greenwich, it is addressed from Wallington. In addition to the characteristics mentioned in

the headnote to *375*, the underlining of the title *New Writing* is not one of Orwell's characteristics. The injury to Orwell's right hand presumably made writing and typing difficult; see *375*.

377. To Leonard Moore

17 July 1937   Typewritten

The Stores   Wallington   Nr. Baldock   HERTS.

Dear Mr Moore,

I enclose a sort of rough plan[1] of my book on Spain, which may perhaps be of use to Secker's. I have got some articles to do, but meanwhile am making out the more detailed plan for the book, and shall then get down to it. No doubt it will be done by Christmas, but I am not going to hurry it.

I also enclose a letter from Duckworth.[2] I am telling them I leave all that kind of thing to you, and possibly we might fall back on them if necessary. But I believe Secker's would be more suitable if we can come to an understanding with them.

Yours sincerely
Eric Blair

1. An annotation made in Moore's office notes that this rough plan was not enclosed.
2 See *375, n. 5*.

378. 'Spilling the Spanish Beans'

New English Weekly, 29 July and 2 September 1937

I

The Spanish war has probably produced a richer crop of lies than any event since the Great War of 1914–18, but I honestly doubt, in spite of all those hecatombs of nuns who have been raped and crucified before the eyes of "Daily Mail" reporters, whether it is the pro-Fascist newspapers that have done the most harm. It is the left-wing papers, the "News Chronicle" and the "Daily Worker," with their far subtler methods of distortion, that have prevented the British public from grasping the real nature of the struggle.

The fact which these papers have so carefully obscured is that the Spanish Government (including the semi-autonomous Catalan Government) is far more afraid of the revolution than of the Fascists. It is now almost certain that the war will end with some kind of compromise, and there is even reason to doubt whether the Government, which let Bilbao fall without raising a finger, wishes to be too victorious; but there is no doubt whatever about the thoroughness with which it is crushing its own revolutionaries. For some time past a reign of terror—forcible suppression of political parties, a stifling censorship of the Press, ceaseless espionage and mass-imprisonment without trial—has been in progress. When I left Barcelona in late June the jails were bulging; indeed, the regular jails had long since overflowed and the prisoners were being huddled into empty shops and any other temporary dump that could be found for them. But the point to notice is that the people who are in prison now are not Fascists but revolutionaries; they are there not because their opinions are too much to the Right, but because they are too much to the Left. And the people responsible for putting them there are those dreadful revolutionaries at whose very name Garvin[1] quakes in his goloshes—the Communists.

Meanwhile the war against Franco continues, but, except for the poor devils in the front-line trenches, nobody in Government Spain thinks of it as the real war. The real struggle is between revolution and counter-revolution; between the workers who are vainly trying to hold on to a little of what they won in 1936, and the Liberal-Communist bloc who are so successfully taking it away from them. It is unfortunate that so few people in England have yet caught up with the fact that Communism is now a counter-revolutionary force; that Communists everywhere are in alliance with bourgeois reformism and using the whole of their powerful machinery to crush or discredit any party that shows signs of revolutionary tendencies. Hence the grotesque spectacle of Communists assailed as wicked "Reds" by right-wing intellectuals who are in essential agreement with them. Mr. Wyndham Lewis,[2] for instance, ought to love the Communists, at least temporarily. In Spain the Communist-Liberal alliance has been almost completely victorious. Of all that the Spanish workers won for themselves in 1936 nothing solid remains, except for a few collective farms and a certain amount of land seized by the peasants last year; and presumably even the peasants will be sacrificed later, when there is no longer any need to placate them. To see how the present situation arose, one has got to look back to the origins of the civil war.

Franco's bid for power differed from those of Hitler and Mussolini in that it was a military insurrection, comparable to a foreign invasion, and therefore had not much mass backing, though Franco has since been trying to acquire one. Its chief supporters, apart from certain sections of Big Business, were the land-owning aristocracy and the huge, parasitic Church. Obviously a rising of this kind will array against it various forces which are not in agreement on any other point. The peasant and the worker hate feudalism and clericalism; but so does the "liberal" bourgeois, who is not in the least opposed to a more modern version of Fascism, at least so long as it isn't called Fascism. The "liberal" bourgeois is genuinely liberal up to the point where his own interests stop. He stands for the degree of progress implied in the phrase "la carrière ouverte aux talents." For clearly he has no chance to develop in a feudal society where the worker and the peasant are too poor to buy goods, where industry is burdened with huge taxes to pay for bishops' vestments, and where every lucrative job is given as a matter of course to the friend of the catamite of the duke's illegitimate son. Hence, in the face of such a blatant reactionary as Franco, you get for a while a situation in which the worker and the bourgeois, in reality deadly enemies, are fighting side by side. This uneasy alliance is known as the Popular Front (or, in the Communist Press, to give it a spuriously democratic appeal, People's Front). It is a combination with about as much vitality, and about as much right to exist, as a pig with two heads or some other Barnum and Bailey monstrosity.

In any serious emergency the contradiction implied in the Popular Front is bound to make itself felt. For even when the worker and the bourgeois are both fighting against Fascism, they are not fighting for the same things; the bourgeois is fighting for bourgeois democracy, *i.e.*, capitalism, the worker, in so far as he understands the issue, for Socialism. And in the early days of the revolution the Spanish workers understood the issue very well. In the areas where Fascism was defeated they did not content themselves with driving the rebellious troops out of the towns; they also took the opportunity of seizing land and factories and setting up the rough beginnings of a workers' government by means of local committees, workers' militias, police forces, and so forth. They made the mistake, however (possibly because most of the active revolutionaries were Anarchists with a mistrust of all parliaments), of leaving the Republican Government in nominal control. And, in spite of various changes in personnel, every subsequent Government had been of approximately the same bourgeois-reformist character. At the beginning this seemed not to matter, because the Government, especially in Cataloñia, was almost powerless and the bourgeoisie had to lie low or even (this was still happening when I reached Spain in December) to disguise themselves as workers. Later, as power slipped from the hands of the Anarchists into the hands of the Communists and right-wing Socialists, the Government was able to reassert itself, the bourgeoisie came out of hiding and the old division of society into rich and poor reappeared, not much modified. Henceforward every move, except a few dictated by military emergency, was directed towards undoing the work of the first few months of revolution. Out of the many illustrations I could choose, I will cite only one, the breaking-up of the old workers' militias, which were organised on a genuinely democratic system, with officers and men receiving the same pay and mingling on terms of complete equality, and the substitution of the Popular Army (once again, in Communist jargon, "People's Army"), modelled as far as possible on an ordinary bourgeois army, with a privileged officer-caste, immense differences of pay, etc., etc. Needless to say, this is given out as a military necessity, and almost certainly it does make for military efficiency, at least for a short period. But the undoubted purpose of the change was to strike a blow at equalitarianism. In every department the same policy has been followed, with the result that only a year after the outbreak of war and revolution you get what is in effect an ordinary bourgeois State, with, in addition, a reign of terror to preserve the status quo.

This process would probably have gone less far if the struggle could have taken place without foreign interference. But the military weakness of the Government made this impossible. In the face of Franco's foreign mercenaries they were obliged to turn to Russia for help, and though the quantity of arms supplied by Russia has been greatly exaggerated (in my first three months in Spain I saw only one Russian weapon, a solitary machine-gun), the mere fact of their arrival brought the Communists into power. To begin with, the Russian aeroplanes and guns, and the good military qualities of the

International Brigades (not necessarily Communist but under Communist control), immensely raised the Communist prestige. But, more important, since Russia and Mexico were the only countries openly supplying arms, the Russians were able not only to get money for their weapons, but to extort terms as well. Put in their crudest form, the terms were: "Crush the revolution or you get no more arms." The reason usually given for the Russian attitude is that if Russia appeared to be abetting the revolution, the Franco-Soviet pact (and the hoped-for alliance with Great Britain) would be imperilled; it may be, also, that the spectacle of a genuine revolution in Spain would rouse unwanted echoes in Russia. The Communists, of course, deny that any direct pressure has been exerted by the Russian Government. But this, even if true, is hardly relevant, for the Communist Parties of all countries can be taken as carrying out Russian policy; and it is certain that the Spanish Communist Party, plus the right-wing Socialists whom they control, plus the Communist Press of the whole world, have used all their immense and ever-increasing influence upon the side of counter-revolution.

II

In the first half of this article I suggested that the real struggle in Spain, on the Government side, has been between revolution and counter-revolution; that the Government, though anxious enough to avoid being beaten by Franco, has been even more anxious to undo the revolutionary changes with which the outbreak of war was accompanied.

Any Communist would reject this suggestion as mistaken or wilfully dishonest. He would tell you that it is nonsense to talk of the Spanish Government crushing the revolution, because the revolution never happened; and that our job at present is to defeat Fascism and defend democracy. And in this connection it is most important to see just how the Communist anti-revolutionary propaganda works. It is a mistake to think that this has no relevance in England, where the Communist Party is small and comparatively weak. We shall see its relevance quickly enough if England enters into an alliance with the U.S.S.R.; or perhaps even earlier, for the influence of the Communist Party is bound to increase—visibly is increasing—as more and more of the capitalist class realise that latter-day Communism is playing their game.

Broadly speaking, Communist propaganda depends upon terrifying people with the (quite real) horrors of Fascism. It also involves pretending—not in so many words, but by implication—that Fascism has nothing to do with capitalism. Fascism is just a kind of meaningless wickedness, an aberration,"mass sadism," the sort of thing that would happen if you suddenly let loose an asylum-ful° of homicidal maniacs. Present Fascism in this form, and you can mobilise public opinion against it, at any rate for a while, without provoking any revolutionary movement. You can oppose Fascism by bourgeois "democracy," meaning capitalism. But meanwhile you have got to get rid of the troublesome person who points out that Fascism and bourgeois "democracy" are Tweedledum and Tweedledee. You do it at the beginning by calling him an impracticable visionary. You tell him that he is confusing the issue, that he is splitting the anti-Fascist forces, that this is not the moment for revolutionary phrase-mongering, that for the moment we have got to fight against Fascism without enquiring too closely what we are fighting *for*. Later, if he still refuses to shut up, you change your tune and call him a traitor. More exactly, you call him a Trokskyist.

And what is a Trotskyist? This terrible word—in Spain at this moment you can be thrown into jail and kept there indefinitely, without trial, on the mere rumour that you are a Trotskyist—is only beginning to be bandied to and fro in England. We shall be hearing more of it later. The word "Trotskyist" (or "Trotsky-Fascist") is generally used to mean a disguised Fascist who poses as an ultra-revolutionary in order to split the Left-wing forces. But it derives its peculiar power from the fact that it means three separate things. It can mean one who, like Trotsky, wishes for world-revolution; or a member of the actual organization of which Trotsky is head (the only legitimate use of the word); or the disguised Fascist already mentioned. The three meanings can be telescoped one into the other at will. Meaning No. 1 may or may not carry with it meaning No. 2, and meaning No. 2 almost invariably carries with it meaning No. 3. Thus: "XY. has been heard to speak favourably of world-revolution; therefore he is a Trotskyist; therefore he is a Fascist." In Spain, to some extent even in England, *anyone* professing revolutionary Socialism (*i.e.*, professing the things the Communist Party professed until a few years ago) is under suspicion of being a Trotskyist in the pay of Franco or Hitler.

The accusation is a very subtle one, because in any given case, unless one happened to know the contrary, it might be true. A Fascist spy probably *would* disguise himself as a revolutionary. In Spain, everyone whose opinions are to the Left of those of the Communist Party is sooner or later discovered to be a Trotskyist, or at least, a traitor. At the beginning of the war the P.O.U.M., an Opposition Communist party roughly corresponding to the English I.L.P., was an accepted party and supplied a minister to the Catalan Government; later it was expelled from the Government; then it was denounced as Trotskyist; then it was suppressed, every member that the police could lay their hands on being flung into jail.

Until a few months ago the Anarcho-Syndicalists were described as "working loyally" beside the Communists. Then the Anarcho-Syndicalists were levered out of the Government; then it appeared that they were not working so loyally; now they are in the process of becoming traitors. After that will come the turn of the Left-wing Socialists. Caballero, the Left-wing Socialist ex-premier, until May, 1937, the idol of the Communist Press, is already in outer darkness, a Trotskyist and "enemy of the people." And so the game continues. The logical end is a régime in which every opposition party and newspaper is suppressed and every dissentient of any importance is in jail. Of course, such a régime will be Fascism. It will not be the same as the Fascism Franco would impose, it will even be better than Franco's Fascism to the extent of being worth fighting for, but it will be Fascism. Only, being operated by Communists and Liberals, it will be called something different.

Meanwhile, can the war be won? The Communist influence has been against revolutionary chaos and has therefore, apart from the Russian aid,

45

tended to produce greater military efficiency. If the Anarchists saved the Government from August to October, 1936, the Communists have saved it from October onwards. But in organizing the defence they have succeeded in killing enthusiasm (inside Spain, not outside). They made a militarized conscript army possible, but they also made it necessary. It is significant that as early as January of this year voluntary recruiting had practically ceased. A revolutionary army can sometimes win by enthusiasm, but a conscript army has got to win with weapons, and it is unlikely that the Government will ever have a large preponderance of arms unless France intervenes or unless Germany and Italy decide to make off with the Spanish colonies and leave Franco in the lurch. On the whole, a deadlock seems the likeliest thing.

And does the Government seriously intend to win? It does not intend to lose, that is certain. On the other hand, an outright victory, with Franco in flight and the Germans and Italians driven into the sea, would raise difficult problems, some of them too obvious to need mentioning. There is no real evidence and one can only judge by the event, but I suspect that what the Government is playing for is a compromise that would leave the war-situation essentially in being. All prophecies are wrong, therefore this one will be wrong, but I will take a chance and say that though the war may end quite soon or may drag on for years, it will end with Spain divided up, either by actual frontiers or into economic zones. Of course, such a compromise might be claimed as a victory by either side, or by both.

All that I have said in this article would seem entirely commonplace in Spain, or even in France. Yet in England, in spite of the intense interest the Spanish war has aroused, there are very few people who have even heard of the enormous struggle that is going on behind the Government lines. Of course, this is no accident. There has been a quite deliberate conspiracy (I could give detailed instances) to prevent the Spanish situation from being understood. People who ought to know better have lent themselves to the deception on the ground that if you tell the truth about Spain it will be used as Fascist propaganda.

It is easy to see where such cowardice leads. If the British public had been given a truthful account of the Spanish war they would have had an opportunity of learning what Fascism is and how it can be combatted. As it is, the "News Chronicle" version of Fascism as a kind of homicidal mania peculiar to Colonel Blimps bombinating in the economic void has been established more firmly than ever. And thus we are one step nearer to the great war "against Fascism" (cf. 1914, "against militarism") which will allow Fascism, British variety, to be slipped over our necks during the first week.

1. J. L. Garvin was the right-wing editor of *The Observer*, 1908–42.
2. Percy Wyndham Lewis (1882–1957) was a painter, author, satirist, and critic. His review, *Blast* (1914 and 1915), espoused Vorticism. He supported Franco and flirted with Nazism, recanting in 1939; see *Time and Tide*, 17 January and 14 February, and *The Hitler Cult, and How it will End* (1939). In Orwell's words, 'Lewis attacked everyone in turn; indeed, his reputation as a writer rests largely on these attacks'; see 'Inside the Whale,' *600*.

378A. Eileen Blair to John McNair

29 July 1937   Typewritten; carbon copy

Although the letters written by George Kopp to Laurence O'Shaughnessy, Lieutenant-Colonel Burillo, and Eileen that follow this letter are dated 7 and 8 July, their contents were only known to Eileen (and Orwell) on 29 July, and they are therefore best placed here, to provide a context for letters written thereafter (for example, Orwell's letter of 6 August in response to the request by *Left Review* for its booklet *Authors Take Sides on the Spanish War*; see 386A).

The Stores,
Wallington,
Near Baldock, Herts.

Dear John,

Herewith two enclosures. Number 1 is a copy of an ultimatum sent by George Kopp to the Chief of Police in Barcelona, together with the letter which accompanied it to my brother. Number 2 is an extract from a letter written by George Kopp to me, which is to some extent repetition of Number 1 but which gives more details of the conditions of imprisonment and will interest you personally by its reference to individuals.

You will see that the important facts emerging from all the documents are that George intended to go on hunger strike on the 9th or 10th July unless he obtained some satisfaction from the Chief of Police and that he wishes his action to be given publicity. Partly because you know the conditions in Spain, I think you will be best able to decide the manner of this publicity—there is of course a strong possibility that George will be made to suffer for it however it is done, but he will have considered that himself; the main doubt appears to be whether his name should be given or not.

It seems almost certain that the hunger strike has occurred, but actually these letters, although written on the 7th and 8th of July, only reached me this morning. In any case, if there is no further news before the next issue of the New Leader, we may assume that he is on strike and unable to communicate. As for publicity outside the New Leader, you and Fenner will know better than we what hope there is. Judging from Eric's experiences in attempting to publish the most conservative truth, we shall not find the English press at least enthusiastic.[1]

Jock Branthwaite[2] proposed to come over to Letchworth on Monday[3] on a bicycle to hear you speak and to see you. We only have one bicycle; so he will represent the whole party on that day, but you could perhaps tell him what you think. Apparently George Tioli[4] is still being helpful, which is really a magnificent gesture.

I hope to see you myself some time during next week—indeed I hope to see you *here*. Apart from all the sentimental considerations, there are a few hundred things I want to know.

Yours ever,
[Unsigned]

I forgot to say that the two earlier letters to which George refers never arrived.

George Kopp to Dr. Laurence O'Shaughnessy
7 July 1937   Handwritten

Dear Mr O'Shaughnessy,
Will you please transmit to your sister the enclosed copy of a letter I am sending to the Chief of Police and tell her that if I have not received a satisfactory reply to same within 48 hours I shall begin a hunger strike. The way myself and my friends are treated makes it a duty for me to volunteer in the only way of protest which is left to us. In the case I am reduced to this measure, I want my friends in England and the I.L.P. people to give this fact the publicity without which it would be useless. You will receive further news after the 48 hours have elapsed. In the case you have no news within a week, it means I am on strike but put in a place where unable to send messages from.

I have written two letters to Eileen which have been posted at[5] your address and I hope you have been able to forward at least the first; the second, perhaps, never reached you, Ethel Macdonald,[6] who took care of my mail, having been arrested without my knowing if this particular message has been posted before her detention.

I am sorry to have to trouble you with all this, but I agreed with your sister to communicate with her through you. Tell her I am intensely thinking of her and give her my love. Shake hands to Eric.

Sincerely yours
(Signed) George Kopp.

Translation of letter written in Spanish by George Kopp to Lieutenant-Colonel Burillo,[7] Chief of Police, Barcelona, 7 July 1937

I was arrested on the 20th June when I had just got back from Valencia on a military commission and was prepared to carry out the orders of my superior officers. The police-agents who detained me told me that it was a question of furnishing the police with certain information which they believed it was in my power to give them, in order to help them with the investigation of a case of espionage, which I am always ready and delighted to do.

In the course of the day on which I was arrested I addressed to you a letter which I entrusted to the Captain of Assault Guards who was charged with my detention. The reason for this letter was that, in spite of the urgency of the military mission that had been entrusted to me, I had not yet been interrogated at 6 in the evening. I asked you to have me interrogated immediately or, if that was not possible, to do me the favour of receiving me personally.

I presume that my letter has been duly delivered to you, but your answer has never reached me.

It is now eighteen days that I have been imprisoned and I [have] not yet been interrogated, nor have I been told the reason for my arrest—I should rather say the supposed reason, for there is no reason for it in my actions.

I am detained in conditions which are intolerable for any decent individual, and which, in the case of an officer of the Spanish Army who has served for eight months at the front, amount to an insult. I am mixed up with pickpockets, tramps, thieves, fascists and homosexuals. I am, like the rest of the principal prisoners, confined in room where as many as 18 persons are put and where there is only room for 3 or 4; all species of exercise is denied us; the food, consisting of 2 plates of soup and 150 grammes of bread, is distributed at unsuitable hours (4 in the afternoon and 11 at night); the guards, although I personally have no serious ground for complaint and though some of them carry out their duties in a decent manner, treat us like cattle, beating the prisoners and insulting them even to the point of insulting their mothers.

It appears to me that a foreign volunteer, an officer of the Belgian Army, who, after aiding the legal Government of Spain by secretly manufacturing munitions in his own country, comes to enlist in the anti-fascist militia and fights at the front where he is successively commander of a company, a battalion and a regiment, does not merit this kind of treatment. Nor is such treatment merited by the prisoners whom I have seen here and who after weeks of imprisonment do not know why they have been arrested.

I do not know how far the patience of these other prisoners will stretch, nor do I know what opinion they entertain of your sense of justice, but for my own part I have come to the end of the time when I could regard my experiences with good humour, and I have no reason for doubting your integrity. I therefore address you for the second time, asking you to give me the chance of clearing myself of any accusations that can be made against me, and to do so without loss of time, since I am needed at the front.

Awaiting your reply, I remain your servant and that of the anti-fascist cause.

(Signed) Commandante Jorge Kopp.

George Kopp to Eileen Blair
8 July 1937   Typed copy of handwritten original (which has not been traced)

Barcelona, in jail.

I have written you two letters c/o Laurence O'Shaughnessy but am not sure the second one reached you because Ethel Macdonald has been arrested and part of the mail she was in charge of had to be destroyed; it is not known if my letter was in that case.

I still have not been interrogated which is very bad sign; all the others have and most of the questions aimed to establish *my* attitude during the May Days. Absolutely frightened people have made wild statements and some of the Moka's guards state that on each of the Poliorama's towers[8] I had a machine gun and that a heavy barrage of fire and bombs was unceasingly produced from this position during three days. I have written yesterday a sort of ultimatum to Lt. Colonel Burillo, chief of the police, and if I do not get a proper answer within 48 hours, I shall start a hunger strike as a protest not only for my case but principally for the way we all are treated here. The prisoners are beaten and insulted and I know that if actual offence should be done to me, I shall kill the guard with bare fists, which will not be a solution for the rest of us. I have sent to Laurence (for you) the copy of my ultimatum and a short note stating that I want this hunger strike business to be given a broad publicity in England and France and that further news will be sent to let you know if really I was compelled to this measure. Without publicity, my sacrifice will be useless. We are now 18 in the 10′ by 15′ room and not allowed even to take a short walk in the passage. Nobody visits me; David[9] has sent me a French poetry book with the mention "from an almost subterranean swine"; no news from George who is my only hope for sending out of Spain my correspondence. I sent out messages to the Hotel Victoria to be transmitted but do not know if they are duly forwarded. My money has got out last week but Harry Milton[10] lets me share some of his. We are all mixed up with thieves, confidence-tricksters, lousy tramps and homosexuals—and 18 to a small apartment! I am not at all downhearted but feel my patience has definitely gone; in one or another way I shall fight to freedom for my comrades and myself. Harry Milton wins° to be known; I promoted him from a gamma minus to an alpha plus status.

1. Eileen refers to Kingsley Martin's refusal to publish Orwell's review of Franz Borkenau's *The Spanish Cockpit* in *The New Statesman and Nation* because it 'controverts the political policy of the paper.' For a full account of this rejection, see *424*.
2. Jock Branthwaite served with Orwell in Spain. His father was a miner and he recalled copies of *The Road to Wigan Pier* arriving at the front. The book 'didn't seem to offend his working-class sensibilities.' Branthwaite thought Orwell had no political leanings when he arrived in Spain, 'except he was more left than right . . . leaning slightly towards the communists.' He told Stephen Wadhams that Orwell was not a snob: 'I thought he was a wonderful man.' Branthwaite got out of Spain on the last refugee boat from Barcelona for Marseilles. See *Remembering Orwell*, 83–84, 93, 99.
3. For the ILP Conference, 1–13 August 1937; see *385*. Monday was the 1 August.
4. George Tioli is described by Orwell in *Homage to Catalonia* as 'an Italian journalist, a great friend of ours.' He was wounded whilst tending a wounded man in Barcelona in May 1937 (116).
5. at = to
6. Ethel Macdonald (1909–1960), leading social activist in Scotland. During Spanish War English-speaking announcer for CNT in Barcelona; arrested in purge of POUM and CNT, 1937, but escaped and helped others to escape, earning nickname of 'Spanish Pimpernel'.
7. Col. Ricardo Burillo Stolle (1891–1939), described by Thomas as 'a left-wing aristocrat, puritanical, anti-clerical, and romantic, soon became virtually a communist' (245, n. 1). After the Events of May in Barcelona, effective control of the police was handed over to Burillo, who became director-general of security in Catalonia (672). He later commanded the army of Estremadura (779). After Franco's victory, he was one of many who was executed (925).
8. See *Homage to Catalonia*, *CW*, VI, 110 ff.
9. Possibly David Murray, the ILP representative in Valencia at the time of Bob Smillie's death, allegedly from appendicitis. Murray was refused permission to see Smillie's body. See *Homage to Catalonia*, 170.
10. Harry Milton was the only American serving with the British ILP group on the Aragon front.

It was to him ('The American sentry') that Orwell was talking when he was shot through the throat (*Homage to Catalonia*, 138). He regarded Orwell as 'politically virginal' on arrival in Spain. Stafford Cottman recalls that only Milton was proud to boast of being a Trotskyist. Milton and Orwell spent hours discussing politics. He tried, very forcefully, to argue Orwell out of his determination to transfer to the International Brigade on the Madrid front, convinced that the Communists would kill him: 'But he was cool as a cucumber, and he just walked away from me. He was a very disciplined invididual.' See *Remembering Orwell*, 81, 85, 90.

379. Review of *The Spanish Cockpit* by Franz Borkenau; *Volunteer in Spain* by John Sommerfield

Time and Tide, 31 July 1937[1]

Dr. Borkenau has performed a feat which is very difficult at this moment for anyone who knows what is going on in Spain; he has written a book about the Spanish war without losing his temper. Perhaps I am rash in saying that it is the best book yet written on the subject, but I believe that anyone who has recently come from Spain will agree with me. After that horrible atmosphere of espionage and political hatred it is a relief to come upon a book which sums the situation up as calmly and lucidly as this.

Dr. Borkenau is a sociologist and not connected with any political party. He went to Spain with the purpose of doing some "field work" upon a country in revolution, and he made two trips, the first in August, the second in January. In the difference between those two periods, especially the difference in the social atmosphere, the essential history of the Spanish revolution is contained. In August the Government was almost powerless, local soviets were functioning everywhere and the Anarchists were the main revolutionary force; as a result everything was in terrible chaos, the churches were still smouldering and suspected Fascists were being shot in large numbers, but there was everywhere a belief in the revolution, a feeling that the bondage of centuries had been broken. By January power had passed, though not so completely as later, from the Anarchists to the Communists, and the Communists were using every possible method, fair and foul, to stamp out what was left of the revolution. The pre-revolutionary police-forces had been restored, political espionage was growing keener and keener, and it was not long before Dr. Borkenau found himself in jail. Like the majority of political prisoners in Spain, he was never even told what he was accused of; but he was luckier than most in being released after a few days, and even (very few people have managed this lately) saving his documents from the hands of the police. His book ends with a series of essays upon various aspects of the war and the revolution. Anyone who wants to understand the Spanish situation should read the really brilliant final chapter, entitled "Conclusions."

The most important fact that has emerged from the whole business is that the Communist Party is now (presumably for the sake of Russian foreign policy) an anti-revolutionary force. So far from pushing the Spanish Government further towards the Left, the Communist influence has pulled it violently towards the Right. Dr. Borkenau, who is not a revolutionary himself, does not particularly regret this fact; what he does object to is that it is being deliberately concealed. The result is that public opinion throughout Europe still regards the Communists as wicked Reds or heroic revolutionaries as the case may be, while in Spain itself—

> It is at present impossible . . . to discuss openly even the basic facts of the political situation. The fight between the revolutionary and nonrevolutionary principle, as embodied in Anarchists and Communists respectively, is inevitable, because fire and water cannot mix. . . . But as the Press is not even allowed to mention it, nobody is fully aware of the position, and the political antagonism breaks through, not in open fight to win over public opinion, but in backstairs intrigues, assassinations by Anarchist bravos, legal assassinations by Communist police, subdued allusions, rumours. . . . The concealment of the main political facts from the public and the maintenance of this deception by means of censorship and terrorism carries with it far-reaching detrimental effects, which will be felt in the future even more than at present.

If that was true in February, how much truer it is now! When I left Spain in late June the atmosphere in Barcelona, what with the ceaseless arrests, the censored newspapers and the prowling hordes of armed police, was like a nightmare.

Mr. Sommerfield was a member of the International Brigade and fought heroically in the defence of Madrid. *Volunteer in Spain* is the record of his experiences. Seeing that the International Brigade is in some sense fighting for all of us—a thin line of suffering and often ill-armed human beings standing between barbarism and at least comparative decency—it may seem ungracious to say that this book is a piece of sentimental tripe; but so it is. We shall almost certainly get some good books from members of the International Brigade, but we shall have to wait for them until the war is over.

1. Translated by Yvonne Davet for a French journal; see *388* and *399*.

380. To Leonard Moore

31 July 1937   Typewritten

The Stores   Wallington

Dear Mr Moore,

I don't know whether the enclosed[1] is any use to us. I have told the people I am referring the matter to you. Possibly they might care for either "Keep the Aspidistra" or "Wigan Pier," and if so it might be worth coming to an agreement with them, as Harper's seem to have lost interest.

Yours sincerely
Eric A. Blair

1. What this was can only be surmised. It was probably a letter or circular suggesting that Orwell's work might be published by or through the sender in the United States.

381. To Rayner Heppenstall

31 July 1937   Typewritten

The Stores   Wallington   Nr Baldock   HERTS.

Dear Rayner,[1]

Thanks so much for your letter. I was glad to hear from you. I hope Margaret[2] is better. It sounds dreadful, but from what you say I gather that she is at any rate up and about.

We had an interesting but thoroughly bloody time in Spain. Of course I would never have allowed Eileen to come nor probably gone myself if I had foreseen the political developments, especially the suppression of the P.O.U.M., the party in whose militia I was serving. It was a queer business. We started off by being heroic defenders of democracy and ended by slipping over the border with the police panting on our heels.[3] Eileen was wonderful, in fact actually seemed to enjoy it. But though we ourselves got out all right nearly all our friends and acquaintances are in jail and likely to be there indefinitely, not actually charged with anything but suspected of "Trotskyism." The most terrible things were happening even when I left, wholesale arrests, wounded men dragged out of hospitals and thrown into jail, people crammed together in filthy dens where they have hardly room to lie down, prisoners beaten and half starved etc., etc. Meanwhile it is impossible to get a word about this mentioned in the English press, barring the publications of the I.L.P., which is affiliated to the P.O.U.M. I had a most amusing time with the New Statesman about it. As soon as I got out of Spain I wired from France asking if they would like an article and of course they said yes, but when they saw my article was on the suppression of the P.O.U.M. they said they couldn't print it. To sugar the pill they sent me to review a very good book which appeared recently, "The Spanish Cockpit," which blows the gaff pretty well on what has been happening. But once again when they saw my review they couldn't print it as it was "against editorial policy," but they actually offered to pay for the review all the same— practically hush-money. I am also having to change my publisher, at least for this book.[4] Gollancz is of course part of the Communism-racket, and as soon as he heard I had been associated with the P.O.U.M. and Anarchists and had seen the inside of the May riots in Barcelona, he said he did not think he would be able to publish my book, though not a word of it was written yet. I think he must have very astutely foreseen that something of the kind would happen, as when I went to Spain he drew up a contract undertaking to publish my fiction but not other books. However I have two other publishers on my track and I think my agent is being clever and has got them bidding against one another. I have started my book but of course my fingers are all thumbs at present.

My wound was not much, but it was a miracle it did not kill me. The bullet went clean through my neck but missed everything except one vocal cord, or rather the nerve governing it, which is paralysed. At first I had no voice at all, but now the other vocal cord is compensating and the damaged one may or may not recover. My voice is practically normal but I can't shout to any extent. I also can't sing, but people tell me this doesn't matter. I am rather glad to have been hit by a bullet because I think it will happen to us all in the near future and I am glad to know that it doesn't hurt to speak of. What I saw in Spain did not make me cynical but it does make me think that the future is pretty grim. It is evident that people can be deceived by the anti-Fascist stuff exactly as they were deceived by the gallant little Belgium stuff, and when war comes they will walk straight into it. I don't, however, agree with the pacifist attitude, as I believe you do. I still think one must fight for Socialism and against Fascism, I mean fight physically with weapons, only it is as well to discover which is which. I want to meet Holdaway and see what he thinks about the Spanish business. He is the only more or less orthodox Communist I have met whom I could respect. It will disgust me if I find he is spouting the same defence of democracy and Trotsky-Fascist stuff as the others.

I would much like to see you, but I honestly don't think I shall be in London for some time, unless absolutely obliged to go up on business. I am just getting going with my book, which I want to get done by Xmas, also very busy trying to get the garden etc. in trim after being so long away. Anyway keep in touch and let me know your address. I can't get in touch with Rees. He was on the Madrid front and there was practically no communication. I heard from Murray[5] who seemed in the weeps about something. Au revoir.

Yours
Eric

1. Rayner Heppenstall; see *238, n. 2*.
2. Mrs. Rayner Heppenstall.
3. In *Homage to Catalonia*, Orwell tells how his hotel room was searched by six plain-clothes policemen, who took away "every scrap of paper we possessed," except, fortunately, Eileen's and his passports and their cheque-book. He learned later that the police had seized some of his belongings, including a bundle of dirty linen, from the Sanatorium Maurín; see *CW*, VI, 164. More than fifty years later, a document was discovered by Karen Hatherley in the National Historical Archive, in Madrid, that confirmed this precisely; see *374A*.
4. *Homage to Catalonia*.   5. John Middleton Murry; see *95*.

382. 'Eye-Witness in Barcelona'
Controversy: The Socialist Forum,[1] Vol. 1, No. 11 August 1937

This article was published as 'J'ai été témoin à Barcelone . . . ,' translated by Yvonne Davet, in *La Révolution Prolétarienne: Revue Bimensuelle Syndicaliste Révolutionnaire*, No. 255, 25 September 1937. It was this article that *The New Stateman* refused to publish; see Orwell's letters to Rayner Heppenstall, *381*; Geoffrey Gorer, *387*; and Yvonne Davet, *389*.

Orwell's article was preceded in *Controversy* by this note:

George Orwell, author of *The Road to Wigan Pier*, has been fighting with the ILP Contingent on the Aragon front. Here he contributes a personal account of events in Barcelona during the May Days and of the suppression of the POUM in the following month.

I.

Much has already been written about the May riots in Barcelona, and the major events have been carefully tabulated in Fenner Brockway's pamphlet, *The Truth About Barcelona*, which so far as my own knowledge goes is entirely accurate. I think, therefore, that the most useful thing I can do here, in my capacity as eye-witness, is to add a few footnotes upon several of the most-disputed points.

First of all, as to the purpose, if any, of the so-called rising. It has been asserted in the Communist press that the whole thing was a carefully-prepared effort to overthrow the Government and even to hand Catalonia over to the Fascists by provoking foreign intervention in Barcelona. The second part of this suggestion is almost too ridiculous to need refuting. If the P.O.U.M. and the left-wing Anarchists were really in league with the Fascists, why did not the militias at the front walk out and leave a hole in the line? And why did the C.N.T.[2] transport-workers, in spite of the strike, continue sending supplies to the front? I cannot, however, say with certainty that a definite revolutionary intention was not in the minds of a few extremists, especially the Bolshevik Leninists (usually called Trotskyists) whose pamphlets were handed round the barricades. What I can say is that the ordinary rank and file behind the barricades never for an instant thought of themselves as taking part in a revolution. We thought, all of us, that we were simply defending ourselves against an attempted *coup d'état* by the Civil Guards,[3] who had forcibly seized the Telephone Exchange and might seize some more of the workers' buildings if we did not show ourselves willing to fight. My reading of the situation, derived from what people were actually doing and saying at the time, is this:—

The workers came into the streets in a spontaneous defensive movement, and they only consciously wanted two things: the handing-back of the Telephone Exchange and the disarming of the hated Civil Guards. In addition there was the resentment caused by the growing poverty in Barcelona and the luxurious life lived by the bourgeoisie. But it is probable that the opportunity to overthrow the Catalan Government existed if there had been a leader to take advantage of it. It seems to be widely agreed that on the third day the workers were in a position to take control of the city; certainly the Civil Guards were greatly demoralised and were surrendering in large numbers. And though the Valencia Government could send fresh troops to crush the workers (they did send 6,000 Assault Guards when the fighting was over), they could not maintain those troops in Barcelona if the transport-workers chose not to supply them. But in fact no resolute revolutionary leadership existed. The Anarchist leaders disowned the whole thing and said "Go back to work," and the P.O.U.M. leaders took an uncertain line. The orders sent to us at the P.O.U.M. barricades, direct from the P.O.U.M. leadership, were to stand by the C.N.T., but not to fire unless we were fired on ourselves or our buildings attacked. (I personally was fired at a number of times, but never fired back.) Consequently, as food ran short, the workers began to trickle back to work; and, of course, once they were safely dispersed, the reprisals began. Whether the revolutionary opportunity *ought* to have been taken advantage of is another question. Speaking solely for myself, I should answer "No." To begin with it is doubtful whether the workers could have maintained power for more than a few weeks; and, secondly, it might well have meant losing the war against Franco. On the other hand the essentially defensive action taken by the workers was perfectly correct; war or no war, they had a right to defend what they had won in July, 1936. It may be, of course, that the revolution was finally lost in those few days in May. But I still think it was a little better, though only a very little, to lose the revolution than to lose the war.

Secondly, as to the people involved. The Communist press took the line, almost from the start, of pretending that the "rising" was wholly or almost wholly the work of the P.O.U.M. (aided by "a few irresponsible hooligans," according to the New York *Daily Worker*). Anyone who was in Barcelona at the time knows that this is an absurdity. The enormous majority of the people behind the barricades were ordinary C.N.T. workers. And this point is of importance, for it was as a scapegoat for the May riots that the P.O.U.M. was recently suppressed; the four hundred or more P.O.U.M. supporters who are in the filthy, verminous Barcelona jails at this moment, are there ostensibly for their share in the May riots. It is worth pointing, therefore, to two good reasons why the P.O.U.M. were not and could not have been the prime movers. In the first place, the P.O.U.M. was a very small party. If one throws in Party members, militiamen on leave, and helpers and sympathisers of all kinds, the number of P.O.U.M. supporters on the streets could not have been anywhere near ten thousand—probably not five thousand; but the disturbances manifestly involved scores of thousands of people. Secondly, there was a general or nearly general strike for several days; but the P.O.U.M., as such, had no power to call a strike, and the strike could not have happened if the rank and file of the C.N.T. had not wanted it. As to those involved on the other side, the London *Daily Worker* had the impudence to suggest in one issue that the "rising" was suppressed by the Popular Army. Everyone in Barcelona knew, and the *Daily Worker* must have known as well, that the Popular Army remained neutral and the troops stayed in their barracks throughout the disturbances. A few soldiers, however, did take part as individuals; I saw a couple at one of the P.O.U.M. barricades.

Thirdly, as to the stores of arms which the P.O.U.M. are supposed to have been hoarding in Barcelona. This story has been repeated so often that even a normally critical observer like H. N. Brailsford accepts it without any investigation and speaks of the "tanks and guns" which the P.O.U.M. had "stolen from Government arsenals" (*New Statesman*, May 22).[4] As a matter of fact the P.O.U.M. possessed pitifully few weapons, either at the front or in the rear. During the street-fighting I was at all three of the principal strongholds of the P.O.U.M., the Executive Building, the Comité Local and the Hotel Falcón. It is worth recording in detail what armaments these buildings contained. There were in all about 80 rifles, some of them defective, besides a few obsolete guns of various patterns, all useless because there were no cartridges for them. Of rifle ammunition there was about 50 rounds for each weapon. There were no machine-guns, no pistols and no pistol ammunition. There were a few cases of hand-grenades, but these were sent to us by the C.N.T. after the fighting started. A highly-placed militia officer afterwards gave me his opinion that in the whole of Barcelona the P.O.U.M. possessed about a hundred and fifty rifles and *one* machine-gun. This, it will be seen, was barely sufficient for the armed guards which at that time all parties, P.S.U.C., P.O.U.M., and C.N.T.-F.A.I. alike, placed on their principal buildings. Possibly it may be said that even in the May riots the P.O.U.M. were still hiding their weapons. But in that case what becomes of the claim that the May riots were a P.O.U.M. rising intended to overthrow the Government?

In reality, by far the worst offenders in this matter of keeping weapons from the front, were the Government themselves. The infantry on the Aragon front were far worse-armed than an English public school O.T.C.,[5] but the rear-line troops, the Civil Guards, Assault Guards and Carabineros, who were not intended for the front, but were used to "preserve order" (i.e., overawe the workers) in the rear, were armed to the teeth. The troops on the Aragon front had worn-out Mauser rifles, which usually jammed after five shots, approximately one machine-gun to fifty men, and one pistol or revolver to about thirty men. These weapons, so necessary in trench warfare, were not issued by the Government and could only be bought illegally and with the greatest difficulty. The Assault Guards were armed with brand-new Russian rifles; in addition, every man was issued with an automatic pistol, and there was one sub-machine-gun between ten or a dozen men. These facts speak for themselves. A Government which sends boys of fifteen to the front with rifles forty years old, and keeps its biggest men and newest weapons in the rear, is manifestly more afraid of the revolution than of the Fascists. Hence the feeble war-policy of the past six months, and hence the compromise with which the war will almost certainly end.

II.

When the P.O.U.M., the Left Opposition (so-called Trotskyist) off-shoot of Spanish Communism, was suppressed on June 16–17, the fact in itself surprised nobody. Ever since May, or even since February, it had been obvious that the P.O.U.M. would be "liquidated" if the Communists could bring it about. Nevertheless, the suddenness of the suppressive action, and the mixture of treachery and brutality with which it was carried out, took everyone, even the leaders, completely unaware.

Ostensibly the Party was suppressed on the charge, which has been repeated for months in the Communist press though not taken seriously by anyone inside Spain, that the P.O.U.M. leaders were in the pay of the Fascists. On June 16 Andrés Nin, the leader of the Party, was arrested in his office. The same night, before any proclamation had been made, the police raided the Hotel Falcón, a sort of boarding-house maintained by the P.O.U.M. and used chiefly by militiamen on leave, and arrested everybody in it on no particular charge. Next morning the P.O.U.M. was declared illegal and all P.O.U.M. buildings, not only offices, bookstalls, etc., but even libraries and sanatoriums for wounded men, were seized by the police. Within a few days all or almost all of the forty members of the Executive Committee were under arrest. One or two who succeeded in going into hiding were made to give themselves up by the device, borrowed from the Fascists, of seizing their wives as hostages. Nin was transferred to Valencia and thence to Madrid, and put on trial for selling military information to the enemy. Needless to say the usual "confessions," mysterious letters written in invisible ink, and other "evidence" were forthcoming in such profusion as to make it reasonably likely that they had been prepared beforehand. As early as June 19 the news reached Barcelona, via Valencia, that Nin had been shot. This report was, we hope, untrue, but it hardly needs pointing out that the Valencia Government will be obliged to shoot a number, perhaps a dozen, of the P.O.U.M. leaders if it expects its charges to be taken seriously.[6]

Meanwhile, the rank and file of the Party, not merely party members, but soldiers in the P.O.U.M. militia and sympathisers and helpers of all kinds, were being thrown into prison as fast as the police could lay hands on them. Probably it would be impossible to get hold of accurate figures, but there is reason to think that during the first week there were 400 arrests in Barcelona alone; certainly the jails were so full that large numbers of prisoners had to be confined in shops and other temporary dumps. So far as I could discover, no discrimination was made in the arrests between those who had been concerned in the May riots and those who had not. In effect, the outlawry of the P.O.U.M. was made retrospective; the P.O.U.M. was now illegal, and therefore one was breaking the law by having ever belonged to it. The police even went to the length of arresting the wounded men in the sanatoriums. Among the prisoners in one of the jails I saw, for instance, two men of my acquaintance with amputated legs; also a child of not more than twelve years of age.

One has got to remember, too, just what imprisonment means in Spain at this moment. Apart from the frightful overcrowding of the temporary jails, the insanitary conditions, the lack of light and air and the filthy food, there is the complete absence of anything that we should regard as legality. There is, for instance, no nonsense about Habeas Corpus. According to the present law, or at any rate the present practice, you can be imprisoned for an indefinite time not merely without being tried but even without being charged; and until you have been charged the authorities can, if they choose, keep you "incommunicado"—that is, without the right to communicate with a lawyer or anyone else in the outside world. It is easy to see how much the "confessions" obtained in such circumstances are worth. The situation is all the worse for the poorer prisoners because the P.O.U.M. Red Aid, which normally furnishes prisoners with legal advice, has been suppressed along with the other P.O.U.M. institutions.

But perhaps the most odious feature of the whole business was the fact that all news of what had happened was deliberately concealed, certainly for five days, and I believe for longer, from the troops on the Aragon front. As it happened, I was at the front from June 15 to 20. I had got to see a medical board and in doing so to visit various towns behind the front line, Siétamo, Barbastro, Monzón, etc. In all these places the P.O.U.M. militia headquarters, Red Aid centres and the like were functioning normally, and as far down the line as Lérida (only about 100 miles from Barcelona) and as late as June 20, not a soul had heard that the P.O.U.M. had been suppressed. All word of it had been kept out of the Barcelona papers, although, of course, the Valencia papers (which do not get to the Aragon front) were flaming with the story of Nin's "treachery." Together with a number of others I had the disagreeable experience of getting back to Barcelona to find that the P.O.U.M. had been suppressed in my absence. Luckily I was warned just in time and managed to make myself scarce, but other[s] were not so fortunate. Every P.O.U.M. militiaman who came down the line at this period had the choice of going straight into hiding or into jail—a really pleasant reception after three or four months in the front line. The motive for all this is obvious: the attack on Huesca was just beginning, and presumably the Government feared that if the P.O.U.M. militia knew what was happening they might refuse to march. I do not, as a matter of fact, believe that the loyalty of the militia would have been affected; still, they had a right to know the truth. There is something unspeakably ugly in sending men into battle (when I left Siétamo the fight was beginning and the first wounded were jolting in the ambulances down the abominable roads) and at the same time concealing from them that behind their back their party was being suppressed, their leaders denounced as traitors and their friends and relatives thrown into prison.

The P.O.U.M. was by far the smallest of the revolutionary parties, and its suppression affects comparatively few people. In all probability the sum total of punishments will be a score or so of people shot or sentenced to long terms of imprisonment, a few hundreds ruined and a few thousands temporarily persecuted. Nevertheless, its suppression is symptomatically important. To begin with it should make clear to the outside world, what was already obvious to many observers in Spain, that the present Government has more points of resemblance to Fascism than points of difference. (This does not mean that it is not worth fighting for as against the more naked Fascism of Franco and Hitler. I myself had grasped by May the Fascist tendency of the Government, but I was willing to go back to the front and in fact did so.) Secondly, the elimination of the P.O.U.M. gives warning of the impending attack upon the Anarchists. These are the real enemy whom the Communists fear as they never feared the numerically insignificant P.O.U.M. The Anarchist leaders have now had a demonstration of the methods likely to be used against them; the only hope for the revolution, and probably for victory in the war, is that they will profit by the lesson and get ready to defend themselves in time.

1. Raymond Challinor, in *Bulletin of the Society for the Study of Labour History*, 54, Winter 1989, 40, states: 'Originally, *Controversy* was begun after the Independent Labour Party disaffiliated from the Labour Party in 1932. At first, it functioned as the Party's internal bulletin. . . . In 1936, however, its character completely changed. From then onwards, *Controversy* sought to be—and largely was—a journal where the many diverse views held within the working-class movement could be openly discussed without rancour.' To acknowledge that its readership was much wider than that of the ILP, it changed its name in 1939 to *Left Forum* and then to *Left*. It ceased publication in May 1950. Challinor attributes much of its success to the character of its editor, Dr. C. A. Smith, a London headmaster and later a University of London lecturer. Among those writing for the journal he lists Frank Borkenau (see *379*), Max Eastman, Sidney Hook, Jomo Kenyatta, Victor Serge (see *1046, n. 7*), August Thalheimer (see p. 398, *n. 6*), Jay Lovestone, George Padmore, Marceau Pivert (see *386*), and Simone Weil.
2. For the significance of the groups represented by initials, see *Homage to Catalonia, CW*, VI, Appendix I. Relevant extracts and part of a letter from Hugh Thomas to the editors of *CJEL* are reprinted as a note to Orwell's 'Notes on the Spanish Militias'; see *439*.
3. Orwell later realised that it was not the Civil Guards, but a local section of Assault Guards, who seized the Barcelona Telephone Exchange. Shortly before he died, he gave instructions that the text of *Homage to Catalonia* be changed; see *CW*, VI, Textual Note, especially 253.
4. For Orwell's later thoughts, see letters to H. N. Brailsford, 10 and 18 December 1937, *413A* and *414B*, vol xx, final appendix.
5. Officers' Training Corps, associated with the public-school system in England.
6. For Andrés Nin (1892–1937), see *519, n. 31*. He 'underwent the customary Soviet interrogation' suffered by those who were claimed to be 'traitors to the cause' and then murdered, possibly in the royal park just north of Madrid. In later months the remaining POUM leaders were interrogated and tortured, some in the convent of Saint Ursula in Barcelona, 'the Dachau of republican Spain,' as one POUM survivor described it. Nin was the only POUM leader to be murdered, however. Bob Smillie was thrown into jail in Valencia without just cause (see *Homage to Catalonia, CW*, VI, 149), where he died, according to his captors, of appendicitis; see *385. n. 3*. Thomas gives this account of Nin's probable fate: 'He . . . refused to sign documents admitting his guilt and that of his friends. . . . What should they do? . . . the Italian Vidali (Carlos Contreras) suggested that a 'nazi' attack to liberate Nin should be simulated. So, one dark night, probably 22 or 23 June, ten German members of the International Brigade assaulted the house in Alcalá where Nin was held. . . . Nin was taken away and murdered. . . . His refusal to admit his guilt probably saved the lives of his friends' (705).

383. Abstracts of Reports on the Spanish Civil War in the *Daily Worker* and the *News Chronicle*, 1936–37

[July and August 1937?]

In a footnote to *Homage to Catalonia*, Orwell remarks, 'In connection with this book I have had to go through the files of a good many English papers' (*CW*, VI, 208). Some of the notes he made in his search have survived; see *519*.

The *Daily Worker*, founded 1 January 1930, supported the Communist Party. It was suppressed by government order from 29 January 1941 to 6 September 1942, and incorporated in the *Morning Star* 23 April 1966. The *News Chronicle* began life as the *Daily News* 21 January 1846 and, after various amalgamations, became the *News Chronicle* 2 January 1930; it ceased publication 17 October 1960. When Orwell summarised its reports, it was, unofficially, a Liberal newspaper.

384. To Amy Charlesworth

1 August 1937   Typewritten

The Stores   Wallington   Nr. Baldock   HERTS.

Dear Miss Charlesworth,[1]

Once again a long delay in answering your letter, I am afraid. I can only excuse myself by saying I had a lot to do in the month after getting back from Spain, and that I have only recently got my health back. The damaged hand and Spain were only indirectly connected—ie. I had blood-poisoning at the front and this recurred. It is all right now. The wound I got in Spain was a bullet through the neck, but it is all healed up and well except that I have lost part of my voice.

You asked about the situation in Spain, and whether the rebels had not a case. I should not say that the rebels had *no* case, unless you believe that it is always wrong to rebel against a legally-established government, which in practice nobody does. Roughly speaking I should say that the rebels stand for two things that are more or less contradictory—for of course Franco's side, like the Government side, consists of various parties who frequently quarrel bitterly among themselves. They stand on the one hand for an earlier form of society, feudalism, the Roman Catholic Church and so forth, and on the other hand for Fascism, which means an immensely regimented and centralised form of government, with certain features in common with Socialism, in that it means suppression of a good deal of private property and private enterprise, but always ultimately in the interest of the bigger capitalists, and therefore completely unsocialistic. I am wholeheartedly against both of these ideas, but it is fair to say that a case can be made out for both of them. Some of the Catholic writers, such as Chesterton, Christopher Dawson etc., can make out a very appealing though not logically convincing case for a more primitive form of society. I would not say that there is any case for Fascism itself, but I do think there is a case for many individual Fascists. I had a lot to say about this in my last book. Roughly speaking I would say that Fascism has a great appeal for certain simple and decent people who genuinely want to see justice done to the working class and do not grasp that they are being used as tools by the big capitalists. It would be absurd to imagine that every man on Franco's side is a demon. But though the Fascist atrocities have probably been exaggerated, some of them undoubtedly happened and I think one can be certain that the Government has conducted the war much more humanely than the Fascists, even to the point of losing military opportunities, eg. by being unwilling to bomb towns where there were civilian populations.

Meanwhile on the Government side there is a very complicated situation and the most terrible things are happening, which have been kept out of the English papers and which I can't properly explain without expanding this letter into the size of a pamphlet. Perhaps I can summarise it like this: the Spanish war was not only a war but a revolution. When the Fascist rising broke out, the workers in various of the big towns, especially in Catalonia, not only defeated the local Fascists but took the opportunity of seizing land, factories etc. and setting up a rough form of workers' government. Ever since then, and especially since about December of last year, the real struggle of the Spanish Government has been to crush the revolution and put things back to where they were before. They have now more or less succeeded and there is now going on a most dreadful reign of terror directed against everyone who is suspected of genuinely revolutionary leanings. It is a little difficult for English people to understand, in so much that the Communist Party, which we are accustomed to regard as revolutionary, has been the principal mover in this, and is now more or less in charge of the Spanish Government, though not officially, and is conducting the reign of terror. This had begun when I left Spain on June 23rd. The party in whose militia I had been serving, the P.O.U.M., was suppressed and every person connected with it whom the police could lay their hands on, including even wounded men in the sanatoriums, was thrown into jail without any kind of trial. I was lucky enough to get out of Spain, but many of my friends and acquaintances are still in jail and I am afraid there is the greatest fear that some of them will be shot, not for any definite offence but for opposition to the Communist Party. If you want to keep in touch with Spanish affairs, the only paper you can more or less rely on the° tell you the truth is the New Leader. Or if you come across it read an excellent book that appeared recently called "The Spanish Cockpit," by Franz Borkenau. The chapters at the end of this sum up the situation much better than I could.

This seems to be quite a long letter after all. I must apologise for lecturing you about Spain, but what I saw there has upset me so badly that I talk and write about it to everybody. I am doing a book about it, of course. I suppose it will be out about next March.

Yours very sincerely,
Eric Blair
("George Orwell".)

P.S. [handwritten] I might have told you before that George Orwell is only a pen-name. I would much like to meet you some time. You sound the kind of person I like to know, but goodness knows when I shall be in your part of the world. I am keeping your address. Let me know if you ever move down London-way.

1. Amy Charlesworth (1904–1945), in a letter to Orwell of 6 October 1937, from Flixton, near Manchester, told him she had been married young, had had two children, had left her husband because he struck her so often, and was training to be a health visitor. She remarried, and when she wrote to Orwell in June 1944, she signed herself Mrs. Gerry Byrne; see Orwell's replies to her 23 June and 28 October 1944, *2493, 2569*. Her husband wrote to Orwell in June 1945 to tell him that his wife had died three months earlier, see *2688*. He may have been Gerald Byrne (1905–), a crime reporter for the *Daily Herald* in the mid-1930s.

385. ILP Conference, 1–13 August 1937

The Independent Labour Party held its annual conference at Letchworth in August 1937. The opening lecture was given on Sunday morning, 1 August, by the party chairman, James Maxton, M.P.[1] on 'The Nature of Capitalism.' Other speakers during the fortnight included Jack Huntz, of the London Divisional Council, on 'The Fight for Socialism'; Campbell Stephen, M.P.,[2] on 'Palestine'; C. A. Smith, editor of *Controversy* (see *382, n. 1*), on 'The State'; and a 'Mr. White' (a pseudonym), described in the *Hertfordshire Express*, 14 August 1937, as 'a prominent German revolutionary,' on 'The International Working Class struggle.' Mr. White reported that a simple American friend of his with no political interest maintained after talking to 'all sorts of people in the Rhineland . . . that at least 70 per cent of the people were against Hitler.' In response to questions, he said that 'while there was a growing feeling against the Nazi regime, the anti-Hitler illegal organisations were getting weaker.'

Spain figured largely at the conference. John McNair, ILP representative in Spain, (see *363, n. 5*), gave a report on 2 August, on nine months of fighting. Bob Edwards, commander of ILP contingent (see *363, n. 2*), was in the chair and 'there were several men from the fighting lines present including Mr. Eric Blair ('George Orwell,' author of 'The Road to Wigan Pier'), who is recuperating from wounds' (*Hertfordshire Express*, 7 August 1937). An hour-long film, *Fury Over Spain*, made under the auspices of the Confederación Nacional del Trabajo (CNT), was shown twice, on 6 and 11 August. (Orwell noted in *Homage to Catalonia* that the POUM militiamen with whom he served were mostly CNT members, *CW*, VI, 203.) Douglas Moyle told Ian Angus, 18 February 1970, that Orwell was very unwilling to get on the platform and talk about his time at the front. He did not stay at Letchworth overnight, refused to be lionised, and did not wish to be used for political purposes. He was much opposed to what Fenner Brockway had been putting into *New Leader* articles.

On Thursday, 5 August, there was a two-minute silence for two ILP members: Arthur Chambers, killed attempting to bring in wounded men, and Bob Smillie, twenty-two, 'who died in Hospital.' Smillie had spoken at the ILP Letchworth Conference in 1935.[3] At this meeting, eye-witnesses gave accounts of experiences in the front line. They were: Orwell, Douglas Moyle, John Branthwaite, and Paddy Donovan, 'a former member of the Irish Republican Congress, who went to Spain as a supporter of the Communist Party but returned a supporter of the policy of the P.O.U.M.' (*Hertfordshire Express*, 14 August 1937). Plate 17 in Crick shows Orwell at the conference with some of those who fought in Spain.

1. James Maxton (1885–1946) was an Independent Labour M.P., 1922–46, and Chairman of the ILP, 1926–31, 1934–39. See also *397, 470, 2405, n. 4*.
2. Campbell Stephen (1884–1947) was Minister of the United Free Church, Ardrossan, 1911–18, a barrister, and Independent Labour M.P., 1922–31, 1935–47.
3. Orwell gives an account of Smillie's death in *Homage to Catalonia, CW*, VI, 170–71. He assumed that Smillie had been shot in prison, but it was later stated that he had died of appendicitis. The local ILP representative, David Murray, was refused permission to see Smillie's body, which 'may have been due to pure spite.' Orwell concludes: 'Smillie's death is not a thing I can easily forgive. Here was this brave and gifted boy, who had thrown up his career at Glasgow University in order to come and fight against Fascism, and who, as I saw for myself, had done his job at the front with faultless courage and willingness; and all they could find to do with him was to fling him into jail and let him die like a neglected animal.'

386. To Charles Doran

2 August 1937   Typewritten

The Stores   Wallington   Nr. Baldock   <u>HERTS</u>.

Dear Doran,[1]

I don't know your address, but I expect they will know it at the I.L.P. summer school, where I am going on Thursday. I was also there yesterday, to hear John MacNair° speak.

I was very relieved when I saw young Jock Branthwaite, who has been staying with us, and learned that all of you who wished to had got safely out of Spain. I came up to the front on June 15th to get my medical discharge, but couldn't come up to the line to see you because they kept sending me about from hospital to hospital. I got back to Barcelona to find that the P.O.U.M. had been suppressed in my absence, and they had kept it from the troops so successfully that on June 20th as far down the line as Lerida not a soul had heard about it, though the suppression had taken place on the 16th–17th. My first intimation was walking into the Hotel Continental and having Eileen and a Frenchman named Pivert,[2] who was a very good friend to everyone during the trouble, rush up to me, seize me each by one arm and tell me to get out. Kopp had just recently been arrested in the Continental owing to the staff ringing up the police and giving him away. MacNair, Cottman and I had to spend several days on the run, sleeping in ruined churches etc., but Eileen stayed in the hotel and, beyond having her room searched and all my documents seized, was not molested, possibly because the police were using her as a decoy duck for MacNair and me. We slipped away very suddenly on the morning of the 23rd, and crossed the frontier without much difficulty. Luckily there was a first class and a dining car on the train, and we did our best to look like ordinary English tourists, which was the safest thing to do. In Barcelona one was fairly safe during the daytime, and Eileen and I visited Kopp several times in the filthy den where he and scores of others, including Milton,[3] were imprisoned. The police had actually gone to the length of arresting the wounded P.O.U.M. men out of the Maurin, and I saw two men in the jail with amputated legs; also a boy of about ten. A few days ago we got some letters, dated July 7th, which Kopp had somehow managed to send out of Spain. They included a letter of protest to the Chief of Police. He said that not only had he and all the others been imprisoned for 18 days (much longer now, of course) without any trial or charge, but that they were being confined in places where they had hardly room to lie down, were half starved and in many cases beaten and insulted. We sent the letter on to MacNair, and I believe after discussing the matter Maxton has arranged to see the Spanish ambassador and tell him that if something is not done, at any rate for the foreign prisoners, he will spill the beans in Parliament. MacNair also tells me that there is a credible report in the French papers that the body of Nin, also I think other P.O.U.M. leaders, has been found shot in Madrid. I suppose it will be "suicide," or perhaps appendicitis again.[4]

Meanwhile it seems almost impossible to get anything printed about all this. As soon as I crossed the French frontier I wired to the New Statesman asking if they would like an article, and they wired back Yes, but when they saw my article (on the suppression of the P.O.U.M.), they said they were sorry but they could not publish the article, as it would "cause trouble." To sugar the pill they sent me to review a very good book that was published recently, "The Spanish Cockpit." But once again when they saw the review they were sorry they could not publish it as it "controverted editorial policy," but they actually offered to pay for the article though unprinted— practically hush-money, you see. I am also having to change my publisher. As soon as Gollancz heard I had been with the P.O.U.M. he said he was afraid he would not be able to publish my book on Spain, though not a word of it was written yet. I haven't definitely fixed up, but shall probably take it to Secker. It ought to come out about March if all is well.

I went up to Bristol with some others to take part in a protest meeting about Stafford Cottman being expelled from the Y.C.L.[5] with the words "we brand him as an enemy of the working class" and similar expressions. Since then I heard that the Cottmans' house had been shadowed by members of the Y.C.L. who attempt to question everyone who comes in and out. What a show! To think that we started off as heroic defenders of democracy and only six months later were Trotsky-Fascists sneaking over the border with the police on our heels. Meanwhile being a Trotsky-Fascist doesn't seem to help us with the pro-Fascists in this country. This afternoon Eileen and I had a visit from the vicar, who doesn't at all approve of our having been on the Government side. Of course we had to own up that it was true about the burning of the churches, but he cheered up a lot on hearing they were only Roman Catholic churches.

Let me know how you get on. Eileen wishes to be remembered.

Yours
Eric Blair

P.S. [handwritten] I forgot to say that when in Barcelona I wanted greatly to write to you all & warn you, but I dared not, because I thought any such letter would simply draw undesirable attention to the man it was addressed to.

1. This letter and that dated 26 November 1938, *505*, were donated by Doran's widow, Mrs. Bertha Doran, to Waverley Secondary School, Drumchapel, Glasgow, in December 1974. They are reproduced here with her kind permission. She and Dr. James D. Young supplied details of Doran's life. Charles Doran (1894–1974) was born in Dublin and moved to Glasgow in 1915. After serving in World War I, he became active in Guy Aldred's Anti-Parliamentary Communist Federation. He joined the ILP in the early 1930s and served with Orwell in the POUM in Spain in 1937. They exchanged letters in 1938–39; but no others have been traced. Doran opposed World War II and joined a small anarchist group led by Willie MacDougall that engaged in anti-militarist and revolutionary socialist propaganda throughout the war. He also contributed to MacDougall's newspaper, the *Pioneer News*. In 1983 Mrs. Doran told Dr. Young that her late husband was impressed by Orwell's modesty and sincerity. 'I remember Charlie saying that Orwell was not an argumentative sort of person. He [Charlie] might voice an opinion about something, hoping to provoke Orwell into agreeing or disagreeing, but Orwell would just say: "You might be right, Doran!" Orwell at that time had not read Marx.' Alex Zwerdling, in *Orwell and the Left* (1974, 20), states that Orwell's work shows he had read Marx with care and understanding; he quotes from Richard Rees, *George Orwell: Fugitive from the Camp of Victory* (1961), who tells how Orwell astonished everyone at the Adelphi Summer

School, 1936, by his knowledge of Marx (147). See Crick, 613, n. 49. By the mid-1940s, according to Mrs. Doran, 'Charlie *classed* him [Orwell] as a rebel—not a revolutionary—who was dissatisfied with the Establishment, while remaining part of it' (*Bulletin of the Society for the Study of Labour History*, 51, pt. 1, April 1986, 15–17). When typing this letter, Orwell ran its first words on immediately after 'Dear Doran.'

2. Marceau Pivert was a contributor to *Controversy*; see *382, n. 1.*

3. Michael Milton, of the ILP contingent.

4. See *382, n. 5.*

5. Young Communist League.

386A. Unpublished Response to *Authors Take Sides on the Spanish War*

[3–6 August 1937]   Typewritten copy

In June 1937, *Left Review* solicited reactions of writers to the Spanish civil war. A questionnaire, prefaced by an appeal to writers to take sides, 'For it is impossible any longer to take no side,' was sent out by Nancy Cunard.[1] The appeal was issued over the names of twelve writers, who included Louis Aragon, W. H. Auden, Heinrich Mann, Ivor Montagu, Stephen Spender, Tristan Tzara, and Nancy Cunard (who processed the replies). Lawrence & Wishart published the result as a pamphlet, *Authors Take Sides on the Spanish War*, in December 1937. Authors were asked, 'Are you for, or against, the legal Government and People of Republican Spain? Are you for, or against, Franco and Fascism?' Authors were asked to answer in half a dozen lines. Although many wrote briefly (Samuel Beckett especially so, turning three words into one: '¡UPTHEREPUBLIC!', and Rose Macaulay in two words, 'AGAINST FRANCO'), many wrote more fully (the number of lines of some is given after their names in the list that follows). Five writers supported the Nationalists (including Edmund Blunden, Arthur Machen, and Evelyn Waugh); sixteen were neutral, including Vera Brittain, T. S. Eliot, Charles Morgan, Ezra Pound, Alec Waugh, H. G. Wells, and Sean O'Faolain, who began, 'Don't be a lot of saps,' and concluded, 'Yours contemptuously'; and 127 supported the Republic, including Mulk Raj Anand, W. H. Auden, Cyril Connolly (12 lines), Douglas Goldring (17), Victor Gollancz, Aldous Huxley (10), Hugh Macdiarmid (14), Louis MacNeice, Arthur Koestler, Naomi Mitchison, Raymond Mortimer, John Middleton Murry, George Padmore, Raymond Postgate (14), Herbert Read, Stephen Spender (16), and Clough Williams-Ellis.[2] A Publisher's Note said that, in order to sell the pamphlet for sixpence, it had been impossible to include all the answers received, but 'in no instance has an answer been omitted on the grounds of "policy".' In his letter to Spender, 2 April 1938 (see *434*), Orwell referred to his having been sent this 'bloody rot' by Nancy Cunard—that is, the appeal—and having sent back 'a very angry reply in which I'm afraid I mentioned you uncomplimentarily, not knowing you personally at that time,' but his letter to Nancy Cunard was believed to have been lost. On 18 March 1994, *The New Statesman* published an article by Andy Croft, 'The Awkward Squaddie,' which included part of Orwell's reply to Nancy Cunard; it had been written on the back of the appeal. She typed a copy (or had a copy typed) of Orwell's reply and sent it to the editor of *Left Review*, Randall Swingler (see *3091, note c*), among whose papers it was found by Andy Croft (who is preparing a critical biography of Swingler), together with a covering letter from Nancy Cunard to Swingler. The copy of Orwell's letter is headed 'Letter received, addressed to me, at Paris address, Aug 6. 1937'; it is not clear whether the 6 August is the date Orwell sent his letter or the date of its receipt.

Will you please stop sending me this bloody rubbish. This is the second or third time I have had it. I am not one of your fashionable pansies like Auden and Spender, I was six months in Spain, most of the time fighting, I have a bullet-hole in me at present and I am not going to write blah about defending democracy or gallant little anybody. Moreover, I know what is happening and has been happening on the Government side for months past, i.e. that Fascism is being rivetted on the Spanish workers under the pretext of resisting Fascism; also that since May a reign of terror has been proceeding and all the jails and any place that will serve as a jail are crammed with prisoners who are not only imprisoned without trial but are half-starved, beaten and insulted. I dare say you know it too, though God knows anyone who could write the stuff overleaf would be fool enough to believe anything, even the war-news in the Daily Worker. But the chances are that you—whoever you are who keep sending me this thing—have money and are well-informed; so no doubt you know something about the inner history of the war and have deliberately joined in the defence of "democracy" (i.e. capitalism) racket in order to aid in crushing the Spanish working class and thus indirectly defend your dirty little dividends.

This is more than 6 lines, but if I did compress what I know and think about the Spanish war into 6 lines you wouldn't print it. You wouldn't have the guts.

By the way, tell your pansy friend Spender that I am preserving specimens of his war-heroics and that when the time comes when he squirms for shame at having written it, as the people who wrote the war-propaganda in the Great War are squirming now, I shall rub it in good and hard.

In her covering letter to Swingler, which also mentioned that E. M. Forster would not respond because he did not believe in signing manifestoes, and the need to abridge Sylvia Pankhurst's reply (of which 13 lines were printed), she asked Swingler what he knew about Orwell. She thought he belonged to the *New Writing* group and 'was connected with [the] Spender-Auden group.' She had his name from Roger Senhouse (a director of Secker & Warburg), whom she knew personally. Senhouse told her that 'Orwell had walked into his office a few days before . . . with a wound in his throat, arm in a sling, and the request that they should publish his new book.' (Orwell had probably visited Secker & Warburg, at Warburg's request, to discuss the publication of *Homage to Catalonia*, on 7 July; see 375). She was, she wrote, 'really curious to know what kind of a man he was before he became a trotskist,° as shown' and she wondered 'what kind of damage he had been doing, or trying to do, in Spain.' She decided that, 'As this is not in any sense an "answer" we are spared the mere query, even, of how to deal with it.' Although Orwell was not represented in the pamphlet, Fenner Brockway, C. L. R. James, and Ethel Mannin were. Croft states that each pushed 'the ILP-POUM line against "bourgeois democracy" in Spain.' James did use the phrase 'bourgeois democracy,' but it is slightly exaggerated to say they pushed the ILP-POUM line.

In his article, Croft correctly sets the context of this letter between the publication of the two parts of 'Spilling the Spanish Beans,' 29 July and 2 September 1937 (see *378*). But there is a more specific, and more significant, context, revealed by the letters published here. Orwell was desperately anxious about the fate of his former colleagues rotting in jails in Spain as a result of the 'reign of terror' to which he refers in his letter to Nancy Cunard. (This section, from 'also that since May . . .' to '. . . war-news in the Daily Worker,' was omitted from his article by Mr. Croft.) Orwell had received Kopp's letters on 29 July (see *378A*), and these are clearly reflected in the passage about the 'reign of terror': note especially the references in the letters from Spain and in Orwell's reply to Nancy Cunard to prisoners being held without trial; jails 'crammed with prisoners,' half-starved (two plates of soup and 150 gr. of bread a day), and their being 'beaten and insulted'—the same phrase appears in Kopp's letter to Eileen and Orwell's to Nancy Cunard; the letter from Kopp to Lt. Col. Burillo specifies the nature of the insults: 'beating the prisoners and insulting them even to the point of insulting their mothers.' On 1 August he told Amy Charlesworth that there was 'the greatest fear that some of them will be shot . . . for opposition to the Communist Party' (see *384*). The next day he told Charlie Doran that *The New Statesman* had rejected his review of *The Spanish Cockpit* because it controverted its policy (see *424*); that Stafford Cottman had been expelled from the Young Communist League as an enemy of the working class, and his house was being 'shadowed' by its members; and he feared that Andrés Nin would be murdered by the Communists (as indeed he was), though it might be called '"suicide", or perhaps appendicitis again' (see *386*), evidence that Bob Smillie's fate still hurt him deeply (see *Homage to Catalonia*, 39, 171). Orwell's letter may now appear to be tactless, but it marks the depths of bitterness and despair he felt at the time, prompted by those he held responsible for betraying the Spanish people and conducting a reign of terror.

The editor is grateful to Andy Croft for making photocopies available of the copy of Orwell's letter and of Nancy Cunard's letter, and to Judith Williams, the owner of the letters, for permission to reproduce them.

1. Nancy Cunard (1896–1965), was the daughter of the wealthy shipping magnate who gave his name to the Cunard line; hence the reference in Orwell's letter to her of defending 'your dirty little dividends.' She wrote poetry and literary reminiscences and devoted herself to socialist issues and the cause and arts of the blacks.
2. Names have been selected that are of interest in connexion with Orwell.

387. To Geoffrey Gorer[1]

16 August 1937   Typewritten

The Stores   Wallington   Nr.Baldock   HERTS.

Dear Geoffrey,

How are things? I gather from your stuff in Time and Tide that you are back in England. Can't you come out and see us some time? We can always put you up, except perhaps during the next week or so when my wife's mother will be in our midst. We got back from Spain about six weeks ago, having had a pretty bloody time and finally sneaking over the border with the police just one jump behind. You cannot conceive the awfulness of the things that are happening in Spain. It is a real reign of terror, Fascism being imposed under the pretence of resisting Fascism, people being flung into jail literally by hundreds and kept there for months without trial, newspapers suppressed etc., etc. The most disgusting thing of all is the way the so-called anti-Fascist press in England has covered it up. I wonder if you saw my review in Time and Tide of a book called "The Spanish Cockpit" (which by the way you ought to read)? The author wrote and told me that I was the only reviewer who had mentioned the essential point of the book, ie. that the Communist Party is now the chief anti-revolutionary party. But the interesting thing was that I had also reviewed it for the New Statesman and was, of course, able to treat it more seriously than for Time and Tide. But the N.S., having previously refused an article of mine on the suppression of the P.O.U.M. on the ground that it would "cause trouble", also refused to print the review as it "controverted editorial policy," or in other words blew the gaff on the Communist Party. They then offered to pay for the review, though unprinted, then asked me by telegram to review another book. They are evidently very anxious to prevent me giving away the fact that they are covering up important pieces of news. However they will get a nasty jar when my book on Spain comes out, as I intend to do an appendix on the lies and suppressions in the English press. Whatever you do don't believe a word you read in the News Chronicle or Daily Worker. The only daily paper I have seen in which a gleam of truth sometimes gets through is the Express—their reports are silly and full of mistakes, of course, but seem honest in intention.

I got wounded by a sniper outside Huesca. It wasn't much but it ought to have killed me, in fact for a few minutes I thought it had, which was an interesting experience. The bullet went through my neck from front to back but skidded round both the carotid artery and the backbone in the most remarkable way. I have one vocal cord paralysed so I can't shout very loud or sing, but my voice is pretty normal. I am getting pretty well going with my book and we are very busy trying to do something about the garden, which was in a ghastly mess when we got back and is now empty of everything. We are going to get some more hens. We have some young ducks but they didn't do well, owing I think to improper feeding in their first week, and we lost several.

Let us know how you are getting on and if you can come and see us. I shall be in town some time next month I think. Eileen sends love.

Yours
Eric A. Blair

1. See 257, n. 6.

388. To Leonard Moore

19 August 1937   Typewritten

The Stores   Wallington   Nr. Baldock   HERTS.

Dear Mr Moore,

I am sending back the French translation of that review,[1] with one mistranslation corrected. I enclose a letter for the translator, which perhaps you would be kind enough to send on as I have not her[2] address. I am afraid one cannot expect any payment for this kind of stuff, in fact in France it seems nobody ever gets paid for anything they write, but I am most anxious to get all publicity possible for the real facts about the Spanish war. I am telling the translator about another article that might interest her, and perhaps if you could let me have her address I could keep in touch with her paper, whatever it is, and supply them directly with anything they want, as there is no reason why you should be troubled with this kind of unprofitable stuff.

Of course I should be delighted if Madame Davet chose to translate any of my books that she thought she could find a publisher for.

Yours sincerely
Eric A. Blair

1. Of *The Spanish Cockpit* by Franz Borkenau, reviewed by Orwell in *Time and Tide*, 31 July 1937; see *379*.
2. Madame Yvonne Davet; see *389*.

389. To Yvonne Davet

19 August 1937   Typewritten

Orwell often wrote to Yvonne Davet[1] in French. Therefore, priority is given to Orwell's French; the translations, by Janet Percival, follow. Orwell, not having a typewriter with accents, had to add these afterwards. If he overlooked one or two, these have been supplied silently; when he added none in a letter (see, for example, *407*), none have been added.

The Stores   Wallington   Nr. Baldock   HERTS. Angleterre.

Camarade,

Vous m' excuserez sans doute d'écrire très mal le français.[2] J'ai reçu de mon agent littéraire votre traduction de mon article; j'ai corrigé une expression, autrement la traduction me semble excellente. J'ai ajouté aussi à la tête de l'article le nom etc. du livre[3] dont je faisais critique; il me semble que ça vaut la peine, car c'est un livre que tout le monde doit lire pour comprendre la situation actuelle en Espagne. Il vous intéressera peut-être d'entendre qu'au même temps j'ai fait critique de ce livre pour le "New Statesman and Nation," journal Liberal-Socialist, et qu'ils ont refusé d'imprimer mon article parce-qu'il n'était pas assez favourable au Gouvernement actuel de l'Espagne. Quand je suis sorti de l'Espagne à la fin de Juin j'ai envoyé au

"New Statesman" un article qui racontait les faits de la suppression du
P.O.U.M., mais pour la même raison ils ont refusé de l'imprimer. Les
journaux anglais, surtout ceux de la Gauche, ou bien ce qui s'appelle la
Gauche, n'ont presque rien dit de la suppression du P.O.U.M., quoiqu'il
s'agissait des centaines de gens imprisonnés, d'autres fusillés, des journaux
supprimés, etc., etc. Ils ont tous l'idée que pour gagner la guerre il faut cacher
les vrais faits de ce qui se passe en Espagne. L'article sur la suppression du
P.O.U.M. que le "New Statesman" a refusé a été publié dans un journal
mensuel du I.L.P., "Controversy." Si il vous intéresserait de le voir, je peux
vous en envoyer un exemplaire.

En conclusion, si vous connaissez des camarades qui sont sortis de
l'Espagne plus tard que moi (je suis sorti le 23 Juin) je serais très content
d'entendre aucunes nouvelles de ce qui arrive la-bàs. Il est longtemps que
nous n'avons pas de nouvelles, et nous avons beaucoup d'amis qui sont en
prison. Surtout nous voulons des nouvelles de Georges Kopp, un Belge,
brave soldat et très bon camarade qui était commandant de ma battaillon° au
front. Il est en prison depuis le 19 Juin à l'hotel Falcón, Barcelona, et nous
avons grand peur qu'il sera fusillé. Il est possible qu'il y aura des caramades
français qui l'ont vu en prison.

Très fraternellement
Eric Blair
("George Orwell")

Translation

Comrade,
Please excuse my very bad, written, French.[2] I have received your translation
of my article from my literary agent; I have corrected one sentence, otherwise
the translation seems excellent. I have also added at the head of the article the
name etc. of the book[3] I was reviewing; I think it is worth it, as it is a book
that everyone should read to understand the present situation in Spain. You
will perhaps be interested to hear that at the same time I reviewed the book for
the "New Statesman and Nation," a Liberal-Socialist weekly, and that they
refused to print my article because it wasn't sufficiently favourable to the
present Government in Spain. When I got out of Spain at the end of June I sent
the "New Statesman" an article recounting the facts concerning the
suppression of the POUM, but they refused to print that for the same reason.
The English papers, especially those on the Left, or what calls itself the Left,
have said very little on the suppression of the POUM, although people were
flung into jail by the hundred, others shot, newspapers were suppressed etc.
etc. They all think that to win the war you must hide the real facts of what is
going on in Spain. The article on the suppression of the POUM which the
"New Statesman" refused was published in the ILP monthly,
"Controversy." If you would like to see it, I can send you a copy.

Lastly, if you know any comrades who got out of Spain later than I did (I
got out on 23 June), I should be very glad to hear any news of what is
happening there. We have had no news for a long time, and we have several

friends in prison. We should especially like news of Georges Kopp, a Belgian, a brave soldier and a very good comrade, who was commandant of my battalion at the front. He has been imprisoned since 19 June in the Hotel Falcón, Barcelona, and we are very afraid that he will be shot. There may be some French comrades who have seen him in prison.

Yours fraternally,
Eric Blair
("George Orwell")

1. Yvonne Davet (c. 1895–) was for many years secretary to André Gide; she and Orwell corresponded before World War II and again thereafter. She translated several of his books in the hope that she might find a French publisher for them. Her translation of *Homage to Catalonia*, completed before the outbreak of war and read by Orwell, was not published until after Orwell died. See Textual Note to *Homage to Catalonia*, *CW*, VI, 251–61. She also translated Jean Rhys, Graham Greene, and Iris Murdoch.
2. By stressing that his written French is relatively weak, Orwell implies, probably correctly, that his spoken French was good.
3. *The Spanish Cockpit*.

390. To Victor Gollancz

20 August 1937   Typewritten

The Stores   Wallington   Nr. Baldock   HERTS.

Dear Mr Gollancz,

I do not expect you will have seen the enclosed cutting,[1] as it does not refer to anything you published for me.

This (see underlined words) is the—I think—third reference in the "Daily Worker" to my supposedly saying that the working classes "smell." As you know I have never said anything of the kind, in fact have specifically said the opposite. What I said in Chapter VIII of "Wigan Pier," as you may perhaps remember, is that middle-class people are brought up to *believe* that the working classes "smell," which is simply a matter of observable fact. Numbers of the letters I received from readers of the book referred to this and congratulated me on pointing it out. The statement or implication that I think working people "smell" is a deliberate lie aimed at people who have not read this or any other of my books, in order to give them the idea that I am a vulgar snob and thus indirectly hit at the political parties with which I have been associated. These attacks in the "Worker" only began after it became known to the Communist Party that I was serving with the P.O.U.M. militia.

I have no connection with these people (the "Worker" staff) and nothing I said would carry any weight with them, but you of course are in a different position. I am very sorry to trouble you about what is more or less my own personal affair, but I think perhaps it might be worth your while to intervene and stop attacks of this kind which will not, of course, do any good to the books you have published for me or may publish for me in the future. If therefore at any time you happen to be in touch with anyone in authority on the "Worker" staff, I should be very greatly obliged if you would tell them two things:

1. That if they repeat this lie about my saying the working classes "smell" I shall publish a reply with the necessary quotations, and in it I shall include what John Strachey[2] said to me on the subject just before I left for Spain (about December 20th.) Strachey will no doubt remember it, and I don't think the C.P. would care to see it in print.

2. This is a more serious matter. A campaign of organised libel is going on against people who were serving with the P.O.U.M. in Spain. A comrade of mine, a boy of eighteen whom I knew in the line,[3] was recently not only expelled from his branch of the Y.C.L. for his association with the P.O.U.M., which was perhaps justifiable as the P.O.U.M. and C.P. policies are quite incompatible, but was also described in a letter as "in the pay of Franco." This latter statement is quite a different matter. I don't know whether it is libellous within the meaning of the act, but I am taking counsel's opinion, as, of course, the same thing (ie. that I am in Fascist pay) is liable to be said about myself. Perhaps again, if you are speaking to anyone in authoritative position, you could tell them that in the case of anything actionable being said against me, I shall not hesitate to take a libel action immediately. I hate to take up this threatening attitude, and I should hate still more to be involved in litigation, especially against members of another working-class party, but I think one has a right to defend oneself against these malignant personal attacks which, even if it is really the case that the C.P. is entirely right and the P.O.U.M. and I.L.P. entirely wrong, cannot in the long run do any good to the working-class cause. You see here (second passage underlined) the implied suggestion that I did not "pull my weight" in the fight against the Fascists. From this it is only a short step to calling me a coward, a shirker etc., and I do not doubt these people would do so if they thought it was safe.

I am extremely sorry to put this kind of thing upon you, and I shall understand and not be in any way offended if you do not feel you can do anything about it. But I have ventured to approach you because you are my publisher and may, perhaps, feel that your good name is to some extent involved with mine.

Yours sincerely
Eric Blair

1. A review of *The Road to Wigan Pier* by Harry Pollitt, leader of the Communist Party of Great Britain, published in the *Daily Worker*, 17 March 1937. The direct cause of Orwell's letter and Gollancz's response is given by Crick, 343–45, the source of this extract from Pollitt's review: 'Here is George Orwell, a disillusioned little middle-class boy who, seeing through imperialism, decided to discover what Socialism has to offer . . . a late imperialist policeman. . . . If ever snobbery had its hallmark placed upon it, it is by Mr Orwell. . . . I gather that the chief thing that worries Mr Orwell is the 'smell' of the working-class, for smells seem to occupy the major portion of the book. . . . One thing I am certain of, and it is this—if Mr Orwell could only hear what the Left Book Club circles will say about this book, then he would make a resolution never to write again on any subject that he does not understand.' Gollancz told Orwell he was passing his letter on 'to the proper quarter.' That proved to be the Communist Party's offices in King Street, London. To Pollitt, he wrote, 'My

dear Harry, you should see this letter from Orwell. I read it to John [Strachey] over the telephone and he assures me that he is quite certain that he said nothing whatever indiscreet.' What Strachey said is not known. However, the attacks did, for the moment, cease.
2. John Strachey (see *304, n. 2*) had been a Labour Party M.P., stood unsuccessfully for Parliament for Oswald Mosley's New Party (of Fascist inclination) then supported Communism.
3. Stafford Cottman. For the picketing of his home by members of the Young Communist League, see Orwell's letter to Charlie Doran, 2 August 1937, *386*.

391. To Leonard Moore

27 August 1937   Typewritten

The Stores   Wallington   Nr. Baldock   HERTS.

Dear Mr Moore,

I am sorry I didn't answer your letter earlier.[1] Yes, of course, the terms with Secker's are very satisfactory. I am getting on fairly fast with the book.

There is of course no need to worry about a counsel's opinion at present, but it is a possibility to be kept in mind. There was a most filthy attack on me, though not legally libellous, in the Daily Worker of a week ago. I sent it on to Gollancz, asking him to silence the D.W., as of course he can if he wishes to. I trust there won't be any more of the same kind. It is more important than it sounds, because these people are well aware that I am writing a book about the Spanish war and would if they could get me written off beforehand as a liar, so as to discredit anything I say.

I am sending separately a copy of the monthly[2] paper "Controversy."[3] I should be greatly obliged if you would send it on to the Frenchwoman[4] who translated that other article. I don't know her address, but she might be able to use some of the stuff in it.

Yours sincerely
Eric A. Blair

1. letter earlier] letter
2. monthly] weekly *typewritten*
3. Presumably the August issue, in which Orwell's 'Eye-Witness in Barcelona' appeared; see *382*.
4. Madame Yvonne Davet; see *389*.

392. Review of *The Men I Killed*, by Brigadier-General F. P. Crozier, CB, CMB, DSO

The New Statesman and Nation, 28 August 1937

General Crozier is a professional soldier and by his own showing spent the years between 1899 and 1921 in almost ceaseless slaughter of his fellow-creatures; hence as a pacifist he makes an impressive figure, like the reformed burglar at a Salvation Army meeting. Everyone will remember his earlier books, with their clipped telegram-like style and their tales of colonial wars in which eager young officers smack their chops over the prospect of "real slaughter". In parts these books were disgusting, but they were completely straightforward and were of great value as illustrating the spirit in which the dirty little wars of that period were waged. Evidently when you are twenty years old it is great fun to turn a machine-gun on a crowd of unarmed "natives". But European war is a different matter, and after much experience of both kinds General Crozier has decided that the only remedy is complete refusal to fight in any circumstances. The only question is, can he advance any argument which will drive the general public an inch farther in the direction of active resistance to war?

Here, on the whole, the book fails. It is a rambling, incoherent book, circling vaguely round two anti-war arguments, one of them good so far as it goes, the other doubtful. The first is the fact that the actual process of war consists in doing things which are instinctively felt to be disgusting, such as shooting your own men to prevent them running away. It is right to insist upon this kind of thing, for war still remains "glorious" in the secret imaginations of most people who have not fought. The other is the fact that all known methods of defence against the aeroplane are more or less useless and that the German bombers could probably reduce England to chaos and starvation in a few weeks. It is doubtful whether this has much value as an argument against war; though true, it amounts to scaremongering and, coupled with the consciousness of German rearmament, it simply induces in most people a desire to see England "stronger" (i.e., possessed of more bombing 'planes) than ever. The two facts which even now are not very widely grasped, and which should be made the centre of all anti-war agitation, are quite different from these. General Crozier is aware of them, but only intermittently aware. They are:

1. That war against a foreign country only happens when the moneyed classes think they are going to profit from it.[1]

2. That every war when it comes, or before it comes, is represented not as a war but as an act of self-defence against a homicidal maniac ("militarist" Germany in 1914, "Fascist" Germany next year or the year after).

The essential job is to get people to recognise war-propaganda when they see it, especially when it is disguised as peace-propaganda.

The test for any pacifist is, does he differentiate between foreign war and civil war?[2] If he does not, he is simply saying in effect that violence may be used by the rich against the poor but not by the poor against the rich. This test General Crozier passes, and if not a completely logical pacifist he is at least a very engaging one. As a living contradiction of the widespread notion that every pacifist is a Creeping Jesus, he should be of great value to his cause.

1. *The New Statesman and Nation* published a letter on 4 September 1937 from Russell Sidebottom, who was astonished that an author of so intelligent and objective a book as *The Road to Wigan Pier* 'should trot out that hoary chestnut of socialist propaganda that: "War against a foreign country only happens when the moneyed classes think they are going to profit from it." ' Orwell might think capitalists were scoundrels, he said, but they were not necessarily fools. Orwell's statement was 'a silly libel' on the intelligence and humanity of such people.

2. Sidebottom said he entirely agreed with Orwell's distinction between foreign and civil war. 'A pacifist,' he wrote, 'is a man who will fight for what he really believes to be worth fighting for, but not for what he is merely told to believe.'

393. To Amy Charlesworth

30 August 1937   Typewritten

The Stores   Wallington   Nr. Baldock   HERTS.

Dear Miss Charlesworth,

Many thanks for your letter, which at present I can't find, but no doubt it will turn up presently, and then I will get your address from it. I enquired where you could get the "New Leader" in Manchester, and am told that you can get it at any of the following:

Garner, 56 Worthington Street, Old Trafford, Manchester 16.

Lewis, 379 Ashton New Road, Bradford, Manchester.

J. Hodgetts, 57 Lynn Street, West Gorton, Manchester.

I think you will find it worth an occasional 1d. It is a poor little paper, but often has the truth in it when other papers don't.

As to the P.O.U.M., the Communist Party in Spain etc. It is not exactly true that the P.O.U.M. was trying to "set up a soviet" in opposition to the Government. Where the P.O.U.M., and you might also say the Anarchists, differed from the Government and the Communist Party, was in saying that Franco must be resisted not in the name of democracy as it exists in England, France etc., but in the name of workers' government. This is not so theoretical as it sounds, because it meant an actual difference of policy. When the revolution broke out the workers did in many parts of Spain establish the beginnings of a workers' government, seizing land and factories, setting up local committees, etc., etc. The Government, which is largely under control of the Communist Party, has managed to undo most of this, at first by appealing to the workers not to endanger the war, later, when they felt themselves stronger, by force. I think the P.O.U.M. and the others were quite right to resist this process and would perhaps have been right to resist it even by open rebellion, though they never did so. It is quite true that we ought all to combine against Fascism, but then one has got to decide what Fascism is. If Fascism means suppression of political liberty and free speech, imprisonment without trial etc., then the present regime in Spain *is* Fascism; so in apparently fighting against Fascism you come straight back to Fascism. I don't mean that the rule of the present Government is no better than what Franco would set up if he won, but it is only different in degree, not in kind. What emerges from this—or so it appears to me—is that Fascism has no real opposite except Socialism. You can't fight against Fascism in the name of "democracy," because what we call democracy in a capitalist country only remains in being while things are going well; in time of difficulty it turns immediately into Fascism. The only thing that can prevent this is for the workers to keep the power in their own hands. Obviously one can't have complete workers' control and Socialism all in a moment, but the workers ought to cling onto every scrap of power they possess, whether, as in England, it is in the form of democratic institutions, or, as in Spain at the beginning of the war, in the fact that the workers have arms in their hands and have seized some of the means of production. If they listen to anyone who says to them, "You must give up this, that and the other for the common good," they will be cheated every time. This is what happened in Spain. The Communist Party propagandists said that the workers had no need to keep direct control on factories, transport etc., because they were adequately represented in the Government, which contained ministers representing the trade unions. Later, of course, when the arms had for the most part been got out of the workers' hands and the Communist-Liberal clique was in a stronger position, the trade-union representatives were turned out of the Government and you now have a Government which does not contain one minister representing any working-class party. The only thing that could excuse this is military necessity, and of course this excuse has been used all along. But as a matter of fact the present Government (the Negrin Government, dating from May) has been much less successful in a military sense than the previous ones. It has worked itself into a position of absolute power and put most of its opponents in jail, but it is not winning the war. I doubt indeed whether the war can now be won unless France intervenes. To win a war you have either got to have a preponderance of arms, which the Government has not got and is not likely to have, or you have got to arouse enthusiasm among the people. But no one can get up much enthusiasm for a Government which puts you in jail if you open your mouth.

Excuse me always lecturing you about this. But what I saw in Spain has upset me so much that I talk about it to everybody. And the English papers have told such frightful lies about the whole business, the left-wing papers (News Chronicle and Daily Worker) almost worse than the right-wing ones. It is desperately necessary to get people to see through the humbug that is talked about "fighting against Fascism," or the next thing we know we shall find ourselves fighting another imperialist war (against Germany) which will be dressed up as a war "against Fascism," and then another ten million men will be dead before people grasp that Fascism and so-called democracy are Tweedledum and Tweedledee.

I think you asked about my voice. It is much better, in fact I can shout to quite a distance now, but I still can't modulate it enough to sing, so I suppose one vocal cord is permanently paralysed.

Yours sincerely
Eric Blair

[Handwritten at top of letter:] Still can't find your address! Am sending this to the hospital—hope they will forward.

394. Excise Duty Notice

Among the documents that survive in the Orwell Archive is a Notice to Pay Excise Duties addressed to Eric Arthur Blair from the Collector of Customs and Excise, Northampton. This indicates that Orwell's licence as a 'Patent Medicine Vendor' had expired on 1 September 1937, and he was required to pay six shillings (30 pence) if this business was to be continued. There is no indication of renewal on the form, which had to be returned with a remittance. The range of patent medicines held at The Stores, Wallington, must have been extremely limited indeed, and the sale scarcely worth the licence fee, but there is a touch of irony that the author of *Keep the Aspidistra Flying* provided this modest service for his neighbours in the village.

The Excise records for this period have been destroyed; no earlier application or payment on this occasion can be traced.

395. To Leonard Moore

1 September 1937   Typewritten

The Stores   Wallington   Nr. Baldock   <u>HERTS</u>.

Dear Mr Moore,

Herewith the signed draft of the agreement,[1] for which many thanks. I trust I shall get the book done by December 31st, as agreed. If Secker and Warburg want to know how it is getting on I could let them have some specimen chapters in a few weeks, provided they understand that this is the rough draft and I always alter it a good deal in rewriting.

Yours sincerely
Eric Blair

1. The contract with Secker & Warburg to publish *Homage to Catalonia*. Gollancz hoped that this would be an isolated exception to his publishing Orwell's work, and had reminded Orwell on 5 July 1937 of their agreement for Gollancz to publish his next three novels; see *375*. In fact, Gollancz published only one more novel by Orwell—*Coming Up for Air*, in 1939—but he was the publisher of Orwell's *Inside the Whale* (1940) and *The Betrayal of the Left* (1941), for which Orwell wrote two chapters. See Crick, 339.

396. Review of *Forbidden Journey* by Ella K. Maillart; translated from the French by Thomas McGreevy

Time and Tide, 4 September 1937

No doubt everyone will remember Mr. Peter Fleming's *News from Tartary*, published about a year ago.[1] It was the record of a journey across Central Asia, first from Pekin to Lanchow by train and lorry, then onwards by horse, camel and donkey to Kashgar and over the Himalayas into India. It took six months and covered two thousand miles of the most inaccessible territory in the world. Now his companion on the journey, Miss Maillart, has published her own account, and so we have the slightly unusual experience of seeing the same story told from two different angles.

As a matter of fact, the outward record of events is very similar. The deserts and mountains, the heat and cold, the ceaseless hunger, the struggles with body-vermin and with wretched pack-animals that collapse and have to be left to die in the mountain-passes—all this is very much the same as in Mr. Fleming's narrative. The difference is in the manner of approach. I hesitate to say that Miss Maillart's approach is "feminine" for women who walk and ride across Central Asia are not exactly typical of the softer sex, if there is a softer sex; but her attitude throughout is more passive, less intellectual, ultimately more receptive. She is, perhaps, the perfect traveller, the kind of person who never wants the journey to end, who is genuinely more interested in marching through empty steppes and past ruined temples than in getting home to write a book about it; but at the same time, of course, sufficiently civilized to retain a sense of strangeness in the wilderness.

In a sense I was only prolonging the journey I had made in Russian Turkestan. I was familiar with the smell of camels and of their fetid breathing as they ruminated. I had already joined in the halt at the watering-place, already seen the gathering of dung for fuel. . . . I knew the silence at night, when one's eyes are burning after marching against the wind all day. I loved the primitive way of living which gave me back that hunger that transforms every morsel one puts under one's tooth into solid satisfaction.

It is an unusual gift to be able to endure that kind of thing and also to appreciate it. Such people, carrying round the world a mentality which at bottom is that of a child, are the only ones who can travel in remote countries without having them debunked in the process. Part of their secret, of course, is physical toughness, not to say callousness. It is fatal to travel if you have the slightest feeling for comfort; it simply means that names which were once like magic emblems call up nothing but memories of insects and boredom. People like Miss Maillart live a good life, and it is a pity that they are a doomed race. For that kind of travel, snooping round the world to see what you can see, is not going to be permitted much longer. As communications improve, foreign countries not only become less worth visiting, but also harder to visit. Keeping alive in the desert is easier than crossing a frontier, and it is already impossible to make any journey of the slightest interest unless you either have limitless money or are ready to break the law. Meanwhile, Miss Maillart has written a very interesting book, less witty than Mr. Fleming's, but revealing, in my opinion, a more engaging personality. The photographs are good but not exciting.

1. Reviewed by Orwell on 15 August 1936; see 322A.

397. To Geoffrey Gorer

15 September 1937   Typewritten

The Stores   Wallington   Nr. Baldock   HERTS.

Dear Geoffrey,

Thanks so much for your letter. I am glad you are enjoying yourself in Denmark, though, I must admit, it is one of the few countries I have never wanted to visit. I rang you up when I was in town, but of course you weren't there. I note you are coming back about the 24th. We shall be here till the 10th October, then we are going down to Suffolk to stay at my parents' place for some weeks. But if you can manage it any time between the 24th and the 10th, just drop us a line and then come down and stay. We can always put you up without difficulty.

What you say about not letting the Fascists in owing to dissensions between ourselves is very true so long as one is clear what one means by Fascism, also who or what it is that is making unity impossible. Of course all the Popular Front stuff that is now being pushed by the Communist press and party, Gollancz and his paid hacks etc., etc., only boils down to saying that they are in favour of British Fascism (prospective) as against German Fascism. What they are aiming to do is to get British capitalist-imperialism into an alliance with the U.S.S.R. and thence into a war with Germany. Of course they piously pretend that they don't want the war to come and that a French-British-Russian alliance can prevent it on the old balance of power system. But we know what the balance of power business led to last time, and in any case it is manifest that the nations are arming with the intention of fighting. The Popular Front boloney boils down to this: that when the war comes the Communists, labourites etc., instead of working to stop the war and overthrow the Government, will be on the side of the Government provided that the Government is on the "right" side, ie. against Germany. But everyone with any imagination can foresee that Fascism, not of course called Fascism, will be imposed on us as soon as the war starts. So you will have Fascism with Communists participating in it, and, if we are in alliance with the U.S.S.R., taking a leading part in it. This is what has happened in Spain. After what I have seen in Spain I have come to the conclusion that it is futile to be "anti-Fascist" while attempting to preserve capitalism. Fascism after all is only a development of capitalism, and the mildest democracy, so-called, is liable to turn into Fascism when the pinch comes. We like to think of England as a democratic country, but our rule in India, for instance, is just as bad as German Fascism, though outwardly it may be less irritating. I do not see how one can oppose Fascism except by working for the overthrow of capitalism, starting, of course, in one's own country. If one collaborates with a capitalist-imperialist government in a struggle "against Fascism," ie. against a rival imperialism, one is simply letting Fascism in by the back door. The whole struggle in Spain, on the Government side, has turned upon this. The revolutionary parties, the Anarchists, P.O.U.M. etc., wanted to complete the revolution, the others wanted to fight the Fascists in the name of "democracy," and, of course, when they felt sure enough of their position and had tricked the workers into giving up their arms, re-introduce capitalism. The grotesque feature, which very few people outside Spain have yet grasped, is that the Communists stood furthest of all to the right, and were more anxious even than the liberals to hunt down the revolutionaries and stamp out all revolutionary ideas. For instance, they have succeeded in breaking up the workers' militias, which were based on the trade unions and in which all ranks received the same pay and were on a basis of equality, and substituting an army on bourgeois lines where a colonel is paid eight times as much as a private etc. All these changes, of course, are put forward in the name of military necessity and backed up by the "Trotskyist" racket, which consists of saying that anyone who professes revolutionary principles is a Trotskyist and in Fascist pay. The Spanish Communist press has for instance declared that Maxton[1] is in the pay of the Gestapo. The reason why so few people grasp what has happened in Spain is because of the Communist command of the press. Apart from their own press they have the whole of the capitalist anti-Fascist press (papers like the News Chronicle) on their side, because the latter have got onto the fact that official Communism is now anti-revolutionary. The result is that they have been able to put across an unprecedented amount of lies and it is almost impossible to get anyone to print anything in contradiction. The accounts of the Barcelona riots in May, which I had the misfortune to be involved in, beat everything I have ever seen for lying. Incidentally the Daily Worker has been following me personally with the most filthy libels, calling me pro-Fascist etc., but I asked Gollancz to silence them, which he did, not very willingly I imagine. Queerly enough I am still contracted to write a number of books for him, though he refused to publish the book I am doing on Spain before a word of it was written.

I should like to meet Edith Sitwell[2] very much, some time when I am in town. It surprised me very much to learn that she had heard of me and liked my books. I don't know what° I ever cared much for her poems, but I liked very much her life of Pope.

Try and come down here some time. I hope your sprue[3] is gone.

Yours
Eric

1. James Maxton, ILP M.P.; see *385, n. 1.*
2. Edith Sitwell (1887–1964; DBE, 1954), poet and literary personality. Her first book of poems was published at her own expense in 1915, and she continued to write throughout her life. She achieved lasting and widespread recognition for *Façade*, which was read in a concert version, with music by William Walton, in January 1922. She encouraged many young artists and was greatly interested in Orwell's work; see *653, n. 2.*
3. Here, a throat infection.

398. To [the Editor], *Manchester Guardian*

22 September 1937   Typewritten

The Stores   Wallington   Nr. Baldock   <u>HERTS</u>.

PRIVATE

Dear Sir,[1]

If it is not an impertinence I would like to congratulate the *Manchester Guardian* on being the only English daily paper, so far as my own knowledge goes, which has endeavoured to tell the truth about the events in the Spanish war. In connection with a book I am writing I have had to examine the accounts in a number of newspapers of the May riots in Barcelona, and while I do not agree in all respects with the *Manchester Guardian* reports, they are the only ones that at all correspond to events as I witnessed them.

What I particularly want to refer to, however, is the courageous protest by your Barcelona correspondent—I suppose it is Frank Jellinek[2]—in the number of June 29th, against the persecution of the P.O.U.M. Knowing what the political conditions in Spain are like, I realise that he risked something in sending this despatch through the censorship. If you have any way of conveying my gratitude and admiration to him, I would be greatly obliged if you would do so. I do not care to write to him personally, as I was serving in the P.O.U.M. militia, my name is probably on the list of political suspects, and it might not do him any good to receive a letter from me.

Yours truly
George Orwell

1. The editor was William P. Crozier (1879–1944), who thanked Orwell on 24 September and told him that 'a good many people take the opposite view and express it with vigour.'
2. Crozier said, in his letter to Orwell, that he would pass on Orwell's commendation to Frank Jellinek, who, he said, would be away in the United States and Mexico for a considerable time. For Jellinek, see 513. Orwell reviewed his book *The Civil War in Spain*, 8 July 1938; see 462.

399. That Mysterious Cart: George Orwell Replies to F. A. Frankfort

The New Leader, 24 September 1937

On 14 September 1937, the *Daily Worker* published a long statement over the name 'F. A. Frankfort' (Frank Frankford) dated 21 August 1937 from Barcelona. He had been in the front line with Orwell and was present when Orwell was shot. Later he was imprisoned in Barcelona, not for a political offence, but because, as he explained in an 'Arena' television programme broadcast to mark 1984, he had been 'trying to get away with a load of pictures.' The *Daily Worker* quoted Frankford as asserting that the POUM was working for Fascism: 'The real reason for the shortage of weapons at the front was the fact that they were being kept hidden by the POUM.' It was also asserted that 'every night,' when the contingent of which Orwell was a member was near Alcubierre under the command of George Kopp, 'at 11 p.m. the sentries heard the rattle of a cart' and he stated that they had been given instructions never to shoot at it, though they could tell from its light that it was within the Fascist lines.

Two days after publication of Frankford's article, the *Daily Worker* said it had been asked to make some corrections: to correct the spelling of Frankford's name; to say that he had not been kept in the POUM by force; that he was not certain the carts about which he wrote had actually crossed the Fascist line; and that he had never seen Kopp returning from the Fascist lines.

In the TV broadcast, Frankford admitted he had not got along with Orwell, because of his attitude to the working class as expressed in *The Road to Wigan Pier*, and he repeated the accusation about smell that Orwell took up in his letter to Victor Gollancz, 20 August 1937; see *390*. When the words were read back to him regarding the POUM supplying weapons to the Fascists, as printed over his name in the *Daily Worker*, he said, 'I don't remember that. . . . I don't think I ever said that . . . that wasn't true and I wouldn't have said that.' When questioned about the legitimacy of printing such accusations, he responded: 'Certain tactics are legitimate when you are fighting a battle like this.' As for stating that the 'POUM's pro-Fascist activities emerged clearly,' he maintained 'I never said anything like that.' He was not, he said, horrified that such statements could be attributed to him; indeed, he said, 'it rather amuses me.'

At the time, a response to Frankford's account (as attributed to him by the *Daily Worker*) was first given by John McNair, representative of the ILP in Barcelona, in *The New Leader*, 17 September 1937. He reported that Frankford had come to the ILP office in London on 4 and 7 September, on the latter occasion to receive that financial assistance 'which we give to all the comrades of the contingent on their return home.' He went on: 'On both these occasions we had long friendly talks with him, and while he was talking to us he knew he had allowed to be printed a number of statements which he knew perfectly well to be absolutely false and misleading, some of which could do tremendous harm to one of his comrades actually imprisoned in Barcelona.' McNair took up various points, and his answer to the accusation of trading, by cart, with the enemy was printed in bold-face type: 'Naturally a cart going to the Fascist lines would carry lights and rattle as much as possible!!! If there were the slightest reason to believe that traffic was going on between the lines it was Frankfort's° duty to mention it then to the leaders of the contingent, not to make rambling statements six months afterwards.'

This is the setting in which Orwell took up the cudgels. See Crick, 346–48 and especially his note 63 on 619–20. Orwell's article was preceded by the editorial note given below. His name is given as 'Frankfort'.

We have received the following statement from George Orwell, who is not a member of the I.L.P., regarding the slanders uttered by Frankfort, to which we referred in last week's NEW LEADER. *It is with reluctance that we refer to this dirty business again, but we want it to be clearly understood that there are limits to our patience. Neither the I.L.P. nor the comrades of the contingent have any intention of submitting to such calumnious campaigns as were used against our comrades of the P.O.U.M. in Spain. We know exactly where we stand, and fortunately the British working class know us, and can judge such attacks at their real value.*

We find that already in the "Daily Worker" of September 16, Frankfort has commenced to climb down. He finds now that he is not certain about "the light." Of course he's not.

GEORGE ORWELL'S STATEMENT

I am not going to waste time and space by replying to F. A. Frankfort's article in the September 14 "Daily Worker" with angry recriminations. The best thing I can do is to deal in order with some of the points on which I happen to have special knowledge:—

1. *"Every night at 11 p.m. the sentries heard the rattle of a cart, and we could tell from its light that it was crossing the space between the positions on our left and the Fascist lines. We were ordered never to shoot at this light."*

The suggestion here is that there was treasonable communication between our headquarters and the enemy. The facts are these: There was some talk at the time about a mysterious light that was said to be seen on certain nights moving along the ravine between us and the Fascists. There was no talk whatever about the "rattle of a cart," nor any suggestion that the light seemed to issue from our lines. In any case, the idea of a cart crossing no man's land from the position on our left is nonsense, as the ground between was a steep ravine where there was no track and no wheeled vehicle could have travelled. No order against firing at the light was ever issued, nor was it suggested from any quarter that rations, etc., were being sent from our lines to the Fascists. If Frankfort had any suspicions it seems strange that he never mentioned them at the time.

2. *"Near Huesca . . . one night we saw Commandant Kopp returning from the Fascist lines."*

This is pure imagination. To see a man "returning from the Fascist lines," i.e., coming out of their trenches, at night, you would have to be at most thirty yards from their parapet. To my knowledge, Frankfort never went out on night-patrol at Huesca, and it is very unlikely that he had any exact idea of how the Fascist lines ran. In any case, he says that "we" saw it. Can he find anyone else to corroborate this? The possible foundation of the story is that he once saw Kopp coming in over our own parapet from patrol. Kopp often went on patrol. So did I, and so did others of us. Is it suggested that every man who went out on patrol was in communication with the enemy?

3. *"The political report given by a representative of the P.O.U.M. always painted defeat as inevitable."*

This is a lie. I challenge Frankfort to produce any evidence to substantiate it. It will be found that he can produce none.

4. *". . . the numerous rifles, machine-guns and tanks which were placed at our disposal in Barcelona"* (during the May fighting).

This is a direct lie. Frankfort was with me during several days of the May disturbances, and he knows as well as I do that there were no machine-guns or tanks, and very few rifles, in the possession of the P.O.U.M. He and I were together at the Comité Local on the first night of the fighting, and he will remember that neither he nor I could obtain a rifle, as there were not enough to go round.

5. *"I am proud that I realised the crime the P.O.U.M. and some of its Anarchist friends were committing* **WITHIN A COUPLE OF DAYS OF GETTING BACK TO BARCELONA,** *and managed to get out of the affair without having the blood of anti-Fascists°workers on my hands."*

My emphasis. Two lies are contained here. First, the remark about "within two days" implies that Frankfort (and the other I.L.P. militiamen) only got back to Barcelona at the beginning of the fighting, i.e., on May 3. Actually, they got back on April 26. This can be proved by documentary evidence as well as by testimony. Secondly, Frankfort is asserting that during the May riots he decided that the P.O.U.M. were in the wrong and turned against them. This is so far from being the case that on the third day of the fighting, when we were on guard on a roof opposite the P.O.U.M. building, I had the greatest difficulty in restraining him from irresponsibly opening fire on some Civil Guards—our orders being not to fire unless fired on ourselves.

6. *"When I got back to the front it was obvious that there was open fraternisation between the P.O.U.M. troops and the Fascists."*

I went back to the front with Frankfort, and was there with him till May 20, the day I was wounded. There was no fraternisation, nor did Frankfort ever speak of any such thing.

7. *"I must say the P.O.U.M. seemed very glad to get rid of me."*

Quite rightly. The truth is that Frankfort refused duty and walked out of the line without leave, at a time when men were desperately short. He then seemed astonished that he was arrested as a deserter. In the circumstances he was lucky not to be shot.

To conclude. It is quite obvious that all these wild statements, and the many others which I have not had space to answer, were put into Frankfort's mouth by the Barcelona journalists, and that he chose to save his skin by assenting to them, because at that time it was extremely dangerous to be known to have any connection with the P.O.U.M. Obviously, if he had had any genuine suspicions of treachery he would have mentioned them earlier.

There is no hope of the "Daily Worker" printing this or any other adequate reply to Frankfort's article, for a paper which will descend to publishing that kind of stuff is not likely to let its opponents have a fair hearing. I suggest, however, that those who knew Frankfort in Spain sign some kind of statement that his charges are completely untrue and are in direct contradiction of all that he was saying at the time.

The above statement has been signed by every member of the contingent with whom we were able to communicate, including:

Bob Edwards.	**John Branthwaite.**
Charles Doran.	**Stafford Cottman.**
John Donovan.	**Harry Thomas.**
Douglas Moyle.	**Phillip Hunter.**
George Gross.	**Urias Jones.**
Charles Justessen.	**Tom Coles.**
Mike Milton.	**John Ritchie.**

400. Review of *Journey to Turkistan* by Sir Eric Teichman

Time and Tide, 25 September 1937

Sir Eric Teichman's journey across Sinkiang began and ended in the same places as that of Mr. Fleming and Mlle. Maillart earlier in the year,[1] but he followed a more northerly route and travelled the greater part of the distance in Ford trucks, one of which broke down and had to be abandoned on the way. From Kashgar onwards he travelled by yak, pony and aeroplane.

On the whole, this is a less interesting book than those of Mlle. Maillart and Mr. Fleming; the reason is probably that the author was travelling with a definite official purpose and, like all people in such positions, says less than he knows. Obviously, though he does not say so, he was sent to Sinkiang to report upon the extent and nature of the Russian influence. From what he says it is evident that though the Russians have not officially absorbed Sinkiang they are in a position to do so whenever it suits them. Economically the province is dominated by the U.S.S.R.—as, for geographical reasons, it must be and ought to be—and the weak Chinese administration is only kept in place by the aid of Russian troops. It is also evident from what Sir Eric does *not* say that this state of affairs is acceptable to Great Britain. From our point of view this is the important fact.

Ten years ago the news that the U.S.S.R. was in virtual control of Chinese Turkistan would have been greeted with a howl of dismay. Now—though Sir Eric has an anti-Communist prejudice which he scarcely conceals—Soviet expansion is regarded with a friendly smile, or something that is meant to look like a friendly smile. The reason, we need not doubt, is that British policy is ceasing to be anti-Russian because Russia is a potential ally against Germany and Japan. And for any thinking person this is a very sinister fact. For if our ruling class is becoming pro-Russian, it is certainly not becoming pro-Socialist. It may be that we are headed for a military alliance with the U.S.S.R. which would give the National Government, or some faked-up Popular Front Government, the one perfect alibi for an imperialist war. Moreover, the mere fact that British imperialism can regard Soviet expansion without dismay gives one a hint of the immense changes that are taking place, not in British policy but in Russian policy.

Sinkiang is at the other end of the world and is practically barred to European travellers, so it will probably be a long time before we learn the whole story of what has been happening there during the past few years. Meanwhile this is a very readable book, written by a person who, unlike most travellers, tends to minimise the dangers and difficulties of his journey. The photographs are admirable.

1. See *322A* and *396*.

401. Review of *Red Spanish Notebook* by Mary Low and Juan Brea; *Heroes of Alcazar* by R. Timmermans; *Spanish Circus* by Martin Armstrong

Time and Tide, 9 October 1937

Red Spanish Notebook gives a vivid picture of Loyalist Spain, both at the front and in Barcelona and Madrid, in the earlier and more revolutionary period of the war. It is admittedly a partisan book, but probably it is none the worse for that. The joint authors were working for the P.O.U.M., the most extreme of the revolutionary parties, since suppressed by the Government. The P.O.U.M. has been so much vilified in the foreign, and especially the Communist press, that a statement of its case was badly needed.

Up till May of this year the situation in Spain was a very curious one. A mob of mutually hostile political parties were fighting for their lives against a common enemy, and at the same time quarrelling bitterly among themselves as to whether this was or was not a revolution as well as a war. Definitely revolutionary events had taken place—land had been seized by the peasants, industries collectivized, big capitalists killed or driven out, the Church practically abolished—but there had been no fundamental change in the structure of government. It was a situation capable of developing either towards Socialism or back to capitalism; and it is now clear that, given a victory over Franco, some kind of capitalist republic will emerge. But at the same time there was occurring a revolution of ideas that was perhaps more important than the short-lived economic changes. For several months large blocks of people believed that all men are equal and were able to act on their belief. The result was a feeling of liberation and hope that is difficult to conceive in our money-tainted atmosphere. It is here that *Red Spanish Notebook* is valuable. By a series of intimate day-to-day pictures (generally small things: a bootblack refusing a tip, a notice in the brothels saying, "Please treat the women as comrades") it shows you what human beings are like when they are trying to behave as human beings and not as cogs in the capitalist machine. No one who was in Spain during the months when people still believed in the revolution will ever forget that strange and moving experience. It has left something behind that no dictatorship, not even Franco's, will be able to efface.

In every book written by a political partisan one has got to be on the look-out for one or another class of prejudice. The authors of this book are Trotskyists—I gather that they were sometimes an embarrassment to the P.O.U.M., which was not a Trotskyist body, though for a while it had Trotskyists working for it—and, therefore their prejudice is against the official Communist Party, to which they are not always strictly fair. But is the Communist Party always strictly fair to the Trotskyists? Mr. C. L. R. James, author of that very able book *World Revolution*, contributes an introduction.

Heroes of the Alcazar re-tells the story of the siege last autumn, when a garrison mainly of cadets and Civil Guards held out for seventy-two days against terrible odds, until Toledo was relieved by Franco's troops. There is no need because one's sympathies are on the other side to pretend that this was not a heroic exploit. And some of the details of siege-life are very interesting; I particularly liked the account of the ingenious way in which a motor-bicycle engine was hitched onto a hand-mill to grind corn for the garrison. But the book is poorly written, in a glutinous style, full of piety and denunciations of the "Reds." There is an introduction by Major Yeats Brown, who generously concedes that not *all* the "Red Militia" were "cruel and treacherous." The photographs of groups of defenders bring home one of the most pathetic aspects of the civil war. They are so like groups of Government militiamen that if they were changed round no one would know the difference.

Finally, Spain of a hundred years ago. *Spanish Circus* recounts the reign of Carlos IV. Godoy[1] (the "Prince of Peace"), Napoleon, Trafalgar, palace intrigues, Goya's portraits—it is that period. At this particular moment I find it rather hard to read such a book. Spain is too much bound up in my mind with flooded trenches, the rattle of machine guns, food-shortage and lies in the newspapers. But if you want to escape from that aspect of Spain, this is probably the book you are looking for. It is written with distinction and, as far as I can judge, it is a piece of accurate historical research. The way in which Mr. Armstrong has *not* exploited the scandalous story of Godoy and Maria Luisa should be an example to all popular historians.

1. Manuel de Godoy (1767–1851) was twice Prime Minister of Spain. When a member of the royal bodyguard, he became the lover of Maria Luisa of Parma, wife of future King, Charles IV. He sided with the French in the Napoleonic Wars, and in 1807 agreed to the partition of Portugal. The following year, Charles was forced to abdicate in favour of the heir apparent (later Ferdinand VII), and by a device, Godoy, with Charles and Ferdinand, became a prisoner of Napoleon. Martin Armstrong was to be one of the contributors to Orwell's 'Story by Five Authors,' 30 October 1942 (*1623*; and see *1465, n. 1*).

402. To Cyril Connolly

12 October 1937   Typewritten

At. 36 High Street   Southwold   Suffolk[1]

Dear Cyril,

I wonder if you are back in England. I haven't seen your name in the New Statesman lately. When in town I enquired after you but was told you were abroad. As far as I remember I wrote to you from Spain but not many letters were getting through at that time. If you are going to be in town during the winter, try and come out and see us some time. You know our address (The Stores, Wallington, Near Baldock, Herts.), it is a bore to get to by train but easy enough if you have a car—about 45 miles from town. We can always put you up. I wonder if you have been back to Spain and how things are going there. It is almost impossible to get any real news. Owing to having served in the P.O.U.M. militia I had to leave in haste with the police on my heels and most of the people I knew there are in jail, or were when I last had news. We were there about six months and had a most interesting time, but it is heart-breaking to see the way things have gone, nearly a million men dead in all, they say, and obviously it is going to be all for nothing. I was about four months in the line, got badly wounded at Huesca but am now completely all right. My wife really had the worst time, being in the middle of that awful nightmare of political intrigue in Barcelona. Richard Rees was on the Madrid front with an ambulance and got back just recently, but I haven't seen him yet. I am doing a book on Spain, of course, and writing against time to try and get it done to come out in March. It doesn't do one any good to have been mixed up with the P.O.U.M.—I have already had to change my publisher, among other things. The only decent book on Spain I have seen hitherto was that one by Franz Borkenau called "The Spanish Cockpit." I dare say if Jellinek does one it might be good.[2] Do you know where he is? He has left Spain and the Manchester Guardian couldn't tell me his address.

Write if you get time.[3] I shall be at the above address till about the 25th, then at the usual.

Yours
Eric Blair

1. Orwell's parents' home.
2. Orwell reviewed Jellinek's *The Civil War in Spain*; see *462*.
3. Connolly replied on 13 October. He said he had spent all summer in the Balkans, had heard Orwell had been wounded, and had tried to see him in Spain but could not get beyond Fraga.

He was anxious to talk to Orwell about Spain and was 'very depressed by the treatment of the P.O.U.M.' 'The moment one expresses any anti-communist feelings or shows any sympathy with anarchist or Trotskyist down and outs who are far more interesting and also far more Spanish than the people who replace them, it gets increasingly hard to find a publisher or an editor who will print one.' Having no car, he wondered if there was any chance of Orwell coming to London. He had enjoyed *The Road to Wigan Pier* 'enormously' and thought that if Orwell had difficulty finding a publisher (for what was to be *Homage to Catalonia*), he was 'sure Secker would jump at you.'

403. To Yvonne Davet

14 October 1937   Typewritten

The Stores   Wallington   Nr. Baldock   <u>HERTS</u>.

Dear Comrade,

I am going to write in English this time, so as to make sure of being understood. I know your English is much better than my French. Thank you so much for the newspaper cuttings, the copy of "La Revolution Proletarienne," and for your own labour of translation,[1] which I liked very much. There was really only one mistake. You translated "There is no nonsense about habeas corpus" as "Rien de plus legitime . . . que l'habeas corpus," "No nonsense" is an ironical English expression, meaning simply that something or other is more than one can expect. I only meant that habeas corpus doesn't exist in Spain at present. But it didn't matter, any way. You mentioned that the expression "O.T.C." puzzled you. It stands for Officers' Training Corps. In England each public school (ie. the expensive boarding-schools to which the rich send their sons) has a training corps which the boys are more or less compelled to join and in which they receive a fairly high degree of military training and are taught to use rifles, machine-guns, etc. In a country like England where military service is not universal, these O.T.Cs are of great importance, as they are a means of ensuring that the sons of the rich are trained in the use of weapons while the sons of the workers are not. One result of this is that when war breaks out and conscription becomes necessary the officers are mainly drawn from the richer classes.

I took the liberty of taking out a year's subscription of "Controversy" for you, and I hope they will send it along each month. If you like I can also arrange to have sent the "New Leader," which is the weekly paper of the I.L.P. It seems to me that at this moment it is most important for the revolutionary parties in all countries to keep in touch as well as they can, and one way they can do so is by exchange of newspapers. I wonder therefore whether you can let me know which French weekly paper represents the viewpoint of the Left Socialists—this I suppose is the party corresponding to the I.L.P. and P.O.U.M. If you can let me know which paper is the most suitable I can arrange to take it in, and then when there is an article or news-item of importance I can pass it on to "Controversy" or the "New Leader." "Controversy" has articles from Germany at present, but doesn't seem to have any from France, where the situation is really more important.

Yours sincerely
Eric Blair

1. This must be 'Eye-Witness in Barcelona,' *Controversy*, August 1937 (see *382*); published in French in *La Révolution Prolétarienne*, 25 September 1937, translated by Yvonne Davet.

404. Review of *The Booster*,[1] September 1937

New English Weekly, 21 October 1937

Mr Robert Graves tells somewhere or other of a man who settled in a large Midland town and devoted an entire year to making the acquaintance of everyone in the town with the name of Ramsbottom, Sidebottom, Winterbottom, Shufflebottom, Higginbottom, Wagginbottom, and plain Bottom. Having made their acquaintance he invited them all to a dinner-party from which he absented himself at the last moment. The dinner when served was found to consist of nothing but rump-steak.

Is this funny? No, it isn't, and perhaps that was the point. If you wanted to do anything so completely futile as wasting a year of life on a practical joke, surely it would be all the *more* futile if the joke was not even funny? And that is one of the possible attitudes, though perhaps not the most satisfactory one, towards modern life: to make some gestures of supreme futility, something so unutterably meaningless and stupid that Caligula making his horse consul would seem sensible by comparison. It is one way, though rather a safe and feeble way, of hitting back at Hitler, Stalin, Lord Rothermere, etc.

I mention this because I believe that it is the motive, if any, that lies behind "The Booster." It seems to me an effort to produce something finally and unsurpassably pointless. "The Booster," we are told in the typewritten prospectus, was previously "the more or less official organ of the American Country Club," but has now passed into the hands of Alfred Perlès, Lawrence Durrell, Henry Miller and others. The editorial staff are modest about themselves:—

"We are mostly renegade, *métèque*, treacherous. No sound moral fibre, no stamina, no honesty, no loyalty, no principles. . . . When we lack material we will borrow from the newspapers, or from other magazines, or even from that Morgue of information, the Encyclopaedia Britannica. Why not? We are not afraid to dish up second-hand stuff. . . .

"We have no plans for reforming the world, no dogmas, no ideologies to defend. We are strictly neutral, peaceful and negative. Also abortive. We do not intend to make a 'success' of 'The Booster.' On the contrary, our aim is to run it into the ground as quickly as possible. . . .

"If you wish to see the editor in person ring the bell at No. 7, Villa Seurat, under the name of Madame Kalf. . . . If you must call, call with dough. . . ."

And so on. Having received a prospectus of this kind, you are all set for a practical joke. When you have swallowed the bait and sent your five francs you look forward to receiving (for instance) a magazine with entirely blank pages, or one which explodes a squib when you open it. But nothing of the kind. All you get is a perfectly ordinary, dam-silly° magazine of the pseudo-artistic type that used to appear and die with the rapidity of May flies in Montparnasse in the 'twenties.

And what does it contain? A not bad fantasy-portrait called "Benno, the Wild Man from Borneo," by Henry Miller, some poems (you can guess what those are like, for how many kinds of poem are there nowadays?), an excellent photograph of an iron armchair, a not altogether disagreeable drawing by Abe Rattner, some stuff in French which I did not bother to read, a burlesque article on sport and some society notes ("Mlle Lefebure and M. J. Lefebure, of Paris, were recent tea guests of Mme France Racine," etc.), which are not even burlesque. Also, as a special supplement, a long letter, written in 1925 and vouched for as authentic, to the New York Park Commissioner, complaining that the trees in the public parks need trimming. The only definitely comic feature in the magazine is the advertisements. There is a vast number of these, and I know by bitter experience[2] what a job it must have been to canvass them. The entire tribe of Paris-American snob-shops—the beauty-specialists, fashionable shoe-makers, etc.—seem to have been caught hopping. No doubt they imagined that their advertisements were to appear in some smart society journal which would lie about in hotel lounges and catch the eye of wealthy American tourists. For "The Booster's" sake let us hope they paid cash in advance.

So much for "The Booster." Is it funny? It is not, and, as I have suggested above, that is perhaps the point. Is it worth buying? It might be, because anything of this kind is liable to develop a scarcity value sooner or later. Meanwhile, "The Booster" offers you a yearly subscription for seventy-five francs and a "life subscription" for five hundred francs. Whether your life or "The Booster's" is not stated; but the point seems to be of importance, for I do not imagine that "The Booster" is exactly a "good life."

1. *The Booster* was a monthly magazine published in French and English in Paris from September 1937 to Easter 1939 (from April 1938 as *Delta*). In addition to those mentioned in the review, William Saroyan and Anaïs Nin were associated with it.
2. What this bitter experience was has not been recorded. Orwell does not mention canvassing for advertisements in his letters or books, though canvassers for newspaper subscriptions appear in *The Road to Wigan Pier*. Perhaps this was one of the 'varied jobs' mentioned in the jacket copy of the U.S. edition of *Down and Out in Paris and London* (1933), which refers to his earning his living by schoolmastering and private tutoring, working in a Paris hotel, picking hops, pushing a barrow in Billingsgate Fish Market, and 'other varied jobs.' Denys King-Farlow (see *29, n. 2*) says in a far from bitter reference to Orwell at Eton that receipts from the sale of *Election Times*, 3 June 1918 (see *29–32*) seemed 'rather laughable contrasted with the £128 that Blair and I netted from publishing *College Days* No 4 (see *37, 43–46*), heavy with snob-appeal advertisements, in 1920 for the Eton–Harrow Match at Lord's' (*Orwell Remembered*, 55). That sum would include sales and advertising revenue.

The Booster's response to this review appeared in *New English Weekly*, 4 November 1937. In it, Alfred Perlès (1897–1990), Managing Editor and

Director, included a lengthy extract from 'a forthcoming editorial which may throw a little light on the muddled situation created by our George.' He maintained that Orwell was wielding not a hatchet but 'one of the smaller calibres of water-pistol' and that he was not an enemy worthy of attack with a bayonet. 'Would you have us set the bed afire because we find a flea in it?' it concluded.

Before its publication, Perlès, on 29 October, wrote to Philip Mairet, who had taken over the editing of *New English Weekly* when A. R. Orage, who founded it, died. He accepted some 'perfectly legitimate' charges, and said that he would have preferred it if Orwell had seen the second issue before writing a review; he might have liked it better. He argued that Orwell's review had lost the journal the 'moral' (his quotation marks) support of the American Country Club, and he expected advertising revenue to drop. He concludes: 'However, no hard feelings. We all like Orwell.'

There would hardly have been time for the American Country Club to break its association with *The Booster*, and Henry Miller, writing to Orwell on 7 November, thought that 'it was purely a coincidence,' though 'it was natural to think there might have been some connection.' Had that and a drop in advertising resulted, it would suggest that Orwell had used something more damaging that a small-calibre water-pistol. Miller enclosed a draft of a letter to the editor of *New English Weekly*, 24 October 1937, 'as a little souvenir.' He invited Orwell to continue the attack: 'You have full permission to slam the shit out of us,' and suggested, with fine generosity, two agents who might help place *Homage to Catalonia*. Orwell's reply was published on 11 November 1937:

Sir,—I note that the letter from "The Booster" in your issue of November 4 describes me as a flea. No doubt this hits me off very neatly, but at least it would appear from the length and tone of the letter that some of my bites have taken effect. However, what I want to say is this: It would appear that I was badly mistaken about "The Booster." I took it for a designedly bad joke, and said so. But it may well be that there is some deep meaning in it which I failed to divine, and in that case it seems rather a pity that it should have been reviewed by such an unsuitable person. I still cannot see any sense in "The Booster," but perhaps somebody else could. The second issue appeared a week or two ago. May I suggest, if you can spare the space, that you allow someone better qualified than myself (Mr. Porteus,° for example) to do a review of this one, or of both together?

In the next issue of *New English Weekly*, novelist and critic Oswell Blakeston, who also wrote poetry and, later, books on film technique and scriptwriting, suggested that beneath its seemingly irresponsible surface, *The Booster* had 'a message which might easily be of importance in the present crisis.'

The 'Mr. Porteus' Orwell suggested was Hugh Gordon Porteous (1906–1993). He contributed reviews and articles to every issue of *New English Weekly* from 1935 to 1938. He took a special interest in visual art.

405. To Jack Common

Tuesday, [October? 1937]   Typewritten

The Stores   Wallington   Nr. Baldock   HERTS.

Dear Jack

I was so glad to hear from you. I had tried and failed to get your address. Had I known you were still in Datchworth, I could probably have evolved it out of my inner consciousness, but I had vaguely heard you had gone to London. Do come across any time you can summon the energy. Of course it is a bloody cross-country journey. Have you got a bike? We can always put you up. As I remember it it isn't the kind of journey one wants to make twice in one day. Come any time except this week-end, when someone else is coming, which uses up our only spare room.

I would like to do something for the Penguin people very much, only the devil of it is that at present I simply can't write about anything but Spain and am struggling with a bloody book on it which I have contracted to do by the end of the year. Of course I could detach something from the book—I think there is at any rate one chapter that would do—but that mightn't be the kind of thing they want and also I don't know that my publishers would want it. It is a devil of a business. It seems only yesterday that nobody would print anything I wrote, and now I get letters from all quarters saying won't I write something; and except for the thing I actually have on hand I am as empty as a jug. Of course I never could and never have written short stories proper. This Spain business has upset me so that I really can't write about anything else, and unfortunately what one has to write about is not picturesque stuff but a blasted complicated story of political intrigue between a lot of cosmopolitan Communists, Anarchists etc. Beyond the book I am not doing anything except the usual hack-work of reviews which I don't count as writing.

We had a devil of a time in Spain but very interesting. I had the bad luck to be heavily mixed up in the political business owing to serving in the P.O.U.M. militia via the I.L.P., so I was also mixed up in the Barcelona fighting in May and finally had to flee from Spain with the police in hot pursuit. Had I gone to Spain with no political affiliations at all I should probably have joined the International Column and should no doubt by this time have had a bullet in the back for being "politically unreliable," or at least have been in jail. If I had understood the situation a bit better I should probably have joined the Anarchists. As it was I went there with I.L.P. papers and was thus drafted into the P.O.U.M. militia, so am being denounced from time to time as a Fascist, Trotskyist etc. in the Daily Worker, also have had to change my publisher as Gollancz won't have any more to do with me now I am a Trotskyist. I got badly wounded at Huesca but had a very lucky escape and am now perfectly all right. A bullet went through my neck but missed all the vital spots and only left one vocal cord paralysed, which doesn't matter as the other cord is "compensating" and my voice is normal again. I haven't seen Richard Rees yet but have heard from him and I hope he will come down here later. He got back about a month ago. I gather he got somehow mixed up in the political business too, I really don't know how, as he was with the Communist Party, but of course we are all Trotskyists nowadays.

Come across when you feel like it. Might be better to drop a card in advance but it doesn't matter very greatly as we are generally here. Please remember me to your wife.

Yours
Eric Blair

406. Review of *Broken Water* by James Hanley; *I Wanted Wings* by Beirne Lay

Time and Tide, 6 November 1937

Mr. James Hanley's novel, *The Furies*, showed considerable talent and a genuine intensity of feeling, but it had the fault, common in "non-stop" novels, of making no visible distinction between trivial and important incidents. It is perhaps not widely enough recognized that every imaginative writer is trying to induce in his reader a series of quite different states of consciousness. There are the passages that describe a general atmosphere extending over long periods of time, the passages where the tempo changes and a minute may occupy pages, the passages where a visual impression has to be evoked or avoided, and so on. The writer's main difficulty is at the points of transition—the joints, so to speak—and the "non-stop" way of writing is an unconscious device for avoiding this. But in *Broken Water*, though it does start in a manner slightly reminiscent of *The Furies*, Mr. Hanley has shed many of his earlier faults. It is a much more selective book, written in a more varied tone of voice, and the subject-matter is undoubtedly better.

It is a sort of autobiography, though obviously it does not contain the whole of Mr. Hanley's life-history. Mainly it is about his experiences as a sailor in the years immediately before and during the war; it is significant of his increased power of selection that though he served as a soldier during the last year or two of war, he says little or nothing about the fighting. There are two passages of wonderful and even shocking intensity. One is a description of a transport full of panic-stricken soldiers waiting for a German submarine to discharge its torpedo. The other is a description of how Mr. Hanley, then a boy of about fourteen, saw a steward slip over the ship's rail, caught his hand, held on to him for a long time, and then, his strength giving out, had to watch him drop into the dark water and drown. This last is a really remarkable piece of writing. Mr. Hanley writes much better about the sea than about the land, perhaps because the narrow limits of a ship confine his imagination.

Some queer characters pass across the pages of the book. "One never strikes a deep friendship at sea," Mr. Hanley says; "all is coming and going, there is no time to consolidate a liking for a particular person, faces just come and go like gusts of wind." The result is that the sailors here, as in most books about the sea, are mainly grotesques, though Mr. Hanley is at any rate not guilty of exploiting them for humorous purposes.

I Wanted Wings has just this much affinity with *Broken Water*, that the author pined to be an airman just as Mr. Hanley, at an earlier age, pined to be a sailor. For the rest it is quite a different kind of book—a slick, cleverly-written book, partly reprinted from American magazines of the type of *Esquire*. The author got his wish in the end, managing by desperate efforts to pass into the American Air Force; it appears that the enormous majority of candidates fail to pass the various tests, physical, mental and psychological. All through his account of his struggles at the flying school there runs the same spirit of savage competition and neurotic dread of failure that one sees in the efficiency advertisements in the American magazines. The most interesting part of the book is an appendix at the end, explaining some of the technicalities of flying. The photographs are terrible.

407. To Yvonne Davet

14 November 1937   Typewritten

The French of this letter lacks all accents and is so reproduced. Orwell presumably forgot to add them by hand after typing the letter—as would appear, from some of the other letters, to have been his more usual practice; see *389, headnote*. Salutations and complimentary closes are omitted from translations hereafter.

The Stores   Wallington   Nr. Baldock   HERTS. Angleterre.

Chere° Camarade,
Je vous remercie beaucoup pour m'avoir envoye "La Revolution Proletarienne" et "La Fleche." Voulez vous me dire combien ca vous a coute pour les abonnements? Je ne veux pas que vous fassiez des depenses pour moi. Je vais vous faire envoyer le "New Leader." Ce n'est pas grand' chose comme journal, mais il est quand meme le seul journal, meme hebdomadaire, en Angleterre qui mene une campagne pour le Socialisme de type revolutionnaire. Je serais tres content de recevoir des Cahiers de la "gauche revolutionnaire" quand ca vous sera possible.

Il me semble que quand vous avez occasion de traduire quelquechose de "Controversy"[1] ou du "New Leader" il n'est pas tres important de demander l'autorisation de l'auteur en cas d'urgence. Peut-etre quand il y a le temps il serait mieux de la demander; mais en tous cas en ces journaux de ce type-la il n'y a pas question d'argent.

Je comprends tres bien qu'il est difficile de placer une traduction d'un livre anglais en France. C'est la meme chose en Angleterre—les editeurs ne s'interessent pas aux livres francais. Les livres allemands ont beaucoup plus de succes en Angleterre que les livres francais—voir par example les livres de Feuchtwanger, Remarque et Ludwig[2] qui ont ete des "best sellers." Peut-etre quand j'aurai fini mon livre sur la guerre en Espagne—il doit paraitre au mois de mars—nous pourrons trouver un editeur francais, car c'est un sujet dont on s'interesse plus en France qu'en Angleterre.

Vous m'avez dit que vous etiez souffrante. J'espere que ca va mieux maintenant.

Veuillez croire, chere camarade, a mes sentiments devoues.

Eric Blair

Translation

Thank you very much for sending me "La Révolution Prolétarienne" and "La Flèche." Could you tell me how much the subscriptions cost you? I do not want you to be put to expense on my behalf. I will have the "New Leader" sent to you. It is not much of a newspaper, but it is the only newspaper, even among the weeklies, in England which is campaigning for revolutionary Socialism. I should be very glad to receive journals of the "revolutionary left" when you can send them.

I think that when you are translating something from "Controversy"[1] or the "New Leader" it is not very important to ask the author's permission if there isn't much time. It would probably be better to get it if you do have time; but in any case with newspapers like these there is never a question of a fee.

I can well understand that it is difficult to place a translation of an English book in France. It is the same in England—the publishers are not interested in French books. German books meet with much greater success in England than French books—look, for example, at books by Feuchtwanger, Remarque and Ludwig,[2] which have been "best sellers." Perhaps when I have finished my book on the war in Spain—it is due to come out in March—we shall be able to find a French publisher, as that is a subject which arouses greater interest in France than in England.

You said you had been ill. I hope you are feeling better now.

1. 'Eye-Witness in Barcelona'; see 382.
2. Lion Feuchtwanger (1884–1958) became particularly famous for his novel *Jud Süss* (1925; English translation, *Jew Süss*, 1926). With the rise of Nazism, he was forced out of Germany and went to France, where he was imprisoned in a concentration camp until he escaped to the United States in 1940, where he died. Erich Maria Remarque (1898–1970) achieved fame with his anti-war novel *All Quiet on the Western Front* (1929 in German and English). A film, distributed with certain shocking scenes (e.g., rats in the trenches) cut, was made in Hollywood in 1930. *The Road Back* (1931) described the collapse of Germany following the war. He left Germany in 1932, to live first in Switzerland, and from 1939 in the United States. He became an American citizen in 1947. He returned to Switzerland with his second wife, film star, Paulette Goddard, and died there. Emil Ludwig (1881–1948) was a prolific biographer. His books, in English translations, included *Napoleon* (1927), *Bismark* (1927), *Goethe* (1928), *Lincoln* (1929), and a controversial life of Christ, *The Son of Man* (1928). He also wrote two plays about World War I. His *Conversations with Mussolini* appeared in 1933.

408. George Barber to Orwell

20 November 1937   Erroneously attributed to Orwell

This letter is recorded in the Register of Modern British Literary Manuscripts as being written by Orwell (Eric Blair) to Eric O'Shaughnessy. However there is no doubt that it was written by George Barber, who mistakenly signed himself Eric Blair—the name of the person to whom he was writing. Barber then lived at 178 Hurst Grove, Bedford. Douglas Moyle,[1] before he went to Spain, knew Barber, who was working for Standard Telephones and Cable, North Woolwich. Barber moved to Bedford, whilst Moyle was in Spain, to work for the Air Ministry at Henlow. On 6 April 1968, he wrote to Moyle and said, 'Clearly I must have been writing the envelope just before [signing the letter] and absentmindedly put Eric's name for my own at the end of the letter' (Barber's letter to Moyle and Moyle's letter to Ian Angus, 9 April 1968; the identifications in the notes come from these letters and from an interview with Ian Angus, 18 February 1970).

178, Hurst Grove,
Bedford.
20th. Nov. '37.

Dear Eric,

Thanks ever so for your letter of a while ago. I'm very sorry I haven't answered it before.

I quite understand that you would rather not engage in a debate, though I think it most unlikely that you would bring other than glory to the I.L.P. However we have fixed up for the moment that John will be speaking on the 30th as originally suggested,[2] and other plans are for the moment set aside. I hope you will be able to come along to that meeting. If you can I suggest that you let me come over and fetch you at about 4.45 pm on my way home from work, and that you bring Eileen to have a meal with John here before we go to the meeting. How about it? I have not definitely found out yet what time he will be here but I expect we shall be able to persuade him to come early. I'll write again with fuller details.

Are you going to the Xmas school[3] at Matlock? Douglas and I are intending to go along for a day or so starting on the 26th. I'm going over with Cyril and Mike to see him at Coventry tomorrow.[4] He seems to be thriving there though I believe he lost a lot of time as a result of the strike there recently. He seems to be in the thick of the struggle at the moment.

I'm sorry I haven't been able to get over to see you lately but look forward to doing so in the near future.

Sincerely,
Eric Blair [mistakenly, for George Barber]

1. Douglas Moyle (c. 1911–) served with Orwell in Spain; see *Homage to Catalonia*, *CW*, VI, 77–78. In *Remembering Orwell* he gives an account of going on night patrol with Orwell, and of Orwell's reading Shakespeare in quiet moments in the trenches (80–81). After serving in Spain, and working in Coventry, first for GEC and then for Armstrong Whitworth on the

Whitley bomber, he inclined toward pacifism, but Orwell's influence led to his abandoning this point of view (interview with Ian Angus, 18 February 1970).
2. John McNair (see *363, n. 5*), spoke at the Left Book Club on 30 November 1937. For Orwell's unwillingness to speak, see *366, headnote*.
3. An ILP 'School' held at Crich, near Matlock. Moyle spent Christmas with Barber at the latter's parents' home in Bristol and then they both went to the ILP School.
4. Cyril Wright and his girl-friend, Mikeal (which Moyle also spelt Michael) Smith. Wright, though not a member of ILP, once canvassed for the Labour Party. His father was a manufacturer of sweets in Bedford, for whom he worked in 1937–39 as a salesman. Smith was an assistant dispenser in Boots the Chemist's. Wright's strong interest in literature formed the basis for his friendship with Orwell and he and Smith frequently drove to see the Orwells at Wallington. Moyle stayed for a short time with Barber, in Bedford, on his return from Spain, before Barber went to Coventry to work. Wright followed him there and shared his rooms whilst he worked as a sales representative for Dean's, a manufacturer of shop blinds. It is possible that Orwell gained some knowledge of a salesman's life (used in *Coming Up for Air*) from Wright, as well as from John Sceats; see *498, 504*.

409. Review of *The Problem of the Distressed Areas* by Wal Hannington; *Grey Children* by James Hanley; *The Fight for the Charter* by Neil Stewart

Time and Tide, 27 November 1937

As everyone knows—or ought to know—Mr. Hannington[1] has worked harder and more effectively for the unemployed than anyone else in England. He knows the derelict areas inside out, he has been prominent in every demonstration and hunger march, his activities have got him into prison at least five times, and above all he is largely responsible for the existence of the N.U.W.M.,[2] an organization which has not only helped the unemployed to fight back against victimisation but has also done a great deal to prevent them from being converted, as they so easily might have been, into a huge army of blacklegs.

His book is partly a survey of the present condition of the distressed areas, partly an enquiry as to what has been done by successive governments to solve the unemployment problem—the answer, of course, being "Nothing." Periodically there is talk of "land settlement"—smallholdings for the unemployed—which, as Mr. Hannington perceives, is plain eyewash. The only positive move has been the establishment of the so-called social service centres, which at best are a charitable sop and at worst are dangerously like a device for providing the local authorities with free labour. Meanwhile unemployment continues almost unabated, the Means Test breaks up families and brings into existence an army of spies and informers, and it is estimated that twenty million people in Great Britain are under-nourished.

There are one or two points on which I do not agree with Mr. Hannington. He sees clearly enough the danger of large-scale unemployment leading to Fascism, but he is too ready to think of Fascism in terms of Hitler and Mosley. English Fascism, if it ever comes, is likely to be a lot subtler than that; Sir Oswald is, in fact, merely a red herring in a black shirt. Also Mr.

Hannington's "immediate programme" for dealing with the distressed areas, which he sets out in detail, is too optimistic. On paper it is a workable scheme and it would no doubt go a long way towards solving the problem, but it involves taxing the rich out of existence, which is simply not thinkable under our present system of government. But perhaps Mr. Hannington is aware of that and hopes that the moral will point itself.[3]

Mr. Hanley's book deals only with South Wales, but it dovetails neatly into Mr. Hannington's, the one supplying what the other lacks. Mr. Hannington gives you the facts and figures; Mr. Hanley tells you, by recording a series of conversations with unemployed people, what it *feels* like to be on the Means Test. By its cumulative effect this is a terribly moving book. Mr. Hanley's writing is certainly improving by leaps and bounds. In some ways, although his range is smaller, he sees more deeply into the problem than Mr. Hannington—is more interested in what the people in the distressed areas actually feel and think. Also he grasps the tragic failure of theoretical Socialism to make any contact with the normal working class, especially at present, when the whole movement is losing itself in internecine struggles. As he says, it is a terrible thing that in the midst of squalor and degradation the Socialist parties should be flying at one another's throats upon the question of whether Trotsky is guilty. This book leaves behind it an even deeper feeling of hopelessness than Mr. Hannington's. And perhaps that is all to the good, for, as Mr. Hanley says, "the thing *is* terrible, and the only way of forcing it home on people is to keep on saying so."

The Fight for the Charter is a good short history of the Chartist movement. As Marx pointed out, if the essential point of the People's Charter (manhood suffrage) had been won at the time when it was demanded, it would in effect have meant revolution, because in the "hungry forties" the bulk of the population was a definitely revolutionary working class. Later, when universal suffrage became law, it made no difference, because by that time England was prosperous and large sections of the working class had "turned respectable." In spite of renewed misery their respectability remains with them, and the job-swapping game of English politics continues almost unchanged. Incidentally, the behaviour of the of the middle-class leaders of the Chartist movement is worth study by those who believe in the Popular Front.

1. For Orwell's comments on Hannington as an orator, see Wigan Pier Diary, *274, 11.2.36.*
2. National Unemployed Workers' Movement.
3. *The Problem of the Distressed Areas*, which Gollancz published in the Left Book Club series, had a thirty-two-page insert of plates, in the manner adopted for *The Road to Wigan Pier.*

410. To Cyril Connolly

Sunday [28 November 1937]   Typewritten

The Stores   Wallington   Nr. Baldock   HERTS.

Dear Cyril,

Are you in town nowadays? I am going to be in town on 2nd-third and would much like to meet if we could arrange it—perhaps some time on the third if you could manage it?

Yours
Eric Blair

411. To Cyril Connolly

[1 December 1937]   Handwritten; dated from lettercard postmark

At. 56 Upper Park Rd.   Hampstead   NW. 3[1]

Dear Cyril,

Thanks, I would like to come to lunch on Friday very much. I would also like to meet Stephen Spender[2] if he is free. I've often said rude things about him in print etc, but I daresay he won't know or won't mind.

Yours
Eric Blair

1. Richard Rees's home. For Rees, see *95*.
2. Stephen Spender (1909–1995; Kt., 1983), prolific poet, novelist, critic, and translator. He edited *Horizon* with Cyril Connolly, 1940–41, and was a coeditor of *Encounter*, 1953–65, remaining on the editorial board until 1967, when it was discovered that some of the money to launch *Encounter* had been provided surreptitiously by the U.S. Central Intelligence Agency. Orwell attacked Spender personally in his letter to Nancy Cunard, *386A*. He also included him among those parlour Bolsheviks and 'fashionable successful persons' whom he castigated from time to time; see Crick, 351. In his letter to Spender of 15? April 1938 he explained why 'I attacked you not having met you'; see *435*. They were then to become friends. See also *856*, n. 3.

412. To Leonard Moore

6 December 1937   Typewritten

The Stores   Wallington   Nr. Baldock   HERTS.[1]

Dear Mr Moore,

Many thanks for your letter. I am glad Gollancz is already showing such solicitude about my next book, but I have only a vague idea of it as yet, as you may well imagine. All I have thought of is this: it will be a novel, it will not be about politics, and it will be about a man who is having a holiday and trying to make a temporary escape from his responsibilities, public and private. The title I thought of is "Coming Up for Air." I am afraid this is a very vague indication, but if it is any use for the catalogue they can have it. At any rate they can publish that title, as it indicates the general idea of what I want to write about.[2]

I have finished the rough draft of the Spanish book and begun revising. I am afraid it is going to be late as usual, but I think it should be done about the middle of January. I suppose they can get it through the press fairly quickly if they want to, can't they? In connection with this book, the Frenchwoman[3] who was wanting to translate some of my work has asked me to send her various wads of it as they get done, so that she can immediately translate it on spec. and begin hawking it round the French publishers. I think her idea is that one of the left-wing papers might publish it, or part of it, in serial form. If so I am afraid there would not be a penny of money in it, but I should like it done for various reasons.

As to the Gollancz book, barring accidents I think I can promise to have something done about next October.

Yours sincerely
Eric Blair

1. For the first time in the surviving correspondence, a telephone number, Baldock 172, is typed at the head of a letter from The Stores.
2. The section from 'I have only a vague idea' to 'what I want to write about' has been marked by heavy double quotation marks in Moore's office. That section was presumably forwarded to Gollancz.
3. Yvonne Davet.

413. To Yvonne Davet

6 December 1937   Typewritten

The Stores Wallington Nr. Baldock HERTS. Angleterre.

Chère Camarade,
Je suis très content d'entendre que vous n'avez du rien payer pour "La Revolution Prolétarienne." Il m'a interessé beaucoup, dans le dernier numéro, d'avoir des nouvelles de Landau,[1] qui a disparu and qu'on croit assassiné en prison. Ma femme connaissait sa femme à Barcelone. Quant au livre que je suis en train d'écrire, quand j'aurai fini la première moitié (probablement un peu après Noel), je le vous enverrai, et la dernière moitié deux ou trois semaines plus tard. Je crois qu'il sera probablement la dernière moitié qu'un éditeur français trouverait le plus intéressant, car c'est là que j'ai écrit mes impressions des jours de Mai en Barcelone, la crise politique en Catalogne etc., etc. Il est tres gentil de votre part de vouloir risquer faire la traduction pour rien.[2]

Très fraternellement
Eric Blair

Translation

I am very glad to hear that you did not have to pay anything for "La Révolution Prolétarienne." I was very interested to see, in the latest number, news of Landau,[1] who had disappeared; we thought he had been killed in prison. My wife knew his wife in Barcelona. As for the book I am writing, when I have finished the first half (probably soon after Christmas), I will send it to you, with the second half two or three weeks later. I think a French publisher will probably find the second half more interesting; that is where I have written my impressions of the May fighting in Barcelona, the political crisis in Catalonia etc., etc. It is very kind of you to be willing to risk doing the translation for nothing.[2]

1. Kurt Landau, Austrian socialist, was to die 'in mysterious circumstances,' as did a number of other international sympathizers of the POUM; see Thomas, 706 and *3733*, Vol XX, 280, item 2.
2. Although a translation was completed and read by Orwell before the outbreak of World War II, Madame Davet's translation of *Homage to Catalonia* was not published until 1955.

413A. To H. N. Brailsford, 10 December: see Vol XX, final appendix

414. Review of *Storm Over Spain* by Mairin Mitchell; *Spanish Rehearsal* by Arnold Lunn; *Catalonia Infelix* by E. Allison Peers; *Wars of Ideas in Spain* by José Castillejo; *Invertebrate Spain* by José Ortega y Gasset
Time and Tide, 11 December 1937

Storm Over Spain sounds like a war-book, but though it covers a period that includes the civil war the author says very little about the war itself—a subject which is obviously distasteful to her. As she very truly remarks, the atrocity-stories that are so eagerly circulated by both sides are an indictment not of Right or Left, but simply of war.

Her book is valuable for a number of reasons, but especially because, unlike almost all English writers on Spain,[1] she gives a fair deal to the Spanish Anarchists. The Anarchists and Syndicalists have been persistently misrepresented in England, and the average English person still retains his eighteen-ninetyish notion that Anarchism is the same thing as anarchy. Anyone who wants to know what Spanish Anarchism stands for, and the remarkable things it achieved, especially in Catalonia, during the first few months of the revolution, should read Chapter VII of Miss Mitchell's book. The pity is that so much of what the Anarchists achieved has already been undone, ostensibly because of military necessity, actually in order to prepare the way for the return of capitalism when the war is over.

Mr. Arnold Lunn writes as a supporter of General Franco and believes life in "Red" Spain (which he has not visited) to be one continuous massacre. On the authority of Mr. Arthur Bryant, who, "as an historian, is well accustomed to weigh evidence," he puts the number of non-combatants massacred by the "reds" since the beginning of the war as 350,000. It would appear, also, that "the burning of a nun in petrol or the sawing off of a Conservative tradesman's legs" are "the commonplaces of 'democratic' Spain."

Now, I was about six months in Spain, almost exclusively among Socialists, Anarchists and Communists, and if I remember rightly I never even once sawed off a Conservative tradesman's legs. I am almost certain I should remember doing such a thing, however commonplace it may seem to Mr. Lunn and Mr. Bryant. But will Mr. Lunn believe me? No, he will not. And meanwhile stories every bit as silly as this are being manufactured on the other side, and people who were sane two years ago are swallowing them eagerly. That, apparently, is what war, even war in other countries, does to the human mind.

Professor Allison Peers is the leading English authority on Catalonia. His book is a history of the province, and naturally, at the present moment, the most interesting chapters are those towards the end, describing the war and the revolution. Unlike Mr. Lunn, Professor Peers understands the internal situation on the Government side, and Chapter XIII of his book gives an excellent account of the strains and stresses between the various political parties. He believes that the war may last for years, that Franco is likely to win, and that there is no hope of democracy in Spain when the war is over. All of them depressing conclusions, but the first two are quite probably correct and the last is most assuredly so.

Finally, two books which really belong to an earlier period, but are relevant to the civil war in so much that they give certain glimpses of its origins. *War° of Ideas in Spain* is primarily a treatise on Spanish education. I am not competent to judge it, but I can admire the intellectual detachment that has been able to produce it amid the horrors of civil war. Dr. Castillejo is a professor at the University of Madrid and for thirty years past has worked for educational reform in Spain. He is now watching his life-work going down into a sea of rival fanaticisms; for, as he rather sadly recognizes, whatever else survives the war, intellectual tolerance will not. *Invertebrate Spain* is a collection of essays, most of them first published about 1920, on various aspects of the Spanish character.[2] Sr. Ortega y Gasset is one of those writers of the type of Keyserling, who explain everything in terms of race, geography and tradition (in fact, of anything except economics), and who are constantly saying illuminating things without reaching any general conclusion. Open *Invertebrate Spain* and you realize immediately that you are in contact with a distinguished mind; go on reading it, and you find yourself wondering what the devil this is all about. Still, it *is* a distinguished mind, and if the book as a whole leaves behind an impression of vagueness, or even chaos, each separate paragraph is capable of starting an interesting train of thought.

1. Mairin Mitchell wrote to Orwell following the publication of this review (letter undated) thanking him for the generosity with which he had treated her book, especially because, from her reading of *The Road to Wigan Pier*, she did not think they were in the same political camp. However, she did point out that she was 'unlike almost all English writers on Spain,' in being Irish!
2. See also Orwell's 'The Lure of Profundity'; *415*.

414A. Peace Pledge Union
12 December 1937

Orwell is said to have 'paid a membership subscription to the Peace Pledge Union' in December 1937. However, because 'there is no record of his renewing it' he may 'only have wanted their pamphlets' (Crick, 366). In her *Beloved Quixote* (1986), Kathleen Middleton Murry, John Middleton Murry's daughter, states that her father 'had joined the Peace Pledge Union along with Richard Rees, George Orwell, Aldous Huxley and many others' in 1937 (177). Although Orwell bought a number of PPU pamphlets about this time (see *3733* under 'Pacifism'), the evidence that he joined the PPU is based on a misreading of a receipt in the Orwell Archive. This acknowledges the receipt of 2s 6d from Mrs E. Blair – Eileen, not Eric. The receipt, No. 20194, is dated 12 December 1937. There can be little doubt she was buying pamphlets for her husband (and pamphlets were sold to non-members). Kathleen Middleton Murry gives no evidence that Orwell and Rees joined. Rees was not a pacifist. Indeed, he withdrew as editor and financial backer of *The Adelphi* in 1936 because he 'disapproved strongly of Murry's conversion to pacifism' (letter to Ian Angus, 10 June 1967).

414B. To H. N. Brailsford, 18 December 1937: see Vol XX, final appendix

415. 'The Lure of Profundity'
New English Weekly, 30 December 1937

There is one way of avoiding thoughts, and that is to think too deeply. Take any reasonably true generalization—that women have no beards, for instance—twist it about, stress the exceptions, raise side-issues, and you can presently disprove it, or at any rate shake it, just as, by pulling a table-cloth into its separate threads, you can plausibly deny that it is a table-cloth. There are many writers who constantly do this, in one way or another. Keyserling is an obvious example. Who has not read a few pages by Keyserling? And who has read a whole book by Keyserling? He is constantly saying illuminating things—producing paragraphs which, taken separately, make you exclaim that this is a very remarkable mind—and yet he gets you no forrarder. His mind is moving in too many directions, starting too many hares at once. It is rather the same with Señor Otega y Gasset, whose book of essays, "Invertebrate Spain,"[1] has just been translated and reprinted.

Take, for instance, this passage which I select almost at random:—

> "Each race carries within its own primitive soul an ideal of landscape which it tries to realize within its own borders. Castile is terribly arid because the Castilian is arid. Our race has accepted the dryness about it because it was akin to the inner wastes of its own soul."

It is an interesting idea, and there is something similar on every page. Moreover, one is conscious all through the book of a sort of detachment, an intellectual decency, which is much rarer nowadays than mere cleverness. And yet, after all, what is it *about*? It is a series of essays, mostly written about 1920, on various aspects of the Spanish character. The blurb on the dust-jacket claims that it will make clear to us "what lies behind the Spanish civil war." It does not make it any clearer to me. Indeed, I cannot find any general conclusion in the book whatever.

What is Señor Ortega y Gasset's explanation of his country's troubles? The Spanish soul, tradition, Roman history, the blood of the degenerate Visigoths, the influence of geography on man and (as above) of man on geography, the lack of intellectually eminent Spaniards—and so forth. I am always a little suspicious of writers who explain everything in terms of blood, religion, the solar plexus, national souls and what not, because it is obvious that they are avoiding something. The thing that they are avoiding is the dreary Marxian "economic" interpretation of history. Marx is a difficult author to read, but a crude version of his doctrine is believed in by millions and is in the consciousness of all of us. Socialists of every school can churn it out like a barrel-organ. It is so simple! If you hold such-and-such opinions it is because you have such-and-such an amount of money in your pocket. It is also blatantly untrue in detail, and many writers of distinction have wasted time in attacking it. Señor Ortega y Gasset has a page or two on Marx and makes at least one criticism that starts an interesting train of thought.

But if the "economic" theory of history is merely untrue, as the flat-earth theory is untrue, why do they bother to attack it? Because it is *not* altogether untrue, in fact, is quite true enough to make every thinking person uncomfortable. Hence the temptation to set up rival theories which often involve ignoring obvious facts. The central trouble in Spain is, and must have been for decades past, plain enough: the frightful contrast of wealth and poverty. The blurb on the dust-jacket of "Invertebrate Spain" declares that the Spanish war is "not a class struggle," when it is perfectly obvious that it is very largely that. With a starving peasantry, absentee landlords owning estates the size of English counties, a rising discontented bourgeoisie and a labour movement that had been driven underground by persecution, you had material for all the civil wars you wanted. But that sounds too like the records on the Socialist gramophone! Don't let's talk about the Andalusian peasants starving on two pesetas a day and the children with sore heads begging round the food-shops. If there is something wrong with Spain, let's blame it on the Visigoths.

The result—I should really say the *method*—of such an evasion is excess of intellectuality. The over-subtle mind raises too many side-issues. Thought becomes fluid, runs in all directions, forms memorable lakes and puddles, but gets nowhere. I can recommend this book to anybody, just as a book to read. It is undoubtedly the product of a distinguished mind. But it is no use hoping that it will explain the Spanish civil war. You would get a better explanation from the dullest doctrinaire Socialist, Communist, Anarchist, Fascist or Catholic.

1. Reviewed briefly by Orwell in *Time and Tide*, 11 December 1937; see *414*.

1938

416. Anonymous Review[1] of *Burmese Interlude* by C. V. Warren

The Listener, 12 January 1938

Mr. Warren was an assistant in one of the big timber firms and was in Burma five years, including the bad period of the rebellion. Between 1928 and 1930 the price of paddy dropped from Rs. 150 to Rs. 70 a hundred baskets, there was widespread misery and bands of men who had been thrown out of employment took to the forests and swore oaths of rebellion. As in previous wars in Burma it was guerilla fighting, and Mr. Warren tells pathetic stories of men armed only with dahs and spears being mown down by the machine-guns of the British troops, and believing to the last in the magic tattoo-marks which were supposed to make them proof against bullets. Like every European who is not tied to the big towns, Mr. Warren conceived a deep affection for the Burmese. Social relations have always been friendlier in Burma than in India, party because of the native geniality of the Burmese, partly because of the fewness of European women.

1. This review is one of ten, all anonymous, printed on a single page. The records of *The Listener* show that Orwell was paid £1 for it.

417. Customs Declaration

21 January 1938   Form completed by hand

Among the items of Orwelliana that have survived is one indicating that Orwell still had in mind his friend and commanding officer in Spain, George Kopp (see *359, n.2*). This is a Customs Declaration form, stamped 21 January at Greenwich (where Eileen's family lived), giving details of a small package sent to Kopp in the Prisión Provisional del Ministerio de Gubernación, Calle Valencia 5, Segorbe (Castellan), Spain. (In a later report, this is described as a forced-labour camp; see *535, n. 1*.) The package contained two four-ounce slabs of chocolate, three ounces of tobacco, and a cake of soap, the whole being valued at 2s 11d (not quite 15p). Orwell gave his name as Eric Blair and his address as The Stores, Wallington, which tallies with his letter to Rayner Heppenstall of this same date.

418. To Rayner Heppenstall

21 January 1938   Handwritten lettercard

As from. The Stores   Wallington   Nr. Baldock   Herts.

Dear Rayner.[1]

I saw Warburg[2] yesterday. He said (I didn't mention I was emissary for you, so this is between you & me & the g.p.) that Senhouse[3] liked your novel & they were "considering" publishing it. I don't know how much that really means. We then got talking as to how there was room for a pacifist book not from the normal turn the other cheek angle but from a we won't bloody well fight angle, & I said you might be the person to write it as I knew you had some interest in pacifism. He said he would be very interested in that. Today I saw Max Plowman[4] who is sorry he hasn't written to you as he has been very busy but will do so. I'll let you have a line about the best day to come down to our place but it would probably be about the 3rd. Love to M.[5]

Yours
Eric

1. See *238*.
2. Fredric Warburg, a director of Secker & Warburg, publisher of *Homage to Catalonia*; see *375, n. 1*.
3. Roger Senhouse, a director of Secker & Warburg; see *375, n. 2.*; 'g.p.' = gatepost.
4. Max Plowman (see *95*), journalist and author, and close associate of John Middleton Murry and the *Adelphi* group, was at this time General Secretary of the Peace Pledge Union.
5. Margaret, Mrs. Rayner Heppenstall.

419. To Rayner Heppenstall

2 February 1938   Typewritten

The Stores   Wallington   Nr. Baldock   HERTS.

Dear Rayner,

What about you and Margaret coming here next Tuesday week, ie. the 15th, but if that doesn't suit, any week except next week (week starting the 6th.) It is best to come Tuesday [or][1] Saturday, because those are the only two days when there are buses. The way you get here is this. Take either the train from King's Cross or the Green Line bus[2] (cheaper), which you can catch at Golders Green station, and book to Baldock. You have to get to Baldock in time to catch the bus to Wallington. There are two buses on Tuesday, one at 3.30 and the other at 4.15. Better to take the second, and if we definitely know you are coming on the second one of us could probably meet you. In any case book to the Stores, Wallington. The return fare on the Green Line bus is about 5/– and the fare to Wallington 4d. Let us know any way which day would suit you and when arriving.[3] I shall have to post this now to catch the post so excuse haste.

Yours
Eric

1. Orwell mistakenly typed 'to.'
2. A limited-stop service that, in the main, runs from the country areas on one side of London to those on the other through central London.
3. In his *Four Absentees*, Heppenstall gives a brief account of this visit: 'I went to Wallington on 15th February, travelling by a Green Line 'bus which reached Baldock at a quarter past four. This was a Tuesday. The Stores was not a pretty cottage, and the village seemed desolate. There were two goats in a stinking shed at the back, and the Blairs rented a strip of ground, across the road at the front and above road-level, in which they grew vegetables and in which Eric and I dug together. He and Eileen behaved with conspicuous affection, fondling each other and sitting, if not on each other's knees, at any rate in the same armchair' (145–46).

420. Len Lye [?] to Orwell

2 February [1938?]

Among Orwell's papers is a letter addressed 'dear° Eric' and signed 'Len.' It is on GPO Film Unit stationery and was identified by Jack Common as from Len Lye (1903–1980). There is an attractive design drawn at the end of the letter, which helps confirm this.

Len Lye was an active innovator in the world of documentary film in the 1930s. He had made a film on his own initiative, *Colour Box*, in 1935 by painting abstract designs on the film. John Grierson, of the GPO Film Unit, adapted it for publicity purposes by adding the words 'G.P.O.—CHEAPER PARCEL POST' at the end. With Grierson's encouragement, Lye made a number of short films, mainly using this technique, including *Rainbow Dance*, *Trade Tattoo*, *Conga*, and *N. or N.W.* (in black and white) in 1936–37. In 1939 he made *Swinging the Lambeth Walk*, one of several films 'illustrating' popular music, and in 1942 a film on unarmed combat, *Kill or be Killed*. In the United States, he worked for the 'March of Time' and, in Grierson's words, made 'five-, seven-, nine-dimensional sculpture, sculpture that plays tunes and sculpture that turns itself upside down and bares its breast to the skies' (Elizabeth Sussex, *The Rise and Fall of British Documentary*, 1975, 84; and see Rachael Low, *Documentary and Educational Films of the 1930s*, 1979, especially 103–07). Lye was associated with Shell-Mex, which had formed the first industrial documentary film unit in Britain, and in 1936 made a puppet film for them, *The Birth of the Robot*, to music by Gustav Holst.

It is impossible to date the year of this letter with certainty. Lye had been asked to conjure up another film for Shell and was seeking Orwell's co-operation. He wrote to say that 'Shell are beginning to get cold on the stuff as I've had a month to supply them with an idea so if you can let's have something to work on soon O.K.' He hopes Orwell has not been ill, since everyone he knows has had flu or similar ailments. That could point to any winter, but might be especially applicable to 1937–38, when there was a severe flu epidemic in London.

421. Review of *The Tree of Gernika*° by G. L. Steer; *Spanish Testament* by Arthur Koestler

Time and Tide, 5 February 1938

It goes without saying that everyone who writes of the Spanish war writes as a partisan. What is perhaps less obvious is that, because of the huge discords that have shaken and threatened to split the Government side, every pro-Government writer is really involved in several distinct controversies. He is writing *for* the Government, but he is also (though he generally pretends otherwise) writing *against* the Communists, or the Trotskyists, or the Anarchists, or what-not. Mr. Steer's book is no exception to the general rule, but he carries a different set of prejudices from the majority of pro-Government writers, because he happens to have seen the war not in eastern Spain but in the Basque country.

In a way the problems here were simpler. The Basques were Catholic and Conservative, the Left Wing organizations were weak even in the large towns (as Mr. Steer says, "there was no social revolution in Bilbao"), and what the Basques chiefly wanted was regional autonomy, which they were likelier to get from the Popular Front Government than from Franco. Mr. Steer writes entirely from the Basque standpoint, and he has, very strongly, the curious English characteristic of being unable to praise one race without damning another. Being pro-Basque, he finds it necessary to be anti-Spanish, i.e., to some extent anti-Government as well as anti-Franco. As a result his book is so full of jibes at the Asturians and other non-Basque loyalists as to make one doubtful of his reliability as a witness—a pity, for he has had opportunities that were shared by very few Englishmen.

His book is sub-titled "A Field Study of Modern War," but as a matter of fact it is not at all clear how much he has seen with his own eyes and how much he is repeating from hearsay. Nearly every incident is described as though by an eye-witness, but it is obviously impossible that Mr. Steer can have been in all places at once. However, there is one very important and much-disputed event upon which he speaks with undoubted authority—the bombing of Guernica (or Gernika). He was in the immediate neighbourhood at the time of the aeroplane-raids, and his account leaves no doubt that the little town was *not* "burnt by Red militiamen" but systematically destroyed from the air, out of sheer, wanton brutality. Guernica was not even of much importance as a military objective. And the most horrible thought of all is that this blotting-out of an open town was simply the correct and logical use of a modern weapon. For it is precisely to slaughter and terrify the civilian population—not to destroy entrenchments, which are very difficult to hit from the air—that bombing aeroplanes exist. The photographs in this book are very good. All photographs in books on the Spanish war have a certain similarity, but these have much more character in them than most.

Mr. Arthur Koestler, a *News Chronicle* correspondent, stayed in Malaga when the Republican troops had departed—a bold thing to do, for he had already published a book containing some very unfriendly remarks about General Queipo de Llano. He was thrown into jail by the rebels, and suffered what must have been the fate of literally tens of thousands of political prisoners in Spain. That is to say, he was condemned to death without trial and then kept in prison for months, much of the time in solitary confinement, listening at his keyhole night after night for the roar of rifle-fire as his fellow-prisoners were shot in batches of six or a dozen. As usual—for it really does seem to be quite usual—he knew that he was under sentence of death without knowing with any certainty what he was accused of.

The prison part of the book is written mainly in the form of a diary. It is of the greatest psychological interest—probably one of the most honest and unusual documents that have been produced by the Spanish war. The earlier part is more ordinary and in places even looks rather as though it had been "edited" for the benefit of the Left Book Club. Even more than Mr. Steer's, this book lays bare the central evil of modern war—the fact that, as Nietzsche puts it, "he who fights against dragons becomes a dragon himself."

Mr. Koestler says:

> I can no longer pretend to be objective. . . . Anyone who has lived through the hell of Madrid with his eyes, his nerves, his heart, his stomach—and then pretends to be objective, is a liar. If those who have at their command printing machines and printer's ink for the expression of their opinions, remain neutral and objective in the face of such bestiality, then Europe is lost.

I quite agree. You cannot be objective about an aerial torpedo. And the horror we feel of these things has led to this conclusion: if someone drops a bomb on your mother, go and drop two bombs on his mother. The only apparent alternatives are to smash dwelling houses to powder, blow out human entrails and burn holes in children with lumps of thermite, or to be enslaved by people who are more ready to do these things than you are yourself; as yet no one has suggested a practicable way out.[1]

1. This anticipates the argument over area bombing; see 2473 and 2473, nn. 2 and 5.

422. To the Editor, *Time and Tide*

5 February 1938

'*Time-Tide* Diary' of 22 January 1938 included these paragraphs over the pen-name Sirocco:

'That nine thousand Left Book Club's members rallied to the Albert Hall on Sunday is gratifying or alarming, according to whichever way you look at it. Here is an organisation both subtle and widespread, an embryo Catholic Church with Mr. Gollancz as Pope. I can imagine him seated at his desk with a map of England in front of him. Everytime the telephone rings he sticks in a red flag—a new member for Blackpool, five for Manchester, a married couple for Stow-on-the-Wold. Presently there is no map left—only red flags.

'It is hard to see why a club with such excellent principles should give one such a nightmare. The Left is kind. The Left has good intentions. Mr. Gollancz is only the spokesman of the Left. But is he also the censor? Why are there no orange volumes by anarchists? Who publishes the perorations of those nice young

Trotskyites one meets at parties? What galvanises all Left Book Club writers into total and unnatural agreement? Is the English intellectual already in training for the critical apathy of post-revolution?'

Orwell responded two weeks later:

"TROTSKYIST" PUBLICATIONS

SIR,—In "Time-Tide Diary" of January 22nd, Sirocco remarks upon the "unnatural agreement" of Left Book Club writers, and adds, "Why are there no orange volumes[1] by anarchists? Who publishes the perorations of those nice young Trotskyites one meets at parties?"

As a matter of fact, a certain number of political books written from a Left Wing but non-Communist standpoint do get published, in particular by Messrs. Secker & Warburg, who are coming to be known rather inaccurately as "the Trotskyist publishers." I have had the honour of reviewing several books of this type, dealing with the Spanish war, in your columns. One was *Red Spanish Notebook*, which was written actually by Trotskyists. I thought it, as I said at the time, a prejudiced book, but interesting in detail and giving a good picture of Catalonia in the early months of the war. Another was Mairin Mitchell's *Storm Over Spain*, written by a Catholic, but very sympathetic to the Spanish Anarchists. And above all there was Franz Borkenau's *The Spanish Cockpit* (published by Faber's), which was written from a strictly non-party standpoint, except insomuch that the author was pro-Government and anti-Franco. This in my opinion is by a long way the ablest book that has yet appeared on the Spanish war or is likely to appear until the dust of conflict has died down. But the sequel to my review of it is rather interesting, and gives one a glimpse of the kind of censorship under which we are now suffering and of which the Left Book Club is a symptom.

Shortly after my review of *The Spanish Cockpit* appeared in TIME AND TIDE, the author wrote and thanked me, saying that though the book had been widely praised I was the only reviewer who had drawn attention to one of its central themes, i.e., to the real part played by the Communist Party in Spain. Simultaneously I had had the book to review for another well-known weekly paper, and had said much the same as I said in TIME AND TIDE, but at greater length. My review was refused publication on the ground that it "controverted editorial policy."[2] Meanwhile I had already discovered that it was almost impossible to get any publicity in the English press for a truthful account of what had been happening in Catalonia in May-June, 1937. A number of people had said to me with varying degrees of frankness that one must not tell the truth about what was happening in Spain, and the part played by the Communist Party, because to do so would be to prejudice public opinion against the Spanish Government and so aid Franco. I do not agree with this view, because I hold the outmoded opinion that in the long run it does not pay to tell lies, but in so far as it was dictated by a desire to help the Spanish Government, I can respect it. But what I think is interesting is this. The pro-Government papers covered up the disreputable happenings in Spain, the mass imprisonments without trial, assassinations by the secret police, etc., but so did the pro-Franco papers. The huge "Trotsky-Fascist" plot which the Communist press claimed to have discovered was given wide publicity; the fact that Prieto and other members of the Government denied that there was any truth whatever in the "plot" story, and said roundly that the police were practically an independent body under Communist control, was carefully unmentioned. It will be seen, therefore, that the pro-Communist censorship extends a great deal further than the Left Book Club. The newspapers of the Right, although professing to lump all "Reds" together and to be equally hostile to all of them, are in fact perfectly well aware which parties and individuals are or are not dangerous to the structure of Capitalism. Ten years ago it was almost impossible to get anything printed in favour of Communism; today it is almost impossible to get anything printed in favour of Anarchism or "Trotskyism." Did not Miss Ellen Wilkinson remark in your number of January 22nd that in Paris "one can meet a Pertinax and a former Chef du Cabinet, Poincaré, at a lunch with Communist leaders without any sense of strain"?[3] And does she really see no more in this than that Pertinax and Thorez[4] are both frightened of Hitler?

1. Left Book Club copies intended for members were bound in limp orange-coloured covers.
2. See *387*, and also *424*.
3. Ellen Cicely Wilkinson (1891–1947), was a leading Labour Party M.P., first elected in 1924; see *1471, n. 2.* She had written: '. . . there is an influential section of French opinion which, though completely reactionary at home, is passionately patriotic as against the old enemy Germany. M. de Kerillis° and Pertinax are the best-known voices of this current of opinion. In France today, however, one cannot be anti-German without also being anti-Fascist. Anti-Fascism immediately links up with the most uncompromising anti-Hitlerites who are the Communists. So one can meet a Pertinax and a former Chef du Cabinet, Poincaré, at a lunch with Communist leaders without any sense of strain.' Henri de Kérillis was a journalist and right-wing politician. He was the only non-Communist member of the Chamber of Deputies to vote against ratification of the Munich pact with Hitler. Pertinax was the pen-name of journalist André Géraud (1882–1956). He was London correspondent of the right-wing *Echo de Paris*, 1905–14, and foreign-affairs editor, 1917–38. He went to the United States after the fall of France in 1940. After the war, he became diplomatic correspondent for *France-Soir.* Raymond Poincaré (1860–1934), a lawyer, was both Premier and Foreign Minister of France from January 1912 to January 1913, and President from 1913 to 1920. Again Premier, 1926–29, he resigned because of ill health. His politics were conservative. See *3515, n. 5.*
4. Maurice Thorez (1900–1964), a miner at the age of twelve, became Secretary-General of the Pas de Calais Communist Federation in 1923 and Secretary-General of the Communist Party of France in 1930. He went to the Soviet Union in 1939 and returned only in 1944. He had been elected a deputy in 1932, and from 1945 to 1946 was a minister of state. In 'As I Please,' 48, 17 November 1944, Orwell devoted a section to Thorez and the falsification of history; see *2579.*

423. To Jack Common

5 February 1938   Typewritten

The Stores   Wallington   Nr. Baldock   HERTS.

Dear Jack,
I'm bloody sorry, but Max[1] got it wrong about my having any sort of job. At least all it was was this. I had to have some help with heavy digging and various other things I couldn't do unaided, so had to have a chap stay here a

week and give me a hand. He is gone now. I enclose cheque for £2. God knows I wish it was more but perhaps it will pay some bill or other.[2] It is a pity you are so far away. There is a lot of things I would like to talk about. If you ever manage to come over here again, come so that you can stay. It seems a pity to come all that way just for a day. My book thank God is done and gone to press. It ought to be out in March. I think the title will be "Homage to Catalonia", because we couldn't think of a better one. I'm not starting another for a few weeks. Please remember me to the wife and kid.

Yours
Eric Blair

1. Max Plowman.
2. It is difficult to be precise, but in 1938 Orwell probably earned about £190 (excluding the loan to enable him to go to Morocco). Thus, £2 was more than half Orwell's average weekly earnings. (The average pay in the mid-1930s was about £4.50 a week.)

424. To Raymond Mortimer

9 February 1938   Typewritten with handwritten addition

On reading Orwell's letter of 5 February 1938 (422) to the editor of *Time and Tide*, Raymond Mortimer, critic and literary editor of *The New Statesman and Nation* (see *301, n.3*) and one of the best that paper had, wrote to Orwell, on 8 February 1938, in protest, saying: 'It is possible of course that the 'well known weekly paper' to which you refer is not the *New Statesman*, but I take this as a reference to us, and so no doubt will the majority of those who read your letter.' The offices of *The New Statesman* were bombed during the war, so all the correspondence of that time has been lost. But among his papers Orwell kept the originals of letters from Kingsley Martin, editor of *The New Statesman* (see *496, n. 4*), and Raymond Mortimer and a carbon copy, reprinted here, of his reply to Mortimer.

The Stores   Wallington   Nr. Baldock   HERTS.

Dear Mortimer,

With reference to your letter of February 8th. I am extremely sorry if I have hurt your or anybody else's feelings, but before speaking of the general issues involved, I must point out that what you say in it is not quite correct. You say, "Your review of *The Spanish Cockpit* was refused, because it gave a most inadequate and misleading description of the book. You used the review merely to express your own opinions and to present facts which you thought should be known. Moreover, last time I saw you, you acknowledged this. Why then do you now suggest, quite mistakenly, that the review was refused because it 'controverted editorial policy'? Are you confusing the review with the previous refusal of an article, which you submitted, and which the editor turned down because we had just printed three articles on the same subject."

I attach a copy of Kingsley Martin's letter. You will see from this that the review *was* refused because it "controverts the political policy of the paper" (I should have said "political policy" not "editorial policy".) Secondly, you say that my previous article had been turned down "because we had just printed three articles on the same subject". Now, the article I sent in was on the suppression of the P.O.U.M., the alleged "Trotsky-Fascist" plot, the murder of Nin,[1] etc. So far as I know the New Statesman has never published any article on this subject. I certainly did and do admit that the review I wrote was tendentious and perhaps unfair, but it was not returned to me on those grounds, as you see from the letter attached.

Nothing is more hateful to me than to get mixed up in these controversies and to write, as it were, against people and newspapers that I have always respected, but one has got to realise what kind of issues are involved and the very great difficulty of getting the truth ventilated in the English press. So far as one can get at the figures, not less than 3000 political prisoners (ie. anti-Fascists) are in the Spanish jails at present, and the majority of them have been there six or seven months without any kind of trial or charge, in the most filthy physical conditions, as I have seen with my own eyes. A number of them have been bumped off, and there is not much doubt that there would have been a wholesale massacre if the Spanish Government had not had the sense to disregard the clamour in the Communist press. Various members of the Spanish Government have said over and over again to Maxton, McGovern, Felicien Challaye[2] and others that they wish to release these people but are unable to do so because of Communist pressure. What happens in Loyalist Spain is largely governed by outside opinion, and there is no doubt that if there had [been] a general protest from foreign Socialists the anti-Fascist prisoners would have been released. Even the protests of a small body like the I.L.P. have had some effect. But a few months back when a petition was got up for the release of the anti-Fascist prisoners, nearly all the leading English Socialists refused to sign it. I do not doubt that this was because, though no doubt they disbelieved the tale about a "Trotsky-Fascist" plot, they had gathered a general impression that the Anarchists and the P.O.U.M. were working against the Government, and, in particular, had believed the lies that were published in the English press about the fighting in Barcelona in May 1937. To mention an individual instance, Brailsford in one of his articles in the New Statesman was allowed to state that the P.O.U.M. had attacked the Government with stolen batteries of guns, tanks etc.[3] I was in Barcelona during the fighting, and as far as one can ever prove a negative I can prove by eye-witnesses etc. that this tale was absolutely untrue. At the time of the correspondence over my review I wrote to Kingsley Martin to tell him it was untrue, and more recently I wrote to Brailsford to ask him what was the source of the story. He had to admit that he had had it on what amounted to no authority whatever. (Stephen Spender[4] has his letter at present, but I could get it for you if you wanted to see it). Yet neither the New Statesman nor Brailsford has published any retraction of this statement, which amounts to an accusation of theft and treachery against numbers of innocent people. I do not think you can blame me if I feel that the New Statesman has its share of blame for the one-sided view that has been presented.

Once again, let me say how sorry I am about this whole business, but I have got to do what little I can to get justice for people who have been imprisoned without trial and libelled in the press, and one way of doing so is to draw attention to the pro-Communist censorship that undoubtedly exists. I would keep silent about the whole affair if I thought it would help the Spanish Government (as a matter of fact, before we left Spain some of the imprisoned people asked us *not* to attempt any publicity abroad because it might tend to discredit the Government), but I doubt whether it helps in the long run to cover things up as has been done in England. If the charges of espionage etc. that were made against us in the Communist papers had been given a proper examination at the time in the foreign press, it would have been seen that they were nonsense and the whole business might have been forgotten. As it was, the rubbish about a Trotsky-Fascist plot was widely circulated and no denial of it was published except in very obscure papers and, very half-heartedly, in the *Herald* and *Manchester Guardian.* The result was that there was no protest from abroad and all these thousands of people have stayed in prison, and a number have been murdered, the effect being to spread hatred and dissension all through the Socialist movement.

I am sending back the books you gave me to review. I think it would be better if I did not write for you again. I am terribly sorry about this whole affair, but I have got to stand by my friends, which may involve attacking the *New Statesman* when I think they are covering up important issues.

Yours sincerely

Handwritten on a separate sheet is a note by Orwell which, because there is no salutation, was almost certainly sent to Raymond Mortimer with the type-written letter above. Orwell enclosed the letter from H. N. Brailsford which he said Spender had. Brailsford's letter here follows this addendum.

I add this letter from H. N. Brailsford because I think it is of interest as showing how stories get made up. In the *New Statesman* he spoke of P.O.U.M. adherents during the Barcelona fighting attacking the Government with stolen tanks & guns. I wrote & asked where he learned this, and it appears from his answer:

<u>a</u>. That he accepted Antonov-Ovseenko's[5] statements about the Friends of Durruti,[6] though obviously no Russian dare speak otherwise than unfavourably about a "Trotskyist" organisation.

<u>b</u>. That on the same authority he assumed that the F. of D. was "acting with" the P.O.U.M.

<u>c</u>. That he added this onto some statements in *Inprecorr*[°7] & elsewhere & so produced the story about guns in the streets of Barcelona.

Meanwhile it is always possible that guns *were* stolen, only for use at the front, not in Barcelona. Every unit was constantly stealing weapons from others, when it could, owing to the general shortage & in one case (the P.O.U.M.) because we were systematically starved of weapons & at times were not far from unarmed. About April 2 batteries of Russian guns did arrive, & conceivably they were stolen ones, as no Russian weapons had been allowed to get to us till then.

17 Dec. '37

Dear Mr. Blair,
The story about the theft of guns & tanks from an arsenal in the rear of the Aragon front came from the Russian Consul-General Ossienko,° who has since been purged. He had his notes before him & gave me date, place & the details of the forged order by which it was worked. I also took notes but haven't got them now. The people who actually did this were Friends of Durrutti° but I gathered they were acting then & later with Poum. I had this from him at the end of April, before the rising. I accepted it, because the Consul-General struck me as a fair-minded man, who had much good to say about Anarchists. About Poum he said very little, but was in general less prejudiced than most Communists. I had confirmation later of this story from the latter.

I'm puzzled when you now tell me that no guns were used in the rising. I hope I haven't been unwittingly unfair.

I hope your wife is well after her very trying time in Barcelona. You must both feel very sore.

Sincerely Yours
H. N. Brailsford
P.S. Is it conceivable that the guns *were* stolen, but were recovered before the rising?

1. See *382, n. 5.*
2. James Maxton, ILP M.P., see *385, n. 1.* John McGovern (1887–1968), ILP M.P., 1930–47; Labour M.P., 1947–59, led a hunger march from Glasgow to London in 1934. Félicien Challaye, French left-wing politician, member of the committee of La Ligue des Droits des Hommes, a liberal, anti-Fascist movement to protect civil liberty throughout the world. He resigned in November 1937, with seven others, in protest against what they interpreted as the movement's cowardly subservience to Stalinist tyranny.
3. Henry Noel Brailsford (1873–1958) was a socialist intellectual, author, political journalist, and leader writer for the *Manchester Guardian, Daily News,* and *The Nation;* editor of *The New Leader,* weekly organ of the ILP, 1922–26. His article in *The New Statesman and Nation* was published in two parts. In the first, 'Anarchists and Communists in Spain,' 22 May 1937, he said that the POUM 'represented the older and now heretical Communist position. It opposed any alliance with the middle-class even for the salvation of the Republic: for the sake of political as distinct from social democracy it would make no sacrifices to unity. Against it, far more fiercely than against the Anarchists, the Communists waged a merciless feud, and charged it with all the treasons ascribed to Trotsky . . . the Anarchists with whom [the POUM] allied itself stand farther from its unbending Marxism than do the Socialists whom it assailed with its tanks and guns stolen from Government arsenals.' See also *413A* and *414B* in Vol XX, final appendix and *1293, n. 1.*
4. See *411, n. 2.*
5. Vladimir Antonov-Ovsëenko (1884–1937), Soviet Consul-General in Barcelona; see *374A,* endnote and *426, n. 6.*
6. The Friends of Durruti were an extreme anarchist group; see Thomas, 656, n. 1. Orwell refers to them in *Homage to Catalonia, CW,* VI, 219, 220, and 237. For Durruti, see *519, n. 24.*
7. For Orwell's references to *Inprecor* in *Homage to Catalonia,* see *CW,* VI, 228 and 231–33.

Raymond Mortimer quickly sent Orwell a handwritten note saying, 'Dear Orwell, Please accept my humble apologies. I did not know Kingsley Martin had written to you in those terms. My own reasons for refusing the review were those that I gave. I should be sorry for you not to write for us, and I should like to convince you from past reviews that there is no premium here on Stalinist orthodoxy.' On 10 February, Kingsley Martin wrote to Orwell: 'Raymond Mortimer has shown me your letter. We certainly owe you an apology in regard to the letter about *The Spanish Cockpit*. There is a good deal else in your letter which suggests some misunderstanding and which, I think, would be better discussed than written about. Could you make it convenient to come and see me some time next week? I shall be available on Monday afternoon, or almost any time on Tuesday.' It is not known whether Orwell accepted Martin's invitation, but he probably did; his letter to Moore (see *425*) indicates that he expected to be in London on that Tuesday, 15 February. Orwell's review of Galsworthy's *Glimpses and Reflections* was published in *The New Statesman* on 12 March 1938 (see *430*), and he contributed reviews to the journal from July 1940 to August 1943. However, as is recorded in conversation with friends, he never forgave Martin for his 'line' on the Spanish civil war. The review of Borkenau's *The Spanish Cockpit* was published by *Time and Tide*, 31 July 1937; see *379*. See also Crick, 340–42.

425. To Leonard Moore

Sat., [12 February 1938]   Handwritten

[No address]

Dear Mr Moore,
I have brought another copy of "Homage to Catalonia," as you suggested. Of course it is only a carbon copy. In two chapters there are some scribblings in the margin, but I have crossed them out & they have nothing to do with the text, as they are only some notes I made for a friend who was reading the chapters.

Yours sincerely
Eric Blair

P.S. [at top of letter] I may be able to drop in sometime on Tuesday.

426. To Alec Houghton Joyce

12 February 1938   Typewritten

Desmond Young, editor of the *Pioneer*, a newspaper in Lucknow, India, wrote on 28 December 1937 inviting Orwell to 'write leaders, "sub" letters & produce book reviews—which ought not to occupy the whole of your time unless you develop a taste for this business as most newspapermen unfortunately do.' He could offer Orwell only something 'rather ridiculously small,' so he would be worse off than he was in the Indian Imperial Police, but he was writing 'on the probably mistaken assumption that even Rs. 400 a month might be useful,' and living in Lucknow was not expensive. (When Orwell left Burma, he was earning £696 a year; Rs. 400 per month was £360 a year.) With the *Pioneer*, 'although it is to-day the property of landlords & "vested interests," ' he had a free hand: 'I don't think that it is so dull or reactionary that its policy would turn your stomach.' He enclosed recent leaders and suggested that Leonard Barnes (though Orwell would not like his Bloomsbury friends) could tell Orwell about him. He concluded with a brief résumé: Oxford just before World War I; service, mainly in France, 1914–18; salvaging wrecked ships, 1919–24 (which led to the publication of his *Ship Ashore*, 1932); 'unfortunate episode with a successful night club' in London; newspaperman in South Africa, 1925–32; and with the *Pioneer* from March 1933. Orwell was evidently interested, since on 27 January 1938 Young wrote to Joyce to ask about Orwell. It is plain that Orwell had explained to Young that he had had 'a good deal to do with left-wing politics and politicians in England' and had fought on the side of the government in Spain. Young told Joyce that he had suggested to Orwell a meeting between the two, in which Orwell could 'explain the position so that you can judge whether there is any likelihood of difficulties being created.'

The Stores   Wallington   Nr. Baldock   <u>HERTS</u>.

Dear Mr Joyce,[1]

The Pioneer newspaper (Lucknow) recently wrote asking me to take up an appointment with them for a year or two years, and in case there should be any difficulty about my entry into India they advised me to consult you. For the purpose of any enquiries you might have to make, perhaps it will be simpler if I give you full particulars about myself, my political record etc.

I was born in 1903 (by mistake this has been entered as 1902 on my passport), educated at Eton 1917–1921, served in the Indian Imperial Police in Burma 1922–1927 and resigned at the beginning of 1928 because the work was not suited to me. During 1928–9 I lived in Paris, was then teaching in England for about four years, and since about 1933 have earned my living by writing. At the end of 1936 I went to Spain, joined the militia and was serving until June 1937, when I was wounded and returned to England. I have never been a member of any political party, but I am of Socialist sympathies, have been associated to some extent with the I.L.P., and when in Spain was with the I.L.P. contingent on the Aragon front.[2]

The books I have published are as follow: *Down and Out in Paris and London, Burmese Days, A Clergyman's Daughter, Keep the Aspidistra Flying* and *The Road to Wigan Pier*. All these were published by Victor Gollancz. *The Road to Wigan Pier* was the Left Book Club choice for March 1937. My next book, *Homage to Catalonia*, is to be published in March by Secker and Warburg. I have also contributed to The *New Statesman, Time and Tide, The Listener*, the *New English Weekly* and other papers.

My object in going to India is, apart from the work on the Pioneer, to try and get a clearer idea of political and social conditions in India than I have at present. I shall no doubt write some book on the subject afterwards, and if I can arrange it I shall probably contribute occasional articles on Indian affairs to Time and Tide or some other English paper.

I hope these notes may be of use to you. I am very sorry to put you to inconvenience and greatly obliged for your help.

Yours sincerely
Eric Blair

P.S. I should have said that I normally write under the name of "George Orwell."

1. Alec Houghton Joyce (1894–1982; OBE, 1938) had been appointed information officer at the India Office in December 1937. He was made a Companion of the Order of the Indian Empire in January 1943. His and Orwell's paths crossed again in November 1941, when Orwell was at the BBC; see 882.
2. 'Indian Imperial Police' to 'not suited to me' and 'At the end of 1936' to 'Aragon front' have been underlined and marked in the margin, presumably in Joyce's office.

Joyce saw Orwell on 18 February 1938 and telegraphed Young: 'Blair keen for twelve months. Leadering ability undoubted but probably temperamental, unbusinesslike. Writing.' He wrote to Young the same day (Crick, 355–56) that 'there is no question of obstacles being put in the way of his going to India, but in view of his record official circles there will no doubt be somewhat apprehensive.' He thought Orwell had not merely a determined left-wing, 'but probably an extremist outlook, plus definite strength of character for difficulties when there is a conflict of views.' He reported that Orwell also intended to write on Indian affairs for papers in Britain and to gather material for a new book, and recommended that if Young decided to offer Orwell an appointment that he 'make the arrangement as tentative as possible' until he could satisfy himself that Orwell 'fits into the picture.' Joyce advised Orwell, on 21 February, that he did 'not anticipate any difficulties from the official side' in his taking up this appointment. India Office records show that the government of India feared that if Orwell's appointment with the *Pioneer* was terminated, 'he might end up doing extremist work at a very small salary.' Joyce was asked 'to try tactfully to discourage Young from making the appointment' and probably to convey to him the views of the Indian government.

Young intended to meet Orwell when he came to England in the spring of 1938, but, as he wrote to Orwell from Lucknow on 29 July 1938, after his return, he had spent most of his time in Scandinavia and in his one day in Hertfordshire 'had not the time to try to set out and find you.' He had had time to meet Joyce in May, however, and had told him he had turned Orwell down on medical grounds. Crick remarks that Young was 'probably only trying to get credit for "acting responsibly", for Orwell had already turned himself down on medical advice' (357–58).

427. To Jack Common

16 February 1938   Typewritten

The Stores   Wallington   Nr. Baldock   HERTS.

Dear Jack,

About Saturday. How about meeting in Hitchin on Saturday at 3.30 pm which will be in comfortable time for tea which might stretch out till pub-opening time and then I can take the late bus home. I think the best place to meet would be Woolworth's, so unless I hear from you to the contrary will look out for you at Woolworth's (inside) at 3.30 pm Saturday.

As to taking a book to Gollancz, if you do do so, keep it dark that you have one coming out with Secker. So long as that fact is hidden until it is too late, ie. until the book has gone to press, G. is, of course, very enterprising about "left" stuff, and as he is not too bright intellectually doesn't necessarily see Trotskyist or other heretical implications if they are not on the surface. I think myself it is rather a good idea to have a foot in both the Gollancz and the Secker camps. Warburg, of course, doesn't mind, and on the other hand if Gollancz has your name on his list and one of your books appearing shortly, it is liable to make his hirelings pull their punches a bit when the Secker book appears. I'm glad about the job with Mitrinovic[1] and hope it turns out well. Unless the India Office take steps to prevent it, I am in all probability going to India for about a year quite shortly. It is a frightful bore and I have seldom wanted to do anything less, but I feel that it is an opportunity to see interesting things and that I should afterwards curse myself if I didn't go. I wish it didn't come at this moment, because I particularly wanted to vegetate for a few months, look after the garden etc. and think about my next novel.[2] I am afraid I don't just at the moment see how exactly you connect up with the Aryan Path.[3] I always had a vague idea it had to do with theosophy. The only bit of advice I can give is that on a number of occasions when someone suddenly turned the light up the ectoplasm turned out to be butter-muslin. But I have always thought there might be a lot of cash in starting a new religion, and we'll talk it over some time. Looking forward to seeing you on Saturday. Remember me to your wife. By the way do you know of anyone else who might take on this fish job[4] (which I really don't think is a swindle) because they have written again.

Yours
Eric Blair

1. Probably Dimitrije Mitrinović (1887–1953), a writer and publicist who spent much time in London, and died there. He was connected with the New Europe group and, in 1933, with the weekly *New Britain*.
2. *Coming Up for Air.*
3. *Aryan Path: An international review of philosophy, mysticism, comparative religion, psychical research, brotherhood and Theosophy* was founded in Bombay in 1930 but published monthly in London in 1938.
4. What 'this fish job' was is not known.

428. Review of *Workers' Front* by Fenner Brockway[1]

New English Weekly, 17 February 1938

For the past year or two every Socialist, whether he likes it or not, has been involved in the savage controversy that rages over the policy of the Popular Front. Hateful in every way as this controversy has become, it raises questions that are too important to be ignored, not merely by Socialists but also by those who are outside or even hostile to the whole Socialist movement.

Mr. Brockway's book is written from the standpoint that it is now usual to denounce as "Trotskyist." His plea is that a Popular Front (*i.e.*, a line-up of capitalist and proletarian for the ostensible purpose of opposing Fascism) is simply an alliance of enemies and must always, in the long run, have the effect of fixing the capitalist class more firmly in the saddle. There is very little doubt that this is true, and a short time ago few people would have bothered to deny it. Until about 1933 any Socialist, or any anti-Socialist in an unbuttoned moment, would have told you that the whole history of class-collaboration (and "Popular Front," or "People's Front," is only a polite name for this) is summed up in the limerick about the young lady of Niger.[2] But unfortunately the menacing rise of Hitler has made it very difficult to view the situation objectively. Rubber truncheons and castor oil have scared people of the most diverse kinds into forgetting that Fascism and capitalism are at bottom the same thing. Hence the Popular Front—an unholy alliance between the robbers and the robbed. In England the Popular Front is as yet only an idea, but it has already produced the nauseous spectacle of bishops, Communists, cocoa-magnates, publishers, duchesses and Labour M. Ps. marching arm in arm to the tune of "Rule Britannia" and all tensing their muscles for a rush to the bomb-proof shelter when and if their policy begins to take effect.

Against all this Mr. Brockway urges that Fascism can only be combatted by attacking capitalism in its non-Fascist as well as its Fascist forms; and that therefore the only real enemy Fascism has to face is the class that does not benefit from capitalism, *i.e.*, the working class. It is a pity that he tends to use the expression "working class" in a rather narrow and restricted sense, being, like nearly all Socialist writers, too much dominated by the concept of a "proletarian" as a manual labourer. In all western countries there now exists a huge middle class whose interests are identical with[3] those of the proletariat but which is quite unaware of this fact and usually sides with its capitalist enemy in moments of crisis. There is no doubt that this is partly due to the tactlessness of Socialist propaganda. Perhaps the best thing one can wish the Socialist movement at this moment is that it should shed some of its nineteenth-century phraseology.

Much of Mr. Brockway's book is taken up in criticising the tactics of the Communist Party—necessarily so, because the whole manoeuvre of the Popular Front is bound up with the Franco-Russian alliance and the volte-face performed by the Comintern in the past few years. Underlying this is a much larger question, always more or less present when the Popular Front is discussed, though it is seldom brought into the foreground. This is the question of the huge though inscrutable changes that are occurring in the U.S.S.R. As the destinies of all of us are involved here, directly or indirectly, this book, written from what is at the moment the most unpopular angle, ought not to be neglected even by those who are hostile to its main implications.

1. For Fenner Brockway, see *363, n. 4.* His book was published by Secker & Warburg; see *375A.*
2. There was a young lady from Niger [or Riga] / Who went for a ride on a tiger. / They returned from the ride / With the lady inside / And a smile on the face of the tiger.
3. Original has 'which.'

429. Anonymous Review[1] of *Trials in Burma* by Maurice Collis

The Listener, 9 March 1938

This is an unpretentious book, but it brings out with unusual clearness the dilemma that faces every official in an empire like our own. Mr. Collis was District Magistrate of Rangoon in the troubled period round about 1930. He had to try cases which were a great deal in the public eye, and he soon discovered the practical impossibility of keeping to the letter of the law and pleasing European opinion at the same time. Finally, for having sentenced a British Army officer to three months' imprisonment for criminal negligence in driving a car, he was reprimanded and hurriedly transferred to another post. For the same offence a native would have been imprisoned as a matter of course.

The truth is that every British magistrate in India is in a false position when he has to try a case in which European and native interests clash. In theory he is administering an impartial system of justice; in practice he is part of a huge machine which exists to protect British interests, and he has often got to choose between sacrificing his integrity and damaging his career. Nevertheless, owing to the exceptionally high traditions of the Indian Civil Service, the law in India is administered far more fairly than might be expected—and, incidentally, far too fairly to please the business community. Mr. Collis grasps the essential situation clearly enough; he recognises that the Burman has profited very little from the huge wealth that has been extracted from his country, and that the hopeless rebellion of 1931 had genuine grievances behind it. But he is also a good imperialist and it was precisely his concern for the good name of English justice that got him into hot water with his fellow-countrymen on more than one occasion.

In 1930 he had to try Sen Gupta, one of the leaders of the Congress Party and at that time Mayor of Calcutta, who had paid a flying visit to Rangoon and made a seditious speech. The account of the trial makes curious reading—an Indian crowd roaring outside, Mr. Collis wondering whether he would be knocked on the head the next moment, and the prisoner sitting in the dock reading a newspaper to make it clear that he did not recognise the jurisdiction of an English court. Mr. Collis' sentence was ten days' imprisonment—a wise sentence, for it deprived Sen Gupta of a chance of martyrdom. Afterwards the two men were able to meet privately and talk the affair over. The description of the Indian and the Englishman meeting in perfect amity, each fully aware of the other's motives, each regarding the other as an honourable man and yet, in the last resort, as an enemy, is strangely moving and makes one wish that politics nearer home could be conducted in an equally decent spirit.

1. As with all reviews published anonymously in *The Listener*, attribution to Orwell has been made from the journal's records.

430. Review of *Glimpses and Reflections* by John Galsworthy
The New Statesman and Nation, 12 March 1938

John Galsworthy was an Old Harrovian with one skin too few, and towards the end of his life the missing skin renewed itself. It is a process almost drearily normal, but interesting in Galsworthy's case because of the fact that the bitterness of his earlier vision of life gave his books an undeniable power.

Glimpses and Reflections is a collection of short essays and letters to the press, largely on such subjects as the caging of songbirds and the traffic in worn-out horses. No one would guess that the man who wrote them once wrote books which were considered dangerously subversive and which were, in fact, morbidly pessimistic. Much of Galsworthy's later writing is tripe, but some of the early plays and novels (*The Man of Property, The Country House, Justice, Fraternity*, and some others) do at least leave behind them a kind of flavour, an atmosphere—a rather unwholesome atmosphere of frustration and exaggerated pity, mixed up with country scenery and dinners in Mayfair. The picture he was trying to build up was a picture of a money-ruled world of unspeakable cruelty—a world in which an obtuse, beef-eating race of squires, lawyers, bishops, judges and stockbrokers squatted *in saecula saeculorum* on the backs of a hypersensitive race of slum-dwellers, servants, foreigners, fallen women and artists. It was not an altogether untrue picture of the Edwardian days when English capitalism still seemed unassailable. But quite suddenly something happened; Galsworthy's private quarrel with society (whatever it may have been) came to an end, or perhaps it was merely that the oppressed classes began to seem less oppressed. From then on it was obvious that he was in no essential way different from the people he had made his name by attacking.

In the letters and essays in this book he emerges as the perfect Dumb Friends' Leaguer, seeing virtually nothing wrong in contemporary society except over-population and cruelty to animals. His solution for all economic troubles is emigration—abolish unemployment by getting the unemployed out of sight: he goes into frenzies over the sufferings of pit ponies, but is conspicuously less sorry for coal-miners: he quotes Adam Lindsay Gordon's "Life is mostly froth and bubble,"[1] and states that it is his "philosophic and religious motto." And it is interesting to note that he seems anxious to explain away the apparent revolutionary implications of some of his plays.

Probably many people, opening this book at random and coming upon the quotation from Adam Lindsay Gordon or an essay entitled "Playing the Game with Birds and Animals," would turn away in disgust, thanking God that they are post-war and post-Eliot. But there is more to it than that. Galsworthy was a bad writer, and some inner trouble, sharpening his sensitiveness, nearly made him into a good one; his discontent healed itself, and he reverted to type. It is worth pausing to wonder in just what form the thing is happening to oneself.

1. Adam Lindsay Gordon (1833–1870), educated in England, emigrated to Australia and wrote poetry with a distinctly Australian 'voice.' It was not well received at the time, and, in despair, he committed suicide. This line is from 'Ye Wearie Wayfarer,' Fytte 8.

431. To Cyril Connolly

14 March 1938   Handwritten

The Stores   Wallington   Nr. Baldock   Herts.

Dear Cyril,

I see from the N.S. & N.[1] list that you have a book coming out sometime this spring.[2] If you can manage to get a copy sent me I'll review it for the New English, possibly also Time & Tide. I arranged for Warburg to send you a copy of my Spanish book[3] (next month) hoping you may be able to review it. You scratch my back, I'll scratch yours.

I am writing this in bed. I may not be going to India after all & any way not before the autumn. The doctors don't think I ought to go. I've been spitting blood again, it always turns out to be not serious, but it's alarming when it happens & I am going to a Sanatorium in Kent[4] to be X rayed.° I've no doubt they'll find as before that I am O.K. but any way it's a good excuse for not going to India, which I never wanted to. This bloody mess-up in Europe has got me so that I really can't write anything. I see Gollancz has already put my next novel[5] on his list tho' I haven't written a line or even sketched it out. It seems to me we might as well all pack our bags for the concentration camp. King Farlow was here the other day & I am going to stay next week-end with him after leaving the Sanatorium. When in town I'll try & look you up. Could you be kind enough to write me a line to 24 Croom's Hill, Greenwich S.E.10,[6] to let me know your telephone address, which of course I've lost again, & then if occasion arises I can ring you up. Please remember me to your wife.

Yours
Eric Blair

1. *The New Statesman and Nation.*
2. *Enemies of Promise*; see Orwell's letter to Connolly of 14 December 1938 from Marrakech about a review copy, *512.*
3. *Homage to Catalonia.*
4. Orwell's Case Record at Preston Hall Sanatorium shows that he coughed up blood when ill in 1929, 1931, and 1934; that he had pneumonia in 1918, 1921, 1933, and 1934; and dengue fever when in Burma.
5. *Coming Up for Air.* Orwell is not being quite fair here: he had suggested that this be done; see his letter to Leonard Moore, 6 December 1937, *412.*
6. Home of Eileen's brother.

432. Eileen Blair to Jack Common

Monday [Monday–Tuesday, 14–15 March 1938?]

The sequence of events leading to Orwell's admission to Preston Hall Sanatorium is uncertain and complicated by doubts about the dating of Eileen's letter to Jack Common. Orwell's Case Record (found by Michael Shelden) shows that Orwell was admitted to Preston Hall on Tuesday, 15 March, and discharged that same day; and that he was re-admitted on Thursday, 17 March, and remained until 1 September 1938. The records also include an analysis of X-rays of Orwell's lungs dated 16 March. It might reasonably be assumed that he was rushed to the hospital on 15 March; that the heavy bleeding described by Eileen was then stopped, and that X-rays were taken; after these were examined on the following day, he was admitted for treatment. This involved complete rest, colloidal calcium injections and vitamins A and D until pulmonary tuberculosis could be definitely excluded. Fitting Eileen's letter and its content, into this time scheme is difficult. Writing to Richard Rees on 25 May, Eileen said that Orwell was taken ill—'laid up'—on 8 March (see *445*). On Monday, 14 March, Orwell wrote to Connolly, from Wallington, to say that he would be going to a sanatorium in Kent to be X-rayed (see *431*). Eileen's letter refers to a crisis of such proportions that occurred 'yesterday,' causing her to contact Jack Common ('hysterically') asking him to come at once to Wallington, even though the journey was difficult and the weather appalling. When he arrived, they had gone. Since the letter is dated Monday, those events should have taken place on Sunday the 13th (presumably the day when 'everyone agreed that Eric must be taken somewhere,' and Eileen would have had experts to consult and would not have needed to turn in desperation to Jack Common). And if the drama took place on that Sunday, Orwell could hardly have written as he did to Connolly on Monday (unless he got the date wrong), and Orwell would surely have arrived at Preston Hall not later than that Monday the 14th, rather than Tuesday the 15th. It looks, therefore, as if Orwell had become progressively worse between 8 and 13 March and on the 13th (Sunday) it was decided 'active steps' must be taken. Then late on the 14th (after he had written to Connolly), he became very seriously ill and was taken from Wallington by ambulance to Preston Hall (whence the Case Record shows he was admitted) where the bleeding was stopped. It could well be that he was taken ill in the night of the 14th–15th, which would partly explain Eileen's desperate call to Common and the uncertainty in dating her letter (written from her brother's home, 24 Croom's Hill, Greenwich).

Although Eileen's brother, Laurence O'Shaughnessy, was a consultant at Preston Hall and would later treat Orwell there, from the impersonal tone of Eileen's reference to 'a specialist . . . who's very good at this kind of thing' it is unlikely she is referring to her brother. A tiny clue that this might be so is that although Orwell's address on admission is given as 'The Stores,' his residential address is given as c/o 24 Croom's Hill, Greenwich, where Eileen was then staying; next to this, but typed in later (using a blacker ribbon) is the word 'Brother'—as if, when admitted, Orwell was not associated with Laurence O'Shaughnessy. (Orwell's occupation, typed in at the same time, is given as 'Writer (Novelist).'

Preston Hall Sanatorium, Aylesford, Kent, was a mile or two north of Maidstone. It was a British Legion hospital for ex-servicemen (hence the name of Orwell's ward, after the World War I Admiral Jellicoe). Initially Orwell was given a single room; this aroused comments about preferential treatment, but he insisted on mixing with the others and got on easily with them. See Crick, 358–60; Shelden, 316–19; U.S.: 289–92.

Dear Jack,
You'll probably have heard about the drama of yesterday. I only hope you didn't get soaked to the skin in discovering it.[1] The bleeding seemed prepared to go on for ever & on Sunday everyone agreed that Eric must be

taken somewhere where really active steps could be taken if necessary—artificial pneumothorax to stop the blood or transfusion to replace it. They got on to a specialist who visits a smallish voluntary hospital near here & who's very good at this kind of thing & he also advised removal, so it happened in an ambulance like a very luxurious bedroom on wheels. The journey had no ill-effects, they found his blood pressure still more or less normal—& they've stopped the bleeding, without the artificial pneumothorax. So it was worth while. Everyone was nervous of being responsible for the immediate risk of the journey, but we supported each other. Eric's a bit depressed about being in an institution devised for murder, but otherwise remarkably well. He needn't stay long they say,[2] but the specialist has a sort of hope that he may be able to identify the actual site of haemorrhage and control it for the future.

This was really to thank you for being so neighbourly from such a distance, & in such weather. One gets hysterical with no one to speak to except the village who are not what you could call soothing.

I'll let you know what happens next. I have fearful letters to write to relations.

Love to Mary & Peter,[3]

Eileen

1. Common lived some half-dozen miles from Wallington, but the journey was awkward; see Orwell's letters to him, 5 October 1936, *327*, and October ? 1937, *405*.
2. He did not leave the sanatorium until 1 September 1938.
3. Jack Common's wife and son.

433. To Jack Common

Wed., [late March? 1938]   Handwritten

Jellicoe Ward[1]   Preston Hall   Aylesford   Kent

Dear Jack,

Warburg has just sent me along a copy of "Seven Shifts",[2] which I know I shall read with great interest. He also asked me to give it a bit of a boost. I'll do so, but I admit this business of sending out books to be boosted, which W. has now done to me 3 or 4 times, makes me a bit uneasy. The trouble is I've always got at the back of my mind a picture of myself as a sort of Gerald Gould[3] selling my intellectual virtue at constantly-decreasing prices. A year to two ago Eileen said I should never be quoted in a blurb because what I said about people's books was always too offensive, & though it wasn't meant as such I took this as a compliment. But now I've been on two blurbs, one of them one of W.'s, & I don't want to become a sort of fixture on the backs of his dust-covers with " 'Genius'—George Orwell" kept permanently in type. The trouble is that everyone in writing is torn between three motives, *i.* Art for art's saking in the ivory tower, *ii.* political propaganda & *iii.* pulling in the dough. But any way I'll say what I can about the book & I'll also see if I can review it for the New Leader.

129

I expect Eileen wrote & told you I was in this place. I'm afraid I'll have to be here about another two months. I don't think there's really much wrong with me, evidently I have an old lesion in one lung which has been there at any rate 10 years & was never discovered before because I am non-infectious, ie. no bacteria to show. The bore is that I can't work, & what with having slacked for about 2 months on the strength of finishing my last book,[4] my next,[5] which Gollancz has hopefully put on his list, I see, will be some time coming along. I am studying botany in a very elementary way, otherwise mainly doing crossword puzzles. It is a very nice place & everyone is very good to me.

Please remember me to the wife & Peter.[6] I hope all goes well with you. I'm going to send this to care of Warburg because I'm not certain whether you've changed your address.

Yours
Eric Blair

P.S. Where is Rees?[7] Is he in Spain? I hope to Christ he'll get out before Franco gets to the coast. No doubt they wouldn't shoot him if he's only with an ambulance, but there's bound to be some unpleasantness.

1. Jellicoe Ward (or Pavilion) was where patients went for tests and operations. For Orwell's time at Preston Hall, as recalled by Victor Stacey, see *Remembering Orwell*, 107–08.
2. *Seven Shifts*, was edited and prefaced by Jack Common; there were seven contributions.
3. Gerald Gould was an influential reviewer for *The Observer*, who typified to Orwell much that was wrong with reviewing. See *219, n. 2*.
4. *Homage to Catalonia*.
5. *Coming Up for Air*.
6. Jack Common's son.
7. Richard Rees was driving an ambulance for the government side in Spain.

434. To Stephen Spender

2 April 1938   Handwritten

Jellicoe Ward   Preston Hall   Aylesford   Kent

Dear Spender,
I hope things go well with you. I really wrote to say I hoped you'd read my Spanish book (title *Homage to Catalonia*) when it comes out, which should be shortly. I have been afraid that having read those two chapters you would carry away the impression that the whole book was Trotskyist propaganda, whereas actually about half of it or less is controversial. I hate writing that kind of stuff and I am much more interested in my own experiences, but unfortunately in this bloody period we are living in one's only experiences *are* being mixed up in controversies, intrigues etc. I sometimes feel as if I hadn't been properly alive since the beginning of 1937. I remember on sentry-go in the trenches near Alcubierre I used to say Hopkins's poem Felix Randall, I expect you know it, over and over to myself to pass the time away in that bloody cold, & that was about the last occasion when I had any feeling for

poetry. Since then it's gone right out of my head. I don't know that I can give you a copy of my book because I've already had to order about 10 extra ones and it's so damned expensive, but you can always get it out of the library.

I have been in this place about 3 weeks. I am afraid from what they say it is TB. all right but evidently a very old lesion and not serious. They say I am to stay in bed and rest completely for about 3 months and then I shall probably be O.K. It means I can't work and is rather a bore, but perhaps is all for the best.

The way things are going in Spain simply desolates me. All those towns & villages I knew smashed about, & I suppose the wretched peasants who used to be so decent to us being chased to & fro & their landlords put back onto them. I wonder if we shall ever be able to go back to Spain if Franco wins. I suppose it would mean getting a new passport anyway. I notice that you and I are both on the board of sponsors or whatever it is called of the S.I.A.[1] So also is Nancy Cunard,[2] all rather comic because it was she who previously sent me that bloody rot which was afterwards published in book form (called *Authors Take Sides*). I sent back a very angry reply in which I'm afraid I mentioned you uncomplimentarily, not knowing you personally at that time.[3] However I'm all for this S.I.A. business if they are really doing anything to supply food etc., not like that damned rubbish of signing manifestos to say how wicked it all is.

Write some time if you get time. I'd like to meet again when I get out of here. Perhaps you will be able to come and stay with us some time.

Yours
Eric Blair

1. Solidaridad Internacional Antifascista, subtitled, on its letterhead, 'International Anti-Fascist Solidarity.' Other sponsors included W. H. Auden, Havelock Ellis, Sidonie Goosens, Laurence Housman, C. E. M. Joad, Miles Malleson, John Cowper, Llewelyn Powys, Herbert Read, Reginald Reynolds, and Rebecca West. Ethel Mannin (see *575*) was the Honorary Treasurer; Emma Goldman, the Honorary Secretary. Goldman wrote to Eileen (as 'Miss Blair') on 14 April 1938 thanking her for her kind contribution and for help in distributing fifty of SIA's folders and bulletins. She also sent wishes for Orwell's recovery. The periodical *Spain and the World* for 8 April 1938 advertised, with Reg Groves's *But We Shall Live Again* (on Chartism) and Rudolf Rocker's *Anarcho-Syndicalism*, Ethel Mannin's *Women and the Revolution*, the last advertised as 'Biographies of great women rebels from Charlotte Corday to Emma Goldman, from Mary Wollstonecraft to Mme. Sun Yat Sen and Maria Spridonova.' For Rudolf Rocker's *Anarcho-Syndicalism*, there was a commendation by Orwell: 'Of great value. It will do something towards filling a great gap in political consciousness.' See Nicolas Walter, 'Orwell and the Anarchists,' *Freedom*, 42, No. 2, 30 January 1981; Crick, 351.
2. For Nancy Cunard and *Authors Take Sides on the Spanish War*, see *386A*.
3. See *386A*.

435. To Stephen Spender

Friday, [15? April 1938]   Handwritten

On receiving Orwell's letter of 2 April, Spender, in an undated letter to Orwell, said that he had arranged to review *Homage to Catalonia* for the *London Mercury*. He then broached the matter of Orwell's attacks on him. Knowing nothing of Spender, Orwell had, he said, attacked him, but he was 'equally puzzled as to why when still knowing nothing of me, but having met me once or twice, you should have withdrawn those attacks,' and wanted to discuss this. In the meantime, saying how sorry he was to hear Orwell was ill, he sent him his play *Trial of a Judge*, which he thought Orwell might care to read if he had little else to do: 'If you can't bear the thought of it, don't look at it: I won't be offended.'

Jellicoe Pavilion   Preston Hall   Aylesford   Kent

Dear Spender,

Thank you so much for your letter and the copy of your play. I waited to read the latter before replying. It interested me, but I'm not quite sure what I think about it. I think with a thing like that one wants to see it acted, because in writing you obviously had different scenic effects, supplementary noises etc. in mind which would determine the beat of the verse. But there's a lot in it that I'd like to discuss with you when next I see you.

You ask how it is that I attacked you not having met you, & on the other hand changed my mind after meeting you. I don't know that I had ever exactly attacked you, but I had certainly in passing made offensive remarks about "parlour Bolsheviks such as Auden & Spender" or words to that effect. I was willing to use you as a symbol of the parlour Bolshie because *a*. your verse, what I had read of it, did not mean very much to me, *b*. I looked upon you as a sort of fashionable successful person, also a Communist or Communist sympathiser, & I have been very hostile to the C.P. since about 1935, & *c*. because not having met you I could regard you as a type & also an abstraction. Even if when I met you I had not happened to like you, I should still have been bound to change my attitude, because when you meet anyone in the flesh you realise immediately that he is a human being and not a sort of caricature embodying certain ideas. It is partly for this reason that I don't mix much in literary circles, because I know from experience that once I have met & spoken to anyone I shall never again be able to show any intellectual brutality towards him, even when I feel that I ought to, like the Labour M.Ps. who get patted on the back by dukes & are lost forever more.

It is very kind of you to review my Spanish book. But don't go & get into trouble with your own Party—it's not worth it. However, of course you can disagree with all my conclusions, as I think you would probably do anyway, without actually calling me a liar. If you could come & see me some time I would like it very much, if it's not much of an inconvenience.[1] I am not infectious. I don't think this place is very difficult to get to, because the Green Lines° buses stop at the gate. I am quite happy here & they are very nice to me, but of course it's a bore not being able to work and I spend most of my time doing crossword puzzles.

Yours
Eric Blair

1. Spender did visit Orwell at Aylesford. Others who made what was often a long and difficult journey were former ILP comrades from the Spanish contingent, who hitchhiked there, Jack Common, Rayner Heppenstall, and Max and Dorothy Plowman, who brought the novelist L. H. Myers. See Shelden, 322–24; U.S.: 294–96.

436. To Geoffrey Gorer

18 April 1938   Handwritten

Homage to Catalonia was published on 25 April 1938, but, as is customary, review copies had been sent out in advance. On a Saturday before Orwell's letter to Gorer, probably 16 April, Gorer sent him a short note to say how 'absolutely first-rate' he thought *Homage to Catalonia*, as well as a carbon copy of his review for *Time and Tide*, 'in case they object to its inordinate length,' and so that Orwell could let him know before the proof arrived if there were any errors. The review appeared on 30 April.

Jellicoe Pavilion   Preston Hall   Aylesford   Kent

Dear Geoffrey,
I must write to thank you for your marvellous review. I kept pinching myself to make sure I was awake, but I shall also have to pinch myself if T. & T. print it—I'm afraid they'll think it's too long & laudatory. I don't think they'll bother about the subject-matter, as they've been very good about the Spanish war. But even if they cut it, thanks ever so for the intention. There were just one or two points. One is that you say the fighting in Barcelona was started by the Assault Guards. Actually it was Civil Guards.[1] There weren't any Assault Guards there then, & there is a difference, because the Civil Guards are the old Spanish Gendarmerie dating from the early 19th century & in reality a more or less pro-Fascist body, ie. they have always joined the Fascists where it was possible. The Assault Guards are a new formation dating from the Republic of 1931, pro-Republican & not hated by the working people to the same extent. The other is that if you are obliged to shorten or otherwise alter the review, it doesn't particularly matter to insist, as you do now, that I only took part in the Barcelona fighting to the extent of doing sentry. I did, as it happens, but if I had been ordered to actually fight I would have done so, because in the existing chaos there didn't seem anything one could do except obey one's own party & immediate military superiors. But I'm so glad you liked the book. Various people seem to have received review copies, but I haven't had any myself yet & am wondering uneasily what the dust-jacket is like. Warburg talked of decorating it with the Catalan colours, which are easily mistaken for *a*. the Spanish royalist colours or *b*. the M.C.C.[2]

Hope all goes well with you. I am much better, in fact I really doubt whether there is anything wrong with me.[3] Eileen is battling with the chickens etc. alone but comes down once a fortnight.

Yours
Eric Blair

1. Orwell was wrong about this. He was later to ask that if a second edition of *Homage to Catalonia* were ever published—there was one English edition in his lifetime; the U.S. and French editions did not appear until after his death—this error should be rectified. The correction has been made in the *Complete Works* edition; see *CW*, VI, 253 and note 102/15.
2. Marylebone Cricket Club, the then ruling cricket authority. Its tie has broad red and yellow stripes.
3. According to Orwell's Blood Sedimentation Test on 27 April (and on 17 May), his disease was 'moderately active.' It was not until 4 July that it became 'quiescent.' It is never shown as normal.

437. To Jack Common
20 April 1938   Handwritten

Jellicoe Pavilion   Preston Hall   Aylesford   Kent

Dear Jack,

Thanks so much for yours. I'm really writing to say that I liked "Seven Shifts" very much, especially Watson's contribution.[1] I wrote Secker's a note some of which might be used for a blurb & I've also asked the New Leader if they'd like it reviewed. Of course it's very difficult for a small publishing firm like that ever to score a thumping success, tho' I suppose by specialising along certain lines they can at any rate keep going. It's not only that without thousands to whack about you can't advertise, but that if you don't advertise no one will review you decently if at all. Then again with S. & W's there's the political issue & Communists sabotaging their books as far as they can manage it. My own book I have no doubt will be ignored in a number of places on that issue, but I've pulled a few strings which may ring a bell here & there. As to the great proletarian novel, I really don't see how it's to come into existence. The stuff in "Seven Shifts" is written from a prole point of view, but of course as literature it's bourgeois literature. The thing is that all of us talk & write two different languages, & when a man from, say, Scotland or even Yorkshire writes in standard English he's writing something quite as different from his own tongue as Spanish is from Italian. I think the first real prole novel that comes along will be spoken over the radio.

I'm glad to hear Richard's[2] coming home. From your saying so I gather he's in Catalonia—I thought he'd be at Madrid again, in which case it wouldn't be so easy to get away.

Love to all
Yours
Eric Blair

1. J. H. Watson's 'The Big Chimney.'
2. Richard Rees; see *445, n. 1.*

438. Publication of *Homage to Catalonia*

Homage to Catalonia was published by Secker & Warburg on 25 April 1938; 1,500 copies were printed. The first U.S. edition was published by Harcourt, Brace and Company, in New York on 15 May 1952. A French translation, by Yvonne Davet—about which Orwell corresponded with her before World War II; see *413, 442, 479*—was not published until 1955, five years after Orwell died.

Philip Mairet in *New English Weekly* and Geoffrey Gorer in *Time and Tide* gave it 'understanding and appreciative reviews'; the anonymous reviewer in *The Listener* praised the description of war but said it was politically muddle-headed and accused Orwell of offering a defence of Trotskyist tactics that 'amounted to treachery'; the *Daily Worker*, unsurprisingly, 'savaged it in a few words.' For these summaries, see Crick, 363. Desmond Flower (see *447, n. 1*) in *The Observer* described Orwell as 'the giant of . . . any other writers on the Spanish war.' He went on: 'My admiration for him is unqualified. At the end of his book he says "beware of my partisanship": he is the only one who has been frank enough to say that, and he is the only one who need not have bothered.' Ethel Mannin, in *Spain and the World*, 20 May 1938, gave the book a long and enthusiastic review, calling it honest, careful, passionately sincere, and exciting. *The Times Literary Supplement* published an adverse review, anonymous, as was the custom then, but by M. P. Ashley. For Orwell's letters in response, see *441, 446*.

Among the many letters Orwell received following publication were those warmly approving his book from Naomi Mitchison, Richard Rees, Herbert Read, and the author of *The Spanish Cockpit*, Franz Borkenau, who wrote, 11 June 1938, that Frank Jellinek's *The Civil War in Spain* lacked 'all those qualities which make the value of your book.'

Jon Kimche (with whom Orwell had shared rooms over Booklovers' Corner, 1934–35) told Tosco Fyvel that in 1945, after the war, he had remaindered the copies of *Homage to Catalonia* he still had in the ILP bookshop (Fyvel, *George Orwell: A Personal Memoir*, 1982, 96). Fredric Warburg said 683 copies were sold in the first six months after publication; thereafter, about 50 copies annually. The first edition had not been sold out by the time Orwell died. (*An Occupation for Gentlemen*, 238).

439. 'Notes* on the Spanish Militias'

These notes may have been written when Orwell was working on *Homage to Catalonia*, but more probably after its publication. The watermark of the paper on which they are typed is the same as that of letters to Lady Rees, 23 February 1939, and Herbert Read, 5 March 1939, and different from that of the letter to Read of 4 January 1939 and all earlier letters from Morocco. The ink in which Orwell wrote the footnotes and the few emendations (included here without notice) is similar to that of the letter to Lady Rees and one to Geoffrey Gorer, 20

* N.B. that these notes refer only to the POUM militia, exceptional because of the internal political struggle, but in actual composition etc. probably not very dissimilar from the other militias in Catalonia in the first year of war [Orwell's handwritten footnote].

January 1939, but is different from that of the letters to Read of 4 January and 5 March. It is possible, therefore, that they were typed early in 1939, but they could have been written earlier. Gorer, in a letter to Sonia Orwell, 4 July 1967, guessed their date of composition as summer 1940, after Dunkirk, for someone at the War Office interested in the experience of militias as resistance fighters.[1]

The relevant portion of text from *Homage to Catalonia*, Appendix I (formerly chapter V), is reprinted here as note 1, with part of a letter to the editors of *CEJL* from Hugh Thomas, whose *The Spanish Civil War* (cited as Thomas) has been a major source of reference for this edition. There are a few errors suggesting the unpolished nature of the text; these have been left uncorrected, but are annotated.

I joined the POUM militia at the end of 1936. The circumstances of my joining this militia rather than any other were the following. I had intended going to Spain to gather materials for newspaper articles etc., and had also some vague idea of fighting if it seemed worth while, but was doubtful about this owing to my poor health and comparatively small military experience. Just before I started someone told me I should not be able to cross the frontier unless I had papers from some leftwing organisation (this was untrue at that time although party cards etc. undoubtedly made it easier). I applied to John Strachey who took me to see Pollitt. P after questioning me evidently decided that I was politically unreliable and refused to help me, also tried to frighten me out of going by talking a lot about Anarchist terrorism. Finally he asked whether I would undertake to join the International Brigade. I said I could not undertake to join anything until I had seen what was happening. He then refused to help me but advised me to get a safe-conduct from the Spanish Embassy in Paris, which I did. Just before leaving England I also rang up the I.L.P., with which I had some slight connections, mainly personal, and asked them to give me some kind of reccommendation°. They sent me to Paris a letter addressed to John McNair at Barcelona. When I crossed the frontier the passport people and others, at that time Anarchists, did not pay much attention to my safe-conduct but seemed impressed by the letter with I.L.P. heading, which they evidently knew by sight. It was this that made me decide to produce my letter to McNair (whom I did not know) and through this that I joined the P.O.U.M. militia. After one glimpse of the troops in Spain I saw that I had relatively a lot of training as a soldier and decided to join the militia. At that time I was only rather dimly aware of the differences between the political parties, which had been covered up in the English leftwing press. Had I had a complete understanding of the situation I should probably have joined the CNT militia.

At this time the militias, though theoretically being recast on an ordinary army basis, were still organised in column, centuria, seccion, the centuria of about 100 men more or less centring round some individual and often being called "So-and-so's bandera". The commander of the centuria ranked more or less as captain, but below that there was no well-defined rank except corporal and private. People wore stripes etc. of rank in Barcelona but it was "not done" to wear them at the front. Theoretically promotion was by election, but actually the officers and NCOs were appointed from above. As I shall point out later this does not in practice make much difference. One peculiar feature however was that a man could choose which section he should belong to and as a rule could also change to another bandera if he wanted to. At that time men were being sent into the line with only a few day's° training and that of a parade-ground kind, and in many cases without ever having fired a rifle. I had brought with me ordinary British Army ideas and was appalled by the lack of discipline. It is [of] course always difficult to get recruits to obey orders and becomes much more so when they find themselves thrust into trenches and having to put up with cold etc. which they are not accustomed to. If they have not had a chance to familiarise themselves with firearms they are often much more afraid of bullets than they need be and this is an added source of indiscipline. (Incidentally a lot of harm was done by the lies published in the leftwing papers to the effect that the Fascists were using explosive bullets. So far as I know there is no such thing as an explosive bullet,[2] and certainly the Fascists weren't using them.) At the beginning one had to get orders obeyed (a) by appealing to party loyalty and (b) by force of personality, and for the first week or two I made myself thoroughly unpopular. After about a week a man flatly refused to go to a certain place which he declared was exposed to fire, and I made him do so by force—always a mistake, of course, and doubly so with a Spaniard. I was immediately surrounded by a ring of men calling me a Fascist. There was a tremendous argument, however most of the men took my side and I found that people rather competed to join my section. After this, for some weeks or months, both among the Spaniards and the few English who were on this front, this kind of thing recurred over and over again. Ie. indiscipline, arguments as to what was justifiable and what was "revolutionary", but in general a consensus of opinion that one must have strict discipline combined with social equality. There was always a lot of argument as to whether it was justifiable to shoot men for desertion and disobedience, and in general people agreed that it was, though some would never do so. Much later, about March, near Huesca, some 200 CNT troops suddenly decided to walk out of the line. One could hardly blame them as they had been there about five months, but obviously such a thing could not be allowed and there was a call for some POUM troops to go and stop them. I volunteered though not feeling very happy about it. Fortunately they were persuaded to go back by their political delegates or somebody, so it never came to violence. There was a lot of argument about this, but again the majority agreed that it would be justifiable to use one's rifle against men doing this if necessary. Throughout this period, ie. January-April 1937 the gradual improvement in discipline was brought about almost entirely by "diffusion of revolutionary conscious-ness", ie. endless arguments and explanations as to *why* such and such a thing was necessary. Everyone was fanatically keen on keeping social equality between officers and men, no military titles and no differences of food etc., and this was often carried to lengths that were rather ridiculous, though they seemed less ridiculous in the line where minute differences of comfort were very appreciable. When the militias were theoretically incorporated in the Popular Army[3] all officers were expected to pay their extra pay ie. anything over 10 pesetas a day, into the Party funds, and everyone agreed to do so, though whether this actually happened I don't know, because I am not certain whether anyone actually began drawing extra pay before the POUM militia was redistributed. Punishments for disobedience were, however, being used even at the time when I first reached the front. It is extremely difficult to punish men who are already in the front line, because short of killing them it is hard to make them more uncomfortable than they are already. The usual punishment was double hours of sentry-go—very unsatisfactory because everyone is already short of sleep. Occasionally men were shot. One man who attempted to cross to the Fascist lines and was clearly a spy was shot. Another caught stealing from other militiamen was sent back supposedly to be shot, though I don't think he actually was. Courts martial were supposed to consist of one officer, one NCO and one militiaman, though I never saw one in action.

Periodically political delegates used to be sent round by the Party to visit the men in the line and, when possible, deliver [some] sort of political discourses. In addition every centuria had one or more men in its own ranks who were called its political delegates. I never grasped what the function of these men had originally been—they had evidently at the beginning had some function for which there was afterwards no need. When with the ILP English I was appointed their political delegate, but by this time the political delegate was simply a go-between who was sent to headquarters to complain about rations etc., and therefore so far as the English were concerned it was simply a question of choosing among the few men who spoke Spanish. The English were stricter than the Spaniards about electing officers and in one or two cases changed an NCO by election. They also appointed a committee of 5 men who were supposed to regulate all the affairs of the section. Although I was voted onto the committee myself I opposed its formation on the ground that we were now part of an army being commanded from above in more or less the ordinary way, and therefore such a committee had no function. Actually it had no important function but was occasionally useful for regulating very small matters. Contrary to what is generally believed the political leaders of the POUM were very hostile to this committee idea and were anxious to prevent the idea spreading from the English to the Spaniards.

Before joining the English I was some weeks in a Spanish bandera, and of about 80 men in it some 60 were completely raw recruits. In these weeks the discipline improved a good deal, and from then on till the end of April there was a slow but fairly steady improvement in discipline throughout the militia. By April a militia unit when it had to march anywhere still *looked* like a retreat from Moscow, but this was partly because the men had been experienced solely in trench warfare. But by this time there was no difficulty in getting an order obeyed and no fear that it would be disobeyed as soon as your back was turned. Outwardly the special "revolutionary" characteristics remained the same till the end of May, but in fact certain differences were showing themselves by this time. In May when I was commanding a seccion (which now meant a platoon) the younger Spaniards called me "usted". I pulled them up about it but the word was evidently coming back, and no doubt the universal use of tu in the early months of the war was an affectation and would seem most unnatural to a Latin people. One thing that seemed to stop abruptly about March was the shouting of revolutionary slogans to the Fascists. This was not practiced° at Huesca, though in many cases the trenches were very close together. On the Zaragoza front it had been practised regularly and probably had its share in bringing in the deserters who were very numerous there (at one time about 15 a week on a section of front held by about 1000 men). But the universal use of "camarada" and the notion that we were all supposed to be equals persisted until the militia was redistributed. * It was noticeable that the first drafts of the Popular Army who came up to the line conformed with this. Between the POUM and PSUC militias, up to the time when I last saw the latter at the beginning of March, there was no perceptible difference in state of discipline and social atmosphere.

The general organisation was in some ways very good but in others quite unnecessarily incompetent. One striking feature about this war was the good food organisation. Up till May 1937 when certain things began to give out the food was always good, and it was always regular, a thing not easy to arrange even in a very stationary war. The cooks were very devoted, sometimes bringing food up under heavy fire. I was impressed by the food-organisation behind the lines and the way in which the peasants had been got to co-operate. The men's clothes were laundered from time to time, but it was not done very well or very regularly. The postal arrangements were good and letters which had started from Barcelona always got to the front promptly, though an extraordinary number of letters sent into Spain went astray somewhere on the way to Barcelona. Ideas of sanitation practically did not exist and no doubt only the dry climate prevented epidemics. There was no medical service worth mentioning till one got about 10 miles behind the lines. This did not matter so long as there was only a small trickle of casualties, but even so many lives were lost unnecessarily. Trenches were at the beginning extremely primitive but about March a labour battalion was organised. This was very efficient and able to construct long sections of trench very rapidly and without noise. Nevertheless up to about May there was not much idea of communication-trenches, even where the front line was near the enemy, and it was not possible, eg., to get wounded men away without carrying them under fire. No effort was made to keep the roads behind the line in repair, although, no doubt, the labour to do so was available. The POUM Red Aid, to which it was voluntary-compulsory to subscribe, were very good about looking after wounded men in hospital etc. In regard to stores, there was probably some peculation and favouritism, but I think extremely little. When cigarettes began to run short the little English section received rather more than their fair share, a tribute to the Spanish character. The grand and inexcusable mistake made in this war, at any rate on the Aragón front, was to keep the men in the line for unnecessarily long

* My medical discharge-ticket, signed by a doctor at Monzón (a long way behind the line) about 18th June refers to me as "Comrade Blair" [Orwell's handwritten footnote].

periods. By Xmas 1936 the war was almost entirely stationary and for long periods during the next six months there was little fighting. It should therefore have been perfectly possible to organise the four days in four days out, or even four days in two days out, system. On this arrangement men do not actually get more hours of rest but they do periodically get a few nights in bed or at any rate with the chance to take their clothes off. As it was men were sometimes kept as long as five months in the line continuously. It sometimes happened that trenches were a long way from the enemy, say 1000 yards, but this is more boring and therefore worse for morale than being at 50-100 yards. Meanwhile they were sleeping in trenches in intolerable discomfort, usually lousy and up till April almost always cold. Moreover even when one is 1000 yards from the enemy one is under rifle and occasional shell fire, causing a trickle of casualties and therefore fear which is cumulative. In these circumstances it is difficult to do more than keep on keeping on. During February–March, the period when there was little fighting round Huesca, attempts were made to train the men in various things, use of the machine gun, signalling, open-order work (advancing by rushes etc.) etc. These were mainly a failure because everyone was suffering from lack of sleep and too exhausted to learn. I myself at this time tried to master the mechanism of the Hotchkiss machine gun and found that lack of sleep had simply deprived me of the power to learn. In addition it would no doubt have been feasible to grant leave at shorter intervals, but the failure to do so probably had reasons other than incompetence. But it would have been quite easy to take the men in and out of trenches as I have indicated, and to provide some kind of amenities for the troops not in the line. Even as far back as Barbastro the life of the troops was much drearier than it need have been. With a little organisation it would have been possible to arrange immediately behind the lines for hot baths, delousing, entertainments of some kind, cafes (actually there were some very feeble attempts at these) and also women. The very few women who were in or near the line and were getatable were simply a source of jealousy. There was a certain amount of sodomy among the younger Spaniards. I doubt whether troops can simultaneously engage in trench warfare and be trained for mobile warfare, but more training would certainly have been possible if more care had been devoted to resting the men. As it was they were exhausted for nothing at a period when the war was stagnant. Looking back I see that they stood it extremely well, and even at the time it was the fact that they did *not* disintegrate or show mutinous tendencies under these intolerable conditions that converted me (to some extent) to the notion of "revolutionary discipline". Nevertheless the strain that was put upon them was partly unnecessary.

As to jealousies between the different militias, so far as the rank and file were concerned I myself did not see serious signs of these till May 1937. To what extent the Aragón front was sabotaged from political motives I suppose we shall learn sooner or later. I do not know how important the capture of Huesca would have been, but there is little doubt that it could have been taken in February or March with adequate artillery. As it was it was surrounded except for one gap about a km. wide, and this with so little artillery that

preliminary bombardments were an impossibility, as they would only have
served as a warning. This meant that attacks could only be surprise attacks
delivered by a few hundred men at most. By the beginning of April Huesca
appeared to be doomed, but the gap was never closed, the attacks petered out
and a little later it became clear that the Fascist trenches were more strongly
held and that they had improved their defences. At the end of June the big
attack on Huesca was staged, clearly from political motives, to provide the
Popular Army with a victory and discredit the CNT militia. The result was
what could have been forseen—heavy losses and an actual worsening of the
position. But as far as rank and file were concerned party-feeling did not
usually get beyond vague rumours that "they", usually meaning the PSUC,
had stolen guns etc. meant for ourselves. On the Zaragoza front where
POUM and PSUC militia were distributed more or less alternately relations
were good. When the POUM took over a sector from the PSUC at Huesca
there were signs of jealousy, but this I think was purely military, the PSUC
troops having failed to take Huesca and the POUM boasting that they were
going to do so. The Guadalajara victory in February could be regarded as,
and in fact was, a Communist victory, but everyone was unaffectedly glad
and in fact enthusiastic. A little later than this one of our aeroplanes,
presumably Russian, dropped a bomb in the wrong place and killed a number
of POUM militiamen. Later, no doubt, it would have been said that this was
"done on purpose", but at the time this did not occur to anybody. About
May, perhaps following on the Barcelona trouble, relations worsened. In
Lérida, where large numbers of the new Popular Army formations were in
training, when detachments of Popular Army marched past, I saw militiamen of I do not know what militia giving them raspberries and bleating in
imitation of sheep. As to victimisation of men known to have served with the
POUM, I doubt whether it began until after the alleged espionage
discoveries. Immediately after these there appear to have been one or two
serious incidents. About the end of June it seems that a detachment of PSUC
militia were sent or came of their own accord to attack one of the POUM
positions outside Huesca, and the men at the latter had to defend themselves
with their machine guns. I have not either the exact date or more than general
facts of this, but the source from which I had it leaves me in no doubt that it
happened. It was no doubt the result of irresponsible statements in the press
about espionage, desertion, etc., which had caused or almost caused trouble
on earlier occasions.

The fact that the militias were organised by and owed loyalty to different
parties had bad effects after a certain date. At the beginning, when everyone
was full of enthusiasm, inter-party rivalry was perhaps not a bad thing—this
impression at least I derived from those who were in the earlier fighting when
Siétamo etc. were taken. But when the militias were dwindling as against the
Popular Army the effect was to make every party anxious to keep its strength
up at no matter what cost. I believe that this was one reason for the fact, noted
above, that leave was not granted as often as it might have been. Up till about
June there was in reality no way of making a man who had gone on leave
rejoin his unit, and conscription into the Popular Army, if[4] passed into law (I

forget when exactly it was passed) was completely ineffective. Therefore a militiaman once on leave could simply go home, and he had the more motive to do so as he had just drawn a big wad of back-pay, or he could join another organisation, which was often done at that time. In practice most men returned from leave, but some did not, so that every spell of leave meant a dwindling of numbers. In addition, I am certain that anxiety to keep up numbers made local commanders over-anxious not to incur casualties when they could not gain eclat° by incurring them. On the Zaragoza front valuable minor opportunities—the kind of thing that would not have got into the papers but would have made a certain difference—were lost owing to this, while such casualties as did occur were completely pointless. Also the useless riff-raff, amounting to five or ten per cent, who are to be found in all bodies of troops and who should be got rid of ruthlessly, were seldom or never got rid of. In January when I complained about the state of discipline a higher-up officer gave me his opinion that all the militias competed in slackness of discipline in order the[5] detach recruits from the others. I don't know whether this was true or said owing to momentary fed-upness.

As to the personnel of the POUM militia, I doubt whether it was much different from the others. In standard of physique, which is a rough test, they were about equal to the PSUC. The POUM did not ask party affiliation from their militiamen, doubtless because being a minority party they found it hard to attract recruits. When the men were in the line efforts were made to get them to join the party, but it is fair to say that there was no kind of pressure. There was the usual proportion of riff-raff, and in addition a certain number of very ignorant peasants and people of no particular political alignment who had probably joined the POUM militia more or less by accident. In addition there was a certain number of people who had simply joined for the sake of a job. The fact that in December 1936 there was already a serious bread shortage in Barcelona and militiamen got bread in plenty had a lot to do with this. Nevertheless some of these nondescripts afterwards turned into quite good soldiers. Apart from a rather large number of refugee Germans there was a sprinkling of foreigners of many races, even including a few Portuguese. Putting aside the Germans, the best soldiers were usually the machine-gunners, who were organised in crews of six and kept rather apart from the others. The fetichistic attitude which men in this position develop towards their gun, rather as towards a household god, is interesting and should be studied. A few of the machine-gunners were old soldiers who had done their service over and over again owing to the Spanish substitute system, but most of them were "good party men," some of them men of extremely high character and intelligence. I came to the conclusion, somewhat against my will, that in the long run "good party men" make the best soldiers. The detachment of in all about 30 English and Americans sent out by the ILP were divided rather sharply between old soldiers of no particular political affiliations and "good party men" with no military experience. As I am nearer to the first type myself I am probably not prejudiced in saying that I believe the second to be superior. Old soldiers are of course more useful at the beginning of a campaign, and they are all right when there is any fighting, but they have more tendency to go to pieces under inaction and physical exhaustion. A man who has fully identified with some political party is reliable in *all* circumstances. One would get into trouble in leftwing circles for saying so, but the feeling of many Socialists towards their party is very similar to that of the thicker-headed type of public school man towards his old school. There are individuals who have no particular political feelings and are completely reliable, but they are usually of bourgeois origin. In the POUM militia there was a slight but perceptible tendency for people of bourgeois origin to be chosen as officers. Given the existing class-structure of society I regard this as inevitable. Middle-class and upper-class people have usually more self-confidence in unfamiliar circumstances, and in countries where conscription is not in force they usually have more military tradition than the working class. This is notably the case in England. As to age, 20 to 35 seems to be the proper age for front-line soldiers. Above 35 I would not trust anybody in the line as a common soldier or junior officer unless he is of known political reliability. As for the younger limit, boys as young as 14 are often very brave and reliable, but they simply cannot stand the lack of sleep. They will even fall asleep standing up.

As to treachery, fraternisation, etc., there were just enough rumours about this to suggest that such things happened occasionally, and in fact they are inevitable in civil war. There were vague rumours that at some time pre-arranged truces had been held in no man's land for exchange of newspapers. I do not know of an instance of this but once saw some Fascist papers which might have been procured in this manner. The stories circulated in the Communist press about non-aggression pacts and people coming and going freely between our lines and the Fascists were lies. There was undoubtedly treachery among the peasants. The reason why no attack on this front ever came off at the time scheduled was no doubt partly incompetence, but it was also said that if the time was fixed more than a few hours ahead it was invariably known to the Fascists. The Fascists always appeared to know what troops they had opposite them, whereas we only knew what we could infer from patrols etc. I do not know what method was used by spies for getting messages into Huesca, but the method of sending messages out was flash-lamp signalling. There were morse code signals at a certain hour every night. These were always recorded, but except for slogans such as Viva Franco they were always in cipher. I don't know whether they were successfully deciphered. The spies behind the lines were never caught, in spite of many attempts. Desertions were very rare, though up to May 1937 it would have been easy to walk out of the line, or with a little risk, across to the Fascists. I knew of a few desertions among our men and a few among the PSUC, but the whole number would have been tiny. It is noticeable that men in a force of this type retain political feeling against the enemy as they would not in an ordinary army. When I first reached the front it was taken for granted that officer-prisoners taken by us must be shot, and the Fascists were said to shoot all prisoners—a lie, no doubt, but the significant thing was that people believed it. As late as March 1937 I heard credibly of an officer-prisoner taken by us being shot—again the significant thing is that no one seemed to think this wrong.

As to the actual performance of the POUM militia, I know of this chiefly from others, as I was at the front during the most inactive period of the war. They took part in the taking of Siétamo and the advance on Huesca, and after this the division was split up, some at Huesca, some on the Zaragoza front and a few at Teruel. I believe there was also a handful on the Madrid front. In late February the whole division was concentrated on the eastern side of Huesca. Tactically this was the less important side, and during March–April the part played by the POUM was only raids and holding attacks, affairs involving at most two hundred men and a few score casualties. In some of these they did well, especially the refugee Germans. In the attack on Huesca at the end of June the division lost heavily, 4-600 killed. I was not in this show but heard from others who were that the POUM troops behaved well. By this time the campaigns in the press had begun to produce a certain amount of disaffection. By April even the politically uninterested had grasped that except in their own press and that of the Anarchists no good would be reported of them, whatever their actual performance might be. At the time this produced only a certain irritation, but I know that later, when the division was redistributed, some men who were able to dodge the conscription did so and got civilian jobs on the ground that they were tired of being libelled. A number of men who were in the Huesca attack assured me that General Pozas[6] deliberately withheld the artillery to get as many POUM troops killed as possible—doubtless untrue, but showing the effect of campaigns like that conducted by the Communist press. I do not know what happened to the division after being redistributed, but believe they mostly went to the 26th division. Considering the circumstances and their opportunities, I should say that the performance of the POUM militia was respectable though in no way brilliant.

1. 'From the point of view of political theory there were only three parties that mattered, the PSUC, the POUM and the CNT [Confederación Nacional de Trabajo]—FAI [Federación Anarquista Ibérica], loosely described as the Anarchists. I take the PSUC first, as being the most important; it was the party that finally triumphed. . . .

'It is necessary to explain that when one speaks of the PSUC "line" one really means the Communist Party "line". The PSUC (Partido Socialista Unificado de Cataluña) was the Socialist Party of Catalonia; it had been formed at the beginning of the war by the fusion of various Marxist parties, including the Catalan Communist Party, but it was now entirely under Communist control and was affiliated to the Third International. Elsewhere in Spain no formal unification between Socialists and Communists had taken place, but the Communist viewpoint and the Right-wing Socialist viewpoint could everywhere be regarded as identical. Roughly speaking, the PSUC was the political organ of the UGT (Unión General de Trabajadores), the Socialist trade unions. . . . They contained many sections of the manual workers, but since the outbreak of war they had also been swollen by a large influx of middle-class members. . . .

'The PSUC "line", which was preached in the Communist and pro-Communist press throughout the world, was approximately this:

'"At present nothing matters except winning the war; without victory in the war all else is meaningless. Therefore this is not the moment to talk of pressing forward with the revolution. . . . At this stage we are not fighting for the dictatorship of the proletariat, we are fighting for parliamentary democracy. Whoever tries to turn the civil war into a social revolution is playing into the hands of the Fascists and is in effect, if not in intention, a traitor."

'The POUM "line" differed from this on every point except, of course, the importance of winning the war. The POUM (Partido Obrero de Unificación Marxista) was one of those dissident Communist parties which have appeared in many countries in the last few years as a result of the opposition to "Stalinism". . . . It was made up partly of ex-Communists and partly of an earlier party, the Workers' and Peasants' Bloc. Numerically it was a small party, with not much influence outside Catalonia, and chiefly important because it contained an unusually high proportion of politically conscious members. . . . It did not represent any block of trade unions. The POUM militiamen were mostly CNT members, but the actual party-members generally belonged to the UGT. It was, however, only in the CNT that the POUM had any influence. The POUM "line" was approximately this:

' "It is nonsense to talk of opposing Fascism by bourgeois 'democracy.' Bourgeois 'democracy' is only another name for capitalism, and so is Fascism; to fight against Fascism on behalf of 'democracy' is to fight against one form of capitalism on behalf of a second which is liable to turn into the first at any moment. The only real alternative to Fascism is workers' control. If you set up any less goal than this, you will either hand the victory to Franco, or, at best, let in Fascism by the back door. . . . The war and the revolution are inseparable" ' (*Homage to Catalonia, CW*, VI, 201–03).

Hugh Thomas comments: '. . . first, that the CNT and FAI were actually different organisations of which the latter was, broadly speaking, the leadership of the former, having been set up in the 'twenties to keep the CNT from revisionism. Secondly, where George Orwell said in *Homage to Catalonia* that the Communists' viewpoint and the right-wing Socialists' viewpoint could everywhere be regarded as identical, this was only the case for quite a short time, since Prieto, the leading right-wing Socialist, moved over into a very strong anti-Communist position quite soon. Thirdly, it is only very 'roughly speaking' that the PSUC was the political organ of the UGT. Indeed, this is nearer a mistake than any of the other points, because the UGT was the nationwide labour organisation, admittedly led by Socialists, whereas the PSUC was simply confined to Catalonia.'

2. Probably the soft-nosed or dumdum bullet was meant, which expands on impact, with appalling effect.
3. 'Since February [1937] the entire armed forces had theoretically been incorporated in the Popular Army [by the Government], and the militias were, on paper, reconstructed along Popular Army lines . . .' (*Homage to Catalonia, CW*, VI, 91.)
4. Presumably 'when' is meant.
5. Should be 'to.'
6. General Sebastián Pozas Perea (1876–died in exile), a Republican, was Director-General of the Civil Guard, and Minister of the Interior for the Republicans in 1936. See also *519, n. 35.*

440. To Cyril Connolly

27 April 1938   Handwritten

Jellicoe Pavilion   Preston Hall   Aylesford   Kent

Dear Cyril,

Thanks for your letter. I'm glad you weren't shot in Spain. It's a bloody mess down there, the game's up I'm afraid. I wish I were there. The ghastly thing is that if the war is lost it will simply lead to an intensification of the policy that caused the Spanish Gov.t to be let down, & before we know where we are we shall be in the middle of another war to save democracy.

Did you manage to get my book to review, or did they give it to someone else? It came out on Monday.

I have been here about 5 or 6 weeks & I am afraid I shall have to be here about another 8 or 10. There isn't really anything very wrong, evidently an old TB. lesion which has partly healed itself & which I must have had 10 years or more. I think if it had been serious the exposure in Spain would have done for me, whereas I came out of that business feeling very well & actually putting on weight until I was wounded.[1] I can't work, of course, which is a bore & will put my next novel back till 1939. I heard from Stephen Spender, who sent me a copy of his play & says he'll come & see me some time. Funny, I had always used him & the rest of that gang as symbols of the pansy Left, & in fact I don't care for his poems to speak of, but when I met him in person I liked him so much & was sorry for the things I had said about him.

Please remember me to your wife.

Yours
Eric Blair

No, don't come & visit me. I know it would depress you—this place I mean—& it's probably a tiresome journey.

1. Orwell's weight on admission to Preston Hall was 159 pounds; by 26 April it had risen to 163 pounds. His 'highest known weight' was recorded as 168 pounds (76.2 kg); he regained this weight on 5 July 1938.

441. To the Editor, *The Times Literary Supplement*

14 May 1938

Sir,—I know it is not usual to answer reviews, but as your review of my book "Homage to Catalonia" in *The Times Literary Supplement* of April 30 amounts to misrepresentation I should be greatly obliged if you would allow me space to answer it.

Your reviewer[1] begins:—

[George Orwell] enlisted in the Militia, took part in the trench warfare round Huesca, was wounded, and after some disheartening experiences in the internal rising in Barcelona in May, 1937, was compelled to flee the country.

The implication here is, *(a)* that I had been wounded before the fighting in Barcelona, and *(b)* that I had to flee the country as a direct result of my "disheartening experiences." As was made perfectly clear in my book, I was wounded some little time *after* the fighting in Barcelona, and I had to leave the country as a result of events which I set out at considerable length and which, so far as I know, had no direct connexion with my "disheartening experiences."

The rest of his review is mainly an attempt to throw discredit upon the Spanish Militias who were holding the Aragon front with inadequate weapons and other equipment during the first year of war. He has distorted various things that I said in order to make it appear that I agree with him. For example:—

Discipline did not exist in the Militia: "if a man disliked an order he would step out of the ranks and argue fiercely with the officer."

I never said that discipline "did not exist in the Militia." What your reviewer failed to mention is that in the passage quoted ("if a man disliked an order," &c.) I was describing the behaviour of raw recruits *their first day at the barracks*, when they behaved as raw recruits always behave, as anyone with military experience would expect.

Yours truly,
George Orwell

* * * The reviewer writes:—

Mr. Orwell is unduly sensitive. I stated that he was wounded in the trench warfare round Huesca and that he was compelled to flee the country after some disheartening experiences in the internal rising in Barcelona—all facts recorded at length in his book. If my necessarily brief sentence implied that he was wounded before the rising this was unintentional and does not seem to reflect on him or anyone else. I did not say he was compelled to flee *because* of his part in the May rising, or that there was any direct connexion between the two events. Actually, however, it seems clear that it was because Mr. Orwell was then, and subsequently, associated with the P.O.U.M. organization, which was officially blamed for the rising, that he was obliged to leave the country.

Of the May rising and the subsequent period Mr. Orwell uses the words "concentrated disgust," "fury," "miserable internecine scrap," "cesspool," "disillusionment" and "a depressing outlook." If that is not disheartenment, what is?

Finally, as to indiscipline, it is a question of point of view. Mr. Orwell speaks of "a mob of ragged children in the front line," one of whom threw a hand grenade into a dugout fire "for a joke"; of slapping generals on the back, of how when men refused to obey orders it was necessary to appeal to them in the name of comradeship, and of how "*You often had to argue for five minutes before you got an order obeyed.*" He says further (p. 34):— "*Actually a newly raised draft of militia was an indisciplined mob. . . . In a workers' army discipline is theoretically voluntary,*" &c. He adds that "it is a tribute to the strength of revolutionary discipline that the Militias stayed in the field at all."

On 28 May 1938, *The Times Literary Supplement* published a second letter from Orwell:

Sir,—I am very sorry to trouble you with this correspondence, but your reviewer has again resorted to misquotation. For example: "Actually a newly raised draft of militia was an undisciplined mob." In my book the sentence ran as follows: "Actually, a newly raised draft of militia was an undisciplined mob not because the officers called the privates 'Comrade' but because new troops are *always* an undisciplined mob."

By suppressing the second half of the sentence he has given it a totally different meaning; and similarly with various other statements which he has picked out of their contexts. As for his rearrangement of the order of events in the book, he pleads that his account was "necessarily brief," this does not seem any reason for altering the chronology.

Yours truly,
George Orwell

1. Reviews in *The Times Literary Supplement* were then customarily unsigned. Records show that the reviewer was Maurice Percy Ashley (1907–1994; CBE, 1978), journalist, author, and historian. He was Winston Churchill's research assistant in 1929, served in the Intelligence Corps, 1940–45, was Deputy Editor of *The Listener*, 1946–58 and Editor, 1958–67.

442. To Yvonne Davet

19 May 1938   Handwritten

Jellicoe Pavilion   Preston Hall   Aylesford   Kent   Angleterre

Chère camarade,

Je vous remercie pour votre lettre. Vous avez du travailler très dur d'avoir fini la traduction litèrale de mon livre[1] et d'autres traductions aussi. Je ferai mon mieux d'expliquer toutes les expressions d'argot, etc. Comme vous pouvez voir pour vous-même, je n'ai pas le moindre idée sur le sujet du *style* français, mais je comprends le français assez bien pour savoir si une phrase est exactement traduite ou non. Pas de besoin d'écrire à Secker & Warburg. Je leur ai dit déjà que vous étiez en train de faire une traduction. Saviez-vous que c'est la N.R.F. qui ont publié une traduction d'un autre livre[2] des miens ("La Vache Enragée", traduction de R. N. Raimbaud.) Ils se souviendront de mon nom, sans doute. En quelques jours, quand ma femme viendra me faire une visite, je vous enverrai une exemplaire de l'édition anglaise de "Homage de Catalonia." Malheureusement je suis depuis deux mois en hôpital. J'ai toussé du sang il y a deux mois, et après m'avoir examiné ils ont découvert que je suis poitrinaire. Mais ce n'est pas grand' chose, seulement ils m'ont dit qu'il ne faut reposer pendant trois ou quatre mois. J'avais promis d'aller aux Indes pour travailler pendant une année pour un journal. Naturellement ça m'est impossible maintenant, et j'en suis assez content, car j'ai vu bien assez des Indes dans ma vie. Je ne pourrai commencer mon prochain roman que quand je sortirai d'ici. Espèrons que j'aurai le temps de le finir avant la guerre!

Bien fraternellement
Eric Blair

Translation

Thank you for your letter. You must have had to work very hard to finish the literal translation of my book[1] and other translations as well. I will do my best to explain all the slang expressions, etc. As you can see for yourself, I haven't the slightest idea of French *style*, but I can understand French well enough to know if a sentence is exactly translated or not. No need to write to Secker & Warburg. I have already told them that you were doing a translation. Did you know that it was the N.R.F. who published a translation of another book of mine ("La Vache Enragée", translated by R. N. Raimbaud).[2] They will no doubt remember my name. In a few days, when my wife comes to visit me, I'll send you a copy of the English edition of "Homage to Catalonia." Unfortunately I've been in hospital for two months. I started spitting blood two months ago, and after examining me they discovered I have consumption. It is not serious, but they've told me to rest for three or four months. I had promised to go to India to work for a year on a newspaper. Naturally that's out of the question now, and I'm quite glad, as I've seen quite enough of India already. I can't start my next novel till I get out of here. Let's hope I have time to finish it before the war!

1. Presumably *Homage to Catalonia*. Orwell's letter to Leonard Moore of 6 December 1937 said that he was sending 'various wads of it as they get done' to Madame Davet. She was translating it 'on spec.' in the hope of finding a publisher. See *412*.
2. *Down and Out in Paris and London*. The French translation was published in 1935.

443. To Jack Common
       Sunday, [22 May 1938][1]   Handwritten

                    Jellicoe Pavilion   Preston Hall   Aylesford   Kent

Dear Jack,
Warburg sent me a copy of your book[2] yesterday, & I think it's bloody good, though there's a lot you say that I don't agree to. I'll do a review of it for the New English Weekly,[3] also send Warburg a note on it as he asked for blurb purposes. As I told you before I'm frankly opposed to this blurb business[4] even when one admires the book in question, because the only way one can get any hearing worth having for one's critical opinions is by being the sort of person who *can't* be quoted on blurbs. Is that your first published book, apart from "Seven Shifts"?[5] Isn't it a grand feeling when you see your thoughts taking shape at last in a solid lump? I don't know if Eileen remembered to send you a copy of my Spanish book, but if not she will when she gets back home on Monday. I don't know how it's sold, but I haven't had as many reviews as usual so I suppose it's been boycotted a bit. Of course apart from any political back-stabbing there is the usual reviewing ramp, ie. the number & favourableness of the reviews you get is directly dependent on the amount your publisher spends on advertising. I think if I was a publisher I wouldn't even do it in such a roundabout way as that, but simply pay the leading hack-reviewers a monthly retaining fee to keep my books to the fore. I hope things go well with you. I am much better though not out of bed yet so I suppose I shall be here another month or two months. It's a bore not being able either to work or to get home & try & salvage what is left of the garden after this bloody weather, but undoubtedly the rest has done me good & incidentally has made me keen to get started with my next novel, though when I came here I had been thinking that what with Hitler, Stalin & the rest of them the day of novel-writing was over. As it is if I start it in August I daresay I'll have to finish it in the concentration camp.
   All the best to Mary & Peter.

                                                          Yours
                                                          Eric Blair

1. This letter is undated, but Eileen's letter to Moore of 24 May (*444*) seems to relate to the

reference to her arranging for Common to have a copy of *Homage to Catalonia* 'when she gets back home on Monday.' 24 May was a Tuesday. Eileen was only able to make the long, awkward, and costly journey from Wallington to Aylesford once a fortnight; see Crick, 360.
2. *The Freedom of the Streets.*
3. In the issue for 16 June 1938; see *453*.
4. See the continuation of Eileen's letter to Moore, 7 June 1938, *450*.
5. It was.

444. Eileen Blair to Leonard Moore

24 May 1938   Handwritten

Wallington,
Near Baldock, Herts.

Dear Mr Moore,

Eric would like two more copies of 'Homage to Catalonia', if possible one to be sent here & one direct to him. I hope I am right in asking you for these— I'm not sure.

I ought to have written to you before but the future remains very vague. However, I think some plan will be settled this week & then I will write to you again.[1]

Yours sincerely,
Eileen Blair.

1. Annotated in Moore's office: 'Get two copies   Send cheque on Friday.' The copy to be sent to Eileen at Wallington was presumably for Jack Common, mentioned in *443*.

445. Sir Richard Rees to Orwell

25 May [1938]   Handwritten

c/o Thos Cook & Sons   Place de la Madeleine   Paris.

Dear Eric

I have just reached Paris from Barcelona,[1] and I learn by a letter from Eileen that you have been laid up since March 8 but are doing very well—which latter I am indeed glad to hear. I knew you had been ill, but didn't realise it was ever since March 8 (before I left for Barcelona). If I had known then I would have tried to get in touch with you before leaving.

I have sent you a book, which I hope you will enjoy—Georges Bernanos' "Les Grands Cimetières sous la Lune".[2] You will, of course, like me, be infuriated by his sentimentality. He's a Royalist and his attitude to "les pauvres" is imbecile. He says they must be "honoured", as the middle ages honoured women, for their "faiblesse". All the same, he's a *very* good chap in many ways, as you'll find if you persevere with the book. His, and his son's experiences with the Phalangistes[3] are in a way analogous to your experience with the P.O.U.M. The fascist treatment of the Phalanges corresponds very much to the C.P. treatment of the P.O.U.M. and the idealistic anarchists.

And, by the way, if you want to read another really good book on Spain—try Elliot Paul's "Life & Death of a Spanish Town".[4] It is about the island of Ibiza before & up to the war and makes a good comparison to Bernanos, which is about the neighbouring island of Majorca and which, more or less, begins just where Elliot Paul's ends, with the first fighting in the Balearic Isles.[5] Both these books really *are* worth reading, and, with yours, they are the only books about Spain that can be said to be written by people with free (i.e. fundamentally honest, if often mistaken) minds. I read your book through at one sitting. It is painful reading, of course, but on the whole it convinced me that you were lucky, in spite of everything, to have got mixed up with the P.O.U.M. & not the C.P.

That short period when the untrained anarchist militia, almost un-armed, were holding the Aragon front, really was the only pure revolutionary experience of the whole sordid business.

However, even my own even more sordid though less exciting experiences were not without flashes of the same thing—and anyway I did not need convincing that "equality" in the anarchist sense *can* work—though whether it ever will be allowed to in this world, God only knows with all respect to God, I find it hard to believe that he will ever allow it to. I get more and more pessimistic.

Chamberlain is going to sell Spain & Eastern Europe to Fascism in return for, a (temporary) immunity for the British Empire & British Capitalism.

During my last visit to Spain I felt ashamed of being English. In my more catastrophically gloomy moods (which are frequent) I find myself hoping that hell will break loose soon. After all, it would be better than a few more decades of ignominious security which Chamberlain hopes to buy by his concessions to Fascism. All the same, your description of hand-to-hand fighting convinces me I could never be a good soldier. I had plenty of bombing & shelling & was sometimes under rifle fire, and I saw plenty of violent death—and I found it all more or less bearable.

But I never had to experience anything like that raid you describe, when the white armlets failed to arrive and somebody said "couldn't we arrange for the fascists to wear white armlets?"! I should never have enough aggressive spirit (i.e. courage) to get through an experience like that, sitting tight while being bombed or machine gunned from the air is *quite* a different matter and infinitely easier.

I hope you are comfortable and have plenty to read. Eileen tells me you have written a Peace pamphlet.[6]

I can't imagine peace, I can only imagine negative war—i.e. the kind of peace you find in Paris & London when you return from Spain. And really I am not sure I don't prefer war to that kind of peace.

But I suppose it is nonsense to talk like that, really.

Well, au revoir, and I hope you'll find Bernanos interesting.

Yours
Richard

1. Rees served in the defence of Madrid, with the Communist Party initially. See Orwell's letter to Rayner Heppenstall, 31 July 1937, *381*. He returned from there 'about a month' before Orwell wrote to Jack Common in October 1937 (see *405*), having somehow got 'mixed up in the political business too.' In his letter to Common of 20 April 1938, Orwell said he was glad Rees was returning home from Catalonia; see *437*.
2. George Bernanos (1888–1948) was a polemical novelist whose passionate stance was expressed with subtlety. *Les grandes cimetières sous la lune* (1938; English title, *Diary of My Times*, 1938) fiercely condemns the atrocities committed in Mallorca by the Fascists and sanctioned by his, the Roman Catholic, church. He is best remembered for his novel *Journal d'un curé de campagne* (1936; English title, *Diary of a Country Priest*, 1937).
3. Falangists. The Falange Española was founded by José Antonio Primo de Rivera (1903–1936), son of Spain's dictator 1923–30, Primo de Rivera (1870–1930). He was tried and executed by the Republicans. The Falangists 'saw themselves as an heroic élite of young men, whose mission was to release Spain from the poison of Marxism, as from what they took to be the second-rate, dull, provincialism of orthodox liberal values' (Thomas, 115). On 18 April 1937 the Falange was united with all other Nationalist groups under Franco, whose brother-in-law, Ramón Serrano Súñer (1901–) was appointed Secretary-General.
4. Elliot Paul (1891–1958) was an American 'autobiographical novelist' and journalist. He served with the American Expeditionary Force in World War I and then worked in Europe for the Associated Press and Paris editions of U.S. newspapers. With Eugene Jolas, he founded the influential journal *transition* (1927–38). His *A Narrow Street* (1942; U.S. title, *The Last Time I Saw Paris*) is chiefly set in the rue de la Huchette, where he lived for eighteen years.
5. 'In the Balearics, while Majorca had been secured by Goded for the [Nationalist] rebels, the NCOs and troops of the garrison at Minorca prevented the success of the rising there. . . . In Ibiza, the rising triumphed, as in the other small Balearic islands' (Thomas, 242; July 1936). Bernanos states that 3,000 were killed by Nationalists (Thomas, 265, who also extracts from Bernanos horrifying details of summary executions, 259–62).
6. This was to be called 'Socialism and War.' See Orwell to Moore, 28 June 1938, *458*.

446. To the Editor, *New English Weekly*

26 May 1938

On 14 April, A. Romney Green had published, in *New English Weekly*, an article on Aldous Huxley, in the series Delinquent Stars. He said that Huxley was 'the arch-exponent of . . . [the] philosophy of "meaninglessness" which was so convenient, as he frankly admits, in its emancipation of their sexual appetites'; and he accused him of taking 'the intolerably smug and absolutely fatal view of his brother pacifists that the abolition of war must precede other social reforms.' Green grouped with Huxley, as 'delinquent stars' and 'false prophets,' C. E. M. Joad, Siegfried Sassoon, Osbert Sitwell 'and the rest of our pacifist philosophers and literati,' and he made sarcastic reference to Huxley's *Ends and Means: An Inquiry into the Nature of Ideals and the Methods Employed for Their Realization* (1937).

Two weeks later, B. J. Boothroyd defended Huxley's position against what he called Green's 'ill-considered attack' on the author of 'this brilliant and inspiring book,' an attack 'ill-mannered and ridiculously inapplicable to such a man' as Huxley. On 12 May, J. S. Collis accused Boothroyd of being himself ill-mannered, showing the 'insolent complacency of a man incapable of grappling with a new idea.' In the same issue, Green said he felt no need to retract anything he had written except for a passing and 'too hasty reference to the Everyman' editions; he had exaggerated the number of misprints he claimed to have found in the Everyman Huxley. At this stage, Orwell joined the debate.

ENDS AND MEANS

Sir,—May I suggest the following considerations to your correspondent, Mr. Romney Green?

(1) He says: "(pacifist) theories are just sufficiently plausible to put to rest the consciences of those well-to-do intellectuals who are rather worried by the social problem but who, if war can otherwise be averted, don't really want to see it solved. It is these people who have the pacifist stars on all their drawing-room tables, and who, since nothing can be done about the social problem till war is abolished, may clearly feel quite justified in doing nothing about it."

Is anything of this kind happening? Is it really pacifist literature that we see on every drawing-room table—is it not, on the contrary, so-called "anti-fascist" literature? Pacifism is so far from being fashionable, or acceptable to the possessing class, that all the big daily newspapers unite to boycott all news of pacifist activities. Virtually the whole of the left-wing intelligentsia, via their mouthpieces in the *News Chronicle*, the *New Statesman, Reynolds*, etc., are clamouring for a Popular Front Government as a prelude to war against Germany. It is true that they are usually too mealy-mouthed to say openly that they wish for war, but that is what they mean, and in private they will often admit that war is "inevitable," by which they mean desirable.

(2) He also says: "I seriously doubt either the intelligence or the sincerity of anyone who goes about England with his eyes open . . . and who . . . professes to think that nothing can be done about the social problem until war is abolished."

The implication is that pacifism is somehow being used, or could be used, as an excuse for blocking social reform. Once again, where is this happening, and how could it happen? In every country except those which are definitely outside the war-orbit, the supposed necessity to prepare for war is being systematically used to prevent every kind of social advance. It goes without saying that this happens in the Fascist countries, but "guns before butter" also rules in the democracies. We have seen how, in the space of two years, the French working class have been swindled out of every advantage they won in 1936,[1] and always by means of the same catchword—"All Frenchmen must unite against Hitler." The truth is that any real advance, let alone any genuinely revolutionary change, can only begin when the mass of the people definitely refuse capitalist-imperialist war and thus make it clear to their rulers that a war-policy is not practicable. So long as they show themselves willing to fight "in defence of democracy," or "against Fascism," or for any other flyblown slogan, the same trick will be played upon them again and again: "You can't have a rise in wages *now*, because we have got to prepare for war. Guns before butter!"

Meanwhile there is considerable possibility of producing an effective anti-war movement in England. It is a question of mobilising the dislike of war that undoubtedly exists in ordinary decent people, as opposed to the hack-journalists and the pansy left. The fact that a book like Mr. Huxley's contains a certain amount of self-righteousness (we are all self-righteous in different ways), and is written too much from the standpoint of a middle-class intellectual, is beside the point. Anyone who helps to put peace on the map is doing useful work. The real enemies of the working class are not those who talk to them in a too highbrow manner; they are those who try to trick them into identifying their interests with those of their exploiters, and into forgetting what every manual worker inwardly knows—that modern war is a racket.

A. Romney Green replied in the issue of 16 June. He reiterated that war was inevitable; that Britain's supremacy as an imperial power 'might very well be challenged by less fortunate races even if we were putting our Empire to reasonably good use'; that if we couldn't have butter and guns it was better to have guns, but 'our victory in the terrific struggle which lies ahead of us depends upon our discovering before it is too late that a people whose gunmaking leaves them still with vast reservoirs of unemployed labour and ill-developed natural resources might have butter also.'

1. The Popular Front government led by the Socialist Léon Blum (see *515, n. 1*), which was elected in June 1936, had enacted a series of reforms which benefitted working men and women.

447. Eileen Blair to Leonard Moore

30 May 1938   Typewritten

Wallington, Near Baldock, Herts.

Dear Mr. Moore,

I promised Eric I would write and tell you the news about him, which is that he is to go abroad for the winter, staying at Preston Hall until he leaves England—that is, probably until August or September. After that we hope he will be able to come home, though not to this house. We think of trying to find somewhere to live in Dorset. All this does not of course mean that he is worse, but only that the position has been made clearer to him. As a matter of fact, the original diagnosis was wrong: he had bronchiectasis and probably no phthisis. Apparently there is no point in treating bronchiectasis by the absolute rest that sometimes cures phthisis, and I think he is going to be allowed up as soon as the weather is reasonable.[1] He ought also to be able to do some gentle work on the novel in July or August. Of course it's not easy to work in a sanatorium, where people constantly walk about and impose a timetable that probably interferes with the work timetable, but the book seethes in his head and he is very anxious to get on with it. I ought to have written to you some time ago about this novel, when Eric first realised that he couldn't finish it by October, but he then wanted Gollancz to be told that it would be ready anyway before Christmas. Now he thinks that it will be ready in the spring and this seems quite probable. I should be very grateful if you could give Gollancz a message about it in whatever terms you think proper.

I hear there is a wonderful review of Homage to Catalonia in the Observer,[2] but I haven't seen it yet. On the whole the reviews have really been very good don't you think? It's interesting that the C.P. have decided not to be rude—and extremely clever of them to be reticent in the definitely Communist press and to say their little piece anonymously in the T.L.S. and the Listener. By the way, do you know when Warburg proposes to pay an advance? We thought he was to pay £75 in January and £75 on publication, but perhaps that's wrong.

Eric is still being extraordinarily amenable and placid about everything, and everyone is delighted with his general condition.

Yours sincerely,
Eileen Blair

1. Orwell was allowed up for one hour a day from 1 June and for three hours a day a week later.
2. The review, on 29 May 1938 (see *438*), was by Desmond Flower (1907–), author, editor, publisher. He was Director of Cassell & Co in 1931, then Literary Director, 1938, and Chairman, 1958–70. He was also founder/editor, with A. J. A. Symons, of *Book Collector's Quarterly*, 1930–34. He served in the war, 1939–45 and was awarded the Military Cross, 1944.

448. To C. D. Abbott, Director, Lockwood Memorial Library, University of Buffalo

4 June 1938

The Lockwood Memorial Library wrote to Orwell, describing him as a poet, to ask if he would let them have, as a gift, any of his manuscripts, since they were making a collection of materials on modern poetry.

New Hostel[1]   Preston Hall   Aylesford   Kent   England

Dear Sir,
With reference to your letter CDA:he dated May 20, I am not a poet, only a novelist. I am afraid perhaps somebody may have misinformed you. If it will interest you to have the MS. of one of my novels, I may still have one by me—I believe the MS. of my latest book, "Homage to Catalonia", has not been destroyed. If so, & if it would be of any use to you, I could send it along.

Yours truly
George Orwell

1. After tests and observation in Jellicoe Ward (or Pavilion), Orwell was moved to New Hostel on 1 June. This was a sort of boardinghouse-cum-dormitory for slow-recovery patients and for recuperation after operations. The sanatorium also had workshops to occupy the patients' time in the later stages of their return to health.

449. To Yvonne Davet

7 June 1938   Handwritten

The doctors at Aylesford advised Orwell to spend the winter in a warm climate for the sake of his lungs. The cost was financed by a gift of £300 given anonymously by novelist L. H. Myers (1881–1944), through Max and Dorothy Plowman. Orwell later repaid this gift, which he regarded as a loan; see letter to Dorothy Plowman, 19 February 1946, *2903*. When Crick wrote his life of Orwell, no evidence had been traced as to why Morocco was chosen (see 369), but since then Madame Yvonne Davet has made available her letters from Orwell; those of 18 and 26 August 1938 (see *474, 477*) reveal the reasons. See also Shelden, 324–25; U.S.: 296–97.

New Hostel   Preston Hall   Aylesford   Kent

Chère camarade,

J'ai fait mon mieux. Je n'ai pas de dictionnaire française ici, mais j'espère que vous pouvez comprendre ce que j'ai écrit. Quand il n'y a rien à changer j'ai marqué votre note ainsi V, autrement j'ai fait mes explications dans les pages ci-jointes.

Je me trouve beaucoup mieux, mais on me dit qu'il me faut rester ici jusqu'à juillet ou août et puis m'en aller au sud de France, car il sera mieux de ne pas passer l'hiver en Angleterre. Je ne sais pas encore si° il ne faudra aller dans un hôpital, ou si on me permettra de prendre un logement et vivre chez moi. Dans le dernier cas, vous pourriez peut-être nous aider à trouver une petite cottage quelconque? En tous cas ma femme et moi serons très contents de vous rencontrer quand nous passons par Paris.

Avec tous mes remerciments pour la peine que vous vous avez donnée en traduisant mon livre,

Très fraternellment
Eric Blair

P.S. Est ce que vous connaissiez Eugène Dabit? Je viens de lire un livre d'André Gide sur la U.R.R.S.,[1] dans lequel il dit que Dabit l'a accompagné en Russie et qu'il est mort là, ce que je ne savais pas. Je savais seulement qu'il était mort. Je l'ai recontré° à Londres. Il était neveu de Mrs Sturge Moore, une dame française qui s'est mariée avec Thomas Sturge Moore,[2] le poète irlandaise. Nous avons diné ensemble et je l'ai trouvé très sympathique.

Translation

I have done my best. I haven't got a French dictionary here, but I hope you can understand what I've written. When there is nothing to alter I've marked your note thus V, otherwise I've made some explanatory notes on the attached sheets.

I am much better, but they say I must stay here till July or August and then go away to the south of France, as it will be better not to spend the winter in England. I don't yet know whether I will have to go into hospital, or whether they will let me rent somewhere and live at home. If the latter, could you possibly help us find some little cottage? In any case my wife and I will be glad to meet you when we go through Paris.

With all my thanks for the trouble you have taken in translating my book.

P.S. Did you know Eugène Dabit? I've just read a book by André Gide on the Soviet Union,[1] in which he says that Dabit went with him to Russia and that he died there, which I did not know. I knew only that he had died. I met him in London. He was the nephew of Mrs Sturge Moore, a Frenchwoman who married Thomas Sturge Moore,[2] the Irish poet. We had dinner together, and I liked him very much.

1. *Retour de l'U.R.S.S.*, November 1936; translated as *Return from the U.S.S.R.* by Dorothy Bussy, April 1937. It is dedicated 'to the memory of Eugène Dabit beside whom, with whom [these pages] were lived and thought.' Fredric Warburg thought this probably the most significant work Secker & Warburg published in 1937. Gide, who had once so warmly supported Soviet Russia, wrote that he doubted whether any other country, 'even Hitler's Germany, thought to be less free' was 'more bowed down, more fearful (terrorized), more vassalized' than the U.S.S.R.
2. Thomas Sturge Moore (1870–1944) was a practising wood engraver who developed into an art historian and poet. He wrote several studies of artists and, in addition to books of poetry published at the turn of the century, a number of verse plays, mainly on classical subjects.

450. Eileen Blair to Leonard Moore

7 June 1938   Handwritten

Wallington,
Near Baldock, Herts.

Dear Mr Moore,

One of my weekend guests tells me that he lost a letter to you that he was going to post for me. So I write again to thank you for the cheque; possibly you will have two acknowledgments but indeed you have earned many. I did not expect to see the second half of the advance for a long time.

I am extremely sorry about Miss Perriam. That business is hell I know. But I also know a woman who had a series of similar operations about eight years ago & has since had no further trouble, so I do hope Miss Perriam may go on resembling her.

You must be terribly overworked. I suppose the summer is your easier time but of course on the other hand it's almost intolerable (to me anyway) to be in London throughout the hot weather.

I am busy too—typing a novel about the Afghan frontier, complete with a 'man-child' being reared to avenge his dead father by a devoted mother & a half-blind grandmother.[1] The grammar is as original as the plot & the punctuation perhaps unique. Does it not surprise you to see what books are completed?

Eric has been allowed up & is very pleased with himself.

With many thanks,

Yours sincerely,
Eileen Blair.

Wednesday.[2]

I missed the postman this morning so have opened this to thank you for the book & letter brought by him. I had to write an almost unintelligible letter to Warburg which did convey I hope the idea that he should stop asking Eric to write blurbs. He persists in doing this & Eric hates getting the books but there is some suggestion (to Eric anyway) that if he doesn't write the blurb he is letting someone down. So I was to tell Warburg that he is not going to write any more 'bits'. Probably he will though. He always enjoys doing things for the New English Weekly as Mairet will print anything he writes & never presses him.[3] I think it's quite good for him to write short articles when he feels like it; it's the compulsion that is exhausting, not the writing. As for the correspondence in the Times Lit. Supp. that you may have seen, it has been a delight.[4]

I'm sorry you've had so hard a time with Warburg. I believe the book ought to sell quite well but I wish he had more money for publicity. The Time & Tide, New Statesman & Observer reviews[5] really warrant a splash.

If you are ever in the direction of Maidstone, Eric would be delighted to see you of course—the place is on the London road about 2½ miles from Maidstone & there are no special visiting hours.

Yours sincerely,
Eileen Blair

1. Unidentified.
2. 8 June 1938.
3. Orwell's enjoyment was despite the fact that *New English Weekly* did not pay contributors.
4. Orwell's letters of 14 and 28 May 1938; see *441*.
5. Orwell wrote to thank Geoffrey Gorer for his review in *Time and Tide* on 18 April 1938; see *436*. V. S. Pritchett (see *750, n. 2*) wrote the review in *The New Statesman*, 30 April 1938, and Desmond Flower that in *The Observer* (with other books on Spain), 29 May 1938; see *438*.

451. Review of *Assignment in Utopia* by Eugene Lyons

New English Weekly, 9 June 1938

To get the full sense of our ignorance as to what is really happening in the U.S.S.R., it is worth trying to translate the most sensational Russian event of the past two years, the Trotskyist trials, into English terms. Make the necessary adjustments, let Left be Right and Right be Left, and you get something like this:

Mr. Winston Churchill, now in exile in Portugal, is plotting to overthrow the British Empire and establish Communism in England. By the use of unlimited Russian money he has succeeded in building up a huge Churchillite organisation which includes members of Parliament, factory managers, Roman Catholic bishops and practically the whole of the Primrose League. Almost every day some dastardly act of sabotage is laid bare—sometimes a plot to blow up the House of Lords, sometimes an outbreak of foot and mouth disease in the Royal racing-stables. Eighty per cent. of the Beefeaters at the Tower are discovered to be agents of the Comintern. A high official of the Post Office admits brazenly to having embezzled postal orders to the tune of £5,000,000, and also to having committed *lèse majesté* by drawing moustaches on postage stamps. Lord Nuffield, after a 7-hour interrogation by Mr. Norman Birkett, confesses that ever since 1920 he has been fomenting strikes in his own factories. Casual half-inch paras in every issue of the newspapers announce that fifty more Churchillite sheep-stealers have been shot in Westmoreland° or that the proprietress of a village shop in the Cotswolds has been transported to Australia for sucking the bullseyes and putting them back in the bottle. And meanwhile the Churchillites (or Churchillite-Harmsworthites as they are called after Lord Rothermere's execution) never cease from proclaiming that it is *they* who are the real defenders of Capitalism and that Chamberlain and the rest of his gang are no more than a set of Bolsheviks in disguise.

Anyone who has followed the Russian trials knows that this is scarcely a parody. The question arises, could anything like this happen in England? Obviously it could not. From our point of view the whole thing is not merely incredible as a genuine conspiracy, it is next door to incredible as a frame-up. It is simply a dark mystery, of which the only seizable fact—sinister enough in its way—is that Communists over here regard it as a good advertisement for Communism.

Meanwhile the truth about Stalin's régime, if we could only get hold of it, is of the first importance. Is it Socialism, or is it a peculiarly vicious form of state-capitalism? All the political controversies that have made life hideous for two years past really circle round this question, though for several reasons it is seldom brought into the foreground. It is difficult to go [to] Russia, once there it is impossible to make adequate investigations, and all one's ideas on the subject have to be drawn from books which are so fulsomely "for" or so venomously "against" that the prejudice stinks a mile away. Mr. Lyons's book is definitely in the "against" class, but he gives the impression of being much more reliable than most. It is obvious from his manner of writing that he is not a vulgar propagandist, and he was in Russia a long time (1928–34) as correspondent for the United Press Agency, having been sent there on Communist recommendation. Like many others who have gone to Russia full of hope he was gradually disillusioned, and unlike some others he finally decided to tell the truth about it. It is an unfortunate fact that any hostile criticism of the present Russian regime is liable to be taken as propaganda *against Socialism*; all Socialists are aware of this, and it does not make for honest discussion.

The years that Mr. Lyons spent in Russia were years of appalling hardship, culminating in the Ukraine famine of 1933, in which a number estimated at not less than three million people starved to death. Now, no doubt, after the success of the Second Five Year Plan,[1] the physical conditions have improved, but there seems no reason for thinking that the social atmosphere is greatly different. The system that Mr. Lyons describes does not seem to be very different from Fascism. All real power is concentrated in the hands of two or three million people, the town proletariat, theoretically the heirs of the revolution, having been robbed even of the elementary right to strike; more recently, by the introduction of the internal passport system, they have been reduced to a status resembling serfdom.[2] The G.P.U. are everywhere, everyone lives in constant terror of denunciation, freedom of speech and of the press are obliterated to an extent we can hardly imagine. There are periodical waves of terror, sometimes the "liquidation" of kulaks or Nepmen, sometimes some monstrous state trial at which people who have been in prison for months or years are suddenly dragged forth to make incredible confessions, while their children publish articles in the newspapers saying "I repudiate my father as a Trotskyist serpent." Meanwhile the invisible Stalin is worshipped in terms that would have made Nero blush. This—at great length and in much detail—is the picture Mr. Lyons presents, and I do not believe he has misrepresented the facts. He does, however, show signs of being embittered by his experiences, and I think he probably exaggerates the amount of discontent prevailing among the Russians themselves.

He once succeeded in interviewing Stalin, and found him human, simple and likeable. It is worth noticing that H. G. Wells said the same thing,[3] and it is a fact that Stalin, at any rate on the cinematograph, has a likeable face. Is it not also recorded that Al Capone was the best of husbands and fathers, and that Joseph Smith (of Brides in the Bath fame) was sincerely loved by the first of his seven wives and always returned to her between murders?

1. Lyons's account of the 'Five Year Plan in Four Years' and his recording of the formula used to express that, $2 + 2 = 5$, directly influenced Orwell's writing of *Nineteen Eighty-Four* (although this formula is to be found at least as early as the mid-eighteenth century, in Sterne's *Tristram Shandy*, a copy of which Orwell had in his possession, and in Dostoevski's *Notes from Underground* (1864).
2. Under the tsars, serfs needed internal passports to leave their villages to take up seasonal work elsewhere.
3. See *Stalin–Wells Talk: The Verbatim Record, and a Discussion* by G. Bernard Shaw, H. G. Wells, J. M. Keynes, Ernst Toller, and others (1934).

452. To the Editor, *The Listener*

16 June 1938

Review of 'Homage to Catalonia'
Your reviewer's[1] treatment of facts is a little curious. In his review of my book *Homage to Catalonia* in THE LISTENER of May 25 he uses about four-fifths of his space in resurrecting from the Communist Press the charge that the Spanish political party known as the P.O.U.M. is a 'fifth column' organisation in the pay of General Franco. He states first that this accusation was 'hyperbolical', but adds later that it was 'credible', and that the leaders of the P.O.U.M. were 'little better than traitors to the Government cause'. Now, I leave on one side the question of how it can be credible that Franco's 'fifth column' could be composed of the poorest of the working class, led by men most of whom had been imprisoned under the regime Franco was trying

to restore, and at least one of whom was on Franco's special list of 'persons to be shot'. If your reviewer can believe in stories of that kind, he is entitled to do so. What he is not entitled to do is to repeat his accusation, which is incidentally an accusation against myself, without even indicating from whom it came or that I had had anything to say about it. He leaves it to be inferred all through that the absurd charges of treachery and espionage originated with the Spanish Government. But, as I pointed out in great detail (Chapter XI of my book), these charges never had any footing outside the Communist Press, nor was any evidence in support of them ever produced. The Spanish Government has again and again repudiated all belief in them, and has steadfastly refused to prosecute the men whom the Communist newspapers denounced. I gave chapter and verse from the Spanish Government's statements, which have since been repeated several times. Your reviewer simply ignores all this, no doubt hoping that he has so effectually put people off reading the book that his mis-representations will pass unnoticed.

I do not expect or wish for 'good' reviews, and if your reviewer chooses to use most of his space in expressing his own political opinions, that is a matter between him and yourself. But I think I have a right to ask that when a book of mine is discussed at the length of a column there shall be at least some mention of what I have actually said.

Aylesford   George Orwell

[*We have sent the above letter to our reviewer, who replies:*
'Mr. Orwell's letter ignores the major fact that conditions in Barcelona at one time became so bad that the Spanish Government was forced to send in armed police to put down what amounted to an insurrection. The leaders of that insurrection were the extreme anarchist elements allied with the P.O.U.M. It is not a question of "resurrecting" charges from the Communist Press, but of historic fact. I have spent a considerable part of the Spanish war in Spain, and have not relied upon newspaper reports for my information.

'As I made clear in my review, it was not the intention of the rank and file of the P.O.U.M. to do other than fight against Franco. Being poor and ignorant men, the complexities of the revolutionary situation were beyond them; their leaders were to blame. As for being part of Franco's fifth column, there is no doubt that whoever declined to co-operate with the central government and to abide by the law was, in fact, weakening the authority of that government and thus aiding the enemy. I submit that in time of war ignorance is as reprehensible as malicious sabotage. It is effect that matters, not the reasons for action.

'I am sorry if Mr. Orwell thinks that I wanted to put readers off a magnificently written book: I didn't: I want people to read it even if, in my opinion, his analysis is wrong. It is the essence of a democracy in peace time that all views should be available to everybody'.

We are bound to say, in printing our reviewer's reply, that we consider it hardly meets the points made by Mr. Orwell, to whom we express our regrets.—Editor, THE LISTENER[2]]

1. Philip Furneaux Jordan (1902–1951) was a journalist, novelist, and reviewer. He had been for a time on the staff of the Paris *Daily Mail* and edited the Riviera edition of the *Chicago Tribune*. In 1936 he joined the staff of the *News Chronicle* and served as its correspondent in Spain, 1936–37. He later became the *News Chronicle*'s features editor and then its foreign correspondent. In 1946–47 he was First Secretary at the British Embassy in Washington, and thereafter Public Relations Adviser to Prime Minister Clement Attlee. He also reviewed for *The Times Literary Supplement*—anonymously, as for *The Listener*.
2. J. R. Ackerley (1896–1967) was literary editor, 1935–59. See *Ackerley* by Peter Parker (1989).

453. Review of *The Freedom of the Streets* by Jack Common
New English Weekly, 16 June 1938

Jack Common, a writer who is at present not so well known as he might be but who is potentially a sort of Chesterton of the Left, approaches the subject of Socialism from an interesting and unfamiliar angle.

He is of proletarian origin, and much more than most writers of this kind he preserves his proletarian viewpoint. In doing so he puts his finger on one of the chief difficulties of the Socialist movement—the fact that the word "Socialism" means something quite different to a working man from what it means to a middle-class Marxist. To those who actually have the destiny of the Socialist movement in their hands, virtually everything that a manual worker means when he says "Socialism" is either irrelevant or heretical. As Mr. Common shows in a series of separate but connected essays, the manual workers in a machine civilization have certain characteristics forced upon them by the circumstances in which they live: loyalty, improvidence, generosity, hatred of privilege. It is out of these that they evolve their vision of a future society, so that the mystique of proletarian Socialism is the idea of equality. This is a very different vision from that of the middle-class Socialist who accepts Marx as his prophet—literally a prophet, a tipster who not only tells you which horse to back, but also provides the reason why the horse didn't win.

The spirit in which Mr. Common writes is the mixture of messianic hope and cheerful pessimism that is sometimes to be found in the quieter corners of the four-ale bar on a Saturday night. He thinks that we are all going to be blown to hell by bombs, but that the dictatorship of the proletariat is really going to happen:

"A time is coming when even the comparatively comfortable will suffer under the terror of lawless governments, created in their own choice or by their acquiescence. The about-to-be-bombed need not fear communism. They will be communists themselves by the time the bombing is over, if they survive . . . For it only needs a turn of the screw, an increase of tension, and the fragile and rather imaginary partitions by which the masses of all the world are allowed to cherish their divisions will blow away."

Yes: but if there were any certainty that this will happen, would it not be the duty of every Socialist to hope and work for war? And dare any thinking person do that nowadays?

There must be very many minds in which that hackneyed phrase, "dictatorship of the proletariat," has been successively a nightmare, a hope and a chimaera. One starts off—for after all, that is how most middle-class people *do* start—by thinking "God help us all when it happens!" and one ends up by thinking "What a pity it can't happen!" Mr. Common writes all the while as though the dictatorship of the proletariat were just round the corner—a pious hope, but the facts do not seem to give much warrant for it. It would seem that what you get over and over again is a movement of the proletariat which is promptly canalised and betrayed by astute people at the top, and then the growth of a new governing class. The one thing that never arrives is equality. The mass of the people never get the chance to bring their innate decency into the control of affairs, so that one is almost driven to the cynical thought that men are only decent when they are powerless.

Meanwhile this is an interesting book, which tells you much less about Socialism as an economic theory and much more about it as a body of belief, one might almost say a way of life, than the average textbook. I particularly recommend the two essays called "The Judgment of the Vulgar" and "Fascism in Men of Good Will." Allowing for the fact that it has found literary expression—which in itself is slightly abnormal—this is the authentic voice of the ordinary man, the man who might infuse a new decency into the control of affairs if only he could get there, but who in practice never seems to get much further than the trenches, the sweatshop and the jail.

454. To Naomi Mitchison

17 June 1938   Handwritten

New Hostel   Preston Hall   Aylesford   Kent

Dear Miss Mitchison,[1]
Many thanks for your letter. I am glad you liked the book. As you say, it is harder than ever before to make sure of the right political line. If one allows a free hand to the Communists & their friends one is, I am certain, allowing the whole Socialist movement to be perverted, whereas if one opposes them there is always the chance that one is, objectively if not intentionally, aiding the Fascists. This last argument is, of course, dragged forth on every occasion. Nevertheless I believe it is right to try & keep alive the older version of Socialism even when it doesn't seem strategically opportune. I have never been much impressed by the C.P. line of talk to the effect, "People's motives do not matter; the only thing that matters is the objective result of their actions." To begin with, it is much easier to be certain about people's motives than to foresee the result of any course of action, & in practice the C.P. prophecies about the results of this & that have often turned out to be wrong. Secondly, their whole line of thought is based on doing evil that good may come, which in my opinion implies thinking that causes do not have effects. On the other hand there is an ever-present danger of becoming simply anti-

Communist, as the Trotskyists do, which is completely sterile even if it isn't harmful. As to the U.S.S.R., I have next to no notion as to what is happening there & I believe less & less of what I read about it. I suppose you have been to Russia? I never have, & I don't suppose I shall be able to now.

My wound healed very quickly & didn't leave much in the way of after-effects. I am in this place for T.B., but it is nothing serious & I shall be out soon, after which I am probably going abroad for the winter.

Thank you for writing.

Yours sincerely
Eric Blair
("George Orwell")

1. Naomi Margaret Mitchison (1897–1999; Lady Mitchison, 1974; CBE, 1985), daughter of J. S. Haldane and sister of J. B. S. Haldane, was the author of some eighty books, mainly novels, often on classical themes, and some books and a play written in collaboration with others. In the year she wrote to Orwell she published *The Moral Basis of Politics*. She served on committees concerned with the Highlands and Islands of Scotland, 1947–76. See also *1361*. She prefers not to use her title.

455. Contract for 'Poverty in Practice'

18 June 1938

Thomas Nelson & Sons Ltd sent Orwell on 18 June, via Eileen, a contract to write a book to be called 'Poverty in Practice.' He was to receive an advance of £50. He was not well enough, however, to be allowed to type, and the contract was not signed. It is possible that, realising the need to husband his strength, he made a choice between 'Poverty in Practice' and the book he was to write in Morocco, *Coming Up for Air*. It may be more than coincidental that one of the consultants treating Orwell at Preston Hall (possibly his brother-in-law, Laurence O'Shaughnessy) wrote in Orwell's Case Record for 21 June 1938: 'I have suggested his immediate future and warned him duly of the risks of literary research!' No letters about this from Orwell have been traced.

455A. Eileen Blair to Denys King-Farlow

22 June 1938   Handwritten

Wallington,
near Baldock, Herts.

Dear Denys,

When I told you on the telephone that I was more or less writing to you it was quite true. But I was also having flu, although at that time incredulously because the time even of this year seems so odd.

I hadn't *forgotten* this money: indeed I have thought of it often with growing appreciation as the 'advance' on the Spanish book went on not coming. Eventually it was extracted by instalments! Poor man—I mean poor publisher. I hope it was time that you didn't need. As a matter of fact I shouldn't have kept the cheque if I'd had any doubt about repaying it almost at once. Or I think not.

Eric isn't so ill as they thought, as you'll have gathered. He of course has never believed that he was 'ill', but for the first two months or so he appeared to have phthisis[1] in both lungs which could have been pretty hopeless. Now it turns out to be bronchiectasis,[2] which people *do* go on having more or less indefinitely under really favourable conditions. I suppose he told you that we can probably go abroad for the winter together instead of his going to a sanatorium, & after that we have to find a perfect cottage in one of the southern counties at an inclusive rental of about 7/6. I shall come back early to do this— They even think that he might leave Preston Hall in August & spend a month or so under normal conditions in England—he must of course be very 'careful' but the treatment really only consists in resting a great deal & eating a lot. We might perhaps stay on a farm somewhere. By that time this cottage will be handed over either to the landlord or to an unfortunate old uncle of Eric's who is suggested as a tenant.[3]

I'm so glad you went to see Eric & took him out. I think it's really more depressing for him to be in this semi-confinement than to be in bed, & he loved having a party.[4] It was particularly nice of you to send that money instead of offering to.

With many thanks,

Yours sincerely,[5]
Eileen Blair

1. Tuberculosis.
2. Chronic viral disease affecting the bronchial tubes.
3. Although Orwell's parents had seventeen brothers and sisters between them, the only uncles to whom Eileen could be referring were Charles Limouzin, at one time secretary of a golf club at Parkstone, Bournemouth; George Limouzin, who was married to Ivy; and Eugène Adam, who was married to Nellie Limouzin. None took the cottage.
4. If the party was to celebrate anything, it might have been for the publication of *Homage to Catalonia* on 25 April; or a party slightly ahead of Orwell's thirty-fifth birthday, 25 June.
5. 'Yours sincerely' is uncertain; Eileen has written a long scrawl.

456. Review of *Spanish Ordeal*[1] by Robert Sencourt; *Franco's Rule* [anonymous]

New English Weekly, 23 June 1938

It is not easy for any thinking person to write in praise of dictatorships, because of the obvious fact that when any dictatorship gets into its stride the thinking person is the first to be liquidated. Possibly Mr. Wyndham Lewis still approves of Hitler, but does Hitler approve of Mr. Lewis? Which side would Hitler have been on in the recent set-to about Mr. Eliot's portrait?[2] It is true that over against the German dictatorship there is the Russian dictatorship, but to a western European that is less immediately menacing.

We are still in the position of being able to admire it from beyond gunshot range.

Consequently, bad as the pro-Government books on the Spanish war have been, the pro-Franco ones have been worse. All or almost all that I have seen—I except those of Professor Allison Peers, who is only rather tepidly pro-Franco—have been written by Roman Catholics. Mr. Sencourt's book does not sink to the level of Arnold Lunn's "Red Rehearsal," but its general thesis is the same. Franco is a Christian gentleman, the Valencia Government are a gang of robbers, the Badajos massacre didn't happen, Guernica was not bombed but wantonly burnt by Red militiamen—and so on and so forth. The truth is that all the haggling about "who started it" and who committed which atrocity that goes on in books of this kind is a waste of time, because it does not tell you anything about the real conflict of motives. It would be much simpler if everyone would say outright, "My money is on Franco (or Negrin), atrocities or no atrocities." For that is what everyone who takes sides really thinks.

Mr. Sencourt at any rate differs from Messrs. Lunn, Yeats-Brown, etc., in that he knows a great deal about Spain and loves the Spaniards, so that though he is hostile to the "Reds" he is not vulgarly spiteful. But like almost everyone who has written of this war he suffers a great disadvantage from having only been able to study conditions on one side of the line. What he says of the pre-war situation is probably sound enough, but his account of internal conditions on the Government side during the war is very misleading. He enormously exaggerates the amount of civil disorder, and though he gives the main outline of the struggle between the various political parties he misunderstands the role and aim of most of them, because he feels himself obliged to equate "Red" with "bad." Communism he speaks of as though it were a disruptive force and nothing else, and he uses "Anarchism" indifferently with "anarchy," which is a hardly more correct use of words than saying that a Conservative is one who makes jam. Still, this is not an ill-natured or dishonest book, and to say that of a book on a political subject is a great deal nowadays.

"Franco's Rule" is simply an enormous list of atrocities committed in all the territories that Franco has over-run. There are long lists of people who have been shot, and such statements as that 23,000 were massacred in the province of Granada, etc., etc. Now, I do not say that these stories are untrue; obviously I have no means of judging, and at a guess I would say that some are true and some are not. And yet there is something that makes one very uneasy about the appearance of books of this kind.

There is no doubt that atrocities happen, though when a war is over it is generally impossible to establish more than a few isolated cases. In the first few weeks of war, especially in a civil war, there are bound to be massacres of non-combatants, arson, looting and probably raping. If these things happen it is right that they should be recorded and denounced, but I am not so sure about the motives of people who are so enthralled by the subject that they will compile whole books of atrocity-stories. They usually tell you that they are trying to stir up hatred "against Fascism" or "against Communism." But you notice that they seldom hate these things sufficiently to fight against them themselves; I believe no soldier has ever compiled a book of atrocity-stories. One is left with the suspicion that some of the atrocity-mongers rather like writing about rapes and summary executions.

And does anyone believe that in the long run this is the best way to combat either Fascism or what is bad in Communism? Mr. Arthur Koestler, whose nerves must have suffered horribly during his imprisonment by Franco, and who is to be forgiven much, tells us in his book, "Spanish Testament," to abandon objectivity and cultivate hatred. The anonymous editor of "Franco's Rule" also speaks contemptuously of "objectivity neurosis." I wish these people would stop to reflect what they are doing. To fight, or even to ask others to fight, is one thing; to go round stirring up maniacal hatred is another. For:

"He who fights too long against dragons becomes a dragon himself: and if thou gaze too long into the abyss, the abyss will gaze into thee."

This book is subtitled "Back to the Middle Ages," which is unfair to the Middle Ages. There were no machine-guns in those days, and the Inquisition was a very amateurish business. After all, even Torquemada only burnt two thousand people in ten years. In modern Russia or Germany they'd say he wasn't trying.

1. The correct title of this book is *Spain's Ordeal*.
2. Lewis's portrait of T. S. Eliot was rejected by the hanging committee of the 1938 Royal Academy Exhibition. In a letter to Lewis of 21 April 1938, Eliot wrote that he would be quite willing to be known to posterity through this portrait. See Walter Michel, *Wyndham Lewis, Paintings and Drawings* (1971), 132 and plate 132.

457. 'Why I Join the I.L.P.'

The New Leader, 24 June 1938

Orwell's membership card for the Independent Labour Party was issued on 13 June 1938. This article[1] was given a position of prominence, running parallel to the leader, or editorial, and on the same page as details of the journal's editorial offices and the name of the editor, Fenner Brockway. See Crick, 364–65.

Perhaps it will be frankest to approach it first of all from the personal angle.

I am a writer. The impulse of every writer is to "keep out of politics." What he wants is to be left alone so that he can go on writing books in peace. But unfortunately it is becoming obvious that this ideal is no more practicable than that of the petty shopkeeper who hopes to preserve his independence in the teeth of the chain-stores.

To begin with, the era of free speech is closing down. The freedom of the Press in Britain was always something of a fake, because in the last resort, money controls opinion; still, so long as the legal right to say what you like exists, there are always loopholes for an unorthodox writer. For some years past I have managed to make the Capitalist class pay me several pounds a week for writing books against Capitalism. But I do not delude myself that this state of affairs is going to last for ever. We have seen what has happened to the freedom of the Press in Italy and Germany, and it will happen here sooner or later. The time is coming—not next year, perhaps not for ten or twenty years, but it is coming—when every writer will have the choice of being silenced altogether or of producing the dope that a privileged minority demands.

I have got to struggle against that, just as I have got to struggle against castor oil, rubber truncheons and concentration-camps. And the only regime which, in the long run, will dare to permit freedom of speech is a Socialist regime. If Fascism triumphs I am finished as a writer—that is to say, finished in my only effective capacity. That of itself would be a sufficient reason for joining a Socialist party.

I have put the personal aspect first, but obviously it is not the only one.

It is not possible for any thinking person to live in such a society as our own without wanting to change it. For perhaps ten years past I have had some grasp of the real nature of Capitalist society. I have seen British Imperialism at work in Burma, and I have seen something of the effects of poverty and unemployment in Britain. In so far as I have struggled against the system, it has been mainly of writing books which I hoped would influence the reading public. I shall continue to do that, of course, but at a moment like the present writing books is not enough. The tempo of events is quickening; the dangers which once seemed a generation distant are staring us in the face. One has got to be actively a Socialist, not merely sympathetic to Socialism, or one plays into the hands of our always-active enemies.

Why the I.L.P. more than another?

Because the I.L.P. is the only British party—at any rate the only one large enough to be worth considering—which aims at anything I should regard as Socialism.

I do not mean that I have lost all faith in the Labour Party. My most earnest hope is that the Labour Party will win a clear majority in the next General Election. But we know what the history of the Labour Party has been, and we know the terrible temptation of the present moment—the temptation to fling every principle overboard in order to prepare for an Imperialist war. It is vitally necessary that there should be in existence some body of people who can be depended on, even in face of persecution, not to compromise their Socialist principles.

I believe that the I.L.P. is the only party which, as a party, is likely to take the right line either against Imperialist war or against Fascism when this appears in its British form. And meanwhile the I.L.P. is not backed by any monied interest, and is systematically libelled from several quarters. Obviously it needs all the help it can get, including any help I can give it myself.

Finally, I was with the I.L.P. contingent in Spain. I never pretended, then or since, to agree in every detail with the policy the P.O.U.M. put forward and the I.L.P. supported, but the general course of events has borne it out.

The things I saw in Spain brought home to me the fatal danger of mere negative "anti-Fascism." Once I had grasped the essentials of the situation in Spain I realised that the I.L.P. was the only British party I felt like joining—and also the only party I could join with at least the certainty that I would never be led up the garden path in the name of Capitalist democracy.

1. As 'Why I Joined the Independent Labour Party' in *CEJL*, I, 132.

458. To Leonard Moore

28 June 1938   Handwritten

New Hostel   Preston Hall   Aylesford   Kent

Dear Mr Moore,

I've just had a letter from Gollancz forwarding one from some Burmans who wish to translate "Burmese Days" into Burmese(!) He suggested that we should let them do it free, & I agreed, as it is obvious there would never be any money in it & at the same time it is an advert. in a small way. I have written to Gollancz to this effect, but if you think otherwise you could get in touch with G. & suggest that we should have a share of the profits *if any*. I don't want them to be put off by thinking they have to pay something in advance.

I can't do any serious work yet. I have sketched out my novel but don't want to start it till I feel completely fit. In the mean time I've been writing a pamphlet more or less on the subject of pacifism, I should say about 5000–6000 words.[1] I suppose it's just conceivable we might find a publisher for it. When done & typed my wife will send it along. I know Faber's used to publish pamphlets about that length (the "Faber Miscellany") & there may be other publishers who do so. It's no use sending it to Gollancz, as it's right off his line.

Hope all goes well with you. I am much better, up & about all day.

Yours sincerely
Eric Blair

P.S. I believe Eileen told me Miss Perriam had been ill.[2] I hope she is better?

1. This pamphlet, 'Socialism and War,' was never published. See letter to Moore, 28 November 1938 (*506, n. 5*), for the possible use of its argument. Richard Rees, in his letter to Orwell of 25 May 1938, indicated that he thought the pamphlet was already written; see *445* and *445, n. 6*. Bob Edwards (see *363, n. 2*), in an early draft of the Introduction to the Folio Society edition of *Homage to Catalonia* (1970), stated that the pamphlet was submitted to the Publications Committee of the ILP, over which he presided. It was rejected as 'too long and absolutist.' He mistakenly dates this 1935.
2. For Miss Perriam's illness, see Eileen's letter to Moore, 7 June 1938, *450*.

459. To Victor Gollancz

29 June 1938   Handwritten

New Hostel   Preston Hall   Aylesford   Kent

Dear Mr Gollancz,

Ref. attached.[1] Of course so far as I am concerned they can translate the thing free. If you are writing to them you might perhaps suggest that it would be better to use the American edition (Harper's), as you may remember that some minor alterations were made in the English edition. However, it's not of great consequence, as they will know what points to correct.

Yours sincerely
Eric Blair

1. A proposed translation of *Burmese Days* into Burmese; see *458*. Two statements are of importance with respect to Orwell's attitude toward what he wrote: 'some minor alterations were made to the English edition,' and, 'it's not of great consequence, as they will know what points to correct.' He regarded the English (Gollancz's) edition of *Burmese Days* as 'garbled' (a damning word in his vocabulary) and may simply have been tactful in writing 'minor alterations,' but his willingness to rely upon others to correct his text is of importance to an editor of his work. No Burmese translation was published, although in his 'Notes on Translations' for his literary executor, 1949 (see *3728*), he listed the French and Italian translations of *Burmese Days* and also 'Burmese? (May exist).'

460. To Leonard Moore

5 July 1938   Handwritten

New Hostel   Preston Hall   Aylesford   Kent

Dear Mr Moore,

I expect I've been putting my foot in it over this Burmese translation business. I ought to have thought of your end of the matter before I wrote to Gollancz. But of course we know in advance that there is never any money in a thing like that, so after all the only important things are:

    i. There ought to be some kind of contract, but

    ii. They ought not to be asked to pay anything, which we know they wouldn't be able to & which would only put them off making the translation.

I'm sorry if I've let you in for any disputes over the matter.

Yours sincerely
Eric Blair

461. To Jack Common

5 July 1938 Handwritten

New Hostel Preston Hall Aylesford Kent

Dear Jack,

You know I have to go abroad for the winter, probably for about 6 months starting about end of August.[1] Well, would you like to have our cottage rent free & in return look after the animals? I'll tell you all the facts & you can work out the pros & cons for yourself.

i. The doctors say I must live somewhere further south. That means giving up the cottage when we come back at latest. But I don't want to scrap the livestock, because we have now worked the flock of fowls up to about 30, which can be worked up to about 100 next year, & it would also mean selling the hen-houses, which cost a lot but which you don't get much for if you sell them. We have therefore the choice of getting someone to inhabit the cottage, or of paying someone to look after the animals, which plus storage of furniture works out at about the same expense as keeping on the rent of the cottage.

ii. You know what our cottage is like. It's bloody awful. Still it's more or less livable. There is one room with a double bed & one with a single, & I fancy there is enough linen etc. to do for 2 people & a kid. When there is sudden rain in winter the kitchen tends to flood, otherwise the house is passably dry. The living room fire, you may remember, smokes, but I think the chimney will have been seen to before we leave—anyway it doesn't need anything very drastic doing to it. There is water laid on, but no hot, of course. There is a Calor Gas stove, which is expensive (the gas, I mean), but there is also a little oil oven that can be resuscitated. As to produce, there won't be many vegetables, as of course Eileen alone couldn't cope with all of the garden, but at any rate there will be potatoes enough to see you through the winter. There'll also be milk, about a quart a day, as the goat has just kidded. A lot of people are prejudiced against goats° milk but really it's no different from cow & is said to be good for kids.

iii. As to the looking after animals. This means feeding etc. about 30 fowls & feeding & milking the goats. I'll leave careful instructions about food etc. & arrange for the corn merchant to deliver supplies & send the bill on to me. You could also sell the eggs (the butcher who calls twice a week buys any quantity) & put the money aside for us. There won't be many eggs at first, as most of the birds are young pullets hatched this year, but by early spring they should be laying about 100 a week.

Let me know would you whether you would like to take this on. It would suit us, & for you at any rate I dare say it would be a quiet place to work in.

All the best to Mary & Peter.

Yours
Eric Blair

1. See headnote to letter to Yvonne Davet, 7 June 1938, *449*.

462. Review of *The Civil War in Spain* by Frank Jellinek

The New Leader, 8 July 1938

Frank Jellinek's book on the Paris Commune[1] had its faults, but it revealed him as a man of unusual mind. He showed himself able to grasp the real facts of history, the social and economic changes that underlie spectacular events, without losing touch with the picturesque aspect which the bourgeois historian generally does so much better. On the whole his present book—*The Civil War in Spain*—bears out the promise of the other. It shows signs of haste, and it contains some misrepresentations which I will point out later, but it is probably the best book on the Spanish war from a Communist angle that we are likely to get for some time to come.

Much the most useful part of the book is the earlier part, describing the long chain of causes that led up to the war and the fundamental issues at stake. The parasitic aristocracy and the appalling condition of the peasants (before the war 65 per cent. of the population of Spain held 6.3 per cent. of the land, while 4 per cent. held 60 per cent. of it), the backwardness of Spanish capitalism and the dominance of foreign capitalists, the corruption of the Church, and the rise of the Socialist and Anarchist labour movements—all these are treated in a series of brilliant chapters. The short biography which Mr. Jellinek gives of Juan March,[2] the old tobacco-smuggler who is one of the men behind the Fascist rebellion (although, queerly enough, he is believed to be a Jew), is a wonderful story of corruption. It would be fascinating reading if March were merely a character in Edgar Wallace; unfortunately he happens to be a real man.

The chapter on the Church does not leave much doubt as to why practically all the churches in Catalonia and eastern Aragon were burnt at the outbreak of war. Incidentally, it is interesting to learn that, if Mr. Jellinek's figures are correct, the world organization of the Jesuits only numbers about 22,000 people. For sheer efficiency they must surely have all the political parties in the world beaten hollow. But the Jesuits' "man of affairs" in Spain is, or was, on the board of directors of forty-three companies!

At the end of the book there is a well-balanced chapter on the social changes that took place in the first few months of the war, and an appendix on the collectivisation decree in Catalonia. Unlike the majority of British observers, Mr. Jellinek does not under-rate the Spanish Anarchists. In his treatment of the P.O.U.M., however, there is no doubt that he is unfair, and—there is not much doubt of this either—intentionally unfair.

Naturally I turned first of all to the chapter describing the fighting in Barcelona in May, 1937, because both Mr. Jellinek and myself were in Barcelona at the time, and this gave me a measure of checking his accuracy. His account of the fighting is somewhat less propagandist than those that appeared in the Communist Press at the time, but it is certainly one-sided and would be very misleading to anyone who knew nothing of the facts. To begin with, he appears at times to accept the story that the P.O.U.M. was really a disguised Fascist organisation, and refers to "documents" which "conclusively proved" this and that, without telling us any more about these mysterious documents—which, in fact, have never been produced. He even refers to the celebrated "N" document[3] (though admitting that "N" probably did not stand for Nin), and ignores the fact that Irujo,[4] the Minister of Justice, declared this document to be "worthless," i.e., a forgery. He states merely that Nin was "arrested," and does not mention that Nin disappeared and was almost certainly murdered. Moreover, he leaves the chronology uncertain and—whether intentionally or not – gives the impression that the alleged discovery of a Fascist plot, the arrest of Nin, etc., took place *immediately after* the May fighting.

This point is important. The suppression of the P.O.U.M. did *not* occur immediately after the May fighting. There was a five weeks' interval. The fighting ended on May 7 and Nin was arrested on June 15. The suppression of the P.O.U.M. only occurred after, and almost certainly as a result of, the change in the Valencia Government. I have noticed several attempts in the Press to obscure these dates. The reason is obvious enough; however, there can be no doubt about the matter, for all the main events were recorded in the newspapers at the time.

Curiously enough, about June 20, the "Manchester Guardian" correspondent in Barcelona sent here a despatch[5] in which he contradicted the absurd accusations against the P.O.U.M.—in the circumstances a very courageous action. This correspondent must almost certainly have been Mr. Jellinek himself. What a pity that for propaganda purposes he should now find it necessary to repeat a story which after this lapse of time seems even more improbable.

His remarks on the P.O.U.M. occupy a considerable share of the book, and they have an air of prejudice which would be obvious even to anyone who knew nothing whatever about the Spanish political parties. He thinks it necessary to denigrate even useful work such as that done by Nin as Councillor of Justice, and is careful not to mention that the P.O.U.M. took any serious part either in the first struggles against the Fascist rising or at the front. And in all his remarks about the "provocative attitude" of the P.O.U.M. newspapers it hardly seems to occur to him that there was any provocation on the other side. In the long run this kind of thing defeats its own object. Its effect on me, for instance, is to make me think: "If I find that this book is unreliable where I happen to know the facts, how can I trust it where I don't know the facts?" And many others will think the same.

Actually I am quite ready to believe that in the main Mr. Jellinek is strictly fair besides being immensely well-informed. But in dealing with "Trotskyism" he writes as a Communist, or Communist partisan, and it is no more possible for a Communist to-day to show common sense on this subject than on the subject of "Social Fascism" a few years ago. Incidentally, the speed with which the angels in the Communist mythology turn into devils has its comic side. Mr. Jellinek quotes approvingly a denunciation of the P.O.U.M. by the Russian Consul in Barcelona, Antonov Ovseenko,[6] now on trial as a Trotskyist!

All in all, an excellent book, packed full of information and very readable. But one has got to treat it with a certain wariness, because the author is under the necessity of showing that though other people may sometimes be right, the Communist Party is always right. It does not greatly matter that nearly all books by Communists are propaganda. Most books are propaganda, direct or indirect. The trouble is that Communist writers are obliged to claim infallibility for their Party chiefs. As a result Communist literature tends more and more to become a mechanism for explaining away mistakes.

Unlike most of the people who have written of the Spanish war, Mr. Jellinek really knows Spain: its language, its people, its territories, and the political struggle of the past hundred years. Few men are better qualified to write an authoritative history of the Spanish war. Perhaps some day he will do so. But it will probably be a long time hence, when the "Trotsky-Fascist" shadow-boxing has been dropped in favour of some other hobby.

Orwell was mistaken in thinking the *Manchester Guardian* correspondent was Jellinek. See his letter to Jellinek, 20 December 1938, *513*. On 13 January 1939, he wrote a letter of correction to *The New Leader*, which was printed under the heading 'A Mistake Corrected.'

In my review of Mr. Frank Jellinek's *Civil War In Spain* I stated that Mr. Jellinek had expressed certain opinions which were in contradiction to one of his own despatches to the *Manchester Guardian*. I now find that this despatch was actually sent not by Mr. Jellinek, but by another correspondent. I am very sorry about this mistake and hope you will find space for this correction.

1. *The Paris Commune of 1871* (1937). Frank Jellinek was *Manchester Guardian* correspondent in Spain. See *513, n. 1*.
2. Primo de Rivera's government sold the Moroccan tobacco monopoly to Juan Ordinas March (1884–1962). See Thomas, 28.
3. The "N" document was a forged letter to Franco, purported by the Communists to be from Andrés Nin (see *382, n. 5*), a prominent member of the POUM, on which they based their charges of conspiracy between the POUM and Franco to justify their suppression of the POUM.
4. Manuel de Irujo y Ollo was a Basque member of the Republican government, as Minister without Portfolio, from 25 September 1936, then Minister of Justice until he resigned in January 1938, remaining Minister without Portfolio. He had attempted to restore 'normal justice'; see Thomas, 701, 778.
5. 'Barcelona after the Rising,' from 'Our Special Correspondent,' *Manchester Guardian*, 26 June 1937.
6. Vladimir Antonov-Ovsëenko was one of those listed by Thomas as having 'either [been] executed or died in concentration camps' following service in Spain. He was for a time rehabilitated, and his death was 'regretted as a mistake, in passing, by Khrushchev in his speech denouncing Stalin in February 1956'; see *374A* and Thomas, 952.

463. To Cyril Connolly

8 July 1938   Handwritten

New Hostel   Preston Hall   Aylesford   Kent

Dear Cyril,

Thanks so much for your letter.[1] I am rather taking you at your word in the matter of asking advice about the S. of France, but don't answer till you feel fit. What I want to know is, can one rent small furnished cottages in small villages? I suppose thousands of people have small summer villas in those parts which they'd be willing to let, but are such places livable in winter? I don't want to go to a pension if I can help it, I hate the places & I must have a place of my own to work in, also I'd rather stay in a very small village which generally don't have pensions in them. I don't of course want you to arrange anything for me, only to let me know whether it is feasible to take such a place as I suggest & what kind of rent.

I'm glad you liked the book[2] & thanks for recommending it to people. I had better reviews than I expected but of course all the best ones in obscure papers. I had Jellinek's book to review for several papers. I thought it was pretty bloody, the usual C.P. stuff of course & obviously written in haste, but he is really very good in a way. I suppose it's true what you say about people not revising their stuff nowadays, though it's incomprehensible to me. What you say about finding old letters of mine makes me apprehensive. I wonder how you can write about St. Cyprian's.[3] It's all like an awful nightmare to me, & sometimes I think I can still taste the porridge (out of those pewter bowls, do you remember?) If you have written about Eton as I should think you might, you'd better watch out you don't get horsewhipped on the steps of your club, if you belong to one.

I wrote to & heard from Denis Dannreuther,[4] who sounded very down in the mouth. It seems he had some job drafting Government bills, which to me sounds too bloody but evidently it fascinated him, & then after a period of probation they chucked him because he couldn't pass a physical test. I never realised they had that sort of nonsense for the higher-up Government departments.

Today is the start of the Eton & Harrow match[5] & it has poured steadily all day. I am much better, & most of the day out of doors. I still haven't done a stroke of work but keep toying with the idea of starting my novel.[6] One good effect the rest has had on me is that it has made me feel I can write a novel again, whereas when I came here I felt my novel-writing days were over.

Please remember me to your wife.

Yours
Eric Blair

1. Connolly had written from Villa Notre Dame de Bon Port, Chemin des Mougins, Antibes. He did not date the letter. He said he had enjoyed *Homage to Catalonia* 'enormously,' having borrowed Stephen Spender's advance copy and having lent it to several people, 'who all devoured it.' Peter Quennell had been 'v. enthusiastic.' Connolly said it was 'as good as anything you have done, and is with Koestler's the only Spanish war book I have read that has

a future. I think the mixture of honesty, imagination, and talent is not usually present in writers on Spain.' V. S. Pritchett's review he thought 'very cagy.' He had found Jellinek's *The Civil War in Spain* boring. He advised shortening the political chapters rather than suggesting they be skipped, 'as no book is improved by skipping.' Orwell later decided to make the two political chapters into appendixes, though that was not done in his lifetime; see *CW*, VI, Textual Note and arrangement of chapters. Connolly also wrote enthusiastically about the area around Nice and offered Orwell information about that part of France. He said he had completed *Enemies of Promise*, but had not included 'an old letter of yours'; see *60*, Easter 1921.

2. *Homage to Catalonia.*
3. Connolly and Orwell were at the private preparatory school St Cyprian's at the same time, and both went on to Eton; see *1*. Connolly was writing about his school experiences, *Enemies of Promise* (1938), around the time of this letter.
4. Dennis Dannreuther (1903–1938) was a lawyer. He was described by Connolly as one of the 'moral leaders' of his, and Orwell's, Election at Eton, 'an exquisite classical scholar, one of those rare people who combine a brilliant and logical mind with genuine moral feeling and who became more than a careerist.' When he became captain of the school, he endeavoured, among other things, to reduce the number of beatings of younger boys to a minimum. His regime was, according to Connolly, 'a shortlived and unpopular experiment in happiness' *Enemies of Promise*, Penguin edition, 1961, 204, 210, 269). At Eton he was top scholar, Davies Scholar, and Newcastle Scholar; he took a double first at Oxford and was Craven Scholar and Jenkyns Exhibitioner, Balliol. In 1926–27 he was Gray's Inn Scholar, Eldon Law Scholar, and was called to the bar; from 1927, he was a Fellow of All Souls, Oxford. He worked on parliamentary drafting in the Treasury Bill Office. Within three weeks of Orwell's letter to Connolly, Dannreuther died of double pneumonia (information from Ion and David Dannreuther).
5. The annual cricket match between the two schools, held at Lord's Cricket Ground in early July; see *37*.
6. *Coming Up for Air.*

464. To C. D. Abbott

12 July 1938   Handwritten

New Hostel   Preston Hall   Aylesford   Kent

Dear Mr Abbott,
I don't think it can possibly have been Geoffrey Grigson who told you I was a poet.[1] It might possibly have been Dylan Thomas or Rayner Heppenstall, both of whom I remember liked a poem of mine, or possibly it was Richard Rees. But anyway I don't really write verse. I am sorry you have had this wild goose chase.

Yours faithfully
George Orwell

1. After Orwell had replied to Abbott on 4 June 1938 (see *448*), regarding a request for his manuscripts under the mistaken belief that Orwell was a poet, Abbott wrote, on 28 June: 'It is somewhat embarrassing to learn you are not a poet.' He had been told, on a recent visit to London, that Orwell was a poet 'it would be most unwise of us to neglect. . . . Geoffrey Grigson, or some other enthusiast, spoke with such praise that I am bewildered at the mistake. We should indeed appreciate the manuscript of *Homage to Catalonia*, but I feel I have no right to ask for it since it is not poetry.' In response to the letter above, Abbott wrote, in a letter dated 26 June, instead of 26 July: 'You are quite right. I remember distinctly now. It was Rayner Heppenstall who spoke with such enthusiasm.' He had not succeeded in finding any of

Orwell's poems, but had found one novel and the sketch 'Shooting an Elephant,' and had liked them. Orwell did not send Abbott the manuscript of *Homage to Catalonia*, which has not survived.

465. To Jack Common

15 July 1938   Typewritten

New Hostel   Preston Hall   Aylesford   Kent

Dear Jack,

Thanks for yours. Please excuse this paper, as I can't find any note paper and I can't go out and get any as it's raining.

I'm afraid there is nowhere in Wallington where one could possibly store furniture. Geary, the second hand furniture dealer in Baldock, probably stores, as he has some very big warehouses, but I don't know what he would charge. You could write and ask him (Geary, Furniture dealer, High St., Baldock). If you are obliged in any case to store your furniture, Pickfords, the removals people in London will probably do it quite cheaply. If I remember rightly, that° they charged for the very small amount of furniture I had at Lawford Road was 2/6 a month, so I suppose they wouldn't charge more than say 5/– a month for your stuff. In any case they'd give you an estimate. I quite agree it's better to hang onto one's furniture if one possibly can. You get nothing for it if you sell it, on the other hand the barest minimum of stuff costs quite a lot to buy, and as for the furnished room business it's such a racket I've often seriously thought of going in for it myself.

Don't go over to Wallington in the near future expecting to see Eileen, as she'll be away. She's in London now and she's going up to Windermere for about a fortnight. Let us know definitely about the cottage fairly soon, won't you, as we've got to make the various arrangements. I don't quite know when I'm coming out of here, but maybe sooner than I thought, though I don't think we shall actually go abroad till about September. I still haven't done a stroke of work. By the way I saw quite a good little review of your book in the New Statesman—rather short but friendly.

The goat[1] successfully kidded, all the local experts including a shepherd having declared until two days before that she wasn't in kid. However there was only one kid, which perhaps accounts for it. It is a billy kid which we will later have destroyed, so if you come there should be a fair amount of milk, 2 to 3 pints a day. A fox got into our place a week or two back and killed a hen and six chicks, and we claimed 25/– from the hunt, who paid up like lambs. It appears that when the locals lose any poultry they never claim less than £10, and the amount normally paid is 5/–. So perhaps honesty does pay.

Excuse bad typing. This is the first time I've handled a typewriter since March. Cheerio. Love to Mary and Peter.

Yours
Eric

1. The goat was called Muriel and features fairly prominently in Orwell's letters, often simply as
'M.' There is a frequently reproduced photograph of Orwell feeding Muriel; e.g., Crick, plate
19; Lewis, 72. Muriel's name lived on, being given to the goat in *Animal Farm*.

466. Review of *Searchlight on Spain* by the Duchess of Atholl;[1] *The Civil War in Spain* by Frank Jellinek; *Spain's Ordeal* by Robert Sencourt

Time and Tide, 16 July 1938

Searchlight on Spain was also reviewed by Orwell in *New English Weekly*, 21 July
1938 (see *469*); *The Civil War in Spain*, in *The New Leader*, 8 July 1938 (see *462*);
and *Spain's Ordeal* (as *Spanish Ordeal*), in *New English Weekly*, 23 June 1938 (see
456).

Although no one who publishes books at seven and sixpence a time (with a
profit of ninepence to the author) can regard such a venture without alarm,
the Penguin Library have shown admirable judgment in their choice of
"specials." The Duchess of Atholl's *Searchlight on Spain* probably contains
less original matter than *Germany Puts the Clock Back* or *Mussolini's Roman
Empire*, but it is a worthy successor. As a short popular history of the Spanish
war, simply written and well documented, it is not likely to be bettered until
the war is over.

Its chief virtue is that it is well-balanced and keeps the main facts in the right
perspective. Its chief fault is the fault of virtually all books on the Spanish
war—political partisanship. As I have pointed out elsewhere, there is not
even among Government supporters one simple and generally-accepted
"version" of the Spanish war. The Loyalists include Socialists, Communists,
Anarchists and "Trotskyists"—one might add Basques and Catalans—who
have never been in quite perfect agreement as to what the war is about. Every
English writer on the Government side adopts more or less unreservedly the
"line" of one or other political party, and unfortunately he usually does so
while claiming to be strictly impartial. The Duchess of Atholl follows the
Communist "line" throughout, and this fact should be borne in mind in
reading her book. So long as she is dealing with the origins of the rebellion,
with the military side of the war and the scandal of non-intervention, all is
well; but I would be a little cautious about accepting her account of the
internal political situation, which is one-sided and very much over-
simplified.

In her final chapter, "What it means to us," she points out the probable
consequence of a Fascist victory in Spain—that England may lose the
command of the Mediterranean and France may be faced with another hostile
frontier. This raises what is perhaps the most mysterious question of the
whole Spanish war. Why has our Government behaved as it has done?
Without any doubt the British Cabinet has behaved as though it wished
Franco to win; and yet if Franco wins it may—to put it as its worst—mean the

loss of India. The Duchess of Atholl states the facts but does not offer any explanation of Mr. Chamberlain's attitude. Other writers have been less cautious. The real meaning of British foreign policy in the last two years will not become clear until the war in Spain is over; but in trying to divine it I believe it is much safer to assume that the British Cabinet are not fools and that they have no intention of giving anything away.

Mr. Jellinek's book has approximately the same angle of approach as *Searchlight on Spain*, but it is much longer, weightier and less "popular." It is at its best in describing the causes that led up to the war, and it is distinguished by some brilliant chapters on the Church, the land-system and the growth of the Spanish labour movement. It has the same qualities and defects as Mr. Jellinek's earlier book on the Paris Commune—a wonderful grasp both of the interplay of political movements and of the motives of individuals, marred by clumsy writing. Mr. Jellinek is qualified to write a really authoritative book on the Spanish war; perhaps some day he will do so; but it will have to be a long time hence, when the guns are silent and several kinds of hatred are less bitter.

Mr. Sencourt is pro-Franco, but—as the advertisements in the *Matrimonial Times* say—not bigoted. Unlike some others who have thundered against the "Reds," he has a deep affection for Spain and does not feel obliged to believe that every Spaniard east of no man's land is a demon. He does, however, completely misunderstand the aims of most of the left-wing parties. He is much too ready to assume that a Communist is necessarily a revolutionary extremist and that Anarchism is the same thing as "anarchy"—which is simply a misuse of words. And once again those phantoms, the Russian volunteers, are produced as realities. Mr. Sencourt appears to accept M. de Kerillis's° estimate of "10,000 to 15,000 Russians, mostly regulars." Now, it has never been denied that there were Russian airmen, technical experts and political agents in Spain; on the other hand, literally everyone who has set foot in Loyalist Spain would testify that there were no Russian infantry. Hundreds have already done so. Is it necessary to go on assuming that all these people are liars?

1. Katharine Stewart-Murray, Duchess of Atholl (1874–1960; DBE, 1918), was trained as a musician, but devoted her life to public service. She became the second woman, and first Conservative, to hold ministerial office: Parliamentary Secretary to the Board of Education, 1924–29. She campaigned ceaselessly against cruelty in many forms and conducted a campaign in 1929 against the practice of female circumcision in Africa. Opposed to her party's policy of appeasement of Hitler, she resigned her seat in Parliament in 1938 and campaigned, unsuccessfully, for re-election on a platform of resistance to Hitler.

467. To Jack Common

Tuesday, [19 or 26[1] July 1938]   Typewritten

New Hostel   Preston Hall   Aylesford   KENT

Dear Jack,

With ref. to your letter. I, of course, being here, can't make any definite decision about dates, and Eileen has just gone away to the north of England[2] and will be away about a fortnight. But I am writing to her about the same time as this and asking her to let you know a definite date when you could move in. I must leave it to her, because, after all, she has to make all the arrangements about moving etc. I think you could move in quite soon, but not so soon as in a week, because Eileen won't even be back. Can you hang on some how° for a bit? You will at any rate hear from Eileen in a few days' time. As to unstorable things, don't dump anything. Tiny as our place is one can generally make room for this and that. At the back there are two small sheds, one of which the goat inhabits while the other has tools and chicken feed and so forth in it. I expect with a bit of tidying up, a thing I never feel strong enough to attempt, you could make room for your tools. I hope we shall be able to fix this thing up. I ought really to have started making arrangements earlier.

It's depressing to hear Warburg isn't selling anything.[3] I hope he doesn't go bust. There's really such need of a publisher who publishes non-official left-wing stuff, and gollancz° is such an octopus you can see his tentacles everywhere. I suppose it'll be months before I find out how my book sold. I should doubt whether it will sell less than 3000, but very likely it won't go to 4000.[4] What is so infuriating is that quite apart from the political racket which causes various people to write deliberate lies about you, there is also the financial racket which prevents any book from a small publisher getting a proper *number* of reviews. What a degradation when one can't even regard reviewers as the canaille they are, but actually has to care whether Ralph Straus[5] says this [is] a work of unforgettable genius or not, because one's livelihood is bound up with it. When I think of what the book trade is like morally, I wonder why we don't go the whole hog and organise it into a proper racket on American lines. Then if Ralph Straus failed to deliver the goods you would just pay so much into the fund and a car would drive past his house and a couple of pineapples[6] would go through his drawing room window. It's what's happening all the time in a genteel way.

Love to Mary and Peter. Yours
Eric

1. This was most probably written just before Eileen's letter to Common, 20 July (see *468*), but it may have been written on the following Tuesday.
2. She was staying at Chapel Ridding, Windermere.
3. See Fredric Warburg's *An Occupation for Gentlemen*, especially chapter 11; he writes: 'the gap between the gross profits and the overheads opened wider, and the capital, though it had increased, was barely enough to support a list half the size of ours' in 'that dreadful year, 1938.' Martin Secker had resigned from the firm, but further capital of £5,000 was raised through a distant cousin of Warburg's, Siegmund Warburg (239–42).

4. Of the 1,500 copies of *Homage to Catalonia* printed, only 683 were sold in the first six months; see *438*. See also Orwell's letter to Moore, 11 October 1938, *495*.
5. Ralph Straus, fiction reviewer for the *Sunday Times*; see *333, n. 6*.
6. Hand grenades.

468. Eileen Blair to Jack Common

20 July 1938   Handwritten

Chapel Ridding[1]   Windermere   Westmorland

Dear Jack Common,

I suppose you have or soon will have my wild telegram. I hope I'll have one from you long before you get this letter but we'll just have to play a peculiarly complicated cat's-cradle for a few days because posts leave here practically never & then at strange hours like 3.30. I haven't yet heard about my letters being delivered anywhere else. Perhaps they aren't. Using the telephone, we can't hear the local exchange, so don't try that.

If you do want the cottage, it's a pity I didn't know last week because you could perfectly well have had it—I really hoped to pack it up one way or the other before coming away. But the difference between packing it up for store & for lending is considerable—e.g. one fills the drawers to store them & empties them to lend—so I couldn't do anything constructive or much destructive. I suppose you, & more importantly your wife, know what the cottage is like—that it hasn't got a bathroom or any hot water, that it frequently absorbs water like a sponge (perhaps very frequently; in some mysterious way the wind seems responsible), that it's $3\frac{1}{2}$ miles from a shop, that the sitting-room chimney is not manageable by me though it may be by someone efficient. That's all I can think of at the moment, except that we never bought any furniture for it. But you saw yourself what it looked like. On the other hand it is habitable & it won't cost money. The goat still has her kid because I like goats & don't like goat's milk, but if you don't like killing kids a man will do it & you'll then have about $2\frac{1}{2}$–3 pints of milk for about $1\frac{1}{2}$d. a day. I didn't stock the garden for the winter because I thought noone would be there, but we can still put in some greens & there are potatoes, parsnips & onions, & a few french & runner beans; also a good crop of cooking apples on one tree & quite a few plums. If you can transport them you could bring things like tools & wheel-barrows—very usefully, because Eric made a wheelbarrow which is permanently in the field as its wheel developed a split personality & I can't persuade it all to go home together. I don't know what Eric has told you about the place. It has the sitting-room you'll remember, a kind of passage-room with a fireplace that we used to have as a sitting-room when we kept the shop, an ill-designed kitchen with a sink & cold water, a Calor-gas oven (this is very convenient for quick heating but the cylinders are expensive & I've always been meaning to combine it with an oil cooker— there is an old Rippingill & a couple of Beatrices[2] that are good for slow boiling); upstairs a square landing we use as a dining-room, which is actually very warm & can be heated enough in any weather by one of the Beatrices,² & two bedrooms opening off it, one with a double bed & one with a single bed. The place isn't over-furnished & you could probably bring anything special, such as an easy chair or/and a chest of drawers etc. I did mean to buy it a number of things but again thinking it would be empty I haven't done so. Heaven knows I don't want to put you off—from my point of view your coming has every advantage. If you wire that you want the place & I hear nothing more I'll be in the cottage on Monday to hand it over. If you could arrive in the afternoon or early evening I could demonstrate the creatures. Goats are not difficult to manage but there are some growing chickens who need special food for a few more weeks. You could send a postcard to Wallington with any last minute alterations—I'll actually arrive some time on Saturday or Sunday morning. A letter posted to me here after Thursday will miss me.

I must say I hope you are strong-minded enough to take Wallington on.

Yours sincerely
Eileen Blair.

1. Why Eileen went to Chapel Ridding is not known. The house is now St Anne's School. Through the headmaster, Michael P. Hawkins, a former owner's niece, Mrs. Mary Varcoe, provided the earlier history of the house. From 1931 it was a guest house run by her aunt, Esther Moss, for semi-permanent and passing visitors and for public-school boys needing a home during vacations. Percy W. Molony, a guest, married Esther Moss, and they ran the guest house jointly until about 1947. No link has been traced between Eileen and either Esther Moss or Percy Molony, although Esther, a nurse during World War I, was also then one of the first women motorcyclists, as was Marjorie Blair, Orwell's sister. Chapel Ridding is a very fine house in beautiful grounds, a sharp contrast with The Stores and the house in Marrakech in which Eileen later lived.
2. Trade names for two types of domestic oil-stove.

469. Review of *Searchlight on Spain* by the Duchess of Atholl[1]

New English Weekly, 21 July 1938

At this time of day it is hardly necessary to point out that there are not merely two versions of the Spanish war. Even among Government partisans there are three at least, the Communist version, the Anarchist, and the "Trotskyist." In England we have learnt a little of the "Trotskyist" version and next to nothing of the Anarchist version, while the Communist version is, so to speak, the official one. The Duchess of Atholl's book follows the familiar lines—in fact, with the excision of not very many sentences it could pass as having been written by a Communist. I doubt whether it contains anything that has not been said before, and therefore, rather than discuss the book itself, perhaps it is more useful to stop and reflect just why it is that books like this are appearing.

There is, of course, nothing surprising nowadays in a pro-Communist duchess. Nearly all monied people who enter the Left-wing movement follow the "Stalinist" line as a matter of course. Neither Anarchism nor "Trotskyism" has much appeal for anyone with more than £500 a year. But the real question is not why monied people are "Stalinists" but why they enter the Left-wing movement at all. They did not do so a few years ago. Why does the Duchess back the Spanish Government and not Franco? It is not as though she were a lonely eccentric. Plenty of other people deeply embedded in the British capitalist system, peers, newspaper proprietors and the higher clergy, have taken the same line. Why? When all is said and done the Spanish war is essentially a class war, and Franco is the defender of the monied class. How is it that these people manage to be such good Socialists abroad and such good Conservatives at home?

At first sight it looks easy: because the Fascist powers menace the British Empire. The Duchess herself supplies this answer in her chapter "What it means to us," in which the dangers of a Fascist domination of Spain are set forth. Germany and Italy will be astride our route to India, France will have another frontier to defend, etc., etc. Here "anti-Fascism," of a kind, and British imperialism join hands. Incidentally, several books pointing this moral have appeared in this same series. It would seem that whoever defends the British Empire also defends democracy—which, to anyone who knows anything about the actual running of the Empire, appears to have a catch in it.

But it is not so simple as that. For though a fairly large section of the British governing class are anti-Franco, the majority are pro-Franco, subjectively and objectively. By a combination of meanness and hypocrisy that would take a lot of beating, Chamberlain[2] and his friends have allowed the Spanish Republic to be slowly strangled. How is one to explain the apparent contradiction? If one believes that the duchesses and deans who quack about "anti-Fascism" are really worrying about British dividends, one has apparently got to believe also that Chamberlain is *not* worrying about British dividends—which is incredible.

It may be that behind the apparent split in governing-class opinion there is a conflict of financial interests. But I think another explanation is possible. Between the "anti-Reds" and the monied "anti-Fascists" there is no fundamental difference. They are all part of the same system and many of them are in the same political party. They will show their essential agreement in any really important crisis—above all, they will show it when England goes to war. When the guns begin to shoot, Chamberlain and the Duchess of Atholl, Lloyd George and Lord Rothermere,[3] will meet on the same recruiting platform. It is quite possible, therefore, that this strange phenomenon of anti-Fascism in high life is simply a part of the national war-preparation.

Chamberlain is preparing for war against Germany. Rearmament, the military understanding with France, A.R.P.[4] and various sinister mumbles about conscription, cannot be explained in any other way. It is quite likely that he has made a mess of things and allowed the strategic situation to worsen, and that this has happened partly because he fears a Russian-controlled Spain as much as Mussolini does; nevertheless, he is preparing for war. And while the Government makes the *physical* preparations for war, the so-called Left, by constantly stirring up a spirit of hatred and self-righteousness, looks after the mental side. The armament factories build the guns, and papers like the "News Chronicle" create the will to use them. We all remember what happened when Delilah said "The Philistines be upon thee, Samson."[5] The first real threat to British interests has turned nine out of ten British Socialists into jingos.

And what is the function of the Conservative anti-Fascists? They are the liaison officers. The average English Left-winger is now a good imperialist, but he is still theoretically hostile to the English ruling class. The people who read the "New Statesman" dream of war with Germany, but they also think it necessary to laugh at Colonel Blimp. However, when the war begins they will be forming fours[6] on the barrack square under Colonel Blimp's boiled blue eye. It is necessary to effect a reconciliation beforehand. That, I think, is the real function of books like this of the Duchess of Atholl's, and Mr. G. T. Garratt's "Mussolini's Roman Empire," and the prophetic utterances of Madame Tabouis, and various others of the same kind. These people are forming—not consciously, of course—the link between left and right which is absolutely necessary for the purpose of war. The war in Spain—indeed, the whole situation since the Abyssinia crisis, but especially the war in Spain—has had a catalytic effect upon English opinion, bringing into being combinations which no one could have foreseen a few years ago. There is much that is not yet clear, but I do not see how patriotic Communists and communistic duchesses can be explained except on the supposition that the ranks are being closed for war.

1. See 466, n. 1.
2. Neville Chamberlain (1869–1940 served several times as a Conservative minister and was Chancellor of the Exchequer. He became Prime Minister in 1937 and was associated with the appeasement of Hitler, though he initiated the rearmament of Britain. Following the failure of the Norwegian campaign in April 1940, he was much criticised and resigned in May. He then served the new prime minister, Winston Churchill. For Eileen's approval of Chamberlain, see 487.
3. David Lloyd-George (1863–1945; Earl Lloyd George of Dwyfor, 1945) was Liberal Prime Minister, 1916–22. He had unsuccessfully advocated a reasonable peace settlement with Germany after World War I. As Chancellor of the Exchequer, 1908–15, he had introduced old-age pensions and national insurance, the foundations of the welfare state. Harold Sidney Harmsworth, Viscount Rothermere (1868–1940), with his brother, Alfred (later Viscount Northcliffe), built up a major newspaper empire, which included the *Daily Mail* (founded in 1896), *Daily Mirror, Sunday Pictorial*, and *Evening News*. During World War I, he was Lloyd George's Air Minister. He later advocated rearmament, but was also sympathetic for a time to Hitler and Mussolini.
4. Air Raid Precautions—civil defence against air attack.
5. Judges, XVI, 9, 12, 14 and 20.
6. The infantry drill of forming fours, introduced in 1889, was modified in 1937, platoons thereafter being ranked in threes. See 560, 29.7.39, n. 4.

470. To the Editor, *Manchester Guardian*
5 August 1938

The same letter was sent by Orwell to the *Daily Herald* (a daily paper supporting the Labour Party) and *The New Statesman and Nation*. The latter acknowledged the letter but did not print it; the *Daily Herald* neither acknowledged nor printed it. For the vilification and suppression of the POUM and the torture of its leaders, see Thomas, Index, 1095.

Espionage Trial in Spain
"Pressure from Outside"

August 1.   New Hostel, Preston Hall, Aylesford, Kent.

Sir,—News has recently reached England that a number of members of the Executive Committee of the Spanish political party known as the P.O.U.M. are shortly to be put on trial on the charge of espionage in the Fascist cause. The circumstances of the case are peculiar, and should, I think, be brought to public notice. The main facts are as follows:—

In June, 1937, following on the fall of the Caballero Government, the P.O.U.M. was declared an illegal organisation and a large number of people were thrown into prison. Simultaneously the Spanish Communist party published accounts of what purported to be a "Trotsky-Fascist spy plot," which was given wide publicity in the Communist press, though treated with reserve elsewhere. Later various delegations from France and England, two of them headed by Messrs. James Maxton, M.P., and John McGovern, M.P.,[1] visited Spain to inquire into the matter.

It appeared that most of the leading members of the Spanish Government disclaimed not only all belief in the alleged plot but also responsibility for the arrest of the P.O.U.M. leaders, which had been undertaken on their own initiative by the Communist-controlled police. Irujo, the then Minister of Justice, Prieto, Zugazagoitia[2] and others all took this line, some stated that they considered the P.O.U.M. leaders responsible for the fighting in Barcelona in May, 1937, but all declared the charge of espionage to be nonsensical. As for the main piece of evidence produced by the Communist press, a document known as the "N document" and supposed to give proof of treasonable activities, Irujo stated that he had examined it and that it was "worthless."[3] More recently, in January, 1938, the Spanish Government, voted by five to two in favour of releasing the P.O.U.M. prisoners, the two dissentients being the Communist Ministers.

I think these facts should make it clear that this prosecution is undertaken not at the will of the Spanish Government but in response to outside pressure, as a part of the world-wide campaign against "Trotskyism." As Zugazagoitia put it in his interview with Mr. McGovern, "We have received aid from Russia, and so we have had to permit things we did not like."[4]

And there are other unsatisfactory features about the case. To begin with, the accused men have been kept in close confinement for thirteen months without the formulation of any clear charge and, so far as is discoverable, without facilities for legal aid. The advocate who at the beginning was engaged for their defence was violently attacked in the Communist press and later forced to leave the country. Moreover, a number of the people arrested have since disappeared in circumstances that leave little doubt as to their fate. Among these was Andrés Nin,[5] who a short time previously had been Minister of Justice in the Catalan Generalite.

In spite of all this it now appears that the accused men are to be tried for espionage after all and that the "N document," previously declared "worthless," is to be revived. I suggest therefore that it is the duty of all who call themselves Socialists to enter some kind of protest. I do not mean that we should protest against the Spanish Government's trying its own political prisoners; obviously it has every right to do that. I mean that we should ask for a clear assurance that these men will be tried in open court and not in secret by a special tribunal set up for the purpose. Given an open trial and the absence of faked evidence or extorted confessions, those of us who happen to know something about the facts will have little doubt that the accused men can clear themselves. But that is a small matter compared with the preservation of ordinary justice, without which all talk of the "defence of democracy" becomes entirely meaningless — Yours, &c.,

George Orwell

1. James Maxton was an ILP M.P., 1922–46; see *385, n. 1*. John McGovern was an ILP M.P., 1930–47; see *424, n. 2*.
2. Manuel de Irujo y Ollo was a Basque minister in the Republican government; see *462, n. 4*. Indalecio Prieto y Tuero (1883–1962) was a Socialist, Minister of National Defence in the Negrín government, and a fountainhead of defeatism; see Thomas, 809. He founded the SIM, counter-espionage police of ill-repute, and died in exile in Mexico. Julián Zugazagoitia was editor of *El Socialista* and Minister of the Interior in Negrín's government. He was shot after being handed over to the Gestapo in Occupied France in 1940.
3. For the 'N document,' see *462, n. 3*.
4. During a cabinet meeting, 'Zugazagoitia demanded if his jurisdiction as minister of the interior were to be limited by Russian policemen,' according to Thomas. 'Had they been able to purchase and transport good arms from US, British, and French manufacturers, the socialist and republican members of the Spanish government might have tried to cut themselves loose from Stalin' (704).
5. For Andrés Nin, see *382, n. 5*.

471. To his mother

8 August 1938   Typewritten

New Hostel   Preston Hall   Aylesford   KENT

Darling Mum,

I hope all goes well. As I haven't heard from you for some days I infer that Father is at any rate not worse and that they haven't decided to operate. We will come down to Southwold before going away, but I am not certain yet of the date, as I have to arrange that with the doctors. Eileen thinks it would be better to come down fairly soon, eg. the week-end after next, and then come back here before going away, which I think we are to do about the end of the month. We'll stay at the Swan or somewhere. Eileen was down for the weekend, now has gone back to town, but next week-end is coming back and I think is going to stay in Aylesford. Our friends have taken over the cottage. She has left me Marx,[1] who sleeps in a shed with a puppy belonging to Dr McDougall.[2] It is a very large golden retriever puppy, almost as large as Marx, and last night they fought fiercely at feeding time, but I think they are settling down a bit. We have at last had some rain which has freshened things up, and in spite of the drought the corn seems good and the fruit not bad. Eileen says at home we had hardly any fruit owing to the late frosts. I am very much better, in fact I really done't° think I have anything wrong with me, and I am anxious to get away and start working, which I can't here. My next novel will be very late of course, but I dare say I'll get it done in time to come out about next March. We have more or less settled to go to Morocco, but haven't decided about what place or how to get there. I am writ[ing][3] to Majorie[4] to ask her if she'll have Marx, and as I have lost her Bristol address I am sending the letter for you to forward. I hope Jane[5] is going along all right. Let me know how Father is getting on and whether it will be all right for you if we come down about week after next. We won't be any nuisance in the house any way, as we'll stay out.

Much love to all
Eric

1. The Orwells' dog, 'a black poodle,' not a lap-dog, but 'the manly hunting-dog sort'; Crick 349.
2. Dr. J. B. McDougall, Medical Director of Preston Hall.
3. Orwell typed 'writ-' at the end of one line but failed to complete the word at the beginning of the next line.
4. Orwell's sister Majorie Dakin.
5. Jane Dakin, Majorie and Humphrey Dakin's daughter. Crick quotes an amusing reminiscence of hers when she was seven or eight (208).

472. Independent Labour Party Conference, Letchworth, 1938

The Spanish civil war had featured prominently at the ILP's 1937 conference, which Orwell had attended; see *385*. Although the 1938 conference was dominated by what the *Hertfordshire and Bedfordshire Express* headline called 'The Black Man's Burden' (13 August 1938), Spain was not forgotten in the discussions of conditions in India, Ceylon, the West Indies, and what was then Kenya (Jomo Kenyatta was one of the speakers). On 8 August 1938 Mari Prado, whose husband, a member of the POUM executive, had been imprisoned by the Communists, spoke on the history of the POUM, and said that, as a result of its suppression, 'the republican government in Spain was now scarcely distinguishable from the capitalist elements,' so far as the workers were concerned. John McNair, the ILP's representative in Spain, was reported as agreeing that 'the time the Spanish workers were united and had control, the Government territory was the happiest, friendliest place in the world.' (See the opening pages of *Homage to Catalonia*.) Prado said that the POUM prisoners 'were vaguely charged with disruption, disloyalty and rebellion through taking part in the May events, and the Communists were keeping in the background vague suggestions that these prisoners were also agents of Hitler and Mussolini.' See Thomas, 702–09; he summarises: 'The crimes against the POUM were acts of barbarity carried out in Spain by Spanish and foreign communists at the behest of the republic's only, and over powerful, ally, Russia' (708).

473. Domestic Diary

9 August 1938—29 April 1940

Orwell kept two diaries in 1938: Domestic Diary, starting on 9 August, and Morocco Diary, from 7 September. The latter is, in this edition, arranged chronologically (see *478*), but the Domestic Diary has been set continuously, in three sections; that for 1938 at *518*; that for 1939 at *582*; and that for 1940 at *729A*.

474. To Yvonne Davet

18 August 1938   Typewritten

New Hostel   Preston Hall   Aylesford   Kent

Dear Comrade,

I am writing in English this time. Very many thanks for your letter, and for several pamphlets, copies of "La Fleche" etc. I greatly hope you and your father have not been at too much trouble in enquiring about a house for us. We had intended to go to the south of France, but they now say I ought to spend the winter in Africa, so as far as we have any definite plan we are arranging to go to Morocco. The only difficulty I fear is that just possibly the French authorities might make difficulties about allowing us to enter Morocco. Normally there is a lot of tourist traffic there, but I suppose that if the European situation gets any more threatening they may object to the entry of foreigners. However, when we have fixed the date of leaving we will enquire at the French consulate before booking passages. I am keeping your father's address in case we should have to consult him after all. We expect to leave England about the beginning of September.

I hope all your trouble in translating the book has not been for nothing. I know it is terribly difficult to get anyone to publish translations nowadays. In England I don't know how many books get translated from the French every year, but I doubt whether there are more than about three or four which have any success. I can also well understand that they don't want books about the Spanish war. There have been so many, and most of them so bad. The trouble is that as soon as anything like the Spanish civil war happens, hundreds of journalists immediately produce rubbishy books which they put together with scissors and paste, and later when the serious books come along people are sick of the subject. Freda Uttley's° "Japan's Feet of Clay", which you tried to get them to publish, had quite a success in England. As to my own book, I don't know yet how it has sold. I should be disappointed if it sold less than 3000 copies, but I don't suppose it would sell more than 4000.[1] It had some good reviews, but the trouble is that books from small publishers never get the same amount of notice as the ones from the big publishers who buy up all the advertisement space. Possibly some paper would publish parts of it serially. I should hate to think of your having all that trouble for nothing. Certainly I would like it very much if Felicien Challaye[2] saw it. I admired him very much for making a stand on behalf of the P.O.U.M. prisoners. I gather that the protests made from France have taken effect, as our latest news is that the Spanish Government has again postponed the trial and that one member of the Government (I suppose either Prieto or Irujo) declared that he would give evidence in favour of the P.O.U.M. prisoners. I wrote recently to three left-wing papers asking people to demand that they should be given a free trial, but only one paper, the Manchester Guardian, printed my letter. In private everyone says to me, "Yes, what you say is quite true, but it is not politic to mention it now." I have nothing but contempt for this attitude.

There is not much news here. The general public is very little interested in the European situation, and I believe that if war were to break out in the near future the English people would refuse to fight, or at any rate would be very apathetic about it. The proposals for forming a Popular Front seem to have fallen through, though I think we may see some such combination on the eve of the next general election. In the form in which it was proposed in England it is a most pernicious idea, because the so-called Liberal party, with which it is proposed that the Labour Party should ally itself, represents some of the most powerful and reactionary sections of the capitalist[3] class.

I hope all goes well with you and that you will manage to find some more congenial and remunerative work.[4] I will let you know later our date of departure and what our address will be abroad.

Yours fraternally
Eric Blair

1. See *467*.
2. Challaye was a French left-wing politician; see *424, n. 2*.
3. capitalist] middle
4. Yvonne Davet was in fairly desperate straits at this time; she was undertaking translations without certainty of payment or publication because of her belief in the value of what she was translating (private communication).

475. To Francis Westrope

25 August 1938   Typewritten

New Hostel   Preston Hall   Aylesford   Kent

Dear Frank,[1]

I hope all goes well with you. I dare say you heard that after it was all fixed up for me to go to India for a year I was taken ill and brought to this sanatorium, where I have been ever since March. I am much better and they have finally decided that I haven't got TB. but something called Bronchiectasis.[2] They now say that I must spend the winter abroad and we are leaving for Gibraltar on Sept. 2nd, after which we are going on to French Morocco, where I suppose we shall stay about six months. It's all rather a bore and waste of time—I haven't, of course, done a stroke of work since being here, and my next novel, which Gollancz put on his list for the autumn, hasn't been begun and won't be done till the spring. I don't know how my Spanish book sold, reasonably well I hope, as it had fairly good reviews.

Meanwhile I would like to know whether you have any guide-books etc. dealing with French Morocco in the shop. What I particularly want, if you have any second hand, is a Baedeker of French Morocco, any maps of the country,[3] and a phrase-book or small dictionary of Arabic—nothing elaborate, but something cheap that would help one to pick up a few words of the language. Also could you let me know if I owe you a bill. I have an uneasy feeling that there was a small bill which wasn't paid.

I hope trade is good. It has been infernally hot, so I suppose London is empty. I managed to get away from the sanatorium for two days and we went down to Southwold to see my father, who has been ill, and found everything there dried up by the drought, and oats and barley being cut which weren't much more than a foot tall.

Please remember me to Mrs. Westrope.

Yours
Eric Blair

P.S. Let me know fairly soon about the books, could you, as I'm leaving here today week.

1. Francis Westrope ran Booklovers' Corner, in Hampstead, and had been Orwell's employer there from the end of 1934 to January 1936. This letter is a clear indication that, despite Gollancz's anxieties, Westrope had taken no offence at any possible reflection on him in *Keep the Aspidistra Flying*; see *279, 283, n. 1*.
2. A chronic viral disease causing dilation of the bronchi (windpipes). In a lengthy report on Orwell's condition, dated 7 November 1938, J. H. Crawford, Assistant Director of Preston Hall, concluded: 'In view of the serological result, the constantly negative cultures of the sputum, and the clinical course and progress, we decided that the condition, in all probability, was one of bronchiectasis of the Left lung, with nonspecific fibrosis of the Right lung.' Nevertheless, Orwell's Case Record also bears a typed statement: 'T.B. confirmed.'
3. In Orwell's pamphlet collection is this map of North Africa (Marrakech); *3733*, Box 41.

476. To Jack Common

25 August 1938   Handwritten

New Hostel   Preston Hall   Aylesford   Kent

Dear Jack,

Thanks for yours. Bad job about the cock. I expect he picked up a bit of poison or something. We won't get another till about next Feb when we start breeding again, as it is no use feeding an idle bird during the winter. He wasn't a bad cock. We called him Henry Ford because he had such a brisk businesslike way of going about his job, in fact he trod his first hen literally within 5 seconds of being put into the run. Muriel should stay in milk for easily a year, ie. till next July, but I expect we'll get her mated again when we come back from Africa. As to the milking you'll probably find it easier by degrees. I did tell you to grease your fingers, didn't I? It makes it easier. She ought to give 2-3 pints a day, & you can generally send the yield up or down a bit according to the amount of fat-producing food (especially flaked maize), but of course they have to have a fair amount of oats etc. to keep up their strength as well. She comes on heat once in 3 weeks & is usually a bit of a nuisance then, stamping round & bleating instead of grazing quietly.

We're going to leave England by Sept. 2nd. We've booked as far as Gibraltar, then we take another boat to Casa Blanca° & then I'm not sure, but I think we head for the Atlas mountains, wherever they may be. Our geography was so poor that both E. & I thought French Morocco gave on the Mediterranean, whereas it's really the Atlantic. As soon as we've a permanent adress° we'll let you know. We've just been down for two days to Southwold to see my father who is very old & has been ill but I am glad to say is rather better.

Love to all.

Yours
Eric

P.S. I don't know whether these milking hints may be of use. Give the goat her food, then get her up against the wall (if she gives trouble you can steady her with your shoulder), & having greased your fingers massage the udder a little & then grip the nearest teat pretty firmly at the root, ie. where it joins the udder. If you are gripping it at the right place you will feel it fill with milk & thicken in your hand. Then, still gripping pretty hard (if you are hurting her she will soon let you know) draw the hand down the teat, being careful not to relax the pressure till you reach the end. When no more milk comes out of this teat, go on to the other. When that is exhausted return to the first & milk each teat a second time. Between the first & second operations it is better to massage the udder again & give a slight upward knocking with your hand, the same as the kid does with its head. The whole operation should take about 5 minutes. It's better to do it at regular times of the day. I used to do it at about 8 am & 7 pm in the winter, but somewhat later in the evenings in the summer as she can go on grazing as long as it is light.

477. To Yvonne Davet

26 August 1938   Typewritten

New Hostel   Preston Hall   Aylesford   KENT

Chère camarade,

Je réponds tout [de] suite à votre lettre, et je vais envoyer ceci par avion. Oui, il serait très gentil de votre part de m'envoyer les chapitres qui sont terminés, et je crois que nous avons le temps. Je vais quitter l'Angleterre vendredi le 2 Septembre, et je quitterai Preston Hall jeudi. Je suppose que cette lettre arrivera chez vous demain, et si vous expédiez le paquet lundi il doit arriver ici mercredi ou jeudi. Dans le cas qu'il arrive ici après mon départ on le pourra renvoyer à Maroc sans grand delai. Il serait très commode d'avoir les chapitres avec moi pour faire les corrections etc. sur le bâteau, c'est à dire si je ne souffre pas trôp de mal de mer.

Je m'étais promis longtemps le plaisir de vous rencontrer en passant par Paris, mais il paraît que nous devons faire tout le voyage au mer. D'ordinaire j'irais à Maroc français par Paris et Marseilles, mais il paraît que par cette route il faut traverser Maroc Espagnol,[1] ce qui est impossible pour nous, car les Franco-istes pourraient savoir par nos passe-ports que nous avons été longtemps en Espagne loyaliste. Donc nous avons pris nos billets à Gibraltar par P. and O.[2] et de là nous prendrons un autre bâteau. Peut-être au printemps je pourrai revenir par Paris. C'est grand dommage de perdre cette occasion de se rencontrer, mais nous l'arrangerons plus tard. Il me faut mettre ceci au poste toute° de suite.

Très fraternellement
Eric Blair

Translation

I am replying at once to your letter, and I will send this by air. Yes, it would be very kind of you to send me the chapters you have finished, and I think there will be time. I am leaving England on Friday 2 September, and I shall leave Preston Hall on Thursday. I suppose this letter will reach you tomorrow, and if you send off the parcel on Monday it should arrive here on Wednesday or Thursday. If it arrives here after I have left it can be sent on to Morocco without much delay. It would be very convenient to have the chapters with me to correct them etc. on the boat, that is, if I am not too seasick.

I had promised myself for a long time the pleasure of meeting you when we came through Paris, but it seems we have to make the whole journey by sea. In the normal way I should go to French Morocco via Paris and Marseilles, but it seems that going this way you have to cross Spanish Morocco,[1] which we cannot do, for the Francoists could see from our passports that we spent a long time in Loyalist Spain. So we have booked our passage to Gibraltar by P. &O.[2] and from there we take another boat. Perhaps I shall be able to come back through Paris in the spring. It is a great pity to miss this opportunity of meeting, but we will arrange a meeting later. I must post this at once.

1. This proved ironic because they travelled via Tangier—then under international control—but had to pass through a Spanish as well as a French zone. Eileen, in a letter to Mrs. Blair of 15 September, told how the Spaniards had collected all the French newspapers they could find, which most people were carrying; they were not allowed in Spanish territory. The Orwells had 'about 20 newspapers, Fascist and anti-Fascist' in their suitcases.
2. Peninsular & Oriental Steam Navigation Company, the company that had carried Orwell back to Europe from Burma eleven years earlier.

478. Morocco Diary

7 September 1938—28 March 1939

Orwell began this diary on the way to Morocco. The diary is typewritten, almost certainly from a handwritten original; the handwritten version for 12 to 28 March 1939 is extant and annotated, in Orwell's hand, 'To be typed into the diary when machine is available.' The text given here, in sloped roman type, is from the typewritten version, but significant differences between the typescript and the manuscript for entries from 12 to 28 March are noted. Orwell annotated his typescript in the margins and wrote longer notes, often illustrated, on blank facing pages. The annotations are marked '[Orwell's note],' and appear as footnotes. Longer passages are included in the body of the text with an indication of their original position. Minor typing errors have been silently corrected. When a letter or other item and a diary entry have the same date, the diary entry is last.

GIBRALTAR 7.9.38:
English newspapers reach Gibraltar by P & O four days late. Local English daily Gibraltar Chronicle & Official Gazette, 8 pages of which about 2½ advertisements, ld. Current number 31,251. More or less pro-Fascist. Local Spanish papers El Annunciador and El Campanse, each four pages largely adverts, ld. daily. No very definite standpoint politically, perhaps slightly pro-Franco. Ten or eleven Franco papers sold here, also three Government papers including Solidaridad Obrera. The latter at least six days old when obtainable here, and much less on evidence. Also two pro-Government Spanish papers published in Tangier, El Porvenir and Democracia. Prices of these stated in Franco exchange.

Impossible to discover sentiments of local Spanish population. Only signs on walls are Viva Franco and Phalangist symbol, but very few of these.

Population of town about 20,000, largely Italian origin but nearly all bilingual English-Spanish. Many Spaniards work here and return into Spain every night. At least 3000 refugees from Franco territory. Authorities now trying to get rid of these on pretext of overcrowding. Impossible to discover wages and food prices. Standard of living apparently not very low, no barefooted adults and few children. Fruit and vegetables cheap, wine and tobacco evidently untaxed or taxed very little (English cigarettes 3/- a hundred, Spanish 10d. a hundred), silk very cheap. No English sugar or matches, all Belgian. Cows' milk 6d. a pint. Some of the shopkeepers are Indians and Parsees.

Spanish destroyer Jose Luis Diez lying in Harbour. A huge shell-hole, probably four or five feet across, in her side, just above water-level, on port side about fifteen to twenty feet behind bow. Flying Spanish Republican flag. The men were at first apparently prevented from going ashore, now allowed at certain hours to naval recreation grounds (i.e. not to mix with local population). No attempt being made to mend the ship.

Overheard local English resident: "It's coming right enough. Hitler's going to have Czecho-Slovakia all right. If he doesn't get it now he'll go on and on till he does. Better let him have it at once. We shall be ready by 1941."

TANGIER 10.9.38:
Papers on sale in Tangier: La Presse Marocaine (morning daily Casablanca), strongly pro-Franco; Le Petit Marocain (ditto), impartial; La Depeche Marocaine (daily Tangier), somewhat pro-Franco; Le Journal de Tanger° (apparently weekly), seemingly non-political, business announcements etc.; Tangier Gazette & Morocco Mail (English weekly Tangier, Fridays), corresponds to above, seems slightly anti-Fascist and strongly anti-Japanese;* also various others, French and Spanish, but seemingly no local Spanish pro-Franco paper.

Two buildings here flying Spanish Republican flag, including one called La Casa de Espana, some sort of club, displaying the usual Government posters. Some shops display Franco posters (the Arriba Espana poster almost exactly like a Government one). Writings on wall not common and pro-Franco and pro-Government ones about equally common, the latter perhaps slightly more so. Generally simply Viva or Muera Franco, or U.H.P., or C.N.T.F.A.I., or very rarely U.G.T. No initials of political parties except the F.A.I., the Phalange and once the J.S.U. All these inscriptions invariably Spanish. No clue to attitude of Moors. (See newspaper cutting Petit Marocain of 15.9.36.)[†1]

Poverty here not extreme for an oriental city. Nevertheless an immense development of mendicancy, the whole town living on the tourist trade. Not many actual beggars but countless touts for curio-shops, brothels etc. Most people speak Spanish, many French and all those connected with the tourist racket speak some English. Local physique very good, especially the young men both Moors and Spaniards etc. In spite of Europeanisation almost all Moors wear the burnous and fez and most of the younger women are veiled. Estimated earnings of longshore fishermen about 3d. an hour.

There are four post offices, one French, one British, and two Spanish, Franco and Government. Stamps are British surcharged Tangier. Coinage as in French Morocco.

---

* N.B. That English trade to Morocco has lost greatly to Japanese since 1934. England was then 2nd largest importer. Japan now 2nd, England 6th. (D. H. Warre, "Present Day Morocco") [Orwell's note].

† 'Le Temps' of 23.1.39 said to have leading article (which I have not seen) seriously suggesting the French might take over Sp. Morocco on the conclusion of the Spanish War [Orwell's note].

1. In 1940, when France fell, Spain took control of the whole of Tangier. After the war it was returned to its international status, until it became part of the Kingdom of Morocco in 1956. For CNT, FAI, and UGT, see 'Notes on the Spanish Militias,' *439, n. 1.* For JSU (Juventudes Socialistas Unificadas; United Youth Movement), see Thomas, xiii. For UHP ('¡Uníos, Hermanos Proletarios!'; 'Unite, proletarian brothers!'), a cry first used at the miners' rising in Asturias in 1934, see Thomas, 136, n. 2.

479. To Yvonne Davet

Dimanche, [11?] September 1938   Handwritten

[Printed] P & O Stratheden

Chère camarade,
Votre traduction[1] me plait beaucoup. J'ai fait des petites corrections aux pages 28, 37, 46, 76, 90, 100, 109 et 118, mais il n'y a rien de très important. Je vais mettre ceci à la poste à Gibraltar, et je vous écrirai de nouveau quand nous aurons une domicile à Maroc.

Très fraternellement
Eric Blair

Translation

I like your translation[1] very much. I have made small corrections on pages 28, 37, 46, 76, 90, 100, 109 and 118, but there is nothing of any importance. I shall post this in Gibraltar, and shall write to you again when we have somewhere to stay in Morocco.

1. Of *Homage to Catalonia.*

480. Morocco Diary

The Orwells arrived in Morocco on 11 September 1938, as the deposition before Robert Parr, the British Consul at Marrakech shows; see p. 196. Orwell's date of birth is given as 1902, not 1903. In his letter to A. H. Joyce of 12 February 1938 (see *426*), he said that by mistake his date of birth had been incorrectly entered as 1902 in his passport. See *3103* for the dates of birth on Orwell's passports.

They were to stay for a little over six months, sailing from Casablanca for England on 26 March 1939. On 18 September, signing as Eric Blair, Orwell accepted the lease of 'une villa et une piece de domestique, route de casa,[1] apartenant° a Monsieur Simont, Boucher a Marrakech' for a minimum period of six months at 550 francs per month, running from 15 October 1938. The villa was about five kilometres from Marrakech. R. L. Bidwell records the French franc as being at 165 to the pound (31 to the dollar) in March 1938, and by January 1939 the rate had become 176.5 to the pound (39.8 to the dollar), a rate maintained at the following January (*Currency Conversion Tables*, 1970, 20). Thus, 550 francs was about £3.25 ($15.50) during these six months. The rent of

Orwell's deposition before the British Consul, Marrakech (Robert Parr), 11 September 1938. (Approximately 55% of original size.)

the cottage at Wallington was 7s 6d per week or £1.50 (in today's coinage, if not value) for four weeks. The Moroccan lease was negotiated by Désiré Bézert of Marrakech-Guéliz.

Until they could take up residence in M. Simont's villa, the Orwells stayed at Madame Vellat's house, rue Edmond Doutte, Marrakech. For Orwell's time in Morocco, see Crick, 368–74; Shelden, 329–34; U.S.: 300–05.

1. 'casa' means Casablanca.

MARRAKECH 13.9.38:

Summer Time observed in Spanish Morocco, not in French. Franco soldiers at the stations dressed almost exactly like those of the Spanish Government. Luggage searched on the train, but very carelessly, by typical Spanish official. Another official entered and impounded all French newspapers, even those favourable to Franco. French travellers much amused by this and ditto the official, who evidently realised the absurdity of it.

Spanish Morocco evidently less developed than French, possibly owing to the barrenness of that particular area. Further South, in French Morocco, great contrast between the areas cultivated by Moors and Europeans. The latter have enormous areas given over to wheat (1,000,000 acres said to be cultivated by 3000 French with coloured labour), fields so vast that they reach the horizon on each side of the railway track. Great contrast in fertility. Soil in places is rich and very black, in others almost like broken-up brick. South of Casablanca the land generally poorer, most of it uncultivated and giving barely any pasture for animals. For about 50–100 km. North of Marrakech actual desert, ground and hills of sand and chipped rock, utterly bare of vegetation. Animals: about the end of Spanish Morocco camels begin to appear, getting commoner until near Marrakech they are almost as common as donkeys. Sheep and goats about equally numerous. Horses not many, mules hardly any. Cows in the better parts. Oxen ploughing near Marrakech but none further north. All animals almost without exception in wretched condition. (This said to be due to two successive famine years.)

Casablanca is in appearance a completely French town (of about 150,000–200,000 inhabitants, a third of these Europeans). Evidently considerable tendency for both races to keep themselves to themselves. Europeans doing manual and menial work of all kinds, but evidently better paid than the Moors. (In the cinematograph only Moors in the cheapest seats, in buses many white people unwilling to sit next to a Moor.) Standard of living seems not exceptionally low. Mendicancy noticeably less than at Tangier or Marrakech.

Marrakech has large European quarters but is more typically a Moorish town. Europeans not doing actual menial work except in restaurants etc. ★ *Cab-drivers Europeans in Casablanca, Moors in Marrakech. Mendicancy so bad as to make it intolerable to walk through the streets. Poverty without any doubt very severe. Children beg for bread and when given it eat it greedily. In the bazaar quarter great numbers of people sleeping in the street, literally a*

★ *A lot of waiters etc. who look like Europeans speak to each other in Arabic & are probably Eurasians* [Orwell's note].

family in every doorway. Blindness extremely common, some ringworm and a certain number of deformities. Large number of refugees camping outside the town. Said to be some of the people who fled north from the famine districts further south.
It is said here to be punishable by law to grow tobacco plants in the garden. *

* *i.e. more than a certain specific area* [Orwell's note].

481. Eileen Blair to Orwell's mother

15 September 1938   Handwritten

Majestic Hotel
Marrakech.

Dearest Mrs Blair,

I think Eric sent postcards today, explaining that I'd been 'upset' as he says. We could both be said to have been upset, partly I expect by the climate & partly by the horror we conceived for this country. My additional achievement was some kind of fever, possibly from food poisoning but more probably from mosquitoes—Eric has eaten the same things but hasn't been bitten to any extent whereas I look as though I were made of brioches.

    The journey until we left Tangier was so pleasant that we were spoilt. It's true that we went to Gib by mistake & then got held up at Tangier because the boats to Casablanca were full, but Gib was quite interesting & Tangier enchanting. Eric's stuff for seasickness worked even on the crossing from Gib. to Tangier, which was rough (he walked round the boat with a seraphic smile watching people being sick & insisted on my going into the 'Ladies' Cabin' to report on the disasters there), & the Continental Hotel in Tangier was very good indeed. If we could have come here by sea as we intended we should probably like Morocco better but we had to come by train which meant having breakfast at 5 a.m., going through endless agonies to satisfy police & customs authorities of all nations before getting into the train at all & then having more police & customs interrogations a) before the train left the International Zone, b) before entering the Spanish zone & c) before entering the French zone. The Spaniards were very pleasant & careless which was as well because at the last minute a man came round & collected the French newspapers that most people had & that were not allowed in Spanish territory. We had in our suitcases a collection of about 20 newspapers, Fascist & anti-Fascist. The French were in character, absolutely refusing to believe that we were not coming to Morocco to break the law. However, they agreed to let the Morocco police do the arresting & we got as far as the junction where we were to change into a train with a restaurant car. By this time it should have been 11 a.m. & was 11.45. Everyone fled across the station surrounded by hordes of Arab porters, aged 10–70, & the train started before we were well in it. Our junior porter, who was about 3′6″, had not unnaturally put the two cases he was carrying down on the platform so that he could catch us to get his tip (he said they were in the dining-car), but to establish this took us hours & to get the cases at Casablanca took two days. Then we came to Marrakech, again leaving at 7 a.m., & went to the Hotel Continental which had been recommended to us & which may have been quite good once. Lately it has changed hands & is obviously a brothel. I haven't much direct knowledge of brothels but as they offer a special service they can probably all afford to be dirty & without any other conveniences. However we stayed for one day, partly because Eric didn't notice anything odd about it until he tried to live in it & partly because my temperature was by that time going up about one degree an hour & I only wanted to lie down, which was easy enough, & to get drinks, which were brought me by a limitless variety of street Arabs who looked murderous but were very kind. Eric of course ate out & this is very expensive in Morocco so we moved here as soon as possible. This is the second most expensive hotel in Marrakech but it's much cheaper to have full pension here (95 fr. a day for two)[1] than to go to restaurants.

Sunday.[2]

Eric made me go to bed at that point, & since then we've been busy. He has written to you this morning while I unpacked, so you'll know about Mme Vellet° & the villa in prospect. I think the villa will be fun from our point of view. It's entirely isolated except for a few Arabs who live in the outbuildings to tend the orange grove that surrounds it. We're going to buy enough furniture to camp with. As it will be the cheapest French furniture obtainable the aesthetic effect may be unfortunate, but we hope to get some decent rugs as we want them to take home. There is a large sitting room, two bedrooms, a bathroom & a kitchen. No provision for cooking but we'll have some little pots with charcoal in them & a Primus. The country is practically desert but may look different after the rains. Anyway we can have a goat & Eric will really get the benefit of the climate. In Marrakech itself he couldn't. The European quarter is intolerable with a second-rate respectability, & very expensive. The native quarter is 'picturesque' but the smells are only rivalled by the noises. Eric was so depressed that I thought we should have to come home but he is now quite excited about the villa & I think will be happy there. According to Dr. Diot (who was recommended by a friend of my brother's in Paris) the climate is ideal for him, or will be in a few weeks when it's cooler. And the villa has a sort of observatory on its roof which will be good to work in.

The second bedroom is of course Avril's when she wants it. If she went to Tangier by sea the fare would be about £12 return. At Tangier one can stay at the Continental for 10/– a day all in. The fare from Tangier to Marrakech by train is 155 fr. second class. Unfortunately the train gets into Casablanca at 3 p.m. or so & the next one to Marrakech leaves at 8 & takes all night. It would be better to stay one night at Casablanca, which I suppose would cost another 10/– altogether, & get the morning train here.

It only takes 4 hours & one sees the country such as it is. We loathed it but that was largely because we were sentenced to live in it for six months. As one approaches Marrakech camels become more & more common until they're as ordinary as donkeys, & the native villages are extraordinary collections of little thatched huts about 5 feet square (but generally round), sometimes surrounded by a kind of hedge of dead wood or possibly a mud wall. We don't know what the walls are for; they aren't strong enough or high enough to keep anything out. Marrakech itself was largely built of mud & has enormous mud ramparts. The earth dries a reddish colour which is very beautiful *in earth* but unfortunate when approximately reproduced in paint by the French, who like to call Marrakech 'la rouge'. Some of the native products are lovely, especially the earthenware pots & jugs they use.

Dr. Diot hasn't really examined Eric yet but intends to. He is not particularly sympathetic but he must be a good doctor & through him we'll be able to know that the chest really is reacting properly.

Please give my love to Mr Blair & Avril. I do hope Mr Blair is getting out & that Avril will get out as far as Morocco. It's said to be a wonderful light here for photography. From her point of view it might have been more interesting to stay in Marrakech but one can walk one way (about 3 miles) in cooler weather & a taxi will cost about 2/6 I think. She might be able to hire a car if she liked to do her International driving test before coming. Anyway there are buses from Marrakech to all the other places.

With love
Eileen.

1. At a rate of exchange of 170 francs to the pound, about 11s 2d.
2. Presumably 18 September 1938.

482. Morocco Diary

MARRAKECH 16.9.38:
The two papers normally read here are the Casablanca dailies, Le Petit Marocain, obtainable about midday, and La Vigie Marocaine, not obtainable till evening. Both are patriotic, more or less anti-Fascist, but neutral as to Spanish Civil War and anti-Communist. The local paper. L'Atlas, weekly, seems utterly insignificant. Yesterday (15th) in spite of sensational news of Chamberlain flying to Berlin, with which the papers made great play, there was utter lack of interest here and evidently no belief in war being imminent. Nevertheless there have been large transfers of troops to Morocco. Two of the French liners which run Marseilles-Tangier-Casablanca were more or less completely filled with troops. There has been a large increase recently in the local Air Force and 125 new officers are said to have arrived.

483. To Dr. J. B. McDougall

18 September 1938   Typewritten

Chez Madame Vellat Rue Edmond Doutte Marrakech French Morocco

Dear Dr MacDougall,[1]
I must apologise for not writing earlier to thank you for your very great kindness to me at Preston Hall. I was extraordinarily happy and comfortable there and I am sure it has done me all the good in the world. This is the first opportunity I have had of writing a proper letter, as I have been travelling more or less continuously for about a fortnight. We went by P. and O. to Gibraltar, then across to Tangier, then here by train. It is still rather hot and touches about 90 or 95 in the daytime, but it will cool down soon and they say the country gets green and full of flowers later on. This is a big French garrison town and also the crossing point of various caravan routes across north Africa. We had a good journey here and not much rough weather, and for the first time in my life I was not seasick, thanks I think to a German seasickness remedy called Vasano which is very good and leaves no after-effects. I have made arrangements to be attended by a French doctor who has been here for many years and says the climate is very good for lung complaints.
My wife is writing to Mrs MacDougall°. I will write again and let you know how we get on. And very many thanks again for all your kindness.
Yours sincerely,
Eric Blair

1. J. B. McDougall (not as spelt by Orwell); see *471, n. 2.*

484. To Leonard Moore, Yvonne Davet, and Cyril Connolly

[18?] September 1938   Handwritten postcards

The postmarks franking the stamps on these cards are badly blurred, but the most likely date is the eighteenth. Moore's office received his card on 22 September. The texts are similar. Each gives the address: 'Chez Madame Vellat / Rue Edmond Doutte / Marrakech / French Morocco,' with these notes:

To Leonard Moore:

The above address will find us from now on. Will write later. All the best.
Eric Blair

To Yvonne Davet:

The above address will find me from now on. Best wishes.
Eric Blair

To Cyril Connolly:

The above address will find me for the time being. Don't forget to send me a copy of your book[1] when it comes out. So looking forward to seeing it. Hope all goes well. All the best to your wife.

Yours
Eric Blair

1. *Enemies of Promise.*

485. Review of *The Communist International* by Franz Borkenau

New English Weekly, 22 September 1938

When Dr. Borkenau's "The Spanish Cockpit" appeared the Spanish war was about a year old and the book dealt only with the events of the first six or seven months. Nevertheless it remains the best book on the subject, and what is more, it is a book different in *kind* from nearly all that have appeared on either side. As soon as one opened it one was aware that here at last, amid the shrieking horde of propagandists, was a grown-up person, a man capable of writing dispassionately even when he knew the facts. It is unfortunate that political books nowadays are almost invariably written either by fools or by ignoramuses. If a writer on a political subject manages to preserve a detached attitude, it is nearly always because he does not know what he is talking about. To understand a political movement one has got to be involved in it, and as soon as one is involved one becomes a propagandist. Dr. Borkenau, however, apart from his intellectual gifts, is in the very unusual position of having been for eight years a member of the German Communist Party and for some time an official of the Comintern, and of having finally reverted to a belief in liberalism and democracy. This is a development about as uncommon as being converted from Catholicism to Protestantism, but a sociologist could hardly have a better background.

In the twenty-years' history of the Comintern Dr. Borkenau traces three more or less separate periods. In the first period, the immediate post-war years, there is a genuine revolutionary ferment in Europe, and in consequence the Comintern is an organisation sincerely aiming at world revolution and not entirely under Russian influence. In the second phase it becomes an instrument in Stalin's struggles first against the Trotsky-Zinoviev group, later against the Bukharin-Rykov group. In the third phase, the one we are in now, it becomes more or less openly an instrument of Russian foreign policy. Meanwhile there are the alternate swings of Comintern policy to "left" and "right." As Dr. Borkenau points out, the earlier changes were comparatively insignificant, the more recent ones catastrophic. The swing-over in Communist policy that took place between 1934 and 1936 was in fact so extraordinary that the general public has as yet failed to grasp it. In the "ultra-left" phase of 1928-34, the "social fascist" phase, revolutionary purity was so pure that every labour leader was declared to be in capitalist pay, the

Russian sabotage trials "proved" that M. Blum and other leaders of the Second International were plotting the invasion of Russia, and anyone who advocated a united front of Socialists and Communists was denounced as a traitor, Trotskyist, mad dog, hyena and all the other items in the Communist vocabulary. Social democracy was declared to be the real enemy of the working class, Fascism was dismissed as something utterly without importance, and this insane theory was kept up even *after* Hitler had come to power. But then came German rearmament and the Franco-Russian pact. Almost overnight Communist policy in the non-Fascist countries swung round to the Popular Front and "defence of democracy," and anyone who cavilled at lining up with Liberals and Catholics was once again a traitor, Trotskyist, mad dog, hyena and so forth. Of course such changes of policy are only possible because every Communist party outside the U.S.S.R. gets a new membership every few years. Whether there will be another corresponding swing to the "left" seems doubtful. Dr. Borkenau thinks that Stalin may ultimately be compelled to dissolve the Comintern as the price of a secure alliance with the western democracies. On the other hand it is worth remembering that the rulers of the democracies, so called, are not fools, they are aware that Communist agitation even in its "left" phases is not a serious danger, and they may prefer to keep in being an organisation which plays almost invariably into their hands.

In so far as it aims—and it still professes rather vaguely to aim—at world revolution, the Comintern has been a complete failure. Nevertheless it has done an immense amount of mischief and has been, in Dr. Borkenau's opinion, one of the chief causes of the growth of Fascism. In every Communist party only about five per cent. of the membership—that is to say, a framework of party officials—remains constant; but in each phase of policy there pass through the party some thousands or tens of thousands of people who emerge having learnt nothing save a contempt for democratic methods. They do not emerge with a belief in Socialism, but they do emerge with a belief in violence and double-crossing. Consequently when the critical moment comes they are at the mercy of the man who really specialises in violence and double-crossing, in other words, the Fascist.

Dr. Borkenau thinks that the root cause of the vagaries of Comintern policy is the fact that revolution as Marx and Lenin predicted it and as it happened, more or less, in Russia, is not thinkable in the advanced western countries, at any rate at present. Here I believe he is right. Where I part company from him is when he says that for the western democracies the choice lies between Fascism and an orderly reconstruction through the co-operation of all classes. I do not believe in the second possibility, because I do not believe that a man with £50,000 a year and a man with fifteen shillings a week either can, or will, co-operate. The nature of their relationship is, quite simply, that the one is robbing the other, and there is no reason to think that the robber will suddenly turn over a new leaf. It would seem, therefore, that if the problems of western capitalism are to be solved, it will have to be through a third alternative, a movement which is genuinely revolutionary, *i.e.*, willing to make drastic changes and to use violence if necessary, but which does not lose touch, as Communism and Fascism have done, with the essential values of democracy. Such a thing is by no means unthinkable. The germs of such a movement exist in numerous countries, and they are capable of growing. At any rate, if they don't, there is no real exit from the pigsty we are in.

This is a profoundly interesting book. I have not enough specialised knowledge to judge its accuracy, but I think it is safe to say that it is as little coloured by prejudice as a book on a controversial subject can be. Probably the best way to test its value as a historical work would be to watch its reception in the Communist press—on the principle of "the worse the better," I need hardly say. I hope that Dr. Borkenau will not only go on writing, but that he will find imitators. It is a most encouraging thing to hear a human voice when fifty thousand gramophones are playing the same tune.

486. To Jack Common

26 September 1938   Typewritten

Chez Madame Vellat   Rue Edmond Doutte   Medinah°
Marrakech   French Morocco

Dear Jack,

After October 15th my address will actually be Villa Simont, Sidahan, Route de Casablanca, Marrakech, but in case of doubt better write to the address I am at at present, as the house we're taking is some way out of the town and I'm not certain about their delivering letters.

I don't know whether or not you will be fitting on your gas mask by the time this gets to you, but things look pretty bad and are perhaps even worse than I think because I don't see the English papers and the local French ones are inclined to minimise things. If war does break out it is utterly impossible to foresee what will happen, but unless I am kicked out I don't think I shall come home, at any rate until the time I was supposed to be coming, ie. early next spring. The whole thing seems to me so utterly meaningless that I think I shall just concentrate on remaining alive. In a mess of this kind it's just a case of sauve qui peut, so in the event of war breaking out you must do what you think fit about the cottage and the animals. The bank any way will pay the rent for the next six months, and if you are just keeping out of it you would probably be as safe there as any where, I don't think anyone will drop a bomb on Wallington and it might even be profitable to expand the fowl industry a bit, as eggs are sure to be scarce and sought after, at any rate until chicken food gets even scarcer. On the other hand if you feel impelled either to join the army or go to jail or for any other reason to leave Wallington, will you communicate with my brother in law and put the matter in his hands? His name and address are Laurence O'Shaughnessy, 24 Crooms Hill, Greenwich SE.10. He will see to the disposal of the cottage, which could perhaps be let furnished to bomb-dodgers. And in the interim, if you left and the house hadn't a tenant for the time being, he will arrange for the Hatchetts and Andersons[1] to look after the animals. I just make these arrangements because it is as well to be prepared for the worst and if the worst does happen communication by letter may become difficult almost immediately. But I suppose there is still hope that all may be well. The next week or two will show any way. Hope all is going well with you and all are in good health and not finding the primitive conditions too much of a bore. I don't care much for this country and am already pining to be back in England, always supposing there isn't a war there. Love to Mary and Peter.

Yours
Eric

1. Neighbours at Wallington.

487. Eileen Blair to Marjorie Dakin
27 September 1938   Handwritten

Chez Mme Vellat,   rue Edmond Doutte   Medina,
Marrakech,   French Morocco.

My dear Marjorie,
We've just had our first letter—from Mrs Blair. It was full of good news. I'm so glad you have a well family & that Marx appreciates his good fortune.[1] I only hope he behaves as they say.

Yesterday we were rather hysterically writing semi-business letters in the hope that they'd be delivered before war broke out. Today the papers are somewhat calmer, but it's maddening to see none except those published in Morocco (we can get others but 4 to 8 days late & those at the moment might as well be years old). The extraordinary thing is that no one here seems interested. We were in a café when the evening paper arrived yesterday & only one other person bought one & he didn't open it. Yet there are many young Frenchman° here who would be mobilised for service in France I suppose. The general idea is that Morocco would be very safe, anyway inland. The Arabs don't seem ripe to make trouble & if they did make it the poor wretches would have 15000 regular troops to contend with in Marrakech alone, complete with artillery & all. So long as we're allowed to stay here, & that will probably be as long as we have any money, we probably have a better chance than most of keeping alive. Though what we should be keeping alive for God knows. It seems very unlikely that Eric will publish another book after the outbreak of war. I was rather cheered to hear about Humphrey's dugout.[2] Eric has been on the point of constructing one for two years, though the plans received rather a check after he did construct one in Spain & it fell down on his & his companions' heads two days later, not under any kind of bombardment but just from the force of gravity. But the dugout has generally been by way of light relief; his specialities are concentration camps & the famine.

He buried some potatoes against the famine & they might have been very useful if they hadn't gone mouldy at once. To my surprise he does intend to stay here whatever happens. In theory this seems too reasonable & even comfortable to be in character; in practice perhaps it wouldn't be so comfortable. Anyway I am thankful we got here. If we'd been in England I suppose he must have been in jail by now & I've had the most solemn warnings against this from all the doctors though they don't tell me how I could prevent it. Whatever the solution I do still desperately hope that there won't be war, which I'm sure would be much worse for the Czechs. After all political oppression, though it gets so much publicity, can make miserable only a small proportion of a whole nation because a political régime, especially a dictatorship, has to be popular. We keep seeing & being exasperated by pictures of London crowds 'demonstrating' when we don't know what they're demonstrating for, & there are occasional references to 'extremists' who are arrested but whether the extremists are Communists demonstrating against Chamberlain's moderation or Fascists or socialists or pacifists we don't know. Eric, who retains an extraordinary political simplicity in spite of everything, wants to hear what he calls the voice of the people. He thinks this might stop a war, but I'm sure that the voice would only say that it didn't want a war but of course would have to fight if the Government declared war. It's very odd to feel that Chamberlain is our only hope, but I do believe he doesn't want war either at the moment & certainly the man has courage.[3] But it's fantastic & horrifying to think that you may all be trying on gas masks at this moment.[4]

You'll probably have heard that we don't like Marrakech. It's interesting, but at first anyway seemed dreadful to live in. There are beautiful arches with vile smells coming out of them & adorable children covered in ringworm & flies. I found an open space to watch the sunset from & too late realised that part of the ground to the west of us was a graveyard; I really couldn't bear Eric's conversation about the view as dominated by invisible worms & we had to go away without seeing the sunset. On the whole, however, I get acclimatised & I thought Eric was moving in the same direction, but he says he isn't. But when we have our villa (we move in on the 15th) he is going to be happy. He is even buying things for the house, including a copper tray four feet across that will dominate us for the rest of our lives. We also have two doves. Here they live in a cage but at the villa they are to go free. One can't have any tame animals because on the whole they have dreadful lives here & six months' spoiling would only make the future worse for them. Otherwise we'd have some donkeys—you can buy a donkey for 100 francs.[5]

I expect you can't read a word of this. We only have one table & Eric is typing diary notes on it. He sends his love to everyone, including Marx. So do I.

Eileen.

If there *is* a war I don't know what Bristol,[6] or indeed anywhere, will be like. But if at any time you wanted some place more remote for the children it's quite possible that the cottage will be empty. I don't know what the Commons would do but we've suggested to my brother that the cottage might anyway be kept in statu quo. It could be almost as safe as anywhere in England, & comparatively self-supporting, so we thought someone might be glad of it. Of course the Commons may all stay. Someone at my brother's house (24 Croom's Hill, S.E.10) will know. My brother himself would be mobilised at once I suppose as he's in the RAMC.[7]

[At top of letter] There's no actual news yet about E's health. The doctor says we must allow 3 or 4 weeks for 'acclimatisation' before expecting much.

1. Marx, the Orwells' black poodle, was being cared for by Marjorie and her husband, Humphrey Dakin.
2. An air-raid shelter dug into the back garden. Such a shelter—not much more than a corrugated steel shell covered by earth—was introduced in November 1938 by the Home Secretary, Sir John Anderson, and was named after him. Over two million were erected, or dug out. They were free to those earning £250 a year or less and cost £7 for those earning more. Though subjected to a fair amount of ridicule, they did probably save lives.
3. Early in September 1938, Sudeten Germans, led by Konrad Henlein (1898–1945, by suicide), organised rallies demanding the reunification of Czech border areas with Germany. By 14 September, the Czech government had declared martial law in the Sudetenland, the French had reinforced the Maginot Line, and on 26 September mobilisation of the Royal Navy was ordered. The French and British governments urged the Czechs to accede to German demands, but on 23 September the Czech government ordered general mobilisation, and war seemed inevitable. The day after Eileen wrote, Hitler called a conference of the Czechs, French, and British, and Prime Minister Neville Chamberlain flew to Munich to attend. For the sake of a short breathing space, the Czechs were forced to accept German demands, and annexation of the Sudetenland began on 1 October. Poland seized the opportunity to take over Czech Silesia. In the light of Chamberlain's much criticised statement in a radio broadcast on 1 October that he believed 'it is peace in our time . . . peace with honour,' Eileen's comment is particularly telling, and probably reflects what many people, without the benefit of hindsight, felt at the time. Compare Orwell's comment on Chamberlain, p. 239, last paragraph.
4. Gas masks were distributed in late September 1938.
5. About 11s 2d.
6. Where Marjorie and her family were living.
7. Royal Army Medical Corps. Laurence O'Shaughnessy was called up as soon as war was declared one year later.

488. Morocco Diary

MARRAKECH 27.9.38:
The other local daily paper read here is La Presse Marocaine, which is somewhat more right-wing (at any rate more anti-Russian and more pro-Franco) than the Petit Marocain
There are said to be about 15,000 troops in Marrakech. Apart from officers and N.C.Os, these will all be Arab or negro troops, except for a detachment

of the foreign legion. * The latter are evidently looked on as dangerous ruffians, though good troops, and are debarred from visiting certain parts of the town except with a special permit. The Arab cavalry (from their badges apparently the 2nd Spahis) look pretty good, the Arab infantry less good, probably about equal to a second-rate Indian regiment. There is a large number of Senegalese infantry (called tirailleurs—presumably rifles—the badge is an anchor, †) here. They are of admirable physique and said to be good marchers. They are used for picket duty at certain parts of the town. In addition the local detachment of artillery (do not know how much, but recently saw a battery of largish field guns, probably larger than 75 mm., on the march) is manned by negroes. They only act as drivers etc. under white N.C.Os and are not taught to aim the guns. Arabs are not used for this purpose, obviously because they could not be prevented from learning too much. All the troops here are said to be standing by and ready to move at a moment's notice. On the fortified hill immediately west of the town there are guns which command the Arab quarter "in case of trouble". Nevertheless the local French show an utter lack of interest in the European crisis, so much so as to make it impossible to think that they believe war will break out. There is no scramble for papers, no one broaches the subject of war unless prompted and one overhears no conversations on the subjects in the cafes. A Frenchman, questioned on the subject, says that people here are well aware that in case of war "it will be more comfortable here than in France." Everyone will be mobilised, but only the younger classes will be sent to Europe. The re-opening of schools has not, as in France, been postponed. It is not easy to be absolutely certain about the volume of poverty here. The province has undoubtedly passed through a very bad period owing to two years drought, and on all sides fields which have obviously been under cultivation recently have reverted to almost desert condition, utterly dried up and bare even of weeds. As a result many products, eg. potatoes, are very scarce. There has been a great to and fro of refugees from the dried up areas, for whom the French have made at any rate some provision. The great French wheat estates are said to be worked largely with female labour, and in bad times the unemployed women flock into the towns, which is said to lead to a great increase in prostitution. There is no doubt that poverty in the town itself is very severe by European standards. People sleep in the streets by hundreds and thousands, and beggars, especially children, swarm everywhere. It is noticeable that this is so not only in quarters normally frequented by tourists, but also in the purely native quarters, where any European is promptly followed by a retinue of children. Most beggars are quite satisfied with a sou (twenty sous equal a penny halfpenny). Two illustrative incidents: I asked a boy of about 10 to call a cab for me, and when he returned with the cab gave him 50 centimes (three farthings, but by local standards an overpayment.) Meanwhile about a dozen other boys had collected, and when they saw me take a handful of small change out of my pocket they flung

* Apparently there were some white troops as well as the N.C.Os. [Orwell's note].
† The anchor is the artillery [Orwell's note].

themselves on it with such violence as to draw blood from my hand. When I had managed to extricate myself and give the boy his 50 centimes a number of others flung themselves on him, forced his hand open and robbed him of the money. Another day I was feeding the gazelles in the public gardens with bread when an Arab employee of the local authorities who was doing navvy work nearby came up to me and asked for a piece of the bread. I gave it him and he pocketed it gratefully. The only doubt raised in one's mind about all this is that in certain quarters the population, at any rate the younger ones, have been hopelessly debauched by tourism and led to think of Europeans as immensely rich and easily swindled. Numbers of young men make a living ostensibly as guides and interpreters, actually by a species of blackmail.

When one works out the earnings of the various kinds of petty craftsmen and pieceworkers here, carpenters, metal-workers, porters etc., it generally comes to about 1d or 2d an hour. As a result many products are very cheap, but certain staple ones are not, eg. bread, which is eaten by all Arabs when they can get it, is very expensive. ¾lb of inferior white bread (the European bread is dearer) costs 1 franc or 1½d. It is habitually sold in half cakes. The lowest sum on which an Arab, living in the streets with no home, can exist is said to be 2 francs a day. The poorer French residents regard 10 francs or even 8 francs a day as a suitable wage for an Arab servant (out of this wage he has to provide his own food). *

The poverty in the Jewish quarter is worse, or at any rate more obtrusive than in the Arab quarters. Apart from the main streets, which are themselves very narrow, the alleys where the people live are 6 feet or less across and most of the houses have no windows at all. Overcrowding evidently goes on to an unbelievable extent and the stench is utterly insupportable, people in the narrowest alleys habitually urinating in the street and against the wall. Nevertheless it is evident that there are often quite rich people living among this general filth. There are about 10,000 † Jews in the town. They do most of the metal work and much of the woodwork. Among them are a few who are extremely wealthy. The Arabs are said to feel much more hostility towards the Jews than towards the Europeans. The Jews are noticeably more dirty in their clothes and bodies than the Arabs. Impossible to say to what extent they are orthodox, but all evidently observe the Jewish festivals and almost all, at any rate of those over 30, wear the Jewish costume (black robe and skull-cap.) In spite of poverty, begging in the Jewish quarters not worse than in the Arab quarters.

Here in Marrakech the attitude of the French towards the Arabs is noticeably more like the Anglo-Indian attitude than, eg., in Casablanca. "Indigene" exactly corresponds to "native" and is freely used in the newspapers. The French here do not, as in Casablanca, do menial jobs such as cab-driving, though there are French waiters in the cafes. In the Jewish quarter there is a very poor French population some of whom appear to have "gone native", but these are not altogether distinguishable from the Jews, most of whom are

---

* Female servants receive 3–5 Fr. a day [Orwell's note].
† 13000 [Orwell's note].

quite white. There is an immensely higher proportion of French-speaking Arabs than of English-speaking Indians, indeed every Arab who is much in contact with Europeans speaks a certain amount of French. The French almost always tu-toi the Arabs in speaking to them, and the Arabs do so in return whether or not understanding the implication (2nd person in Arabic has not this implication). Most French people of long standing here speak some Arabic, but probably not a great deal. A French officer speaking to his N.C.O. speaks in French, at any rate some of the time.

489. To Jack Common

29 September 1938   Typewritten

Chez Madame Vellat Rue Edmond Doutte Marrakech French Morocco

Dear Jack,

I wrote yesterday making suggestions as to what you should do in case of war, then this morning received your letter in which you didn't sound as though war were really likely, so write now in a more normal mood. At this end of the world I can't make out about this war business. The troops are standing by more or less in full kits, the artillery is trained on the proletarian end of the town "in case of trouble" and this afternoon we had some kind of air-raid practice which I couldn't get the hang of, but meanwhile the French population is utterly uninterested and evidently doesn't believe that war is coming. Of course they are out of all danger here, except for the young ones who will be mobilised, and perhaps that affects their attitude. The whole thing is so utterly insane that it just sickens me. One thing I am certain of. Unless there is some tremendous loss of prestige, such as Hitler seizing the whole of Czechoslovakia while England and France do nothing, and perhaps at the same time painting the British ambassador's arse green and sending him back to England, Chamberlain is safe to win the next election with a big majority. The so-called left parties have played straight into his hands by their idiotic policy.

I'm sorry to hear the cockerels don't fetch anything. We crossed the hens with a Leghorn because they're good layers and it's much more paying to go in for eggs than for table birds. The best thing to do really is to eat them. They['re] all right to eat, only they're so light they fetch nothing. The earliest pullets ought to lay this month and the others I suppose about November. Try giving them a spot of Karswood, which is quite cheap, to bring them on. I hope Muriel is behaving. I still can't remember what arrangement was made about her food. Are Clarke's delivering the stuff? If so, ask them about their bill. They know I am good to pay, and they could make some suggestion, whether to send the bills on to me here or what not. Yes, have the telephone disconnected if it hasn't been done. I thought my brother in law had had it done. Could you drop him a line about it? I gave you his address in the last letter. I wonder if there are any apples on the tree in the kitchen garden. It gives 30 or 40 pounds some years. They're very good cookers but you want to use them up because they don't keep.

It makes me sad to hear you say you've never been out of England, especially when I think of the bastards who do travel, simply going from hotel to hotel and never seeing any difference anywhere except in the temperature. At the same time I'm not sure how much good travel does to anyone. One thing I have always believed, and that is that one really learns nothing from a foreign country unless one works in it, or does something that really involves on[e] with the inhabitants. This trip is something quite new to me, because for the first time I am in the position of a tourist. The result is that it is quite impossible, at any rate at present, to make any contact with the Arabs, whereas if I were here, say, on a gun-running expedition, I should immediately have the entree to all kinds of interesting society, in spite of the language difficulty. I have often been struck by how easy it is to get people to take you for granted if you and they are really in the same boat, and how difficult otherwise. For instance, when I was with the tramps, merely because they assumed that I was on the bum it didn't make a damn's worth of difference to them that I had a middle-class accent and they were willing to be actually more intimate than I wanted. Whereas if, say, you brought a tramp into the house and tried to get him to talk to you it would just be a patron-client relationship and quite meaningless. I am as usual taking careful notes of everything I see, but am not certain what use I shall be able to make of them afterwards. Here in Marrakech it is in some ways harder to find out about conditions in Morocco than it would be in a less typical Arab town. In a town like Casablanca you have a huge French population and a white proletariat, and consequently local branches of the Socialist Party and so forth. Here with not very important differences it is very like Anglo-Indian society and you are more or less obliged to be a pukka sahib or suffer the consequences. We're staying in the town itself for another two or three weeks, then we're taking a villa outside. That will be slightly more expensive but quieter to work in and I simply have to have a bit of garden and a few animals. I shall also be interested to see a little of how the Arab peasants live. Here in the town conditions are pretty frightful, wages generally work out at about 1d or 2d an hour and it's the first place I've seen where beggars do literally beg for bread and eat it greedily when given it. It's still pretty hot but getting better and we're both pretty well in health. There's nothing wrong with me really, but much as I resent the waste of time it's probably done me good to lay off work for seven months. People who don't write think that writing isn't work, but you and I know the contrary. Thank God I've just begun to work again and made a start on my new novel, which was billed for this autumn but might appear in the spring perhaps. Of course if war comes God knows if the publishing of books will even continue. To me the idea of war is a pure nightmare. Richard Rees was talking as though even war couldn't be worse than the present conditions, but I think what this really means is that he doesn't see any peace-time activity for himself which he feels to be useful. A lot of intellectuals feel like this, which I think is one explanation of why the so-called left-wingers are now the jingoes. But I personally do see a lot of things that I want to do and to continue doing for another thirty years or so, and the idea that I've got to abandon them and either be bumped off or depart to some filthy concentration camp just infuriates me. Eileen and I have decided that if war does come the best thing will be to just stay alive and thus add to the number of sane people.

The above address will find me for a bit. I'll give you the new one when I have it—probably a poste restante address, as I don't think they will deliver letters where we are going to. Best love to Mary and Peter. Eileen also sends love.

Yours
Eric

P.S. [handwritten at top of first page] Yes, I did once just meet Alec Henderson[1] at a party. The village people are really very nice, especially the Hatchetts, Mrs Anderson, Titley, Keep, Edie (Mrs Ridley's daughter) & her husband Stanley, & Albert, Mrs R's other son in law. I don't know what one can really do for old H. except occasionally to give him eggs when his hens don't lay. He is a dear old man. Tell them all you've heard from me & I wanted to be remembered to them.

1. Possibly this was a neighbour at Wallington, but since he is separated from the 'village people' he may not be local. 'Alec' could be an error for 'Arthur.' Arthur Henderson, Sr. (1863–1935) had died the previous year. His son (1893–1966), like his father, was a Labour M.P., 1923–24, 1929–31, and 1935–66.

489A. Manifesto: If War Comes, We Shall Resist

The New Leader, 30 September 1938

This manifesto, printed in *The New Leader*, the paper of the Independent Labour Party, on 30 September 1938, was signed by 149 people, forty-eight of whose names were printed. Orwell was listed among 'Authors,' the others being Vera Brittain (see *2473, n. 1*), Havelock Ellis, Laurence Housman, C. E. M. Joad, and Ethel Mannin. Five M.P.s signed: James Maxton, H. G. McGhee, Alfred Salter, Campbell Stephen, and Cecil H. Wilson. Among others listed were: Frank Horrabin, Fenner Brockway, Fred. W. Jowett (Treasurer, ILP), J. H. Hudson (Chairman, Parliamentary Pacifist Group), Tom Stephenson (Cumberland Miners), H. A. Moody (Chairman, League of Coloured Peoples), George Padmore (Chairman, International African Service Bureau), C. H. Norman, and J. S. Rowntree. See P. J. Thwaites, 'The Independent Labour Party, 1938–1950,' unpublished Ph.D. thesis, London University, 1976.

The European crisis has arisen from larger issues than those which centre on Czechoslovakia. Should war break out, now or later, Czechoslovakia or some other country (like Belgium in 1914) would provide only the incidental occasion for it.

The danger of war arises from the injustices of the Treaties which concluded the last war and the imperialist economic rivalries which they embodied. The danger will remain, even though war be avoided now.

The threat of war will continue until world supplies are made available to all peoples on a basis of co-operation and social justice.

By its policy of economic imperialism during recent years the British Government has aggravated the evils of world distribution, and thereby has a heavy responsibility for the present crisis.

We repudiate, therefore, all appeals to the people to support a war which would, in fact, maintain and extend imperialist possessions and interests, whatever the incidental occasion.

For the democratic countries which resort to war the immediate result would be the destruction of the liberties of the people and the imposition of totalitarian regimes.

If war comes, it will be our duty to resist, and to organise such opposition as will hasten the end of that war, not by Treaties which represent the triumph of one imperialism over another, and which would only sow the seeds of future wars, but by the building of a new world order based on fellowship and justice.

490. To *Controversy*

October 1938

WE, THE UNDERSIGNED

We, the undersigned, urge all who value a free Socialist Press to respond to the appeal made by J. F. Horrabin and C. A. Smith for immediate financial assistance to *Controversy*.

No one of us is in agreement with all that has appeared in its columns. That is inevitable, since both its contributors and we ourselves hold varying and often conflicting views. But in this magazine each of these views has found repeated expression—by members of the Labour Party, Independent Labour Party and Communist Party, by Anarchists, Trotskyists and Pacifists. Its disappearance would be a loss to Left journalism.

The value of an open forum, convenience of having all Socialist opinion represented between the covers of one magazine, the need for resisting political censorship and the suppression of truth—these are worthy of some small sacrifice.

Members, ourselves of different Parties, we unitedly endorse the appeal, and hope that readers will respond generously enough and quickly enough to save *Controversy*.[1]

W. Ballantine
  (*N.U.R. Executive*)
Leonard Barnes
Aneurin Bevan, M.P.
R. Bhavan
Julius Braunthal
  (*Asst. Sec., L.S.I.*)

Naomi Mitchison
W. H. Morris
  (*Labour Candidate, Hampstead*)
C. H. Norman
George Orwell

Fenner Brockway
W. J. Brown
F. W. Chandler
W. T. Colyer
  (Labour Candidate,
  Chislehurst)
Edward Conze
Sydney Elliott
Lionel Elvin
Alan Flanders
  (British Leader, M.S.I.)
W. Fox
C. E. M. Joad
A. Creech Jones, M.P.
Satish Kalelkar
F. L. Kerran
  (Labour Candidate,
  Luton)²
Norman Leys
Conrad Noel
Ethel Mannin
James Maxton, M.P.
G. R. Mitchison

George Padmore
  (Chairman of
  International African
  Service Bureau)
Leslie Paul
  (Editor of "Plan")
Roger Pugh
Reginald Reynolds
F. A. Ridley
Henry Sara°
Mary Saran
H. Allen Skinner
Jack Tanner
  (A.E.U. Executive)
W. N. Warbey
  (N.C.L.C. District
  Organiser)
Wilfred Wellock
J. R. White
E. E. Williams
  (Chairman, Women's
  Co-op. Guild)
Tom Wintringham
Geraldine Young

1. In an 'S.O.S.' published alongside this letter was a statement signed by J. F. Horrabin and C. A. Smith, the editor, on behalf of the Editorial Committee, explaining the periodical's desperate case. There was urgent need for £150, two-thirds of which was required to pay off existing debts. If that amount were not raised by 31 October, there would not be a November issue. The journal did survive, becoming *Left Forum* in June 1939. See Orwell's letter to John Sceats, 24 November 1938, *504*.
2. Kerran supported David L. Wickes's application to serve in an ambulance unit in Spain; see *374A*.

491. To Leonard Moore

1 October 1938   Typewritten

Chez Madame Vellat Rue Edmond Doutte Marrakech French Morocco

Dear Mr Moore,

I wonder if there is any chance of getting anyone to print that pamphlet, "Socialism and War", that I sent you.¹ The present seems a suitable time for it. Possibly Warburg² might consider doing it if he ever goes in for pamphlets. I don't want any money for it. If anyone does print it, you might get them to add a note at the beginning stating that it was written in May 1938.

We have been here about a fortnight and are having a very interesting time. We are staying in the town another fortnight, then going to a small villa we are taking outside. The above address will find me for the time being and I'll give you the other one later. I am very well and have made a good start on my novel.[3] I'll be finished about March, I suppose. Thank goodness the war danger seems to be over, at any rate for the time being, so we can breathe again. For several days we had almost given up hope, though the people here were quite calm about it and apparently uninterested. It is still rather hot but I believe it gets quite chilly in the winter. This is an old Arab town with labyrinthine bazaars full of camels and donkeys, awful dirt and poverty everywhere, of course, but all very interesting. I'm taking notes of all I see and no doubt shall be able to write something on it when I get back.

Do you know how "Homage to Catalonia" sold? I suppose Warburg has had some returns by this time. It was boycotted in certain places but got very good reviews on the whole.

My wife sends all the best. I hope Miss Perriam is a bit better.[4]

Yours
Eric Blair

1. Sent from Preston Hall, Aylesford, on 28 June 1938. From the annotation made in Moore's office on the letter, Hogarth Press was suggested.
2. Warburg] *handwritten for typed* Seckker°
3. *Coming Up for Air*.
4. See Eileen's letter to Moore, 7 June 1938, *450*.

492. Marjorie Dakin to Eileen Blair and Orwell

3 October 1938   Typewritten

166 St. Michael's Hill   Bristol.

My dear Eileen and Eric,
Thanks very much for your letters, and the £1 enclosed. Marx is being perfectly good except for such natural wickedness as will never be eradicated. He is very obedient out of doors, and comes directly when called, also is learning to keep on pavements, as we let him off the leash in quiet roads to train him. He has simply terrific games with the children, especially on the downs. A sword of Damocles has been hanging over his head, he was threatened with being made into sausages if there was a food shortage, also Tor, though he is getting a bit tough.

As you will have gathered there has been complete wind-up about war, everybody thought it had really come this time, as indeed it may yet. All preparations are being pushed on just the same. I took the children down to get their gas-masks the other day, not that I have much faith in them, but still it is the correct thing to do. I have heard that the A.R.P. is a farce so far, if there was a really bad bombing raid, there would be practically nobody who knew what to do.[1] I also heard that all the warning that Bristol would get would be four minutes, and London only 25 seconds, but I don't know if this is true.[2] If it is it hardly seems worth while to do anything, as I don't see myself getting the children into gasmasks and shelter in four minutes.

Humph has been transferred pro. tem. into the Ministry of Transport, and has been sent off to Salisbury, but I imagine he will be back quite soon now. As far as he could make out all the high officials in London (in transport) moved out in a body to the south of England with their wives and families. The head man took over the Truro district. Humph as the only outsider was given Salisbury, it being the most dangerous place.

Everything here was perfectly calm, no meetings of any kind. All the parks and gardens have been dug up into shelters, and England is swept clean of corrugated iron and sand bags. I believe the grocers have done a roaring trade "better than Christmas". I didn't go in for a food hoarding myself, except to buy a sack of potatoes, which the grocer offered me.

Devon and Cornwall are simply packed, there is not a house or rooms to be had for love or money, people who went up to London on friday° said it was practically empty, Hyde Park and Kensington Gardens have miles of trenches in them. The bill has now to be paid.

I hope Chamberlain rounds off the thing properly, and offers to give back Germany her mandated colonies, also tries to do something about removing tariffs. Otherwise I think we shall have everything to be ashamed of, in saving our skins at the expense of the Czechs. But I bet he won't. It looks as if poor France has had a kick in the pants, to be vulgar, agreements being signed without reference to her. Personally I think there is going to be a most awful row over the whole thing, when the hysteria has died down a bit. One school of thought says that we shall not be ready for war for another two years and that the Govt. will do anything to put it off till then,[3] others, that now that the great ones of the earth realise that it is really going to be a 'free for all' and that is not just a case of "giving" one's son it puts a different complexion on things.

I think if there is another war, I shall have Humph in a lunatic asylum in two twos,[4] his nerves are in an awful state, I was really quite glad when he went off to Salisbury poor dear, as he was adding to the horrors of the situation very considerably and of course the children[5] didn't care two hoots, and were enjoying the whole thing, Hen went round and really had his fill of looking at searchlights and machine guns, and Jane was perfectly indifferent, except that she hoped they wouldn't turn the Art School into a Hospital.

My heart goes out to you over the four foot tray, I have one of the same ilk, but I had a trestle made to go under it and use it as [a] table. I have had some pretty B.[6] furniture landed on me from Dr. Dakin's[7] house, things I have loathed from my childhood, but I am hoping to be able to discreetly jettison them soon. Excuse typing faults, I am doggedly practising on all my friends and relations.

Have you read any books by a man called R. C. Hutchinson.[8]

I have just read a book of his called "Shining Scabbard" which I thought was awfully good. I believe his latest one "Testament" is even better.

Thanks very much for the offer of the cottage, but if things become really desperate, I expect we should try to get up to Middlesmoor, the cottage there is still furnished, a friend of mine took it over, and I daresay we could all fit in, as it is a magic cottage, and will hold an unlimited amount of people.

Best love to you both
Marge.

1. In January 1938 the government decreed that children be issued gas masks and in April 1938 the rest of the population be measured for them, many months before the Munich crisis.
2. It was not correct: there was invariably adequate time to seek shelter.
3. This was a reasonable approximation of the position.
4. In the 1930s this meant the brief time necessary to add dabs of rouge and powder to each cheek before dashing out. In the nineteenth century it referred to an overrouged overpowdered street woman.
5. Marjorie and Humphrey Dakin had three children: Jane, born 1923; Henry, 1925; and Lucy, 1930.
6. Bloody.
7. Humphrey's father. Both served in World War I, and were on the Somme together. Humphrey was wounded and lost an eye. His father, who was a captain in the Royal Army Medical Corps, patched him up.
8. Ray Coryton Hutchinson (1907–1975). *Shining Scabbard* was published in 1936 and *Testament* had just appeared.

493. Eileen Blair to Geoffrey Gorer

4 October 1938   Handwritten

chez° Mme. Vellat, rue Edmond Doutte,
Medina, Marrakech, French Morocco.

Dear Geoffrey,
Your letter has just arrived. Of course *we* are blameworthy. I thought Eric had written to you & now I see he can't have done so. For myself I don't remember the last few weeks in England except that they were spent almost entirely in trains. People had to be said good-bye to & things (including Eric) collected from all over the country & the cottage had to be handed over furnished but nakedly to the Commons who are spending the winter there & mustering the goats etc. We were thrust out of England very hurriedly partly in case war broke out & partly because Eric was getting rebellious & I had rebelled. As it turns out this was rather a pity. Marrakech is the dernier cri of fashionable medicine. Certainly it is dry. They've had three years' drought, including 17 months entirely without rain. But the climate doesn't get tolerable in any year until the end of September & this year the hot weather still persists. We are both choosing our shrouds (the Arabs favour bright green & don't have coffins which is nice on funeral days for the flies who leave even a restaurant for a few minutes to sample a passing corpse), but have now chosen instead a villa. It's in the middle of an orange-grove in the palm-tree country at the foot of the Atlas from which the good air comes. I think Eric really will benefit when we get there but it isn't available until the 15th. We've bought the furniture—for about £10. I've only seen the place once for five minutes & I

wasn't allowed to open the shutters & there was no artificial light, but I believe it could be very attractive. Garnished with us & our ten pounds' worth it may be odd to the eye but will be comforting to the spirit. We shall even have goats who will be physically as well as emotionally important because fresh milk is otherwise unobtainable. It's five kilometres from Marrakech.

Do you know Morocco? We found it a most desolate country—miles & miles of ground that is not technically desert, i.e. it could be cultivated if it were irrigated but without water is simply earth & stones in about equal proportions with not even a weed growing. We got all excited the other day because we found a dock. The villa is in one of the more fertile bits. Marrakech itself is beautiful in bits. It has ramparts & a lot of buildings made of earth dug up about five feet below ground level. This dries a soft reddish colour so the French call Marrakech 'la rouge' & paint everything that isn't earth a dreadful salmon-beige. The best thing is the native pottery. Unfortunately it generally isn't glazed (except some bits painted in frightful designs for the tourist trade) but we're trying to get some things made watertight. There are exquisite white clay mugs with a very simple black design inside. They cost a franc & it seems to us that people here generally earn about a franc to two francs an hour.

Eric is going to write to you & I shall leave him the crisis. I am determined to be pleased with Chamberlain because I want a rest. Anyway Czecho-Slovakia ought to be pleased with him; it seems geographically certain that that country would be ravaged at the beginning of any war fought in its defence. But of course the English Left is always Spartan; they're fighting Franco to the last Spaniard too.

I hope the old book & the new go well.[1] Are you going to America? If you happen to come to the south of Europe, call on us. It isn't very difficult—indeed there's an air service from Tangier—& we have a spare room (quite spare I should say, not even furniture in it) & we could go & look at the country on donkeys & possibly at the desert on camels, & we should enjoy it very much.

I'd better send love from us both in case Eric's letter gets delayed. He has begun his novel[2] & is also carpentering—there is a box for the goats to eat out of & a hutch for the chickens though we have no goat yet & no chickens.

Yours ever
Eileen.

The villa is not in any postal district & I think we have to have a 'box'. We'll let you know the proper address when we discover it.

1. Probably *Hot Strip Tease and Other Notes on American Culture* (1937) and *Himalayan Village: An Account of the Lepchas of Sikkim* (1938; U.S., 1967).
2. *Coming Up for Air.*

494. Morocco Diary

MARRAKECH 9.10.38:
The other daily paper sometimes obtainable is *Maroc Matin*, illustrated, Casablanca. Much more left wing than the others. Poor paper and print, evidently not prosperous and not much in evidence, in fact seldom obtainable.

After the crisis was over everyone here showed great relief and was much less stolid about it than they had been during the trouble itself. Educated Frenchwoman in official position, known to us personally, writes letter of congratulation to Daladier. It is perfectly evident from the tone of the press that even in the big towns where there is a white proletariat there was not the smallest enthusiasm for the idea of going to war for the sake of Czechoslovakia.

I was wrong in thinking the brass-work etc. was done exclusively by Jews. Actually Jews and Arabs seem to do much the same class of work. Much of the work of making wooden ploughs, wooden spoons, brass and copper utensils, and even some classes of blacksmithing, is done by very young children. Children certainly not older than 6 work at some of the simpler parts of these jobs. Children of about 8-10 work with adze and chisel, very diligently and with great skill. Children almost too young to stand are set to such jobs as keeping flies off piles of fruit. Arab woodwork, though rather rough and done with extremely primitive tools, is quite good, but they seem almost always to use unseasoned wood, which of course is liable to warp. Shafts for ploughs are cut straight out of green boughs. This is presumably due to lack of capital and storage space. It is also evident that peasants have to buy a new plough every year.

Women servants receive less than men. Madame V. pays her cook-general Aicha Frs. 6.50 a day, but it appears that Frs. 5 is more usual, and in some cases Frs. 3.50 or even 3. In no case would the servant getting these wages receive any food or lodging. A. is an extremely good plain cook who in England would be considered worth £50 a year and her keep.[1]

Most riding and baggage animals here are exceedingly cheap. The following prices quoted at the Bab el Khemis animal fair (some of these subject to reduction if one bargained). Full-grown but smallish camel Frs. 300. Riding horse, 15-16 hands, apparently good, Frs. 275. Donkeys Frs. 75-150. Cow in milk Frs. 650. Mules Frs. 250-1000. * High price of mules is due to their being ridden by rich men, the mule being in fact the badge of wealth. Goats (very poor) 30-50 Frs.[2]

Immense prevalence of blindness here. In some of the poorest quarters it is possible to pass three or four blind people in 50 yards. A few of the blind beggars are probably impostors, but the main cause is no doubt the flies which which° every child's eyes are constantly crusted. Curiously enough children below a certain age, say 5, appear not to notice the flies.

* 10% tax paid by purchaser on each sale [Orwell's note].

The Arab women, though almost invariably veiled, are anything but shy, do not object to going about alone and in quarrels, bargaining etc. do not seem at all inhibited by their veils. Arabs seem to attach less importance than most orientals to touching and being touched. Arab men often go about hand in hand, and sometimes hand in hand with a woman (unthinkable in some oriental races.) In the buses mild flirtations between Arab women and European men. The Mahometan rules about not drinking seem to be strictly kept and drunkenness unheard of. On the other hand there is much smoking of a sort of drug called kiff, which is at any rate supposed to have narcotic effects, It is said to [be] illegal but is obtainable everywhere. No Europeans are admitted to the mosques here.

The French authorities enrol a sort of special constables,° a force known as the surete,° who are armed with truncheons and called out when criminals are to be rounded up. I have not yet got reliable particulars but it appears that either these or the regular police can summarily order flogging of thieves etc. and that savage floggings are administered without trial.

Have seen a good many of the Foreign Legion. Do not look very dangerous ruffians. Almost universally poor physique. Uniforms even worse than those of the conscripts.

Offical advertisement of post for girl teacher of native girls in state school, teacher evidently expected to be daughter of army officer or something of the kind, wage to be Frs. 900 a month (about 25/– a week.)

French film "Legion d'Honneur", propaganda film corresponding to 'Bengal Lancer', dealing with the French Sahara. Certain social differences interesting. French officer speaks to Touareg tribesmen largely through interpreter. Calling for two men for special duty he refers to them by their numbers instead of their names. Officers (represented as more or less aristocratic) smoke cigars with bands on and wear uniform off duty, eg. on ship going home.

On getting the English newspapers of the period of the crisis, it was evident that the local French press had systematically minimised the whole thing, for obvious reasons.

In the bazaar a tiny screw of tea (green China tea, of which the Arabs drink a great deal), perhaps ¼ to ½ oz., and about 1 oz. of sugar, can be bought for 25[3] *centimes. Utterly impossible to buy things in such quantities in most European countries. Price of a cup of water 1 sou. This may be taken as meaning that the sou has no other purchasing power.*

Have not yet seen a single sign of any hostility towards Europeans as such, of the kind one is constantly seeing in an Indian city.

1. If she worked a seven-day week, Aicha would have been paid Frs. 45 a week; £50 a year was about Frs. 170 a week.
2. 'Goats' to 'Frs.' is handwritten by Orwell.
3. '2c' typed; '25' is marginal emendation.

495. To Leonard Moore

11 October 1938   Handwritten

> Chez Madame Vellat   Rue Edmond Doutte   Medinah
> Marrakech   Fr. Morocco

Dear Mr Moore,
Many thanks for your letter which I've just received. You say in it:
"Verbally from Warburg I learn that there are about 700 copies of H. to C. sold to date. . . . That, I think, in all the circumstances is very good."
Was it really 700?[1] I ask because it seems to me that 700 would be a terribly bad sale & incidentally would mean a heavy loss for Warburg, & it struck me that it may have been a typist's error.
Hope all goes well & trust Miss Perriam is improving. I'll let you have our permanent address when we make quite sure what it is, but meanwhile the above will find us.

> Your sincerely
> Eric Blair

1. Only 683 copies were sold in the six months after publication on 25 April 1938. Someone in Moore's office evidently checked the sales figures; at the head of the letter is written 'Ask Warburg again,' which is crossed out.

496. To Jack Common

12 October 1938   Typewritten

> Chez Madame Vellat   Rue Edmond Doutte   Medinah
> Marrakech   French Morocco

Dear Jack,
Thanks for yours. There were several important items I wanted to talk to you about but they were chased out of my mind by the European situation. The first is, I think we forgot to warn you not to use thick paper in the WC. It sometimes chokes the cesspool up, with disastrous results. The best to use is Jeyes paper which is 6d a packet. The difference of price is negligible, and on the other hand a choked cesspool is a misery. Secondly, if you find the sitting room fire smokes intolerably, I think you can get a piece of tin put in the chimney, which is what it needs, for a very small sum. Brookers in Hitchin would tell you all about it. Or you could probably do it yourself. I was always meaning to but put it off. Thirdly, I enclose cheque for £3. Could you some time get this cashed and pay £2 to Field, the postmaster at Sandon, for the rent of the field. It's a lot overdue as a matter of fact but F. never remembers about it. Field goes past in his grey car, which he uses to carry cattle in, every Tuesday on his way to Hitchin Market, and one can sometimes stop him if one jumps into the middle of the road and waves. As to the remaining £1, could you some time in the winter get some or, if possible, all of the ground in the vegetable garden dug over? Old H.[1] is getting so old that I don't really

like asking him to do that kind of work, but he's always glad of it and, of course, willing to work for very low rates. There's no hurry, it's just a question of getting the vacant ground turned over some time in the winter and preferably some manure (the goat's stuff is quite good if there isn't too much straw in it) dug in. The official theory is that we are to give up the cottage next spring, so I suppose on good business principles one ought to exhaust the soil by taking an enormous crop of Brussels off it and then let it go to hell. But I hate starving soil and in addition I'm not so certain of giving up the cottage. As I expect you've discovered by this time it's truly a case of be it never so humble, but the fact is that it's a roof and moving is so damned expensive besides being a misery. I think I would rather feel I had the cottage there to move into next April, even if when the time comes we don't actually do it, because I don't know what my financial situation will be next year. I don't believe my book on Spain sold at all, and if I have to come back to England and start on yet another book with about £50 in the world I would rather have a roof over my head from the start. It's a great thing to have a roof over your head even if it's a leaky one. When Eileen and I were first married, when I was writing "Wigan Pier", we had so little money that sometimes we hardly knew where the next meal was coming from, but we found we could rub along in a remarkable manner with spuds and so forth. I hope the hens have begun laying. Some of them have by this time, I expect, at any rate they ought to. We've just bought the hens for our house, which we're moving into on Saturday. The hens in this country are miserable little things like the Indian ones, about the size of bantams, and what is regarded as a good laying hen, ie. it lays once a fortnight, costs less than a shilling. They ought only to cost about 6d, but at this time of year the price goes up because after Yom Kippur every Jew, of whom there are 13000 in this town, eats a whole fowl to recompense him for the strain of fasting 12 hours.

Well, the mortal moon hath her eclipse endured till 1941, I suppose. I don't think one need be surprised at Chamberlain's stock slumping a bit after the danger is over. Judging from the letters I get from home I should say people feel as you feel when you are just going to dive off the springboard and then think better of it. The real point is what will happen at the election, and unless the Conservative Party splits right up I prophecy they will win hands down. Because the other bloody fools can't produce any policy except "We want war", and however ashamed people may feel *after* we've let down Czechoslovakia, or whoever it may be, they'll shy away from war when it comes to a show-down. The only hope of Labour getting in is for some downright disaster to happen, or alternatively, for the elections to be held a year hence with another million unemployed. I think now we're in for a period of slow fascisation,° the sort of Dollfuss-Schussnig Fascism[2] which is what Chamberlain and co would presumably introduce, but I would sooner have that than have the Left parties identified in the public mind as the war party. The only hope is that if Chamberlain wins and then begins seriously to prepare for war with Germany, as of course he will, the L.P.[3] will be driven back to an anti-war policy in which they will be able to exploit the discontent with conscription etc. The policy of simultaneously shouting for a war policy and pretending to denounce conscription, rearmament etc. is utter nonsense and the general public aren't such bloody fools as not to see it. As to the results if war comes, although *some* kind of revolutionary situation will no doubt arise, I do not see how it can lead to anything except Fascism *unless* the Left has been anti-war from the outset. I have nothing but contempt for the fools who think that they can first drive the nation into a war for democracy and then when people are a bit fed up suddenly turn round and say "Now we'll have the revolution." What sickens me about left-wing people, especially the intellectuals, is their utter ignorance of the way things actually happen. I was always struck by this when I was in Burma and used to read anti-imperialist stuff. Did you see Kingsley Martin's[4] ("Critic") article in last week's N.S. about the conditions on which the L.P. should support the Government in war. As though the Government would allow any conditions. The bloody fool seems to think war is a cricket match. I wish someone would print my anti-war pamphlet I wrote earlier this year,[5] but of course no one will.

All the best. Love to Mary and Peter. E. sends love.

Yours
Eric

P.S. [handwritten at top of first page] This address will find us.

1. Hatchett, a neighbour at Wallington.
2. Engelbert Dollfuss (1892–1934) was Chancellor of Austria, 1932–34. He was largely responsible for the establishment of a quasi-fascist regime on the Italian pattern, which brought to an end parliamentary government in Austria, not without bloodshed. He was assassinated by members of the Nazi Party. Kurt von Schuschnigg (1897–1977), Austrian Minister of Justice and then of Education, became chancellor after the assassination of Dollfuss and attempted to maintain Austria's independence. After annexation by Germany in 1938, he was imprisoned until the end of World War II. See his *The Brutal Takeover* (1969).
3. Labour Party.
4. Basil Kingsley Martin (1897–1969), left-wing writer and journalist, was editor of *The New Statesman and Nation*, 1931–60. See headnote to Orwell's letter to Raymond Mortimer, 9 February 1938, *424*, and also *1209, n. 3*.
5. 'Socialism and War'; see letters to Moore, 28 June and 28 November 1938, *458, 506*.

497. To Raymond Postgate

21 October 1938   Typewritten draft

Boite[1] Postale 48   Gueliz   Marrakech   French Morocco

Dear Mr Postgate,[2]

You may perhaps remember meeting me once at a party of Warburg's. You also wrote to me once about a book of mine, a letter that never got answered because I was in Spain at the time.

The trial of the Executive Committee of the P.O.U.M., which the Spanish Government has been postponing for about[3] sixteen months, has just begun, and from such reports as I can obtain here I see that, as was to be expected, they are being accused of things which everyone with any knowledge of the facts knows to be untrue. I do not think that we can assume as yet that they will not get a fair trial, and obviously we have no right to obstruct or interfere with the Spanish Government even if we were able to do so. But at the same time in the French press (and I have no doubt it will be the same in the English) all kinds of untruthful statements are being made and it is extremely difficult to get an opportunity of answering them. I expect you have some inner knowledge of this affair and are aware that the accusations against the P.O.U.M. in Spain are only a by-product of the Russian Trotskyist trials and that from the start every kind of lie, including flagrant absurdities, has been circulated in the Communist press. It has been almost impossible to answer these because the Communist press, naturally, does not publish letters from opponents and the rest of the left-wing press has been held back by a desire not to embarrass the Spanish Government. At the same time it is difficult to see what good is done by malicious lies directed against innocent people. The accusation (which seems to be fully accepted by the French press of this country – pro-Franco, by the way) which especially troubles me is that the 29th division (the P.O.U.M. troops) deserted from the Aragon front. Everyone with any knowledge of the facts, including those who make the accusation, knows that this is a lie. I myself served with the 29th division from December 30 1936 to May 20 1937, and the I.L.P. could give you the addresses of from ten to twenty other Englishmen, some of whom remained at the front a good deal longer than I did—this in addition to the thousands of Spaniards who could contradict the story. This cowardly libel against brave men can only be circulated because of the perhaps well-meaning refusal of the left-wing press to have this affair properly ventilated.

If this accusation is also flung about in the English press, and any opportunity of contradicting it arises, could you not lend your weight to it? Any statement from such a person as yourself would come much better than from anyone like me, who am obviously a prejudiced witness. The I.L.P. can give you all the details of the affair. You would be perfectly safe in saying that you know on good authority that all the stories of desertion, collaboration with the enemy etc. are untrue.

I enclose a summary of an article from La Fleche° giving the views of various members of the Spanish Government on the case. So far as I know it contains no inaccuracies. In any case Maxton and others can verify. Even if you cannot see your way to doing anything about this, please forgive me for writing.

Yours sincerely
[Not signed]

Orwell made two copies of this summary from *La Flèche*:

Summary of article in "La Fleche" of October 14 1938, by L-P. Foucaud.

The act of accusation against the P.O.U.M. repeats the charge of espionage formulated by the Communist press. On this subject two international delegations have obtained statements from the principal members of the Spanish Government.

To the first delegation, composed of Fenner Brockway, general secretary of the I.L.P., Charles Wolff and R. Louzon, editor of "La Revolution Proletarienne":

M. Irujo, Minister of Justice, declared: "That the accusations of espionnage° brought against the P.O.U.M. were not founded on any fact that could be taken seriously" (aucun fait serieux).

M. Miratvilles, general secretary of the Department of Propaganda of the Catalan Generalite, declared: "That the 'Golfin' document* was for him and for President Companys a forgery so obvious that at the moment when it was presented to him, he burst into such a shout of laughter that no one dared make use of it any longer."

M. Largo Caballero stated: "That if at present the P.O.U.M. was being prosecuted for espionage, this was solely for political reasons and because the Communist Party wished the P.O.U.M. to be suppressed."

To a second delegation, composee° of Mr Maxton, M.P., M. Weill-Curiel, M. Yves Levy and M. L-P. Foucaud, various Spanish ministers made similar declarations.

M. Irujo, at 12 o'clock on the 20 August 1937 at the Ministry of Justice in Valencia, stated: "That there was no proof of espionage against the P.O.U.M. and that the 'Golfin' document was valueless."

M. Ortega y Gasset expressed his disbelief in the P.O.U.M. leaders being Fascist spies. M. Prieto, then Minister of War, received the delegation on August 23 1937. Not having seen the dossier, he refused to speak of the accusation of espionage, but added that: "The arrest of the P.O.U.M. leaders had not been decided by the Government, but by the police, which the Communists had infiltrated (noyautée) according to their usual custom."

All these statements, in particular Prieto's, can be obtained in the report on the Maxton delegation published by "Independent News." In addition there is the pamphlet "Terror in Spain" by Mr John McGovern M.P., dealing with a later delegation and confirming the above.

The fate of this draft is given in Orwell's own handwritten note at the head of the letter:

Draft of letter sent to Raymond Postgate at the time of POUM trial. Similar letters sent to J. F. Horrabin & C. E. M. Joad.[4] All, of course, unable to do anything, but all answered sympathetically & appeared to accept my version. R. P. offered to give part of "Fact"[5] to publicity about the 29th division if J. McNair[6] supplied the facts.

---

* Generally referred to in the English press as 'the N document' [Orwell's note]. See *462, n. 3* for brief details.

On 14 November 1938, a letter by the General Secretary of the ILP, Fenner Brockway,[7] was published in the *Manchester Guardian*. This summarised a full report of the trial. He stated that the charge of espionage made against the prisoners 'completely collapsed during the trial' and was dropped by the prosecution. The charge that the POUM divisions 'had deserted the front was also dropped.' Whatever the rights and wrongs of the final indictment (that members of the POUM 'had joined the uprising provoked by rebellious elements in Barcelona in May, 1937'), that was the only charge upon which anyone was found guilty. Four prisoners were sentenced to fifteen years' internment and one to eleven years'. Thus, he concluded, 'the accusations against the P.O.U.M. of Fascist espionage and desertion at the front, which have been spread throughout the world by the Communist International and some of its innocent allies, have been shown to have no basis in fact.' Full accounts of those accused, the trial, the dropping of the principal charges, and the sentences for involvement in the May Events of Barcelona are given in various issues of *The New Leader*; see, for instance, 21 October, 4 and 11 November 1938. The accused sentenced to eleven years' imprisonment was Jordi Arquer, to whom Orwell had Leonard Moore send a copy of the Italian translation of *Homage to Catalonia* (published in December 1948); see *3651*.

1. Orwell regularly omits the circumflex over the 'i' of 'Boite'; 'Boite' = maturity; 'Boîte' = (post)box.
2. Raymond Postgate (1896–1971) edited *Tribune*, 1940–42 (to which Orwell contributed). Among his best-known books was *The Common People, 1746–1938* (1938), written in collaboration with G. D. H. Cole. He also wrote on food and wine. Cole (1889–1959) was an economist and novelist whose writing on economics was often effectively directed to the general reader—for example, *The Intelligent Man's Guide Through World Chaos* (1932) and *What Everybody Wants to Know About Money* (1933).
3. 'some time' was typed before 'about' but was crossed out.
4. J. F. Horrabin was a journalist, illustrator, Labour M.P., 1929–31, and a member of the editorial board of *Controversy*. See *952, n. 1*. C. E. M. Joad (1891–1953) was a philosopher and writer. He achieved particular fame as a member of the team of the BBC's radio programme 'The Brains Trust.' From 1930 until his death, he was head of the Department of Psychology and Philosophy, Birkbeck College, University of London.
5. *Fact*, subtitled *A Monograph a Month*, was published, in twenty-seven issues, from April 1937 to June 1939.
6. John McNair, the Independent Labour Party's representative in Spain; see *363, n. 5*.
7. For Fenner Brockway, see *363, n. 4*, and *428*.

498. To John Sceats

26 October 1938   Typewritten

Boite° Postale 48   Gueliz   Marrakech   French Morocco

Dear Sceats,[1]

I hope all goes well with you. I had meant to look you up before leaving England, but as it turned out I went almost straight from the sanatorium to the boat and only had one day in London, which of course was pretty full. I'm writing to you now for some expert advice. The chap in the novel I'm writing is supposed to be an insurance agent. His job isn't in the least important to the story, I merely wanted him to be a typical middle-aged bloke with about £5 a week and a house in the suburbs, and he's also rather thoughtful and fairly well-educated, even slightly bookish, which is more plausible with an insurance agent than, say, a commercial traveller. But I want any mention that is made of his job to be correct. And meanwhile I have only very vague ideas as to what an insurance agent does. I want him to be a chap who travels round and gets part of his income from commissions, not merely an office employee. Does such a chap have a "district" and a regular round like a commercial traveller? Does he have to go touting round for orders, or just go round and sign the people up when they want to be insured? Would he spend all his time in travelling or part of it in the office? Would he have an office of his own? Do the big insurance companies have branch offices all over the place (this chap lives in a suburb which might be Hayes or Southall) or do they only have the head office and send all the agents out from there? And would such a man do valuations of property, and would the same man do life insurance and property insurance? I'd be very glad of some elucidation on these points. My picture of this chap is this. He spends about two days a week in the branch office in his suburb and the rest of the time in travelling round in a car over a district of about half a county, interviewing people who've written in to say that they want to be insured, making valuations of houses, stock and so forth, and also touting for orders on which he gets an extra commission, and that by this he is earning round about £5 a week after being with the firm 18 years (having started very much at the bottom). I want to know if this is plausible.

Well, "The mortal moon hath her eclipse endured and the sad augurs mock their own presage"[2] and some of them are very sad indeed to judge by the New Statesman. However, I suppose they'll get the war they're longing for in about two years. The real attitude of the governing class to this business is summed up in the remark I overheard from one of the Gibraltar garrison the moment I set foot there: "It's pretty clear Hitler's going to have Czechoslovakia. Much better let him have it. We shall be ready in 1941." Meanwhile the net result will be a sweeping win for the Conservatives at the General Election. I judge from letters from more or less conservative relatives at home that now that it is all over people are a bit fed up and saying "What a pity we didn't hold on a bit longer and Hitler would have backed down." And from this the bloody fools of the L.P. infer that after all the English people *do* want another war to make the world safe for democracy and that their best line is to exploit the anti-fascist stuff. They don't seem to see that the election will revive the spirit of the crisis, the word will be Chamberlain and Peace, and if the L.P. go round saying "We want war", which is how ordinary people, quite rightly, interpret the firm line with Hitler stuff, they will just be eaten up. I think a lot of people in the last two years have been misled by phenomena like the Left Book Club. Here you have about 50,000 people who are willing to make a noise about Spain, China etc., and because the majority of people are normally silent this gives the impression that the Left Bookmongers are the voice of the nation instead of being a tiny minority. No one seems to reflect that what matters is not what a few people say when all is quiet but what the majority do in moments of crisis. The only hope is that if the L.P. gets a knock at the election, as it's almost certain to do, this will gradually force them back to their proper policy. But I am afraid it may be a year or two years before this happens.

I've got to go down to a meal that's getting cold, so au revoir. I'd be enormously obliged if you'd let me know about those points some time, but there's no immediate hurry.

Yours
Eric Blair

1. John Sceats (1912–), an insurance agent, had written articles for the socialist monthly *Controversy*. Orwell had admired these and invited Sceats to visit him at Preston Hall in 1938. In a letter to Malcolm Muggeridge, 24 April 1955, Sceats described this, their only, meeting, probably in May or June 1938, since it was shortly after *Homage to Catalonia* was published (25 April): 'We talked chiefly of politics and philosophy. I remember he said he thought "Burmese Days" his best book (excluding, sans dire, the latest). At the time he was reading Kafka. Despite his recent association with POUM, he had already decided he was not a Marxist, and he was more than interested in the philosophy of Anarchism. As he saw things then, it was a matter of months before either Fascism or War landed him in the Concentration Camp (British); whatever the future held he could not believe it would allow him to go on writing. He was of course anti-Nazi, but could not (at the time) stomach the idea of an anti-German war: in fact, talking to Max Plowman (who called in the afternoon) he implied that he would join him in opposition to such a war with whatever underground measures might be appropriate.' Sceats marked the last sentence with an asterisk and added a footnote: 'Indeed, it was Max who put the views of common sense.' For Plowman, see 95 and 418, *n. 4*.
2. Shakespeare, Sonnet 107; quoted in part in *496*.

499. To his mother

29 October 1938　　　Handwritten postcard

Boite° Postale 48　Gueliz　Marrakech　French Morocco

[No salutation]

Thanks so much for your last letter. I hope the slight improvement you spoke about in Father is continuing. In case our last p.c. didn't get to you, the above is the safest postal address to find us.

Love to all
Eric

500. Morocco Diary

VILLA SIMONT, ROUTE DE CASABLANCA　1.11.38:

Cannot yet get any definite idea as to the land system here. All the land round here is either cultivated or what passes as cultivable, except for a few spurs of hills. We are just within the edge of the huge palm plantation which runs round the northern side of Marrakech and must be thousands of acres. The land between the palm trees is mostly cultivated the same as the fields. But there are no or very few boundaries and I cannot find out whether the peasants own their own plots or rent it, whether everyone owns a plot, and whether any land is owned communally. I suspect that some must be, as the fields lying fallow count as pasture for the sake of the few patches of weeds growing on them, and the flocks of sheep and goats are grazed everywhere. Possibly there are private plots for cultivation but common grazing rights. The palms grow in a completely haphazard way and it is difficult to believe that they can be privately owned. Immediately round our house it is an area mainly of vegetable and fruit gardens. There appear to be some peasants who cultivate fairly considerable plots and keep them in fairly good order. There are also large and well-ordered market gardens, generally walled off and owned by Europeans or rich Arabs—generally the latter, I think. Contrasting their ground with that of the ordinary peasants, one sees the enormous difference made here by having the capital to run water conduits.

Ploughing is now going on everywhere after the recent heavy rain. From the size of the plots evidently for some cereal crop. Here and there a little wheat or some other grain coming up, presumably winter wheat sown at much the same time as in England. The local plough is a wretched thing made entirely of wood except for the share, which is merely a kind of iron point fitted over a wooden bar. The whole apparatus can easily be carried on one's shoulder. The share stirs the ground about 4" to 6" deep, and presumably most of the soil is never cultivated deeper than this. Nevertheless some of it does not look bad, and in places, eg. the orange grove round our house, it is extremely deep, about 4 feet (ie. the top-soil.) The lack of a wheel on the plough makes it much harder for the men and beasts and almost impossible to plough straight furrows. Oxen are mostly used, but also all the other beasts except camels, and an ox and a donkey sometimes yoked together. Should say a yoke of oxen could plough about half an acre in a day.

Chief crops round here: palms, olives, pomegranates, maize, chilis,° lucerne, most of the European vegetables (beans, cabbages, tomatoes, marrows, pumpkins, peas, radishes[1]), brinjals, oranges, and some cereals, I do not yet know which. Oranges seem chiefly grown by Europeans, also lemons. Pomegranates are about over, dates coming to an end. I fancy that lucerne, which grows quickly and is cropped when about a foot high, is grown all the year round. It is the principal fodder here and is sold[2] at 10 c. for a bundle about 3" thick. Maize, used for fodder, probably also grown all the year round, and most of the vegetables. Quality of most of the plants very poor, owing no doubt to poor soil and still more to lack of capital for equipment. Eg. tomatoes are grown without sticks and are wretched plants. Of the animals, the sheep seem to do best on the miserable pasture, and besides making quite good mutton have excellent fleeces. Most of the other animals wretched, and no milk-yielding animals have udders of any size on them. A good class Spanish goat costs almost the same as a cow, which gives one a hint of the latter's milking qualities. Fowls are like the Indian fowl. All animals abominably treated but astonishingly docile. Tools are extremely primitive. No spades or European forks, only hoes of the Indian style. Cultivation is made much more laborious by the lack of water, because every field has to be

partitioned off into tiny plots with earth banks between, to conserve water.
Not only small children but very old women work in the fields, women who
must be at least 60, probably 70, clearing roots etc. with pick-axes.
The typical Arab village is a large enclosure with high mud walls, which
looks like one huge house. Inside are the usual miserable huts, mostly of
straw or palm thatch, shaped like beehives, about eight feet wide and seven
high. All the people round here seem to fear robbers and like to feel
themselves shut in at night. Except in the temporary field huts used for
watching ripe crops, no one sleeps outside the enclosure of the village.
Have not yet got to the bottom of the reason for the very high price of cereals.
Eg. in the market a decalitre of wheat, weighing about 40 lb. costs Frs. 30 or
over 1d a pound even in English money. Bread is correspondingly expensive.
(Last month price of wheat officially fixed at Frs. 158 the quintal. See cutting
V.M. [3] 9.10.38.)
Ramadan has begun. The Arabs here seem fairly strict about their obser-
vances, but I gather they sometimes eat forbidden things, eg. I suspect they
will sometimes eat an animal that has died a natural death. Our servant and
M. S's caretaker thought it all right to eat a fowl pecked to death by the
others. They appear to be strict about not drinking. [4]
Troops often passing on their way to the rifle range nearby. They look pretty
good, spirits very good and marching style better than I had expected, better
than ordinary French conscripts. Harold Maral, who did his military service
in the Zouaves, says the latter are largely Algerian Jews and greatly looked
down on by other regiments. I gather that in Morocco proper Jews are not
recruited. One meets everywhere here with signs of hostility to Jews, not
only among Arabs but also Europeans. Jews are said to undercut, cheat, take
other people's jobs etc., etc. (See cutting P.M. [5] 18.10.38).

1. In the margin is a note in Orwell's hand, with no indication of where it fits: *'potatoes (poor).'*
2. *Sold*] used
3. *La Vigie Marocaine*, a local newspaper.
4. Marginal note in Orwell's hand (though not precisely related to this paragraph): *'M. also eats*
   left-over scraps from our table.' Eating such scraps is forbidden during Ramadan. M. stands
   for Mahdjoub Mahommed, 'our servant'; see *502*.
5. *Le Petit Marocain*, a Casablanca daily morning newspaper.

501. To Jack Common

2 November 1938   Handwritten

Boite° Postale 48   Gueliz   Marrakech   French Morocco

Dear Jack,
Thanks for yours. I am handwriting this as Eileen has the typewriter. I'm
sorry about the hens, but I suppose they *must* lay soon. I don't think the cock
makes any difference. At any rate it's common knowledge that he makes no
difference when they *are* laying, though I suppose conceivably they start

more readily when there's a cock. As to Muriel's[1] winter feed. The chief difference is that she must have hay after the grass ends, ie. about end of October. I used to find a truss of meadow hay lasts 2 goats 3 weeks, so should last M., who is a hearty eater, say 5. It's best to give it several times a day in small quantities, as they are very wasteful with it, tear it out of the manger & shy it on the floor, after which they won't eat it.

The other thing is green stuff. After October there's no good in the grass, though on fine days I generally peg a goat out to get the air. But a thing that does stay green & which goats love is ivy. One can sometimes cut a strand of it out of the hedge & hang it up in the stable. Ditto if there are any run-to-seed cabbages etc. about. I used to hang them on a meat-hook you'll find in the shed, because the goat eats them best & wastes least that way. They should never have more than a little cabbage as it gives them diarrhea. As to hard food, I don't know that it varies much summer or winter, it's mainly a question of whether the goat's in milk. I expect you've discovered that the more fattening food, eg. flaked maize, the more milk, while oats etc. keeps the strength up. I don't know if there were any runner or other beans in the garden. If there were, there are always some foods which ripen & dry up on the plant. These, especially broad beans, are very good. I used to just shell a few pods each time I fed the goats, & give them about a handful of the beans, which are very good food & economise grain a little. Once or twice in very cold weather I've given a hot bran mash, & sometimes in bad weather when a goat is confined all day & bored a good idea is to bulk out the hard food with chaff (the dark nice-smelling, chaff, sanfoin[2] I think) which costs next to nothing & gives the goat the illusion of eating large quantities. Towards the end of winter, ie. Jan–Feb, a goat *ought* to have mangles or some kind of turnip, but M. won't eat them. I fancy what a goat will eat depends on early training, & when we go in for them properly as we intend to do when back in England, I shall train the kids to eat things easy to grow, such as swedes & cow-cabbage. Our idea when we get up to a respectable number of fowl, say 200, is to keep goats, good ones not scrubs like M., in conjunction & feed milk to the fowls in place of meat meal. Then if goats' milk ever gets onto the map, as I hope it may some day, you could start in as a dairy at any given moment. But that's all in the far future & supposing there aren't any wars.

No news here. It's cooler, thank God, about like English summer. We've got a few flower seeds coming up, phloxes & sweet peas & things. *Our* miserable hens have started laying, at least one has. The eggs aren't much bigger than pigeon's eggs. The goats give about ½ pint of milk a day each! Poor brutes, the goats in this country feed chiefly on things like cactus, & when we first showed ours barley they didn't know what it was, but they know now & yell when they see the feeding boxes coming. (Incidentally, it might be worth asking the price of barley to see if it's cheaper than oats. It seems a pretty good feed.) You can buy a camel here for Frs. 300 or about 35/- & a donkey for Frs. 100, which gives you an idea how the wretched brutes are treated. But though the Arabs underfeed & overwork their animals they live in great intimacy with them, & most animals here are driven without a bridle & follow like dogs.

Love to all.   Yours
Eric

P.S. Congratulations on pinching the bricks. I've had my eyes on them for years but had sentimental scruples about robbing a church.

1. Muriel was Orwell and Eileen's goat, abbreviated as 'M' in this letter.
2. Sanfoin, or, more properly, sainfoin (wholesome hay) is the perennial herb *Onobrychis saliva*, or *viciaefolia*, a leguminous fodder plant, sometimes known as everlasting grass or French grass. Orwell mentions it several times in *Coming Up for Air*: for example, 'My favourite place for reading was the loft behind the yard. . . . There were huge piles of sacks to lie on, and a sort of plastery smell mixed up with the smell of sainfoin . . .'; *CW*, VII, 92.

502. Morocco Diary

VILLA SIMONT   22.11.38:
Some days back visiting the British consul. The latter (name Robert Parr) is man of about 40, cultivated, very hospitable, married, appears to be in easy circumstances. Speaks French, very careful and grammatically very correct, but very strong English accent and manner while speaking of mentally going over grammar rules. The Assistant Consul or Vice Consul is young Englishman son of missionary, who has apparently been brought up in Morocco. Nevertheless has more characteristically English manner and accent than, eg. an Englishman brought up in India.
Parr considers I was wrong about the local French attitude to the crisis. Thinks they really believed war was coming and were prepared to go through with it though thoroughly fed up. Their apparent indifference was mere surface stolidity. He believes that there will be no general election for sometime to come. Says the scandals about the Air Ministry were very bad and known to everybody,[1] and the Government would prefer to make this good before risking an election. Says he has been struck by the number of more or less ordinary Conservatives he has met who are becoming perturbed by the Government's foreign policy. Thinks a likely development in the near future would be an attempt to revive the old Liberal Party. His own opinions seem to be moderately conservative. Could not be sure, whether, as a Government servant, he has any inside knowledge of what is going on, but gather not.
Ref. note on wheat prices above, a quintal equals about 2 cwt. Recently paid Frs. 31.50 for a measure, a decalitre I think, which appears to weigh about 40 lbs. This works out at nearly the same price, ie. about 70 centimes a pound. Seventy centimes equals about a penny in English money, so that the price of wheat here is at about the English price-level. Have not yet been able to secure full price lists, but it would appear that the things cheaper here (ie. when the franc is taken as being equal to its exchange value) are meat, certain fruits and vegetables, most of the products of the local hand-workers (leather, earthenware, certain kinds of metal work and heavy-quality

woollen cloth) and, of course, rent. Imported goods, especially manufac-
tures, are all expensive. Oil of all descriptions notably expensive.
It appears that the negroes in Senegal are French citizens, the Arabs in
Morocco not, this province being still called by a fiction the Cherifien
Empire. All negroes are liable for military service just the same as
Frenchmen. In Morocco only French subjects, ie. mostly Europeans, do
compulsory service. The Arab troops are voluntarily engaged men and enlist
for long periods. They appear to get a (by local standards) respectable pension
for long service. Eg. our servant Mahdjoub Mahommed, who served about
15 years in an Arab line regiment, gets a pension of about Frs. 5 a day.
Forgot to mention earlier that at the entrance to Marrakech there is a toll-
station where all incoming lorries etc. have to unload and pay a tax on any
goods being brought in for sale. This applies to all the vegetables taken in to
market by the peasants. Do not know amount of tax, but it makes an
appreciable difference to the price if one buys vegetables etc. outside the
town.

1. Possibly a reference to the demand by M.P.s on 12 May 1938 for an inquiry into the state of Britain's air defences.

503. Review of *The Church in Spain, 1737–1937* by E. Allison Peers; *Crusade in Spain* by Eoin O'Duffy

New English Weekly, 24 November 1938

Professor Allison Peers,[1] though a Franco partisan and of late rather an acrimonious one, is a writer who can be taken seriously. He is also, I gather, a Catholic, and he is quite naturally and rightly concerned about the fate of the Church in Spain. No one would blame him for being angry when churches are burned and priests murdered or driven into exile. But I think it is a pity that he has not looked a little more deeply into the reasons why these things happen.

In recounting the various persecutions of the Church in Spain, from the Middle Ages onward, he traces four main causes. The first three are the struggle between Church and King, the struggle between Church and State, and the liberal anticlericalism of the nineteenth century. The last is the "development of what is broadly termed Communism, *i.e.,* a number of related[2] but not identical proletarian movements, one common factor of which is disbelief in, and denial of, God." All church-burning, priest-shooting and anticlerical violence generally are supposed to have their roots in Communism and its Spanish variant, Anarchism, which are inseparable from "hatred of God." It is not, Professor Peers thinks, a question of hostility to a corrupt church, but of "a cold, calculated, determined attempt to destroy institutional religion throughout the country."

Now, it is no use denying that churches have been destroyed all over Government Spain. Various Government partisans, in their efforts to make their cause respectable, have pretended that churches were only demolished when they had been used as fortresses in the street fighting at the beginning of the war. This is merely a lie. Churches were destroyed everywhere, in town and village, and except for a few Protestant churches none were allowed to open and hold services till about August, 1937. It is also useless to deny that both Anarchism and Marxian Socialism are hostile to all religion. But this does not really tell us why the Spanish churches were destroyed. Professor Peers's *Catalonia Infelix*[3] made it clear that he understands the internal political situation in Government Spain a great deal better than most writers on the Spanish war, and there are two facts bearing on this question which he is probably aware of. One is the fact that during the present war the Russian Government has used its influence in Spain *against* and not *for* anticlerical violence and revolutionary extremism generally. The other is that the sacking of churches happened during the early period when the proletariat were in control, and the churches began to re-open and the priests to come out of hiding, when the Caballero Government fell and the middle class was back in the saddle. In other words the anticlerical movement, in its violent form, is a popular movement and a native Spanish movement. It has its roots not in Marx or Bakunin,[4] but in the condition of the Spanish people themselves.

In Catalonia and Aragon, in the first year of war, there were two things that impressed me. One was the apparent absence of any religious feeling whatever among the mass of the people. Admittedly at the time it might have been dangerous to admit openly to religious belief—still, one cannot be altogether deceived about a thing like that. The second was the fact that most of the wrecked or damaged churches that I saw were new ones; their predecessors had been burnt down in earlier disturbances. And this raises the thought, when was the last church burnt down in England? Probably not since Cromwell. A mob of English farm hands sacking the parish church would be something next door to unthinkable. Why? Because at present the conditions of class warfare simply do not exist in England. In Spain, for a century past, millions of people had had to live in conditions that were beyond bearing. Over huge tracts of country peasants who were serfs in everything but name worked enormous hours for wages of sixpence a day. In these conditions you get something that we have not got in England, a real hatred of the status quo, a real willingness to kill and burn. But the Church was part of the status quo; its influence was on the side of the wealthy. In many villages the huge garish church, with the cluster of miserable mud huts surrounding it, must have seemed the visible symbol of property. Naturally, Catholic writers have of late been denying this. The Church was not corrupt, it was anything but wealthy, the priests were often good Republicans, etc., etc. The answer is that the Spanish common people, whose opinion on this matter is worth something, did not think so. In the eyes of at any rate very many of them, the Church was simply a racket and the priest, the boss and the landlord were all of a piece. The national church had lost its hold on them because it had failed in its job. Catholics would probably do their Church a better service by facing this fact than by tracing everything to mere wickedness, or to Moscow, which persecutes its own religious believers but has its reasons for being slightly pro-clerical elsewhere.

General O'Duffy's adventures in Spain do seem in one way to have resembled a crusade, in that they were a frightful muddle and led to nothing in particular. Otherwise his book does not tell one much. For the most part it consists of the usual vapid tributes to General Franco ("the great leader and patriot, General Franco, at the head of the Nationalist Movement, composed of all that is great and noble in Spanish national life, fighting for Christian civilization," etc., etc.) and the usual ignorant misrepresentations of what is happening on the other side. General O'Duffy's information is so sketchy that he even gets the names of some of the Spanish trade unions and political parties wrong. Franco propaganda is often less irritating than the rather subtler type of lie that has been evolved by the other side, but I confess to getting tired of that story of the "Russian troops" (it is not recorded whether they had snow on their boots[5]) who are supposed to have fought on the Madrid front.

After what I saw in Spain, and what I have read about it in England, I understand why Sir Walter Raleigh burned his History of the World.[6] If

> "The truth is great and will prevail
> "When none cares whether it prevail or not,"[7]

then the sooner people stop feeling strongly about this Spanish struggle, the better it will be. At present the atmosphere of lies that surrounds every aspect of it is suffocating. Meanwhile O'Duffy's is a badly written and uninteresting book.

Orwell's review drew protests from both authors. For that from General O'Duffy, see *n. 8* below. Professor Peers's letter was published on 8 December 1938. He made three points: he was not a Roman Catholic; he was not a 'Franco partisan,' but had maintained that the Spanish conflict could be resolved permanently only by agreement; his conclusions as to 'why these things happen' were not the product of a visit of a few months but of twenty years' study of many aspects of Spanish life. Orwell's response, headed 'Spanish Clericalism,' was published in the *New English Weekly* on 22 December 1938:

Sir,—I am very sorry to see that I have hurt Professor Peers' feelings. I did not mean to do so. But perhaps I had better answer the three points he raises:

1. I only said that I "gathered" that Professor Peers was a Catholic. My reason was simply that he is much more friendly in his attitude to the Catholic Church than is usual in non-Catholics, even including Anglicans. But I freely admit that his not being a Catholic makes his testimony in favour of the Spanish Church stronger.

2. I described Professor Peers as "a Franco partisan and of late[9] rather an acrimonious one." I do not think Professor Peers would deny that the tone of *The Church in Spain* is a good deal more bitter than that of *Catalonia Infelix*. As to the question of partisanship, Professor Peers claims to be impartial on the ground that he has 'continually maintained . . . that the only solution to the Spanish conflict that can be permanent is a solution by agreement." Well, I should regard that as being pro-Franco. After all, Franco is, at least

technically, a rebel. What should we say of a person who suggested a "solution by agreement" between the burglar and the policeman? We should say that he was at any rate to some extent pro-burglar. But I never for an instant meant to suggest that Professor Peers was unfair or dishonest. When I read *Catalonia Infelix*, I regarded it as a book written from the Franco standpoint but written with extreme fair-mindedness. I believe I said something to this effect in a short review that I did of it. Incidentally, it may amuse Professor Peers to learn that I have been in trouble in "left" circles for not attacking him more severely.

3. I quite agree that Professor Peers knows infinitely more about the Church in Spain, and everything else in Spain, than I am ever likely to know. But I think that his explanation of modern anti-clericalism is altogether too simple to be true, and I do not see why my own observations, small as they are, should not be advanced as evidence.

1. E. Allison Peers (1891–1952), an Anglican scholar of English and French literature, was appointed in 1920 to the chair of Spanish at Liverpool University. His knowledge of Spain was extensive, and he wrote several distinguished studies on that country. He wrote on contemporary Spain from well before the outbreak of the civil war for the *Bulletin of Spanish Studies*. Under the pseudonym Bruce Truscot he wrote the influential *Redbrick University* (1943).
2. 'related' was set as 'relegated.'
3. This book was favourably reviewed by Orwell in *Time and Tide*, 11 December, 1937; see *414*. 'Peers's' was set as 'Peer's.'
4. Mikhail Aleksandrovich Bakunin (1814–1876), Russian anarchist and political writer, opposed Karl Marx.
5. Orwell refers to one of the famous, and more incongruous, myths of World War I. At a critical period on the Western Front, rumours abounded that Russian troops were being transferred there from the Eastern Front. The 'evidence' purported to be sightings of Russian troops travelling in darkened trains from the north of Britain 'with snow on their boots.'
6. This was written by Sir Walter Raleigh (1552?–1618) when he was imprisoned in the Tower of London; it was published in 1614. Orwell writes of Raleigh's imprisonment and his *History* in 'As I Please,' 10, 4 February 1944, *2416*.
7. "Magna et Veritas", lines 9–10, by Coventry Patmore (1823–1896).
8. On 4 December General O'Duffy wrote to the editor of *New English Weekly*, asking that his letter not be published, but describing Orwell's review as scurrilous. The word 'review' is underlined and placed in single quotations marks, evidently to indicate an anomalous, to him, use of the word. His book had, he said, received twenty-four favourable reviews and only one other (in a 'Communist organ') that was critical. He enclosed copies of typical reviews and claimed that his book had 'a *record* circulation here & abroad,' strange if, as Orwell claimed, the book was 'an ignorant representation and badly written.' The letter is marked 'Came while you were in Africa' and was evidently not sent to Orwell at the time, but the letter was answered. O'Duffy replied on 6 December to the effect that the editor's letter merely added insult to injury, and he asked that his name be removed from *New English Weekly*'s circulation list.
9. 'late' was set as 'later.'

504. To John Sceats

24 November 1938   Typewritten

Boite° Postale 48   Gueliz   Marrakech   French Morocco

Dear Sceats,

Thanks so much for your letter with the very useful information about insurance offices. I see that my chap will have to be a Representative and that I underrated his income a little. I've done quite a lot of work, but unfortunately after wasting no less than a fortnight doing articles for various papers fell slightly ill so that properly speaking I've done no work for 3 weeks.[1] It's awful how the time flies by. What with all this illness I've decided to count 1938 as a blank year and sort of cross it off the calendar. But meanwhile the concentration camp looms ahead and there is so much one wants to do. I've got to the point now when I feel I could write a good novel if I had five years peace and quiet, but at present one might as well ask for five years in the moon.

This is on the whole rather a dull country. Some time after Xmas we want to go for a week into the Atlas mountains which are 50 or 100 miles from here and look rather exciting. Down here it's flat dried-up country rather like a huge allotment patch that's been let "go back", and practically no trees except olives and palms. The poverty is something frightful, though of course it's always a little more bearable for people in a hot climate. The people have tiny patches of ground which they cultivate with implements which would have been out of date in the days of Moses. One can get a sort of idea of the prevailing hunger by the fact that in the whole country there are practically no wild animals, everything edible being eaten by human beings. I don't know how it would compare with the poorer parts of India, but Burma would seem like a paradise compared to it, so far as standard of living goes. The French are evidently squeezing the country pretty ruthlessly. They absorb most of the fertile land as well as the minerals, and the taxes seem fairly heavy considering the poverty of the people. On the surface their administration looks better than ours and certainly rouses less animosity in the subject race, because they have very little colour-prejudice. But I think underneath it is much the same. So far as I can judge there is no anti-French movement of any size among the Arabs, and if there were one it would almost certainly be nationalist rather than Socialist, as the great majority of the people are at the feudal stage and the French, I fancy, intend them to remain so. I can't tell anything about the extent of the local Socialist movement, because [it] has for some time only existed illegally. I asked the I.L.P. to get the French Socialist party to put me in touch with any Socialist movement existing here, if only because I could thus learn more about local conditions, but they haven't done so, perhaps because it's too dangerous. The local French, though they're quite different from the British population in India, mostly petty traders and even manual workers, are stuffily conservative and mildly pro-Fascist. I wrote two articles on local conditions for the Quarterly which I hope they'll print[2] as they were I think not too incorrect and subtly Trotskyist. I hope by the way that "Controversy" has not succumbed.[3] It would be a disaster if it did, and still more if the N.L.[4] had to turn into a monthly. As to Controversy I'm sure the sale could be worked up with a little energy and a certain willingness to distribute back numbers, and I'll do what I can in my nearest town when I get back.

Have you heard any rumours about the General Election? The only person I can make contact with here who might conceivably know something is the British consul, who thinks the Government are going to defer the election as long as possible and that attempts may also be made to resuscitate the old Liberal party. Personally I don't think anything can prevent Chamberlain winning unless there is some unforeseen scandal. Labour may win a few by-elections, but the general election will be fought in a completely different emotional atmosphere. The best one can hope is that it may teach Labour a lesson. I only get English papers rather intermittently and haven't seen the results of some of the by-elections. I see Labour won Dartford but gather the Conservatives won Oxford.[5]

Let me have a line some time to hear how things are going.

Yours
Eric Blair

1. Orwell originally typed 'months,' but altered this in handwriting.
2. Despite a thorough search, these have not been traced.
3. It did survive, but became *Left Forum* in June 1939; see *490, n. 1*.
4. *The New Leader*. For Orwell's contributions, see *457, 462*. For his financial contribution, see *510A*.
5. In its issue for 9 December 1938, *The New Leader* reported what it described as 'Amazing Stories' of how Labour candidates had been 'ousted' at selection meetings for the constituencies of Bridgwater and Oxford by 'Independent Progressives.' At Bridgwater, the 'alleged Independent candidate' was introduced to the constituency by Sir Richard Acland; see *609, n. 2*, and *2095* for Orwell's profile in *The Observer*. There was also intervention by 'the new political party, the Left Book Club.' At Oxford, academics were blamed for manipulating the selection of an Independent Progressive, even though that meant the Labour candidate withdrew and wealthy members of the Oxford Labour Party had to find £350 to meet the Liberal candidate's expenses when he also agreed to withdraw. The report concluded: 'These "intelligentsia" and their Left Book Clubs are the new instrument of the Communist Party.' This manoeuvring was to little effect, since the Conservative, Quintin Hogg, took the seat; see *512, n. 3*.

505. To Charles Doran

26 November 1938   Typewritten

Boite° Postale 48   Gueliz   Marrakech   French Morocco

Dear Charlie,[1]

Thanks so much for your letter with the copy of "Solidarity" and the too kind review of my book. I see from the front page of "Solidarity" that those bloody liars in the "News Chronicle" reported the result of the P.O.U.M. trial under the heading "spies sentenced" thus giving the impression that the P.O.U.M. prisoners were sentenced for espionage. The "Observer" also did something of the kind, though more circumspectly, and the French press of this country, which is in the main pro-Franco, reported the act of accusation against the P.O.U.M., stated that it had been "all proved" and then failed to report the verdict at all! I admit this kind of thing frightens me. It means that the most elementary respect for truthfulness is breaking down, not merely in the Communist and Fascist press, but in the bourgeois liberal press which still pays lip-service to the old traditions of journalism. It gives one the feeling that our civilization is going down into a sort of mist of lies where it will be impossible ever to find out the truth about anything. Meanwhile I've written to the I.L.P. asking them to send me a copy of the issue of Solidaridad Obrera[2] which reported the case, so that if necessary I can write to the press, that is to say such papers as would print my letter, stating quite clearly what the P.O.U.M. prisoners *were* sentenced for. I trust, however, that someone has already done so. It's difficult for me to get hold of foreign papers here, especially a paper like Solidaridad Obrera, which I couldn't get nearer than Gibraltar and there only with difficulty.

As perhaps you know I was told to spend the winter here for the sake of my lungs. We've been here nearly three months now and I think it has done me a certain amount of good. It is a tiresome country in some ways, but it is interesting to get a glimpse of French colonial methods and compare them with our own. I think as far as I can make out that the French are every bit as bad as ourselves, but somewhat better on the surface, partly owing to the fact that there is a large indigenous white population here, part of it proletarian or near-proletarian. For that reason it isn't quite possible to keep up the sort of white man's burden atmosphere that we do in India, and there is less colour-prejudice. But economically it is just the usual swindle for which empires exist. The Poverty° of most of the Arab population is frightful. As far as one can work it out, the average family seems to live at the rate of about a shilling a day, and of course most of the people are either peasants or petty craftsmen who have to work extremely hard by antiquated methods. At the same time, so far as one can judge, there is no anti-French movement on any scale. If one appeared it would I think be merely nationalist at the beginning, as the great majority of the people are still at the feudal stage and fairly strict Mahommedans. In some of the big towns such as Casablanca there is a proletariat, both white and coloured, and there the Socialist movement just exists. But as for the Arab Socialist parties, they were all suppressed some time ago. I feel reasonably sure that unless the working class (it really depends on them) in the democracies change their tactics within a year or two, the Arabs will be easy game for the Fascists. French opinion here is predominantly pro-Franco, and I should not be greatly surprised to see Morocco become the jumping-off place for some French version of Franco in the years to come.

I don't altogether know what to think about the crisis, Maxton etc. I think Maxton put his foot in it by being too cordial to Chamberlain, and I also think it would be absurd to regard Chamberlain as really a peace-maker. I also quite agree with what anybody chooses to say about the way in which the Czechs have been let down. But I think we might face one or two facts. One is that almost anything is better than European war, which will lead not only to the slaughter of tens of millions but to an extension of Fascism. Certainly Chamberlain and Co. are preparing for war, and any other government that is likely to get in will also prepare for war; but meanwhile we have got perhaps two years' breathing space in which it *may* be possible to provoke a real popular anti-war movement in England, in France and above all in the Fascist countries. If we can do that, to the point of making it clear that no government will go to war because its people[3] won't follow, I think Hitler is done for. The other fact is that the Labour Party are doing themselves frightful harm by getting stamped in the public mind as the war party. In my opinion they can't now win the general election[4] unless something very unforeseen turns up. They will therefore be in the position of an opposition pushing the government in the direction in which it is already going. As such they might as well cease to exist, and in fact it wouldn't surprise me in the next year or two to see Attlee and Co. cave in and take office in some new version of a national government.[5] I admit that being anti-war probably plays Chamberlain's game for the next few months, but the point will soon come when the anti-wars, of all complexions, will have to resist the fascising° processes which war-preparation entails.

I hope things are prospering with you. After all the frightful waste of time due to being ill I got started on my novel, which I suppose will be ready to come out about April. Eileen sends love.

Yours
Eric Blair

P.S. [at top of letter] Thanks so much for your good offices about my Spanish book. That's what sells a book—getting asked for in libraries.

1. Extracts from this letter were read to a meeting of the John MacLean Society in Glasgow, 6 February 1983, by Mrs. Bertha Doran, Charles Doran's widow. It was reproduced in full in the *Society for the Study of Labour History Bulletin*, 51, Pt. 1 (April 1986), 15–17, by Dr. James D. Young. For Charles Doran, see *386* and *386, n. 1*.
2. A Spanish Anarchist daily newspaper of the time.
3. people] government *handwritten marginal correction*
4. A largely Conservative government—with National Liberal and National Labour adherents—had assembled on 16 November 1935, with a majority of 247, for a maximum five-year term. Orwell is expecting a general election in 1939 or 1940, but because of the outbreak of war none was held until 1945.
5. With the fall of Neville Chamberlain and the appointment of Winston Churchill as Prime Minister in May 1940, Labour joined a genuinely national government, Clement Attlee becoming deputy prime minister. The Labour Party was to win the 1945 general election with a majority of 146.

506. To Leonard Moore

28 November 1938   Typewritten

Boite° Postale 48   Gueliz   Marrakech   French Morocco

Dear Mr. Moore,

I have just had a letter from Allen Lane, who apparently runs the Penguin Series.[1] He says:

"I am writing to you to know whether it would be possible to include some of your work in my series. As a matter of fact I was very much impressed by one of your stories which I published some time ago in NEW WRITING when I was at the Bodley Head.[2] If it is not possible for us to get one of your novels have you a collection of short stories sufficient for one volume?"

I think we ought to cash in on this if possible. Of course I haven't any short stories for them. I simply can't write short stories. But I gather from this that they would prefer one of my novels, and I have replied suggesting DOWN AND OUT,[3] BURMESE DAYS[4] and KEEP THE ASPIDISTRA FLYING. I don't know which if any of these they'd be likely to choose. But I have asked Mr Lane to get in touch with you if he is interested, and said you would supply him with copies of any book he wanted. If it is a question of DOWN AND OUT, I haven't a copy and I believe you have not either. The only person I know has one is my mother. If there should be a demand for one, could you write and ask for it from her, which would save time? Her address is Mrs R W Blair, 36 High Street, Southwold, Suffolk. I am writing to her asking her to hand it over if she hears from you. If the Penguin people *do* seem inclined to take one of these books, I don't in the least know on what terms they deal. But I think it would be well worth letting them have one on not very advantageous terms for us, if necessary, because it is first-rate publicity.

Please don't give yourself any more trouble with that wretched pamphlet.[5] I am sorry you have had so much already. As you say, there is no sale for pamphlets, and in any case the Hogarth Press is in the hands of Communists (at any rate Lehmann is one)[6] who won't publish my work if they can help it.

The weather has got a lot cooler and I think the climate is doing me good. The novel is going pretty well. I think I can promise it for the beginning of April, which perhaps you could tell Gollancz if he makes further enquiries. If he does, tell him I was very sorry to let him down about the time, but I suppose he knows I was actually in the sanatorium till the end of August.

I hope Miss Perriam[7] is making some progress. My wife sends all the best.

Yours sincerely
Eric Blair

1. Allen Lane (1902–1970; Kt., 1952), one of the most influential British publishers of the twentieth century, was apprenticed to his uncle, John Lane, at the Bodley Head Press in 1919. He resigned in 1936 and founded Penguin Books, which revolutionized paperback publication in Britain—and, indeed, more widely. See J. E. Morpurgo, *Allen Lane: King Penguin, a Biography* (1979). See Orwell's review of the third batch of ten volumes (nine titles) of the Penguin Books series in *New English Weekly*, 5 March 1936, *290*, for his opinion of this series.
2. *New Writing* had published 'Shooting an Elephant' in its second number, Autumn 1936.

Orwell's 'Marrakech' appeared in the Christmas 1939 issue, and 'Shooting an Elephant' was reprinted in the first number of *Penguin New Writing*, November 1940.

3. Published by Penguin Books in December 1940. '? in print' has been written on the letter beside this title in Moore's office and answered 'O.P.' (out of print).

4. Published by Penguin Books in May 1944.

5. 'Socialism and War': see letter to Moore, 28 June 1938, *458*. The pamphlet was never published, but possibly some of its ideas, and even some of its text, appeared in 'Not Counting Niggers,' a July 1939 review article that took Clarence Streit's *Union Now* as its starting point; see *552*.

6. John Lehmann was probably not, at least formally, a Communist, but he had been associated with Lawrence & Wishart briefly and he reviewed for the *Daily Worker*. Samuel Hynes, *The Auden Generation* (1976), quotes a section of Lehmann's review of *Overtures to Death* by Cecil Day Lewis, *Daily Worker*, 19 October 1938 (335, n. 7). These links would suffice to convince Orwell that Lehmann was a Communist. Lehmann was manager of the Hogarth Press, 1931–32, and became a partner in 1938. See J. H. Willis, Jr., *Leonard and Virginia Woolf as Publishers: The Hogarth Press, 1917–41* (1992), 183–4, 295–96. Willis does not mention the submission of 'Socialism and War' to the Hogarth Press, nor does Peter Alexander in *Leonard and Virginia Woolf: A Literary Partnership* (1992).

7. See Eileen's letter to Moore, 7 June 1938, *450*.

507. 'Political Reflections on the Crisis'

The Adelphi, December 1938

In all the controversies over the Popular Front, the question least often debated has been whether such a combination could actually win an election.

It was obvious enough from the start that a Popular Front in England would be something quite different from the French Popular Front, which was brought into being by an *internal* Fascist threat. If it were formed it would be, more or less avowedly, for the purpose of war against Germany. What was the use of saying that collective security and so forth meant peace and not war? Nobody believed it. The point really under debate was whether left-wingers ought to support a war which meant bolstering up British imperialism. The advocates of the Popular Front shouted "Stop Hitler!" and its opponents shouted "No line-up with capitalists!" But both seem to have taken it for granted that if a Popular Front were formed the British public would vote for it.

Then came the war crisis. What happened? It is too early to say with absolute certainty, but if the signs are worth anything the crisis revealed two things. One, that the British people will go to war if they are told to; the other, that they don't want war and will vote against any party which stamps itself as a war party. When Chamberlain came back from Munich he was not booed and execrated but greeted by miles of cheering people. And it does not greatly matter that afterwards, when all was safe, there was a certain revulsion, on the strength of which Labour may win a few by-elections. In the decisive moment the mass of the people swung over to Chamberlain's side, and if the General Election revives the spirit of the crisis, as in all probability it will, they will do the same again.[1] And yet for two years past the *News Chronicle*, the *Daily Worker*, *Reynolds's*,° the *New Statesman*, and the sponsors of the Left Book Club had been deluding themselves and part of their public that the entire British nation, barring a few old gentlemen in West End Clubs, wanted nothing better than a ten-million-dead war in defence of democracy.

Why was it possible for a mistake of such magnitude to be made? Mainly because a small body of noise-makers can for a while give the impression that they are more numerous than they are. The mass of the people are normally silent. They do not sign manifestoes, attend demonstrations, answer questionnaires or even join political parties. As a result it is very easy to mistake a handful of slogan-shouters for the entire nation. At first sight a membership of 50,000 for the Left Book Club *looks* enormous. But what is 50,000 in a population of 50,000,000? To get a real idea of the balance of forces one ought not to be watching those 5,000 people who are making a noise in the Albert Hall: one ought to be watching those 5,000,000 outside who are saying nothing, but who are quite possibly thinking, and who will cast their votes at the next election. It is just this that propaganda organisations such as the Left Book Club tend to prevent. Instead of trying to assess the state of public opinion they reiterate that they *are* public opinion, and they and a few people round them end by believing it.

The net result of Strachey[2] and Company's efforts has been to give a totally false estimate of what the English people were thinking, and to push the leaders of the Labour Party a little further on the road to war. In doing so they have gone some distance towards losing Labour the election.

(ii)

So far as one can judge from the French Press, it seems clear that nobody in France, except the Communists and M. Kerillis,[3] seriously wished for war. I think events showed that the English people did not wish for war either; but it would be absurd to pretend that there was not in England an influential minority which wished very ardently for war and howled with disappointment when they did not get it. And by no means all of these people were Communists.

A type that seems to be comparatively rare in France is the war-hungry middle-class intellectual. Why should this type be commoner in one country than in the other? One can think of several subsidiary reasons, but the question can probably be answered satisfactorily with a single word: Conscription.

Compared with England, France is a democratic country, there are fewer privileges attaching to status, and military service is not at all easy to dodge. Nearly every adult Frenchman has done his service and has the harsh discipline of the French army well fixed in his memory. Unless he is over age or in an exceptionally sheltered position, war means to him something quite different from what it means to a middle-class Englishman. It means a notice on the wall, "Mobilisation Generale," and three weeks later, if he is unlucky, a bullet in his guts. How can such a man go about irresponsibly declaring that "we" ought to declare war on Germany, Japan and anyone else who happens to be handy? He is bound to regard war with a fairly realistic eye.

One could not possibly say the same of the English intelligentsia. Of all the left-wing journalists who declare day in and day out that if this, that and the other happens "we" must fight, how many imagine that war will affect them personally? When war breaks out they will be doing what they are doing at present, writing propaganda articles. Moreover, they are well aware of this. The type of person who writes articles for the political Left has no feeling that "war" means something in which he will actually get hurt. "War" is something that happens on paper, a diplomatic manoeuvre, something which is of course very deplorable but is "necessary" in order to destroy Fascism. His part in it is the pleasantly stimulating one of writing propaganda articles. Curiously enough, he may well be wrong. We do not yet know what a big-scale air-raid is like, and the next war may turn out to be very unpleasant even for journalists. But these people, who have been born into the monied intelligentsia and feel in their bones that they belong to a privileged class, are not really capable of foreseeing any such thing. War is something that happens on paper, and consequently they are able to decide that this or that war is "necessary" with no more sense of personal danger than in deciding on a move at chess.

Our civilisation produces in increasing numbers two types, the gangster and the pansy. They never meet, but each is necessary to the other. Somebody in eastern Europe "liquidates" a Trotskyist; somebody in Bloomsbury writes a justification of it. And it is, of course, precisely because of the utter softness and security of life in England that the yearning for bloodshed—bloodshed in the far distance—is so common among our intelligentsia. Mr. Auden can write about "the acceptance of guilt for the necessary murder"[4] because he has never committed a murder, perhaps never had one of his friends murdered, possibly never even seen a murdered man's corpse. The presence of this utterly irresponsible intelligentsia, who "took up" Roman Catholicism ten years ago, "take up" Communism to-day and will "take up" the English variant of Fascism a few years hence, is a special feature of the English situation. Their importance is that with their money, influence and literary facility they are able to dominate large sections of the Press.

(iii)

Barring some unforeseen scandal or a really large disturbance inside the Conservative Party, Labour's chances of winning the General Election seem very small. If any kind of Popular Front is formed, its chances are probably less than those of Labour unaided. The best hope would seem to be that if Labour *is* defeated, the defeat may drive it back to its proper "line."

But the time-factor is all-important. The National Government is preparing for war. No doubt they will bluff, shuffle and make further concessions in order to buy a little more time—still, they are preparing for war. A few people cling to the belief that the Government's war preparations are all a sham or even that they are directed against Soviet Russia. This is mere wish-thinking. What really inspires it is the knowledge that when Chamberlain goes to war with Germany (in defence of democracy, of course) he will be doing what his opponents demand and thus taking the wind out of their sails. The attitude of the British governing class is probably summed up in the remark I overheard recently from one of the Gibraltar garrison: "It's coming right enough. It's pretty clear Hitler's going to have Czechoslovakia. Much better let him have it. We shall be ready by 1941." In fact, the difference between the warmongers of the right and the warmongers of the left is merely strategic.

The real question is *how soon* the Labour Party will start effectively opposing the Government's war plans. Suppose that war actually breaks out. Some of the more soft-boiled left-wing papers have recently been discussing the "conditions" on which the Labour Party should "support" the Government in case of war. As though any Government at war could permit its subjects to make "conditions"! Once war has started the left-wing parties will have the choice of offering unconditional loyalty or being smashed. The only group large enough to be capable of resisting, and perhaps even of scaring the Government away from war, is the Labour Party. But if it does not begin soon it may never do so. Two years, even a year, of tacit acquiescence in preparation for war, and its power will have been broken.

When and if Labour loses the election, the cry will be raised that if we had had a Popular Front the election could have been won. This may obscure the issue for a long time, perhaps even for two years. Hence more Popular Frontism, more brandishing of fists and shouts for a "firm line," more clamour for overwhelming armaments—in short, more pushing of the Government in the direction in which it is going. So long as Labour demands a "firm line" which entails the risk of war, it cannot make any but a sham resistance to the fascising° process which war-preparation implies. What is the use of asking for a "strong" foreign policy and at the same time pretending to oppose increased working hours, reduced wages, Press censorship and even conscription? The retort will always be the same: "How can we keep Hitler in check if you obstruct rearmament?" War, and even war-preparation, can be used as an excuse for anything, and we may be sure the Government will make full use of its opportunities. In the end a perception of what is happening may drive the Labour Party back to its proper "line." But how soon will that end come?

On September 28th the National Council of Labour made one of the few sensible moves that were made during the whole war-crisis. It appealed over the radio to the German people to resist Hitler. The appeal did not go far enough, it was self-righteous in tone and contained no admission that British capitalism, like German Nazism, has its faults; but it did at least show some perception of the right method of approach. What hope is there of that method being followed up if the Labour Party continues much longer on the path of jingoism and imperialism? It may be that sooner or later the mere fact of being in opposition will drive the Labour Party back to an anti-militarist and anti-imperialist line. But it will have to be sooner and not later. If it continues much longer in its present anomalous position, its enemies will eat it up.

1. Orwell is anticipating a general election in 1939 or 1940; see *505, n. 4.*
2. For John Strachey, see *304, n. 2.*
3. Henri de Kérillis was the only non-Communist member of the French Chamber of Deputies to vote against the ratification of the Munich pact; see *422, n. 3.* When Germany reoccupied the Rhineland in March 1936 he published *Français! voici la guerre*: in effect, the war has started (Eugen Weber, *The Hollow Years*, 243).
4. Wystan Hugh Auden (1907–1973), poet and critic, was associated at the time with Christopher Isherwood, Stephen Spender and Louis MacNeice. He left for America in January 1939 and became a U.S. citizen in May 1946. He was Professor of Poetry at Oxford University, 1956–61. For Orwell's attack on him and 'the necessary murder,' see 'Inside the Whale,' *600.*

508. Review of *Gypsies* by Martin Block; translated by Barbara Kuczynski and Duncan Taylor

The Adelphi, December 1938

M. Martin Block's book deals mainly with the gypsies of south-eastern Europe, who are far more numerous and evidently live at a much more primitive level than those of England. They use tents, oxen and pack animals rather than horses and caravans, never sit on chairs, are dirty beyond belief, speak Romany among themselves and follow hereditary trades such as locksmithing, bear-leading and the making of wooden spoons and basins. Rather unfortunately M. Block does not include a chapter on the Romany language, but much of the information he has compiled is profoundly interesting, and his photographs, unlike the "illustrations" in the majority of books, do really illustrate. It is a pity that, so far as I know, no one has produced an equally detailed and up-to-date book on the gypsies of England.

As a matter of fact, the existence of this primitive nomadic people, with strongly marked racial characteristics, in a crowded country like England is a very curious thing. Why do they continue being gypsies? According to all precedent they ought long ago to have been seduced by the delights of civilisation. In England the "true" gypsies probably own rather more property and live at a slightly higher level than the average farm labourer, but they can only follow their distinctive way of life by constantly breaking the law. One is obliged to conclude that they do it because they like it. A gypsy makes part of his living by begging, and consequently, when he thinks he can get anything out of you, he is offensively servile, pours out gross flatteries and exploits his picturesqueness and even his bad English. But if you happen to meet gypsies on equal terms—or, at any rate, when they have nothing to gain by flattering you—you get a totally different impression. So far from being envious of the industrial civilisation which they see about them, they are merely contemptuous of it. They despise the "gorgios" for their physical softness, their bad sexual morals and, above all, their lack of liberty. To serve in the army, for instance, seems to them merely a despicable slavery. They have preserved most of the mental characteristics of a nomadic people, including a complete lack of interest in the future and the past. Hence the curious fact that though they first appeared in Europe as late as the fifteenth century, no one knows for certain where they came from. Perhaps it is not fanciful to say that the gypsy is, in the West, the nearest existing approach to the Noble Savage. And considering their admirable physique, their strict morals—strict according to their own peculiar code, that is—and their love of liberty, one must admit that they have a strain of nobility.

They also appear to be fairly successful in surviving. M. Block estimates that the number of gypsies in the world, if one includes the gypsy tribes of India, is about five millions, and that in Europe alone, counting only "true" gypsies, *i.e.*, those who are wholly or partly of gypsy blood, the number would be from one to one-and-a-half million. There are supposed to be 18,000 in Great Britain and 100,000 in the U.S.A. Considering that any nomadic population is necessarily small, these are respectable numbers.

Will they survive? M. Block's book seems to have been originally published in 1937, but unfortunately it says nothing about the effect on the gypsies of the recent political changes in Europe. There seem to be very few gypsies in Germany proper, but there is a considerable number in Austria and also in Russia. What is Hitler doing about the gypsies? Or Stalin? It seems almost impossible that the totalitarian régimes will fail to persecute these people on the pretext of civilising them. In the past they have survived countless attempts to stamp them out. "There is no country in western or central Europe," says M. Block, "which has not tried to get rid of gypsies by means of cruelty and persecution. None, however, has succeeded." But the terrifying thing about modern methods of persecution is that we cannot be sure, as yet, that they will not succeed. The Inquisition failed, but there is no certainty that the "liquidation" of Jews and Trotskyists will fail. It may be that the wretched gypsies, like the Jews, are already serving as a corpus vile, and it is only because they do not have friends who own newspapers that we hear nothing about it. Perhaps the concentration camps are already crowded with them. If so, let us hope that they survive it.[1] No civilised person would wish for an instant to imitate the gypsies' habits, but that is not the same as saying that one would like to see them disappear. Existing in the teeth of a civilisation which disapproves of them, they are a heartening reminder of the largeness of the earth and the power of human obstinacy.

1. More than 400,000 Gypsies were killed in the concentration camps.

509. To his father

2 December 1938   Typewritten

Boite° Postale 48   Gueliz   Marrakech   French Morocco

Dear Father,

I am glad to hear from Mother that you have been a little better and getting up occasionally. If your appetite is very bad, did you ever think of trying Haliborange? I have taken it occasionally, and it is not at all unpleasant to take, nourishing in itself and seems to improve one's appetite after a while. I should think Doctor Collings would approve of it. It's only halibut's liver oil flavoured with orange and a few other things.

The weather here has got a lot cooler and is rather like the cold weather in Upper Burma, generally fine and sunny but not hot. We have a fire most days, which one doesn't actually need till the evening, but it is nice to have it. There is no coal in this country, all the fires are wood and they use charcoal to cook on. We have tried to do a bit of gardening but not been very successful because it's hard to get seed to germinate, I suppose because it is generally so dry. Most English flowers do pretty well here once they are established, and at the same time there are tropical plants like Bougainvillea. The peasants are just getting in their crops of chilis,° like the ones they used to grow in Burma. The people here live in villages which are surrounded by mud walls about ten feet high, I suppose as a protection against robbers, and inside they have miserable little straw huts about ten feet wide which they live in. It is a very bare country, parts of it almost desert, though it's not what is considered true desert. The people take their flocks of sheep, goats, camels and so forth out to graze on places where there seems nothing to eat at all, and the wretched brutes nose about and find little dried up weeds under the stones. The children seem to start work when they are five or six. They are extraordinarily obedient, and stay out all day herding the goats and keeping the birds off the olive trees.

I think the climate is doing me good. I was a little unwell last week, but on the whole feel much better and am putting on a little weight. I have done quite a lot of work. We are going to take some more photographs, including some of the house, and will send them to you when developed. Look after yourself and get well soon.

With love
Eric

510. Eileen Blair to Mary Common

5 December 1938   Typewritten

Boite° Postale 48   Marrakech-Gueliz   French Morocco

Dear Mary,

We have just got back from a Christmas shopping. It began by my bicycle having a puncture. The next stage was my arrival in Marrakech, entirely penniless, two minutes after the bank had shut. By the time Eric arrived for lunch I had scoured the town (in which we know no one) for succour and had succeeded in cashing a cheque and in collecting a retinue of guides, porters etc., all of whom had most charmingly waited for money so long that they might be said to have earned it. After lunch we began to shop and we went on for two and a half hours, surrounded by as many as twenty men and boys, all shouting and many of them weeping. If either of us tried to speak, long before we had mentioned what we were talking about everyone present cried "Yes, yes. *I* understand. The others don't understand." We bought a lot of things in one shop because the people there will post to England—at least so they say. The things are being sent in three lots, to three key recipients who are to distribute them. You are a key recipient, and you ought to get a dish for Mrs. Hatchett, a brass tray for Mrs. Anderson, and a "couverture" for yourself (and Jack). You may of course get something quite different, or nothing at all. A porter is engaged if he succeeds in laying hands on any piece of property, and as I put each thing on its appropriate pile it was instantly seized by one to four helpers and put somewhere else, or the pieces in several different places. Supposing you do get something, there may be duty to pay. I don't think it can be more than three or four shillings and I hope it will be nothing. We have sent a few things home already without trouble (by which I mean paying money) and they should be kind at Christmas, but it is perfectly probable that they put on for Christmas a special staff to be unkind. Anyway if there is duty of course we'll refund it when we get back or before by proxy, but meanwhile we can't think of any better arrangement than that Peter[1] should pay it. Peter, like all our younger friends, is having money for Christmas because we can't get anything here for children unless we pay about thirty francs for something that Woolworth makes better. Money means 5/-. I hope that will arrive, but naturally we are doing all this much too late. We should have done it too late in any case, but in fact Eric was ill and in bed for more than a week and as soon as he was better I had an illness I'd actually started before his but had necessarily postponed. I enjoyed the illness: I had to do all the cooking as usual but I did it in a dressing-gown and firmly carried my tray back to bed. Now we are both very well, or I remember thinking that we were very well last night. This evening we are literally swaying on our feet and the menu for supper, which once included things like a mushroom sauce and a souffle, has been revised to read: Boiled eggs, bread, butter, cheese; bread, jam, cream; raw fruit. The servant goes home after lunch. He was supposed to sleep here in a kind of stable, but he prefers to cycle the five or six miles to Marrakech morning and evening. I like it much better. There is nothing for him to do in the evening except wash up the supper things, and until they were dirty he used to sit on the kitchen step, often in tears, getting up every ten minutes or so to tidy the kitchen and put away (generally in the cellar) the things I was just about to use for the cooking. It is customary, among the French as well as among the Arabs, to get up at five o'clock at the latest, and he arrives here about seven with fresh bread and milk for breakfast. It is early enough for us. We come to understand each other fairly well, though I seldom know whether he is speaking French or Arabic and often talk to him myself in English. The weather has got quite cold, which is delightful. Indeed it's a good climate now and I think we sha'n't die of it, which until recently seemed probable in my case and certain in Eric's. His illness was a sort of necessary stage in getting better; he has been worse here than I've ever seen him. The country is, or was anyway, almost intolerably depressing, just not desert. Now it's better because a few things are growing, and according to the guide books by February or so the whole land will be covered with a carpet of wild flowers. We found a wild flower the other day with great excitement and as it was a kind of lilyish thing without any stalk we suppose it was the first shred of the carpet. In our own garden we have had heartrending experiences. I suppose we have sowed about twenty packets of seed and the result is a few nasturtiums, a very few marigolds and some sweet peas. They take about three or four weeks to germinate and either grow at the same pace or don't grow higher than half an inch. But generally of course they don't germinate. The two goats are more satisfactory now because they went right out of milk and that saves trouble. Until recently they were milked twice a day, with Mahjroub[2] holding head and hind leg, Eric milking and me responding to cries of agony while some good cows' milk boiled over; and the total yield of the two per day was well under half a pint. The hens however have become very productive—they've laid ten eggs in four days. We started with twelve hens but four died immediately, so if you like you can do the sum I was thinking of doing but find too difficult. I hope all those great hens at Wallington will be ashamed. They really ought to be laying pretty well (i.e. about four each a week) now. Last Christmas we had great numbers of eggs and sent quite a lot away, with the result that all the lucky recipients got letters from the P.M.G.[3] who regretted that a parcel addressed to them had had to be destroyed because it was offensive. I must write some Christmas letters, which is why I go on typing this. I get intolerably melancholy if I have to say exactly the same thing twice, so at about the tenth or fifteenth Christmas letter I am sending people the most surprising greetings, but by the twentieth I am resigned to intolerable melancholy and wish the rest a happy Christmas. That's what I wish you, and a bright New Year of course. And Eric, I am sure, does the same. And we both send our love.

Yours,
Eileen.

1. Son of Mary and Jack Common.
2. The Orwells' servant, Mahdjoub Mahommed.
3. Postmaster-General.

510A. Financial Contribution to *The New Leader*

9 December 1938

The New Leader depended, as did many left-wing journals, upon voluntary subscriptions from its readers to help bridge the gap between its costs and its income from sales and advertising. As Orwell's letter to John Sceats, 24 November 1938, *504*, indicates, *Controversy* and *The New Leader* were both in danger of ceasing to publish or having to publish less frequently. In this issue of *The New Leader*, considerable space was devoted to an appeal to 'raise a huge sum by February.' Readers were promised that in the next issue they would be told what that amount was. A list was also given of seventy-seven groups and individuals who had contributed to the costs of that week's paper, raising, in addition to £63 already acknowledged, the sum of £51 6s 7d. One contributor gave almost half that amount—£25—and the average amount contributed by the other seventy-six groups and individuals was 6s 11d. Orwell was recorded as having sent 5s 7d. See also *490*.

511. Morocco Diary

VILLA SIMONT   10.12.38:
Cannot get any definite idea of the system of land tenure here, whether the peasants own their plots, whether they rent them etc. Land appears to be held in plots of two or three acres upwards. Evidently there are common grazing grounds, and there must obviously be some communal arrangement for the distribution of water. The small streams are diverted in different directions according as they are wanted, and by means of the channels and small dykes which exist in the fields water can be run to almost any spot. Nevertheless there is an obvious great difference in the water supply between peasants' plots and the plantations of Europeans and wealthy Arabs. The difficulty about water makes an immense amount of work. The soil in parts here is a sort of soft chalk which has streams running through it about twenty feet down. In order to get at this—often a stream of a few inches deep—wells are sunk at intervals. One sometimes finds such wells all along the edge of a field a few yards apart—why so many I do not know, but I have seen this in a number of fields, eg. one field had 12 wells along its edge. There is evidence of great shrinkage in the water supply in recent years. Some streams have three beds, ie. one they run in now, a wider one they presumably run in after the rainiest season, and a much larger one they ran in at some time in the past. Some recently cultivated fields seem to have gone out of cultivation. It seems very difficult to get small seeds to germinate without constantly watering the soil.
The peasants here evidently do not use harrows, but they appear to plough it over several times in different directions. At the end of course it is still in furrows. This has the advantage that it gives the seed (broadcast) a certain tendency to lie in straight lines. Also perhaps conserves water better.
   The winter grain (I suppose barley) is now about 4–6" high. Trees seem to do better here than small crops, eg. the olives (black and known for their bitterness) are good. Nevertheless there are practically no trees except cultivated ones, palms, olives etc. Firewood,* ready chopped and good quality, costs about 70–80 frs. (about 8/–) for 1000 kilos (about 1 ton). The only fuel here wood and charcoal. Near here a large new plantation of olives etc. run by Frenchmen. A sort of cooly barracks for the Arab workers. Quite good, very much better than the corresponding kind of thing would be in India. Except for a few wealthy ones the Arabs in their villages almost all live

* *Always olive-wood, mostly roots* [Orwell's note].

in tiny straw or palm-thatch huts, like beehives, about 8-10 feet wide. A few wild-looking people living in tiny tents which are simply a piece of cloth stretched over a pole, no walls or flaps. Evidently more or less permanent, as they had built little enclosures round. Normally a village is surrounded by a mud wall about 10 feet high with thorns on top. As in Burma, only men plough but women do all other jobs in the fields, especially tiresome jobs like weeding. Children working, usually at herding animals, when they are almost too young to speak. They are extraordinarily good, never stray away from work and seem to understand exactly what they have to do. Many of the peasants one sees come out and beg as one passes. With some of them this seems to be a reflex action on sight of a European. Generally quite satisfied with 20c. None of the peasant women, at least those one sees working, are veiled.

Examining the Petit Marocain, find its make-up is as follows. 10 pages (some days 12) ie. 60 columns. Of this just over one third is filled with advertisements. Back page and last page but one entirely advertisements. Principal adverts are Persil and other Lever products (note it is always stated on the packet that Lever's stuff is French product), Nestle's milk, various shipping companies, several eye-tonics and other patent medicines. Special pages are set aside for Moroccan news, which does not as a rule figure on the front page. No book reviews, and though get-up etc. is good the general tone of writing is dull compared with ordinary French papers.

All the papers here heavily patriotic. Eg. when Marshall° Lyautey's[1] statue was being brought to Casablanca, both Petit and Presse for over three weeks gave never less than a column and often most of a page to the subject, ie. to adulations of Lyautey. On the actual day of the installation the Presse gave its entire front page to this. La Presse frequently demands the suppression of the Communist Party, the Petit not, tho' Daladier[2] is its hero and it reports de la Rocque[3] sympathetically. The most widely-read French paper in Marrakech seems to be the weekly Candide, which is sold on the streets everywhere. On buying it find it is virtually Fascist. Left-wing French papers seem unobtainable here.

M. Simont has sacked Hussein, evidently on the ground that he was lazy. The job here (for one man) is to look after about 2 acres planted with orange[4] and lemon trees, and part of the ground between the trees, perhaps 20-30 rods, down under marrows etc. Also to look after a few sheep. By European standards it would be said that Hussein worked hard. M. Simont complaining that Hussein (who evidently also had some negro blood) is a Cleuh.[5] They are said to be stupid, shiftless etc. Arabs also accuse them of avarice. Apparently Europeans share the prejudice. Do not know what the pay for this job would be, but probably not more than 10 frs. a day and quarters.

1. Marshal Louis-Hubert-Gonzalve Lyautey (1854–1934) was, as French Resident-General of Morocco, largely responsible for the development of the country. He was French Minister of War 1916–17, and organised the Colonial Exhibition in Paris in 1931.
2. Edouard Daladier (1884–1970), Socialist Premier of France, 1938–40, signed the Munich pact, with Chamberlain, Hitler, and Mussolini, surrendering the Sudetenland to Germany, on 30 September 1938. For Churchill's account of Daladier's visit to London on 18 September to

discuss Hitler's demands with Chamberlain, see *The Second World War*, I, 270–72; U.S.: *The Gathering Storm*, 301.
3. Colonel François de la Rocque was a leading figure of the extreme right who led the Croix de Feu, an anti-Marxist and anti-capitalist group. It was banned but reconstituted as the Parti Social Français. He was anti-German and did not become a collaborator. See also *562*, Diary of Events, *6.8.39, Party Politics*.
4. 'orange' was preceded by 'olive trees,' which was then crossed out.
5. Cleuh (which Orwell also spells as Chleuh) is probably Shluh, which is the Hamito-Semitic language of the Berbers of Morocco; see *Encyclopaedia Britannica*. See *530* for Orwell's reference to their speaking 'their own Berber dialect' and also Arabic.

512. To Cyril Connolly

14 December 1938   Typewritten

Boite° Postale 48   Gueliz   Marrakech   French Morocco

Dear Cyril,

I see your book[1] is out. Send me a copy, won't you? I can't get English books here. The New English were going to send it to me to review, but they haven't done so, perhaps haven't had a copy. I have been in this place about three months, as it is supposed to do my lungs good to spend the winter here. I have less than no belief in theories about certain climates being "good for" you, on enquiry they always turn out to be a racket run by tourist agencies and local doctors, but now I am here I suppose I shall stay till about April. Morocco seems to me a beastly dull country, no forests and literally no wild animals, and the people anywhere near a big town utterly debauched by the tourist racket and their poverty combined, which turn them into a race of beggars and curio-sellers. Some time next month we are going into the Atlas for a bit, which may be more interesting. I am getting on with my novel which was listed to come out in the autumn but, owing to this bloody illness, didn't get started till two or three months ago. Of course I shall have to rush it as I must get it done in time for the spring. It's a pity, really, as it's a good idea, though I don't think you'll like it if you see it. Everything one writes now is overshadowed by this ghastly feeling that we are rushing towards a precipice and, though we shan't actually prevent ourselves or anyone else from going over, must put up some sort of fight. I suppose actually we have about two years before the guns begin to shoot. I am looking forward to seeing your book, I gather from the reviews that a lot of it is about Eton, and it will interest me very much to see whether the impressions you retain are anything like my own. Of course you were in every way much more of a success at school than I, and my own position was complicated and in fact dominated by the fact that I had much less money than most of the people about me, but as far as externals go we had very much the same experiences from 1912 to 1921. And our literary development impinged at certain points, too. Do you remember one or other of us getting hold of H. G. Wells's "Country of the Blind" about 1914, at St. Cyprian's, and being so enthralled with it that we were constantly pinching it off each other? It's a very vivid memory of mine, stealing along the corridor at about four o'clock on a midsummer morning into the dormitory where you slept and pinching the book from beside your bed. And do you remember at about the same time my bringing back to school a copy of Compton Mackenzie's "Sinister Street", which you began to read, and then that filthy old sow Mrs Wilkes found out and there was a fearful row about bringing "a book of that kind" (though at the time I didn't even know what "sinister" meant) into the school. I'm always meaning one of those days to write a book about St. Cyprian's.[2] I've always held that the public schools aren't so bad, but people are wrecked by those filthy private schools long before they get to public school age.

Please give all the best to your wife. I hope I'll see you when I get back.

Yours
Eric Blair

P.S. [handwritten] I suppose the Quintin Hogg[3] who won the Oxford election was the little squirt who was a fag when I left school.

1. *Enemies of Promise*. Although primarily concerned with aspects of life that work against the creative writer, it also describes life at St Cyprian's (called St Wulfric's) and Eton. Connolly was at both schools with Orwell, who is quite frequently mentioned. Orwell and Christopher Isherwood are described 'as the ablest exponents of the colloquial style among the young writers.'
2. For Orwell's letters from St Cyprian's, the preparatory school attended by Connolly and Orwell, see *CW*, X. For his account of his time there, see 'Such, Such Were the Joys,' *3409*.
3. Quintin Hogg (1907–; 2nd Viscount Hailsham; peerage disclaimed for life, 1963; created life peer, Baron Hailsham of St Marylebone, 1970; PC, 1956; KG, 1988; CH, 1974), lawyer, Conservative Party politician, and writer, had entered Eton shortly after Orwell. He was elected to the House of Commons for Oxford City in 1938. Edward Hulton's *Picture Post* reported that Hogg's platform was 'Unity: solid behind Chamberlain.' Hogg later served variously as First Lord of the Admiralty, Minister of Education, Minister for Science and Technology, Lord Privy Seal, and Lord Chancellor.

513. To Frank Jellinek

20 December 1938   Typewritten

Boite° Postale 48   Gueliz   Marrakech   French Morocco

Dear Jellinek,[1]

Many thanks for your letter. I am extremely sorry that I attributed that note in the Manchester Guardian to you, but my reason for doing so was that the M.G. had not denied it. The facts were these. I was apparently semi-disabled by my wound (though actually it got all right soon afterwards) and had decided to go back to England, and on June 15 I went up to Sietamo to get my discharge-papers, which for some reason unknown to me one had to go up to the front to do. When I got there the P.O.U.M. troops besides the others in Sietamo were being got ready for an action which actually took place some days later, and it was only by a bit of luck that I did not get involved in the battle, though at the time I could hardly use my right arm. When I managed to get back to Barcelona on June 20, it was to find that the P.O.U.M. had been suppressed, everyone I knew was in jail or in hiding, I had to sleep two nights in the streets, and the police had been interfering with my wife in the most revolting manner. What really angered me about all this was that it had carefully been kept secret from the men at the front and even from people in Lerida (where I had been on June 20.) On I forget which day I saw you in a cafe near the Hotel Oriente. I was going to cross the road and speak to you, but at this time, as was not unnatural in the circumstanc[es] I was ready to believe that every Communist was a spy, and I simply walked on. Then later in England, when I went through the files of the M.G., I saw the note saying that the P.O.U.M. were not Fascists (or words to that effect), which I naturally attributed to you. I was greatly touched and wrote to the M.G. congratulating them and asking for your address. I suppose the man who replied didn't know who had sent that message, and he merely said that you were in Mexico and they didn't know your address. I am going to send a note to the New Leader saying I was wrong about who sent the message.[2] If they don't insert it, please believe it is only for lack of space. They are quite honest, though often no doubt mistaken, but with only 8 pages per week one hasn't much space to spare.

I am writing at the same time as this asking my agent to send you a copy of my book on the Spanish war. Parts of it might interest you. I have no doubt I have made a lot of mistakes and misleading statements, but I have tried to indicate all through that the subject is very complicated and that I am extremely fallible as well as biassed. Without answering in detail all the points in your letter, I might indicate more clearly than I could do in the book my position on one or two questions that inevitably come up in a controversy of this kind. I entirely agree with you that the whole business about the P.O.U.M. has had far too much fuss made about it and that the net result of this kind of thing is to prejudice people against the Spanish Government. But my position has always been that this kind of controversy could die a natural death and cause comparatively little harm if people would refrain from telling lies in the beginning. The sequence of events is approximately this. The P.O.U.M. preach a "line" which may or may not make it more difficult to secure military efficiency for the Spanish Government, and which is also rather too like what the C.P. were saying in 1930. The C.P. feel that they have got to silence this at all costs, and therefore begin stating in the press that the P.O.U.M. are Fascists in disguise. This kind of accusation is infinitely more resented than any ordinary polemic could be, with the result that the various people and parties who could be described as "Trotskyist" tend to develop into mere anti-Communists. What complicates it and enormously increases the feeling of bitterness it causes is that the capitalist press will on the whole throw its weight on the Communis[t] side of the controversy. I know that Communists don't as a rule believe this, because they have got into the habit of feeling that they are persecuted and have hardly noticed that since about 1936 (ie. since the change of "line") the attitude towards them in the democratic countries is very different. Communist doctrine in its present form appeals to wealthy people, at least some wealthy people, and they have a very strong footing in the press in both England and France. In England, for instance, the News Chronicle and New Statesman are under direct Communist influence, there is a considerable press which is actually official C.P., and certain influential papers which are bitterly *anti-Socialist* nevertheless prefers° "Stalinism" to "Trotskyism". On the other side, of course, there is nothing, because what is now called "Trotskyism" (using the word very widely) has no appeal to anyone with over £500 a year. The result is that the most appalling lies can be printed and except in a few papers like the M.G. which keep up the old traditions it is quite impossible to answer them. One's only resort is to start miserable little rags like the ones the Trotskyists run, which, necessarily, are nothing but anti-Communist papers. There is no question that appalling lies were published about the P.O.U.M., not only by the official C.P. press, but by papers like the N.C. and N.S. & N., which after publishing refuse to print any answers in their correspondence columns. I don't know whether you have yet seen the accounts of the P.O.U.M. trial. The trial made it clear, as it was bound to do if fairly conducted, that there was no truth in the accusations of espionage, which were for the most part merely silly. One accusation, for instance, had been that several miles of the Aragon front had been entirely deserted for two months—this at a time when I was there myself. This witness broke down in the box. Similarly, after all the statements in papers of the type of the Daily Worker about "two hundred signed confessions" etc., there was complete failure to produce any evidence whatever. Although the trial was conducted more or less in camera, Solidaridad Obrera was allowed afterwards to print a report, and it was made quite clear that the charges of espionage were dismissed and the four men who were sentenced were only convicted of taking part in the May fighting in Barcelona. In the face of all this the C.P. press printed reports that they had been condemned for espionage. In addition this was also done by some pro-C.P. papers, which significantly enough are also pro-Fascist papers. Eg. the Observer reported the verdict in such a way as to let it appear that the verdict was one of espionage, and the French press of this country, which of course is pro-Franco, reported the accusation, stated that it had been "proved" and then failed to report the verdict. You must agree that this kind of thing is likely to cause resentment, and though in the heat of the moment it may seem "realistic" to say "These people are obstructing us—therefore they might as well be Fascists—there we'll say they *are* Fascists", in the end it may do more harm than good. I am not a Marxist and I don't hold with all this stuff that boils down to saying "Anything is right which advances the cause of the Party." On the title page of my book you will find two texts from Proverbs[3] which sum up the two prevailing theories of how to combat Fascism, and I personally agree with the first and not the second.

I think you'll find answers in my book to some of what you say. Actually I've given a more sympathetic account of the P.O.U.M. "line" than I actually felt, because I always told them they were wrong and refused to join the party. But I had to put it as sympathetically as possible, because it has had no hearing in the capitalist press and nothing but libels in the left-wing press. Actually, considering the way things have gone in Spain, I think there was something in what they said, though no doubt their way of saying it was tiresome and provocative in the extreme.

I got over the wound with no ill-effects but now my lungs have been giving trouble and they sent me to spend the winter in this country. I think it's doing me good, and I expect to be back in England in April.

Yours

Eric Blair

("George Orwell")

P.S. I don't agree with you that there was no persecution of P.O.U.M. militiamen. There was a lot—even, later on, in hospitals, as I learned from a man who was wounded later than I. I have today heard from George Kopp, who was my commandant at the front, and who has just got out of Spain[4] after 18 months in jail. Making all allowance for exaggerations, and I know people who have been in those circumstances always exaggerate, there is no question he has been shamefully treated, and there were probably some hundreds of others in the same case.

The chap who told you something about the I.L.P. militiamen signing some kind of statement was probably a man named Parker. If so it was probably a lie. Ditto if it was a man named Frankfort. If it was a man named Hiddlestone[5] it was probably not a lie but might have been some kind of mistake. I know nothing about it as I came to Spain quite independently of them.

1. Frank Jellinek (1908–1975), author of *The Paris Commune of 1871* (1937) and *The Civil War in Spain* (1938), reviewed by Orwell in *The New Leader*, 8 July 1938 (see *462*), was an American correspondent in London for the *New York Herald Tribune* and in Spain for the *Manchester Guardian*. He wrote to Ian Angus, 10 June 1964, to explain that Orwell's letter was prompted by his (Jellinek's) protest that he had not falsified a despatch to the *Guardian* 'for propaganda purposes,' as suggested by Orwell in his review of *The Civil War in Spain*. He had left Barcelona well before 20 June 1937 and he wrote nothing for the *Guardian* about the suppression of the POUM. He believes the article in question 'was more or less planted on the *MG* by F. A. Voigt,' who was a visiting correspondent in Barcelona. Voigt (1892–1957), an outstanding foreign correspondent, early drew attention to the dangers of Nazism; such was his analysis of the rise of National Socialism that he was unable to work for the *Manchester Guardian* in Germany again after Hitler's accession to power in 1933. After his book *Unto Caesar* (1938) was published, he was grouped by Orwell among 'The Pessimists' in 'The Intellectual Revolt', 1, 24 January 1946; see *2875*. Orwell, in 'Notes on Nationalism,' October 1945 (see *2668*), grouped him with other Anglophobes who suddenly became violently pro-British. Voigt edited *The Nineteenth Century and After* from 1938 to 1946.
2. See 'A Mistake Corrected,' *The New Leader*, 13 January 1939, *526*.
3. 'Answer not a fool according to his folly, lest thou also be like unto him. / Answer a fool according to his folly, lest he be wise in his own conceit.' Proverbs 26:4–5. Orwell gave the reference as xxvi, 5–6 in *Homage to Catalonia*. It was not corrected until the Penguin Edition of 1989.
4. 'jail' typed before 'Spain' but crossed out.
5. Buck Parker, Frank Frankfort, and Reg Hiddlestone were members of the ILP contingent linked to the 3rd Regiment, Division Lenin, POUM, of which Orwell was also a member. For Frankfort (Frankford), see Orwell's reply to his accusations, 24 September 1937, *399*.

514. To Leonard Moore

20 December 1938   Typewritten

Boite° Postale 48   Gueliz   Marrakech   French Morocco

Dear Mr Moore,

Would you be kind enough to ask Warburg to send a copy of HOMAGE TO CATALONIA to

Frank Jellinek
Humboldt, 15,
Cuernavaca, Morelos,
MEXICO

and charge it up to me.

The Penguin Library people wrote to say they wanted to see DOWN AND OUT and BURMESE DAYS, and I expect by this time they will have written to you for copies.[1] I think I gave you the address of my mother, who has a copy of DOWN AND OUT, did I not? I hope this business will come to something.

The novel[2] is going quite well. In case this reaches you in time for Christmas, my wife and I wish you a very merry Christmas, and to Mrs Moore. I hope Miss Perriam is better.

Yours sincerely
Eric Blair

1. See *506*.
2. *Coming Up for Air*.

515. Morocco Diary

VILLA SIMONT 22.12.38:

After heavy rain such as that of the last few days the rivers swell enormously. The Oued Tensift, normally about 10 yards wide, has filled the whole valley it runs in, about 300 yards wide. But judging from the vegetation in the valley this does not happen most years.

The Arab funerals here are the wretchedest I have seen. The dead man is carried by friends and relatives on a rough wooden bier, wrapped in a cloth. Don't know whether this is due to poverty, or whether Mahomedans are supposed not to have coffins. A hole not more than two feet deep is hacked in the ground and the body dumped in it with nothing over it except a mound of earth and usually either a brick or a broken pot at one end, presumably the head. The burial places as a rule are not walled in in any way and except when there happens to be the tomb of some rich person there one would never know them for burial-places—they merely look like a rather hummocky piece of ground. No sort of identifying mark over the graves. On one, presumably of a scribe, I found a pen and inkhorn, otherwise only the broken pots etc. On one an enamel tin mug. A few vacant graves always waiting, including little ones for children. Women apparently never attend funerals.

The other widely-read French weekly paper is Gringoire. * Used to be a sort of gossipy literary paper, but now much as Candide. I notice that these papers, though evidently prosperous and having a lot of advertisements, are not above inserting pornographic advertisements. Also that in spite of their politics they publish serial stories etc. by writers who are more or less "left". On a wall in a cafe lavatory, "A mort Blum"[1] in very small letters. The first political inscription I have seen in French Morocco.

* "Gringoire" claims circulation of ½ million, evidently truthfully [Orwell's note; see 1668, n. 1].

1. Léon Blum (1872–1950) was the first Socialist premier of France, 1936–37, 1938, presiding over a popular front government. He was imprisoned in France and Germany from 1942 until the end of World War II, and was again premier, 1946–47.

516. To Jack Common

26 December 1938   Typewritten

Boite° Postale 48   Gueliz   Marrakech   French Morocco

Dear Jack,

Thanks so much for yours. I'm really frightfully sorry about these blasted hens. We seem to have saddled you with a herd of white elephants. I can't think what it can be. It seems to me that if it were any definite illness they would die off and not merely stop laying. As to its being the ground, I don't think there can be anything in that. To begin with, wherever they are in the field they must be on ground they ranged over before with good results. The hens of old Desborough, who had the field up to end of 1935 or so, died of coccidiosis, but I doubt to start with whether the disease germs would remain in the ground so long, secondly why haven't they developed it before, thirdly you probably wouldn't mistake coccidiosis, which makes the fowls weak and droopy even when they don't die, as most of them do. The thing I really don't understand is why the old fowls (there are a few, aren't there?) don't lay. As to the pullets, it does sometimes happen that they just miss coming into lay in August-September, and then what with the moult and the cold weather don't start till spring. But meanwhile you are being saddled with the food-bills. In a few days I'll try and send you a few quid (I'm afraid at best it'll have to be a few) towards ex[pens]es. I've written recently to my bank to know whether I've got any money left, and I'll get their reply in a few days. Of course this journey, which at any rate was made on borrowed money,[1] has been very expensive and I don't think I'll have any money to speak of coming in for three or four months. The novel ought to be done beginning of April. It's really a mess but parts of it I like and it's suddenly revealed to me a big subject which I'd never really touched before and haven't time to work out properly now. I can't tell you how deeply I wish to keep alive, out of jail, and out of money-worries for the next few years. I suppose after this book I shall write some kind of pot-boiler, but I have very dimly in my mind the idea for an enormous novel in several volumes and I want several years to plan it out in peace. Of course when I say peace I don't mean absence of war, because actually you can be at peace when you're fighting, but I don't think what I mean by peace is compatible with modern totalitarian war. Meanwhile the Penguin people are making moves towards reprinting one or other of my books, and I hope they'll do so, because though I don't suppose there's much dough in it it's the best possible advert. Besides it's damned annoying to see your books out of print. One of mine, "Down and Out," is so completely out of print that neither I nor anyone else known to me except my mother possesses a copy—this in spite of the fact that it was the most-taken-out book in the library at Dartmoor. I'm glad Warburg has struck it lucky with at any rate one book. I must say for him that he has enterprise and has published a wider range of stuff than almost anyone. My Spain book sold damn all, but it didn't greatly matter as my agent had got the money out of him in advance and the reviews were O.K.

God knows when that parcel will turn up. From what I know of French post offices it wouldn't surprise me if it was just in time for Xmas 1939.[2] Actually I left it and a lot of others to be sent off by the shopkeeper, because I was fatigued by a long afternoon of shopping, which is really tiring in this country as in most oriental countries. Arabs are even greater bargainers than Indians and one is obliged to conclude that they like it. If the price of an article is a shilling, the shopman starts by demanding two shillings and the buyer starts by offering threepence, and they may[3] well take half an hour to agree on the shilling, though both know from the start that this is the right price. One thing that greatly affects one's contacts in foreign countries is that English people's nerves are not so durable as those of some other races, they can't stand noise, for instance. I like the Arabs, they're very friendly and, considering their position, not at all servile, but I've made no real contact, partly because they mostly speak a kind of bastard French and so I've been too lazy to learn any Arabic. The French in this country seem dull and stodgy beyond all measure, far worse than Anglo-Indians. I doubt whether there's any real political movement among the Arabs. The left-wing parties have all been suppressed (by the Popular Front) but I don't think they can ever have amounted to much. The people are entirely in the feudal stage and most of them seem to think they are still ruled by the Sultan, which by a fiction they are. There've been no echoes of the Tunis business except in the French press. If a big Arab movement ever arises I think it's bound to be pro-Fascist. I am told the Italians in Libya treat them atrociously, but their main oppressors have been the democracies, so-called. The attitude of the so-called left wing in England and France over this imperialism business simply sickens me. If they went on in the same vein they would end by turning every thinking coloured person into a Fascist. Underlying this is the fact that the working class in England and France have absolutely no feeling of solidarity with the coloured working class.

You asked where Marrakech was. It's somewhere near the top left hand corner of Africa and immediately north of the Atlas Mountains. Funnily enough we've been having the cold snap even here and on Xmas eve there was a heavy frost—don't know whether that is usual here, but judging by the vegetation I don't think it can be. I had the queer and rather pleasant experience of seeing the oranges and lemons on the trees frosted all over, which apparently didn't damage them. The effects of the frost were very curious. Some nasturtiums I had sown earlier were withered up by it, but the cactuses and the Bougainvillea, which is a tropical plant from the South Pacific, weren't affected. The mountains have been covered with snow even on their lower slopes for some time past. As soon as I've done the rough draft of my novel we're going to take a week off and go into the mountains. The Romans thought they were the end of the world, and they certainly look as if they might be. It's generally fine and bright in the day time, but we have fires all the time. The only fuel is olive wood, because there simply isn't a wild tree for miles and miles. This is one of those countries which are very nearly desert and which just exactly support a small population of men and beasts who eat every eatable thing and burn every burnable thing on the surface, so that if there were one more person there'd be a famine. And to think that in Roman times North Africa was full of magnificent forests full of lions and elephants. There are now practically no wild animals bigger than a hare, and I suppose even the human population is smaller. I've just been reading about approximately these parts in Flaubert's "Salammbô", a book which for some reason I'd always steered clear of but which is simply stunning.

I'm not surprised at J.M.M entering the Church.[4] But he won't stay in it long. I suppose in the near future there will be a book called "The Necessity of Fascism."[5] But I think it's really time someone began looking into Fascism seriously. There must be more to it than one would gather from the left press. Mussolini has been "just about to" collapse ever since 1926.

The French hardly celebrate Xmas, only the New Year. The Arabs probably celebrate the New Year, but it may not be the same as ours. They are pretty strict Mahomedans, except that owing to poverty they are not overscrupulous about what they eat. We simply haven't celebrated Xmas yet, but shall when we get a pudding that is coming from England. Eileen was ill on Xmas day and I actually forgot till the evening what day it was. It's all very gloomy, because my father is very ill and my sister who was to come out here consequently can't. Two friends have just got back from Spain. One is a chap called Robert Williams[6] who has come out with his guts full of bits of shell. He says Barcelona is smashed out of recognition, everyone is half starved and you can get 900 pesetas for a £. The other is George Kopp,[7] a Belgian, whom there is a lot about in my book. He has just escaped after 18 months in a G.P.U.[8] jail, in which he lost seven stone in weight. They were bloody fools to let him go after what they have done to him, but I suppose they couldn't help themselves. It's evident from several things that the Communists have lost most of their power and the GPU only exists unofficially.

My love to Mary and Peter. Eileen sends love and thanks Mary for the letter. I'll write again when I hear from the bank. I hope the cold will let up. It can be bloody in a small cottage. About February we'll have to think of getting Muriel mated, but there's no hurry. Whatever happens don't let her go to that broken-down old wreck of Mr Nicholls's,[9] who is simply worn out by about twenty years of fucking his own sisters, daughters, grand-daughters and great-grand-daughters.

Yours
Eric

PS. Were you giving the pullets a forcing mash? Clarke's stuff is pretty good.

1. The novelist L. H. Myers, an admirer of Orwell's work, had given Dorothy Plowman £300 to give to Orwell so he could make the journey, but asked her not to reveal his identity. See *449*, *headnote*.
2. Orwell typed '1929' in error for '1939.'
3. Orwell typed 'make' in error for 'may.'
4. John Middleton Murry (see *95*) had become a communicating member of the Church of England.
5. Murry had a predilection for such titles: *The Necessity of Art* (with others), (1924), *The Necessity of Communism* (1932; New York, 1933), and *The Necessity of Pacifism* (1937).
6. A fellow member of the POUM militia.
7. The commander of Orwell's unit in Spain; see *359, n. 2*.
8. Secret police of the U.S.S.R.
9. A neighbour at Wallington.

517. Eileen Blair to Francis Westrope

29 December 1938   Handwritten

Boite° Postale 48, Marrakech-Gueliz, French Morocco.

Dear Mr Westrope,

Eric meant to write to you for Christmas & then he meant to write to you for the New Year & finally this morning he was going to write to you today. But unfortunately he is ill—indeed we have been ill in turn for the last month. It's really my fault because I collected a cold somehow & then of course Eric caught it. I hope he will be all right in a day or two—his general health really is better now but like everyone in the world we've been unlucky in our weather. At first it was so hot as to be very nearly intolerable & this persisted for months after the cool weather generally begins here; then quite suddenly there were violent winds & rains, frosts & so on. Now however the weather is quite perfect, like the best sort of October day in England, but Eric hasn't properly recovered from the first six or eight weeks—indeed no one has, the place is swarming with low fevers & so on. Nevertheless we missed the crisis & are grateful.

In the first place the letter to you was just to wish you a happy Christmas & New Year, & we hope you had the one &, if it isn't too fantastic a hope, will have the other. Then these book tokens arrived. We are desperate for something to read, something *long*. We spent hours with New Statesmans etc. trying to decide on the books & failed, so we wonder whether you would cash the tokens, send us Martin Chuzzlewit & Barnaby Rudge in the ordinary Everyman edition & credit us with any change (we don't know what the postage will be). If you happen to have one of those leaflets giving lists of the Everyman or World's Classics series we should be still more grateful. It seems sad that we cannot remember any books unaided but there it is. If either of us has an inspiration the other has either read the book very recently or doesn't want to read it at all. I am afraid we give you a lot of trouble but perhaps you won't mind being so hard-worked a benefactor & then we shall have the two Dickenses anyway. We had Our Mutual Friend with us but are now competent to pass the most searching examination on it.

Eric really will write very soon.

With all best wishes
Yours sincerely
Eileen Blair.

APPENDIX 1

518. Domestic Diary

9 August 1938—29 April 1940

Orwell began two diaries in 1938. His Domestic Diary begins on 9 August 1938; his Morocco Diary, on 7 September; see *473* and *478*. Though some diaries are arranged chronologically in this edition, it appeared more useful and less confusing to arrange this in three continuous sections. The Diary from 1938 is printed here; that for 1939 at *582*; and that for 1940 at *729A*.

The Domestic Diary is entirely handwritten. Slight errors have been silently corrected here. Orwell stuck newspaper cuttings into the diary. These are not reproduced, but a heading or brief descriptive note is given within square brackets indicating what had attracted his attention. The texts of these cuttings can be consulted at the Orwell Archive, University College London. Orwell also drew illustrations for certain entries, usually on otherwise blank verso pages. These have been incorporated into the entries they illustrate. Notes are at the end of each month. Dates of entries and paragraphing (in the manuscript, variably indented) have been regularized.

<u>August 9, 1938:</u>   *Caught a large snake in the herbaceous border beside the drive. About 2' 6" long, grey colour, black markings on belly but none on back except, on back of neck, a mark resembling an arrow-head (⌂). Not certain whether an adder, as these I think usually have a sort of broad arrow mark (⌂) all down the back. Did not care to handle it too recklessly, so only picked it up by extreme tip of tail. Held thus it could nearly turn far enough to bite my hand, but not quite. Marx[1] interested at first, but after smelling it was frightened & ran away. The people here normally kill all snakes. As usual, the tongue referred to as the "fangs."[2]*
<u>August 10:</u>   *Drizzly. Dense mist in evening. Yellow moon.*
<u>August 11:</u>   *This morning all surfaces, even indoors, damp as result of mist. A curious deposit all over my snuff-box, evidently result of moisture acting on lacquer.*
Very hot, but rain in afternoon.
Am told the men caught another snake this morning—definitely a grass snake this time. The man who saw them said they had tied a string round its neck & were trying to cut out its tongue with a knife, the idea being that after this it could not "sting."
The first Beauty of Bath apples today.
<u>August 12:</u>   *Very hot in the morning. In the afternoon sudden thunder-*

storm & very heavy rain. About 50 yards from the gate the road & pavement flooded a foot deep after only 1½ hours rain.

Blackberries beginning to redden.

August 16: *Several days past uncertain weather, rainy & sometimes hot. Most of the wheat & barley now cut & stacked. Children picking more or less ripe blackberries two days ago.*

Saw a white owl two nights ago—the first in about two years. Also in the distance another bird probably a little owl.

Horse-chestnuts full-size but not ripe yet. Hops about the size of hazel-nuts. Yesterday went to the Zoo* again. Another litter of lion-cubs, which are a bit bigger than a domestic cat & spotted all over. Those born just a year ago are about the size of a St Bernard dog. The ration of meat for a lion—I suppose its only meal in the day—seems to be about 6 or 7 lbs.

The Sardinian mouflon sheep³ has a large udder like a goat & would probably yield a pint or more. I notice that the zebra's hooves, at least the front ones, are quite perpendicular, but those of the ass-zebra hybrid are like those of a horse. The hybrid has very slightly larger ears, otherwise so far as shape goes almost exactly like the zebra.

August 17: *Warm & fine, rather windy.*

The barley from the 22-acre field is not stacked yet, but the wheat is stacked & makes two stacks measuring so far as I can judge it 30' by 18' x 24' (high) & 18' x 15' x 20' (high). If these estimates are correct, this works out at 14,040 cubic feet of stack for about 14 acres of ground. Allowing 1 ton per acre, it seems 1000 cubic feet of stack represent a ton of grain. NB. to check when the whole field is stacked.

Catmint, peppermint & tansies full out. Ragwort & willow-herb going to seed. A few ripe blackberries. Elder-berries beginning to turn purple.

Oak planks etc. made from the boughs instead of the trunk is known as bastard oak & is somewhat cheaper.

Disused railway sleepers here sold off at £1 = 1 = 0 10 cwt. This probably works out at about 1/– each, ie. 2d a foot.

[Newspaper cutting: short article on greenheart timber]

August 19: *Ref. the stacks in the cornfield. Actually the area under wheat & barley was about the same, & the crop makes 4 stacks, 2 of 30' x 18' x 24' (high) & 2 of 18' x 15' x 20' (high.) This works out at about 28,000 cubic feet of stack for 22 acres. Yesterday fine & rather windy. A fair number of ripe blackberries. Elderberries changing colour rapidly. Hazel nuts almost fully formed. Valerian & mulleins over.*

For improving finish of cement.

[Newspaper cutting describing method to be adopted]

Weather today cold, blowy & rather wet. Haws getting quite red. Some rain in the afternoon.

August 21: *Yesterday fine & fairly warm. Went in afternoon & saw Kit's*

---

* *ie. near Maidstone* [Orwell's note].

Coty,[4] *a druidical altar or something of the kind. It consists of four stones arranged more or less thus:*

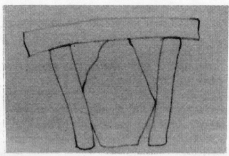

The whole about 8' high & the stone on top approximately 8' square by something over a foot thick. This makes about 70 cubic feet of stone. A cubic yard (27 cubic feet) of coal is supposed to weigh 27 cwt., so the top stone if of coal would weigh about 3½ tons. Probably more if I have estimated the dimensions rightly. The stones are on top of a high hill & it appears they belong to quite another part of the country.

[Newspaper cutting: 'Fruit Bottling Without Sugar, Old-Time Country Method'; see *29.8.38*]

<u>August 22:</u> *Warmish day, with showers. Nights are getting colder & more like autumn. A few oaks beginning to yellow very slightly. After the rain enormous slugs crawling about, one measuring about 3" long. Large holes, presumably ear-holes, some distance behind head. They were of two distinct colours, some light fawn & others white, but both have a band of bright orange round the edge of the belly, which makes one think they are of the same species & vary individually in colour. On the tip of their tails they had blobs of gelatinous stuff like the casing of water-snails' eggs.*
A large beetle, about the size of a female stag-beetle but not the same, extruding from her hindquarters a yellow tube about the length of herself. Possibly some sort of tube through which eggs are laid?

[Newspaper cutting on how to make sloe gin]

<u>August 22.</u>[5] Southwold: *Cool this morning & raining most of the day. Most of the crops in & stacked. Blackberries in Suffolk much less forward than Kent, otherwise little difference in the vegetation.*
When clipping fowls' wings, clip only one wing, preferably the right (left wing keeps the ovaries warm.)
Cold tea is good fertiliser for geraniums.
<u>August 25.</u> Preston Hall: *Everything in Suffolk is much more dried-up than in Kent. Until the day we arrived there had been no rain for many weeks & various crops had failed. Near S'wold saw several fields of oats & barley being harvested which had grown only 1' or 18" high. Ears nevertheless seemed normal. Wheat crop all over the world said to be heavy.*
A bedstraw hawk-moth found in our back garden & mounted by Dr

266

Collings.[6] *Evidently a straggler from the continent. Said to be the first seen in that locality for 50 years.*
Little owl very common round here. Brown owl does not seem to exist.
Dr C. says the snake I caught was the "smooth snake", non-poisonous & not very common.
Today hot again.
Gipsies beginning to arrive for the hop-picking. As soon as they have pitched their caravans the chickens are let loose & apparently can be depended on not to stray. The strips of tin for clothes-pegs are cut out of biscuit boxes. Three people were on the job, one shaping the sticks, one cutting out the tin & another nailing it on. I should say one person doing all these jobs (also splitting the pegs after nailing) could make 10-15 pegs an hour.
Another white owl this evening.
August 26: Hot. Dense ground-mist early this morning. Many blackberries now ripe, very large & fairly sweet. Also fair number of dew-berries. Walnuts now nearly full-sized. Plenty of English apples in the shops.
August 28: Night before last an hour's rain. Yesterday hot & overcast. Today ditto, with a few drops of rain in the afternoon. The hop-picking due to start in about a week.
August 29: Overcast & very chilly. Heavy rain last night. Dahlias now in full bloom.

[Newspaper cutting: response to cutting on fruit bottling (see *21.8.38*), which was 'bound to give unsatisfactory results in many cases'].

August 30: Warmer.
Leaves of the tulip tree beginning to yellow. Sunflowers & gladioli in full bloom. Godetias getting past their best. Montbretias coming into bloom. Elderberries now ripe & bird-shit everywhere deep purple. Purple stains on logs etc. where they have been. Seems difficult to believe that birds digest much of what they eat. The man who keeps the guinea pigs here seems uncertain whether or not they sleep. Says they close their eyes sometimes, but it is uncertain whether they are asleep. First English eating pears today.
August 31: Morning very cold, warm & fine later.

1. The Orwells' dog.
2. It was an ancient belief that a poisonous snake injects its poison by means of its forked tongue and not, as is the case, through two fangs. So Shakespeare, in *Richard II*, 3.2.20–22.
   Guard it, I pray thee, with a lurking adder
   Whose double tongue may with a mortal touch
   Throw death upon thy sovereign's enemies.
   See also 11.8.38.
3. A wild sheep found in the mountains of Sardinia and Corsica but, by extension, any large, wild, big-horned sheep.
4. Kit's Coty House is the chamber of a long barrow (an ancient grave mound) not far to the north of Aylesford.
5. Because the previous diary entry was dated 22 August, it is likely that this was 23 August. Orwell had gone to Southwold to see his parents before leaving for North Africa; see his letter to Jack Common, 25 August, *476*. The diary entry for 25 August indicates a return to Preston Hall; thus the two days at Southwold were 23 and 24 August.
6. The Blairs' family doctor at Southwold from 1921. His son, Dennis, was a friend of Orwell's; see *109, n. 1*.

<u>September 1:</u> *Fine & fairly warm.*
<u>September 2:</u> *Fine & fairly warm.*
<u>September 3:</u> *Writing on P.&O. ss. "Stratheden", 23,500 tons. No of passenger berths 1063. Left Tilbury dock 6 pm yesterday. Position marked this morning (not certain whether 8 am or noon) as 49.25 N, 3.34 W, run being 288 miles. Distance to go 1007 miles. Passed Ushant, about 5-10 miles on port side, about 5 pm Now entering Bay of Biscay & travelling about due South. Should sight land again tomorrow night. Sea at present calm. Once or twice small shoal of fish, pilchards or sardines, leaping out of the water as though something was after them. Small land-bird, bunting or some such thing, came on board this morning when out of sight of land. Also pigeons perching on rigging.*
<u>September 4:</u> *Today crossing mouth of Bay of Biscay. Sea a little rougher, ship rolling somewhat. Not sick (seasickness remedy "Vasano" evidently efficacious.) Passing C. Finisterre about 5 pm but invisible owing to mist. Run of the ship (12–12) 403 miles. Gibraltar is about 5° west of Greenwich. Clocks will be retarded ½ hour on Monday & Tuesday, then put forward again at Marseilles. We are due in at Tangier 7 am on Tuesday (6th) & Gibraltar at 1.30 pm Run of 1007 miles to Tangier takes about 89 hours.*
Today a few porpoises passing the ship. Yesterday saw a gull I did not know, dark brown with white bands on wings. Otherwise no life.
Length of ship is about 250 yards, width at widest about 25 yards. There are 7 decks above water-level. Do not yet know number of crew, who including stewards are mainly lascars.
<u>September 5:</u> *Last night much fog, syren° sounding continually. This morning the sea much smoother, grey & oily, about the colour of lead. Later in the day very hot, & the sea bright blue. Passed Cape Roca about 10 am, but invisible in mist. Passed Cape St. Vincent quite close in, about 2–3 miles, at 6 pm Run of the ship (noon to noon) 342 miles. Due at Tangier early tomorrow.*
Gulls here of a breed I do not know, dark brown or black on top, white below, hawking over the water only a few inches above the surface, just like an owl over grass. Clumps of sea weed° as we got nearer land. Some swallows or martins (different from the English) following the ship when still far from land. Two whales said to have been seen yesterday, but I missed them.
This is not, as I had thought, a steam turbine ship, but an oil turbine. Crew thought to be about 600. The tourist class (really midway between 2nd & 3rd class) has three lounges apart from the dining saloon, two decks where games are played, a small swimming bath & a rather primitive cinematograph. R.C. mass & Anglican H.C. held every day. Tourist fare London-Gibralter £6–10.[1]
<u>Later.</u> *Number of crew 543. Ship carries 8 or 9 thousand tons cargo.*
<u>September 8.</u> Gibraltar: *Weather mostly hot & nights sometimes uncomfortably so. Sea variable mostly rather choppy. When no wind fish visible at least 10 feet below surface.*
The Barbary Ape is said to be now very rare at Gibraltar & the authorities are trying to exterminate them as they are a nuisance. At a certain season of the

year (owing to shortage of food I suppose) they come down from the rock & invade peoples° houses & gardens. They are described as large doglike ape with only a short stump of tail. The same species found on the African coast just opposite.

The breed of goat here is the Maltese, or at any rate is chiefly Maltese. The goat is rather small, & has the top half of its body covered with long & rather shaggy hair which overhangs it to about the knees, giving the impression that it has very short legs. Ears are set low & drooping. Most of the goats are hornless, those having horns have ones that curve back so sharply that they lie against the head, & usually continue round in a semi-circle, the point of the horn being beside the eye. Udders are very pendulous & in many cases simply a bag with practically no teats, or teats barely ½ inch long. Colours black, white & (especially) reddish brown. Yield said to be about a litre a day. Goats apparently will graze on almost anything, eg. the flock I watched had grazed the wild fennel plants right to the ground.

Breed of donkeys here small, like the English. The conveyance peculiar to the place a little partly closed in carriage rather like the Indian gharry with the sides taken out.

Hills steep & animals on the whole badly treated. No cows. Cows' milk 6d a pint. Fruits now in season, apples, oranges, figs, grapes, melon, prickly pear, brinjals & various English vegetables. Prickly pear grows very plentifully on poor soil. Few hens here & eggs small. "Moorish eggs" advertised as though a superior kind.

Cats of Maltese type. Dogs all muzzled.

<u>September 10.</u> Tangier: Temperature here said never to rise above about 85°. Sea is fairly warm, water extremely clear, objects 20 & 30 feet below being visible when there is no wind. There is a tide rise of about a foot. Sea & harbour full of fish, but for some reason only the smaller kinds seem to be caught. There is a largish fish, generally about 6″ to a foot long, brown-coloured & somewhat resembling a pollock, which haunts the stones of the jetties in great numbers, swimming in shoals of 5–20, but all the fishermen say that these cannot be taken on a hook. The method of fishing with rod & line for the smaller fish seems to be foul-hooking. A contrivance made of about half a dozen small hooks set back to back, with a bait of bread or meat just above it, is lowered into the shoal & drawn rapidly up as the fish gather round it. Long-shore fishing with a net is done as follows. A net about 150′ feet° long & 6′ deep, finely meshed in the middle but coarse towards the end,

is carried out to sea by boats & placed in position, being held up by floats. Attached to each end of the net is an immensely long rope, probably half a mile or more. This is gradually hauled in, the men on each rope converging gradually then bring the net into a curve. There is a team of 6 or 8 men & boys on each rope. They do not pull with their hands but have a string round the waist & on the end of it a knot that can be attached immediately to the rope. They then pull with the body, leaning backwards & doing most of the work with the right leg. As the rope comes in it is coiled, & as each man reaches the coils he detaches his string, runs forward & hooks on to the seaward end of the rope. Hauling in takes at least an hour. Of the one I saw hauled in, the bag was about 30 lbs of sardines (or some similar small fish) & about 5 lb. of sundries, including squids, red mullet, long-nosed eels etc., etc. Probably °
value (to the fishermen) about 5/-, & representing about 2 hours work-time to 15 men & boys, say 20 adult work-hours, or 3d an hour.

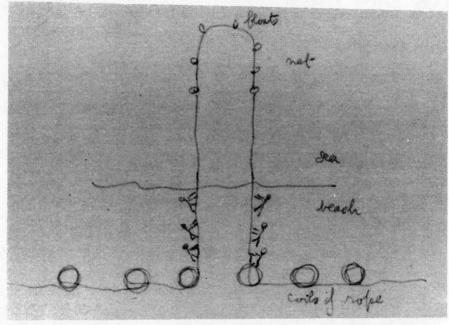

Donkeys here overworked to a terrible degree. They stand about 9–10 hands & carry loads which must often be well over 200 lbs. After putting a considerable load on the donkey's back the driver then perches himself in the middle. Hills here extremely steep, 1 in 5 or 6 in many places, but donkeys go up carrying loads so immense that they are sometimes almost invisible underneath. They are nevertheless extremely patient & willing, usually wear no bridle or halter & do not have to be driven or even led. They follow or walk just in front of their master like a dog, stopping when he stops & waiting outside any house while he is inside. The majority seem to be uncastrated, ditto with many of the horses (all small & in poor condition.)

Smells here not bad, in spite of the heat & labyrinthine bazaars.

Fruits in season, prickly pear, melons of many kinds, grapes, brinjals, otherwise all European. Water carried in goatskins & sold. Large fig-tree here has both green & purple figs on it, a thing I did not know happened. A sort of convolvulus creeper very common here has blue flowers & pinkish flowers on same plant & sometimes on same stem. Flowers now out, cannas, bourgainvillea,° geraniums; peculiar coarse grass for lawns.

Two kinds of swallow or martin here. No gulls in harbour.

Gets dark here well before 7 pm (ie. really 7, summer time not being in operation.)

Butter here all right, but fresh milk apparently almost unobtainable.

September 14. *Marrakesh°: Birds seen on railway journey Tangier-Casablanca-Marrakech.* [2] *Ibis extremely numerous, Kestrels fairly common & also two larger kinds of hawk or kite, a few solitary crows very similar to the English bird. No storks, tho' said to exist here. A very few partridges. Goldfinches, apparently identical with English bird, common in Marrakesh. Saw a man carrying a hare, otherwise no wild quadrupeds at all. There are said to be literally none, except a few hares & jackals, in Fr. Morrocco.° A few camels in Sp. Morocco, but not common till south of Casablanca. In general a camel seems to stand about 18 hands high. All are extremely lean & have calloused patches on all joints. Most are muzzled. Donkies° in Marrakesh slightly less overloaded & slightly less docile than in Tangier.*

Dates are now almost ripe. The partially ripe dates are bright yellow & hang in thick clusters on stems of their own just where the crown of the palm joins the trunk. There are generally about 6 clusters per tree & the whole would weigh about ½ hundredweight. The fallen date looks just like an acorn without its cup. Apparently there are several varieties of date palm including a dwarf one.

The peppercorns on the pepper trees just about ripe. Apparently these are known as "false pepper", although it can be used in the ordinary way. Walnuts, evidently local, just ripe. Pears & peaches rather under-ripe. Lemons here are round & green, more like the Indian lime, only larger & thicker-skinned. Wine grapes in great profusion & very cheap.

The marine life at Casablanca seemed almost exactly the same as in England. Winkles, limpets, barnacles, land-crabs & one kind of anenome apparently identical. Saw no gulls, however. Forgot to mention that at Tangier there were catches of very large mackerel.

Rosemary grows well in Marrakech. Roses do well, petunias grow into huge bushes, as in India. Zinnias also thrive. Apparently good grass can be grown if there is sufficient water.

September 15: *Caught a water-tortoise, about 8" long, outside the small zoological gardens here (evidently it had not escaped from within, though of the same kind as those kept inside.) It was in an irrigation ditch, swimming against the current & only succeeding in remaining about stationary. When turned onto its back it was unable to turn over. It smelt abominably, though active & apparently in good condition.*

No ordinary sparrows here, but a small bird of the finch family, with brown body, bluish head & long tail, very common.

A few michaelmas daisies in flower in the Z[oological]. gardens, which surprised me. Olives almost ripe. Some turning bluish-red, which is perhaps their ripe colour. Oranges still green. These trees evidently need a lot of manure. Runner beans in pod, much as at home. Grapes here are poor, rather dry & tasteless.

Large ants here, half red & half black, enlarging their hole in the ground. One carrying out a bean-shaped stone about ¼" long by ½" thick. Flies here very trying, mosquitoes fairly numerous, but as yet no plagues of flying insects.

Tonight dark by 7 pm

<u>September 19</u>: For sale along with the bright orange half-ripe dates are others equally bright purple, about the colour of brinjals. Pomegranates for sale in large piles everywhere. Some oranges beginning to yellow. Immense vegetable marrows for sale, probably weighing 20-30 lbs. each. Also a kind of smooth pale green extremely elongated marrow—possibly a species of cucumber. Black bread made & sold here in the bazaar; presumably barley but looks like rye.

Goldfinches extremely common here. Storks it appears are migratory & do not appear here till mid-winter. Great variations in temperature. Today & yesterday fairly cool, the day before unbearable, temperature even at 6 pm being 25°C. (ie. 77°F.) & probably about 40°C at midday. Is said to reach 45°C. (ie. 113°F.) as hottest indoor temperature here. After cooling off about 4 pm it generally seems to get hotter again about 6, perhaps owing to the prevailing warm wind. At night a sheet over one is sufficient, but in the early morning one generally pulls up the blanket.

A donkey is said to cost about Fr. 100 (about 12/6d.)

Lettuces said to be very difficult to grow here.

<u>September 20</u>: Lathes used by Jewish carpenters who make the string-seated chairs etc. are of extremely primitive type. There are two clamps, the left hand one fixed, the right sliding upon a metal rod, with a metal point in each. The bar of wood to be turned is fixed upon the two points & turns itself, the points being stationary. Before it is put on the string of a bow is looped once round it. The carpenter holds the movable clamp in place with his right foot & works the bow with his right hand, holding the chisel in his left hand & steadying it with his left foot. In this way he can turn a piece of wood apparently as accurately as on a proper lathe, judging by eye to about 1/100 inch. Working the bow makes the wood revolve at an astounding speed.

The earth walls here are made out of earth which is dug out at a depth of 4-6 feet, either because this is different earth or because at this depth it is easier to find it damp enough to be workable. It is a peculiar chocolate colour & it dries into the light pink distinctive of this town. Having been dug out it is mixed with rubble & a little water, then cast in sections in a wooden frame, just like cement, but when in the frame it has to be packed together very hard with heavy rammers. When one section is hard enough to stand unsupported the next is made, & the joins do not show, the mud setting almost like cement.

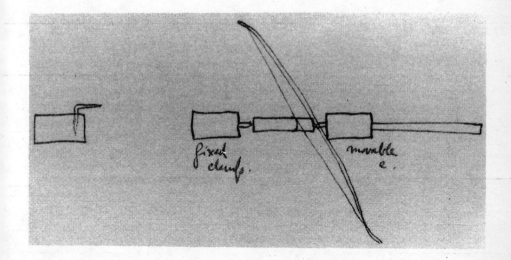

fixed clamp.

movable c.

These mud walls are said to stand many years in spite of torrential rains.
The orange trees which grow in the street here are of an inedible bitter kind.
This kind is used as a stock for grafting the sweet orange on.
Some of the olive trees here have, among the ordinary green olives, a certain
number which are bluish red, though apparently ordinary in every other
respect.
The superstition that it is lucky to touch a hunchback apparently obtains
among the Arabs as well.
Today stifling hot about midday, otherwise somewhat cooler, though we did
not want a coat till about 6-30 pm We have not yet had a day when it was clear
enough to see whether the Atlas mountains have snow on them or not.
September 25: Yesterday morning blowy & overcast, then some fairly
heavy showers of rain. Today no rain, but cooler & still windy.
The reason for the galls always present on camels' joints is that these are what
they kneel down on, usually on stones etc. Nearly all camels here also have
galled backs. It is said that a camel can often only be managed by one man
whom it knows, & that one must at all costs avoid beating them. Relative to
size they carry a much smaller load than a donkey. Some of them have flies &
maggots burrowing into the galls on their backs, without appearing to notice
it. Children also pay very little attention to flies, which are sometimes crusted
in sores all round their eyes.
Hollyhocks just over & sunflowers coming to an end. The former grow 10 or
12 feet high.
Chrysanthemums in the public gardens budding. Cannas are very fine, in 4
colours.
There is no snow at present on the Atlas mountains. At sunset when it is clear
they take on a remarkable purplish-red colour.
The bow which is used for a lathe is also used for a drill. A drill with a
cylindrical wooden handle in the base of which there is a hole is fitted against a

steel point & rotated with the bow. It is kept firm by the other end being in contact with the wood that is drilled. It seems to work as exactly as an ordinary drill & very rapidly.

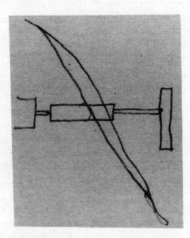

Bought two turtle doves this morning. Two doves 10 Fr. (an overcharge), bamboo cage about 20" by 15" by 20", 15 Fr. Total cost about 3/–. These birds seem to domesticate very easily.
Ordinary blackbird, or some bird extremely similar, is common here. Also the little owl or some very similar owl. Bats here are large, about twice the size of English bat.
It gets dark now at about 6.45 pm
September 27: *Yesterday cooler. Some thunder in afternoon, then an hour's steady rain in the evening. Have not worn dark glasses for several days past.*
September 28: *Distinctly cooler at night. Last night used a blanket all night. Red hibiscus in flower.*

1. Six pounds ten shillings—not £6 to £10.
2. Orwell sometimes writes 'Marrakech' and sometimes 'Marrakesh.' It is not always clear whether 'c' or 's' is intended. The name is given here as Marrakech when there is doubt.

October 1: *Snow on the Atlas today. Evidently it fell last night.*
Camels vary greatly in size, also in colour, some being almost black. Ditto donkeys, which range from reddish fawn to almost black, the latter the commonest colour. Saw yesterday a donkey, evidently full grown, less than 3' high. The man riding it had one foot on the ground.
The Atlas said to go up to 3200 metres (about 10,000 feet.) (Actually about 13,500.)[1]
October 2: *Nightjars here, much as in England. Female donkey today, very heavily in foal, carrying respectable load of wood, & its master. Load something over 200 lb., plus the foal.*
The Spahis ride stallions. Arab saddles, but not blinkers. Horses of different colours. Donkeys here, when male, are always uncastrated.

October 4:   *Still very hot in the middle of the day. Huge lumps of camel-fat (presumably from the hump), very white, like pork-fat, on sale in the bazaar. Said to be only eaten by "people from the mountains."*
Wooden spoons here are cut out with a small adze, which is used with great skill until the spoon is almost entirely hollowed out, after which a gouge-like tool (but with the edge at the side) is used, & then sand paper. Some of these spoons are 2' or 3' feet long & the head as large as a breakfast cup. This work done mainly by children, ditto the work of making wooden ploughs (very primitive, & sold in such numbers as to suggest they have to be renewed every year.)
October 6:   *Yesterday insufferably hot, & this continued till about 6 am this morning, when I felt the need of a blanket on the bed. Flies & mosquitoes still very bad.*
Unbearably hot all day. Apparently this is very unusual for the time of year. Camel cub supposed to be about 6 months old is already about 5' high. They are still sucking when quite a considerable size. Contrary to what I had been told, camels appear to be fairly tractable, as after changing owners they behave quite normally, only the young ones having a tendency to take fright. They vary not only in size & colour (white to almost black, the latter being usually small), but also in the nature of their coats, which are sometimes curly, sometimes smooth, a few camels having a sort of beard all down the neck. They have very little smell.
Horses are sometimes excellent in appearance, always uncastrated. Arab saddle like Mexican, but the Arabs ride with rather short stirrups. The stirrup is a long flat piece of steel with sharp corners which serve as spurs. The Arabs

do not sit very gracefully in the saddle, but have complete mastery of the horse, which goes forward, changes pace & stops all with a loose rein & apparently mostly from the man's voice. The mule is always ridden on the hindquarters. It is evident that the tractability of animals here is due to their being constantly handled from childhood.
October 9:   *Day before yesterday still unbearably hot, yesterday cooler but night very stuffy. Very hot today at midday, in the afternoon a violent dust-storm, much thunder & then fairly heavy rain for about an hour. Fearful mud in the bazaar in consequence. Air much fresher after the rain.*
Primitive drill used by the Arabs—not certain whether merely drill for wood or used for stone & earthenware—constructed as follows. The drill is attached to an upright which passes through a heavy round stone of 5–10 lb. Above this is a cross-piece which fits round the upright but is movable. From the ends of the cross-piece strings go to the top of the upright. These are twisted round the upright & the cross-piece worked up & down, causing the upright & therefore the drill to rotate. The stone serves merely as a weight.

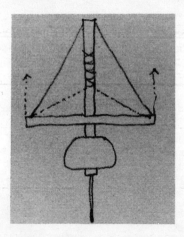

Arab drug kiff,[2] said to have some kind of intoxicating effect, smoked in long bamboo pipe with earthenware head about the size of a cigarette holder. The drug resembles chopped grass. Unpleasant taste &—so far as I am concerned—no effect. Sale said to be illegal, though it can be acquired everywhere for 1 Fr. for about a tablespoonful.

The one smell one rarely encounters here is garlic, which apparently the Arabs do not use much. Almost a majority of the ripe olives now on sale are purple. Possibly these are the ones black olives are made from. Dates getting very ripe. They seem to be a rather dry & inferior kind.

10.10.38: Midday temperature (indoors) today 26°, ie. about 78°F. This is much cooler than the last few days. This evening cool enough to wear a coat.

12.10.38: A lot cooler. No snow now visible on the Atlas, but perhaps obscured by clouds.

Have installed the hens & goats. Hens about the size of the Indian fowl, but of all colours, some with a species of topknot, white ones very pretty. These are supposed to be laying pullets but have not laid yet. Twelve brought crammed together in two small baskets, then sent on donkey back about 5 miles, at the end of which one fowl was dead, apparently pecked to death by others. They appear not to like maize, probably not used to it, or possibly when unbroken it is too big for them. Arabs always keep them in completely grassless runs. Tried giving them some green stuff at which they pecked not very enthusiastically. Hope they may take to it later.

Goats are tiny. Searching all over the market could not find any of decent size or with large bags, though one does see some not actually bad goats in the flocks that graze on the hillsides. The breed here is very shaggy & tends to get its coat dirty. Of ours one, a tiny red goat, is evidently about to kid soon. The other, somewhat larger, supposed to be in milk, but doubt whether she will give more than ½ pint a day at first. After feeding up for 10 days probably a pint. Arabs all scandalised at the idea of giving grain of any kind to goats. Said we should only give them grass. If given grain they drink enormously & swell up. Quite good chopped fodder (lucerne I think) sold in the bazaar for 10c. a bunch. One franc's worth should be enough for 2 goats for a day so far as green food goes. Gave them for their first meal mixture of barley & bran. They had perhaps not seen such a thing before & took no notice of it. Then later smelt it & got to work on it. Goats here do not object to eating off the ground. They are very shy but being so small are easy to handle & do not try to use their horns. They are gentle with each other & do not quarrel over food. Were taken to the house in paniers one on each side of a donkey, the donkey's owner sitting in the middle.

The only form of mash given to fowls here is bran. Grocers here, & apparently everyone else, have never heard of suet—ie. for use in puddings etc.

M. Simont's[3] oranges just beginning to ripen. Dates now ripe, but rather dry & poor. Walnuts very good. Pomegranates exquisite colour inside. The reason why so many dates are gathered when bright yellow is said to be that they are a kind which are used for cooking.

Curiously enough, among the general misery of the animals here, the sheep are very good. They are a long-tailed kind, fairly large, apparently fat (the mutton is quite good & tender) & with very thick, firm coats. They are very docile & tend to huddle all together in a bunch, which makes them easy to manage. When buying a sheep a man carries it across his shoulders, where it lies completely docile like a large slug. A man will ride a bicycle carrying a sheep like this.

13.10.38:   Today fairly cool, & up to about 10 am almost chilly in the shade. This evening another violent dust-storm followed by rain.

14.10.38:   Stuffy, but not very hot. Today milked the small goat (which is probably not in kid) for the first time. For a long time could get no milk at all, though the udder was large & obviously contained milk. Finally discovered that if instead of running my hand down the teat in the ordinary way, I took hold of the whole quarter & squeezed as if squeezing out[4] a sponge, the milk came quite easily. Apparently a different configuration of udder. Wretched yield, about ½ pint from two goats combined. But they are eating well & should improve soon.

Ripe pepper falling from the trees. No eggs.

16.10.38. Villa Simont, route de Casablanca: Yesterday intolerably hot. In the evening thunderstorm & torrential rain, flooding the ground some inches deep.

This morning a disaster. One hen dead, another evidently dying. Forget the name of the disease, which has something to do with the throat. The hen is unable to stand & head droops forward. The dead one had evidently perched for the night & then fallen off the perch. May have something to do with perching in the rain, as they all did so, though I put up another perch for them under cover.

Goats a little tamer. The wife of the Arab who works in the orange plantation & looks after the sheep says that the brown goat is in kid.

18.10.38:   We have now lost 3 fowls in addition to the one which was presumably pecked to death. Symptoms all the same—loss of power of legs & head drooping. Evidently paralysis, tho' attributed by the Arabs to a black parasite infesting the birds. Cause & effect uncertain here. The Arabs' treatment is rubbing with a mixture of charcoal ash, salt & water. Seems effective, at any rate two which were slightly affected seem better to day° & able to run about. The remaining 8 fowls seem now in good condition, but their appetite is very small even allowing for small size. They will never eat maize unless boiled, & do not care greatly for mash.

Goats tamer. Am milking the small one only once a day, & getting about ½ pint a day from the two. Even this is more than a few days back. The small one had slight diarrhea yesterday, probably caused by too much wet green fodder, so am now drying the lucerne into a kind of hay. About the same time one of M. Simont's sheep mysteriously died—attributed to eating too much of the herbage which sprang up after the rain. Goats will eat almost anything, eg. orange peel, & a certain amount of maize can be given them if boiled & mixed with mash. Flaked maize not obtainable here. The goats already follow & know the way to their shed.

Saw a lizard this morning, walking up the window pane. About 4″ long, rather stumpy, resembling an alligator, prickly tail. The first lizard seen in Morocco.

A little cooler, & today very still.

Large ant can drag two peppercorns & the twig connecting them. Ants of various sizes drag a grain of wheat each.

The fowls perched on the new perch for the first time last night.

20.10.38: The turtle doves after about 2 days plucked up courage to leave their house, flew off & presently disappeared. The Arabs said that they would not return. However, they come every day for corn, & sleep in the pepper tree behind the house.

M. Simont's sheep are allowed to browse among the orange trees. Apparently the idea is that they will not eat the leaves of the trees (presumably bitter) but will keep the weeds down. Actually they do nibble at a leaf occasionally.

Cooler. Nice autumnal feeling in the early mornings.

Goats giving distinctly more milk. More than ½ pint, though am only milking the brown one once daily.

Hens all well, but no eggs. These hens, even allowing for size, have extraordinarily small appetites.

Arabs round here growing practically all English vegetables (carrots, radishes, lettuces, cabbages, tomatoes, runner beans, crown artichokes, marrows) besides large green chilis° which are extremely hot. Most of the vegetables rather poor quality. Dates very dry & poor. Sheep here eat half-ripe dates.

The charcoal braziers generally used here are quite satisfactory for cooking. They are generally about 1′ across by 8″ deep & either have very many holes in sides or a double bottom with holes in the top one. The charcoal can be started with very little paper & wood & smoulders for hours. A few strokes with the bellows gets it into a fierce heat. A small tin oven is placed on top & bakes fairly satisfactorily.

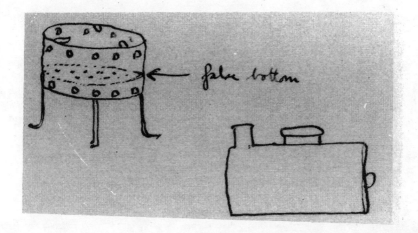

false bottom

21.10.38: _Yesterday went to the Oued Tensift, about 2 Km. from here, the principal river of these parts. About 5 yards wide & 1–3' deep, but lies in a considerable valley & probably rises at some times of the year. Poor water, but said to have small fish in it. Muddy banks & bottom. Fresh water mussels, very similar to those in the Thames, moving to & fro in the mud leaving deep track behind them. Red shank & ringed plover, or extremely similar birds, live on the mud. Feathery shrub which in England is used for making hedges in gardens, arbutus_[5] _I think, growing everywhere. Patches of grass almost like English grass._
Still very hot. Last night unbearably so till quite late at night.
The water here is almost undrinkable, not only tasting of mud but also distinctly salty.
The bitter oranges grown here as grafting stocks said to be good for marmalade, so presumably the same as Seville oranges.
Some of the goats round here a bright silvery-grey colour. First-class Spanish goat said to cost Frs. 500.
23.10.38: _The water here evidently has some mineral in it which is the cause of the almost continuous belly-ache we have had since coming here. Near the Oued Tensift noticed that where the water had receded it had left some white deposit behind. Possibly something akin to Epsom salts—at any rate not an organism as it is not affected by boiling. Arranging to get Marrakech tap water (which is all right & said to come from the Atlas.) Various bottled table-waters impossibly expensive, actually dearer than the cheapest wine._
Soil here is extremely deep, at least 4' without any change of substance. Rather light & reddish, though it dries into a kind of brick, & said to need a lot of manure.
Some of the small oranges ("mandarins") are yellowing. Some lemons almost ripe, others only in blossom—different kinds,[6] _perhaps._
Today the first day we have had when it was cool all the time. Overcast,

279

windy & some rain rather like a damp day in September in England. The day before yesterday a little rain with much thunder.

The doves come to the house from time to time & are very tame, eating from one's hand with a little persuasion. Saw a partridge in the grounds yesterday. Today sowed seeds of nasturtiums, phlox D.[7] & pansies.

Flytox very good & kills flies by the thousand. Otherwise they are utterly intolerable.

Red chilis° spread out to dry in the fields, like huge red carpets.

25.10.38: *Much cooler. Yesterday overcast & cool all day, with occasional sharp showers. Violent wind & storms of rain in the night. Fire last night & this morning, not absolutely necessary but acceptable.*

The brown goat, besides being very difficult to milk, gives little or nothing. Perhaps she is really going off preparatory to kidding, in which case she would probably kid in some weeks' time.

The pigeons this morning of their own accord went into the pigeon-house in which we put them for our first day here. They are now very tame.

Goats eat boiled wheat & maize readily.

27.10.38: *On Tuesday afternoon (25th) tremendous rain, much as in the tropics except that it was very cold rain. Everything flooded feet deep, the earth not dry yet. The Oued Tensift is now quite a considerable stream & low ground all round it has turned into marsh. Today near the Oued Tensift came upon a sort of large pool where there were° a flight of wild duck swimming about. Managed to scare them onto the wing, & after much circling round they came straight overhead. Sixteen in number, & evidently mallards, same as in England, or very similar. Saw another larger flight in the distance afterwards. Almost the first game birds seen here.*

Ordinary sparrows fairly common in the garden here. In Marrakech itself one used not to see them.

Large numbers of black beetles, about 1″ long, crawling everywhere, evidently brought out by the rain. Have sowed sunflowers, sweet peas & marigolds. The other seeds not up yet, as it has been much cooler (we are having fires every evening.) The ground here is lumpy & unpleasant to work, but at present not many weeds—more when this rain has taken effect, perhaps. Some weeds as in England, eg. bindweed & twitch grass, but not growing very strongly. Silver poplar or some very similar tree grows here. Tomatoes here are grown in large patches without sticks. Very poor floppy plants & smallish tomatoes, but plenty of them.

Yesterday on milking the brown goat found her milk had gone sour & came out quite thick. This is because she is only being milked once a day & had not been fully milked for two days owing to her restiveness. Squeezed the bad milk onto the ground & tonight her milk was all right again. Another hen bad in the legs this evening. Examined & found enormous black lice. Hope treatment will be effective as before. The stripey goat's milk increases, but very slightly, still not much over ½ pint a day. She is very thin, though she eats well. The present ration of hard food is 2 handfuls of barley & 2 of bran morning & evening, with a mash of boiled maize & bran about once a week. The doves readily eat maize if it is broken.

Today saw some doves in an aviary which had eggs.

The fountain in front of the house filled up after the rain & mosquito larvae are multiplying rapidly.

One egg (the first) yesterday, none today.

28.10.38:   One egg. Many black beetles squashed in the road. Inside they are brilliant vermilion. Men ploughing with teams of oxen after the rain. Wretched ploughs, with no wheel, which only stir the soil.

30.10.38:   Fine, not very hot. One egg.

31.10.38:   Ditto. One egg. Inside bad again.

Fruit on sale here much resembling a strawberry, but full of pips & has an unpleasant sour taste.

Put paraffin on the water in the fountain yesterday. About 30 square feet, & about a cupful of paraffin covered it. Mosquito larvae all dead by this morning.

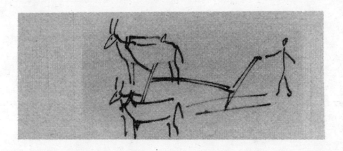

The plough used here has a crossbar which passes under the bellies of the two draft animals, & to this are attached the yokes – wooden for oxen & sackcloth for horses etc. Oxen, mules, horses & even donkeys used for ploughing. Two different animals sometimes yoked together.

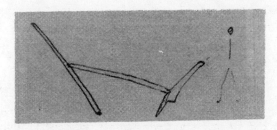

The ploughman walks on the already ploughed side & holds the handle with one hand, changing at each furrow. The share is only a sort of hollow iron point fitted over a wooden rod. The whole structure can be easily carried over the shoulder.[8] Absence of wheel makes it far harder to guide.

1. Copy within second set of parentheses is later addition.
2. kiff (or kef, keef, kif) is Indian hemp, marijuana, marihuana, *cannabis sativa* (or *indica*), from Arabic 'kaif,' meaning enjoyment, well-being, state of dreamy intoxication.
3. M. Simont, the butcher, owned the villa the Orwells rented from 15 October. It was set in an orange grove.
4. 'out' is difficult to distinguish from 'at.'
5. It is not certain what Orwell is describing, since arbutus has leathery, rather than feathery, leaves. The most likely possibility is tamarisk, which could grow in the situation Orwell describes.
6. Orwell was evidently unaware that in the lemon all stages of flowering and fruiting occur at the same time. He does know this later; see Domestic Diary, 4.3.39.
7. Perhaps this was the annual phlox drummondii, which is found in several varieties.
8. The two illustrations and the copy below the second are on the page facing the diary entries. The positioning here has been arranged by the editor.

1.11.38: *Fine, not at all hot. People ploughing everywhere. The plough stirs the soil about 4" to 6" deep. The soil varies greatly & some of it looks rather good. Large patches which were perhaps cultivated a few years ago have been eroded till the rock is sticking through. After the rain some kind of weed (dicotyledon) is springing up everywhere very rapidly & will no doubt give a lot of pasture soon. The fallen olives are quite black. Pomegranates now about over. The pomegranate tree is small & very unimpressive, much like a hawthorn bush. Some wheat (or some other grain) just coming up, evidently winter wheat sown about the same time as in England.*
Passing a flock of sheep & goats today, a goat had just given birth to a kid. The shepherd picked the kid up & carried it & the mother hobbled after them, crying to the kid, with the placenta still hanging out of her. Goats will eat leaves of prickly pear. Others grazing at thorn bushes go down on all fours & creep under the thorns almost like a cat, to get at a few green leaves.
The nasturtium & marigold seeds germinating, the others not yet.
Inside still very bad.
Another kind of orange coming into season, but still not completely ripe. A largish sour kind, rather thick skin & lots of pith, but good flavour.
3.11.38: *Yesterday one egg. Fine sunset, with green sky.*
The nasturtiums & marigolds well up.
Inside terribly bad in the night.
Fairly warm. On silver poplar tree found puss–moth caterpillar about 1" long. Found shell of dead tortoise. Some time in life it had had some kind of injury which had crushed in a portion of the shell, forming a dent, & had set & grown in that position.
The half-starved donkey which I think was bought recently by M. Simont has discovered that the goats are given barley & comes across to rob them of it.
The pool where I saw the wild duck has already largely dried up.
One egg today.
The barley about at an end. There was about 20-25 lbs, & it has lasted 3 weeks, ie. each goat gets about ½ lb. a day.
4.11.38: *One egg.*
5.11.38: *One egg.*

<u>6.11.38</u>:   *Two eggs.*
Fairly considerable rain recently at nights. In the daytime fine & rather warm. This afternoon some raindrops out of a completely clear sky, then a thunderstorm & fairly heavy rain.
After the recent rain the streams in the fields are much swollen, & water tortoises are everywhere. Today saw 10-20 of them, & often 3 or 4 at a time. They are generally sitting on the mud & leap into the water when one approaches. After a while they come to the surface & remain with eyes & nose just out of the water, like the frogs in Spain, diving at once at any alarm. They seem able to move very rapidly.
The goats almost out of milk, possibly because they have had no barley for a couple of days, though pending the arrival of the barley I have given them other things, eg. boiled maize.
The nasturtiums now quite large. 1 sweet pea showing. No phlox or pansies (about a fortnight), so evidently dud seed.
Some of the local dates quite good, very shiny & sticky, & roundish shape, about size & shape of large walnuts.
Inside better.
<u>7.11.38</u>:   *No rain today. A little cooler. Very yellow moon.*
Today in among the orange trees they were ploughing with 1 donkey. They have a small light plough, no wheel but share as in Europe & quite sharp, made in Czechoslovakia & probably costing £1–£2. It is hard work but evidently not too much for a strong donkey, & he can plough up a fair-sized patch (this was about 25 yards by 5 yards of ground that had more or less gone back to grass) at one go.

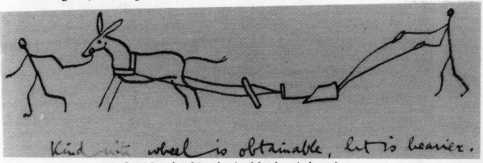

Kind with wheel is obtainable, but is heavier.

The oranges practically ripe now. We had a few of them (tangerine type) the other day.
Fresh barley today, about 30 lb. for Frs. 17.50 or a little less than 1d a lb. This is less than I paid before.
In an old stone tank near the house found the decayed head of what may be a dog but I think is a jackal. There are said to be some in this country. In either case a very complete skull, so have put it up on a stick for the insects to get it clean.
<u>8.11.38</u>:   *Fine, rather warm. Some rain last night. A few sweet peas up.*

One egg.
Footmarks of tortoises in the mud could easily be mistaken for those of a rabbit.
9.11.38: *Sowed sweet peas (only about ½ dozen of the others have come up) carnations & violas.*
10.11.38: *Sowed pinks, godetias & clarkia.*
Rainy & overcast all day, but fairly warm. Fine sunset. Green sky. Large flocks of starlings flying everywhere.
12.11.38: *One egg.*

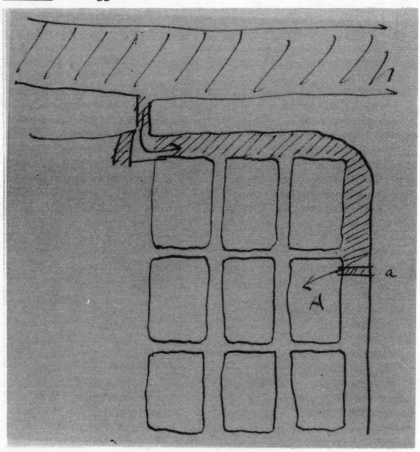

Method of irrigation used here. The soil in any field growing crops that require irrigation is divided into small beds about 4 yds–3 yds. The irrigation ditch which can be connected up with the stream, runs round the edge. If it is desired to water bed A, the ditch is damned then & a chunk cut out of A's surrounding bank. The water runs into A, & when enough has run in the bank is closed again, the dam across the ditch removed, & the water can be run to any other place required.

<u>13.11.38:</u> One egg.
The striped goat now completely out of milk.
On the whole very hot in the daytime lately. Fire at nights but not really necessary. Immense flocks of starlings, probably as many as 5000 in a flock, all the while attacking the olives, which are now ripe on the trees. Arabs out all day in the olive groves, shouting to scare the starlings away. E. compares the sound of the starlings' twittering to the rustle of a silk dress.
In an irrigation tank the other day saw quantities of tortoises, ranging from 3" long to nearly a foot. Caught a small one. These cannot swim fast enough to get away if you wade after them. Compared with land tortoises they are not very retractile, keep their heads & limbs out even when you are holding them, & have no power to withdraw the tail. They draw their head into a kind of cylinder of skin like a muffler. They do not seem able to stay under water long without coming up for air.[1] In the same tank, underneath a stone, found some tiny leeches about ¼" long. The first I have seen in this country.
Last night found a huge toad in the flower bed. The first I have seen here. Nearly twice the size of an English toad, very warty & able to leap a considerable way.
Shallots in the fields almost ripe. Peasant brought us some young leeks.
Today saw a dead dog by the roadside. I am afraid the same one as came asking for food a few days back, & I am afraid probably dead of starvation. The peasants here evidently use no harrows or cultivators, merely plough the soil & then sow on the rough ridges. Curiously enough the result is to give the impression that the grain is sown in rows, though of course actually broadcast. A good deal of wheat coming up now. Broad beans about 6" high.
<u>14.11.38:</u> Planted out nasturtiums.
<u>16.11.38:</u> One egg.
<u>17.11.38:</u> One egg.
<u>19.11.38:</u> Two eggs.
<u>21.11.38:</u> Two eggs.
<u>22.11.38:</u> One egg.
<u>23.11.38:</u> One egg.
Weather fine & warm, not particularly hot. Fires some evenings. When it is reasonably clear the snow peaks of the Atlas now seem so close that one would think them only a few miles away (actually 50–100 miles I suppose.) Nearly all the seeds, except marigolds, sweet peas & nasturtiums have done very badly & most have failed to germinate, no doubt owing to having been kept for years in stock. It seems very difficult here to grow any small flowers, which are easily killed by the heat & drought. Gardens mostly specialise in shrubs.
Paid Frs. 31.50 for a measure of wheat (round about 40 lb. = about 1d a lb.)
Have been ill (chest) since 16th. Got up yesterday & somewhat better today.
<u>24.11.38:</u> One egg.
Cylinder of Butagaz gave out yesterday. That makes 5 weeks. It has supplied pretty regularly 3 gas-jets (one of them higher candle-power—I think 60—than the others) & a fourth occasionally.
<u>25.11.38:</u> Two eggs.

<u>27.11.38</u>:   *One egg.*
<u>28.11.38</u>:   *Two eggs.*
<u>29.11.38</u>:   *One egg.*
<u>30.11.38</u>:   *Two eggs.*

1. Compare this reference to the tortoises with the passage in *Coming Up for Air* that gives that novel its title, *CW,* VII, 177. Orwell does not mention a title for this novel before its publication, 12 June 1939.

<u>1.12.38</u>:   *Two eggs. (This makes 30 since 26.10.38.)*
<u>2.12.38</u>:   *The weather has been much cooler, some days clear & fine, much like English spring, sometimes heavy mist. The day before yesterday fairly heavy rain. On clear days the Atlas mountains look extremely close, so that you can distinguish every contour, on other days completely invisible.*
Very poor success with the flower seeds. Only nasturtiums, sweet peas, marigolds, carnations & a very few pinks & clarkia germinated. Phlox, pansies, violas, godetias, poppies & sunflowers failed entirely to come up, though soil conditions etc. were all right. Presumably due to seed having been in stock for years.
Find that the weaker of the two catapults will throw a stone (less satisfactory than buckshot) 90 yards at most. So a powerful catapult ought to throw a buckshot about 150 yards.
Three eggs.
<u>3.12.38</u>:   *Two eggs.*[1]
The tallest palms are about 25 yards high (to the base of the leaves.)
<u>4.12.38</u>:   *Two eggs.*
<u>5.12.38</u>:   *Three eggs.*
On a patch which I saw being ploughed 30th October or a day or two earlier, the grain is now 4–6" high.
Oranges now ripe & on sale everywhere. Pomegranates now on sale are over-ripe & quite a different colour, brown instead of red.

Form of donkey shoe used here.

<u>6.12.38</u>:   *Two eggs.*
Nights now are distinctly chilly.
<u>7.12.38</u>:   *Two eggs.*
Yesterday afternoon much hotter.
Looking at the beds of streams here, it is evident that the streams have shrunk very greatly, though whether recently or not I do not know. The stream along which we walked yesterday had in effect three beds. The bed in which it was actually running; perhaps 6' wide & 1' deep, a bed about 10' wide into

which it evidently swells at the wettest season of the year, & outside this a wide bed channelled out of the chalk which showed that at some time in the past what is now a tiny stream was a considerable river.

Many more small birds about now. I suppose some of them migrants.

Leaves of the pomegranate trees yellowing.

8.12.38:   Two eggs.

In the morning dust-storms, then fairly heavy rain. The afternoon cold & misty, just like England.

9.12.38:   Two eggs.

Notice that ibises always collect round a man digging & are very tame then. Presumably after worms etc. They did not do this in Burma. Probably there is next to no food in the streams here.

10.12.38:   One egg.

11.12.38:   Two eggs.

Chilly & overcast, rain in afternoon.

12.12.38:   Heavy rain all night. Cold & overcast, much like November weather in England. E. has neuralgia, probably owing to going out in the rain yesterday.

Raining most of the day.

Two eggs. (53 since 26.10.38, 23 since 1.12.38. One hen is now broody.)

13.12.38:   Two eggs.

14.12.38:   Three eggs.

Chilly & fine. Very heavy dew these days.

15.12.38:   Two eggs.

Clear, fine & not hot.

16.12.38:   Two eggs.

Fine & cool. Domestic animals here eat almost anything. Donkey eating old dried-up vegetable marrow leaves off a rubbish heap. Cows, goats & sheep being fed on waste leaves from crown artichokes. Notice that when goats & sheep are herded together, the goats fight among themselves but do not go for the sheep.

Picked up pellet of some fairly large hawk. Only wing-cases etc. of insects, mostly woodlice. Have not yet seen a snake in Morocco, though recently we picked up a fresh slough of one.

Oranges when ripe enough to pick can apparently be left on the trees for some time without falling. Wholesale price of oranges (at any rate locally) Frs. 2.50 or 3 a dozen.

Saw a dead donkey the other day—the first I have seen. The wretched brute had simply dropped & died beside one of the tracks leading from Marrakech to the Oued, & was left lying there by the owner. A few dogs hanging round waiting to start on it, but with a guilty air.

17.12.38:   One egg.

Very heavy rain in the night. Cold during morning, about ½ hour's sun in the afternoon, then more rain. Everything flooded, the Oued Tensift swollen to considerable size—bed is 50 yards wide in places.

The donkey (actually seen dead on 11.12.38.) now an almost completely clean skeleton. Notice that they leave the head till last.

<u>18.12.38</u>:   *Two eggs.*
<u>19.12.38</u>:   *Three eggs.*
Heavy rain in the night. Today cold & cloudy, with heavy showers & violent wind.
<u>20.12.38</u>:   *Two eggs.*
Heavy rain at night, raining on & off all day. The little stream we followed up some time back, then a tiny trickle of water, is now a rushing torrent about 10 yards wide. Today saw two rainbows parralel°in the sky, a thing I have not seen before.
<u>21.12.38</u>:   *Two eggs.*
Finer, cool, a few spots of rain.
One of the pigeons is dead – cause unknown.
<u>22.12.38</u>:   *Three eggs.*
Finer in the morning, rain in the afternoon.
The surviving pigeon (presumably the hen) is sitting on a nest. Do not know whether it can survive, but possibly we may be able to get another cock for it.
The Oued Tensift has now filled up the whole of the valley it runs in, so that at the bridge it is about 300 yards wide (previously about 10 yards). Judging from the vegetation in the valley I should say this is unusual.
<u>23.12.38</u>:   *The pigeon has laid two eggs & is sitting on them.*
Cold & fine. The Oued Tensift has shrunk to about twice its original size.
Three eggs.
<u>24.12.38</u>:   *Four eggs.*
Both the pigeons eggs broken—do not know how, possibly a cat tried to get up to the nest & scared the bird off. Evidently fertile eggs, as they were streaked with blood.
Clear & fine.
<u>25.12.38</u>:   *Quite a heavy frost in the night, everything white this morning, & a little cat-ice on the pools. Curious sight of oranges & lemons on the trees frosted over, & lemon blossom frozen stiff. Do not yet know whether it has done much damage. Bourgainvillea° blossoms look all right. Should not think frosts can be common here, but at the moment there is a wave of cold all over the world. The mountains have for sometime past been covered with snow even on the lower slopes.*
Four eggs.
<u>26.12.38</u>: ⎫ *Have been ill. Not certain number of eggs,*
<u>27.</u>   ⎬ *but about 9.*
<u>28.</u>   ⎭ *Weather clear & fine.*
Second cylinder of Butagaz ended 27.12.38. Exactly 3 weeks (same as last time.)[2]
<u>29.12.38</u>:   *Two eggs.*
Clear & fine. We have got a cock-pigeon (Frs. 4.50) & put him in the cage with the hen to get acquainted. She started pecking his head gently, I think picking out lice.
<u>30.12.38</u>:   *Large flight (about 200) of storks or cranes passing over. Large white birds, apparently with black edges to their wings. Flying*

288

northward, but probably merely circling round to find a place to settle, as
they must be migrants from Europe.
Very fine, clear & chilly. No wind.
Two eggs.
<u>31.12.38:</u> *Three eggs. (102 eggs since 26.10.38,[3] or nearly 12 a week).*

1. Two eggs] One egg
2. The previous cylinder lasted five weeks; see 24.11.38
3. '28' typed in error.

The Domestic Diary continues at *582*.

APPENDIX 2

519. Abstracts of Reports on the Spanish Civil War from the
Daily Worker and the *News Chronicle*, 1936–37
[July 1936–August? 1937]

Orwell remarks in a footnote to *Homage to Catalonia*: 'In connection with this book I have had to go through the files of a good many English papers. Of our larger papers, the *Manchester Guardian* is the only one that leaves me with an increased respect for its honesty' (*CW*, VI, 208); see also his letter to the editor of the *Manchester Guardian*, 22 September 1937, *398*. The notes below were made when Orwell went through the newspaper files. It is obvious they were of direct use to him in writing *Homage to Catalonia*. Thus, one long section, 'A Trotskyist Revolt,' *News Chronicle*, 10 May 1937, was reprinted almost word for word; see *n. 22* and *CW*, VI, 235–36. The notes, taken from only two newspapers, are almost certainly incomplete; one exercise book of notes from the *Daily Worker*, 6–28 May 1937, has not survived. From Orwell's list of desiderata ('Wanted for 1937') and his letter to the *Manchester Guardian* (*398*), it is likely he searched that paper, too.

The extant manuscript notes, which follow one another within the same notebook, comprise: *Daily Worker*, 22 July–20 August 1936, 8 pages; *News Chronicle*, 20 July–4 September 1936 and 5–10 May, 19 June 1937, 12 pages. The typewritten notes comprise: *News Chronicle*, 5–10 May 1937, 3 pages; *Daily Worker*, 6–28 May 1937, 7 pages.

The manuscript notes are written on twenty recto leaves of a lined school exercise book measuring 8½ × 6 inches. The typed sections are on paper with the watermark PLANTAGENET BRITISH MAKE with a coat of arms. Characteristics of the typing suggest that it is Orwell's work. There was, presumably, an earlier handwritten version of the *Daily Worker*, 6–28 May 1937. A rough calculation based on a comparison of the number of typed pages required to reproduce the equivalent handwritten pages of notes from the *News Chronicle*, 5–10 May 1937, suggests that the seven pages of the report would have taken about twenty pages—presumably another exercise book.

Orwell crossed the border from Spain into France on 23 June 1937 and was back in Wallington in the first week of July. On 17 July he mentioned to his agent, Leonard Moore, a rough plan he had made for what was to become *Homage to Catalonia*. He said he was working on a more detailed plan, and would then set about writing the book; see *377*. On 29 July the *New English Weekly* published the first of two articles, 'Spilling the Spanish Beans' (see *378*), in which he wrote, 'It is the left-wing papers, the "News Chronicle" and the "Daily Worker," with their far subtler methods of distortion, that have prevented the British public from grasping the real nature of the struggle.' Orwell might have come to this conclusion without having made a systematic search through newspaper files, but it may have been that search that prompted his castigation of these two newspapers. On 16 August 1937 he wrote to Geoffrey Gorer and advised him not to believe a word he read in those newspapers (see *387*); and on 27 August he told Moore he was getting on 'fairly fast' with his book (see *391*). It seems likely, therefore, that these notes were compiled in July and perhaps early August 1937.

Orwell variously underlined and punctuated dates; these have been regularised. Minor errors (such as mistypings) have been corrected silently, and false starts have not been noted apart from two important exceptions; see *ns. 14* and *28*. When the *sic* sign used for this edition,°, is given after a closing square bracket, such brackets are Orwell's. Some of the more important references to *Homage to Catalonia* are given in the notes. Double diagonals (//) are Orwell's.

Daily Worker, 22 July–20 August
Handwritten

(Quiroga, Barrio, Giralt.°)[1]
D. W.[2] 1936
July 22. (Pitcairn[3] from Barcelona.) "Streets here are being patrolled by cars filled with armed workers who are preserving order & discipline.// Preparations are going forward for the organisation of a permanent Workers' Militia.// Negotiations have been opened for the formation of a committee of public safety including some members of the present Government, with all the workers' parties including the Communists & Anarchists.// Such a committee would have supreme control in Catalonia . . ." (1st mention of Anarchists.)
July 22. (F. P.[4]) "Thousands of armed workers are guarding every road. A control of permits is being carried out strictly & efficiently.// Local committees along the road distributed cards directing the hotels & cafes to supply food. . . . // The moment the first news of the attack was heard in the city the workers dashed into the streets. . . . Within a couple of hours of the first attack the streets were defended by a network of barricades manned by Communists, Anarchists, Socialists & Republicans alike. . . ."
July 24. (F. P. Barcelona.) "[Communist]° position has been immensely strengthened here because *i*. Only party who accurately foretold coming Fascist attack. (Anarchists did not take seriously.) *ii*. Played vital part in fighting. *iii*. Taken lead in organisation of workers' militias."
First mention on this date of attacks on churches. Explained by churches being used as fortresses. Spanish worker quoted as saying:
"We did not want to harm the priests," etc.
Same date, Kay Beauchamp's[5] article, C.P. in Asturias alone said to number 5000 members.
July 27. (H. Pollitt[6]) Fascists described as "gangs of parasites, moral perverts & murderers." Later in speech demands united campaign between 2nd International, I.F.T.U., & 3rd International.[7]
Spanish Foreign Legion are "composed of murderers, white slavers, dope fiends & the offal of every European country."

Same date, Pitcairn's despatch, much talk of workers' militias but only Communist militia specifically mentioned. Eg. "Columns of armed workers are still leaving here for Saragossa. I watched a column 600 strong leave with banners from the Communist headquarters. . . . Several hundred Asturian miners arrived here yesterday to join the Communist militia detachments for Saragossa."

"The Hotel Colon & the Hotel Ritz have been completely taken over by the militia & the C.P. has occupied the big Rambla Palace" etc. No mention of buildings taken over by other parties.

July 29th. (H. Pollitt from Paris.) Loyalist worker quoted as saying: "Yes, churches have been burnt. The anger of the people at discovering the use to which these supposed sacred places were put manifested itself in their burning them. . . . Wouldn't you have done the same[?]"

H. P. "Of course we would, & every decent person who wishes to defend democracy would support you."

Aug. 3. Caballero[8] is "man of steel."

Aug. 5. Middle page article by André Marty (French Communist Deputy.) "In a country like Spain . . . [feudalism etc.]°—the working class & all the people have the immediate & urgent task, *the only possible task*—& all the recent appeals of the C.P. repeat it & approve it—not to bring about the Socialist revolution, but to defend, consolidate & develop the bourgeois democratic revolution. . . . The few confiscations which have been made— for example, those of the offices & journals of the rebels—constitute sanctions against enemies of the State . . . & were undertaken not as Socialist measures, but as measures of defence by the Republic." [Later, during months preceding rebellion, Communists repeatedly called attention of Gov.t to danger.]°

Aug. 6. Large-print across middle-page article, (with pictures of barricades etc. "Their aim is not Soviets but defence of democracy."

H. Pollitt in this article: "The people of Spain are not fighting to establish Soviets or the proletarian dictatorship. Only downright lying scoundrels, or misguided self-styled 'Lefts', declare that they are—& both contrive to help the aims of the Fascist rebels."

Pollitt's suggestions as to way Spanish Gov.t can be helped:

1. "Demanding & enforcing our will" (not stated how enforced) that proper help be given to Spanish Gov.t & none to Fascists. (Help here means facilities to buy arms etc.)

ii. "Demanding an immediate mobilisation of the forces & power at the disposal of the League of Nations."

3. Deputation of the N.C.L.[9] to the Government to demand support for "People's Gov.t." (about 1st time this term used) in Spain.

4. Red Cross to be asked to organise ambulances, Co-op. movement to organise food-ships. (This repeated on Aug. 7.) (Aug. 8.).

On next page of paper statement that democracy not Soviets is the objective is repeated with telegram from Central Committee of Spanish C.P. to the same effect.

Above: "Confiscation, nationalisation, seizure of factories, land, etc., are

all proclaimed [all]° day & daily: 'Soviets' in Spain has become a standing headline.// Yet it is untrue, completely untrue."
Aug. 11. (Isobel° Brown[10]) "Spanish Foreign Legion, composed of murderers, pimps & dope-fiends fleeing from justice in every European country." Headline on this date: "How Communists saved Spain."
Aug. 12. (Pitcairn). "5th Regiment" composed entirely of workers under democratically elected section-, company- & battalion commanders. Later in article, as before, no proletarian revolution.
Aug. 13. (from a Barcelona correspondent) "Workers' organisations—Unified Socialists & Communists, Anarchists & the Marxist Party—are co-operating with the Gov.t both in the fight against the rebels & in maintaining order. . . . Enterprises abandoned by their owners, such as the tramways in Barcelona, are being run by the workers. Workers' organisations are at present housed in the big luxury hotels, palaces & royalist clubs."
Aug. 14. 1st mention of "People's Army." In same article. "Kazanevas°[11] (the head of Catalan Gov.t) laid stress on the fact that the Catalonian Gov.t were taking every possible measure to organise normal life both in the capital & throughout the province.// Special care in being given by the Gov.t & by the workers' militia to enterprises & houses owned by foreigners."
Aug. 20. Militias mentioned as being first legalised as "People's Army" on Aug. 19.

(Wanted for 1937.   Issues   March 10th–20th   May 5th–20th
June 15th to 30th[12]
News Chronicle.   May 5th–20th
                  June 15th–30th
M. Guardian.   May 5th–20th
                  June 15th–30th

News Chronicle, 20 July–4 September 1936
Handwritten

News Chron. 1936
July 20th. "Revolutionary workmen's committees have been formed in the towns of Northern Spain & share control with the civil authorities." (Correspondent in Hendaye.)
    Same date, middle-page article by Eric Siepmann[13] stating that actual proletarian revolution, under leadership of Caballero, is fairly likely, also that "Caballero's Socialism has seemed during the last few months to be well ahead of the official Communism, which has been giving the appearance of holding back under the orders of the Third International."
July 22. ("Special Correspondents"). "The part of Catalonia adjoining the French frontier is in the hands of a revolutionary committee composed partly of Anarchists & partly of Communists.// The Soviet flag is flying on the Town Hall of Puiccerda°."[14]
July 23. Casualties at Barcelona estimated at 500 killed & 3000 wounded.

July 24. (Special Corresp. at Gibraltar.)

"It is becoming daily clearer here that whoever wins, both will lose. // . . . The Republicans see the regime already smashed. The Popular Front is ancient history now.// It is hard to imagine the Socialist, Communist & Syndicalist elements that have borne the brunt of the fighting for the defence of the Republic in the South, continuing under the tutelage of a handful of purely bourgeois Republicans."

July 25th. Eye witness from Barcelona reports to N.C. correspondent: "Señor Companys,[15] the head of the Government, has become a mere cypher.// The real power is in the hands of the anti-Fascist Committee of Public Safety. This is composed of 3 trade unionists, 3 Socialists, 3 Anarchists, 1 Communist, 1 Trotskyist & 1 Liberal Republican.// All important decisions are taken by this body.// The big danger comes from the Anarchists, who are reported to constitute about 65% of the Barcelona workers."

Sep. 3. Landon-Davies°[16] article, Catalan Gov.t described as "bourgeois." Later, "two thirds of the columns fighting on the Saragossa front are 100 per cent anarcho-syndicalist columns." Later, "What would change the whole situation in a moment would be a real threat to Madrid from the Moorish invaders in the South. Should they pursue their path of blood to the gateway of the capital every bourgeois life would be in danger."

Sep. 4. J. Langdon-Davies estimates that the "error" in Barcelona has led to about 200 murders in something over a month. Stated to be mostly factory-owners, wealthy bourgeois etc. L.-D. declares no organised political party, Socialist, Anarchist, Communist etc., is responsible. Later in article, blame put by implication on Anarchists.

News Chronicle, 5–10 May 1937
Typescript (with variants from handwritten version)

"News Chronicle" reports on Barcelona riots.[17]

May 5. Headline: Barcelona Quells Anarchist Revolt.// Troops Recalled from the Front.// (From correspondent in Perpignan.)

After bitter fighting in the streets of Barcelona, in which hundreds were killed and wounded, an Anarchist revolt against the Government of Catalonia was crushed tonight.[18]

. . . The trouble began this morning when the Anarchists handed an ultimatum to the Government demanding full control of all Government departments and full command over the whole of Catalonia on the ground that they were conducting the war.

To this demand the Government replied with a counter-ultimatum, requesting the Central Committee of the F.A.I. (Iberian Anarchist Federation) to put an end to its activities and ordering all civilians to give up their arms at once.

At the same time the Government recalled troops from the front.

Following this armed Anarchists appeared in the streets and arrested all the soldiers, guards and civilians whom they could find.

Armed with hand-grenades, bands of Anarchists terrorised the people in many parts of the city, driving them back into the suburbs, where they were imprisoned in many buildings. Others built up barricades in the streets.

One powerful band of Anarchists stormed and took possession of the Post Office and several other Government buildings. etc.

May 6. Headline: Barcelona Rebels Beaten.// Public Safety Cabinet.// Diehards at Barricades.

Late last night a few bands of Anarchist die-hards were still holding out behind the barricades in the streets of Barcelona . . . British cruiser Despatch and the destroyers Gipsy and Hostile are now on their way to Barcelona to protect British interests . . .[19]

Lower Headline: Troops Capture Anarchist Guns.

. . . The Anarchists have been turned out of the Government buildings. Hundreds of machine-guns have been captured by the troops.

. . . Some 1500 or 2000 Anarchists, however, most of them belonging to the extremist F.A.I. (Iberian Anarchist Federation),[20] failed to obey the order of their chiefs to lay down their arms and are still holding several barricades in certain quarters . . . Groups of a few hundred of them have appeared at intervals in the streets firing their rifles and revolvers. . . . etc.

In stop-press: Valencia Government decrees that Republican Government assumes charge of public order and services in Catalonia.

May 7 & 8. no mention.

May 10. Headline. First Inside Story of Barcelona Rising.// By John Langdon-Davies.

The net effect of Barcelona's new Tragic Week has been to bring realities into the open and to reinforce the need to control the "uncontrollables."[21]

It has been the worst uprising that even Barcelona has ever seen. Four hundred killed, according to the Minister of Propaganda, and thousands wounded; and it took three days for most of the combatants to discover who was fighting what.

New Headline: A Trotskyist Revolt.[22]

. . . This has not been an Anarchist uprising. It is a frustrated putsch by the "Trotskyist" P.O.U.M,[23] working through their controlled organisations, "Friends of Durrutti,°"[24] and the Libertarian Youth . . .

The tragedy began on Monday afternoon when the Government sent armed police into the Telephone building, to disarm the workers there, mostly C.N.T.[25] men. Grave irregularities in the service had been a scandal for some time.

A large crowd gathered in the Plaza de Catalunya outside, while the C.N.T. men inside resisted, retreating floor by floor to the top of the building . . .

The incident was very obscure, but word went round that the Government was out against the Anarchists. The streets filled with armed men . . .

By nightfall every workers' centre and Government building was barricaded, and at ten o'clock the first volleys were fired and the first ambulances began ringing their way through the streets.

By dawn on Tuesday all Barcelona was under fire. The Government buildings were isolated; the workers' district around the Parallel was rapidly dominated by the National Guard . . .

As the day wore on and the dead mounted to over a hundred, one could make a guess at what was happening.

The Anarchist C.N.T. and Socialist U.G.T.[26] were not technically 'out in the street.' So long as they remained behind the barricades they were merely watchfully waiting, an attitude which included the right to shoot at anything armed in the open street . . .

(The) general bursts were invariably aggravated by "pacos"[27]—hidden solitary men, usually Fascists, shooting from roof-tops at nothing in particular, but doing all they could to add to the general panic . . .[28]

By Wednesday evening, however, it began to be clear who was behind the revolt. All the walls had been plastered with an inflammatory poster[29] calling for an immediate revolution and for the shooting of Republican and Socialist leaders. It was signed by the "Friends of Durrutti°."

On Thursday morning the Anarchist daily denied all knowledge or sympathy with it, but "La Batalla," the P.O.U.M. paper, reprinted the document with the highest praise.

Barcelona, the first city of Spain, was plunged into bloodshed by agents provocateurs using this subversive organisation . . .

On Thursday "La Batalla" was raided and confiscated, but it did not prevent its reappearance. Its flaring Headline, "For Three Days the Streets of Barcelona belonged to the People," reads curiously, seeing that for three days, thanks largely to the P.O.U.M., the streets of Barcelona belonged to no one.

Two practical consequences of the rising will be: First, the elimination of the P.O.U.M., and, secondly, a definite challenge to the "uncontrollable" element within[30] the Anarchist F.A.I.

(Below are explanations of the various parties etc. P.O.U.M. defined thus: P.O.U.M. Partido Obrero de Unificacion Marxista. Small party formed by amalgamation of Left Communists (Trotskyists) and Workers' and Peasants' Bloc.)

News Chronicle, 19 June 1937
Handwritten

June 19. "In Madrid, following the round-up of the Trotskyist P.O.U.M. leader, Andreas° Nin,[31] & other leading members of the Party, a new purge has started.//

Two hundred persons, many holding high rank in the Army, have been arrested & are stated to have confessed to being direct agents of General Franco.// "A large number of documents bearing on the case were found in the recent raid on the Peruvian Consulate building in Madrid," says the official statement.// Julien° Gorkin,[32] one of the leaders of the P.O.U.M. in Barcelona, was put on trial yesterday, charged with "incitement against public order," according to a statement issued by the Independent Labour Party in London.// The I.L.P. has cabled a protest to the Valencian Gov.t."

Reuter, British United Press & Spanish Press Agency.

Daily Worker, 6–28 May 1937
Typewritten

"Daily Worker" reports on May riots.

———————

May 6. CRIMINAL PUTSCH FAILS TO SHAKE CATALAN UNITY.// Disorders have taken place in Barcelona, following an attempt by a minority of extreme members of the Anarchist organisation and under-cover agents of Franco to break up the unity of the Popular organisations forming the Catalan Government.// All organisations collaborating in the reconstructed Government . . . agreed on the paramount necessity for single authority in the prosecution of the struggle . . . Unity was opposed only by a small minority in the C.N.T. and F.A.I. (political anarchist organisation), a grouping which includes many members who joined only last July, and who are "Fifth Column" hidden agents of Franco, in closest touch with the rebels.// In the decision of the Catalan Government, supported unanimously by all the organisations comprising it, that civilians should surrender their arms, and in the rising feeling for unity, these elements saw the termination of their influence.// Last week the Catalan U.G.T. secretary was taken from his car and shot by an "anarchist" group.[33] Disorders were precipitated also by requisitions demanded from the farmers of Bellver in the Llobrega valley, by other "anarchists."// This proving unsuccessful, and all the workers' organisations remaining calm, a minority group of Anarchists on Monday and Tuesday seized and attempted to hold the telephone and telegraph buildings, and started firing into the street. The confusion thus caused appears to be under perfect control . . . Details of the developmnt of the situation are not available, but the plot to split the workers' parties comprising the Government appears to have failed, and the "coup" attempted by irresponsible minority elements egged-on by Franco agents to be completely isolated.// Barcelona was calm yesterday, etc.

May 7. FIFTH COLUMN IN BARCELONA RISING. (Paris, Thursday.) In reply to numerous questions which have been submitted about the character and scope of the rising[34] in Barcelona, the Spanish Embassy in Paris has issued the following statement:—// "The rising was not so exclusively anarchist as has been alleged by various foreign newspapers, who seek to discredit the ability of the Government of the Republic to maintain order and to impose respect for the law.// (Leaded type.) "A significant feature of the uprising has been that the old monarchist flag was flown from the balcony of various houses in Barcelona, doubtless in the belief that those who took part in the rising had become masters of the situation.// "It is a well-known fact that numerous enemies of the regime had gained a footing in various syndicalist organisations since the outbreak of Franco's rebellion, in order to have a better opportunity of putting into practice their subversive aims. These men have been called by the rebels themselves the 'Fifth Column. . . . etc. (See earlier story on Page Three.)

(Same date, p. 3.) ALL CATALONIA IS CALM.// COUNCIL OF fiVE SET UP. (Repeats manifesto of the Valencia Gov.t stating that that gov.t will assume charge of order in Catalonia and that armed forces on the Aragon front will be attached to 4th Army Division under General Pozas.[35] Also gives list of new Catalan Directorate: Justice & Hygiene, Valerio Mas (CNT.) Defence, Vidiella (UGT.) Labour & Public Services, Joachime Pou (Peasants' Smallholders' Union). Public Order & Security, Marti Feced (Catalan Left.)

May 8. ANARCHIST DISORDER IN CATALONIA.// The serious disorders in Catalonia are not yet completely ended, it is clear from reports received from Barcelona yesterday. In Barcelona itself, all is quieter. Telephone and telegraph communication was resumed. In certain suburbs there are groups of Anarchists who have not laid down their arms, but there was little firing yesterday . . . In the countryside, however, Anarchists are in possession of two small towns, and have seized certain villages.// A strong feature of the situation is that the Anarchist leaders and the main organisation support the Government. Senorita Montsenys,°[36] one of the most popular anarchists, came from Valencia yesterday and broadcast an appeal, to those who are still making difficulties.// General Pozas, the new commander appointed by the Government, arrived in Barcelona and was welcomed in the streets.// Every possible effort is being made by undercover Franco agents to prevent rank-and-file anarchists in the countryside from realising their organisation's support of the Government, and thus prolong the disorder.

May 11. PITCAIRN LIFTS BARCELONA VEIL.// FASCIST PLOT TO LAND TROOPS.// TROTSKYIST RISING AS SIGNAL.// (From our Special Correspondent, Frank Pitcairn, Valencia, Monday.)

This will turn out to have been fateful days in the history of Spain. It is one of the most critical moments of the war. The Germans and Italians are at the gates of Bilbao. Catalonia is full of German and Italian agents working desperately to reorganise the rebellion against the People's Front Government, which was crushed last week by the forces of the People's Army, co-operating with the people of Catalonia. (etc. then a statement that the CP. had broadcast a message all over Spain.)

THE FASCIST PLAN.// There is a specially dangerous feature about the situation in Catalonia. We know now that the German and Italian agents, who poured into Barcelona ostensibly in order to "prepare" the notorious "Congress of the Fourth International,"[37] had one big task. It was this:—// (Leaded type.) They were—in co-operation with the local Trotskyists—to prepare a situation of disorder and bloodshed, in which it would be possible for the Germans and Italians to declare that they were "unable to exercise naval control of the Catalan coasts effectively, because of the disorder prevailing in Barcelona," and were, therefore, "unable to do otherwise" than land forces in Barcelona.// In other words, what was being prepared was a situation in which the German and Italian Governments could land troops or marines quite openly on the Catalan coasts, declaring that they were doing so "in order to preserve order."// That was the aim. Probably that is still the aim. The instrument for all this lay ready to hand for the Germans and Italians in the shape of the Trotskyist organisation known as the P.O.U.M.// The

P.O.U.M., acting in co-operation with well-known criminal elements, and with certain other deluded persons in the Anarchist organisations planned, organised and led the attack in the rearguard, accurately timed to coincide with the attack on the front at Bilbao.// In the past, the leaders of the P.O.U.M. have frequently sought to deny their complicity as agents of a Fascist cause against the People's Front. This time they are convicted out of their own mouths as clearly as their allies, operating in the Soviet Union, who confessed to the crimes of espionage, sabotage, and attempted murder against the Government of the Soviet Union.// Copies of La Battalla, issued on and after May 2, and the leaflets issued by the P.O.U.M. before and[38] during the killings in Barcelona, set down the position in cold print.// IN PLAINEST TERMS./ In the plainest terms the P.O.U.M. declares it is the enemy of the People's Government. In the plainest terms it calls upon its followers to turn their arms in the same direction as the Fascists, namely, against the Government of the People's Front and the anti-Fascist fighter.// (Leaded type.) Nine hundred dead and 2,500 wounded[39] is the figure officially given by Diaz as the total in terms of human slaughter of the P.O.U.M. attack in Barcelona.// It was not, by any means, Diaz pointed out, the first of such attacks. Why was it, for instance, that at the moment of the big Italian drive at Guadalajara, the Trotskyists and their deluded Anarchist friends attempted a similar rising in another district? Why was it that the same thing happened two months before at the time of the heavy Fascist attack at Jarama,[40] when, while Spaniards and Englishmen, and honest anti-Fascists of every nation in Europe, were being killed holding Arganda Bridge, the Trotskyist swine suddenly produced their arms 200 kilometres from the front, and attacked in the rear?// There are, as a matter of fact, a lot of our lads lying dead behind the trenches on the Jarama who would be alive today if the Poumsters had not chosen that moment to stab the Government heroes in the back. //... At the moment when the leaders of the CNT. were imploring to put an end° to the fighting in Barcelona, the P.O.U.M. through its illegally circulated La Battalla, were (sic) calling on its men to keep up the fighting against the People's Government.// DRASTIC LIQUIDATION./ This was the final statement in a long series of similar statements, as open as we want.// Throughout a large part of Catalonia the Fascists and their allies have been disarmed. They were disarmed, in most cases easily, because the village people and the peasants rushed to assist the men of the People's Army to disarm the enemy.// (Leaded type.) What the Communist Party demands is a final drastic liquidation of the organisation responsible. The Communist Party demands the immediate suppression of the P.O.U.M. as an avowed enemy of Spain and its Government, and a collaborator with the Fascists of Spain and the invading Fascist Powers.//

(Same day, page 3.) BARCELONA FIGHTING: DOCUMENTS REVEAL RESPON-SIBILITY.//TROTSKYISTS INCITEMENT: FORGED LEAFLETS.// (Slightly smaller type.) The Daily Worker is able to publish today documentary and other evidence of the complicity of the Trotskyist P.O.U.M. (Workers' Party of Marxist Unity) in the recent Barcelona disorders.// (Leaded type.) Yesterday the News Chronicle, through its special correspondent John Langdon-

Davies, gave an account of the events of the last days in Barcelona, an account which declared that there had "not been an Anarchist rising. It is a frustrated putsch by the Trotskyist P.O.U.M."// The evidence we print below leaves no doubt that it is at the door of the P.O.U.M. that the responsibility for the bloodshed in Catalonia must be laid, thereby affording a further example of the way in which the Trotskyists are playing the role of Fascism's agents in the ranks of the working and democratic people.// UNITY OF ALL FOR ORDER.//(From a special correspondent.) (Statement that the P.O.U.M. had intensified its campaign against P.S.U.C. and U.G.T.)// SEIZE POWER.// The May First appeal of the P.O.U.M. was significant enough. It called openly upon its followers to "destroy the existing bourgeois institutions and seize power," ie., to take up arms against the Popular Front Government and overthrow it.// In a May First article the P.O.U.M. leader Nin declared, "Today it is still possible. Tomorrow may be too late."// On Monday, May 3rd, the attack was launched.// That afternoon the Left Catalan Minister of Public Security, Aiguade, and the United Socialist General Commissar for Public Order, Rodrigue Salas, sent the armed republican police into the Telefonica building, to disarm the employees there, most of them members of CNT. unions. For a considerable time the telephone service had been run in a way which was open to the gravest criticism, and it was imperative to the whole conduct of the war that the defects in[41] the service should be remedied.// The Telefonica employees resisted this order of the Government, and a large crowd collected in the streets, most of them completely unaware of what was going on.// RUMOUR STARTED.// Then the rumour was started that the Government was out gunning after the Anarchists. Who exactly started this rumour cannot, of course, be ascertained.// By the evening Barcelona was an armed camp and the first shots were being fired.// The next day (Tuesday 4th) the P.O.U.M. paper appealed to the citizens of Barcelona "to be in a position of constant mobilisation."// At the same time leaflets and stickybacks appeared all over the town, under the initials of the CNT., FAI., the POUM. and a body called "The Friends of Durutti.°"// CNT.-FAI. DENIAL.// The day following (Wednesday, May 5th) the CNT. paper, Solidaridad Obrera, published the following denial:—// "Yesterday there circulated through Barcelona leaflets with the initials of the POUM., the CNT. and the FAI., in which were expressed conceptions incompatible with our point of view.// "We wish to state that neither the CNT. nor the FAI. has ever issued any kind of leaflet, manifesto, etc., of any kind in conjunction with the Workers' Party of Marxist Unity."// "We are making this public that it shall be known to all workers."// (Leaded type.) The statement is signed by the Regional Committee of the CNT., the Regional Committee of the FAI., the Peninsular Committee of the FAI., local Confederation of United Syndicates, the Regional Committee of the Libertarian Youth and the local Federation of Anarchist Groups.// The same day the following document, again under the initials of the CNT. and FAI., was circulated in Barcelona:—//

CNT.   FAI.
GROUP OF THE FRIENDS OF DURR-
UTI.

WORKERS! A revolutionary junta. Shoot the guilty. Disarm all the armed organisations (ie., the police.) Socialisation of the economy. Dissolution of the political parties which have allied themselves with the working-class. We shall not surrender the streets. The revolution before everything. We salute our comrades of the P.O.U.M., who have fraternised in the streets with us.// LONG LIVE THE SOCIAL REVOLUTION! DOWN WITH THE COUNTER-REVOLUTION!// The following morning (Thursday, May 6th) the P.O.U.M. paper, La Battalla, republished this document under the comment:// (italics.) "The comrades of the Group 'Friends of Durruti' published yesterday the following leaflet, of really extraordinary interest, which we are exceedingly glad to reproduce."// The same day the Solidaridad Obrera issued a further denial over the signatures of the Regional Committees of the CNT. and FAI.// "ABSOLUTELY INTOLERABLE."// The contents of this leaflet were declared to be "absolutely intolerable," and the two committees disassociated themselves entirely, disavowing it. At the same time they warned against "authentic agents provocateurs," and declared: // (Leaded type) "The Council of the Generalidad has been established. All should accept its decisions, since all of us are represented in it."// The declaration was dated May 5th.// In the same issue of (sic) the paper published the following:// NATIONAL REPUBLICAN UNIFORMS. The delegation of Public Order of the Government of the Republic has learnt that a group of people has raided a shop which stocks uniforms of the National Republican Guard. This is made known to all loyal followers of the Republic and all workers, so that they may be on their guard.// Here it should be noted:-// (a.) That the publication of this statement by the Anarchist paper proves the innocence of the CNT.FAI.// (b) That one of the easiest ways of provoking the Anarchist and Syndicalist workers against the Government would be for the elements who stole the uniforms to dress in them and then shoot down an Anarchist worker.// ENCOURAGED BY FASCISTS.// Meanwhile, while through the columns of Solidaridad Obrera the CNT. was declaring itself in complete unity with the Government and the UGT., was calling for arms to be given up and work to be resumed, the POUM paper La Battalla demanded that their arms should be kept for use "against the counter-revolution."// And almost in the same terms Quiepo° de Llano[42] broadcast encouragement, "We sympathise with you and will render help. Stand fast."// He was joined by the Lisbon radio station: "Continue the attack. Don't stop firing."
May 17. (From despatch of Frank Pitcairn dated 16th May.) (Starts by stating that Gov.t is to start rounding up hidden arms.) With (the decree), the struggle to "put Catalonia on a war footing", which has been going on for months and was resisted with open violence by the P.O.U.M. and its friends in the first week of May, enters a new phase.// . . . If the decree is successfully carried out it means:—// FIRST: that the groups led by the P.O.U.M. who rose against the Government last week will lose their main source of strength, namely, their arms.// SECOND: That, as a result of this, their ability to hamper

by terrorism the efforts of the anti-Fascist workers to get the war factories on to a satisfactory basis will be sharply reduced. THIRD: That the arms at present hidden will be available for use on the front, where they are badly needed.// FOURTH: That in future those who steal arms from the front or steal arms in transit to the front will be liable to immediate arrest and trial as ally of the Fascist enemy.// ARMS STOLEN FOR MONTHS// Included in the weapons which have to be turned in are rifles, carbines, machine-guns, machine-pistols, trench mortars, field guns, armoured cars, hand-grenades, and all other sorts of bombs.// The list gives you an idea of the sort of armaments accumulated by the Fascist conspirators and brought into the open for the first time last week.// There were actually all sorts of arms used by them in the outrage. There were the arms which they have been stealing for months past, and hidden, and there were arms such as tanks, which they stole from the barracks just at the beginning of the rising.// It is clear that scores of machine-guns and several thousand rifles are still in their possession . . .// It is the size and character of the armaments they have accumulated, rather than the number of men involved in the attack which accounts for the heavy loss of life in Barcelona during the fighting.// It accounts for the fact that they were able to create violent disorder without, as a matter of fact, any mass support worth speaking of—that and the fact that the Government was extraordinarily and, as some think, excessively anxious to avoid drastic action until drastic action was forced upon them.// etc.

May 22. IS THE ILP. FOR WINNING THE WAR OR AIDING FRANCO? // by J. R. Campbell.[43]// For 50 days, Franco, assisted by Italian and German Fascism, has been waging bloody warfare against the Basque people. Whole towns have been blotted out by aerial bombardment.[44]// This was the moment chosen by the Spanish I.L.P. (the P.O.U.M.) to participate in a rebellion of anarchists and to call for bloody and relentless war—not against Franco—but against the People's Government of Catalonia.// The reply of the Spanish ILP. (the P.O.U.M.) to the Fascist civil war against the Spanish people was to support a civil war of uncontrollable anarchists against the People's Front Government of Catalonia . . . (Defended by the I.L.P.)// The time has therefore come for a show-down. The British I.L.P. has to tell the British workers plainly where it stands. Is it for the defence of the existing Governments° of Spain which are fighting Franco? Or is it for assisting anarchist rebellion against these Governments—anarchist rebellion which coincides with a heightened Franco offensive?// . . . (Much more to same effect.) In justification for this counter-revolutionary attitude we are told (in the New Leader) that the Government was placing the control of the police and the military in charge of officers of the old regime. A lie often repeated in the New Leader, but nevertheless a lie for which not an iota of proof has ever been advanced.// (Later again, "rebellion of anarchist uncontrollables.")

Same day, middle page article by R. Palme Dutt.[45] . . . With shame it must be confessed that a section of the British working class, even though a small one, represented by the I.L.P., was involved in the criminal armed attempt against the Spanish People's Front.// The I.L.P. contingent of volunteers to Spain, according to the report of McNair in the New Leader, travelled from the front to Barcelona, arrived in Barcelona on May 3, the day of the rising "just as it started," and served under the P.O.U.M. in this armed rising against the Spanish People's Front and its constituted authorities—an act of treason which in any war would be punishable by death, but all the more terrible when committed by those who have been received by the Spanish People's Front as friends and fellow-fighters.// Volunteers whom the British working-class movement had supported and assisted to go to Spain to fight Franco, were thus used to bear arms against the Spanish People's Government, ie., on the same side as Franco.// . . . The I.L.P. defenders of the P.O.U.M. claim that it is "not Trotskyist." This verbal alibi is valueless. Every argument, every policy every incitement and provocation of the P.O.U.M. is drawn from the treasury of Trotskyism. . . . // First, the incitement came from the P.O.U.M. It was on May 1 that the P.O.U.M. called on its followers to "seize power", and its leader Nin declared that "tomorrow it may be too late."// It was on May 2 that the P.O.U.M. organ, "La Battalla," declared its agreement with the anarchist group, 'Friends of Durruti' (in whose name the rising was conducted).// "We entirely agree with one of the anarchist groups, the 'Friends of Durruti' group . . . Against the Generalitad° of Barcelona we set up the Revolutionary Junta. // . . . The P.O.U.M. was only able to play on the support of the most doubtful, irresponsible, unorganised elements especially the gunmen and racketeering elements on the fringes of Anarchism (the same that shot the leader of the UGT., Sese,[46] outside the doors of the Anarcho-Syndicalist Amusements Syndicate), in the face of the repudiation of the organised working-class.// . . . The criminal is Trotskyism.// etc.

May 28. (From Frank Pitcairn's message.) Frente Rojo, organ of the Communist Party in Valencia, has issued a serious warning against the present plans of the P.O.U.M. which are directed towards the organisation of acts of individual terrorism against various working-class and anti-Fascist leaders.// "Following the attempt at rebellion carried out in Catalonia, the pistols of the Fascist Falangists, stamped with the mark of the P.O.U.M., are getting ready to fire.// (Leaded type.) Trotskyism is not a political doctrine. Trotskyism is an official capitalist organisation, a Fascist terrorist band, occupied in sabotage and crime against the people.// Financed by the Fascist powers, they are invading our country. The Trotskyists have come to Spain to fill an important role. The payment they expect to get from the Gestapo. It is for the justice of the people to work to prevent them getting in."

1. Casares Quiroga was Minister of Public Works and later Prime Minister in the Catalan Regional Government (the Generalidad), 1936. Martínez Barrio (d. 1962) was Speaker of the Cortes and Prime Minister for a short time after Quiroga; he assumed the role of president of the Republic in exile; see Paul Preston, *The Spanish Civil War 1936–39* (1986), 56. José Giral, a professor of chemistry, was responsible for the Admiralty in the Catalan Regional Government, 1936. In *Homage to Catalonia, CW*, VI, 191. fn., Orwell notes that the first two refused to distribute arms to the trade unions.
2. The *Daily Worker*, a Communist daily newspaper; see *145, n. 6, 383.*
3. Frank Pitcairn (Claud Cockburn, 1904–1981) was a Communist journalist and editor of *The Week*, 1933–46, a Communist newsletter for private subscribers. It was suppressed, as was the *Daily Worker* (see 383) during World War II. In March 1938, with Otto Katz, he

fabricated a news story that there had been a military uprising against Franco in Tetuán. This Communist propaganda was designed to give the impression that Franco might still be defeated and so persuade the French to open their border; see Thomas, 805, n. 3. He was implacably opposed to the POUM. In a televised interview, broadcast in the BBC programme 'Arena' to mark 1984, he said, 'Any damage I could do them [the POUM] I would do. Certainly. No bones about that at all. In the same way after all you are prepared to shoot people with a gun. Well then—as in my case, the typewriter was somewhat more mighty than the rifle.' See his *Reporter in Spain* (1936) and *Crossing the Line* (1956), which refers to this fraud (27–28).

4. Frank Pitcairn.
5. Kay Beauchamp (1899–), one of eight founders of the *Daily Worker*, was for many years its women's-page editor and Managing Director of Utopia Press.
6. Harry Pollitt, a founder-member of the Communist Party of Great Britain, was later its General Secretary; see *364, n. 1*. He reviewed *The Road to Wigan Pier* in the *Daily Worker*, 17 March 1937; see *390, n. 1*.
7. The Second International, established in Paris in 1889, was, in time, composed of the socialist parties of all European countries, the United States, Canada, and Japan. It campaigned within the limits of parliamentary democracy. The International Federation of Trade Unions was founded 1901. The Third International (or Comintern) was founded by the Soviet Communist Party in 1919, to organise Communist and left-wing socialist parties for revolution against capitalist governments. It opposed the Second International and was dissolved by Stalin in 1943 to allay fears among the Allies of Communist subversion. See and *n. 37*.
8. Francisco Largo Caballero was Prime Minister of Spain, September 1936–May 1937; see *370, n. 4*.
9. The National Church League.
10. Isabel Brown, a Communist, was the moving spirit behind the British Committee for the Relief of the Victims of Fascism. She inspired the despatch of a British medical-aid unit to Spain, left-wing but non-Communist; see Thomas, 457, n. 1.
11. Juan Casanovas was the Catalan Premier. In the autumn of 1936, he escaped to Paris after the failure of a plot to agree to a victory for Franco that would allow an autonomous Catalonia; see Thomas, 424–25 and 925.
12. Closing bracket crossed out.
13. Eric Siepmann was a journalist working for the *News Chronicle*. The article was 'Behind the Censorship in Spain.' Siepmann was said to have 'just returned from Andalusia.'
14. Puigcerdá; see *Homage to Catalonia, CW*, VI, 98. After 'Puiccerda' a new line begins with 'From correspondent at Gibraltar,' but this is crossed out; see 24 July.
15. Luis Companys (1883–1940) was President of the Catalan Regional Government (the Generalidad), 1933–40. He was shot by Franco's supporters after he was handed over by the Gestapo; see Thomas, 925.
16. John Langdon-Davies (1897–1971), journalist and author, wrote for the *News Chronicle* in Spain and was joint secretary with the Communist lawyer Geoffrey Bing of the Comintern-sponsored Commission of Inquiry into Alleged Breaches of the Non-Intervention Agreement in Spain, on which sat a number of 'respectable persons'; see Thomas, 397–98. Following his experience in Barcelona, he wrote *Air Raid* (1938), in which he advocated large-scale evacuation and underground highways. According to the *New Leader* review, 8 July 1938, 'Municipal underground shelters were useless because they could not be reached [by the populace]' owing to the ability of bombers to approach silently (a forecast that radar proved incorrect). Orwell's 'refusal to accept the politics of liquidation and elimination' led to sneering by 'harder Communists'—of which Langdon-Davies was one—at *Homage to Catalonia*; see Valentine Cunningham, *British Writers of the Thirties* (1988), 427. Among Orwell's books when he died was Langdon-Davies's *Russia Puts the Clock Back* (1949).
17. The manuscript has only '1937' for this line.
18. The manuscript is written continuously, with paragraphs separated by double diagonals. The typescript also uses these but sometimes, as here, starts a new paragraph omitting the diagonals. Such changes are not noted hereafter.

19. See *Homage to Catalonia, CW*, VI, 220.
20. The manuscript does not give the explanation of F.A.I.; it simply has, within parentheses, 'expl.'—explain.
21. Thomas notes that 'Uncontrollables,' at the orders of the CNT, 'robbed the *Generalidad* of 18,000 pounds of flour, 5 lorry-loads of wheat, 40 of potatoes' (652, n. 3).
22. The section from 'A Trotskyist Revolt' to 'Barcelona, the first city of Spain . . . subversive organisation' was quoted almost word for word in *Homage to Catalonia, CW*, VI, 235–36. The omissions are from paragraph six: 'on Tuesday' and 'The Government buildings . . . the National Guard.'
23. For Orwell's description of the POUM (Partido Obrero de Unificación Marxista), Revolutionary (anti-Stalinist) Communists, see *360, n. 2*.
24. Friends of Durruti was a small extremist group within the FAI (Federación Anarquista Ibérica); see *Homage to Catalonia, CW*, VI, 219, 237. It was named after Buenaventura Durruti (1896–1936), who was mortally wounded fighting in Madrid and thereafter became a 'legendary anarchist warrior'; see Thomas, 36.
25. Confederación Nacional de Trabajadores, the Anarcho-Syndicalist trade union.
26. Unión General de Trabajadores, the Socialist trade union.
27. Snipers; also used for policemen.
28. After 'general panic . . .' in the manuscript, Orwell begins a new line with 'After three days of battle' but then crosses it out.
29. See *Homage to Catalonia, CW*, VI, 220, 236 for reference to this 'inflammatory poster.'
30. The manuscript has 'within'; Orwell typed 'in' but altered it by hand to 'within.'
31. Andrés Nin, leader of the POUM, had once been Trotsky's private secretary in Moscow, but broke with him when Trotsky spoke critically of the POUM; see Thomas, 523. He was murdered by the Communists in May 1937; see *382, n. 5*.
32. Julián Gorkin (1901–died in exile) was a leader of the POUM.
33. This may refer to Roldán Cortada, who, on 25 April 1937, was found shot dead, presumably by anarchists; see Thomas, 652–53.
34. 'rising' typed as 'riding'
35. General Sebastián Pozas Perea (see *439, n. 6*) was Minister of the Interior for the Republicans. On taking over command of the Catalan army, Thomas notes, 'he seems to have actually joined the communists (PSUC).' Though the PSUC was the United Catalan Socialist Party it was pseudonymous with the Communists (Thomas, 672, xiii).
36. Federica Montseny (1905–1994) was the first woman minister in a Spanish government. An anarchist, she served as Minister of Health, 1936–37; see Thomas, 471–73. With García Oliver, Minister of Justice, she broadcast an appeal to their anarchist followers to lay down their arms and return to work on 4 May; see Thomas, 657. She fled from Spain after the civil war and lived for many years in exile.
37. The Fourth International was formed in 1938 by the followers of Trotsky. See *n. 7* above.
38. 'and' mistyped as 'the.'
39. Thomas quotes a contemporary press estimate that 500 were killed and 1,000 wounded, and another source, Diego Abad de Santillán, as speaking of 1,000 dead and several thousand wounded: 'The anarchist leaders regretted afterwards that they had secured this ceasefire, since it led to their final surrender before the communists' (Thomas, 660 and 660, n. 2).
40. The Battle of the Jarama River took place near Madrid in February 1937. It was the first in which the 15th International Brigade took part, and suffered heavy casualties. According to the commander of the British battalion, Tom Wintringham (see *721, n. 1*), who was wounded, 225 of the original 600 members of the battalion were left at the end of the day's fighting on 12 February. The writer Christopher Caudwell was among the dead; see Thomas, 590–96.
41. Orwell typed 'of' but wrote 'in' over it.
42. General Gonzalo Queipo de Llano y Serra (1875–1951) was a Nationalist who, Thomas notes, was capable of thinking independently of Franco (861). He made very effective use of the radio in the Nationalist cause, coining some effective turns of phrase—for instance, 'tonight I shall take a sherry and tomorrow I shall take Málaga' (Thomas, 520). See also *558, 22.7.39, n.2*.
43. John Ross Campbell (1894–1969) was a member of the Executive Committee of the Communist Party, 1926–64. In October 1924, when he was acting editor of the Communist

paper *Worker's Weekly*, it published an open letter to the armed forces, urging them not to be used to break strikes. This led to his being charged with incitement to mutiny, and, owing to its mishandling of the incident, to the fall of the minority Labour government, led by Ramsay MacDonald. Campbell was editor of the *Daily Worker*, 1949–59. In 1917 he was awarded the Military Medal for bravery.

44. The infamous bombing of Guernica by forty-three German planes took place on 26 April 1937. The number of casualties is uncertain—perhaps a thousand were killed—and, as Thomas notes, even the Nationalist commission of inquiry found that 70% of the houses were destroyed and a further 20% damaged. At first, attempts were made by Nationalists to say that the Basques had themselves blown up Guernica, but the large number of foreign correspondents present, and the evidence of the British Consul, made it clear where the responsibility lay, though the full story did not emerge for some time. See Thomas, 623–29, who gives a particularly well-balanced account of this attack, including the Nationalist case for attacking the area—there was an arms factory outside the town—and the possibility for error.

45. Rajani Palme Dutt (1896–1974), a prolific author, had been expelled in 1917 from Oxford University for disseminating Marxist propaganda. He was a member of the Executive Committee of the Communist Party, 1922–65, and editor of the London *Daily Worker*, 1936–38.

46. Thomas records: 'Antonio Sesé, the communist general-secretary of the Catalan UGT, and a member of the new provisional council of the *Generalidad*, was killed on his way to take up his appointment (perhaps accidentally, since all moving cars were shot at, though possibly as a reprisal for the death of the anarchist, Domingo Ascaso, killed earlier on)' (659–60).

APPENDIX 3

519A. Orwell's Marrakech Notebook
Handwritten

This little notebook measures 5¼ x 3⅜ inches. Its leaves are perforated at the top and each has twenty-five faint lines. It was presumably carried by Orwell as he went about Marrakech so that he could note down prices. He numbered each page (as here). Six pages have been filled in. There were about 175 francs to the £; 40 francs to the U.S. dollar. For more precise details, see *480, headnote*.

1

* Copper tray about 2' across, weight about 15 lb, F. 175.
* Donkey Fr. 75–150.
* Camel (small) Fr. 300. Prices probably go up to about Fr. 1000
* Mule Fr. 250–1000 (or more.)
* Cow in milk, about Fr. 600
* Horse (riding). Fr. 200 upwards.
* Lantern for candle Fr. 4–5.
* Women's soft leather slippers 10–15 Fr. (goodish quality.)
* Copper tray about 1' 6" across, second hand, worn & not heavy, Fr. 35.
* Couverture about 6' by 4', all wool, Fr. 40.

2

* Wheat, Frs. 30 the large measure, about a bushel & weight about 40 lb. Not certain whether overcharge (decalitre).
* Goats, young female, very poor but of about average standard, Frs. 30 & 35. Good goat (if obtainable) said to cost Frs. 60.
* Chopped lucerne 10c. a bunch about 3–4" thick.
* Hire of a donkey about 2–3 Fr. an hour.
* Laying pullets, considered good specimens, Frs. 7.50 each (said to be rather high price.)

3

Hire of bicycle, Frs. 6 a day (probably overcharge, should be Frs. 4 or 5.)
Bran Frs. 1.35 a kg.
¾" x ¾" wood (presumably imported pine, sawn but not planed) 2 Fr. a metre.

6″ x ¾″ (ditto) Frs. 5 a m.
Plywood (poor quality) about Fr. 1.75 the.° square foot.
Firewood (more or less chopped) Frs. 80 for 1000 kg. (a ton.)
Hire of lorry, Frs. 125 for about 2 hours & 10 miles.

4

Cylinder of Butagaz (somewhat smaller than Calorgas) Frs. 85 (ie. price of gas only.)
Table waters, various, roundabout Frs. 3.50 a litre.
★ "Mandarin" oranges, & lemons (October 20) about 50c. each.
★ Other type of orange (Oct. 21, just coming in) Frs. 3.50 for 6.
Canadian apples about Frs. 7 a kg.
★ Oranges (10.11.38) 10 for Frs. 3.50
Candles (cheapest) 10 for 3.50. Better quality 8 for 6.50
Peas (13.11.38) Frs. 5 a kilo.

5

★ (native workmanship.)
± (belongs to country.)[1]
★ All-wool (probably camel) dyed couverture, handspun & woven, about 8′ by 6′, 150 Fr.
★ Copper tray, about 2′ 6″ across, weight about 25 lb. 300 Fr.
★ String bottomed chairs (estimated 7 work-hours) 7 Frs. (Fr. 4 (?))
[2] Second-hand axe-head, about 6 lb., 7 Fr.
★ Basket of type priced 2/– – 3/6 in England. 5 Fr. (overpayment.)
★ Spherical unglazed earthenware-bowl with fitted lid, 4 Fr.
★ 1 pint unglazed white earthenware cup, 1 Fr.
★ 1½ pint red earthenware vase, roughly glazed inside 3 Fr. (probably overpayment.)

6

★ Slightly cheaper all-wool couverture, same measurements as above, 100 Fr.
+ Cheaper style, part wool part cotton, 6′ by 4′, 30 Fr.
Small kettle (not tin, which apparently are not sold here) Fr. 9.50.
★ Bellows (style 2/– to 3/6.) Fr. 7
Nails, 1½″, 2 Fr. kilo.
Cup of water, 5c.
‡ Common wine, 3–4 Fr. litre (French price about the same.)
‡ Common cigarettes, "Favorites", Fr. 1.50 for 20. (French price about Fr. 2.50–3.)
★ Leather sandals, made to measure, (English price about 5/–), Fr. 25 (probably overcharge.)

1. The symbol varies but the intention is always clear.
2. An asterisk (or possibly the ±) crossed out.

1939

520. Review of *Power: A New Social Analysis* by Bertrand
Russell

The Adelphi, January 1939

If there are certain pages of Mr. Bertrand Russell's book, *Power*, which seem
rather empty, that is merely to say that we have now sunk to a depth at which
the restatement of the obvious is the first duty of intelligent men. It is not
merely that at present the rule of naked force obtains almost everywhere.
Probably that has always been the case. Where this age differs from those
immediately preceding it is that a liberal intelligentsia is lacking. Bully-
worship, under various disguises, has become a universal religion, and such
truisms as that a machine-gun is still a machine-gun even when a "good" man
is squeezing the trigger—and that in effect is what Mr. Russell is saying—
have turned into heresies which it is actually becoming dangerous to utter.

The most interesting part of Mr. Russell's book is the earlier chapters in
which he analyses the various types of power—priestly, oligarchical,
dictatorial and so forth. In dealing with the contemporary situation he is less
satisfactory, because like all liberals he is better at pointing out what is
desirable than at explaining how to achieve it. He sees clearly enough that the
essential problem of to-day is "the taming of power" and that no system
except democracy can be trusted to save us from unspeakable horrors. Also
that democracy has very little meaning without approximate economic
equality and an educational system tending to promote tolerance and
toughmindedness. But unfortunately he does not tell us how we are to set
about getting these things; he merely utters what amounts to a pious hope
that the present state of things will not endure. He is inclined to point to the
past; all tyrannies have collapsed sooner or later, and "there is no reason to
suppose (Hitler) more permanent than his predecessors."

Underlying this is the idea that common sense always wins in the end. And
yet the peculiar horror of the present moment is that we cannot be sure that
this is so. It is quite possible that we are descending into an age in which two
and two will make five when the Leader says so.[1] Mr. Russell points out that
the huge system of organised lying upon which the dictators depend keeps
their followers out of contact with reality and therefore tends to put them at a
disadvantage as against those who know the facts. This is true so far as it goes,
but it does not prove that the slave-society at which the dictators are aiming
will be unstable. It is quite easy to imagine a state in which the ruling caste
deceive their followers without deceiving themselves. Dare anyone be sure
that something of the kind is not coming into existence already? One has only

to think of the sinister possibilities of the radio, State-controlled education and so forth, to realise that "the truth is great and will prevail"[2] is a prayer rather than an axiom.

Mr. Russell is one of the most readable of living writers, and it is very reassuring to know that he exists. So long as he and a few others like him are alive and out of jail, we know that the world is still sane in parts. He has rather an eclectic mind, he is capable of saying shallow things and profoundly interesting things in alternate sentences, and sometimes, even in this book, he is less serious than his subject deserves. But he has an essentially *decent* intellect, a kind of intellectual chivalry which is far rarer than mere cleverness. Few people during the past thirty years have been so consistently impervious to the fashionable bunk of the moment. In a time of universal panic and lying he is a good person to make contact with. For that reason this book, though it is not so good as *Freedom and Organisation*, is very well worth reading.

1. See *Nineteen Eighty-Four*, *CW*, IX; e.g. 261–71 and 303.
2. From Coventry Patmore, 'The Unknown Eros'.

521. To John Lehmann

4 January 1939   Typewritten

Boite° Postale 48   Gueliz   Marrakech   French Morocco

Dear Lehmann,

Thanks very much for your letter. I'll try and do you something for New Writing. I don't expect you knew, but I have been badly ill, was in a sanatorium for a long time and now have to spend the winter in this place. But I am a lot better and getting on with some work again. I have seen some interesting things in this country and had thought of doing some sketches of them, and I dare say I could do something that might suit New Writing. Just at this moment I am rather submerged with the novel I am doing,[1] but perhaps in three or four weeks from now I could send you something. Would that be soon enough?[2]

Yours sincerely
George Orwell

1. *Coming Up for Air*.
2. Acknowledging this letter on 12 January 1939, Lehmann said he knew Orwell had been ill but did not know he was in Morocco. He was delighted that Orwell might send 'some sketches' for *New Writing*. They proved to be 'Marrakech,' acknowledged by Lehmann on 12 April 1939 and published in *New Writing*, Christmas 1939; see 579.

522. To Herbert Read

4 January 1939   Typewritten

Boite° Postale 48   Gueliz   Marrakech   French Morocco

Dear Read,[1]

Thanks for your letter and the manifesto.[2] Funnily enough I'd already seen it in "La Flèche" and had thought of making further enquiries. I'll certainly sign it, though if you merely want a few names to represent England you could get some much better-known people. But any way use my name for anything it is worth. You asked if I wanted to suggest any changes in the manifesto. The only point I am a bit doubtful about, though I don't press it, is this. On p. 2 you say "To make Russia safe for bureaucracy, first the German workers, then the Spanish workers, then the Czechoslovakian workers, have been left in the lurch." I've no doubt this is true, but is it strategically wise for people in our position to raise the Czech question at this moment? No doubt the Russians *did* leave the Czechs in the soup, but it does not seem to me that they behaved worse or very differently from the British and French Governments, and to suggest by implication that they ought to have gone to war to defend the Czechs is to suggest that Britain and France ought to have gone to war too, which is just what the Popular Frontiersmen would say and what I don't believe to be true. I don't press this point, I merely suggest it and any way add my name to the manifesto.

I am spending the winter here for the sake of my lungs, which I think it is doing a little good to. Owing to this blasted health business I have had what is practically a wasted year, but the long rest has done me good and I am getting on with a new novel,[3] whereas a year ago, after that awful nightmare in Spain, I had seriously thought I would never be able to write a novel again. Meanwhile, curiously enough, I had for some time past been contemplating writing to you about a matter which is much on my mind. It is this:—

I believe it is vitally necessary for those of us who intend to oppose the coming war to start organising for illegal anti-war activities. It is perfectly obvious that any open and legal agitation will be impossible not only when war has started but when it is imminent, and that if we do not make ready *now* for the issue of pamphlets etc. we shall be quite unable to do so when the decisive moment comes. At present there is considerable freedom of the press and no restriction on the purchase of printing presses, stocks of paper etc., but I don't believe for an instant that this state of affairs is going to continue. If we don't make preparations we may find ourselves silenced and absolutely helpless when either war or the pre-war fascising° processes begin. It is difficult to get people to see the danger of this, because most English people are constitutionally incapable of believing that anything will ever change. In addition, when one has to deal with actual pacifists, one generally finds that they have a sort of lingering moral objection to illegality and underground work. I quite agree that people, especially people who have any kind of notoriety, can get the best results by fighting in the open, but we might find it extremely useful to have an underground organisation *as well*. It seems to me that the commonsense thing to do would be to accumulate the things we should need for the production of pamphlets, stickybacks etc., lay them by in some unobtrusive place and not use them until it became necessary. For this we should need organisation and, in particular, money, probably 3 or 4 hundred pounds, but this should not be impossible with the help of the people one could probably rope in by degrees. Would you drop me a line and let me know whether you are interested in this idea? But even if you are not, don't speak of it to anyone, will you?

I enclose the manifesto, which I have signed.

Yours
Eric Blair

P.S. [handwritten] I'm keeping the leaflet of "Clé"[4] & will send in a subscription as soon as I can get into Marrakech & buy a money-order.

1. Herbert Read (1893–1968; Kt., 1953), poet, critic, educator, and interpreter of modern art, served in World War I (DSO, MC) and was particularly influential in the thirties and forties. He was assistant keeper at the Victoria and Albert Museum, taught at Edinburgh University, 1931–32, and edited the *Burlington Magazine*, 1933–39. He wrote a series of major works including *Form in Modern Poetry* (1932), *Art Now* (1933), *Art and Society* (1936), and *Poetry and Anarchism* (1938; reprinted in *Anarchy and Order*, 1954). His *Education through Art* (1943) had an important post-war influence. He was the most prominent British intellectual to support anarchism before World War II and was closely associated with anarchism until he was knighted.
2. *Towards a Free Revolutionary Art*. This called for the formation of an Internationaal Federation of Independent Revolutionary Art. It was signed by André Breton, founder and leader of the Surrealist movement, and Diego Rivera, painter of the Mexican revolution, when they rejected the Third International politically and culturally. See also draft letter to Raymond Postage, *497*
3. *Coming Up for Air.*
4. *La Clé* was the monthly bulletin of the International Federation of Independent Revolutionary Art.

523. Morocco Diary

VILLA SIMONT 8.1.39:

Cost of sending four rather heavy parcels to England, about Frs. 400. Two others not quite so heavy about Frs. 100 the two. The red tape in post offices here even worse than in France. The two which E. and I despatched personally took us over two hours. First about half an hour's wait to get a place at the counter. This not due to Xmas, as it is always much the same. Then endless filling up of forms and the usual search by the officials through large books to find out which forms should be used. Then the usual complaint that the parcels were insufficiently secure. One had not thick enough string, the other which was enveloped in cloth had to be sewn up. Went out and bought string, needles and thread and did the sewing up. Then a complaint because the parcels were not sealed. Fresh journey to buy sealing wax. This kind of thing seems inseparable from French post offices. Notice that most of the minor officials here, of the type who in India would be Indians, are French. Eg. all the post-office clerks and clerks in the other offices, and even most of the traffic policemen. Supply of native clerks evidently does not exist. Most Arabs who are in contact with Europeans speak a little French, but have not yet met an Arab whose French seemed to be perfect.

On Xmas Eve there was a very heavy frost here, which did a good deal of damage. From the type of vegetation and what the Arabs say I do not think this can be usual. Notice, however, that oranges and lemons were quite unaffected by it.

The French here seem to take even less notice of Xmas than in France. They celebrate New Year. Arabs all acquainted with New Year and use it as a pretext for begging. There are said to be less tourists than usual this year.

People gathering lucerne draw it up with their hands instead of cutting with the sickle, thus saving an inch or two on each plant. The people in the little walled village near the house give the impression of owning their land communally, as they all turn out and do the same jobs, weeding, ploughing etc., together.

Examined recently the grave of what was evidently a fairly rich man, in a little mud enclosure. A concrete grave of the usual pattern, with a sort of little oven evidently for burnt offerings at the head. No name on the grave. On a tree over the grave various little charms, bunches of wool etc., hanging. Stole one of the charms, a sort of little leather purse. Inside it a bunch of wool and a paper with writing.

524. Review of *Russia under Soviet Rule* by N. de Basily

New English Weekly, 12 January 1939

"Russia under Soviet Rule" falls definitely into the "anti" class of books on the U.S.S.R., but for once it is not Trotskyist. The author—an exile, of course—holds approximately the same opinions as Kerensky[1] and the others of the Provisional Government of 1917, with which he was associated in an official capacity. He is therefore attacking the Bolshevik experiment not from a Socialist but from a liberal-capitalist standpoint, rather as Gaetano Salvemini[2] attacks the Fascist experiment of Italy. His book might almost, in fact, be a companion-volume to "Under the Axe of Fascism." In the last analysis it is doubtful whether any liberal criticism of a totalitarian system is really relevant; it is rather like accusing the Pope of being a bad Protestant. However, as the dictators are generally dishonest enough to claim the liberal virtues on top of the totalitarian ones, they certainly lay themselves open to attacks of this kind.

The author, it should be noticed, though hostile to the Bolshevik régime, does not think that it is going to collapse in the near future. His main thesis is that it has functioned inefficiently and that the loss of liberty and enormous suffering which it has caused were largely unnecessary. The modernisation of industry and agriculture which Stalin has undertaken is, according to Mr. de Basily, simply a continuation of something that was already happening in pre-war Russia, and the rate of progress has actually been slowed down rather than advanced by the revolution. It is of course obvious that a statement of this kind cannot be finally proved or disproved. Even to begin to examine it is to sink into a bog of statistics—and incidentally this book contains more figures, mainly from Soviet sources, and longer footnotes than any book I have read for years. But it is worth being reminded that Russia was already being fairly rapidly modernised in the ten years or so preceding the revolution. It is now, perhaps, beginning to be possible to see the Russian revolution in some kind of historical perspective, and the hitherto-accepted version of a barbarous feudal country turning overnight into a sort of super-America is something that will probably have to be revised.

But is life—life for the ordinary person—any better in Russia than it was before? That is the thing that it seems almost impossible for an outsider to be certain about. Statistics, even when they are honestly presented (and how often does that happen nowadays?), are almost always misleading, because one never knows what factors they leave out of account. To give a crude illustration, it would be easy to show, by stating the figures for fuel-consumption and saying nothing about the temperature, that everyone in Central Africa is suffering from cold. Who does not know those Soviet statistics, published by Mr. Gollancz and others, in which the curve of everything except mortality goes up and up and up? And how much do they really tell one? Mr. de Basily's statistics, naturally, point a different moral, but, without in the least questioning the accuracy of his figures, I would not infer too much from them. As far as the material side of life goes, all that seems to emerge fairly certainly is this: that the standard of living was rising during the N.E.P. period, dropped during the period 1928–33, and is now rising again but is still low by western European standards. This is denied by Soviet apologists, but not very convincingly. The average wage in 1936 was only 225 roubles a month—the purchasing-power of the rouble being about threepence. Moreover, it is well-known that it is next door to impossible for a Soviet citizen, unless on some kind of official mission, to visit any foreign country—a silent admission that life is more comfortable elsewhere.

If Mr. de Basily were merely claiming that twenty years of Bolshevik rule had failed to raise the general standard of living, his criticism would be hardly worth making. After all, one could not reasonably expect an experiment on such a scale to work perfectly at the beginning. Economically the Bolsheviks have been far more successful than any outsider would have prophesied in 1918. But the intellectual, moral and political developments—the ever-tightening party dictatorship, the muzzled press, the purges, the oriental worship of Stalin—are a different matter. Mr. de Basily devotes a good many chapters to this. He is, nevertheless, comparatively optimistic, because, as a liberal, he takes it for granted that the "spirit of freedom" is bound to revive sooner or later. He even believes that this is happening already:

"The thirst for liberty, the notion of self-respect . . . all these features and characteristics of the old Russian élite are beginning to be appropriated by the intellectuals of to-day . . . The moment the Soviet élite opens its fight for emancipation of the human individual, the vast popular masses will be at its side."

But will they? The terrifying thing about the modern dictatorships is that they are something entirely unprecedented. Their end cannot be foreseen. In the past every tyranny was sooner or later overthrown, or at least resisted, because of "human nature," which as a matter of course desired liberty. But we cannot be at all certain that "human nature" is constant. It may be just as possible to produce a breed of men who do not wish for liberty as to produce a breed of hornless cows. The Inquisition failed, but then the Inquisition had not the resources of the modern state. The radio, press-censorship, standardised education and the secret police have altered everything. Mass-suggestion is a science of the last twenty years, and we do not yet know how successful it will be.

It is noticeable that Mr. de Basily does not attribute all the shortcomings of the present Russian régime to Stalin's personal wickedness. He thinks that they were inherent from the very start in the aims and nature of the Bolshevik party. It is probably a good thing for Lenin's reputation that he died so early. Trotsky, in exile, denounces the Russian dictatorship, but he is probably as much responsible for it as any man now living, and there is no certainty that as a dictator he would be preferable to Stalin, though undoubtedly he has a much more interesting mind. The essential act is the rejection of democracy—that is, of the underlying values of democracy; once you have decided upon that, Stalin—or at any rate something *like* Stalin—is already on the way. I believe this opinion is gaining ground, and I hope it will continue to do so. If even a few hundred thousand people can be got to grasp that it is useless to overthrow Tweedledum in order to set up Tweedledee, the talk of "democracy versus Fascism" with which our ears are deafened may begin to mean something.

1. Aleksandr Kerensky (1881–1970), Socialist Premier of the Provisional Government of Russia, July–October 1917, fled to France, and lived in Australia from 1940 and in the United States from 1946, where he died.
2. Gaetano Salvemini (1873–1957), historian of contemporary Italy, was forced to leave Italy in 1925 because of his attacks on Fascism. He taught at Harvard University, 1933–48, and became a U.S. citizen in 1940. See also *533, n. 1* and *2548, n. 2*.

525. To Jack Common

12 January 1939   Typewritten

Boite° Postale 48   Gueliz   Marrakech   French Morocco

Dear Jack,
I enclose cheque for £2 towards the hens' grub. I wish it were more but we are damned hard up and it's bloody to find yourself pinched for money in a foreign country. Any way it'll pay for their grub for a few weeks. I wonder if

that parcel turned up. One that we sent has done so, so I suppose there's hope that the others will, though the mental and moral atmosphere of a French post office is such as always to convince me that they have a large furnace somewhere on the premises into which they chuck all correspondence entrusted to them. This particular parcel I left to the shopman to send, and I see by the voucher that it was addressed to a place called Balderk, but I should think the English post office would be equal to that.

I hope you are getting on all right and the weather isn't being too bloody. I shall finish the rough draft of my novel[1] tomorrow, then in a few days we are going to the mountains for a week to see the Berber villages, and then I can get down to rewriting the novel, which generally takes me about two months. So probably at worst I'll get it done before the war breaks out. I wonder if the political situation will hold up? It's getting harder and harder for the English public. I suppose 50 per cent of them knew whereabouts Austria was and about 20 per cent knew where Czechoslovakia was, but where is the Ukraine? And where are Memel and Eupen Malmedy, not to mention Russian Subcarpathia?[2] The only people who can really keep up with affairs nowadays are philatelists. One reason why I so particularly don't want war to break out is that I have been bitten with the desire to write a Saga. I don't know that in a novelist this isn't a sign of premature senile decay, but I have the idea for an enormous novel in three parts which would take about five years to write and there wouldn't have to be a war going on in the background.

I wonder if some time you could make a sort of preliminary demarche about Muriel's mating. The thing is this. There is a woman called Miss Woods who lives at Woodside not far from Sandon and keeps a fattening plant. She uses goat's milk to fatten the birds, and she has a very superior breed of goats, Nubians I think. Her billy is a beauty. I wanted to take Muriel to him last year. Miss W. wasn't too keen because she is very proud of her goats and has a vague feeling that it defiles her billy to have to do with crossbred females, and she is always shooing off the Sandon villagers who want a mate for five shillings. Finally however she consented to do it for a guinea, but then the foot and mouth epidemic intervened and you weren't allowed to send animals about, so it fell through, and finally we sent M. to a dreadful scrub goat somewhere else. But if you could drop Miss W. a post card saying we want a mate say some time in February, and perhaps mentioning last year, she might consent. I wouldn't mind paying the guinea because in that case it's worth keeping the kids and I know her goats are a first class milking strain.

Love to Mary and Peter. Eileen sends love.

Yours
Eric

1. *Coming Up for Air.*
2. Orwell refers to places which Germany might claim or where it stirred up discontent. Eupen and Malmédy in Belgium, close to the border with Germany, and the Memel area of Lithuania had German populations. Memel was demanded by Germany in December 1938 and ceded on 21 March 1939. There was a nationalist movement in the Ukraine, and Hitler mischievously

suggested that the Ukraine be made an independent state; see *527*. After Munich, a weakened Czechoslovakia allowed an autonomous government to be set up in sub-Carpathia (Ruthenia). On 15 March 1939 this area declared itself independent, but that same day it was annexed by Hungary.

526. A Mistake Corrected

On 13 January 1939 *The New Leader* published a letter from Orwell explaining that in his review of Frank Jellinek's *The Civil War in Spain* he had attributed a despatch to him that was sent by someone else; see *462*, and also Orwell's letter to Jellinek, 20 December 1938, *513*.

527. To Francis Westrope

15 January 1939   Typewritten

Boite° Postale 48   Gueliz   Marrakech   French Morocco

Dear Frank,

I wonder if you could be kind enough to send us the following:

Thackeray's *Pendennis* (Nelson Double Vol. 2/–).

Trollope's *Eustace Diamonds* (World's Classics).

H. James' *Turn of the Screw* (Everyman No. 912.)

J. S. Mill's *Autobiography* (World's Classics.)

I think that about exhausts our credit, but if we owe you anything, let me know, won't you?

I am afraid it is a long time since I have written, and I never answered the letter Mrs Westrope[1] wrote me about the time we left England. We have been in this country about four months now and expect to be here till about the beginning of April. We have a little villa a few miles out of Marrakech, which is a big town of about 200,000 inhabitants, mostly Arabs of course. We are about 1000 feet above sea level, and though it was beastly hot when we first came here the winter weather is beautifully sunny and cool, about like a spring day in England. There is the most ghastly poverty here, of course, most of the population, so far as I can work it out, living at the level of about a shilling a day. Most of the peasants round here are too poor even to have a pair of oxen for ploughing and plough with an ox and a donkey yoked together. The country is very poor, not quite desert but dried up and more or less treeless except for cultivated trees. What rivers there are seem to have shrunken greatly in the last few years, and I suppose ever since Roman times this country has been drying up. Here round Marrakech it is fairly green as they grow the date palm here, but in the train you pass over enormous areas of what looks like broken-up brick where nothing will grow except the prickly pear. Needless to say the French have grabbed all the best soil. Wages of labourers etc. in the towns generally work out at about a penny an hour,

319

and the children begin begging literally as soon as they can walk. Nevertheless there seems to be very little discontent and, at any rate on the surface, no organised movement against the French rule. All the Arab left-wing parties have been suppressed, but it is evident that they never amounted to very much, as one meets with no hostility towards Europeans as such, which makes a great contrast to India. The people are still almost entirely in the feudal stage and most of them seem to imagine that they are still ruled over by the sultan.

I must say I was very thankful to be out of Europe for the war crisis. Here the people paid very little attention to it, partly I think because they did not want to excite the Arabs but also because they evidently didn't believe war was coming. I think one of the determining factors of the situation is that the French people can't be got into war unless France is invaded, and their politicians are aware of this. I suppose the next bit of trouble will be over the Ukraine, so perhaps we may get home just in time to go straight into the concentration camp if we haven't been sunk by a German submarine on the way. I hope and trust it won't be so. I have just finished the rough draft of my novel,[2] and then we are going into the Atlas mountains for a week before I begin the revision, which will take till about the beginning of April. I think the climate has done me good. I cough very little now and I have put on a bit of weight, about half a stone already. It does seem so infuriating to be interrupted all the time by these wars and things.

I don't think by the way I ever thanked you for very kindly sending me that book of Arabic. I'm sorry to say Eileen and I have learned practically no Arabic, except the few words one can't help learning, because all the Arabs speak a kind of pidgin French, at any rate if they are at all in contact with Frenchmen. They also, of course, in these parts, speak a kind of dialect with Berber and even Spanish words mixed up in it. A lot of the people round here are Chleuh,[3] a race the French only conquered quite recently, and there is also a certain amount of negro blood. We had to pass through Spanish Morocco coming down here. I didn't of course get more than glimpses, but I saw a few Franco troops, who looked indistinguishable from the Government troops I used to see a year earlier. The French here are mainly pro-Franco, and I think when all is known it will come out that they have given Franco a good deal of help, direct and indirect. There is a huge Jewish population here and in consequence a lot of anti-Jewish feeling, though most of the Jews are terribly poor and live much the same life as the Arabs. I hadn't realised before that much of the characteristic Moroccan work, coppersmithing and so forth, is done by Jews. Most of the native work is lovely and, of course, extremely cheap, though unfortunately many of the best things aren't portable.

Please give all the best to everyone. I trust when we next meet it won't be behind the barbed wire.

Yours
Eric Blair

1. Myfanwy Westrope, wife of Francis Westrope, proprietor of Booklovers' Corner, where Orwell had worked as a part-time shop assistant in 1934–35; see *212*. For the attribution of the addressee as Frank Simmonds, see Crick, 373, n. 37.

2. *Coming Up for Air*.
3. For Chleuh, which Orwell also spelled Cleuh, see *511, n. 5*.

528. To Geoffrey Gorer

20 January 1939   Handwritten

Boite° Postale 48   Gueliz   Marrakech   French Morocco

Dear Geoffrey,

I've been meaning to write to you for ages, & here I am doing it at last. We have been in this country ever since September & I think it has done my lungs a good deal of good. I don't cough much now & have put on about ½ a stone. Eileen is also thriving. In September the climate was foul, unbearably hot & every kind of insect pest, but as winter comes on it gets to be a lovely clear kind of weather like spring in England. I am writing this 5 or 6 thousand feet up in the Atlas.[1] I'd finished the rough draft of my novel[2] & wanted to take a week off, so we came up here. It's wonderful country, enormous limestone gorges & ravines full of frozen snow, & little Berber villages of mud huts with flat tops. The Berbers—the kind round here are called Chleuh—are fascinating people, often more or less white with red cheeks, & the women have the most wonderful eyes. But what fascinates me about them most of all is that they are so dirty. You will see exquisitely beautiful women walking about with their necks almost invisible under dirt. Of course the poverty is such as you would expect & you have only to produce a packet of cigarettes to be more or less buried under a pile of people of all ages & both sexes. But that seems to be the same everywhere in Morocco. It is funny that all hill people have a certain resemblance, perhaps in their walk, & there is something about the people here that slightly reminds me of the Kachins in Burma.

I hope your book[3] on the Lepchas went off all right. I'm not displeased with parts of my novel, which I hope to have finished by the beginning of April. I don't know what I shall do next. Nelson's wanted me to do a book[4] for that series they are bringing out, then it fell through owing to my being ill, but if I can connect up with them again I should like to do that before doing another novel. I have an idea for a very big novel, in fact 3 in series, making something about the size of War & Peace, but I want another year to think over the first part. I suppose it's a sign of approaching senile decay when one starts projecting a Saga, but in my case it may merely be another way of saying that I hope war won't break out, because I don't think I could write a Saga in the middle of a war, certainly not in the concentration camp. I must say we were very glad to be out of England for the war crisis. One gets so fed up with arguing with people about this war business, & everything that could conceivably be said has been said already. I think you are a bit younger than me & probably don't remember the great war very vividly, but I have a very retentive memory & often when I hear people tirading against Hitler nowadays I often think the clock has somehow slipped back twenty years. In Morocco the French simply paid no attention & obviously didn't think war conceivable. I think the absolutely bottomless selfishness of the French may help to save the situation, because it is obvious that they would not fight unless French soil is invaded & the higher-ups presumably know this. What a mess in Spain! A friend who recently came out tells me that Barcelona is smashed out of recognition, all the children are hungry & you could buy 900 pesetas for an English pound note. I keep hearing in roundabout ways of Spaniards I knew, always that they are killed. It does seem so meaningless. George Kopp, whom you may remember reading about in my book on the war, recently escaped, having lost 7 stone of weight thanks to what the G.P.U. had done to him during 18 months. I hope he publishes his experiences, because it is time this kind of thing was put a stop to.

I have no idea where you are, but shall send this to Highgate, of course. I hope you'll be in England in the spring & that we'll see you when we get back. Eileen sends love.

Yours
Eric

1. Orwell wrote on letterhead from the Auberge 'Les Noyers,' where he was staying in Taddert. He wrote his address in Gueliz, reverting to his childhood spelling, 'Adress.'
2. *Coming Up for Air.*
3. *Himalayan Village: An Account of the Lepchas of Sikkim* (1938; New York, 1967, with a new foreword).
4. 'Poverty in Practice,' 18 June 1938; see *455.*

529. Review of *Communism and Man* by F. J. Sheed

Peace News, 27 January 1939

This book—a refutation of Marxian Socialism from the Catholic standpoint—is remarkable for being written in a good temper. Instead of employing the abusive misrepresentation which is now usual in all major controversies, it gives a fairer exposition of Marxism and Communism than most Marxists could be trusted to give of Catholicism. If it fails, or at any rate ends less interestingly than it begins, this is probably because the author is less ready to follow up his own intellectual implications than those of his opponents.

As he sees clearly enough, the radical difference between Christian and Communist lies in the question of personal immortality.[1] Either this life is a preparation for another, in which case the individual soul is all-important, or there is no life after death, in which case the individual is merely a replaceable cell in the general body. These two theories are quite irreconcilable, and the political and economic systems founded upon them are bound to be antagonistic.

What Mr. Sheed is not ready to admit, however, is that acceptance of the Catholic position implies a certain willingness to see the present injustices of society continue. He seems to claim that a truly Catholic society would contain all or most of what the Socialist is aiming at—which is a little too like "having it both ways."

Individual salvation implies liberty, which is always extended by Catholic writers to include the right to private property. But in the stage of industrial development which we have now reached, the right to private property means the right to exploit and torture millions of one's fellow-creatures. The Socialist would argue, therefore, that one can only defend private property if one is more or less indifferent to economic justice.

The Catholic's answer to this is not very satisfactory. It is not that the Church condones the injustices of Capitalism—quite the contrary. Mr. Sheed is quite right in pointing out that several Popes have denounced the Capitalist system very bitterly, and that Socialists usually ignore this. But at the same time the Church refuses the only solution that is likely to make any real difference. Private property is to remain, the employer-employee relationship is to remain, even the categories "rich" and "poor" are to remain—but there is to be justice and fair distribution. In other words, the rich man is not to be expropriated, he is merely to be told to behave himself.

"(The Church) does not see men primarily as exploiters and exploited, with the exploiters as people whom it is her duty to overthrow . . . from her point of view the rich man as sinner is the object of her most loving care. Where others see a strong man in the pride of success, she sees a poor soul in danger of hell . . . Christ has told her that the souls of the rich are in special danger; and care for souls is her primary work."

The objection to this is that *in practice* it makes no difference. The rich man is called to repentance, but he never repents. In this matter Catholic capitalists do not seem to be perceptibly different from the others.

It is obvious that any economic system would work equitably if men could be trusted to behave themselves but long experience has shown that in matters of property only a tiny minority of men will behave any better than they are compelled to do. This does not mean that the Catholic attitude toward property is untenable, but it does mean that it is very difficult to square with economic justice. In practice, accepting the Catholic standpoint means accepting exploitation, poverty, famine, war and disease as part of the natural order of things.

It would seem, therefore, that if the Catholic Church is to regain its spiritual influence, it will have to define its position more boldly. Either it will have to modify its attitude toward private property, or it will have to say clearly that its kingdom is not of this world and that feeding bodies is of very small importance compared with saving souls.

In effect it does say something of the kind, but rather uneasily, because this is not the message that modern men want to hear. Consequently for some time past the Church has been in an anomalous position, symbolized by the fact the Pope almost simultaneously denounces the Capitalist system and confers decorations on General Franco.

Meanwhile this is an interesting book, written in a simple style and remarkably free from malice and cheap witticisms. If all Catholic apologists were like Mr. Sheed, the Church would have fewer enemies.[2]

1. *Peace News* printed 'immortality' as 'immorality,' and also duplicated 'almost' in the last sentence of the penultimate paragraph.
2. This review attracted two letters printed in *Peace News*, 3 February 1939, one signed 'A Roman Catholic,' the other from John Nibb. Among points raised by what Nibb called an 'apt review' were that 'Catholics are not tied to a belief in the necessary permanence of indigence' and that, although the Catholic church taught and upheld 'the lawfulness of private property,' that right might be abrogated 'to avoid worse evils and in the interests of a whole people.' Indeed, some responsible Catholics, according to 'A Roman Catholic,' advocated 'that ownership of the means of production should be in the hands of the workers (*all* workers, not simply the "proletarians").' Referring to what he described as the anomaly Orwell saw in the Pope denouncing the evils of capitalism yet approving of Franco, Nibb said 'most Catholics find it impossible to view the Spanish war as an episode caused by wicked militarists and capitalists attacking a beneficient government . . . the wrong people are suffering for the actions of other individuals, and . . . the religion of the Franco element seems to be as much nationalism (and even imperialism) as Christianity.'

530. Morocco Diary

VILLA SIMONT   27.1.39:

Have just returned after spending a week at Taddert in the Atlas, about 95 km. from Marrakech. T. is at 1650 metres elevation, ie. about 5000 ft. When one gets about 2000 feet above the plain (itself about 1000 feet above sea level) one gets to a different type of vegetation, oaks and firs, more or less stunted, fairly good grass, of the downland type, and above about 4000 feet walnut trees, which grow profusely and very well, but evidently don't grow wild. The fig tree does grow at about 5000, but evidently doesn't do well. Almonds seem to do well. On the whole the mountain slopes are exceedingly bare and only begin to be well forested when one gets about 1000 feet above the valleys through which the main road runs. The lower slopes for about 500 feet above a village are often completely bare, mere chipped-up limestone like a slag-heap. Probably this is partly due to goats. The French Gov.t is now apparently beginning to do something about reafforestation, and is going to prohibit grazing on some of the hills. Evidently this area, even round the motor-road, is only in process of being accurately surveyed, as the landmarks for the survey people have only been newly set up. Road is good though not too wide. The bus does the journey from Marrakech to Taddert in 3 hours and the return in about 2½. There is a great deal of what appears to be iron ore in the mountains, but evidently quite unexploited. In the inhabited valleys there does not seem to be so much shortage of water as down here.

If one looks round from a high peak one sees that only about one valley in twenty, even round the motor road, is inhabited. Most of the valleys are mere clefts, and evidently the soil is only cultivable in those into which the sun gets for a good deal of the day. At this time of year there is frost every night, which hangs on in shady places for most of the day. Snow drifts everywhere, but nowhere below about 6000 ft. where the hills are impassable because of snow. Cultivation is of the terrace type, much as in the hills in Burma. The terraces are very skilfully done, walled up with limestone, as in Spain, and the soil appears to be deep, 4 feet or so, though of course it is artificially made up.

In moderately shady valleys and along banks of streams there are small but quite good pastures for the cows, the goats being grazed right on the tops of the hills. Goats are as down here, the sheep mostly of a quite different breed, with exceedingly silky wool. From what people say locally and from general appearances it appears that all the villagers own a small piece of land, and of course grazing is free, though evidently each village has its recognized beat. Could not make an accurate judgement, but I should not say that more than one acre is cultivated per head of population. It appears that barley is grown in winter-spring (the barley is coming up now, though not so advanced as down here), this is cut in June and then maize is sown. The local French consider that the Chleuh are good cultivators, and they evidently use plenty of manure. Ploughing is done with a cow and donkey, as here. The people have plenty of animals, and no doubt their staple food is barley and goats milk.

The villages are quite different from those in the plains, as they are not walled in. The houses are of mud, very occasionally limestone, and square, with flat roofs. These are thatched over with wild broom and then covered with earth, which is possible owing to the dryness. When one looks down at a village from above one sees that as a rule all the houses on the same level have a common roof, though inside they are separate. This points to a certain amount of communal life. Practically none have glass windows. What woodwork there is is mostly crude.

The Chleuh seem to be rather remarkable people. The men are not greatly different in appearance from Arabs, but the women are exceedingly striking. In general they are rather fair, sometimes fair enough to have red in their cheeks, with black hair and remarkable eyes. None are veiled, and all wear a cloth round their heads tied with blue or black cords, the dominant colours of their dress being red and blue. All the women have tattooing on their chins and sometimes down each cheek. Their manner is much less timid than that of most Arab women. Virtually the whole population is ragged and there is no evidence of any being much richer than the others. The children for the most part have nothing on but a ragged blanket. Begging is almost universal, and the women have discovered that their jewellery (amber and rough silver, some of it exceedingly well worked) is liked by Europeans and will sell it for prices that cannot be much above the value of the silver. The children beg as soon as they can walk and will follow for miles over mountain tracks in hopes of a sou. Tobacco is greatly appreciated by those who do smoke, but I notice that a great many do not, and none of the women. Children beg for bread and are glad to get it. Nevertheless it is difficult to be certain about the real amount of poverty. Probably there is no actual destitution, at any rate no one is homeless or quite propertyless. I notice under the walnut trees quantities of nuts which have been left to rot, which does not suggest serious hunger. But evidently everyone's life is at a low level. In some parts of the mountains carpets, leatherwork etc. are made. Near Taddert the chief trade apart from agriculture seems to be charcoal-burning. The people can of course get good wood (mostly oak) free, though possibly the Gov.t will interfere with this later, and they cook it in exceedingly primitive earth ovens and sell it at

Frs. *12 for a large sack (about Frs. 35 in Marrakech.) Local physique is pretty good, though the people are not particularly large or very athletic in appearance. All walk well, and the women easily walk up steep hillsides carrying a huge bundle of wood or a three-gallon stone jar of water. Apart from their own Berber dialect all speak Arabic, but few or none French. A few have reddish hair. There seems to be a Jew or two in most of the villages, not easily distinguishable from the rest of the population.*

Graveyards not quite the same as the Arab ones, though the people are Mahomedans. The graveyard is generally a patch of good grass and the cattle browse among the graves. Owing to plentiful stone the graves are generally covered with a cairn, not a mere mound of earth, as here, but they have no names or other indications of individuals. Judging from a few that had fallen in, it seems usual to make the grave as a kind of cave with flat slabs of rock, and then cover this over, originally perhaps as a protection against wild animals. Some of the graves are immensely long, 8 or 10 feet. I saw one funeral. It was done in the usual way by a party of friends, one of whom kept up a sort of mumbling recitative noise. The women as usual were not present, but a group sat on a rock within sight 100 yards away and kept up a rather perfunctory kind of wailing.

Talked a number of times in Taddert with a German in the Foreign Legion, who is there on some job I could not understand, something to do with some electric installation. A friendly intelligent man, who speaks French well. Has been eight years in the Legion and does not seem particularly discontented. Intends to stay his full time to get his small pension. Says they do not give you free tobacco in the French army and that you have to serve some time before your pay reaches even a franc a day, so that newcomers generally cannot smoke. No particular political opinions. Says there were 5 million unemployed when he left Germany and that he cannot go back as he is wanted for desertion. Did not express any opinion about Hitler. Seemed mildly pro-Government in the Spanish war.

Today the news of the fall of Barcelona has come. Nobody in Marrakech seems much interested, though the papers are splashing it. I note that there are at least 2 Socialist weeklies in Morocco, the Depeche de Fez and another whose name I forget. Not extreme and evidently (this is really why French Socialist papers are allowed to run and Arab ones not) not anti-imperialist. But both they and the P.S.F.[1] "Presse" keep up the abusive and scurrilous tradition of French newspapers, which the more moderate papers do not. Eg. the Depeche de Fez makes accusations of German corruption of the French press, naming names. This could not be done in newspapers either in England or in India without a prosecution, though the papers would probably only be fined. On the other hand, evidently no paper in Morocco can suggest that Morocco should be independent, without being suppressed. If the papers are reporting truthfully, there were demonstrations among the Spaniards in Tangier to celebrate the fall of Barcelona, without any kind of counter-demonstrations. Yet I had had the impression that the pro-Government Spaniards in Tangier slightly outnumbered the others. The hotel at Taddert exactly like a cheap Paris hotel, and ditto with the one or two cafes on the route. The people one met, also, completely [like] the ordinary lower-middle-class French, living exactly the same life as in France except that they are obliged to speak a little Arabic.

1. Parti Social Français; see *511, n. 3.*

531. Review of *The Clue of History* [by John Macmurray][1]
The Adelphi, February 1939

The main argument of Professor Macmurray's book can be stated thus:

The necessary and inevitable movement of human society is towards world-communism. The chief obstacle is the persistence of "dualism," from which only the Jewish consciousness has shown itself free. Consequently the Jewish mind, chiefly *via* its offspring, Christianity, has been the sole agent of human progress. Fascism, especially Hitler's version, is the last effort of the western world to escape its destiny. It will inevitably frustrate itself, and Hitler's special function is to destroy the bases of western life and usher in the Jewish Kingdom of Heaven in the form of a society of free and equal human beings.

I personally would agree with Professor Macmurray that humanity must move in the direction of Communism or perish, and that in practice it will not perish. But it is impossible not to take notice of the special rôle he assigns to the Jews. This is the central theme of the book, and as at this moment it has a particular importance, it is worth pointing out what very shaky grounds it rests upon.

Professor Macmurray begins by saying that the Hebrew culture is the only example of a religious culture that the world has seen. He makes no mention of Hinduism, though clearly one can only say that the Hebrew culture was religious and the Hindu culture un-religious if one argues in a circle and adds that by "religious" one means "Hebrew." Some such argument is, in fact, necessary to Professor Macmurray, because he is also claiming that the "religious consciousness" is incompatible with acceptance of class-divisions. Obviously this would rule out Hinduism, though caste ought not to be identified with class. But here one comes on a serious difficulty. What evidence is there that the "Jewish consciousness" either is or ever has been freer from "dualism" than any other? The Palestine Jews may have been free from the familiar dualism of this world—next world; certainly there is no clear mention of an after life in the Old Testament; but in their attitude towards *this* world they seem to have been slaves to the most incorrigible dualism of all, because they saw everything in terms of Jew–Gentile. So far from having more sense of human brotherhood than most nations, they appear to have had none whatever. The Old Testament is largely a literature of hatred and self-righteousness. No duties towards foreigners are recognised, extermination of enemies is enjoined as a religious duty, Jehovah is a tribal deity of the worst type. Finally there appears the arch-heretic Jesus, whom Professor Macmurray describes as the culminating point of the "Jewish consciousness." And yet it was precisely the Jews who rejected Jesus more decisively than any of the pagan nations.

When it comes to the rôle of the Jews in modern times, Professor Macmurray seems at times to be in danger of succumbing to a kind of racial mysticism. To begin with he speaks throughout of the "Jewish consciousness," the "Greek consciousness," and so forth, as though these were entities of known worth like coins or chessmen. Moreover, he seems to be suggesting that the "Jewish consciousness"—developing, no doubt, but recognisably the same thing—has persisted from Biblical times until the present. If this is true it makes nonsense of Marxism, which Professor Macmurray seems to accept. After all, how much has a typical modern Jew, a New York solicitor, say, in common with some bloodthirsty nomad of the Bronze Age? Is there really such a thing as the "Jewish consciousness"? According to Professor Macmurray, the great truth which Hitler has discovered is that "the source of all this pressure towards progress, equality, freedom and common humanity is—the Jew." A little later he seems to contradict this by accusing the Jews of "exclusive racialism" by which they are "self-isolated from the community of mankind." But in any case, what evidence is there that the Jews have done more or less for human progress than anyone else? One might perhaps argue that the motive force behind every progressive movement has been the teaching of Jesus, and that Jesus was a Jew; but the first statement is very doubtful and the second needs a lot of qualification. There have always been Jews in the Socialist movement, and Marx was a Jew of sorts, but one could hardly call Socialism a Jewish movement. How little Russian Communism is a Jewish movement has just been strikingly illustrated. In the middle of an atrocious persecution, the Jewish refugees show no desire whatever to go to Russia; in fact, they will go anywhere else in preference. And in this, of course, they are reacting not as Jews but as western Europeans. In fact, is not the truth about the Jews something like this: that because in the past they have been persecuted and have followed the oriental practice of not intermarrying with foreigners, they are just different enough from their neighbours to be unpopular and to make useful scapegoats?

As to Professor Macmurray's interpretation of Christianity, it is coherent in itself but hardly seems to be borne out by the recorded teachings of Jesus. Briefly, he represents Christianity as entirely *this-worldly* and seems to assert that Jesus did not believe in personal immortality, which is negatived not only by what Jesus said but still more decisively by what he failed to say. I do not know whether this matters greatly, because, in practice, every reading of the Gospels depends on an arbitrary selection of texts. But the fathering of human progress on to the Jews, because of the results which it is capable of having, is rather a different matter.

It will be seen that Professor Macmurray is saying that Hitler is right. This he readily admits. The "Jewish consciousness" is "poison" to the Aryan races and Hitler's perception of this is "the proof of his genius." The only difference is that whereas Hitler disapproves of what is happening, Professor

Macmurray approves. I do not know whether it has occurred to him that if this issue really existed, or were believed to exist, nearly everyone would side with Hitler. Professor Macmurray says, "the thought of the triumph of the Jewish consciousness fills me with joyous exhilaration." It would not have that effect upon other people. If one could popularise the idea that western civilisation is being sapped away through the influence of an alien race, the result would be to make the whole world throw itself at Hitler's feet. One does not damage a theory by standing it on its head. To say that Hitler has discovered the truth but is playing the part of Lucifer is simply to encourage anti-semitism. This is the worst possible moment for airing theories about "the Jews" as a mysterious and, from a western point of view, sinister entity. Even more at this moment than at most times it is important to remind people that the Jews are human beings before they are Jews.

Of course this does not invalidate Professor Macmurray's theory. He may be right, and Hitler after his fashion may be right. But considering the evil results of saying so, I doubt whether one ought to advance a theory of this kind if one is obliged to base it on such very shadowy evidence as the "Jewish consciousness," the "Greek consciousness" and the "Roman consciousness"—things which it is impossible to define and which probably do not exist.

1. Orwell's review was the second in a symposium devoted to Macmurray's book. In 1943 Orwell invited Macmurray to broadcast to India; see *2071*.

532. To Lady Rees

23 February 1939   Typewritten

Boite° Postale 48   Gueliz   Marrakech   French Morocco

Dear Lady Rees,[1]

I do so hope all is well with Richard. The last I heard from the Plowmans some months back was that he was still in Barcelona, but since the retreat I have had no news of him, of course. I hope and trust he got out all right and isn't too overcome by all he must have been through. If he is home and cares to write, our address is the above until about the end of March. I think my wife told you I had been ill with what they finally decided after a lot of X-raying was not tuberculosis but something with a long name. I spent about six months in a sanatorium and then they told me I should spend the winter here. I don't know how much good it has done me, but I have no doubt it was as well to be out of England for this winter, which seems to have been a very severe one. Of course this business has set my work back a lot, however I have nearly finished another novel[2] and we are going to come home as soon as it is done, about the beginning of April. They said I ought to live further south, so I dare say we shall settle in Dorset or somewhere like that when we can find another cottage.

It is very quiet and peaceful here. We have a little house a few miles out of

Marrakech and we don't see any other Europeans except when some of the soldiers from the Foreign Legion come and see us. A short while back we spent a week about 5000 feet up in the mountains, where the Berber race called the Chleuh live. They are rather interesting people, very simple, all free and equal, very dirty but splendid to look at, especially the women. They have beautiful little pastures with grass almost like England, and you can lie about on the snow in blazing sunshine. Down here the country is flat and very dried up, with no natural trees, much like northern India, I should think. The Arabs are terribly poor and most of the people work for about a penny an hour. For Europeans living isn't very cheap, not so cheap as France, I should say, though certain things are fantastically cheap, for instance you can buy a camel for three hundred francs, supposing that you wanted one. The brass &[3] copper work that they do here is beautiful, but the most attractive thing of all is the very cheap native pottery, which unfortunately it is almost impossible to bring away.

We were most thankful to be out of England during the war crisis, and I trust we shan't get back just in time to meet another. The idea of war is just a nightmare to me, and I refuse to believe that it can do the slightest good or even that it makes much difference who wins. If Richard is back and doesn't feel up to writing, could you give him all our love and say we hope to see him when we get back?

Yours sincerely
Eric Blair

1. Lady Rees was Sir Richard Rees's mother; he was serving as an ambulance driver in Spain. For his leaving Spain, see letter to Jack Common, 19 March 1939, *539*.
2. *Coming Up for Air.*
3. &] a

533. To Jack Common

23 February 1939   Typewritten

Boite° Postale 48

Dear Jack,

Did you write to Miss Woods about Muriel's mating? If not, could you be good enough to drop her a card? I don't remember the exact address, but I think it's Woods, Woodcotes, Nr. Sandon, and any way they'll know at the pub. You remember the circumstances—Muriel was to have been mated last year, fee a guinea, then it fell through owing to the foot and mouth. If I could get a mating from Miss W's billy it would be worth keeping the kids, if female. Failing that we must arrange one elsewhere. In either case Field (Post Office, Sandon) will do the transporting for five bob. Let me know what Miss W. says and I'll send you the money. Incidentally I hope there's no foot and mouth this year. I suppose they are right in not letting animals be moved about while it is on, though they don't stop men and dogs, but it is really time they stopped that insane business of slaughtering a whole flock of cattle because of one case.

I don't know exactly when we'll be back, but some time in April, and will let you know the exact date later. I've got to finish the novel,[1] which has been set back because I have again been ill and was in bed a fortnight, though I'm all right now, and then there's the question of a boat. If possible we want to go all the way from Casablanca by boat, but there's only one a month and I can't obtain the date yet. After we get back I must go straight down to Southwold and see my father, and Eileen as soon as possible is going to look for a new house. This is all supposing war hasn't broken out by then, because if it has I don't want to be caught with my pants down and shall keep the cottage. But if it would suit you to stay on at the cottage till about the end of April, it would suit us. On the other hand if you wished to leave a bit earlier we could fit that in as well, because in any case either E. or I will have to come down to Wallington to superintend moving the stuff. We shall take the hens, of course, in spite of their failure to make good, but shall probably dump the fowl houses and buy new ones, which would not be dearer than transporting and less fag. I wonder if anything is coming up in the garden. There ought to be a few snowdrops and crocuses soon.

I don't know whether the world situation is better or worse. I look at it now simply with a meteorological eye, is it going to rain or isn't it?, though I suppose once it's started one will fail as usual to keep out of it. If I was biologically a good specimen and capable of founding a new dynasty I would devote all my energies during the war to keeping alive and keeping out of sight. I haven't heard of or from Richard, but I've just written to his mother to know what the news is. I suppose he got out all right. It's all a ghastly mess, and if one is not personally involved the most ghastly thing of all will be the complete failure of left-wingers to learn anything from this disaster, the awful sterile controversies which will go on for years, everyone laying the blame on everybody else.

I wonder if Murry's ordination is going through all right? I suppose as he's got a degree[2] already he won't have to study for very long. But is he quite sound on the 39 articles[3] etc.? I shouldn't have thought so. It would be comic if he ended up as a bishop. By the way, have you run across the rector of Rushden cum Wallington, Mr Rossborough. Although not very prepossessing he's a nice little man and has a very nice son. The son, Rob, is at Haileybury and he joined the P.P.U.[4] and refused to enter the O.T.C.[5] What impressed me was not so much this as that his father after thinking it over decided to back him up. He has been a missionary in Africa and seen the way the natives are treated, and this has given him slightly heterodox views on some questions, as often happens with missionaries. His wife though very nice impresses me as being a bit off her rocker. By the way her praying circle pray regularly for my health (don't tell anyone this as it's supposed to be a secret even from me, Mrs R. having told Eileen in confidence).

Best love to Mary and Peter. Eileen sends love.

Yours
Eric

1. *Coming Up for Air.*
2. For Murry's entering the church, see Orwell's letter to Jack Common, 26 December 1938, *516*.
3. Those ordained as priests of the Church of England must assent to the Thirty-nine Articles. These encapsulate the doctrinal position of the church following the Reformation.
4. Peace Pledge Union, founded 1934. Max Plowman (see *95*) was its General Secretary, 1937–38. It published *Peace News*, for which Orwell wrote a review; see *529*.
5. Officers' Training Corps, formed by Lord Haldane, Lord Chancellor, 1912–15, before World War I as a means of training a pool of officers; it is chiefly to be found in public schools.

534. 'Caesarean Section in Spain'

The Highway,[1] March 1939

When General Franco raised his rebellion in July, 1936, he threw a spanner into the works of a machine which was travelling in a fairly well-defined direction. How seriously he jammed it is still uncertain.

The revolution of 1931 had got rid of the Spanish monarchy but had failed to solve any of the country's fundamental economic problems. One of its effects, however, had been to create an atmosphere of liberalism and free speech in which ideas hitherto frowned upon could circulate widely. From then onwards it was clear to many observers that civil war in Spain was inevitable. The decisive moment came when a Government which could roughly be described as "left" was returned by a rather narrow majority at the elections of February, 1936. This Government—the Government of the Popular Front—was not by any means under the control of extremists. It did not precipitate a crisis by violence towards its political opponents; on the contrary, it actually weakened itself by its moderation. A more rigidly "left" Government would have dealt earlier with the military plot which everyone knew was being prepared, and would probably have made some promise of independence to the Arabs in Spanish Morocco, thus preventing them from throwing in their lot with Franco. Nevertheless the Government's programme of reform menaced the big landowners and the Church, as any radical reform was bound to do. In the existing state of Spain it was not possible to move nearer to a real democracy without colliding with powerful vested interests. Consequently, the mere appearance of the Popular Front Government was enough to raise the most difficult problem of our time: the problem of making fundamental changes by democratic methods.

Parliamentary democracy, and especially the party system, developed in a period when no dispute between the different factions was really irreconcilable. Whigs and tories, or liberals and conservatives, are conducting what is in effect a family quarrel, and they will abide by one another's decisions; but when the issue is, for instance, between capitalism and socialism, the case is altered. Actually, in slightly varying guises, the same situation has arisen over and over again. A democratically elected government proceeds to make radical reforms; it is acting perfectly legally, but its opponents "won't play"; they rise in rebellion, either by open violence, as in Spain, or, more usually, by financial sabotage. The peculiarity of this case was that the Spanish Government fought back.

The war has now lasted two-and-a-half years and caused perhaps a million deaths, besides unheard-of-misery. How much damage has it done to the cause of democracy? One has only to consider the possibilities of modern war, the kind of things that governments will have to do to hold their peoples together, to feel very doubtful whether there will be much democracy left anywhere after several years of "all-in" warfare between great nations. Yet it is a fact that the Spanish war, in nearly every way so terrible, has been a hopeful portent in this respect. In Government Spain both the forms and the spirit of democracy have survived to an extent that no one would have foreseen; it would even be true to say that during the first year of the war they were developing.

I was in Catalonia and Aragon from Christmas, 1936, until about the middle of the following year. To be in Spain at that time was a strange and moving experience, because you had before you the spectacle of a people that knew what it wanted, a people facing destiny with its eyes open. The rebellion had plunged the country into chaos and the Government nominally in power at the outbreak of war had acted supinely; if the Spanish people were saved, it had got to be by their own effort. It is not an exaggeration to say that practically the whole resistance of the opening months was the direct and conscious action of the ordinary people in the street, via their trade unions and political organisations. Transport and major industries had devolved directly into the hands of the workers; the militias which had to bear the brunt of the fighting were voluntary organisations growing out of the trade unions. There was plenty of incompetence, of course, but also there were astonishing feats of improvisation. The fields were tilled, trains ran, life away from the fighting line was for the most part peaceful and orderly, and the troops, though poorly armed, were well fed and cared for. With all this there was a spirit of tolerance, a freedom of speech and the press, which no one would have thought possible in time of war. Naturally the social atmosphere changed, in some ways for the worse, as time went on. The country settled down to a long war; there were internal political struggles which resulted in power passing from the hands of socialists and anarchists into the hands of communists, and from the hands of communists into the hands of radical republicans; conscription was imposed and censorship tightened up—two inevitable evils of modern war. But the essentially voluntary spirit of the opening months has never disappeared, and it will have important after-effects.

It would be childish to suppose that a Government victory could have instantly brought a democratic regime into existence. Democracy, as we understand it in Western Europe, is not immediately workable in a country so divided and exhausted as Spain will be when the war is over. Certainly any Government which triumphs over Franco will be of liberal tendency, if only because it will have to sweep away the power of the great landowners and most if not all of the power of the Church. But the task of governing the whole of Spain will be completely different from that of governing the present loyal fraction. There will be large dissident minorities and enormous problems of reconstruction; inevitably this implies a transition period during which the regime will be democratic chiefly in name. On the other hand, if Franco wins even the name will be abandoned. He has made perfectly clear his intention of setting up a corporative state on the Italian model—that is to say, a state in which the majority of people are openly and cynically excluded from having any voice in affairs.

And yet the situation may be less desperate than it looks. Obviously if Franco wins the immediate prospects are not hopeful; but the long-term effects of a Franco victory are hard to foresee, because a dictator in Franco's position would almost certainly have to depend on foreign support. And if the Government can win, there is reason to think that the evil results necessarily following on civil war may disappear quite rapidly. Wars are normally fought by soldiers who are either conscripts or professionals, but who in either case are essentially in the position of victims and who have only a very dim idea as to what they are fighting about. One could not possibly say the same of the armies of Government Spain. Instead of the usual process of conscripts being fed into a military machine, a civilian people has voluntarily organised itself into an army. It is the psychological after-effects of this that may make a return to democracy more easy.

It was impossible to travel in Spain in early 1937 without feeling that the civil war, amid all its frightful evil, was acting as an educational force. If men were suffering, they were also learning. Scores of thousands of ordinary people had been forced into positions of responsibility and command which a few months earlier they would never have dreamed of. Hundreds of thousands of people found themselves thinking, with an intensity which would hardly have been possible in normal times, about economic theories and political principles. Words like fascism, communism, democracy, socialism, Trotskyism, anarchism, which for the vast mass of human beings are nothing but words, were being eagerly discussed and thought out by men who only yesterday had been illiterate peasants or overworked machine-hands. There was a huge intellectual ferment, a sudden expansion of consciousness. It must be set down to the credit side of the war, a small offset against the death and suffering, and it is doubtful whether it can be completely stamped out, even under a dictatorship.

It is true that things have not fallen out as we expected them to do at that time. To begin with, up till the summer of 1937 everyone in Government Spain took it as a thing assured that the Government was going to win. I would be far from saying that the Government is beaten even now, but the fact is that a Government victory cannot any longer be regarded as certain. Secondly, great numbers of people took it for granted that the war would be followed by a definitely revolutionary movement in the direction of socialism. That possibility has receded. Given a Government victory, it seems much likelier that Spain will develop into a capitalist republic of the type of France than into a socialist state. What seems certain, however, is that no regression to a semi-feudal, priest-ridden regime of the kind that existed up to 1931 or, indeed, up to 1936, is now possible. Such regimes, by their nature, depend upon a general apathy and ignorance which no longer exist in Spain. The people have seen and learned too much. At the lowest estimate, there are several million people who have become impregnated with ideas which make them bad material for an authoritarian state. If Franco wins, he will hold Spain's development back, but probably only so long as it pays some foreign power to keep him in place. Shooting and imprisoning his political opponents will not help him; there will be too many of them. The desire for liberty, for knowledge, and for a decent standard of living has spread far too widely to be killed by obscurantism or persecution. If that is so, the slaughter and suffering which accompany a modern civil war may not have been altogether wasted.

1. *The Highway* was subtitled, *A Review of Adult Education and the Journal of the Workers' Educational Association.* W. E. Williams, editor of a special number, called 'Democracy at Work,' had written to Orwell, 22 November 1938, asking if he could contribute an article with this title. A note preceded the article: 'Two at least of Mr. Orwell's books are familiar to W.E.A. members: *The Road to Wigan Pier*, and *Down and Out in London and Paris*°. This article was witten° before Catalonia collapsed.' Various dates for the collapse can be used. Hugh Thomas's *The Spanish Civil War* (1977) has a map showing the advances made by nationalist forces in the campaign for Catalonia, December 1938–January 1939 (870); Barcelona was occupied on 26 January 1939; nationalist troops reached the French border at all points by 10 February (873, 881).

534A. To Lydia Jackson

1 March 1939   Handwritten

Lydia Jackson (née Jiburtovitch, 1899–1983) was educated at Leningrad University, worked for the Society of Friends in Moscow and, in 1925, came to England, not intending to stay permanently. In 1929 she married Meredith Jackson, a lecturer in law at Cambridge University (and later Professor of Law); they divorced in 1935. In the preceding year she had started studying psychology at University College London; she graduated in 1942 and was awarded a D.Phil. by Oxford University in 1949. She then lectured in psychology, practised child psychotherapy, and, under the name, Elisaveta Fen, translated Chekhov's plays, 1951–54, published in a single Penguin volume in 1959. Whilst at UCL she became a close friend of Eileen O'Shaugnessy and often visited her home. She knew Orwell from the time he met Eileen and went to their wedding. Her autobiography (written under her pen-name), *A Russian's England* (1976), gives good accounts of Eileen (341–44), life at the Orwells' cottage at Wallington (347–48, 377–78), and Eileen's and Orwell's relationship (348 and 349). She also states that Karl Schnetzler (see *2893*), a friend of the O'Shaughnessys and the Blairs, used to accompany her on visits to Eileen in 1937 when Eileen was at Wallington minding the shop whilst Orwell was in Spain. She says, 'Eileen genuinely thought that Karl was in love with me . . . [Karl and I] were good friends, but neither of us was in love with the other. . . . There was a look which came over his face when Eileen appeared on the scene which left me in no doubt that he was in love with *her*' (417).

Lydia Jackson had visited Orwell at Aylesford Sanatorium in 1938 and she gave this account of her visit:

I found George fully dressed sitting in a deck chair outside; on my arrival, he got up and suggested we should go for a walk in the park. We did not go very far. When we were out of sight of the buildings, we sat on the grass and he put his arms around me.

It was an awkward situation. He did not attract me as a man and his ill health even aroused in me a slight feeling of revulsion. At the same time, the fact that he was a sick man, starved of intimacy with his wife, made it difficult for me to repulse him. I did not want to behave like a prude or to treat the incident as a serious matter. Why should I push him away if kissing me gave him a few minutes of pleasure? I was convinced that he was very fond of Eileen and I was in no sense a rival to her (419).

Boite° Postale 48 Gueliz Marrakech French Morocco

Dear Lydia,

I am afraid it is a very long time since I have written to you & I don't think you have written to me either, have you? I hope all is going well with you. We are in all probability leaving this country on the 23rd March, in which case we should get back about the 30th. I suppose I shall be in London for a bit before going down to see my people etc. So looking forward to seeing you! So try & keep a date or two open a few days after the 1st of April. How is your work getting on? I hope to get my novel finished before we sail, though it will hardly be typed before then. Parts of it I am quite pleased with, others not. Eileen is well though she has had one or two spells of being a little off colour. I was recently quite ill & in bed for a fortnight with what was evidently flu, however I'm all right again now. I don't believe in the alleged marvellous qualities of this climate which I think is neither better nor worse than any other. All our spending the winter here has really meant is that we have spent immense quantities of borrowed money, however, we were out of England for the war-crisis & that was a blessed relief. Let's hope we aren't going to bump into another just when we get back.

I wonder who your young man is now? I have thought of you so often – have you thought about me, I wonder? I know it's indiscreet to write such things in letters, but you'll be clever & burn this, won't you? I am so looking forward to seeing you & having a good talk with you. Eileen too is longing to get back to England. We'll have to give up the Wallington cottage, I suppose, but if possible we're going to get one in Dorset or somewhere. Take care of yourself. Hoping to see you early in April.[1]

With love
Eric

---

1. In *A Russian's England*, which reproduces a few lines of this letter Lydia Jackson says she read this letter with mixed feelings: 'I was looking forward to seeing Eileen again, but not George, especially as the tone of his letter suggested a renewal of the amorous behaviour I had been too soft-hearted to repel at the Maidenhead hospital' (that is, Aylesford Sanatorium, near Maid*stone*). Further, 'I had several men friends at the time whom I found more attractive than George, and his masculine conceit annoyed me. Least of all did I want to disturb his relationship with Eileen, or have anything to conceal from her' (430).

Whilst the proofs of this edition were being corrected, the existence of twenty-four letters from Orwell to Lydia Jackson, one from Eileen to her, and one letter from Lydia Jackson to

Orwell, in the possession of Mrs Rosemary Davidson and the Russian Archive, Brotherton Library, University of Leeds, was drawn to the attention of the editor by Richard D. Davies, Archivist at Leeds. These letters, written over a period of ten years, from 1 March 1939 to 27 June 1949, can be identified by the 'A' following their item numbers (except for 'B' after *542*). The editor is deeply grateful to Mrs Davidson and Richard Davies for making them available and for allowing them to be included in this edition.

535. To Jack Common

5 March 1939   Typewritten

                Boite° Postale 48   Gueliz   Marrakech   French Morocco

Dear Jack,

Hope all goes well with you. About our arrangements. If the bank sends us the money in time we're going to take a boat which sails from Casablanca on the 22nd or 23rd and ought to get to London about the end of March. After that I've got to go down to Southwold and see my people and there will be other odds and ends to see to. After much thought we've decided to go on living in the cottage for the rest of the summer and not move till the autumn. Apart from anything else we shall have no money at any rate till my book comes out, which would make it very awkward to move, and in any case one can find a better place if one takes one's time looking for it. Barring war we shall no doubt move, as they say I oughtn't to spend the winter there and by going further afield one could get a much more sanitary cottage at not much more rent, but we might as well spend the summer there as anywhere else. Also if we go in the autumn we can take certain fruit bushes etc. which we have put in. So, any work you've done or had old Hatchett to do won't have been wasted, rather a barren consideration for you, I'm afraid.

Meanwhile can you do us a great favour, which might, however, ease things up if there happened to be an interval between your finding somewhere else to go to and our coming in. You may remember reading in my book on the Spanish war about Georges Kopp,[1] who was commander of my brigade for a while. He's been for some time staying with Eileen's brother at Greenwich, but we can't ask them to have him stay there indefinitely, because they've got the house full already and it's awkward for them. So if necessary could you put him up at Wallington? I don't mean in the cottage, he can stay at Mrs Anderson's, but could you see about his meals? Gwen O'Shaughnessy, Eileen's sister in law, will see about the money for his grub etc., so that you shan't be out of pocket, and perhaps it wouldn't be so much trouble for Mary to have one extra person at meals? You'll find him very easily satisfied. I think you'll like him also. Of course this might turn out not to be necessary, some job might turn up for him in the mean while, but I doubt whether he's fit to work yet after being 18 months in jail and starved and so forth. Then if it so happened that you wanted to clear out before we could move in, he could keep the place warm for us. But in any case he'd be there till we come and could then stay for a while until he can get a job, which

I expect he can ultimately. If this *should* turn out to be necessary, I hope it won't put you out too much.

I'm longing to see England again. It's starting to get hot here. This is the only time of the year when there's a bit of greenness, and all the camels, donkeys etc. are gorging themselves while the going's good. Quite a lot of the wildflowers are the same as in England. The cherry trees are in flower and the apple trees just coming into leaf. It's nice that we shall see this over again in England. I wonder if there were any snowdrops and crocuses in the garden. I think I shall just finish my novel[2] before we board the boat, but it will probably have to be typed on the sea. There's about 100 pages I'm pleased with, the rest is a failure. I haven't heard any more about the Penguin business[3] and hope it hasn't fallen through.

Did you drop a card to Miss Woods about Muriel? I haven't heard a word about Richard but I wrote to his mother to ask about him. If writing, don't send any letter later than the 15th, as it might miss us. Love to Mary and Peter,

Yours
Eric

P.S.[4] Eileen sends love—& the postscript, really to Mary. I think you might find George Kopp quite an asset, especially if you can bear to be separated from the gas oven. He is quite handy in the house & *adores* cooking. But the thing is this: if you can have him will you write & ask him to come? Without of course mentioning that anyone is going to pay for his food. We feel Gwen may be getting a bit down as she's just had a baby & the house is full of it & its nurse & the locum it necessitates (Gwen is a doctor). On the other hand she can't suggest that George should go somewhere else; but she could let him accept our invitation. It could be given on the grounds that he'd be staying with us if we were in England & he might like to see our village (he would). He's the sort of man who's happy anywhere if people are pleased to see him & you'd find him interesting to talk to—he speaks English quite fluently. If you don't want to write to George but don't mind having him, write to Gwen & she can pass on the invitation. The only important thing is that he should be allowed to think that you're inviting him spontaneously.

[In Eileen's hand at the top of the first page of the letter:]
Gwen's address:
Dr. Gwen O'Shaughnessy,
24 Crooms Hill,
Greenwich,
London S.E.10

1. Among Orwell's papers were three issues of *Independent News:* a special number of, probably, late November or early December 1938 devoted to 'The P.O.U.M. Trial in Barcelona'; No. 59, 16 December 1938, with an article titled 'After the P.O.U.M. Trial'; and No. 60, 23 December 1938, which included a report on George Kopp's imprisonment and release. Kopp was Orwell's commander in Spain, and Orwell and his wife visited him in prison; see *359, n. 2* and *CW*, VI, 171–78. The account given must have been derived from Kopp, who was not the most reliable of witnesses, but Orwell would have taken it at face value. It shows that Orwell had a close friend who had suffered at the hands of the Cheka (the Soviet secret police), knew

about false confessions, and had read of 'torture by rats' in a confined space. In view of its significance this account is given in full (with two or three slight styling corrections). It should be noted that Kopp was questioned in Russian and that an interpreter was required, which seems natural. Kopp, however, was born in Russia and went to Belgium only when he was ten. He may have been able to speak Russian but not have revealed this to his captors. *Independent News*, 'Service de Presse Hebdomadaire du Bureau d'Informations Franco-Britanniques,' was issued from Paris; its editor was Lucien Weitz. It presented the POUM point of view. For Weitz, see *562*, *Diary of Events, 11.8.39, Party Politics, n. 3*.

GEORGE KOPP RELEASED

After an intensive campaign for the release of George Kopp our Belgian comrades have succeeded in saving one more revolutionary militant from the claws of the Spanish stalinists.

George Kopp has been saved but for a long time he will carry on his body the marks of the sadistic cruelty of these twentieth century inquisitors. When George Kopp came to Spain he was a robust strapping young man, radiantly healthy and strong. Today he has emerged from his long calvary, thin, feeble and bent, walking slowly with the aid of a cane. His body is covered with scabs and bruises, the marks of the diseases he has contracted in the subterrenean° dungeons of the stalinist "checas", in the damp, airless holds of the prison ships, and in the Forced Labor Camps.

Kopp was arrested June 20, 1937 at the height of the P.O.U.M. repression. Arrested without a warrant, without the knowledge of any authority, he was released in the same manner, without an order from any Spanish Court,—but for the past year and a half he has been under the vigilance of the Communist Party watch dogs.

During this time Kopp has been in the following jails, hideouts, secret prisons etc. First, upon his arrest he was taken to Police Headquarters; from there to the Hotel Falcón; then to the "checa" of Puerta del Angel; from there to Vallmajor (clandestine prison). He was later sent to Segorbe (near Valencia) to a Forced Labor Camp; then back again to Vallmajor; then to the prison ship "Uruguay"; then to Falset (Labor Camp N°6); then to the Palacio de Misiones; back again to the "Uruguay"; then to the Barcelona Seminary; afterwards to the Preventorium of Colell; then to Tamarite in Bonanova (suburb of Barcelona); and back to the Seminary. He was finally released December 7, 1938.

In the "checa" of Puerta del Angel he was interrogated 27 times during a total of ONE HUNDRED AND THIRTY FIVE hours. The questions were put in Russian and the Russian Communist agents in charge had to use an interpreter both for the questions and the answers.

When Kopp was taken to the Falcón Hotel (the POUM hotel stolen by the "unofficial" police and turned into a prison), he was so exasperated with the entire situation and with his arbitrary arrest that he decided to go on a hunger strike as a protest. During 6 days he touched no food but was obliged to give it up as it only endangered his situation.

In the Vallmajor prison the stalinists put on their best performance. They started by cajoling, then intimidation and finally coercion and open threats. They placed before him three documents to sign,—one, his promotion to Lieutenant Colonel; another, his affiliation to the Communist Party; and the third, a "confession" saying that the P.O.U.M. was a nest of spies and traitors. When Kopp refused to sign he was put in a coal bin without light, air, or food where enormous rats ran in and out of his legs. For 12 days he remained in the black pit, seeing no one, hearing no one until one day a voice called out, "Tonight we're going to shoot you!"

Kopp's long martyrdom was his reward for a clean revolutionary record in the Workers' Militia. He came to Spain from Belgium when the revolution broke out. He left immediately for the Aragon front with the Miguel Pedrola Column as "Centuria" chief. He took part in the following military operations: Casetas (9-10-36); Huesca (21-10-36); Insane Asylum of Huesca (11-36); Vedado Zuera (5-12-36); Alcubierre (6-2-37); the Hermitage of Salas (13-4-37); Chimillas (13-6-37). He fought in this last battle only seven days before his arrest. At that time he was Major in the Popular Army and had occupied commanding posts in the 29th. Division.

2. *Coming Up for Air.*

3. See letter to Leonard Moore, 28 November 1938, *506*.
4. The postscript, apart from the first three words, is in Eileen's hand.

536. To Herbert Read

5 March 1939   Typewritten

Boite° Postale 48   Gueliz   Marrakech   French Morocco

Dear Read,

Thanks so much for your letter. I am probably leaving this country about the 22nd or 23rd of March and should be in England by the end of the month. I shall probably be in London a few days and I'll try and arrange to come and see you. If I could help with "Revolt"[1] I'd like to, though till I've seen what kind of paper it is to be I don't know whether I could be any use. The trouble is that if I am writing a book as I generally am I find it almost impossible to do any other creative work, but on the other hand I *like* doing reviews, if they would want anything in that line. If we could keep a leftwing but non-Stalinist review in existence (it's all a question of money, really) I believe a lot of people would be pleased. People aren't all fools, they must begin soon to see through this "antifascist" racket. A thought that cheers me a lot is that each generation, which in literature means about ten years, is in revolt against the last, and just as the Audens etc. rose in revolt against the Squires and Drinkwaters,[2] there must be another gang about due to rise against the Audens.

About the press business. I quite agree that it's in a way absurd to start preparing for an underground campaign[3] unless you know who is going to campaign and what for, but the point is that if you don't make some preparations beforehand you will be helpless when you want to start, as you are sure to sooner or later. I cannot believe that the time when one can buy a printing press with no questions asked will last forever. To take an analogous case. When I was a kid you could walk into a bicycle-shop or ironmonger's and buy any firearm you pleased, short of a field gun, and it did not occur to most people that the Russian revolution and the Irish civil war would bring this state of affairs to an end. It will be the same with printing presses etc. As for the sort of thing we shall find ourselves doing, the way I see the situation is like this. The chances of Labour or any left combination winning the election are in my opinion nil, and in any case if they did get in I doubt whether they'd be better than or much different from the Chamberlain lot. We are therefore in either for war in the next two years, or for prolonged war-preparation, or possibly only for sham war-preparations designed to cover up other objects, but in any of these cases for a fascising° process leading to an authoritarian regime, ie. some kind of austro-fascism.° So long as the objective, real or pretended, is war against germany,° the greater part of the Left will associate themselves with the fascising° process, which will ultimately mean associating themselves with wage-reductions, suppression of free speech, brutalities in the colonies etc. Therefore the revolt against these things will have to be against the Left as well as the Right. The revolt will form itself into two sections, that of the dissident lefts like ourselves, and that of the fascists, this time the idealistic Hitler-fascists, in England more or less represented by Mosley. I don't know whether Mosley will have the sense and guts to stick out against war with Germany, he might decide to cash in on the patriotism business, but in that case someone else will take his place. If war leads to disaster and revolution, the official Left having already sold out and been identified in the public mind with the war-party, the fascists will have it all their own way unless there is in being some body of people who are both anti-war and anti-fascist. Actually there will be such people, probably very great numbers of them, but their being able to do anything will depend largely on their having some means of expression during the time when discontent is growing. I doubt whether there is much hope of saving England from fascism of one kind or another, but clearly one must put up a fight, and it seems silly to be silenced when one might be making a row merely because one had failed to take a few precautions beforehand. If we laid in printing presses etc. in some discreet place we could then cautiously go to work to get together a distributing agency, and we could then feel "Well, if trouble does come we are ready." On the other hand if it doesn't come I should be so pleased that I would not grudge a little wasted effort. As to money, I shall probably be completely penniless for the rest of this year unless something unexpected happens. Perhaps if we definitely decided on a course of action your friend Penrose[4] might put up something, and I think there are others who could be got to see the necessity. What about Bertrand Russell,[5] for instance? I suppose he has some money, and he would fall in with the idea fast enough if he could be persuaded that free speech is menaced.

When I get back I'll write or ring up and try and arrange to meet. If you're going to be in town about the beginning of April, or on the other hand going to be away or something, could you let me know? But better not write to the above as the letter might miss me. Write to: AT: 24 Croom's Hill, Greenwich SE.10.

Yours
Eric Blair

1. *Revolt!*, jointly edited by Vernon Richards in London, ran for six issues, from 11 February to 3 June 1939. It aimed at presenting the Spanish civil war from an anti-Stalinist point of view.
2. John Squire (see *142, n. 3*) founded the *London Mercury*, and edited it, 1919–34. He stood for Parliament for Labour in 1918 and for the Liberals in 1924, unsuccessfully both times. He had a particular interest in architecture and was an early advocate of appointing a minister of fine arts. Among the many books he wrote and edited were *A Book of Women's Verse* (1921) and *The Comic Muse* (1925). John Drinkwater (1882–1937), poet, playwright, and essayist, was evidently an object of particular scorn to Orwell; Gordon Comstock sneeringly refers to him as *Sir* John Drinkwater in *Keep the Aspidistra Flying*, chap. VII, though he was not knighted. See Textual Note to *CW*, IV, 287, 138/5–6.   3. See letter to Read, 4 January 1939, *522*.
4. Roland Penrose (1900–1984; Kt., 1966) was a painter and writer who used his independent means to help many painters and artistic and left-wing projects.
5. Bertrand Russell, 3rd Earl Russell (1872–1970), noted philosopher and Nobel Prize winner, was a prominent advocate for peace, and campaigned vigorously for it. Supported World War II and advocated threatening USSR with Atomic Bomb at start of Cold War. See *3089*, n. 5. See also Orwell's review of his *Power: A New Social Analysis*, *520*.

537. To Leonard Moore

9 March 1939   Handwritten postcard

[No address]

[No salutation]

We are leaving on March 23rd & should be in England at the end of the month. Please don't send any communication here after the 15th or it may miss us. Novel finished & will bring it home with me—quicker & safer than sending it. Look forward to seeing you about beginning of April.

All the best
Eric Blair

538. Morocco Diary

12.3.39   VILLA SIMONT:[1]

Troops[2] returning from manoeuvres[3] passed the house a few days back, to the number of about 5000 men, more than half of[4] these Senegalese. The spahis look pretty good, general physique better than the average of the population. Horses about 14 hands, strong but not much breed, all colours, whites and greys predominating, seemingly some castrated and some not, but no mares (never ridden in this country).[5] Notice at the rifle range that[6] all horses[7] are well accustomed to fire. Seeing them on the march en masse, I do not now think (as I did before) that the Senegalese infantry are superior to the Arabs. They look much of a muchness. With the cavalry were some kind of small-bore quick-firing guns[8]—could not see the mechanism[9] as they were enveloped in canvas, but evidently the bore of the gun was[10] 1" or less. Rubber tyres to wheels. Transport wagons have huge all-steel disc wheels and are pulled by three mules. In addition there were[11] pack batteries (screw guns[12]). These[13] guns were round about 3", perhaps 75 mm, though, of course, different from the quick-firer 75 mm. field gun.[14] To carry the whole gun, ammunition etc. evidently requires 6–8 mules. The breech-piece of the gun is a load for one mule. A column such as we saw could manoeuvre without difficulty anywhere in country such[15] as this, except in the mountains. The men are sent on manoeuvre[16] with their heavy khaki overcoats etc., but do not seem to be overloaded as they used to be. Most seemed to be carrying 40– 50 lb.

Five English and Americans from the Foreign Legion have been to visit us from time to time:

Craig. Glasgow Irish, but Orange. Fairly superior working-class, claims that[17] his father is well-paid office employee[18] and to have been the same himself. Age about 25, healthy and good physique. Distinct signs of paranoia (boasting about past grandeurs etc.) as is usual with these types. Has been about 2½ years in the Legion and spent half of this in prison camps etc., having made two attempts to desert.[19] Speaks little French. Somewhat "anti-red", showed hostility at mention of Maxton. Does not like the French and would try not to fight if war came.[20]

Williams. *American, dark hair, possibly touch of dark blood. Health and physique not very good. Has nearly finished his 15 years, then gets small pension (about 500 francs a month) and expects to remain in Morocco. Is now orderly at the officers' mess. Not well-educated*[21] *but well-disposed and evidently thoughtful.*

Rowlands. *Age about 30–35. "Superior" type and curious accent which might belong to an*[22] *Eurasian. Drinks when possible. Has done 5 years in the Legion, or nearly, and thinks of leaving (they engage*[23] *for 5 years and can then re-engage if they wish). Evidently has not been much in trouble. Gentle disposition, thoughtful type, but not intelligent.*

Smith. *American, age about 40, employed as bandsman. Some tendency to drink. Has a good many years of service. Not intelligent*[24] *but evidently good-hearted.*

Also a young Scotsman whom I only met once. Evidently there are only two or three other Englishmen and Americans in this lot (the 4th). It is clear that[25] *Englishmen etc. don't get on, will not put up with the rough conditions etc., and are also handicapped by inability to learn French, which the Germans are better able to do. All the above-mentioned are still privates. The Legion is predominantly German and the NCOs are usually Germans.*

It is clear that life in the Legion is now thoroughly dull. None of the above has[26] *seen any fighting except innocuous skirmishes. Fights occur among the men sometimes, but the duelling once prevalent has been put down. After a year or so of service a legionnaire*[27] *is still only earning about 2 francs a day (3d), and it never gets much above this unless he becomes an NCO. A sergeant gets 1200 francs a month but has to pay for*[28] *his food and also something for his clothes. Uniforms are badly-fitting but the men get a fair quantity of clothes. They have to launder them themselves. Each man gets ½ litre*[29] *of wine a day. There is no free tobacco issue, and recruits are usually unable to smoke for their first six months.*

After the collapse of[30] *Catalonia the Petit Marocain immediately became much more pro-Franco. Every comparison of French papers with those we receive from England makes it clear that the French and British publics get their news in very different forms, and that one or other press, more probably both, is habitually lying. Eg. the local press did not mention the machine-gunning of refugees*[31] *in Catalonia, alleged in the English press.*

To judge from the legionnaires' rumours there is still some expectation of war. Once the rumour went round that they were to be mobilised tonight. Within the last few days they have received a large consignment of machine guns[32] *and other small-arms at the depot*[33] *here, as though in expectation of fresh drafts of men. Whenever a French warship touches at Casablanca numbers of the sailors are sent*[34] *on voluntary-compulsory trips*[35] *to Marrakech, where they fraternise with the soldiers.*

Some of the crops of barley are now in ear and look fairly good. It appears that by local standards there has been a large rainfall this year and crops are expected to be good.

1. The section of the Morocco Diary from 12 March to 'Japanese and apart' in the fourth sentence of 28 March (see *541*) exists in manuscript and typed forms. Both are Orwell's work. The typed version is given here, except for obvious errors. In the following textual notes, unless stated otherwise the typed version is given first. Orwell invariably uses an ampersand for 'and' when writing, but spells it out when typing; some other words (e.g. 'about' and numerals) are contracted when written but are typed in full. These are not noted. It can be seen that Orwell's practice in such matters as hyphenation varies.

2. *Troops*] *Troops,*
3. *Typescript erroneously spells this 'maneouvres.'*
4. *of*] *omitted*
5. *(never ridden in this country)*] *omitted*
6. *Typescript has 'than.'*
7. *horses*] *the horses*
8. *quick-firing guns*] *quick-firing gun*
9. *the mechanism*] *mechanism*
10. *evidently the bore of the gun was*] *bore of the gun evidently about*
11. *were*] *were were*
12. *screw guns*] *screw-guns*
13. *These*] *The*
14. *quick-firer 75 mm. field gun.*] *ordinary 75 mm.*
15. *country such*] *such a country*
16. *manoeuvre*] *manoeuvres*
17. *that*] *omitted*
18. *office employee*] *office-employee*
19. *desert*] *escape*
20. *came*] *came along*
21. *-educated*] *-educated,*
22. *an*] *a*
23. *engage*] *enlist*
24. *intelligent*] *intelligent,*
25. *that*] *omitted*
26. *has*] *have*
27. *legionnaire*] *légionnaire (The accent, correct in French, is not used in English. Not noted again.)*
28. *pay for*] *pay 300 for (Orwell may have omitted the amount because, on reflection, uncertain of its correctness.)*
29. *litre*] *a litre*
30. *of*] *in*
31. *refugees*] *the refugees*
32. *machine guns*] *machine-guns*
33. *depot*] *dépôt (See n. 27.)*
34. *on*] *on a*
35. *trips*] *trip*

539. To Jack Common

19 March 1939   Handwritten

Marrakech

Dear Jack,

Thanks so much for your good offices re. George Kopp. He wrote telling us you had invited him to go to Wallington & that he wasn't going, at which I dare say you were not unrelieved, though you'd have liked him, I think. It's all rather awkward, Gwen O'Shaughnessy, Eileen's sister in law, has been putting him up for about 2 months now & we can't ask her to do so indefinitely. Meanwhile I don't know if it is going to make difficulties about our moving in—there being no one there, I mean. If so be you wanted to move out before we could get back, ie. that some opportunity of another house arose, or something, I suppose it would be quite simple to arrange with old Hatchett to look after the creatures till we arrive. He knows we'll make it up to him, & anyway, he's very good & kind about undertaking anything like that. I don't think we'll reach London before April 2nd, & then I must go straight down & see my father, who I am afraid is dying, poor old man. It's wonderful how he's lasted through this winter, which must have been beastly cold in Suffolk, & he was too frail to be moved. He's 81, so he's had a pretty good innings, but what a hole it seems to leave when someone you have known since childhood goes. We can't get back earlier because the boat we were to have sailed on on the 23rd has been delayed at sea in some way. Of course if something like that didn't happen on any journey I take this wouldn't be my life. However there's a Japanese boat a few days later which has got to stop off at Casablanca to drop a cargo of tea & we are going to take that instead. I've never been on a Japanese boat before but I'm told they're very good. We could go the way we came, across Spanish Morocco to Tangier, but it is intolerable if one has much luggage. Coming down we lost most of our luggage & didn't get it back for weeks because at every station there is an enormous horde of Arabs all literally fighting for the job of porter, & whenever the train stops they invade it, grab all luggage they can see, carry it off & stow it away in any other trains that happen to be in the station, after which it steams away into various parts of Africa while you try to explain what has happened to people who don't speak anything but arabic. I like to go as far as possible by sea, because on a ship at any rate there's no question of getting out at the wrong station.

My novel's finished,[1] which is why I'm writing in pen, as it is being typed. I've heard from Richard, who's at Perpignan & sounds pretty exhausted, as well he may be. I wonder if we can possibly get 5 years of respite before the next war. It doesn't look like it. Anyway, thank God for a roof over one's head & a patch of potatoes when the fun begins. I hope Muriel's mating went through. It is a most unedifying spectacle, by the way, if you happened to watch it. Love to Mary & Peter. Eileen sends love. Don't write because it would cross us. If any occasion to write, write to the Greenwich address.

Yours
Eric

P.S. Did my rhubarb come up, I wonder? I had a lot, & then last year the frost buggered it up. I don't know whether it survives that or not.

1. *Coming up for Air.*

540. Morocco Diary

<u>21.3.39</u> HOTEL DES NEGOCIANTS, MARRAKECH:
Yesterday the Sultan made an official visit and drove through the town, which had been previously decorated[1] with flags etc. and several thousand troops to line the streets. Obviously this was intended partly as a loyalty-parade in connection with the present crisis. It is evident that the people, ie. Arabs, here have a great feeling of loyalty to the Sultan.[2] There was much enthusiasm even in the Gueliz where normally there is not a large Arab population. Great numbers of the[3] petty chiefs and their retainers, forming[4] a sort of irregular cavalry, all armed with muzzle-loader guns. Evidently the

345

French are not afraid to allow these guns (good up to 2 or 3 hundred yards[5]in all probability) to be freely scattered about the countryside. The Arabs' loyalty to the Sultan, who is completely under the thumb of the French, makes things a lot easier for the French. [6]Madame V. told me that Arabs will even make signs of obeisance when hearing the Sultan's voice over the radio. [7] The Sultan is a small, not very impressive-looking man of 30–40.

Senegalese troops when seen in the mass look very good. Saw a detachment of the Foreign Legion march past. Contrary to my earlier impression, physique and carriage very good.

More attention being paid to the war-crisis this time. French people refer to it spontaneously, which they did not last time. Even Arabs talk about it, eg. our servant Madhjub Mahomed, [8] who informed us that there was "going to be war" and that it was the same as last time, ie. against Germany. Madhjub evidently fought in Europe in the Great War. [9]He cannot read any language, but has some ideas of geography, eg. he[10]knows you have to cross the sea to get to Europe.

E. remarks that Arab children have no toys whatever. This seems to be the case. In the Arab quarters no toys of any sort are on sale, no dolls, kites, tops or what-not, and the very few toys (sometimes a ball) one sees in Arab children's hands are of European manufacture. In any case they don't seem to play much. Great numbers are working from the age of about 6 onward, and most seem to know the value of money almost as soon as they can walk.

Soldiers in the Foreign Legion are not allowed into chemists'[11] shops (because of drugs and poisons) without a special permit.

1. decorated]been decorated
2. Sultan]sultan (and generally)
3. the] omitted
4. forming] formed
5. yards]yards,
6. the French]France
7. Madame V. . . . over the radio] omitted from manuscript
8. Madhjub Mahomed]Mahdjub Mahomet (and Mahdjub again later in manuscript)
9. Great War]great war
10. he] omitted
11. chemists']chemists

541. Morocco Diary

<u>28.3.39</u> ON BOARD SS. YASUKUNIMARU (NYK)[1] CROSSING BAY OF BISCAY:

Yasukuni is 11,950 tons. Do not yet know, but from vibrations[2] judge that she is a motor-ship. Apart from the bridge, only 3 decks above water-level. Cabins and other appointments pretty good, but certain difficulties in that entire[3] crew and personnel are Japanese and apart[4] from the officers the majority do not speak much English. Second class fare Casablanca–London £6.10. As the boat normally goes straight to London from Gibraltar & on this occasion went out of her way to deliver a load of tea, fare from Gibraltar would probably be the same. P. & O. tourist class is £6.10 London–Gibraltar. Food on this ship slightly better than on the P. & O. & service distinctly better, but the stewards here have the advantage that the ship is almost *empty. Facilities for drinking not so good, or for deck games, owing to comparatively restricted space.*

Do not know what the accomodation° for passengers would be, but presumably at least 500. At present there are only 15 in the second class, about 12 in the third, & evidently not many in the 1st, though I don't know how many. One or two of the 2nd & 3rd class are Danes or other Scandinavians, one or two Dutch, the rest English, including some private soldiers who got on at Gibraltar. It appears that for its whole voyage the ship has been as empty as this. Since the Chino-Japanese war English people from the far east will not travel on the Japanese boats. All the P. & O. boats said to be crowded out in consequence.

Run of the ship during the last 24 hours 378 miles. This was in pretty good weather conditions. Left Casablanca 4 pm on 26.3.39, & allowing for waiting for tides etc. in London river should apparently dock on evening of 30th or morning of 31st. (morning of 30th) (in dock about 9 am = 87 hours Casa – dock.)[5]

Ship gives out a cyclostyled sheet of news every day. Movies occasionally (have not seen them yet.)

In Casablanca went to the pictures, & saw films making it virtually certain that the French Gov.t expects war. The first a film on the life of a soldier, following up all the different branches & with some very good shots of the inner arrangements of the Maginot line. This film had evidently been hurriedly constructed & went into much greater detail than is normal in films of this kind. The other was the Pathé news gazette, in which the announcer gave what was practically a political speech denouncing Germany. Then more shots of British & French troops etc. The significant point was the attitude of the audience—utterly unenthusiastic, hardly a clap, & a few hostile comments.

This time all the French people are convinced it is war. A number began talking to us spontaneously about it, all deploring the prospect (eg. in one or two cases, "It does no good to us, it's only the rich who profit out of it", etc., etc.), though sometimes describing Hitler as a "salaud."

A.R.P. (ie F.A.P.A.C.) notices, calling for volunteer helpers, posted in Marrakech for the first time about 20th March. According to Madame M., whose son is at St Cyr, even the cadets there do not want war, though ready for it, of course.

1. *NYK*]*N.Y.K.*
2. *vibrations*]*vibration*
3. *entire*]*the entire*
4. Orwell typed his handwritten diary as far as the word 'apart.' The rest of the diary exists only in handwritten form. The point at which typing should resume is marked in the manuscript with the figure 20—the number of the next page to be typed.
5. (morning of 30th . . . *Casa – dock.*)] *a later addition*

542. To Leonard Moore

30 March 1939   Handwritten postcard

[No address]

Dear Mr. Moore,
I got back this morning & dropped in at your office this afternoon to deposit the ms. of my novel.[1] So sorry to find you are off colour. I hope you don't mind my having asked them to send the novel in to Gollancz right away—it's already six months late & this will save a few days. Hoping to see you some time next week.

Yours
Eric Blair

1. *Coming Up for Air*—although the title of this novel has not yet appeared in surviving letters by Orwell, nor in his diaries.

542A. To Lydia Jackson

[30 March 1939]   Handwritten postcard[1]

[No address]

Dear Lydia,
I knocked at the door of your flat & was very disappointed not to find you at home. I gathered from the hall porter that you weren't actually away from London. I've got tomorrow to go down & see my parents for the week-end, but hope to see you when I get back, about Tuesday. Meanwhile if clever I *may* be able to look in for an hour tomorrow morning, so try & stay at home in the morning will you?

Love
Eric

1. The postcard was of 'A Café in the Faubourg Montmartre' by Edgar Degas. It has been dated by reference to the next letter, 542B; on the same day, 30 April, Orwell left a postcard for Leonard Moore, 542. This, and the other letters, are not quite accurately reproduced in *A Russian's England*, 430–31.

542B. To Lydia Jackson

Friday [31 March 1939][1]   Handwritten

36 High Street Southwold Suffolk

Dear Lydia,
You were mean not to stay at home this morning like I asked you. But perhaps you couldn't. I rang up 3 times. Are you angry with me? I did write to you twice from Morocco & I don't think you wrote to me. But listen. I am

coming back to town Monday or Tuesday, & Eileen is going to stay down here a bit longer. I shall have to be in town several days to see to various things, so we can arrange to meet – unless you don't want to. I'll ring up.

Yours ever.
Eric.

1. Lydia Jackson gives the date as 31 March (which was a Friday) in *A Russian's England*, 431. The Monday and Tuesday referred to were the 3rd and 4th April.

543. To Leonard Moore

6 April 1939   Handwritten

At. 36 High St.   Southwold   Suffolk

Dear Mr. Moore,

I am sorry to say I am in bed again, which is why I haven't been to see you as I said I would. I came down to see my people, & then no doubt caught cold or something, but it is nothing serious & I shall be about again in a day or two. Next week I am going back to our cottage, where we are going to stay for the rest of the summer, & I shall have to stay at any rate a few days to put things in order, but if it is necessary I can come up to town again after that, in fact I shall probably have to in any case. I hope there isn't being° any hitch about the novel. Gollancz you may remember put it on his list of last autumn, & from what he said was evidently anxious to go on publishing my stuff, but if he makes any trouble about this book, other than the minor alterations of names etc. which they always seem to demand, it might be better to change to another publisher.

Did anything finally materialise about the Penguin people?

I hope you are well over your attack of flu. My wife sends all the best. I shall be at this address till the 11th.[1]

Yours sincerely
Eric Blair

1. Annotated in Moore's office: 'Ring Gollancz & Lane.' This would be Allen Lane, of Penguin Books. The Southwold address has been crossed out.

544. To Jack Common

Sunday, [9 April 1939]   Handwritten

36 High St.   Southwold   Suffolk

Dear Jack,

Many thanks for yours, which has been forwarded from London, & please excuse delay both in answering & putting in an appearance. I *was* to have come down to Wallington last Wed. (5th) after making a hasty visit here, then no sooner got here than I became ill again & have spent a week in bed. It's nothing serious, mainly due to the change of temperature no doubt, & Eileen's had a cold too, probably from the same cause. We are coming down to Wallington on Tuesday (the 11th) but probably shan't arrive till 6 or 7 pm I think Eileen's mother is being dropped there earlier & Mrs Anderson[1] has been informed, so doubtless all will be well. I'm sorry if we've thrown you out with this late arrival & hope you haven't had too much [stick][2] & worry coming all the way down from Sandon to look after the beasts. However it's nearly over. I wonder whether Muriel's come on heat yet. I always wanted to get a mate from one of those Govt. stud billies but didn't know there was one anywhere within striking distance. Later when we go in for goats properly I'd like to have one myself. He'd no doubt pay his keep with stud fees. It's possible M. has gone off because it's the spring but she'll come on later, & in any case she's good to stay in milk about 16 months, & I am going to get another milker any way. I hope you're all flourishing & more or less finished with winter colds etc. If you're in one of the Council houses you're no doubt finding it a lot more sanitary than our cottage. We intend to stay the summer, then move. I finished my novel[3] just before we got back & dumped it but haven't heard any repercussions yet. Gollancz was anxious that I shouldn't "leave" him as they call it & by contract he's supposed to publish my next 3 fictions, but if he tries to bugger me about I think I shall leave him, & then there'll be long complications about who else to go to. Love to Mary & Peter—looking forward to seeing you in the near future.

Yours
Eric

1. A neighbour at Wallington.
2. 'stick' is uncertain. If correct, it probably means 'hindrance,' 'nuisance.'
3. *Coming Up for Air.*

545. Eileen Blair to Mary Common

[9? April 1939]   Handwritten

S wold.

Dear Mary,
I hope you aren't cursing us too heartily—or rather that you're now cursing heartily enough to get it over by Tuesday,[1] when we really hope to arrive. What telegrams etc. you have had I can't quite gather. The life here is what you might call hectic. E's father is permanently & very ill, his mother got ill with phlebitis, I came down all in a rush as they say to do a bit of filial-by-law nursing & was met on the doorstep by Eric with a temperature of about 102. Since then all have been in bed & I have spent the whole day creating confusion in one sickroom after another. (There is a visiting nurse for the massages etc. but no maid.) But God willing we'll see

you in two–three days, at Wallington. As Eric's ill (or was—his chest has behaved very nicely & he's convalescent) my mother decided to go & open the house & take the several tons of stuff we have parked in London so that we can go straight from here – but I rather hope you know more than I about these arrangements.

Till Tuesday if you can make it.

Eileen.

By the way, it seems likely to me that we shall arrive about midnight on Tuesday, so I expect it's till Wed. I hope you like the L.H's.[2]

1. Tuesday was 11 April; Orwell has an entry in his Domestic Diary for 12 April at Wallington; see *518*.
2. Possibly 'C.H's.' Unidentified.

545A. To Lydia Jackson

Tuesday [11 April 1939][1]   Handwritten

Southwold

Dear Lydia,

I'm so sorry it fell through about my coming up to London, but, as I dare say you guessed, I started being ill almost immediately after I got here & have spent most of this week in bed. I'm all right now. Today we are going direct to Wallington, but in not many days I'll have to come up to town on business, & we'll meet then. I'll let you know beforehand. So sorry it didn't come off this time.

Best love
Eric

Lydia Jackson records that her annoyance 'was extinguished by compassion. So when we met at last, I could not be unpleasant to him. He, no doubt, chose to think that I let him kiss me because I liked it. I did not' (431). She did not want to deceive Eileen, whose friendship she 'valued much more than his' and she 'resisted throughout [their relationship] becoming a love affair'. One day Eileen arrived in her flat 'in a state of great frustration and anger against her husband'. Eileen told her that on their return from Morocco 'their relationship had been unusually harmonious' but things had begun to go 'seriously wrong'. The cause, Eileen believed, was 'a schoolmistress, or something' whom Orwell had known before he married Eileen. 'The village people saw him meeting her. This affair goes on because she wouldn't sleep with him. If she had, it would have been finished long ago' (431–32). Lydia Jackson makes no more references in her autobiography to Orwell's infatuation for her and the next of the thirteen letters that he wrote to her that have survived is dated 1 April 1945. As she kept these seventeen letters of 1939 and from 1945 to 1949, it may be that these are all but one (see *542B*) he wrote to her. She stayed at Barnhill from 26 March to 2 April 1948 when Orwell was in Hairmyres Hospital, Glasgow, and it is possible that whilst at Barnhill she typed out the final version of 'Such, Such Were the Joys'. She

351

probably visited Orwell at Hairmyres on her way to or from Jura (or on both occasions) in April 1948, and she also arranged to see him at Hairmyres in July 1948 (see *3416A*). The schoolmistress was doubtless Brenda Salkeld; see *107, n. 2*.

1. Dated from last sentence of letter to Moore, *543*, and see *545, n. 1*.

546. To Leonard Moore

25 April 1939   Handwritten

The Stores   Wallington   Nr. Baldock   Herts.

Dear Mr Moore,

Many thanks for your letter. I am afraid you must be very overworked, with Miss Perriam away and having been unwell yourself, and I am sorry to trouble you with all this stuff.

I thought Gollancz might show fight. The book[1] is, of course, only a novel and more or less unpolitical, so far as it is possible for a book to be that nowadays, but its general tendency is pacifist, and there is one chapter (Chapter i. of Part III—I suppose you haven't seen the manuscript) which describes a Left Book Club meeting and which Gollancz no doubt objects to. I also think it perfectly conceivable that some of Gollancz's Communist friends have been at him to drop me and any other politically doubtful writers who are on his list. You know how this political racket works, and of course it is a bit difficult for Gollancz, or at any rate Lawrence and Wishart, to be publishing books proving that persons like myself are German spies and at the same time to be publishing my own books. Meanwhile how does our contract stand? I didn't see our last contract, which you may remember was drawn up while I was in Spain, but I understood from my wife that Gollancz undertook to publish my next three works of fiction and pay £100 in advance on each. He has also had this book in his advance lists three times, owing to the delay caused by my illness. But at the same time I think it would be much better not to pin him down to his contract if he is really reluctant to publish the book. To begin with he has treated me very well and I don't want to make unpleasantness for him, and secondly if he really objects to the book he could hardly be expected to push it once published. It might be better to have a quite frank explanation with him. If we are to go to another publisher, whom do you recommend? I suppose it would be better to go to one of the big ones if they will have me, but meanwhile there will I suppose be considerable delays. It is all a great nuisance. I have earned little or no money since last spring and am infernally hard up and in debt, and I was looking to this book to see me through the summer while I get on with my next. I am also not completely decided about my next book, I have ideas for two books which I had thought of writing simultaneously, and if we are going to change publishers it might be necessary to talk that over too. So perhaps the sooner this business is settled the better. I am sorry to be such a nuisance.

I hope you are quite over your flu. I am very well again and have been putting in some strenuous gardening to make up for lost time. My wife sends all the best.

Yours sincerely
Eric Blair

P.S. [at top of letter] If G. wants alterations in the book, I am willing to make the usual minor changes to avoid libel actions, but not structural alterations.

1. *Coming Up for Air.*

547. Review of *The Mysterious Mr. Bull* by Wyndham Lewis; *The School for Dictators* by Ignazio Silone

New English Weekly, 8 June 1939

I do not think it is unfair to say that Mr. Wyndham Lewis[1] has "gone Left." He says somewhere in his "Mysterious Mr. Bull" at any rate, that he is a "revolutionary" and "for the poor against the rich," things which one would not altogether have inferred from some of his earlier writings, and he even says that he has recently "modified" certain of his opinions, a very brave admission in these days when the sub-title of almost every book on a political subject might as well be "I told you so."

And of course it was inevitable that a man of Mr. Lewis's calibre should "modify" his opinions sooner or later. For how could one go on backing Hitler after Hitler had won? So long as Fascism was on the defensive, or merely struggling for power, it was possible to see it as a kind of enlightened despotism or dynamic conservatism which might save us from the "leftwing orthodoxy" of which Mr. Lewis so justly complained. But the trouble is that as soon as any dictator actually begins to dictate it becomes clear that he is *not* an enlightened despot, and above all is not a conservative; he is merely an end-product of democracy, a sort of Strube's "little man"[2] blown up with a bicycle pump. What chance would a man like Mr. Lewis have under a dictatorship of the modern type? As a painter he would be judaeo-marxist or bourgeois-formalist, and as a writer he would not even last long enough to be bumped off in the first purge. We are at a moment when the only possible choice is between being a democrat and a masochist. At any rate, whatever his motives, the one-time blasphemer against the Left is sitting on the penitent's bench, perhaps even baptised, though not by total immersion, of course.

Like most penitents, he shows a certain tendency to overdo it. Of course he is not attracted by the "News Chronicle's" war-mongering, he foresees and dislikes the "status quo war" towards which we are being driven, and he sees the lack of any real difference between the policies of the so-called Right and Left. But he also shows a curious readiness to believe that the official leaders of the Left are more honest than their opponents, and to take their "antifascist" enthusiasm almost at its face-value. I should have thought that events since 1935 had made it perfectly clear that most (not quite all) of what now goes by the name of "antifascism" is simply a thin disguise for jingo imperialism, complicated in the case of the monied intelligentsia by sheer lack of anything useful to do. Here Mr. Lewis's—in my opinion—far too generous estimate of the English character is of importance. He makes the usual claims for the English—they are peace-loving, kindly, unassuming, etc., etc. The closing paragraph of the book would do almost as it stands for a leader in the "Daily Telegraph." And yet the fact remains that for a hundred years past these kind-hearted English have exploited their fellow-creatures with a callous selfishness unparalleled in history. It is quite true, as Mr. Lewis points out, that every extension of the Empire has been made in the face of a certain amount of popular protest, but the significant fact is that these protests have never been real enough to take issue in action. And at any moment when the Empire is actually menaced, the anti-imperialist of yesterday is always found to be in hysterics about the safety of Gibraltar. The truth is that in a prosperous country, especially an imperialist country, left-wing politics are largely make-believe. The unwritten law is always "Fight as much as you like but don't upset the beer," and the transparent honesty of a few isolated men like Cripps[3] does not alter the general situation.

In the earlier part of the book Mr. Lewis attempts the rather unprofitable tasks of tracing the ancestry of the English. Who are the English? Are the lowland Scots the only real English, and are the South English merely Saxons? English history up to the Norman Conquest is a sort of kaleidoscope,° and even at the present day it is impossible to get hold of reliable statistics about the prevalence of fair hair and blue eyes. Politically this mongrel ancestry of the English has been rather an advantage, because it allows them to be as "racial" as anyone else and at the same time to turn their racialism in any desired direction, like a kind of hosepipe. Thus we were "Teutons" from 1870 to 1914, we ceased being "Teutons" on August 4, 1914, only to become "Nordics" round about 1920 and remain so until the rise of Hitler. But in any case, does it matter?

Perhaps it is an impertinence, but I rather wish Mr. Lewis would read Silone's "The School for Dictators." It deals with the inside of the political mess which Mr. Lewis is handling rather diffidently from the outside. Silone is a revolutionary and an honest man (which rather suggests the old story about "Why did they put them two fellers in the same grave?"), and therefore, needless to say, an exile. His book takes the form of a series of conversations between a Mr. W., who aims at becoming dictator of the United States, an amiable old idiot named Professor Pickup, and Thomas the Cynic, a political refugee who has had so many aliases that he has forgotten his own name. Professor Pickup, the typical academic bore, stuffed with useless learning, honestly believes that authoritarian government is a Good Thing, but the other two are under no illusions. They know that the aim of a dictator is simply to dictate, and they discuss with a wealth of instances ranging from Agathocles[4] to General Franco the only problem that interests Mr. W., that of attaining and keeping power. The great charm of the book is that it is written by a man who is inside the leftwing movement but whose mind has never developed the characteristic diseases of leftwing thought. The intrigues, line-ups, betrayals, putsches, civil wars, purges, riots, murders and libels which have made up European political history since the war are written about with astonishing knowledge, but without any of the dreary slogan-shouting of the ordinary political writer on the one hand, or the smart-aleck omniscience of the Reids and Gunthers[5] and their kind on the other. Silone is certainly one of the most interesting of the writers who have come up in the last five years. His "Fontamara" is one of the brightest spots of the Penguin Library. He is one of those men who are denounced as Communists by Fascists and as Fascists by Communists, a band of men which is still small but is gradually growing. It is not inconceivable that Mr. Lewis himself may belong to it one of these days. Meanwhile I seriously believe he could profit by reading this book, because at present his handling of political problems, in spite of his independence of mind and his characteristic flashes of acumen, shows a certain naiveté.

1. For Percy Wyndham Lewis, see *378, n. 2.*
2. Sydney Strube (1891–1956) was a popular cartoonist for the *Daily Express*, 1912–47. His cartoons prominently featured 'the little man,' a suburban character of modest means, always with an umbrella, which seemed to epitomise all the protection he relied on from an adverse world. He was a long-suffering victim of authority
3. Sir Stafford Cripps was a lawyer who became a Labour M.P. in 1931. His personal austerity and patent integrity won him widespread respect if not affection. See *554, n. 7.*
4. Agathocles (361–289 BC), demagogue, Tyrant of Syracuse and ruler of Sicily.
5. Douglas Reed (not Reid) (1895–1976), author and journalist, was Assistant Berlin Correspondent of *The Times*, 1929–35, and its Central European correspondent, 1935–38. See Orwell's review of *Foreign Correspondent: Twelve British Journalists, 563,* and his 1943 review of Reed's *Lest We Forget, 2347.* John Gunther (1901–1970), a U.S. author and foreign correspondent, was noted for several books that attempted to reveal the inner workings of various places: *Inside Europe, Inside Asia, Inside Latin America, Inside Russia Today.*

548. To Leonard Moore

[11 June 1939[1]]   Handwritten

The Stores   Wallington   Nr. Baldock   Herts

Dear Mr. Moore,
Many thanks for sending the books.[2] I wonder if you could get me 4 extra copies & charge them up to me? And do you think Gollancz could send copies to the "Adelphi" & "New English Weekly" (ie. if he was not going to do so any way)? I can be sure of sympathetic reviews there.

Yours sincerely
Eric Blair

1. Although dated 11.9.39 by Orwell, this letter is stamped as having been received in Moore's office on 12 June. Orwell also misdated his Domestic Diary for 11 July 1939, as 11.9.39.
2. Copies of *Coming Up for Air*, published 12 June 1939.

549. Publication of *Coming Up for Air*

Coming Up for Air was published by Victor Gollancz Ltd on 12 June 1939, and in the United States in 1950 by Harcourt, Brace and Company. Gollancz printed 2,000 copies, and a further 1,000 were required almost immediately. They sold out in a couple of years. A second edition was published in 1948 by Secker & Warburg, as the first volume of their Uniform Edition of Orwell; see Crick, 375–76.

The outline of a contract between Orwell and Gollancz survives for the publication of three 'new and original full-length novels' after *Keep the Aspidistra Flying*; see 357. This gives Orwell's royalty as 10% on the first 1,000 copies; 12½% on the second 1,000; and 15% on the next 3,000; and 20% thereafter. The book sold for 7s 6d. Orwell's royalty on 3,000 copies would amount to £140 12s 6d, less Moore's commission of at least 10%: a net of £126 11s 3d (£126.56). Spread over the two years of the book's sale that averaged about £1 per week.

Ruth Dudley Edwards, in *Victor Gollancz: A Biography* (1987), records that Gollancz 'disapproved of the political aspects of George Orwell's novel, *Coming Up for Air*, which included a parody of an LBC [Left Book Club] meeting. . . . Yet to Orwell's surprise, Victor published the book as it stood . . .'(289).

T. R. Fyvel in 'A Writer's Life,' *World Review*, June 1950, remarked, 'For the first time . . . one of his novels enjoyed a moderate popular success' (18).

Elizabeth Bowen reviewed *Coming Up for Air* in *Purpose*, 11, October–December 1939, with three other novels, advising her readers: 'This is a book to read now.'

550. To Yvonne Davet

19 June 1939   Typewritten

The Stores   Wallington   Nr. Baldock, HERTS.   Angleterre

Chère camarade,

Je vous envois les chapitres 7–10,[1] et je vous enverrai les autres en quelques jours quand je les aurai corrigés. Dans ces quatre chapitres j'ai fait des remarques aux pages: 120, 126, 128, 141, 164, 165, 168, 174, 207. En nul cas il n'y a grand' chose à changer, et il me semble que la traduction exprime très bien le sentiment de l'original. J'espère bien que vous n'aurez pas eu votre travail pour rien. Dans le cas que nous ne trouvons pas un éditeur, je ne vois rien d'inconvenient de faire paraître quelques chapitres dans une revue. L'introduction de Georges Kopp me plait beaucoup,[2] mais quant à ça je suivrai les idées de l'éditeur, si nous en trouvons un. Dans le même cas je serai tout prêt à écrire une introduction moi-même. Je ferai savoir à Warburg qu'il ne faut pas trop demander. Il me surprend qu'il a demandé £40 pour le livre de Freda Uttley°[3]—peut-être parce-qu'il a eu un assez grand succès en Angleterre.

Jusqu'à l'autre jour je ne savais pas que vous n'aviez pas une exemplaire de "Homage to Catalonia". Il y a une année j'ai demandé à Warburg de vous en envoyer une et il m'a promis de le faire mais a peut-être oublié. L'autre jour je vous ai envoyé une exemplaire de preuve, mais je vous enverrai une vraie exemplaire du livre aussitôt que je pourrai en obtenir une. Il n'y a d'ailleurs pas de différence de texte entre le livre et le manuscrit. On pourrait changer le nom de Monte Oscuro à Monte Trazo[4]—sans doute je me suis trompé.

Mon dernier livre[5] est paru il y a une semaine. Je ne sais pas encore comment il a été reçu. Vous aurez remarqué que je suis toujours chez Gollancz, l'éditeur Staliniste!

Très fraternellement
Eric Blair

Translation

I am sending you chapters 7–10,[1] and I shall send the others in a few days when I have corrected them. In these four chapters I have made notes on pages 120, 126, 128, 141, 164, 165, 168, 174, 207. There is not very much to alter anywhere, and I think the translation expresses the feeling of the original very well. I do hope that all your work will not be in vain. If we cannot find a publisher, I do not see why we should not publish some chapters in a magazine. I like the introduction by Georges Kopp very much,[2] but here I shall be guided by the wishes of the publisher, if we can find one. If necessary I am quite prepared to write an introduction myself. I shall let Warburg know he must not ask too much. I am surprised he asked £40 for Freda Utley's book[3]—it is probably because the book was quite successful in England.

Until the other day I didn't know you did not have a copy of *Homage to Catalonia*. A year ago I asked Warburg to send you one and he promised he would, but he probably forgot. The other day I sent you a proof copy, but I shall send you a proper copy of the book as soon as I can get one. Anyway there is no textual difference between the book and the manuscript. The name of Monte Oscuro could be changed to Monte Trazo[4]—I was definitely mistaken.

My latest book[5] came out a week ago. I don't yet know how it will be received. You will have noticed that I am still with Gollancz, that Stalinist publisher!

1. Chapters from *Homage to Catalonia* as originally published; these are chapters 6 to 9 and Appendix I, as rearranged in line with Orwell's wishes in the *Complete Works* edition. Yvonne Davet's translation was not published until 1955, five years after Orwell's death. See Textual Note, *CW*, VI, 251–52.
2. George Kopp evidently wrote an introduction, because Orwell told Moore, 15 April 1947 (see *3216*), that it had been sent to the publisher (Gallimard). By 1947 Orwell thought it 'was not a very suitable one and in any case would have no point now.' Kopp's introduction has not been traced.
3. Freda Utley's *Japan's Gamble in China*, published in June 1938.
4. This change has been made in *CW*, VI, 38.
5. *Coming Up for Air*.

551. To A. P. Watt & Son

21 June 1939   Typewritten

On 19 June A. P. Watt & Son wrote to Orwell to ask if they might act as his literary agent. They enclosed a copy of James Agate's review of *Coming Up for Air* from the *Daily Express*, 15 June 1939, and listed some of their more famous clients, who included John Buchan, Pearl Buck, Rudyard Kipling, W. Somerset Maugham, H. G. Wells, and P. G. Wodehouse.

The Stores   Wallington   Nr. Baldock   <u>HERTS.</u>

Dear Sir,

With reference to your letter dated 19th June, many thanks for the offer, but Messrs. Christy and Moore have been my agents for a good many years.

Yours truly
George Orwell

552. Review of *Union Now* by Clarence K. Streit

The Adelphi, July 1939

It is possible that this review salvages something from Orwell's pamphlet 'Socialism and War,' which was not published and the manuscript of which has not survived. See *458, n. 1*, and *506*.

A dozen years ago anyone who had foretold the political line-up of to-day would have been looked on as a lunatic. And yet the truth is that the present situation—not in detail, of course, but in its main outlines—ought to have been predictable even in the golden age before Hitler. Something like it was bound to happen as soon as British security was seriously threatened.

In a prosperous country, above all in an imperialist country, left-wing politics are always partly humbug. There can be no real reconstruction that would not lead to at least a temporary drop in the English standard of life, which is another way of saying that the majority of left-wing politicians and publicists are people who earn their living by demanding something that they don't genuinely want. They are red-hot revolutionaries as long as all goes well, but every real emergency reveals instantly that they are shamming. One threat to the Suez Canal, and "antifascism" and "defence of British interests" are discovered to be identical.

It would be very shallow as well as unfair to suggest that there is *nothing* in what is now called "antifascism" except a concern for British dividends. But it is a fact that the political obscenities of the past two years, the sort of monstrous harlequinade in which everyone is constantly bounding across the stage in a false nose—Quakers shouting for a bigger army, Communists waving union jacks, Winston Churchill posing as a democrat—would not have been possible without this guilty consciousness that we are all in the

358

same boat. Much against their will the British governing class have been forced into the anti–Hitler position. It is still possible that they will find a way out of it, but they are arming in the obvious expectation of war and they will almost certainly fight when the point is reached at which the alternative would be to give away some of their own property instead of, as hitherto, other people's. And meanwhile the so-called opposition, instead of trying to stop the drift to war, are rushing ahead, preparing the ground and forestalling any possible criticism. So far as one can discover the English people are still extremely hostile to the idea of war, but in so far as they are becoming reconciled to it, it is not the militarists but the "anti-militarists" of five years ago who are responsible. The Labour Party keeps up a pettifogging grizzle against conscription at the same time as its own propaganda makes any real struggle against conscription impossible. The Bren machine guns pour from the factories, books with titles like *Tanks in the Next War, Gas in the Next War,* etc., pour from the press, and the warriors of the *New Statesman* glose over the nature of the process by means of such phrases as "Peace Bloc," "Peace Front," "Democratic Front," and, in general, by pretending that the world is an assemblage of sheep and goats, neatly partitioned off by national frontiers.

In this connection it is well worth having a look at Mr. Streit's much-discussed book, *Union Now.* Mr. Streit,[1] like the partisans of the "Peace Bloc," wants the democracies to gang up against the dictatorships, but his book is outstanding for two reasons. To begin with he goes further than most of the others and offers a plan which, even if it is startling, is constructive. Secondly, in spite of a rather nineteen-twentyish American naivete, he has an essentially decent cast of mind. He genuinely loathes the thought of war, and he does not sink to the hypocrisy of pretending that any country which can be bought or bullied into the British orbit instantly becomes a democracy. His book therefore presents a kind of test case. In it you are seeing the sheep-and-goats theory at its *best* . If you can't accept it in that form you will certainly never accept it in the form handed out by the Left Book Club.

Briefly, what Mr. Streit suggests is that the democratic nations, starting with fifteen which he names, should voluntarily form themselves into a union—not a league or an alliance, but a union similar to the United States, with a common government, common money and complete internal free trade. The initial fifteen states are, of course, the U.S.A., France, Great Britain, the self-governing dominions of the British Empire, and the smaller European democracies, not including Czechoslovakia, which still existed when the book was written. Later, other states could be admitted to the Union when and if they "proved themselves worthy." It is implied all along that the state of peace and prosperity existing within the Union would be so enviable that everyone else would soon be pining to join it.

It is worth noticing that this scheme is not so visionary as it sounds. Of course it is not going to happen, nothing advocated by well-meaning literary men ever happens, and there are certain difficulties which Mr. Streit does not discuss; but it is of the order of things which *could* happen. Geographically the U.S.A. and the western European democracies are nearer to being a unit than, for instance, the British Empire. Most of their trade is with one another, they contain within their own territories everything they need, and Mr. Streit is probably right in claiming that their combined strength would be so great as to make any attack on them hopeless, even if the U.S.S.R. joined up with Germany. Why then does one see at a glance that this scheme has something wrong with it? What is there about it that smells—for it *does* smell, of course?

What it smells of, as usual, is hypocrisy and self-righteousness. Mr. Streit himself is not a hypocrite, but his vision is limited. Look again at his list of sheep and goats. No need to boggle at the goats (Germany, Italy and Japan), they are goats right enough, and billies at that. But look at the sheep! Perhaps the U.S.A. will pass inspection if one does not look too closely. But what about France? What about England? What about even Belgium and Holland? Like everyone of his school of thought, Mr. Streit has coolly lumped the huge British and French empires—in essence nothing but mechanisms for exploiting cheap coloured labour—under the heading of democracies!

Here and there in the book, though not often, there are references to the "dependencies" of the democratic states. "Dependencies" means subject races. It is explained that they are to go on being dependencies, that their resources are to be pooled among the states of the Union, and that their coloured inhabitants will lack the right to vote in Union affairs. Except where the tables of statistics bring it out, one would never for a moment guess what *numbers* of human beings are involved. India, for instance, which contains more inhabitants than the whole of the "fifteen democracies" put together, gets just a page and a half in Mr. Streit's book, and that merely to explain that as India is not yet fit for self-government the *status quo* must continue. And here one begins to see what would really be happening if Mr. Streit's scheme were put into operation. The British and French empires, with their six hundred million disenfranchised human beings, would simply be receiving fresh police forces; the huge strength of the U.S.A. would be behind the robbery of India and Africa. Mr. Streit is letting cats out of bags, but *all* phrases like "Peace Bloc," "Peace Front," etc., contain some such implication; all imply a tightening-up of the existing structure. The unspoken clause is always "not counting niggers." For how can we make a "firm stand" against Hitler if we are simultaneously weakening ourselves at home? In other words, how can we "fight Fascism" except by bolstering up a far vaster injustice?

For of course it *is* vaster. What we always forget is that the overwhelming bulk of the British proletariat does not live in Britain, but in Asia and Africa. It is not in Hitler's power, for instance, to make a penny an hour a normal industrial wage; it is perfectly normal in India, and we are at great pains to keep it so. One gets some idea of the real relationship of England and India when one reflects that the *per capita* annual income in England is something over £80, and in India about £7. It is quite common for an Indian coolie's leg to be thinner than the average Englishman's arm. And there is nothing racial in this, for well-fed members of the same races are of normal physique; it is due to simple starvation. This is the system which we all live on and which we denounce when there seems to be no danger of its being altered. Of late, however, it has become the first duty of a "good antifascist" to lie about it and help to keep it in being.

What real settlement, of the slightest value, can there be along these lines? What meaning would there be, even if it were successful, in bringing down Hitler's system in order to stabilise something that is far bigger and in its different way just as bad?

But apparently, for lack of any real opposition, this is going to be our objective. Mr. Streit's ingenious ideas will not be put into operation, but something resembling the "Peace Bloc" proposals probably will. The British and Russian governments are still haggling, stalling and uttering muffled threats to change sides, but circumstances will probably drive them together. And what then? No doubt the alliance will stave off war for a year or two. Then Hitler's move will be to feel for a weak spot or an unguarded moment; then our move will be more armaments, more militarisation, more propaganda, more war-mindedness—and so on, at increasing speed. It is doubtful whether prolonged war-preparation is morally any better than war itself; there are even reasons for thinking that it may be slightly worse. Only two or three years of it, and we may sink almost unresisting into some local variant of austro-fascism. And perhaps a year or two later, in reaction against this, there will appear something we have never had in England yet—a real Fascist movement. And because it will have the guts to speak plainly it will gather into its ranks the very people who ought to be opposing it.

Further than that it is difficult to see. The downward slide is happening because nearly all the Socialist leaders, when it comes to the pinch, are merely His Majesty's Opposition, and nobody else knows how to mobilise the decency of the English people, which one meets with everywhere when one talks to human beings instead of reading newspapers. Nothing is likely to save us except the emergence within the next two years of a real mass party whose first pledges are to refuse war and to right imperial injustice. But if any such party exists at present, it is only as a possibility, in a few tiny germs lying here and there in unwatered soil.

1. Clarence K. Streit (1896–1986) was an American author and journalist—for the *New York Times*, 1925–39. This review/article, advocating the righting of imperial injustices, was originally published with the ironic title 'Not Counting Niggers.'

553. Diary of Events Leading Up to the War

2 July–1 September 1939

Orwell's 'Diary of Events Leading Up to the War' is, in the main, a listing of extracts from newspapers, especially the *Daily Telegraph*, from 2 July to 1 September 1939, and it concludes with a summary dated 3 September. The manuscript comprises fifty-five pages. Except for 24 August—to which two pages are devoted—there is one page for each day recorded. One page is blank except for its headings—3 July—and for ten days no record was made—18 and 31 July; 3, 5, 9, 13, 16, and 25–27 August. However, items for these dates are sometimes included on later pages. The hiatus 25–27 August is explained, and made up, in the summary dated 28 August.

Each page is divided in half horizontally, the upper half recording events, the lower half, sources of information; and is also divided into five columns, headed Foreign & General, Social, Party Politics, Miscellaneous, and Remarks (capitalisation has been regularised). The allocation of topics to these headings is sometimes arbitrary. The column 'Remarks'—rarely used—gives what might best be termed footnotes. The writing is often small and cramped, and whereas one column might be very full, others may be empty.

The transcription given here is arranged sequentially. Entries are listed under the date they were made by Orwell and beneath the relevant heading. The dates are not repeated as in the original. Whereas Orwell gave a source and date as a footnote to each entry, here the source only is given, in square brackets, after the items, and a date is included only if it differs from that at the head of the section. Orwell's remarks are placed below the item to which they refer and are marked '[Orwell's note].'

Orwell quotes forty-one sources for the 297 items. Of these, 138 (46.5%) are the Daily Telegraph. The others are: Sunday Times, 20; Sunday Express, 16; Manchester Guardian Weekly, 13; News Chronicle and New Leader, 8 each; Socialist Correspondence[1] and The Times, 7 each; radio (BBC), 6; Smallholder, 5; Daily Mirror, File S.P. 1,[2] and private (unspecified), 4 each; Daily Express, Daily Herald, Daily Worker, E. H.,[3] Left Forum, and The Observer, 3 each; C.W.,[4] Daily Mail, Manchester Guardian, Revolutionary Proletarian,[5] and The Week, 2 each; 17 others, 1 each; and 12 unspecified. There is a noticeable increase in references to The Times and the News Chronicle, and a proportionate decrease in references to the Daily Telegraph , when Orwell went to stay with L. H. Myers at Ringwood on 24 August (see 565, 28.8.39, n. 1), confirming what these figures show: that it was to the Daily Telegraph that Orwell looked for factual information during these months.

There is some variation in the way Orwell itemises entries, using Arabic and Roman numerals, underlining once or twice, or not at all; his practice has here been disregarded. He also varies capitalisation of section headings; that has here been regularised.

The diary entries, in conformity with Orwell's other diaries, are printed in sloped roman type. Relevant notes follow each date.

1. Socialist Correspondence was run by a group within the ILP known as 'the right-wing opposition' (though it was only to the right in a left-wing party). Members were followers of Nikolai Bukharin (1888–1938). Prominent among them were W. W. Sawyer, a mathematician at Manchester University and author of the popular Penguin book Mathematician's Delight, and Jack Huntz, who had contributed to The New Leader in the thirties. The group had links with ex-Communists in Germany, among them Heinrich Brandler and August Thalheimer. The other ILP groups were, first, the Trotskyists, including Jim Wood and C. L. R. James, West Indian writer described by Orwell in a 1937 review as 'author of that very able book World Revolution' (see 401); and, second, the Revolutionary Policy Committee, which was pro-Communist and led by Jack Gaster, a lawyer, and Dr. Collen, Health Officer for Poplar, London, E.14. (For a reference to the internal troubles of the ILP, see 558, 21.7.39, Party Politics, 2.) Socialist Correspondence, an octavo of eight to sixteen pages, which were sometimes left blank but marked 'To Let,' described itself as 'An Organ of Marxist Theory and Information.' In 1939, it was edited, printed, and published by J. Collen, 5 Perry's Close, London E.14. The secretary was P. Schofield. In the 1940s it was published by P. Schofield,

51 Hodge Lane, Salford, Lancashire. About 500 copies were printed, and sold at two (old) pence (information from Sam Bernstein (1920–1990) and Stafford Cottman, August 1989). It was linked with the Communist International Opposition, in which August Thalheimer played an important role, and a version of its German journal (on which *Socialist Correspondence* drew) was published in the United States as *The International Class Struggle*, a quarterly. (For Thalheimer, see *565, 22.8.39, Party Politics, n. 6*.) A persistent line adopted by *Socialist Correspondence* was drawing a distinction between imperialism, Hitler, and Stalin, on the one hand, and the fostering of a Socialist workers' revolution on the other. The issues (and special supplements) for July and August 1939, some at least of which Orwell read, raise many matters of considerable interest to him. Thus, the supplement for August was a translation from the German Communist Party's paper, *Die Internationale Klassenkampf*, June 1939, on the use of slogans to advocate war ('Defend the Fatherland') and in the class struggle ('Turn the Imperialist War into Revolutionary War'). Topics discussed include the need for sanctions against Japan to aid the Chinese; the overthrow of Hitler by 'working-class struggle' rather than war; support for a rent strike in the East End of London and a strike of the railways; opposition to the Military Training Act and the bill to allow the deportation of IRA suspects; opposition to conscription as a 'form of class struggle waged by the bourgeoisie'; Labour and Communist Party policies; the Russian–German Non-Aggression Pact; and the effects of the termination of the 1911 United States–Japanese commercial treaty. A long article in the issue for 1 July argues that because 'a revolutionary situation' did not exist in Britain, 'the workers will not be able to prevent the outbreak of the next imperialist war.' In a leaflet published during the Soviet invasion of Finland (30 November 1939–12 March 1940), it argued that the chief responsibility lay with Stalin; that the invasion 'must be condemned as a violation of the principles of Socialism,' but 'WE MUST RESIST, BY EVERY POSSIBLE MEANS any attack on Russia' by Britain; the invasion did not demonstrate that Russia had shown Socialism to be a failure. In an article by Thalheimer, 'Socialist Revolution in Germany,' dated June 1945, he quoted Gaetano Salvemini (see *524, n. 2* and *2548, n. 2*) as saying that 'England and the United States were waging two wars in Italy: one against Nazi and Fascist Imperialism, the other against socialist revolution in Italy,' and arguing that the same applied in Germany. Despite this line, the paper's book recommendations were catholic, and included, for example, *Fascism and Social Revolution* by R. Palme Dutt (associated with the *Daily Worker*), and *Spotlight on Germany* (1933) by Erich Roll (1907–; Lord Roll of Ipsden, 1977), son of an Austrian banker; he went to England in 1925 to study, was Professor of Economics, University College of Hull, 1935–46, and Director of the Bank of England, 1968–77. He and his wife, Freda, organised the Humber Food Ship for victims of the Spanish civil war.

2. File S.P. 1 is unidentified. It might refer to Orwell's own filing system; see *565, 24.8.39, n. 1*.
3. E. H. is unidentified, but presumably a member of the ILP in London.
4. C. W. was probably Cyril Wright, a friend of Orwell's and Douglas Moyle's from their service in Spain; see *408, n. 4*.
5. *Revolutionary Proletarian* was *La Révolution Prolétarienne: Revue bimensuelle syndicaliste révolutionnaire*. It was founded on 1 January 1925 and suspended after issue 301, 25 August 1939—in effect, censored. Issue 302 was published in April 1947. Its line was anti-Stalinist. The French translation of Orwell's 'Eye-Witness in Barcelona' was published in issue 255, 25 September 1937; see *382*.

554. Diary of Events Leading Up to the War

2.7.39

Foreign & General
1. *Poland states that Danzig[1] will be occupied if Danzig Senate declares for the Reich. [Sunday Times]*
2. *N.L.C.[2] of Labour Party broadcast in German in much the same terms as at September crisis. [Observer]*
Party Politics
Sinclair,[3] Ramsay Muir,[4] Amery, [5] Eden,[6] Cripps,[7] Burgin [8] make virtually identical statements re. resistance to German agression.[9] [Sunday Times]

1. Danzig (now Gdansk, Poland), first mentioned some thousand years ago as part of Poland, has since been variously Polish and German (including Prussian). It was made a Free City by the Treaty of Versailles (1919), but became a focus of dispute between Poland and Germany, especially after the rise of the Nazis. This was the pretext for the German invasion of Poland that initiated World War II in 1939. See *525, n. 2.*
2. This is probably an error for NCL (National Council of Labour); see *556, 15.7.39, Party Politics, 2.* The sense is elliptical, but seems to refer to an appeal to the German people under the heading 'Why kill each other?' made by the NCL. Summaries were broadcast by the BBC on the night of Saturday, 1 July 1939, in German, French, Italian, Portuguese, and Spanish. The NCL also arranged broadcasts to German workers from secret radio stations on the Continent and distributed printed copies of the appeal through underground organisations.
3. Archibald Sinclair (1890–1970; 1st Viscount Thurso, 1952), Liberal M.P., 1922–45, was a close friend of Winston Churchill and became political private secretary to him when the latter was Colonial Secretary, 1921–23. He served as Secretary of State for Scotland, 1931–32 but came to disapprove strongly of government policies associated with Chamberlain, sided with Churchill and Eden. He attacked Chamberlain's policy strongly in July 1939; and this developed into a bitter argument, centering on the refusal of *The Times* to print Sinclair's rejoinder; see *556, 12.7.39, Social.* He was Secretary of State for Air in Churchill's wartime coalition government.
4. John Ramsay Muir (1872–1941) was Professor of Modern History at the University of Manchester, 1913–21, and politician, first as a Liberal, and from 1931, after the split within the party, as a National Liberal. He was Chairman and President successively of the National Liberal Federation, 1931–36.
5. Leopold Charles Maurice Amery (1873–1955), Conservative M.P., opposed disarmament and supported the Hoare-Laval proposals for resolving the Abyssinian crisis in 1935. In May 1940, after the fall of Norway to the Germans, he directed, at Chamberlain, Cromwell's words to the Long Parliament (1640–53): 'You have sat too long here for any good you may be doing. . . . In the name of God, go!' His *My Political Life* (1953–55) gives an account of political events of the thirties.
6. Anthony Eden, (1897–1977; Earl of Avon, 1961), Conservative M.P., was Foreign Secretary, 1935–38. He resigned to protest against Chamberlain's policy of appeasement. In 1940 he was Secretary of State for War, then Foreign Secretary in the War Cabinet, 1940–45. He was Prime Minister, 1955–57, but resigned again, as a result of Britain's disastrous involvement in the occupation of the Suez Canal Zone in 1956.
7. Sir Stafford Cripps (1889–1952), lawyer (in 1927 becoming the youngest King's Counsel) and Labour politician, entered Parliament in 1931, but was expelled from the Labour Party from 1939 to 1945. He was Ambassador to the Soviet Union, 1940–42; Minister of Aircraft Production, 1942–45, and Chancellor of the Exchequer in the Labour government, 1947–50. See Orwell's War-time Diary, *637, 8.6.40,* regarding his appointment as ambassador.
8. Dr. Leslie Burgin (1887–1945), lawyer and Liberal (later National Liberal) M.P. from 1930, was Minister of Transport, 1937–39, and Minister of Supply, 1939–40. In *A Prime Minister on Prime Ministers* (1977), Harold Wilson, who worked in the Ministry of Supply for a short time

in 1940, remarked that 'its organization under Burgin's ministerial direction would not have been capable of running a chip-shop' (233).

<u>3.7.39</u>
[Headings only; no entries]

555. To Leonard Moore

14 July 1939 [4 July?][1]   Typewritten

The Stores   Wallington   Nr. Baldock, HERTS.

Dear Mr. Moore,

Many thanks for your letter. I called at your office yesterday and was sorry not to find you there. I am terribly behind with my book of essays[2] which I had hoped to finish by September at latest. These infernal illnesses have of course wasted months of time. Also I am sorry to tell you my father has just died. I was with the poor old man for the last week of his life, and then there was the funeral etc., etc., all terribly upsetting and depressing. However, he was 82 and had been very active till he was over 80, so he had had a good life, and I am very glad that latterly he had not been so disappointed in me as before. Curiously enough his last moment of consciousness was hearing that review I had in the Sunday Times. He heard about it and wanted to see it, and my sister took it in and read it to him, and a little later he lost consciousness for the last time.

About the book. I shan't be starting my novel till after I have done the book of essays, and unless something upsets my plans I intend doing next a long novel, really the first part of an enormous novel, a sort of saga(!) which will have to be published in three parts. I think I *ought* to finish the book of essays in October, but the novel will take a long time and even barring wars, illnesses etc. isn't like[ly][3] to be finished before the late summer of 1940. Those at any rate are my plans. As to the book of essays, I don't know whether Gollancz will want them. They may be a bit off his track, and as they are sort of literary-sociological essays they touch at places on politics, on which I am certain to say things he wouldn't approve of. The subjects are Charles Dickens, boys' weekly papers (the Gem, Magnet etc.), and Henry Miller, the American novelist. I am finishing the rough draft of the Dickens one now, but the others probably won't take so long. I should say it will be a short book, 50–60 thousand words. I don't know whether this is at all the kind of thing to interest Gollancz, but if he wants to have the first refusal that is up to him and you. If he wants to take a chance on the book and put it in his lists I will think of a title, but I can't send a specimen, as it is all rather in a mess as yet.

I see "Coming up for Air" has gone into a second edition, so I suppose it's doing fairly well. It had some wonderful reviews, especially from James Agate. The Frenchwoman[4] who was translating "Homage to Catalonia" has finished it and is hawking it round various publishers, always unsuccessfully, as people are fed up with books on the Spanish war, which well they may be. She has an idea however that she may be able to induce someone to publish it or part of it unpaid. But she is afraid Warburg will kick against this, as he apparently did over some book of Freda Utley's.[5] In case of this coming to anything, I suppose we can get Warburg to agree.[6] It's always a bit of an advert., and in any case one never gets much out of a French publisher. Appropos° of this, can you tell me what if anything ever came of that Burmese translation of "Burmese Days" which those people wrote to me about? It was sometime last year.[7]

I hope all goes well. My wife sends all the best.

Yours sincerely
Eric Blair

1. This date must be incorrect, because the letter was stamped as received in Moore's office on 4 July. Since it was possible for a letter to be posted and delivered on the same day, Orwell may have written on the fourth and by mistake added a one. The letter was annotated in Moore's office: 'Answered in July,' but no date is given. The answer was probably Moore's letter of 17 July to which Orwell replied on 21 July; see *557*.
2. *Inside the Whale.*
3. Orwell typed 'like-' at the end of a line and evidently failed to complete the word at the beginning of the next line.
4. Yvonne Davet.
5. Presumably *Japan's Gamble in China*, mentioned in Orwell's letter to Yvonne Davet, 19 June 1939; see *550*.
6. From an annotation to this letter made in Moore's office, it appears that Warburg agreed to permit this for a 'Nominal fee of £1.'
7. See, especially, letters to Moore of 28 June and 5 July 1938, *458* and *460*. Nothing came of this proposal. By the time Orwell died, only French, Hungarian, and Italian translations had appeared; the French in 1946; the others in 1948.

556. Diary of Events Leading Up to the War

<u>4.7.39</u>

<u>Foreign & General</u>
1. Fighting reported on Manchukuo[1]-Mongolian border. [*Daily Telegraph*]
<u>Social</u>
1. Unemployment now down to about 1,350,000. [*Daily Telegraph*]
2. Egg-production of England & Wales in 1937 about 3,250 million. [*Smallholder, 24.6.39*]

1. Manchukuo was a puppet kingdom of Manchuria when occupied by the Japanese, 1932–45. It was restored to China in 1945.

<u>5.7.39</u>

<u>Foreign & General</u>
1. More fighting reported on Manchukuo border. [*Daily Telegraph*]
<u>Party Politics</u>
1. Conservative M.P.s to petition for Churchill's[1] entry into Cabinet. Following D. T.'s[2] article, many letters to this effect. [*Daily Telegraph*]

1. Sir Winston Churchill (1874–1965), politician, soldier, journalist, author, held high office in Liberal and Conservative governments over nearly half a century, but in the thirties was excluded because of his vigorous opposition to appeasement of dictators; he was branded a warmonger. He was the natural choice for prime minister after the fall of Norway following the German invasion in 1940. Despite his success as a war leader, he was not returned to office in 1945, but he did become prime minister of a peacetime government, 1951–55.
2. *Daily Telegraph*'s.

6.7.39

Foreign & General
1. Britain to grant arms credit of £100 million to Poland, Turkey & Rumania. [Daily Telegraph]
2. Polish, Turkish & Chinese gov.ts said to believe Stalin genuinely desires pact. [Daily Telegraph]
Party Politics
1. McGovern[1] again attacking L.P.[2] in Parliament. [Daily Telegraph]

1. John McGovern was an Independent Labour Party M.P., 1930–47; see *424, n. 2.*
2. Labour Party.

7.7.39

Foreign & General
1. Fighting on Manchukuo border reported this time from Russian sources (Tass agency). [Daily Telegraph]
Party Politics
1. At Zurich conference of I.F.T.U.,[1] British T. U. leaders now advocating affiliation of Russian unions. [Manchester Guardian Weekly]

1. The International Federation of Trade Unions, established in 1901, had failed to survive World War I. Re-established in 1919, it came into conflict with the Soviet-inspired Red International of Labour Unions. Failure to reconcile differences between Communist and non-Communist trade unions continued after World War II. British, Soviet, and U.S. unions combined briefly to establish the World Federation of Trade Unions, but in 1949 the non-Communist unions broke away to form the International Confederation of Free Trade Unions. The news item above is indicative of fundamental disagreement lasting over many decades.

8.7.39

Foreign & General
1. Public Information Leaflet No. 1 (Civil Defence) issued by the Post Office today. Large-scale A.R.P.[1] practice to take place tonight over S.E. England. [No separate reference]
Party Politics
1. I.F.T.U. now apparently refusing Russian affiliation, France, Mexico, Norway & G. Britain voting for (the last two conditionally), U.S.A. & most European countries against. [Daily Telegraph]
2. Trial of Julien* Besteiro[2] begins in Madrid today. (J. B. took part in Casado[3] junta). [Daily Telegraph]
*30 years [Orwell's note].

Miscellaneous
1. Rat population of G. Britain estimated at 4–5 million. [Smallholder, 7.7.39]

1. Air Raid Precautions.
2. Julien Besteiro (properly Julián) (1870–1940), President of the UGT (Socialist Trade Union, Spain) to 1931, was Speaker of the Cortes (the Spanish Parliament) and temporarily President of Spain the same year. He died in prison in 1940, while serving the thirty-year sentence imposed by Franco's government.
3. Colonel Sigismundo Casado López (1893–1968), commander of the Republican Army of the Centre, organised the campaign against Republican Prime Minister Negrín and attempted, towards the end of the civil war, to gain better terms from Franco. He failed and took refuge in Britain, though he later returned to Spain.

9.7.39

Foreign & General
1. Madame Tabouis[1] considers chances of full Russian-French-British pact are now small & hints that Russians wish to regain position of Czarist Empire in the Baltic provinces. [Sunday Dispatch]
Social
1. Population of Scotland now more than 5 million. [Sunday Times]
Party Politics
1. I.F.T.U. rejected motion to invite Russian affiliation, but not v. large majority.* [Sunday Times]
*Majority said to be entirely due to large vote held by Green of the A.F.L.[2] [Orwell's note].

1. Geneviève Tabouis (Paris, 1892–1985) was a diplomatic and international journalist, foreign news editor of *L'Oeuvre* from 1932, and correspondent for the *Sunday Dispatch*. On 23 June 1940 that paper printed her account of her escape to England via Bordeaux after the fall of Paris. This began with a statement attributed to Hitler: 'The speech I am making to-day she knew yesterday.' She directed the weekly *Pour la Victoire*, in New York, 1941–45, and was noted for her uncanny gift for forecasting accurately the outcome of political events.
2. William Green was President of the American Federation of Labor, founded in 1886, which was split in 1935 by the formation of a faction that advocated and then organized industrial unions and in 1938 became the Congress of Industrial Organizations. The two united to form the AFL–CIO in 1955. For the IFTU, see 7.7.39, n. 1.

10.7.39

Foreign & General
1. Germany said to be demanding entire Rumanian wheat crop, also part of what is left over from 1938 crop. [Daily Telegraph]
2. Large-scale practice blackout[1] on Sat. night said to have gone off successfully. [Daily Telegraph]
Social
1. Groups of friends entering militia are being[2] split up, sufficiently noticeably for this to call for explanation by the W.O.[3] [Daily Telegraph]
Party Politics
1. Papers which appealed on July 3 for inclusion of Churchill in cabinet were D. Tel., Yorkshire Post, News-C., M. Guardian & Dy. Mirror. It is alleged that Communist party after demanding C's inclusion for some months are

becoming alarmed now that it appears likely to happen. [*Socialist Correspondence,* 8.7.39]
2. Bela Kun[4] again reported shot in Moscow. [*La Révolution Prolétarienne*]

1. As part of the precautions against air attack, windows had to be completely covered to ensure no light could be seen from the street, street-lights were turned off, and essential lights (such as car headlights and traffic lights) were masked. For a brief but eloquent account of the psychological effect of the blackout, see Malcolm Muggeridge, *The Thirties,* 305. He notes that after two months of war the number of casualties caused by the blackout was nearly twice that of all three services combined. See *562, 10.8.39, Social, 4.*
2. Orwell first wrote 'have been.'
3. War Office. The practice of separating friends, especially from the same locality, was designed to ensure that if a unit suffered heavy losses they were not all felt in the same town or city. This policy was adopted following the terrible casualties inflicted at the Battle of the Somme (July–October 1916), when units of men from the same place (e.g., the Exeter Boys) trained together, went into action together, and were then almost wiped out in a few moments, which concentrated the grief felt at home. The effect of the deaths of the five Sullivan brothers when U.S.S. *Juneau* was sunk, 13 November 1942, is another example.
4. Béla Kun (1886–1939?), Communist revolutionary leader in Hungary, and briefly its Commissar for Foreign Affairs and dominant figure in the government in 1919. After fleeing from Hungary he tried, as a member of the Third International, to foment revolution in Germany and Austria. He fell out of favour and was murdered in one of Stalin's purges. For a later report of his execution, see *562, 7.8.39, Party Politics, 2.*

11.7.39

Foreign & General
1. More reports of fighting on Manchukuo border, sufficient to indicate that fighting (prob. inconclusive) has actually taken place. [*Daily Telegraph*]
2. Chamberlain's[1] speech reiterates that we shall support Poles in case of Danzig coup, but seems to leave initiative to Poles. [*Daily Telegraph*]
3. German reports that Russian submarine fleet is larger than anticipated. Warships using Stalin canal[2] for first time. [*Daily Telegraph*]
Party Politics
1. Further letters in D. Tel. demanding inclusion of Churchill. These however do not imply very strong criticism of Chamberlain. D. Tel. prints a few against. Times said to be printing none for. [*Daily Telegraph*]
Miscellaneous
1. Death of Havelock Ellis,[3] aged 80, gets small front page mention in D. Tel. [*Daily Telegraph*]

1. Prime Minister Neville Chamberlain (see *469, n. 2*) was associated with appeasement of Hitler and Mussolini in the thirties. His stance was probably that of most British citizens, including many who were, with hindsight, to criticise him. Thus, J. L. Garvin (see *296, n. 8*), editor of *The Observer,* on New Year's Day 1939, argued that 'Mr. Chamberlain was a thousand times right in saving the world's peace at Munich even at the price exacted' (quoted by Robert Kee, *The World We Left Behind,* 1984, 8). And see, for example, Eileen Blair's comments in her letter of 27 September 1938, *487.*
2. The Belomor-Baltic Canal connecting Archangel and Leningrad. It was constructed by slave labour in 1931–33 and runs for some 140 miles, saving a sea journey of 2,500 miles. It was built by a quarter of a million prisoners, nearly 200,000 of whom died or were executed.
3. Henry Havelock Ellis (1859–1939), psychologist, editor, and author, noted particularly for his work on sex in relation to society. Orwell reviewed his *My Life* (1939) in May 1940; see *617.*

<u>12.7.39</u>

Foreign & General

1. Expulsion of foreigners from Italian Tyrol does not include Americans. [1]
Rumours that purpose is to cover movements of German troops into Italy. E.
Standard correspondent declares this is a mare's nest. [Daily Telegraph;
London Evening Standard]
2. Chamberlain's speech apparently taken seriously throughout most of
world. [Daily Herald]

Social

1. J. A. Spender published letter in Times attacking Sir A. Sinclair. Sinclair's
reply refused publication. Today various prominent Liberals sent joint letter
to D. Tel. exposing this, which D. Tel. published. [2] *[Daily Telegraph]*
2. Labour amendment to Agricultural Development Bill, to make farm
labourers' minimum wage £2 (present average 35/-) defeated by only 4 votes.
[Daily Herald]

Party Politics

1. Catholic press as represented by the Universe is now strongly anti-Nazi
but scarcely as yet anti-Italian & still strongly anti-red as regards Spain.
[Universe, 7.7.39]

1. The Italian government expelled foreigners from the frontier province of Bolzano. According to Signor Giuseppe Bastiniani, Italian Under-Secretary for Foreign Affairs, foreigners of *all* nations were included in the decree, and the motive was 'political and military.' Those most affected were 200 to 300 Swiss, many of them hotel owners. They were forced to sell, and the lire in which they were paid could not be taken out of Italy.
2. John Alfred Spender (1862–1942), an 'old and respected Liberal' (as the joint letter referred to described him), had attacked Archibald Sinclair, leader of the Liberal Party, for 'assaulting the Prime Minister Neville Chamberlain in unmeasured terms and holding him up to odium as an incompetent man of infirm purpose.' The joint letter, signed first by Lady Violet Bonham Carter (see *14.7.39, n. 1*) followed by eight others, claimed that Sinclair's speech did not bear that interpretation. However, it went on, it was doubted by many (not only those in the Labour and Liberal parties) whether adequate means were being taken 'to convince the outside world that we are unanimous, and that our Government is in earnest.'

<u>13.7.39</u>

Social

1. J. A. Spender continues his attack on Sinclair. Times prints other letters to
same effect, none contradicting. [1] *[The Times]*

Party Politics

1. Labour Party has more or less refused conditional affiliation of I.L.P. [2]
I.L.P. evidently considering all-but unconditional affiliation. [The Times;
New Leader, 14.7.39]

1. *The Times*, in a second leader defending its action, referred also to 'the now familiar clamour . . . for the instant inclusion of Mr. Churchill in the Cabinet,' clamour from which '*The Times* has steadily held aloof.' It felt 'intensely that Mr. Churchill may well be needed in a Government again' but that 'His friends have already done him infinite harm.' Orwell is correct in recording that no 'contradicting' letters were published by *The Times* on 13 July, but a number were published on other days.
2. Independent Labour Party, founded in 1893 by Keir Hardie (see *565, 17.8.39. n. 3*), was older

than the Labour Party, which was formed by the ILP and trade unions in 1900. Orwell was a member of the ILP; see his 'Why I Join the I.L.P.,' *The New Leader*, 24 June 1938, *457*. At this time, the ILP and the Labour Party had split and were separately represented in the House of Commons. See Crick, 255, for some account of the character of the ILP; and *562, 10.8.39, Party Politics, 2*. For subdivisions within the ILP, see *553, n. 1*.

14.7.39

Foreign & General
1. Public Information Leaflet No. 2 (masking windows etc.) issued today. German visitors state gas masks have not been distributed in Germany. [No reference]
Social
1. M. G. Weekly prints facts about the Spender letter, & letter from Bonham Carter[1] etc. [Manchester Guardian Weekly]
Party Politics
1. M. G. Weekly considers pro-Churchill move inside the Conservative party has been checkmated. [Manchester Guardian Weekly]
2. Communist party pamphlet against conscription withdrawn from circulation after 3 weeks. [Left Forum, July 1939]

1. Lady Violet Bonham Carter (1897–1969), daughter of H. H. Asquith, Liberal Prime Minister, 1908–16, and a considerable force in the Liberal Party, was a member of Churchill's group Focus on Defence of Freedom and Peace, 1936–39.

15.7.39

Foreign & General
1. Large demonstration against British Embassy in Tokio. [Daily Telegraph]
2. Celebration of 150th anniversary of taking of Bastille included march-past of 30,000 troops including British. [Daily Telegraph]
3. Conscription of all persons 18–55 ordered in Hong Kong, but evidently so phrased as to apply chiefly to Chinese & allow exemption to most of the whites. [Daily Telegraph]
Social
1. Cmr. Stephen King-Hall's[1] German circular letters thought to have reached 50,000 people in Germany, evading the Gestapo by different-sized envelopes & different methods of folding. [Daily Telegraph]
2. Beginning of what are evidently large spy-revelations in France (cf. U.S.A.) by arrest of various persons connected with rightwing° newspapers. [Daily Telegraph]
Party Politics
1. Economic League accuses P.P.U.[2] of being vehicle of Nazi propaganda. [Daily Telegraph]
2. Individual membership of N.C.L.[3] now said to be 4500. Affiliations: 281 Women's Co-op Guilds, 30 Trades Councils & T.U. branches, 37 Labour parties & Women's sections, 10 Co-op parties etc., 53 P.P.U. branches, & miscellaneous. Communist press accuses N.C.L. of being a Fascist body. [No Conscription, July-August 1939; Daily Worker, 13.6.39]

Miscellaneous

1. Crowds at Eton-Harrow match[4] estimated at 10,000 & said to be smartest gathering for some years. [No reference]

1. Commander Stephen King-Hall (1893–1966) retired from the Royal Navy in 1929. He was elected to Parliament, as an Independent-National, in 1939. In 1936 he started the *K-H News Service Letter* (as *National News Letter* from 1941). Right-wing and outspoken, he was well regarded as a political commentator for his personal interpretation of events.
2. Peace Pledge Union, publishers of *Peace News*, was founded in 1934; Max Plowman (see *95*) was its general secretary, 1937–38. Orwell contributed a review to it; see *529*.
3. National Council of Labour. See *554, 2.7.39, Foreign & General, 2.*
4. The annual cricket game beween these schools, held early in June at Lord's Cricket Ground, London. Orwell had been co-editor of a special issue of *College Days* for this match in 1920; see *37*. For the outcome of this match see *16.7.39, Miscellaneous.* Lord's Cricket Ground has a capacity of about 25,000, achieved only on special occasions.

16.7.39

Foreign & General

1. 12,000 naval reservists to be called up July 31 for about 7 weeks. [*Sunday Times*]
2. General impression that Anglo-Russian pact is going to fall through. [*Sunday Times; Sunday Express*]
3. Sunday Express states that move to include Churchill in Cabinet is really move to get rid of Chamberlain. [*Sunday Express*]

3. Social

1. No mention of dissentients among 30,000 militiamen called up yesterday. [No reference]
2. More or less scaremongering article (submarine menace) by Liddell Hart[1] in Sunday Express. [*Sunday Express*]

Party Politics

1. Liberal retains N. Cornwall seat, slightly increasing previous small majority. Both candidates' polls rose largely. [*Daily Telegraph*, 15.7.39]
2. Beaverbrook press[2] accuses P.P.U. of being pro-Nazi, misquoting article. [*Peace News*, 14.7.39]

Miscellaneous

1. Eton Harrow match ends in a fight, the first time since 1919.[3] [*Sunday Express*]

1. Captain Sir Basil Henry Liddell Hart (1895–1970) was a writer of more than thirty books, including *History of the Second World War* (1970). He had been military correspondent to the *Daily Telegraph*, 1925–35, and to *The Times*, 1935–39, and military editor of the *Encyclopaedia Britannica*, 14th edition, 1929. In 1937 he was personal adviser to the Minister of War. He then wrote infantry training manuals and edited the series The Next War, 6 vols. (1938). Orwell wrote of him, 'The two military critics most favoured by the intelligentsia are Captain Liddell Hart and Major-General Fuller, the first of whom teaches that the defence is stronger than the attack, and the second that the attack is stronger than the defence. This contradiction has not prevented both of them from being accepted as authorities by the same public. The secret reason for their vogue in left-wing circles is that both of them are at odds with the War Office'; see 'Notes on Nationalism,' *Polemic*, 1, [October] 1945, *2668.* See also *784, n. 2.*
2. Right-wing newspapers owned by Lord Beaverbrook (see *628, n. 11*), which included the *Daily Express*, *Sunday Express*, and *Evening Standard*. See Orwell's London Letter of 15 April 1941, *787*.

3. In the annual cricket match between Eton and Harrow, the latter had a notable victory, winning by eight wickets (Harrow 294 and 131 for two; Eton 268 and 156). The front page of the *Sunday Express* carried a story prominently displayed and headed: 'Worst Hat-Bashing for Years / Our 'Gentlemen' enjoy themselves.' It states, 'Top hats were torn to shreds, umbrellas broken in pieces, ties torn up – and even trousers taken off.' It concludes: 'There have not been such scenes since the 1919 match' (when Orwell was at Eton), 'which resulted in a warning that the fixture would be cancelled if fighting occurred again.'

17.7.39

Foreign & General
1. British send cruiser & thus prevent threatened anti-British demonstration at Tsingtao.[1] Tokyo conversations evidently not getting anywhere. [Daily Telegraph]
2. Anglo-Russian pact only just makes front page of D. Tel. [Daily Telegraph]
Social
1. Definitely stated in D. Tel. that Saturday's militia draft (34,000 men) turned up with not one absentee (except cases of illness etc). [Daily Telegraph]
Party Politics
1. Left wing of Indian Congress party (as judged by "Congress Socialist") more vigorously anti-war than before. Publishes vicious attack on C.P.[2] from Trotskyist angle, but another article demands democratic bloc. [Congress Socialist; no date given]
2. Serious trouble in I.L.P. on pacifist-revolutionary controversy & long statement from I.L.P.'ers (London group) published in "Socialist Correspondence", which also takes other opportunities of attacking McGovern. [Socialist Correspondence]

1. Tsingtao (now Qingdao), a port in northern China, built to rival Tientsin (Tianjin) in the 1930s, was occupied by the Japanese, 1938–45. See *558, 24.7.39, n. 1.*
2. Communist Party.

19.7.39

Foreign & General
1. Gov.t advising all householders to lay in supply of non-perishable food. Leaflet on the subject to be issued shortly. [Daily Telegraph]
2. D. Tel. gives over 2 pages to scale pictures of entire British battle fleet. [Daily Telegraph]
3. German economic mission in Moscow said to be making no more progress than Anglo-Russian pact, with implication that 3-cornered bargaining is going on. [No reference]
Party Politics
1. First appearance of People's Party in Hythe by-election. [Daily Telegraph]
2. Appears that Lidell° Hart's book "Defence of Britain" boosts Hore Belisha.°[1] [Daily Telegraph, 18.7.39]
Miscellaneous
1. General estimation that harvest this year will be good, & not (as last year) wheat only. [No reference]

1. B. H. Liddell Hart, see *16.7.39, n. 1*. His *Defence of Britain* was published in 1939. Leslie Hore-Belisha (1893–1957), politician, barrister, and journalist (especially for the Beaverbrook press), was a Liberal M.P., 1923–45, and was instrumental in 1931 in organising the National Liberal Party to support the 'National Government' led by Stanley Baldwin (Conservative) and Ramsay MacDonald (Labour). He served as Secretary to the Board of Trade and then as Minister of Transport, 1934–37. In 1937, Chamberlain appointed him Secretary of State for War, charging him with the task of modernising the armed forces; he served until 1940; see *560, 29.7.39, Miscellaneous, n. 4*.

20.7.39

Foreign & General
1. Public Information Leaflet no. 3 (evacuation[1]) issued today. Never less than 4 searchlights visible at night from this village. [No reference]
2. News from Danzig seems to indicate that all there expect Danzig to fall into German hands in near future. [*Daily Telegraph*]
3. France said to be in favour of acceptance of Russian terms for Anglo-Russian pact, which have not been altered re. the Baltic States. [*Daily Telegraph*]
Social
1. One of the editors of Humanité[2] questioned by the Paris police with ref. to spy revelations, but no indication from report whether merely in advisory capacity or under suspicion of complicity. [*Daily Telegraph*]
2. Recent W.O.[3] regulation has forbidden army officers to resign their commissions & seemingly steps are being taken to prevent N.C.Os buying out[4] from the service (present cost £35). [*Daily Telegraph*]

1. Large numbers of children were dispersed from cities to country areas for safety from air attack. Many stayed in their adopted homes for the duration of the war. See also *565, 29.8.39, Foreign & General, 3; 567, 31.8.39, Foreign & General; 1.9.39, Foreign & General, 2*.
2. Leading French Communist daily newspaper.
3. War Office.
4. A serviceman could, with permission, reduce the time he had agreed to serve at his enlistment by buying his release. The practice continues today.

557. To Leonard Moore

21 July 1939   Typewritten

The Stores   Wallington   Nr. Baldock, HERTS.

Dear Mr Moore,
Many thanks for your letter of the 17th. I enclose a summary of the three essays I am doing,[1] which you can show to Gollancz if you think fit. In the event of his deciding to take a chance at the book I will think of a title. As to the novel, of course it was only the first third I was projecting to have ready by next summer, and that of course barring accidents, such as having to write some kind of potboiler meanwhile. Last year Nelson's approached me to do a book on poverty in England for their series.[2] It fell through owing to my

illness, but I see we are going to be terribly hard up before long and am thinking of writing to them to know whether they are still interested.

Yours sincerely
Eric Blair

1. *Inside the Whale*; see letter to Moore 14 [4?] July 1939, *555*.
2. Thomas Nelson & Sons had sent Orwell a contract for a book to be called 'Poverty in Practice' on 18 June 1938, when he was in the hospital. He was offered an advance of £50. He decided against signing, in order to concentrate on his next novel, *Coming Up for Air*. See *455*.

558. Diary of Events Leading Up to the War

<u>21.7.39</u>

Foreign & General
1. Polish official assassinated on Danzig frontier & consequent "tension."[1]
[*Daily Telegraph*]
Social
1. Times has leading article explaining (not very satisfactorily) the business of the Spender letter. [The Times, 20.7.39]
2. M. G. Weekly prints long letter extolling the Italian régime in Abyssinia & another answering this. [Manchester Guardian Weekly]
Party Politics
1. Conservatives hold Hythe with reduced majority. Only 37% of electorate voted. People's Party candidate polled 5-600 votes. [Daily Telegraph]
2. Internal row in London I.L.P. still obscure, but evidently reduces to a quarrel between the E.C.[2] who wish to attract pacifists into the party & the London Divisional Council who are more or less Trotskyist. Apparently some hope of getting rid of the latter. [New Leader]
3. Parliamentary debate on Palestine, illegal immigration etc., passed off with less row than had been anticipated. [Daily Telegraph]

1. Witold Budziewicz, a Polish customs officer, was shot dead shortly after being challenged by a Danzig customs officer accompanied by two Nazis. At the time, it was not known who fired the shot. This was one of a number of incidents designed to increase tension in the area in order to provide Hitler with a pretext for intervention.
2. Executive Committee; for divisions within the ILP, see *553, n. 1.*

<u>22.7.39</u>

Foreign & General
1. Rumours of impending Anglo-American deal with Germany, which is said to be connected with Herr Wohltat's visit but not as yet sponsored by the Cabinet.[1] Conditions to be loan of £1000 million & access to raw materials, in return for disarmament under international surveyance. [Daily Telegraph]
2. Russian fleet exercises evidently designed to impress Baltic States. [Daily Telegraph]

Social
1. *D. Tel. gossip column notes that nearly 100 Conservative MPs. are officers in the territorials, R.A.F. voluntary reserve etc.* [*Daily Telegraph*]
Party Politics
1. *Queipo de Llano[2] relieved of his post.* [*Daily Telegraph*]
2. *Friendly review of my novel in "Daily Worker."*[3] [*Daily Worker*, 19.7.39]

1. Dr. Helmut Wohltat, Economic Adviser to Hermann Goering, was visiting Britain for a conference on whaling. He undoubtedly also had discussions with R. S. Hudson of the Department of Overseas Trade. It is now known that each was acting on his own initiative, but suspicions were aroused. Prime Minister Chamberlain categorically denied to the House of Commons on 24 July that anything more was involved than informal discussion on matters of joint interest, and assured the House that no proposal for a loan had been made.
2. General Gonzalo Queipo de Llano y Serra (see *519, n. 42*) had commanded Franco's Army of the South. Though a Republican, he accepted the title of marquis in 1947. See also *23.7.39, Party Politics, 1*, for the reason for his dismissal from his post as Inspector-General of the Carabiñeros.
3. *Coming Up for Air.* Orwell's surprise was occasioned by the way the *Daily Worker* had attacked him in 1937; see letter to Victor Gollancz, 20 August 1937, *390*.

23.7.39

Foreign & General
1. *Appears from today's press that the offer referred to in this column yesterday has actually been talked of, but only unofficially. Cabinet disclaim knowledge but evidently know all about it. Presumption is that it has been allowed to leak out to see how the public take it. Terms were: loan (amount not stated) to Germany, raw materials & possible condominium in certain African possessions, against partial disarmament & withdrawal from Czechoslovakia.* [*Sunday Times; Sunday Express*]
2. *Now evident that Russian pact will fall through.* [*Sunday Express*]
3. *Calling up of territorials & naval reservists suggests that danger moment will be first week in August.* [*Sunday Times*]
Party Politics
1. *Cause of Queipo de Llano's dismissal said to be that he protested against tying Spain to the Axis & threatened to declare independence of Andalusia.*[1] [*Sunday Express*]
2. *Nat. Liberals intend to split Gov.t vote in Brecon by-election.*[2] [*Sunday Express*]
3. *Editor (Grey)[3] of pro-Fascist "Aeroplane" has resigned for unexplained reasons.*[4] [*Sunday Express*]
4. *Beaverbrook press now more openly against the Russian pact & for isolationism than for some months past.* [No reference]

1. Queipo had been a member of Spain's National Council in 1937 but was left out of Franco's cabinet early in 1938. See Thomas, 750, 752–54, and 948, n. 2.
2. The National Liberals were close allies of the Conservatives in Baldwin's and Chamberlain's governments. By standing in an election against a Conservative candidate, the National Liberals would split the pro-government vote. See *562, 4.8.39, Party Politics, 1*.
3. Charles Grey (1875–), a journalist with a special interest in aeronautical matters, founded *The Aeroplane* in 1911 and edited it until 1939, when he became air correspondent for several

newspapers. He wrote a number of books on aircraft and edited *All the World's Aircraft*, 1916–41.
4. Claud Cockburn, in his pro-Communist journal, *The Week*, described *The Aeroplane* as 'frankly pro-Nazi.' See *562, 4.8.39, n. 1.*

24.7.39

Foreign & General

1. The conversation with Wohltat was held by R. S. Hudson (Overseas Trade) who reported to the P.M. following day. Obviously the affair has been allowed to leak out intentionally. Italian press reported as suggesting that this (tie-up with Germany) is a threat aimed at impressing U.S.S.R. Anglo-Russian pact back on front page with suggestion that Stalin really wants it. German trade talks are also being resumed, this presumably a threat aimed at England. [Daily Telegraph]
2. Fighting on Mongolia° border evidently genuine. [Daily Telegraph]
3. Japanese press giving advance forecast of terms to Britain over Tientsin[1] which would clearly not be accepted. [Daily Telegraph]

1. Tientsin (Tianjin) was a port in northern China where Britain and France had been granted Concessions by a treaty of 1858, which were extended later to Germany and Japan. It was occupied by the Japanese, 1937–45, but guerrilla and 'terrorist' resistance continued. In one incident, when the Chinese manager of the Japanese-sponsored Federal Reserve Bank was killed, and the Japanese were looking for four Chinese believed to be responsible, the Chinese took refuge in the British Concession. When the British refused to hand them over, the Japanese blockaded the British and French Concessions, starting on 14 June 1939. Supplies were admitted only after careful search. It was reported in *The Times*, 15 July 1939, that milk was at last being allowed into the Concession. See *560, 1.8.39, Foreign & General, 3,* and *565, 18.8.39, Social, 1.*

25.7.39

Foreign & General

1. Brit-Japanese agreement very vaguely worded but amounts to climbing down on Britain's part as in effect it amounts to a promise not to help Chinese.[1] Chamberlain denies any alteration in British policy. [Daily Telegraph]
2. Anglo-Soviet pact back on front page & appears more probable. [Daily Telegraph]
Social
1. Bill to deal with I.R.A. provides for power to prohibit entry of aliens, deportation of aliens, & compulsary registration of aliens. Also emergency power to Sup.ts of Police to search without warrant. Bill said to be for 2 years only. Not seriously opposed (passed 218–17.) [Daily Telegraph]

1. See *24.7.39. n. 1.*

26.7.39

Foreign & General

1. General impression in world press that Gt. Britain has climbed down in Tokyo agreement. [Daily Telegraph]

2. *Another demonstration flight of 240 aeroplanes over France. Joint French-British aeroplane production now claimed to equal German.* [*Daily Telegraph*]

Social

1. *Proposal to affiliate N.U.J.*[1] *to T.U.C.*[2] *lost by very narrow margin (ballot showed actual majority for but not ⅔ majority).* [*Daily Telegraph*]

Party Politics

1. *Franco evidently standing by his Axis commitments & seems about due for his June purge against de Llano, Yague*[3] *& others.* [*Daily Telegraph*]

2. *Litvinoff*[4] *apparently in disgrace.* [*Daily Telegraph*]

1. National Union of Journalists.
2. Trades Union Congress. It was founded in 1868, to represent all unions that choose to be affiliated to it.
3. Colonel Blanco de Yagüe (1891–1952) was a successful Nationalist commander. Thomas reports that at a Falangist banquet on 19 April 1938 he praised the fighting qualities of the Republicans, and described the allies of the Nationalists, the Germans and Italians, as 'beasts of prey' (819).
4. Maxim Litvinov (1876–1951) represented the Soviet Union abroad in many capacities from 1917, when he was unacknowledged Ambassador to Britain, to 1941–43, when he served as Ambassador to the United States. A Jew and a prominent anti-Nazi, who had recommended collective action against Hitler, he was dismissed as Commissar of Foreign Affairs on 3 May 1939.

559. Review of *Stendhal* by F. C. Green

New English Weekly, 27 July 1939

"Stendhal," by Mr. F. C. Green, is said to be the first book on Stendhal written in English for over sixty years. What this probably demonstrates is that the biographer and the novelist need different material to work on. Stendhal's life was of the kind that is absorbingly interesting when one sees it from the inside, as one does in certain passages in his novels, but not particularly suited to biography, because he lived more or less in obscurity and had periods of years on end when nothing particular was happening. He was never a popular idol or a resounding scandal, never even starved in a garret or wrote masterpieces in a debtors' prison. In a fairly active life of fifty-nine years (1783–1842) his experiences seem to have been, on the whole, the kind of experiences that happen to ordinary unsuccessful people.

One of them was to see war at close quarters. For some years Stendhal held a responsible position in the supplies department of Napoleon's army, and he was in the retreat from Moscow, which in itself would be quite enough adventure for one normal lifetime. It was the kind of thing that would never happen to an even potentially successful writer, but undoubtedly it was a bit of luck for all of us that it happened to Stendhal. He seems to have written little or nothing about the Moscow campaign, but without that large-scale demonstration of the boringness of war he might never have written his celebrated description of Waterloo, which must be one of the earliest pieces of *truthful* battle-literature in existence. As a soldier and later as a consular agent Stendhal seems to have been both brave and competent, but it is evident that like most sensitive people he found action boring. Among the flames of Moscow he read an English translation of "Paul et Virginie," and during the revolution of 1830 he sat listening to the gunfire in the streets without, apparently, feeling any impulse to join in. The things that seem to have moved him most deeply were scenery and, of course, an endless succession of love-affairs, in which he was passably successful. He also caught syphilis, a thing that must have affected his outlook to some extent, though, as Professor Green points out, before Ibsen and Brieux had done their worst syphilis was merely a disease like any other.[1]

As a writer Stendhal is in a peculiar position, because everyone has read two of his books and nobody except a small circle of admirers has read any of the others. Professor Green gives long and interesting analyses of his four principal novels, but finds it as difficult as it always is to explain just where Stendhal's charm lies. For of course with Stendhal it is above all a question of *charm*. There is something about him, a kind of mental climate, that makes it possible for him to get away with all the vices that ruin the ordinary sensitive novel. As for the besetting sin of novelists, narcissism, he is able to wallow in it without ever once giving offence. Of the two novels that everyone knows, it is easier to see why "Le Rouge et le Noir" leaves a lasting impression behind, because it has what the other at first sight seems to lack, a central unifying theme. As Professor Green rightly says, its theme is class-hatred. Julien Sorel, the clever, ambitious peasant-boy, at a time when reaction has triumphed and right-thinking is synonymous with stupidity, enters the Church with quite deliberate hypocrisy, because the Church is the only profession in which one can rise. As a poor hanger-on in aristocratic families, he loathes from the bottom of his heart the snobbish half-wits who surround him. But what gives the book its tone is that his hatred is mixed up with envy, as it would be in real life, of course. Julien is in fact the type of° the revolutionary, and nine times out of ten a revolutionary is merely a climber with a bomb in his pocket. After all, the hated aristocrats are deeply fascinating. Mathilde de la Mole is all the *more* fascinating because of her atrocious pride and egoism. "What a frightful character!" Julien thinks, and instantly her frightfulness makes her twice as desirable as before. It is interesting to compare "Le Rouge et le Noir" with another epic of snobbishness, "Great Expectations." Here the whole thing is happening on a lower social level, but there is a certain similarity of theme. Once again it is the fascination of something felt and known to be rotten. The one flaw in "Le Rouge et le Noir" is the shooting of Madame de Rênal, which brings Julien to the guillotine. Professor Green maintains that this too can be explained in terms of class-hatred. It may be so, and yet few people can have read the book without feeling that this is a peculiarly meaningless outrage and has only been put in because Julien has got to die in the limelight. A comparatively probable ending would have been to have him killed in a duel by some jealous relative of Mathilde. Perhaps this would have struck Stendhal as too obvious.

"La Chartreuse de Parme" does not seem at first sight to have an equally

379

seizable theme, and yet one cannot read it without feeling that it *has* a theme, if only because Stendhal is peculiarly adept at producing what Professor Green calls "unity of tone." Without his very delicate feeling for proportion he could not deal so freely in improbabilities. Actually the theme of "La Chartreuse de Parme" is magnanimity. Unlike people in real life, the principal characters in it are spiritually decent. Apart from the Waterloo episode the whole book is an escape from time and space into a sort of Shakespearean never-never land. Admittedly it is a queer kind of magnanimity that the characters show, but that is just where Stendhal's genius comes in. For what one is obliged to feel is not merely that the Duchess of Sanseverina is superior to the ordinary "good" woman, but that she herself *is* a good woman, in spite of a few trifles like murder, incest, etc. She and Fabrice and even Mosca are incapable of acting *meanly*, a thing that carries no weight in the Judaeo-Christian scheme of morals. Like several other novelists of the first rank, Stendhal has discovered a new kind of sensitiveness. He is deeply sentimental and completely adult, and it is perhaps this unlikely combination that is the basis of his peculiar flavour.

In parts, at any rate in the opening chapters, Mr. Green's is not an easy book to read, but it must have been a lot harder to write. Apart from the labour of research it needed a very difficult interweaving of biography and criticism. I doubt whether this could have been more skilfully or conscientiously done than it is here, and what is especially to be praised is the way in which Professor Green has avoided the Maurois touch and ignored the picturesqueness of Stendhal's background—the Revolution, Napoleon, etc., etc. He sticks to his subject, and when he is doubtful about the facts he says so. The book was certainly needed, and it deserves to become the standard English biography of Stendhal.

1. In *Ghosts* (1881), by Ibsen, and *Damaged Goods* (1901), by Brieux.

560. Diary of Events Leading Up to the War

<u>27.7.39</u>

<u>Foreign & General</u>
1. More fighting on Manchukuo border. Japanese said to be contemplating blockade of Russian half of Sakhalin. [*Daily Telegraph*]
2. French-British-Russian staff talks being arranged for. Question of Baltic states apparently unsettled. [*Daily Telegraph*]
3. Public Information leaflet No. 4 (food storage) issued today. [No reference]
<u>Party Politics</u>
1. Conservatives held Monmouth div.n with reduced majority. Both polls dropped. [*Daily Telegraph*]
2. Queipo de Llano appointed ambassador to Argentine.[1] [*Daily Telegraph*]

3. Summary of efforts of the various anti-war groups to be found in New English Weekly 20 & 27.7.39 [New English Weekly, 20–27.7.39]
4. The MP.s (19) who voted against the I.R.A. bill included Gallacher, Pritt,[2] Cripps. [New Leader, 28.7.39]

1. But see *1.8.39, Party Politics, 1.*
2. William Gallacher (1881–1965), Communist M.P. 1935–50. Dennis Noel Pritt (1887–1972), lawyer, author, and Labour M.P., 1935–40. Following policy disagreements, Pritt was expelled from the Labour Party, and was an Independent Socialist M.P. until 1950. A fervent supporter of left-wing causes and of the Soviet Union, in 1954 he was awarded the Lenin Peace Prize. Orwell had little love for Pritt; see his letter to Humphry House, 11 April 1940, *609* and *3732* (XX, 252).

<u>28.7.39</u>

<u>Foreign & General</u>
1. Americans evidently deciding to denounce commercial treaty with Japan. [Daily Telegraph]
<u>Social</u>
1. Gov.t apparently considering raising of old age pension, no doubt with an eye to general election. [Daily Telegraph]
2. Rich gold deposits said to have been found near Great Slave Lake in Canada. [Daily Telegraph]
3. Smallholders & small farmers evidently being incommoded by conscription. First special tribunal under M.T. act[1] had 20 objectors to deal with, none apparently on political grounds. [Smallholder; Daily Telegraph]
<u>Party Politics</u>
1. Fresh purge in Moscow, including Tarioff, Soviet Minister to Outer Mongolia. [Daily Telegraph]
2. French handing over £8 millions of Spanish gold to Franco. [Daily Telegraph]
3. P.P.U., N.C.L, Friends & Fellowship of Reconciliation were able to be represented at first tribunal under M.T. Act. [Daily Telegraph]

1. The Military Training Act permitted the call-up of men for military service and allowed for conscientious objection.

<u>29.7.39</u>

<u>Foreign & General</u>
1. French general election to be postponed by decree for 2 years (ie. until 1942). [Daily Telegraph]
2. Evidently[o] that fairly severe struggle is going on in Spain between Axis supporters (Suñer[1]) & Traditionalists (esp. the generals, Yague etc.) & that there is likelihood of Franco remaining neutral in case of war. [Manchester Guardian Weekly; Daily Telegraph]
<u>Social</u>
1. Editor of Humanité who was tried in test case for printing various allegations about German espionage in France, acquitted. Order of arrest

issued against another journalist for writing anti-Semitic article. * [*Daily Telegraph*]

**Sentence of imprisonment* [Orwell's note].

Party Politics

1. Labour held Colne Valley constituency with increased majority. (Labour vote rose about 1000, Liberal & Cons. each dropped 2–3 thousand.) [*Daily Telegraph*]

2. According to figures given in MG.,[2] *3–500 people a week (Republicans) have been being shot in Catalonia from May onwards.*[3] [*Manchester Guardian Weekly*]

Miscellaneous

1. Guards trooped the colours in 3's[4] *for the first time yesterday.* [*Daily Telegraph*]

1. Ramon Serrano Suñer (1901–), brother-in-law of Franco and, as Minister of the Interior, second in importance to him, until dismissed in 1942. His experience as a prisoner of the Republicans embittered him for life. As Thomas puts it, they were such 'as to make him close his eyes to pity' (924, and see 633–34).
2. *Manchester Guardian.*
3. Count Galeazzo Ciano (1903–1944), Italian Foreign Minister, visited Spain in July 1939 and reported (as quoted by Thomas, 924): 'trials going on every day at a speed which I would call almost summary. . . . There are still a great number of shootings. In Madrid alone, between 200 and 250 a day, in Barcelona 150, in Seville 80.' Thomas comments, 'Seville had been in nationalist Spain throughout the war: how could there be still enough people to shoot at this rate?' In 1944 it was reported that 193,000 people had been executed, but Thomas suggests this might be the number of death sentences, some of which were commuted, or that it includes those executed during the war (925).
4. Infantry regiments formed up in four ranks until the 1937 reforms instituted by Secretary of State for War Hore-Belisha (see *556, 19.7.39, Party Politics, 1.*) Among them were changes in army drill to simplify the often complicated movements and so speed the process of training. The change Orwell notes here is forming up in three ranks, a practice still followed. Hore-Belisha's reforms also included the introduction of battle dress and the abolition of puttees. See *469, n. 5.*

30.7.39

Foreign & General

1. Seems clear that Parliament will adjourn as usual with no previous arrangements for recall before October.[1] [*Sunday Times*]

2. There are now 60,000 German troops (ie. including police, storm troopers etc.) in Danzig. [*Sunday Times*]

3. Seemingly authoritative article in S. Times states that in case of war Jugo-Slavia will certainly be neutral but more likely to be pro-ally if the Russian pact goes through & the Croats are given the degree of autonomy they want. Population of 14 m. includes 5 m. Serbs, 5 m. Croats, ½ m. Hungarians, ½ m. Germans, the rest presumably Slovenes. Pan-Slav feeling strong among the poorer classes. [*Sunday Times*]

Social

1. One of Daladier's[2] *decrees sets up separate propaganda dep.t under P.M.'s control. Working hours of civil service raised from 40 to 45.*

France's gold reserve now said to be second only to that of U.S.A. Gold holding of Bank of France is £560 m. [Sunday Times]
2. I.R.A. suspects already being deported in fairly large numbers (about 20 hitherto). [Sunday Times; Daily Telegraph, 29.7.39]

1. See 565, 30.8.39, Social, 1. for adjournment of Parliament.
2. Edouard Daladier, Socialist Prime Minister of France, 1938–40; see 511, n. 2.

1.8.39

Foreign & General
1. Military mission probably leaving for Moscow this week. Leader (Admiral Plunkett-Ernle-Erle-Drax[1]) took part in mission to Tsarist Russia just before Great War. [Daily Telegraph]
2. Polish Gov.t taking economic sanctions against Danzig amounting to refusal to import products of certain factories. [Daily Telegraph]
3. British authorities apparently agreeing to hand over the 4 Chinese alleged terrorists hiding in the Tientsin concession.[2] [Daily Telegraph]
Social
1. Number of unemployed for July about 1¼ millions, ★½ million less than same period in 1938. Total number in insured employment close on 13 million, more than ½ million more than a year ago. [Daily Telegraph]
★100,000 less than estimate of a month previously [Orwell's note].
2. In first 34,000 militia men° called up only 58 absented themselves without leave. [Daily Telegraph]
3. Prohibition inaugurated in Bombay Presidency.[3] [Daily Telegraph]
Party Politics
1. Queipo de Llano appointed chief of Spanish military mission to Italy. [Daily Telegraph]
2. Socialist Correspondence claims that Labour Members who voted against I.R.A. bill are being threatened with discipline by Parliamentary Group. [Socialist Correspondence, 29.7.39]
3. P.O.U.M.[4] Youth Group managing to issue leaflets. [Socialist Correspondence, 29.7.39]
Miscellaneous
1. New method of bracken destruction by mowing plus sodium chlorate successfully extirpates bracken using only 20 lb. of s.c. per acre. [Daily Telegraph; Farmer & Stockbreeder]
2. This year's European wheat production, excluding U.S.S.R., estimated at 44 million metric tons, slightly above average but 14% less than last year's [Daily Telegraph]

1. Admiral Sir Reginald Plunkett-Ernle-Erle-Drax (1880–1967), Commander-in-Chief, The Nore, 1939–41, was accompanied by a representative of the Army and one of the Royal Air Force. Although a talented man, he was ill-briefed for this mission and was subjected to ridicule in Moscow, Voroshilov ridiculing his being a Knight Commander of the 'Bath'. He signed himself simply as 'Drax' (William Wilson).
2. See 558, 24.7.39, Foreign & General, 3, and 565, 18.8.39, Social, 1.
3. One of the three divisions of India when administered by the East India Company; the others

were Bengal and Madras. The titles were continued after the East Indian Company was superseded.

4. Partido Obrero de Unificación Marxista was the Revolutionary Communist Party of Spain, anti-Stalinist. Orwell fought with it in Spain. See *Homage to Catalonia*, *CW*, VI, especially Appendix II, for the attempt by the Communist Party to eradicate the POUM.

2.8.39

Foreign & General

1. Announced today that ration cards are already printed & ready. [*Daily Telegraph*]

2. Chamberlain's speech broadcast throughout U.S.S.R. [1] [*Daily Telegraph*]

3. Number of Ukrainian leaders arrested in Poland. [*Daily Telegraph*]

Social

1. Labour MPs' complaints in Parliament about conditions in militia turn upon such things as militiamen sleeping 8 in a tent. [*Daily Telegraph*]

2. Appears that German Jewish refugees are settling in great numbers in certain parts of London, eg. Golders Green, & buying houses which they have plenty of money to do. [Private (C.W.)[2]]

Party Politics

1. Rumour of quarrels among Spanish refugee higher-ups in Paris over money & disagreement between Negrin & Prieto. [3] [Private (R.R.)[4]]

2. Col. Wedgwood's[5] Catholic Constituents (to number of 5000, mostly working-class) in Newcastle under Lyne,° have memorialised stating that they will vote against him. [Private (C.W.)]

1. This speech, in the House of Commons, 31 July, announced that a mission was to go to Moscow for discussions with Soviet authorities on military matters. It reiterated the government's aim, summarised in *The Times*, 1 August, as 'peace with justice; its method . . . the formation of the "Peace Front." '

2. Probably from Cyril Wright; see *553, n. 4.*

3. Dr. Juan Negrín (1889–1956) was Socialist Prime Minister of the Republic of Spain, September 1936–March 1938. He fled to France, where he died in exile; see also *2852, n. 3.* Indalecio Prieto y Tuero (1883–1962), Socialist Minister of National Defence in Negrín's cabinet, died in exile in Mexico.

4. Either Orwell's friend Richard Rees (see *95; 2696, n. 2*) or Reginald Reynolds (1905–1958), journalist and author, Quaker and pacifist, who supported the non-Communist Republicans in Spain and was a brilliant speaker for the ILP; see *1060, n. 1.*

5. Josiah Clement Wedgwood (1872–1943; Baron, 1942), M.P. for Newcastle-under-Lyme, 1906–42, first as a Liberal, later for Labour, was Vice-Chairman of the Labour Party, 1921–24.

561. To Leonard Moore

4 August 1939   Typewritten

The Stores   Wallington   Nr. Baldock, HERTS.

Dear Mr Moore,

Naturally I'm delighted about the Albatross business.[1] It was very clever of you to work it. I've always wanted to crash one of those continental editions.

English people abroad always read the few English books they can get hold of with such attention that I'm sure it's the best kind of publicity.

Of course I've no objection to the alterations they want to make, but in two of the four cases I've suggested substituting another phrase instead of just leaving a blank. Of course they can do as they prefer, but in these two cases I felt that simply to cut the phrase out without inserting another would upset the balance of the paragraph. Also as they're going to set up the type anew they might correct two misprints which I let through. I've made notes on all this on the attached,[2] and perhaps you could explain to them.

Yours
Eric Blair

1. The Albatross Modern Continental Library was a paperback series of books in English put out by John Holroyd-Reece (born Johann Herman Riess) for distribution on the Continent. Most were sold in Germany. The first book was issued on 1 March 1932. On 1 October 1934 Holroyd-Reece, with the Albatross printer, Brandsetter, took over the long-established Tauchnitz series. William B. Todd and Ann Bowden's *Tauchnitz International Editions in English 1841–1955* (New York, 1988) lists item 5371, Orwell's *Coming Up for Air*, as unpublished. The entry records that the contract was between Orwell and The Albatross Verlag G.m.b.H., either for itself or on behalf of the Tauchnitz successors (Brandsetter) and was dated 31 August 1939, file no. 275, It stipulated that the book was to be issued not later than August 1940. Although the publishing house was German, the contract was issued from 12 rue Chanoinesse, Paris. See Orwell's letter to Moore of 8 December 1939, *581, n. 3.*
2. These do not appear to have survived. However, see Orwell's Diary of Events Leading Up to the War, *562, 4.8.39, Miscellaneous, 1,* where he records these requested changes.

562. Diary of Events Leading Up to the War

4.8.39

Foreign & General
1. French-Brit. military mission leaving tomorrow on slow liner which will take a week to reach Leningrad. The "Week"[1] suggests that the move is not intended seriously. Quotations from Finnish papers & Swedish Foreign Minister's speech suggest that Baltic States are genuinely nervous. [Daily Telegraph; Manchester Guardian Weekly; The Week, 2.8.39]
2. Germany said to be considering transference of Slovakia from Hungary in order to detach the latter from Poland.[2] Said also to be systematically depleting Slovakia of timber, foodstuffs & machinery. [Manchester Guardian Weekly. Given reference number 3 for 2]
Social
1. Mander M.P. (Lib.)[3] declares Anglo-German Fellowship[4] a pro-German organisation & asks whether Home Sec. can supress it. Hoare[5] replies unable to do anything unless an organisation breaks the law. [Daily Telegraph]
Party Politics
1. Labour won Brecon & Radnor by 2500 majority.[6] Labour vote rose about 750, Gov.t vote dropped about 4000, & total poll dropped. [Daily Telegraph]

Miscellaneous

1. Albatross Press[7] arranging for publication of my last book require excision of certain (though not all) unfriendly references to Hitler. Say they are obliged to do this as their books circulate largely in Germany. Also excision of a passage of about a page suggesting that war is imminent. [F.[8] Personal]

1. *The Week* was a private-circulation, ostensibly independent but pro-Communist newsletter edited by Claud Cockburn (Frank Pitcairn; see *519, n. 3*). It was published from 29 March 1933 to 15 January 1941, when it was suppressed by government order. A new series was allowed from October 1942, and it ran until December 1946. See his book *The Years of The Week* (1968), 262–64.
2. This opaque summary refers to side-effects of the Munich pact. For sense, it should read 'to Hungary.' As Churchill summarised it, after Munich, 'A formal division of the spoils was made by Germany at the beginning of November. Poland was not disturbed in her occupation of Teschen [an area of Silesia opportunely seized by Poland]. The Slovaks, who had been used as a pawn by Germany, obtained a precarious autonomy. Hungary received a piece of flesh at the expense of Slovakia' (*The Second World War*, I, 298; U.S.: *The Gathering Storm*, 332). See *525, n. 2*.
3. Geoffrey Mander (1882–1962; Kt., 1945) was a Liberal M.P., 1929–45.
4. The Link; see *6.8.39, Party Politics, n. 6*.
5. Sir Samuel Hoare (1880–1959; Viscount Templewood, 1944) Conservative, was appointed foreign secretary in June 1935, but resigned in December because of opposition to his plan to settle the Abyssinian crisis. In June 1936 he became first lord of the Admiralty and later home secretary. A supporter of the Munich pact, he fell with Chamberlain in May 1940. Later, as Ambassador to Spain, he negotiated the release from Spanish gaols of some 30,000 Allied prisoners and refugees.
6. See *558, 23.7.39, Party Politics, 2* and *n. 2*.
7. For details of Albatross's proposal to issue *Coming Up for Air*, see *561, 581*.
8. Unidentified.

6.8.39

Foreign & General

1. Purge of Sudeten[1] leaders taking place, evidently as result of Czech pressure & as prelude to milder methods. [Sunday Times]

2. Polish gov.t evidently now ready to allow Russians to use Polish air bases. [Sunday Times]

3. S. Express considers Franco has definitely come down on the side of the Axis, but hints that French & Swiss banks who have hitherto lent him £5 m. are putting pressure on him by withholding further loans. [No reference given, but evidently *Sunday Express*]

Social

1. Evidently there has been trouble about the food in the militia. Number of first draft who declared themselves conscientious objectors stated at 2%. [Sunday Times]

2. Earnings throughout life from cabinet posts etc. of various politicians estimated by Peter Howard[2] thus: Runciman £71, Lloyd George £94, Baldwin £70, Hoare £79, Simon £78, Churchill £92 (all in thousands).[3] [Sunday Express]

Party Politics

1. Peter Howard considers Sir A. Wilson[4] is becoming unpopular in Hitchin Div.n owing to pro-German sentiments. ★ [Sunday Express]

★"Herts Pictorial" (15.8.39) repeats this without comment. [Orwell's note].

2. Mosley's [5] Earls Court Stadium meeting said to have been attended by 25,000. M. said to have lost some of his East End working-class support but gained following among small business men etc. [*Left Forum*, August]
3. "The Link" [6] said to be actively pro-Nazi & also recommended by P.P.U. [*Left Forum*, August]
4. Evidently the French spy scandals are being officially hushed up to some extent. La Rocque [7] asks Daladier to pass decree—law making receipt of foreign money for other than commercial purpose a criminal offence. [*Observer*]
5. Sunday Express prints friendly article about Japan (gossip article). [*Sunday Express*]

1. The Sudetenland, parts of Moravia and Bohemia incorporated into Czechoslovakia by the Treaty of Versailles, led by the Sudeten German Party, under Konrad Henlein, wanted to reunite with Germany. It was aided and abetted by Hitler. The Munich pact of 30 September 1938 required Czechoslovakia to cede the area to Germany by 10 October 1938; see *487, n. 3.*
2. Peter Howard (1908–1965), author, journalist, dramatist, and farmer, was political columnist for Express Newspapers (Beaverbrook group), 1933–41.
3. Walter Runciman (1870–1949; Viscount, 1937), a Liberal M.P., 1899–1931, then a National Liberal, held many offices, including President of the Board of Trade, 1914–16, 1931–37. He led a mission to Czechoslovakia in 1938. For David Lloyd George, see *469, n. 3.* Stanley Baldwin (1867–1947; Earl Baldwin, 1937), was Conservative Prime Minister three times, 1923–24, 1924–29, 1935–37. He successfully negotiated the crisis occasioned by the abdication of King Edward VIII, but is generally blamed for Britain's failure to prepare adequately for the impending war. For Samuel Hoare, see *4.8.39, n. 5.* Sir John Simon (1873–1954; Viscount, 1940) entered the House of Commons as a Liberal in 1906, and was instrumental in forming the National Liberal Party in 1931. He was Foreign Secretary, 1931–35; served at the Home Office, 1935–37, was Chancellor of the Exchequer, 1937–40, and Lord Chancellor, 1940–45. He wanted to avoid entanglements on the Continent. For Winston Churchill, see *556, 5.7.39, n. 1*
4. Sir Arnold Wilson (1884–1940) was Conservative M.P. for Hitchin, 1933–40, and Chairman of the Home Office Committee on Structural Precautions against Air Attack, 1936–38. See *2490* and *2490, n. 4.*
5. Oswald Mosley was head of the British Union of Fascists; see *295, n. 7.*
6. The Link was avowedly an Anglo-German cultural and friendship association. See *4.8.39, Social; 7.8.39, Party Politics.*
7. Colonel François de la Rocque; see *511, n. 3.*

7.8.39

Social
1. "Soc. Corresp." repeats complaints about food etc. in militia camps with implication that the men are being treated rough more or less wilfully. [*Socialist Correspondence*]
2. 57 people reported shot in connection with recent political murders in Madrid (number of people murdered was apparently 3). [*Daily Telegraph*]
Party Politics
1. Members of the P.S.O.P. [1] arrested in France in connection with anti-war activities. C.P. making accusations of Nazi agency etc. [*Socialist Correspondence; The Week, 2.8.39*]
2. Bela Kun [2] again reported shot (from Vienna source this time). [*Daily Telegraph*]

3. Adm.1 Sir Barry Domville°³*chairman of "the° Link", describes statement of Hoare & Mander as a lie*⁴*& hopes they will repeat it outside Parliament.* ⁵ *[Daily Telegraph]*⁶

1. Parti Socialiste Ouvriers et Paysans, a left-wing splinter group of the Socialist Party (SFIO, Section Française de l'Internationale Ouvrière); see *11.8.39, n. 3.*
2. See *556, 10.7.39, n. 4.*
3. Admiral Sir Barry Edward Domvile (1878–1971) retired from the Royal Navy in 1936.
4. See *4.8.39, Social.*
5. A statement made inside the House of Commons is privileged, and an action for slander or libel cannot be prosecuted.
6. A headline in Lord Beaverbrook's newspaper, the *Daily Express*, for 7 August boldly proclaimed, 'No War this Year.'

<u>8.8.39</u>

<u>Foreign & General</u>
1. Chinese dollar has now dropped below 4d. [Daily Telegraph]
2. Danzig senate° appears to have climbed down in dispute over Polish customs officials. [Daily Telegraph]
3. Again reported that largish number of Asturian soldiers are still holding out in the mountains. ¹ *[Daily Telegraph]*
<u>Social</u>
1. Complete column given in D. Tel. to "the° Link", besides extra piece on front page. Statement by organisers that they are not propaganda agents etc. Statement that Prof. Laurie received £150 for "The Case for Germany" from German publishing firm, British firms having refused to publish book which was "pro-German". Statement that Leeds branch of "the° Link" was voluntarily dissolved as organisers considered the German end was under Nazi control. [Daily Telegraph]
2. D. Tel. gives a column (in news section) to summarising "Germany's War Chances", ² *the Gollancz book translated from the Hungarian, for publication of which the author is being persecuted in Hungary. [Daily Telegraph]*
<u>Miscellaneous</u>
*1. Death of Leonard Merrick*³ *makes front page (just) of D. Tel. [Daily Telegraph]*

1. Miners in Asturia, in the north of Spain, had organised revolution in 1934 (see Thomas, 136ff). A feature there during the Spanish civil war, in September and October 1937, was Germany's practice of 'carpet bombing,' regardless of civilians below. Although Franco's forces were successful in getting for the Nationalists the coal resources of the region, *guerrilleros* continued to fight there until 1948 (Thomas, 728–33).
2. The full title of the book, by Ivan Lajos, published by Gollancz in August 1939, was *Germany's War Chances: As Pictured in German Official Literature.*
3. Leonard Merrick (1864–1939), born Miller, was a novelist, now almost forgotten, but in 1918 a collected edition of his novels was published in which each was introduced by a distinguished author. He was described by Sir James Barrie as 'the novelist's novelist,' and William Dean Howells put him next in stature to Jane Austen. *The Position of Peggy Harper* (1911) was to be reissued in the Century Library series, and Orwell wrote an introduction to it. A page proof survives, dated 1948, though Orwell probably wrote the introduction in 1945; see *2957.* The volume was never issued. See Crick, 500.

10.8.39

Foreign & General
1. *Franco assumes more or less full powers of dictator.* [Daily Telegraph]
2. *The King inspects Reserve Fleet of 133 warships.* [Daily Telegraph]
Social
1. *Complaints (not very important) at militia camp in Devon reveal that reservists in large numbers have been called up as instructors.* [Daily Telegraph]
2. *14 C.Os tried by tribunals, not harshly treated but work of national importance insisted on. Questions much as in great war.° No report of C.Os on other than religious-moral grounds. Secretary of S. Wales Miners' Federation on the tribunal.* [Daily Telegraph]
3. *Anti-Hitler jokes in "Eggs".* [1] [Eggs, 8.8.39]
4. *Interior lamps of London buses now fitted with removable blue cowls for use in air-raids.* [Daily Telegraph, 9.8.39]
Party Politics
1. *After 6 weeks of no gov.t, Dutch national gov.t formed of several parties including two social-democrats.* [Daily Telegraph]
2. *Reported that at September conference I.L.P. National Council will advocate* unconditional *affiliation to L.P.* [2] [Daily Telegraph]

1. *Eggs*, the official organ of the Scientific Poultry Breeders' Association, as a weekly founded in 1919. Orwell had been corresponding with the Association about feed for his hens around 26–27 July 1939.
2. See *556, 13.7.39, Party Politics*, for the Labour Party's refusal of conditional affiliation.

11.8.39

Foreign & General
1. *Chinese dollar reaches about 3½d.* [Daily Telegraph]
2. *Twenty Bulgarian MPs. received in Moscow.* [Daily Telegraph]
3. *British-French military delegation arrives Leningrad.* [Daily Telegraph]
Social
1. *Fresh reports of trails of objectors by tribunals do not in any case indicate objection on political lines (normally members of Christadelphian etc. churches).* [Daily Telegraph]
2. *Attack on "the°Link" in "Time & Tide", with implication that it should be suppressed.* [Daily Telegraph]
3. *Again denied that banning of "Time" by Federation of Wholesalers has political motive, though evidently it has.* [Daily Telegraph]
Party Politics
1. *I.L.P. Nat. Council again speaks of unconditional affiliation, but in referring to intentions within L.P. suggests activities which would amount to flatly opposing L.P.'s present line on rearmament etc. & presumably will not be accepted.* [New Leader]
2. *Those present at House of C. reception to Menna Schocat,* [1] *representing League for Jewish-Arab Unity included H. W. Nevinson, Chalmers*

389

Mitchell, Lord Faringdon, Wilson (Cecil), Lansbury, A. Maclaren, M.Ps. [2]
[New Leader]
3. Various arrests in France in connection with anti-war & anti-imperialist activities include Lucien Weitz [3] *& R. Louzon* [4] *(18 months). [New Leader]*

1. Menna Schocat was a pioneer revolutionary in tsarist Russia who suffered imprisonment and exile. She escaped in 1905 and went to Palestine, where she was active in various workers' movements. She insisted on Jewish-Arab workers' unity and championed the cause of Arab peasants. The ILP had proposed to work for the unity of Jewish and Arab masses against British imperialism, in the hope of setting up a workers' state federated with neighbouring Arab states. It also championed the right of persecuted Jewish workers in Europe to enter not only Palestine, but all countries, including Britain and the Dominions.
2. Henry Woodd° Nevinson (1856–1941), prolific author, journalist, and foreign correspondent, was President of the Council for the Defence of Civil Liberties in 1939. Sir Peter Chalmers Mitchell (1864–1945; Kt.,1929), an eminent zoologist, was responsible for rebuilding much of the London Zoo and for the creation of the 'open' zoological garden at Whipsnade. He retired to Málaga, but the civil war forced his return to England. Orwell reviewed his translation of *The Forge,* by Arturo Barea, in *Time and Tide,* 28 June 1941 (see *821*) and in *Horizon,* September 1941 (see *852*). During World War II, Mitchell was Treasurer to the joint committee for Soviet aid. Alexander Gavin Henderson, 2nd Baron Faringdon (1902–1977), a contemporary of Orwell at Eton, was Treasurer of the Committee of Inquiry into Non-Intervention in Spain, 1936; and Treasurer of the National Council for Civil Liberties, 1940– 45. Cecil Henry Wilson (1862–1945) was a Labour M.P., 1922–31, 1935–44. George Lansbury (1859–1940), Leader of the Labour Party, 1931–35, was a pacifist and resigned as leader on that issue. Andrew MacLaren (1883–1975) was an ILP M.P., 1922–23, 1924–31, 1935–45.
3. Lucien Weitz, editor of *Independent News,* published in Paris, was also associated with the journal of Solidaridad Internacional Antifascista, of which Orwell was a sponsor; see *434*. Weitz and a number of others associated with that journal and with the ILP's brother organisation in France, Parti Socialiste Ouvriers et Paysans (see *7.8.39, n. 1*) and its journal, *Juin 36,* were imprisoned as a result of publishing articles exposing clandestine sales by French motor manufacturers to Germany, and antimilitarist tracts.
4. Robert Louzon was imprisoned with Lucien Weitz and others. Of the nine people named in *The New Leader* as being arrested, Orwell picks out these two names presumably because they were known to him personally or by their writings: Weitz in *Independent News,* and Louzon in *La Révolution Prolétarienne* or his book *L'Economie Capitaliste.*

563. Review of *Foreign Correspondent: Twelve British Journalists; In the Margin of History* by L. B. Namier; *Europe Going, Going, Gone!* by Count Ferdinand Czernin

Time and Tide, 12 August 1939

These three rather scrappy books all revolve at varying distances round the same subject. At a moment when Hitler has shoved cricket off the front page and people who hardly know a putsch from a purge are writing books called *Storm Over Blank,* I suppose it is unnecessary to say what that subject is. It is what Lord Castlerosse calls *"the* subject."

Foreign Correspondent consists mostly of "eye stuff," and as it comes from twelve different hands it is of very variable quality. Perhaps the liveliest contributor is Mr. Arthur Koestler, who describes a journey through

Palestine and an unofficial interview with the Mufti of Jerusalem. Mr. Koestler does not and probably would not claim to view the Palestine problem with a completely unbiassed eye (he is pro-Jew and to some extent anti-Arab), but he still writes in the same friendly and sensitive style as in *Spanish Testament*. Mr. Alexander Henderson gives a detailed and pathetic account of life in Prague at the time of the September crisis, and Mr. Karl Robson writes with detachment about Franco's Spain in the early months of 1938. Mr. Douglas Reed's contribution, on the other hand, is merely frivolous and silly, and Mr. Steer spoils anything he has to say about the Emperor of Abyssinia by tiresome efforts to be picturesque. Mr. F. A. Voigt's account of his experiences during the Kapp putsch of 1920 is well worth reading. It brings home to one the nightmare atmosphere of civil war and the impossibility of ever discovering the truth about anything. If one is in the middle of such events as Mr. Voigt is describing (he was in the Ruhr, where the "Reds" seized power for a few days) one knows nothing except that bombs are bursting; if one is at a distance one knows everything, and knows it all wrong. Compare this narrative with some of the others in the book (especially the opening one, where Mr. O. D. Gallagher presents the Chino-Japanese War as a huge joke) and you see the difference between being an eye-witness and merely an I-witness.

Professor Namier does succeed at times in escaping from *the* subject, for his book consists of a series of more or less disconnected essays, about half of which deal with Napoleon and the eighteenth century. Some of them are merely book reviews and were hardly worth reprinting. Perhaps the most interesting section of the book is the section called "Judaica," in which Professor Namier discusses the present state of European Jewry. He is speaking as a Jew, and therefore as a partisan, but he gives every appearance, of knowing his subject, and he makes it quite clear that the position of the Jews, as a racially distinct people, is impossible unless they can have a country of their own. Whether this means that unrestricted immigration into Palestine is desirable seems rather less clear, even on his statement of the case. The first section of the book deals with the present European situation, and towards the end there is a series of essays on von Bülow and on various leading Austrian statesmen of the time of the outbreak of the Great War. Most of the latter were written ten or fifteen years ago, but the earlier ones date from this year or last year, and Professor Namier, for all his knowledge and his independence of approach, does not escape the morass of hatred into which we are all descending. The book ends with some interesting reminiscences of T. E. Lawrence.

Finally, Count Czernin, who begins by trying to laugh at the European situation and ends by finding that it is beyond a joke. He is an Austrian, exiled, of course, and he is the typical decent person who is revolted by totalitarianism without being particularly "left." He thinks that Bolshevism and Fascism are bound to amalgamate in the end, whether by conquest or by mutual agreement:

> The alternative is not, and never can be, Bolshevism or Fascism, but will for ever remain Totalitarianism or Democracy, slavery or liberty. . . . To win, Democracy will have to fight on a clear-cut issue, and that issue can only be: Democracy or Totalitarianism.

If only it were really as simple as that! The earlier part of the book consists largely of this kind of thing:

> The French have Manet and Monet. A Manet is very costly and nearly as beautiful, and monet is French for small change. . . . The Spaniards are wild, have charm, and are unsafe people to leave girls with, particularly if the girl is a blonde, which goes to prove that the Spaniards are gentlemen, etc. etc.

This is described on the dust-jacket as "inimitable wit." As a matter of fact, it is so imitable that *1066 and All That* anticipated it by a good many years. But this is a decent book all the same. Mr. Walter Goetz's numerous illustrations are amusing.

564. To Mrs. Olga Parker

12 August 1939   Typewritten

The Stores   Wallington   Nr. Baldock, HERTS.

Dear Mrs Parker,[1]

I hope you will forgive my very long delay in answering your letter of nearly a month ago, but perhaps you will believe that my time is rather full, as I am struggling with a book[2] which is two months behind time owing to my illness earlier this year. I am glad you liked "Homage to Catalonia". It didn't sell very well, chiefly I expect because by the time it appeared people were getting very tired of books on the Spanish war. As you say, the end of the struggle, after all that suffering that the Spanish people went through, is heartrending. By the time we left, in the middle of 1937, conditions were in many ways not very bad, though certain foodstuffs were running short, but I believe later it was terrible. Robert Williams,[3] whom you may have heard of from Douglas Moyle,[4] was there till nearly the end, and another friend of ours left Barcelona only a few hours before Franco got there, and they said that the people were literally dying of starvation. From Robert Williams I had news of a few of the Spaniards I had known, always that they had been killed.

My recent book[5] has I believe sold fairly well. At any rate it was well reviewed and went into a second editions,° which my books generally don't. Thank you so much for writing.

Yours sincerely
George Orwell

1. Mrs. Olga Parker wrote to Orwell on 15 July 1939 to say how much she had enjoyed *Homage to Catalonia*—though she then qualified her use of 'enjoy.' She had been given the book by Orwell's friend Douglas Moyle, who lived near her in Coventry.

2. *Inside the Whale.*
3. Robert Williams was a Welsh workingman who had married a Spanish girl; see *Homage to Catalonia, CW*, VI, 12. He served in the POUM with Orwell; they joined the 3rd Regiment together; see *CW*, VI, 38. His membership of the POUM led to his serving time in a Spanish jail.
4. Douglas Moyle served with Orwell in Spain; see *408, n. 1.*
5. *Coming Up for Air.*

565. Diary of Events Leading Up to the War

12.8.39

Foreign & General

1. M. G. correspondent reports that German mobilization will be at full strength half way through August & that some attempt to terrorise Poland will be made. War stated to be likeliest issue (as also in yesterday's "Time & Tide"). The striking thing is the perfunctory air with which these statements are made in all papers, as though with an inner certainty that nothing of the kind can happen. [*Manchester Guardian Weekly*, 11.8.39; Orwell incorrectly dates this as 12.8.39]

2. Appearances seem to show that fighting on Manchurian border from Changkufeng[1] incident onwards has been fairly heavy but inconclusive. [*Manchester Guardian Weekly*, 11.8.39; misdated as 12.8.39; *La Révolution Prolétarienne*, undated]

Social

1. Refugee problem stated to be becoming serious in London especially East End. Mosley said to have not greatly increased his following however. [Private]

2. It appears that the P.O. authorities are now able to read a letter, sufficient to determine nature of its contents, without opening it. [Private]

Miscellaneous

1. All my books from the Obelisk Press[2] this morning seized by the police, with warning from Public Prosecutor that I am liable to be prosecuted if importing such things again. They had opened my letter addressed to Obelisk Press[3] evidently at Hitchin. Do not know yet whether because of the address or because my own mail is now scutinised. [No reference]

2. Potato & tomato said to have been successfully crossed in U.S.S.R. [*Smallholder*]

1. On 29 July 1939 some 3,000 Soviet troops with 100 tanks attacked on a four-mile front centred on Changkufeng, about a hundred miles southwest of Vladivostock. They were forced back, losing approximately 400 men to about 120 lost by the Japanese. On 6 August the German and Italian ambassadors in Tokyo intervened to urge moderation by the Japanese to settle the dispute peacefully so the 'Anti-Comintern Triangle' would not become embroiled with Russia (*The Times*, 9 August 1939).
2. Obelisk Press (see *277, n. 3*), in Paris, published books in English for sale on the Continent, some of which British authorities regarded as obscene. Their importation into England was liable to legal proceedings. See Jack Kahane's *Memoirs of a Booklegger* (1939). See also letter to Victor Gollancz, 8 January 1940, *583*.
3. Not traced. See Shelden, 345–47; U.S.: 316–17.

14.8.39

Foreign & General
1. German-Italian "compromise" scheme for Polish problem alleged to have been formulated, in a form that would obviously not be accepted by Poland. [Daily Telegraph]
2. Staff talks in Moscow have begun. [Daily Telegraph]
Social
1. Yesterday's Sunday Express had scare article on the illegal Jewish immigration into Palestine which was in effect anti-Jew propaganda. [Sunday Express, 13.8.39]
2. It appears that the opening of letters to persons connected with leftwing° parties is now so normal as to excite no remark. [E. H.¹]
3. G. K.² claims that the C.P. are so strongly entrenched in the French police & other public services that the gov.t can do nothing against them. [File S.P. 1]
Party Politics
1. According to G. K., membership of the PSOP is now only 4000. [File S.P.1]
2. According to E. H., the Bermondsey anti-war conference was prevented from arriving at anything definite by the action of a few Trotskyists who will have no truck with pacifists & said so so violently as to antagonise the latter. [E. H.]
3. According to E. H., the older members of the I.L.P. are on the whole opposed to affiliation, the newer members in favour, but the only leading I.L.P'er who is uncompromisingly against is C. A. Smith³ [E. H.]

1. Unidentified; possibly someone in the ILP.
2. Probably George Kopp, Orwell's commander in Spain.
3. C. A. Smith was editor of *Controversy*, later *Left Forum* and then *Left*, a socialist monthly dedicated to the realisation of a classless society; see *382, n. 1*. He, with Orwell and others, urged that Rudolf Hess be interrogated at Nuremberg in 1946 regarding an alleged meeting with Trotsky; see *Forward*, 25 February 1946.

17.8.39

Foreign & General
1. Announced that full scheme for national register is now ready.¹ [Daily Telegraph]
Party Politics
1. I.L.P. dissociating itself from P.P.U.'s friendly attitude towards "the° Link." [New Leader, 18.8.39]
2. More evidences° of struggle going on between Negrin & Prieto,² cf. 2.8.39. [File S.P.1 (as 'i')]
3. Speakers at Keir Hardie³ memorial to be: Maxton, Dallas (L.P.E.C.),⁴ Ebby Edwards (T.U.C.), Jas. Barr MP., Duncan Graham MP. [New Leader, 18.8.39]

1. This involved production of identity cards (without photographs for most people), to be

carried at all times. The individual identification numbers are still in use in the 1990s for certain government purposes, although the cards disappeared long since.
2. For Negrín and Prieto, see *560, 2.8.39, n. 3*.
3. James Keir Hardie (1856–1915) was the first Socialist to be elected a Member of Parliament (1892). He led the Labour Party in the House of Commons, 1906–15.
4. Labour Party Executive Committee.

18.8.39

Foreign & General
1. M.G. diplomatic correspondent considers Spain will almost certainly remain neutral in case of war. The new cabinet balances the soldiers fairly evenly against the Falangists. [Manchester Guardian Weekly]
Social
1. Appears now fairly certain that the 4 Chinese alleged terrorists will be handed over to Japanese, in spite of plea in London for writ of habeas corpus. [1]
[Manchester Guardian Weekly]
2. Details of national register now worked out, but announced that actual registration will not take place except on outbreak of war or possibly at 1941 census. [Manchester Guardian Weekly]
3. Spanish immigration into Mexico said to be proving very successful. [File S.P.1]

1. See *558, 24.7.39, n. 1*. It was reported on 12 August that the government had decided that the four Chinese would be handed over to be tried by a Japanese-controlled court. It had been convinced by new evidence the Japanese had produced in Tokyo, after having refused to make it available in Tientsin. This entry and several thereafter are numbered in small roman numerals, as is 'S.P. 1' on occasion. These variations are not here recorded.

19.8.39

Foreign & General
1. Germans are buying heavily in copper & rubber for immediate delivery, & price of rubber rising rapidly. [Daily Telegraph]
2. Indications that difference of some kind has arisen in Moscow staff talks (stated by Tass agency not to be connected with Far East). [Daily Telegraph]
3. Stated more or less officially in Madrid that Spain will remain neutral. [No reference]
Social
1. Inquiries into the activities of the Bund [1] in U.S.A., rather as into those of "the ° Link" here. Evident that i all these associations have been used for Nazi propaganda & ii. that attempts will be progressively made to break down cultural relations between Germany & the democracies. [Daily Telegraph]
2. The police are getting wise to the marriage of convenience (as a way of obtaining Brit. nationality for German women) & are going to recommend deportation in these cases. [Daily Telegraph]
3. Number of I.R.A. suspects expelled up to date is about 90. [Daily Telegraph]
4. Numbers of militiamen said to have been found to be completely illiterate. [News Chronicle]

Miscellaneous
1. *Ministry of Agric. returns for first ½ of 1939 indicate following developments: total acreage under crops & grass about 24¾ mill., decrease of about 80,000 acres, but arable land increased by about 50,000 acres & permanent grass decreased by 130,000 acres. (Change said to have taken place before gov.t's subsidy for ploughing-up took effect.)*
Area under wheat decreased by 150,000 acres, potatoes by about 20,000 acres, peas & cabbages also decreased, field beans increased & oats & barley increased by 56,000 & 25,000 acres resp.
Most stock increased largely, except pigs & work horses, which decreased by about 50,000 & 14,000 resp. Fowls increased by 200,000 head. [Smallholder]

1. The German-American Bund was a Nazi front organization. Its leader, Fritz Kuhn, was imprisoned later in the year, having been found guilty in New York of embezzling the association's funds.

20.8.39

Foreign & General
1. *Lloyd George[1] predicts the Danzig crisis coming to a head very shortly. Also hints (S. Express puts this in leaded type) that if the Poles deliberately back down we are under no obligation to act. [Sunday Express]*
2. *Tokyo conversations suspended, owing to G. Britain declaring necessity of consulting other nations on Chinese currency question. [Sunday Times]*
Social
1. *Row over Spender's articles[2] still reverberating in Sunday Times. [Sunday Times]*
Party Politics
1. *Peter Howard[3] speaks of general election more or less as a certainty & predicts that increased old age pensions will be one of the gov.t's bribes. [Sunday Express]*
2. *In case of general election happening this autumn, a bill will be passed to keep the existing gov.t in being during the election period,[4] owing to the crisis. [Sunday Times]*

1. Former Prime Minister David Lloyd George; see, 469, n. 3.
2. See 556, 12.7.39, n. 2.
3. See 562, 6.8.39, n. 2.
4. Orwell originally wrote 'crisis' for 'period.'

21.8.39

Foreign & General
1. *Fresh enquiries by American I.P.O.[1] indicates that number of people believing U.S.A. would be involved in world war has greatly increased (to about 75%). Number thinking U.S.A. would send troops to Europe still only 25%. [Daily Telegraph]*
2. *Japanese preparing blockade of Hong Kong, obviously in order to put pressure on London over the silver & currency question. [Daily Telegraph]*
3. *£10 m. 2 year trade agreement signed between Germany & U.S.S.R. for*

exchange of German manufactured goods versus Russian raw materials. [Daily Telegraph]
4. Strategic bridge from Danzig into E. Prussia completed. [Daily Telegraph]
Social
1. Railway strike for 50/– minimum wage likely within the next week or two. [Daily Telegraph]
2. Stated that England can now supply herself with optical glass in case of war. [Daily Telegraph]

1. American Institute of Public Opinion, which conducted polls popularly known as Gallup polls, after its founder, statistician George Gallup (1901–1984), beginning in 1935.

22.8.39
Foreign & General
1. Officially stated in Berlin that Ribbentropp°[1] flies to Moscow tomorrow to sign non-agression° pact with U.S.S.R. News later confirmed from Moscow by Tass Agency, in a way that seems to make it clear that pact will go through. Little comment in any of the papers, the news having evidently arrived in the small hours of this morning & the Russian confirmation only in time for the stop press. Reported suggestion from Washington that it may be a Russian manoeuvre (ie. to bring England & France to heel) but everyone else seems to take it at face-value. Shares on the whole have dropped. Germans still buying shellac etc. heavily. The military talks were still proceeding yesterday. [Daily Telegraph; Daily Mail; News Chronicle; Daily Mirror]
Social
1. Illegal radio, somewhat on the lines of German Freiheit movement's radio,[2] has been broadcasting anti-conscription propaganda. Secretary of P.P.U. (Rowntree?)* denies knowledge but does not dissociate himself from the talks. P.O. engineers state that they have tracked down location of radio to within a few houses & will soon run it to earth. Indication is that it takes at least some days to locate an illegal radio. [Daily Telegraph]
*Palmer [Orwell's note].
Party Politics
1. Letchworth "Citizen"[3] reprints long article on Sir A. Wilson[4] from Sunday Pictorial with evident approval. [Letchworth Citizen, no date]
2. Soc. Corresp. prints long statement on war issue by Comm. Opp.[5] setting forth hopelessly complicated programme of supporting anti-Fascist war & at same time disillusioning the working class etc., etc. But makes statement (probably true as Thalheimer[6] & others would have knowledge of Russian conditions of at any rate a few years ago) that tho' the Red Army is now more or less as other armies, the reserves still receive more or less the training of a revolutionary army. Also violent attack on I.L.P. signed by 3 sets of initials one Audrey Brockway's,[7] launching slogan of 4th International.[8] [Socialist Correspondence]

1. Joachim von Ribbentrop (1893–1946) was German Minister of Foreign Affairs, 1938–45. He negotiated the Russo-German Non-Aggression Pact in 1939 with Molotov (see 28.8.39, n. 4). He was hanged as a war criminal after being found guilty by the International Military Tribunal at Nuremberg.

2. See *554, 2.7.39, n. 2*. Three months after note above, 'German Freedom Radio' was reported to be still broadcasting appeals to Germans to liberate themselves from Hitler's régime.
3. *The Letchworth Citizen* was Orwell's local paper at Wallington.
4. See *562, 6.8.39, n. 4*.
5. International Communist Opposition, headquartered in Paris. The decline of the ICO was the subject of the July Supplement of *Socialist Correspondence*.
6. August Thalheimer was one of the leaders of the International Communist Opposition, and was described in *The New Leader*, 20 August 1937 (to which issue he contributed an article, 'A Call for Revolutionary Socialist Unity'), as 'one of the authors of the thesis which formed the basis of the Communist International at its establishment. For many years he was the leader of the Communist Party in Germany, but was deposed from that position by the C. I. Executive because he opposed its disastrous policy of dividing the Trade Union Movement by the formation of rival Red Trade Unions.' *The New Leader* welcomed the chance to publish his views 'because it indicates that there is scope for close co-operation between the parties (including the I.L.P.) attached to the International Bureau for Revolutionary Socialist Unity and the Communist International Opposition.'
7. Audrey Brockway was Secretary to the ILP Guild of Youth, and was married to Jim Wood, a member of the Trotskyist group in the ILP; see *553, n. 1*.
8. The Fourth International was formed in 1938 by followers of Trotsky. They hoped the impending war would create conditions favourable for world revolution. It was reported that as Trotsky lay dying in Mexico City in 1940, victim of an assassin, he said 'I am sure of victory of the Fourth International. Go forward!'

23.8.39

Foreign & General
1. Parliament meeting tomorrow. Emergency Powers Act will be passed. Certain classes of reservists called up. The King returning to London. Reservists being called up in France & Germany. Legislation to be hurried through in Parliament to prevent further buying of nickle,° copper etc. by Germany. Almost all shares have dropped, no doubt in anticipation of this. World press comments as quoted by D. Tel. are very non-committal but the Axis powers evidently greatly pleased by the Russian démarche. [Daily Telegraph]
Social
1. Railway strike now arranged to begin in a few days' time. [Daily Telegraph]
Party Politics
1. Communist Party membership stated as 17,000, * which is increase of 2000 over last year. C.P. again applying for application to L.P.[1] [Daily Telegraph] *40% of this in London, & membership in industrial areas negligible (C.P. pamphlet) [Orwell's note].

1. Labour Party.

24.8.39

Foreign & General
1. Russo-German Pact signed. Terms given in Berlin (File War etc).[1] suggest close pact & no "escape" clause. This evening's radio news gives confirmation in Moscow in same terms. Official statement from Moscow that "enemies of both countries" have tried to drive Russia & Germany into enmity. Brit. Ambassador calls on Hitler & is told no action of ours can influence German decision. Japanese opinion evidently seriously angered by

what amounts to German desertion of anti-Comintern pact, & Spanish (Franco) opinion evidently similarly affected. Rumania said to have declared neutrality. Chamberlain's speech as reported on wireless very strong & hardly seems to allow loophole for escape from aiding Poles.

E. on visiting W.O.[2] today derived impression that war is almost certain. Police arrived this morning to arrange for billeting of soldiers. Some people (foreigners) arrived in afternoon looking for rooms—the second lot in 3 days. In spite of careful listening, impossible in pubs etc. to overhear any spontaneous comment or sign of slightest interest in the situation, in spite of fact that almost everyone when questioned believes it will be war. [The Times; Daily Telegraph; News Chronicle; Manchester Guardian; Daily Express; Daily Herald; Daily Mail; London Evening News]

Social

1. Emergency Powers Act passed evidently without much trouble. Contains clauses allowing preventive arrest, search without warrant & trial in camera. But not industrial conscription as yet. [Wireless 6 pm][3]

2. Moscow airport was decorated with swastikas for Ribbentrop's arrival. M. Guardian adds that they were screened so as to hide them from the rest of Moscow. [Manchester Guardian]

Party Politics

1. C.P. putting good face on Russo-German pact which is declared to be move for peace. Signature of Anglo-Soviet pact demanded as before. D. Worker does not print terms of pact but reprints portions of an earlier Russo-Polish pact containing an "escape" clause, in order to convey impression that this pact must contain the same. [Daily Worker]

2. In today's debate Sinclair & Greenwood[4] spoke strongly in support of Gov.t. Mander[5] spoke demanding "strengthening of Cabinet". Maxton[6] declared I.L.P. would not support Gov.t in war. [Wireless 6 pm]

1. Presumably a file Orwell kept on this subject. Possibly related to his reference 'File S.P. 1.'
2. Eileen was working at the War Office in the Censorship Department; see 2831, final section.
3. National news was broadcast by BBC at 6:00 P.M.
4. Archibald Sinclair; see 554, 2.7.39, n. 3. Arthur Greenwood (1880–1954) was a Labour M.P., 1922–31, 1932–54; Deputy Leader of the party, 1935; Secretary to the party research department, 1920–43. His opposition to totalitarian regimes led to his being singled out for attack by Hitler in 1938.
5. Geoffrey Mander; see 562, 4.8.39, n. 3.
6. James Maxton; see 385, n. 1.

28.8.39

[No section headings]

Have been travelling[1] etc. during the past days & therefore unable to keep up the diary in the ordinary way.

The main developments have been as follow:

Hitler has proposed some or other kind of plan which was flown across by N. Henderson[2] & has been discussed at several Cabinet meetings including one yesterday (Sunday) afternoon, but no statement has been made by the gov.t as to the Nature° of Hitler's communication. H. is to fly back today with the Brit. gov.t's reply, but even so there is no sure indication that either H.'s[3] proposal or the gov.t's reply will be communicated to the public. Various papers have published statements, all of which are officially declared to be unfounded. No clear indication of the meaning of the Russian-German pact as yet. Papers of left tendency continue to suggest that it does not amount to very much, but it seems to be generally taken for granted that Russia will supply Germany with raw materials, & possibly that there has been a large-scale bargain which amounts to handing Europe over to Germany & Asia to Russia. Molotov[4] is to make an announcement shortly. It is clear that the Russian explanation will be, at any rate at first, that the British were playing double & did not really wish for the Anglo-French-Russian pact. Public opinion in U.S.S.R. said to be still somewhat taken aback by the change of front, & ditto left wing opinion in the West. Left wing papers continue to blame Chamberlain while making some attempt to exhonorate° Stalin, but are clearly dismayed. In France there has evidently been a swing of opinion against the Communist Party, from which there are said to be large-scale resignations (D. Tel. repeating Reuter). Humanité has been temporarily suspended. The Anglo-French military mission is already returning.

Germany & Poland now more or less fully mobilised. France has called up several more classes of reservists & is said to have 4,000,000* men under arms. No more reservists yet called up in Britain. Admiralty has taken over control of all shipping. Sale of foreign shares is being controlled by gov.t. Main buildings in London being sandbagged. Practice evacuation of children in evacuation areas today. Little or no excitement in London. For the last day or two it is possible to overhear people in the street discussing the situation, but only in terms of "is there going to be war?" Yesterday afternoon during the Cabinet meeting about 1000 people in Downing St., mostly rubbernecks, & no banners etc. No demonstrations in Hyde Park. The only political speaker there a Troskyist[5] who was getting a good hearing (about 200 people).† No mass-exodus from the railway stations, but immense quantities of luggage waiting to leave, by the look of it the luggage of fairly well-to-do people.

L.M.[6] is of opinion that if we do not involve Italy in the war she will sit tight until we are in difficulties & have alienated the smaller European countries & will then come in on the German side. He is of the opinion that virtually the whole of the wealthy class are entirely treacherous & quite ready to do a deal with Germany, either without war or after a short sham war, which could be presented as an honourable peace, & would allow for the imposition of fascism in England.‡ Spain is at present making declarations of neutrality, & Turkey still declaring she will stand by France & England.

The price of gold has risen to record heights (about 155/– per ounce).[7] Price of wheat still extremely low (price in wholesale markets recently quoted at less than 4/– the cwt.)

P.P.U. evidently completely quiescent & not intending to do anything.

---

* Today (29.8.39) given as 3,000,000 [Orwell's note].

† See 31.8.39 (Party politics) [Orwell's note].

‡ NB. That L. M. says he derived this opinion from Geoffrey Pike, a Communist [Orwell's note; Myers's assessment of Italy's intentions proved accurate].

I.L.P. has issued official declaration that they will not support the government in war.

The Emergency Powers Act passed by over 400 votes to 4. Dissentients were Maxton (the other 2 I.L.P. MPs acted as tellers), Lansbury, Cecil Wilson & an Independent.[8] Gallacher abstained.[9] Some of the extremists, eg. Ellen Wilkinson[10] & A. Bevan,[11] voted for the bill.

[Daily Telegraph; News Chronicle; Daily Mirror; Daily Express; New Statesman; Sunday Times; Observer; Reynolds's News°; Empire News; no dates given][12]

1. On 24 August Orwell travelled to Ringwood in Hampshire, where he stayed with novelist L. H. Myers; see *449, headnote*. He was there until 31 August at least. On 3 September he was in Greenwich, where the O'Shaugnessys lived. It is not possible to be sure where he was on 1 and 2 September.
2. Sir Neville Henderson (1882–1942) was British Ambassador in Berlin, 1937–39. See his *Failure of a Mission* (1940).
3. Hitler's.
4. Vyacheslav Molotov (1890–1986) was President of the USSR's Council of People's Commisars, 1930–41, and Commissar of Foreign Affairs, 1939–49, 1953–56. He negotiated the Russo-German Non-Aggression Pact in August 1939, with Ribbentrop. He was later a delegate to the United Nations General Assembly.
5. Orwell originally wrote 'Communist.'
6. This must be L. H. Myers, with whom Orwell was staying. Myers was a Communist, as was the source of his information. See G. H. Bantock, *L. H. Myers*, 152.
7. In January 1939 the price of gold was 150s 5d (£7.52). By June it had dropped to 148s 6d. In January 1940 it was 168s (£8.40). An official price was in effect from June 1945 (172s 3d) until the free market reopened in March 1954, when the price was 248s (£12.40); see R.L. Bidwell, *Currency Conversion Tables* (1970). There were $4.63 to the pound in January 1939; from January 1940 to September 1949 the rate was $4.03. The pound was then devalued and was worth about $2.80 until 1967.
8. James Maxton; see *385, n. 1*; George Lansbury and Cecil Wilson; see *562, 11.8.39, n. 2*.
9. William Gallacher; see *560, 27.7.39, n. 2*.
10. Ellen Wilkinson was a Labour M.P.; see *422, n. 3*.
11. Aneurin (Nye) Bevan (1897–1960), a collier from Tredegar, was a Labour M.P. representing the Ebbw Vale constituency, South Wales, from 1927 until his death. An impassioned orator, he was the idol of much of the left and was disliked, even feared, by many Conservatives. As Minister of Health, 1945–50, he was responsible for the creation of the National Health Service. He resigned from the second post-war Labour government in 1951 in disagreement over disarmament, and was defeated as leader of the party in 1955. He was a director of *Tribune* when Orwell wrote for that journal, and allowed Orwell complete freedom to say what he wished even against current party policy. His *In Place of Fear* (1952) sets out his philosophy. See also *1064, n. 3*.
12. Orwell listed the newspapers that were his sources between the penultimate and final paragraphs.

29.8.39

Foreign & General

1. N. Henderson has returned to Berlin with Brit. gov.t's reply & Parliament meets this afternoon when presumably the affair will be elucidated.
2. E. P. Act[1] coming into force. Admiralty has not only assumed control of shipping but ordered all British shipping out of the Mediterranean & the Baltic.

3. Practice evacuation of school children said to have gone off successfully. Children to stand by in schools though this is not term time.
4. Japanese Cabinet has resigned as result of Russo-German pact. Evident that Japanese policy will now become pro-British.
[Items 1, 2, 3, and 4 are bracketed and next to them *The Times, News Chronicle*—both 29.8.39—and *Bournemouth Echo*,[2] 28.9.39; separate: *Daily Telegraph*, 29.8.39; and Radio, no date]

Social

1. Private motorists for some days past have been buying up large quantities of petrol. [No reference]

Party Politics

1. Labour Party still declaring against accepting office. Said that in case of war a Labour representative would accept office but only on terms defined by the party & so stringent as to be probably unacceptable to the Nat. gov.t. [*News Chronicle*]

Miscellaneous

1. It appears from reliable private information that Sir O. Mosley is a masochist of the extreme type in his sexual life. [Private]

1. Emergency Powers Act; see *28.8.39*, last paragraph.
2. Ringwood, where Orwell was staying with L. H. Myers, is near Bournemouth.

<u>30.8.39</u>

Foreign & General

1. Virtually no news. Communications are passing to & fro but the Cabinet are revealing nothing. Parliament adjurned° for a week. King of the Belgians offering to mediate, which Poles have accepted & Germans express themselves sympathetic to, but meanwhile troop movements & frontier outrages continue. Rumania is fortifying her Russian frontier. 2-300,000 Russian troops said to be moving to Western frontier.
Soviet Parliament will not ratify the pact till the end of the week, obviously in order to give a different interpretation to it according to the then circumstances. If necessary it is still open to them to refuse ratification which could be used as demonstration of Soviet democracy.
Harold Nicolson[1] claims that U.S.S.R. cannot supply Germany with much oil in case of war. Third-hand information via the Stock Exchange★ indicates that 3 days back the Cabinet were confident Hitler could not move. On the other hand L. M. says that a few weeks back W. Churchill expressed very pessimistic views to him, based on talks with German generals. [*The Times; News Chronicle; Daily Mirror;* undated, Radio; ★Private]

Social

1. Adjurnment° of Parliament for a week passed without a division.[2] [*The Times*]

1. Harold Nicolson (1886–1968; Kt., 1953), diplomat (to 1929), biographer, and novelist, was an M.P., 1935–45. His *Diaries and Letters* (edited by his son Nigel Nicolson, 3 vols., 1966–68) give insight into the political life of the thirties. In *English History 1914–1945*, A. J. P. Taylor records the wild scene that followed Chamberlain's announcement in the House on 28

September 1938 that Hitler had agreed to a four-power conference at Munich: 'Members rose to their feet, cheering and sobbing. Attlee [the Labour leader], Sinclair the Liberal leader, and Maxton of the I.L.P. blessed Chamberlain's mission. Only Gallacher, the Communist, spoke harshly against it.' In a footnote he asks, 'Who remained seated?' Certainly Gallacher and, quoting R. W. Seton-Watson, he adds Churchill, Eden, and Amery. Another source, J. W. Wheeler-Bennett, is quoted as saying that 'Harold Nicolson, despite the threats of those surrounding him, remained seated.' Taylor says that Nicolson remembered only being rebuked the next day by a Conservative M.P. for not rising. Nicolson was a National Labour member of the government. (Revised Pelican edition, 1970, 525.)

2. See *560, 30.7.39, Foreign & General, 1*, for anticipation of adjournment despite the crisis.

566. European Contract for *Coming Up for Air*

31 August 1939

Orwell signed a contract with Albatross Verlag G.m.b.H. for the publication of *Coming Up for Air* by Albatross for distribution on the continent of Europe on 31 August 1939. The contract is now at the Harry Ransom Humanities Research Center, University of Texas at Austin. See *561, n. 1* and *581, n. 3*.

567. Diary of Events Leading Up to the War

31.8.39

Foreign & General
1. No definite news. Poland has called up more reserves but this does not yet amount to full mobilisation. German occupation of Slovakia continues & 300,000 men said to be now at strategic points on Polish frontier. Hitler has set up inner cabinet of 6 not including Ribbentrop.
16,000 children already evacuated from Paris. Evacuation of London children thought to be likely before long. No news one way or the other about ratification of Russo-German pact. Such slight indications as exist suggest pact will be ratified. German persecution of Jews said to be slightly diminished, anti-German film withdrawn from Soviet pavilion at New York world fair°. Voroshilov[1] reported as stating that U.S.S.R. would supply Poland with arms. [Daily Telegraph; News Chronicle; Daily Mirror]
Social
1. Sir J. Anderson[2] requests the public not to buy extra stores of food & to conserve those they have, & states that there is no food shortage. [Daily Telegraph]
2. A.E.U.[3] is now agreeing to dilution of labour. [Daily Telegraph]
Party Politics
1. E's report of speeches in Hyde Park suggest that Communist Party are taking more left wing line but not anxious to thrash out question of Russo-German pact. Speaker (Ted Bramley) claimed that MPs who voted against E. P. Act were Gallacher, Wilkinson & A. Bevan & 1 other.[4] (Actually Maxton, Lansbury, C. Wilson & 1 other). [Private]

1. Kliment Voroshilov (1881–1969), Marshal of the Soviet Union, was People's Commissar for

Defence, 1925–40, and President of the USSR, 1953–60. He was one of those responsible for organising the defence of Leningrad during the 900-day siege, September 1941–January 1944. From 1953 to 1960 he was President of the Soviet Union.

2. John Anderson (1882–1958; Viscount, 1952) was an M.P. representing Scottish universities, 1938–50. Appointed Lord Privy Seal by Chamberlain in November 1938, with special responsibility for manpower and civil defence, he was responsible for what came to be called the 'Anderson' air-raid shelter; see *850, n. 8*. At the outbreak of war, he was made Home Secretary and Minister of Home Security; later, Lord President of the Council, 1940–43, and Chancellor of the Exchequer, 1943–45. In *The Lion and the Unicorn*, Orwell remarked that it took 'the unnecessary suffering of scores of thousands of people in the East End [sheltering in Andersons] to get rid or partially rid of Sir John Anderson'; see *763, II, ii*. The shelters could be extremely uncomfortable and were prone to flooding. On 3 September 1940 Churchill wrote to Anderson to say that 'a great effort should be made to help people to drain their Anderson shelters, which reflect so much credit on your name . . .' (*The Second World War*, I, 313; U.S.: *Their Finest Hour*, 355).

3. Amalgamated Engineering Union.

4. See *565, 28.8.39, last paragraph*.

<u>1.9.39</u>
Invasion of Poland began this morning. Warsaw bombed. General mobilisation proclaimed in England, ditto in France plus martial law. [Radio]
<u>Foreign & General</u>
1. Hitler's terms to Poland boil down to return of Danzig & plebiscite in the corridor,[1] to be held 1 year hence & based on 1918 census. There is some hanky panky about time the terms were presented, & as they were to be answered by night of 30.8.39.,[2] H.[3] claims that they are already refused. [*Daily Telegraph*]
2. Naval reservists and rest of army and R.A.F. reservists called up. Evacuation of children etc. begins today, involving 3 m. people & expected to take 3 days. [Radio; undated]
3. Russo-German pact ratified. Russian armed forces to be further increased. Voroshilov's speech taken as meaning that Russo-German alliance is not contemplated. [*Daily Express*]
4. Berlin report states Russian military mission is expected to arrive there shortly. [*Daily Telegraph*]

1. The Polish Corridor, which gave Poland an outlet to the Baltic Sea between 1919 and 1939; it separated East Prussia from the rest of Germany and, with Danzig, was a source of friction and an ostensible cause of the outbreak of war.
2. Orwell wrote the date as 30.9.39 by mistake.
3. Hitler.

568. 'Democracy in the British Army'
The Left Forum, September 1939

When the Duke of Wellington described the British army as "the scum of the earth, enlisted for drink," he was probably speaking no more than the truth. But what is significant is that his opinion would have been echoed by any non-military Englishman for nearly a hundred years subsequently.

The French Revolution and the new conception of "national" war changed the character of most Continental armies, but England was in the exceptional position of being immune from invasion and of being governed during most of the nineteenth century by non-military bourgeoisie. Consequently its army remained, as before, a small professional force more or less cut off from the rest of the nation. The war-scare of the sixties produced the Volunteers, later to develop into the Territorials, but it was not till a few years before the Great War that there was serious talk of universal service. Until the late nineteenth century the total number of white troops, even in war-time, never reached a quarter of a million men, and it is probable that every great British land battle between Blenheim and Loos was fought mainly by foreign soldiers.

In the nineteenth century the British common soldier was usually a farm labourer or slum proletarian who had been driven into the army by brute starvation. He enlisted for a period of at least seven years—sometimes as much as twenty-one years—and he was inured to a barrack life of endless drilling, rigid and stupid discipline, and degrading physical punishments. It was virtually impossible for him to marry, and even after the extension of the franchise he lacked the right to vote. In Indian garrison towns he could kick the "niggers" with impunity, but at home he was hated or looked down upon by the ordinary population, except in wartime, when for brief periods he was discovered to be a hero. Obviously such a man had severed his links with his own class. He was essentially a mercenary, and his self-respect depended on his conception of himself not as a worker or a citizen but simply as a fighting animal.

Since the war the conditions of army life have improved and the conception of discipline has grown more intelligent, but the British army has retained its special characteristics—small size, voluntary enlistment, long service and emphasis on regimental loyalty. Every regiment has its own name (not merely a number, as in most armies), its history and relics, its special customs, traditions, etc., etc., thanks to which the whole army is honeycombed with snobberies which are almost unbelievable unless one has seen them at close quarters. Between the officers of a "smart" regiment and those of an ordinary infantry regiment, or still more a regiment of the Indian Army, there is a degree of jealousy almost amounting to a class difference. And there is no question that the long-term private soldier often identifies with his own regiment almost as closely as the officer does. The effect is to make the narrow "non-political" outlook of the mercenary come more easily to him. In addition, the fact that the British Army is rather heavily officered probably diminishes class friction and thus makes the lower ranks less accessible to "subversive" ideas.

But the thing which above all else forces a reactionary viewpoint on the common soldier is his service in overseas garrisons. An infantry regiment is usually quartered abroad for eighteen years consecutively, moving from place to place every four or five years, so that many soldiers serve their entire term in India, Africa, China, etc. They are only there to hold down a hostile population and the fact is brought home to them in unmistakable ways.

Relations with the "natives" are almost invariably bad, and the soldiers—not so much the officers as the men—are the obvious targets for anti-British feeling. Naturally they retaliate, and as a rule they develop an attitude towards the "niggers" which is far more brutal than that of the officials or business men. In Burma I was constantly struck by the fact that the common soldiers were the best-hated section of the white community, and, judged simply by their behaviour, they certainly deserved to be. Even as near home as Gibraltar they walk the streets with a swaggering air which is directed at the Spanish "natives." And in practice some such attitude is absolutely necessary; you could not hold down a subject empire with troops infected by notions of class-solidarity. Most of the dirty work of the French empire, for instance, is done not by French conscripts but by illiterate negroes and by the Foreign Legion, a corps of pure mercenaries.

To sum up: in spite of the technical advances which do not allow the professional officer to be quite such an idiot as he used to be, and in spite of the fact that the common soldier is now treated a little more like a human being, the British army remains essentially the same machine as it was fifty years ago. A little while back any Socialists would have admitted this without argument. But we happen to be at a moment when the rise of Hitler has scared the official leaders of the Left into an attitude not far removed from jingoism. Large numbers of Left-wing publicists are almost openly agitating for war. Without discussing this subject at length, it can be pointed out that a Left-wing party which, within a capitalist society, becomes a war party, has already thrown up the sponge, because it is demanding a policy which can only be carried out by its opponents. The Labour leaders are intermittently aware of this—witness their shufflings on the subject of conscription. Hence, in among the cries of "Firm front!" "British prestige!" etc., there mingles a quite contradictory line of talk. It is to the effect that "this time" things are going to be "different." Militarisation is not going to mean militarisation. Colonel Blimp is no longer Colonel Blimp. And in the more soft-boiled Left-wing papers a phrase is bandied to and fro—"democratising the army." It is worth considering what it implies.

"Democratising" an army, if it means anything, means doing away with the predominance of a single class and introducing a less mechanical form of discipline. In the British army this would mean an entire reconstruction which would rob the army of efficiency for five or ten years. Such a process is only doubtfully possible while the British Empire exists, and quite unthinkable while the simultaneous aim is to "stop Hitler." What will actually happen during the next couple of years, war or no war, is that the armed forces will be greatly expanded, but the new units will take their colour from the existing professional army. As in the Great War, it will be the same army, only bigger. Poorer sections of the middle-class will be drawn on for the supply of officers, but the professional military caste will retain its grip. As for the new Militias, it is probably quite a mistake to imagine that they are the nucleus of a "democratic army" in which all classes will start from scratch. It is fairly safe to prophesy that even if there is no class-favouritism (as there will be, presumably), Militiamen of bourgeois origin will tend to be promoted first. Hore-Belisha and others have already hinted as much in a number of speeches. A fact not always appreciated by Socialists is that in England the whole of the bourgeoisie is to some extent militarised. Nearly every boy who has been to a public school has passed through the O.T.C. (theoretically voluntary but in practice compulsory), and though this training is done between the ages of 13 and 18, it ought not to be despised. In effect the Militiaman with an O.T.C. training behind him will start with several months' advantage of the others. In any case the Military Training Act is only an experiment, aimed partly at impressing opinion abroad and partly at accustoming the English people to the idea of conscription. Once the novelty has worn off some method will be devised of keeping proletarians out of positions of command.

It is probable that the nature of modern war has made "democratic army" a contradiction in terms. The French army, for instance, based on universal service, is hardly more democratic than the British. It is just as much dominated by the professional officer and the long-service N.C.O., and the French officer is probably rather more "Prussian" in outlook than his British equivalent. The Spanish Government militias during the first six months of war—the first year, in Catalonia—were a genuinely democratic army, but they were also a very primitive type of army, capable only of defensive actions. In that particular case a defensive strategy, coupled with propaganda, would probably have had a better chance of victory than the methods casually adopted. But if you want military efficiency in the ordinary sense, there is no escaping from the professional soldier, and so long as the professional soldier is in control he will see to it that the army is not democratised. And what is true within the armed forces is true of the nation as a whole; every increase in the strength of the military machine means more power for the forces of reaction. It is possible that some of our Left-wing jingoes are acting with their eyes open. If they are, they must be aware that the *News-Chronicle* version of "defence of democracy" leads directly *away* from democracy, even in the narrow nineteenth-century sense of political liberty, independence of the trade unions and freedom of speech and the press.

569. Review of *Best-Sellers* by George Stevens and Stanley Unwin

The Adelphi, September 1939

This book, jointly written by one publisher and two persons connected with the publishing trade (Mr. Frank Swinnerton contributes the third essay but for some reason is not mentioned on the title page) sets out to discover whether best-sellers are born or made. Needless to say there is no damned nonsense about the *merits* of the books under discussion. It is simply a question of why this or that book "catches on", and the conclusions are largely negative. They could hardly be otherwise, for the simple reason that anyone who knew what makes best-sellers would be producing them as fast as he could, not telling other people how to do it.

Also, there is no discussion of the one thing that is in the slightest degree interesting about most best-sellers, and that is the time-factor. For instance, it is of some interest, and probably tells one something about the psychological after-effects of war, that *Tarzan of the Apes* and *If Winter Comes* both swamped the market round about 1920. What our three authors are chiefly concerned with, however, is to drive home the fact that advertising will not help a book which is not selling already. This piece of information is aimed chiefly at novelists, who, it appears, spend all their spare time in writing to their publishers and clamouring for more and bigger advertisements. On the other hand, it seems that a good deal can be done by wire-pulling and "prepublication build-up", of which this is a fair sample:

> "*Elizabeth and Essex* had been adroitly sampled by serialization of 28,000 words in the *Ladies' Home Journal*. When the publishers submitted the MS. to the editors a phrase popped into the conversation: 'The love life of the Virgin Queen'. This *motif* helped to put the sale over, and, wrapped in delicately suggestive phrases, became the 'angle' on the book".

All three authors insist that advertising does not sell books. Mr. Swinnerton says it several times, always in italics. Why, then, do publishers go on advertising? None of the three mentions the real reason, though Mr. Swinnerton comes somewhere near to hinting at it:

> "It may be that those papers which devote a certain amount of space to book reviews need some proof other than their continued circulation that it is worth while to continue to devote this amount of space to the reviewing of books".

Put in plain English, this means that if a publisher doesn't advertise, his books don't get reviewed. He pays so much an inch for his advertisement-space, but the real advertisement appears a little to the right or left of it and is called a review. Here is a case that came to my own knowledge. A small publisher who specialised in theological works suddenly decided to publish a novel which he believed to be of exceptional merit. (So far as I know it was a mediocre novel but no worse than nine-tenths of those that get published.) He spent a great deal of money on it, prepared special displays, etc., etc. A month later he told me in great distress that the novel had received exactly *four* reviews. Only one of them was of more than a few lines, and this one was in a motoring paper which had seized the opportunity to point out that the part of the country described in the novel would be a delightful spot for a motoring tour. The publisher happened to be outside the usual gang; he was no source of revenue to the big papers of the book-racket, and so they had simply ignored him.

Of course the thing works both ways. If a publisher fails to get good reviews he will stop advertising, and it is this simple fact which accounts for the awful mush that fills the columns of the Sunday papers. It is now quite a common practice for the editors of literary papers to send books out with a message stating, practically in those words, that they are to be either praised or sent back. Seeing that most book reviewers are people to whom a guinea means a good deal, the effects of this kind of thing hardly need pointing out.

Some day somebody will write a book exposing the book racket. For obvious reasons it will have to be circulated in manuscript. Meanwhile the fact that three people in the publishing trade can write a book on the commercial side of publishing, quite frankly treating books as commodities like soap or cheese, and at the same time barely even hint that reviews are also bought and sold, is an interesting sidelight on Anglo-American hypocrisy.

570. Diary of Events Leading Up to the War

3.9.39 (Greenwich).
Have again been travelling etc. Shall close this diary today, & it will as it stands serve as a diary of events leading up to the war.
We have apparently been in a state of war since 11 am. this morning. No reply was received from the German gov.t to the demand to evacuate Polish territory. The Italian gov.t made some kind of last-minute appeal for a conference to settle differences peacefully, which made some of the papers as late as this morning show a faint doubt as to whether war would actually break out. Daladier made grateful reference to the "noble effort" of Italy which may be taken as meaning that Italy's neutrality is to be respected.
No definite news yet as to what military operations are actually taking place. The Germans have taken Danzig & are attacking the corridor from 4 points north & south. Otherwise only the usual claims & counterclaims about air-raids, number of aeroplanes shot down etc. From reports in Sunday Express & elsewhere it seems clear that the first attempted raid on Warsaw failed to get as far as the town itself. It is rumoured that there is already a British force in France. Bodies of troops with full kits constantly leaving from Waterloo, but not in enormous numbers at any one moment. Air-raid practice this morning immediately after the proclamation of state of war. Seems to have gone off satisfactorily though believed by many people to be real raid. There are now great numbers of public air-raid shelters, though most of them will take another day or two to complete. Gasmasks° being handed out free, & the public appears to take them seriously. Voluntary fire-brigades etc. all active & look quite efficient. Police from now on wear steel helmets. No panic, on the other hand no enthusiasm, & in fact not much interest. Balloon barrage[1] completely covers London & would evidently make low-flying quite impossible. Black-out at nights fairly complete but they are instituting very stringent penalties for infringement. Evacuation involving 3 m. people (over 1 m. from London alone) going on rapidly. Train services somewhat disorganised in consequence.
Churchill & Eden are coming into the cabinet. Labour are refusing office for the time being. Labour MPs. in the house make violent protestations of

loyalty but tone of the left press very sour as they evidently realise the wind has been taken out of their sails. Controversy about the Russo-German pact continues to some extent. All the letters printed in Reynolds's[2] extol the pact but have shifted the emphasis from this being a "peace move" to its being a self-protecting move by U.S.S.R. "Action" of 2.9.39. still agitating against the war. No atrocity stories or violent propaganda posters as yet.
M. T. Act[3] extended to all men between 18–41. It is however clear that they do not as yet want large numbers of men but are passing the act in order to be able to pick on anyone they choose, & for purpose of later enforcing industrial conscription.

[Conclusion of Orwell's record of events leading up to the war]

1. Part of the air defence system was provided by barrage balloons. These were flown, unmanned, at a height that made dive-bombing to a low level impracticable owing to the cables anchoring the balloons in position.
2. *Reynold's News* was a Labour-inclined Sunday newspaper.
3. Military Training Act.

571. Application to Enrol for War Service

9 September 1939

Orwell offered his services to help the war effort in some capacity on 9 September 1939, six days after war was declared. His letter has not been traced, but it is referred to in a reply dated 8 December 1939 from the Ministry of Labour and National Service (C.R.B. 1382). This stated that his name had been entered in the section of the Central Register dealing with authors and writers. It went on: 'This entry is regarded as recording your readiness to accept, if invited to do so, suitable employment in war time.' With the letter was sent a leaflet describing the significance of the Central Register. The scheme was voluntary and designed to put suitably qualified people in touch with those who could use their services for 'National Defence.' Enrolment on the Register 'did not mean that any guarantee is given that the services of a particular individual will be called upon by the Government.'

572. To Leonard Moore

6 October 1939   Typewritten

The Stores   Wallington   Nr. Baldock   HERTS.

Dear Mr Moore,
Can you tell me whether there is any channel through which one can find out the circulations of weekly papers? As I think I told you, one of the essays in the book I am doing deals with the boys' twopenny weeklies of the type of the "Gem", "Wizard" etc, and I should like to know their circulations, but don't quite know how to find them out. I suppose if you write and ask the editor he

won't necessarily tell you? I have a dozen papers on my list, and should be greatly obliged if you could help me to find this out.[1]

My wife has already got a job in a government office.[1] I have so far failed to do so. I shall try again later, but for the time being I am staying here to finish the book[2] and get our garden into trim for the winter, as I dare say we shall be glad of all the spuds we can lay hands on next year. The book should be finished some time in November. It ought to have been done already, but of course this war put me right off my stride for some weeks.

Yours
Eric A Blair

1. Eileen was working in the Censorship Department, War Office, Whitehall; see Crick, 382.
2. *Inside the Whale.*

573. To Leonard Moore

16 October 1939   Typewritten

The Stores   Wallington   Nr. Baldock, HERTS.

Dear Mr Moore,

With ref. to your letter, for which many thanks, the papers I want to discover the circulations of are;

Gem	)
Magnet	)
Modern Boy	)
Detective Weekly	) —— Amalgamated Press
Thriller	)
Triumph	)
Champion	)
Wizard	)
Rover	)
Skipper	) —— D. C. Thompson° & Co.
Hotspur	)
Adventure	)

Rough figures would do, and in any case I understand all their circulations are very variable. But I want to get *some* idea of how many people read them, as it is relevant to what I am saying about them. From the numbers of them one sees everywhere I gather their circulations are pretty large, especially the "Wizard" and "Hotspur". Hope this isn't giving you too much trouble.[1]

Yours sincerely
Eric Blair

1. The letter has two annotations. One, very faint, which seems to be in Orwell's hand, says, 'Don't know how you would find my request.' The other gives the name of the publisher D. C. Thomson, and appears to have been written in Moore's office.

574. Review of *Green Worlds* by Maurice Hindus; *I Haven't Unpacked* by William Holt

Time and Tide, 21 October 1939

These two books, both of them in some sense autobiographies, only intersect at one point—Russia.

Mr. Hindus, born the son of a kulak somewhere in western Russia, emigrated with his mother to America at the age of fourteen. His book is really the story of two villages—the medieval village of his childhood, with its endless work and endless hunger, mud, flies, wolves, dancing, singing, superstition and early death, and the trim American village of the prosperous pre-war days, with its high wages, up-to-date machinery, buggy-rides, bob-sleigh parties and meetings in the Baptist Chapel. Years later he made two trips to his old village, one when the wounds of the Civil War had barely healed, the other when the first Five Year Plan was well under way. On the first occasion nothing much had changed, except that the peasants had seized the landlord's estates and immediately ruined miles of beech forest out of sheer destructiveness. On the second, seven years later, the mud was as deep and the houses as wretched as ever, but—

> the children in the schoolhouse know what a toothbrush is, and in the nursery, though not as yet in the home, they are being accustomed to the individual towel and the individual plate. A woman in childbirth no longer has her umbilical cord cut with a kitchen knife. . . . In Moscow, in their battle for power, leaders may conspire and degrade and execute one another, but in the old village the drive for "the hang of things" with the new machine and the new way of life never ceases.

He is convinced that no event, internal or external, can undo the collectivization. Also that if "the revolution" ever happens in America there will be none of the disgusting barbarities that have marked the Stalin régime. The two things that give Mr. Hindus's book a special value are the fact that he went back to Russia with no illusions as to the physical conditions he would find there, and still more that he went there with a knowledge of agriculture. As he says, most of the "romantics" who have rhapsodized over the collective farms are people who would not know a Rhode Island Red if they saw one. But simply as an autobiography, as a story of a boy from the Middle Ages, standing amazed before soda-fountains and threshing-machines and trying to fathom the mysterious mind-processes of the American girl, the book is unusually interesting and, in places, deeply moving.

Mr. Holt's autobiography is of a kind rather more usual nowadays, although it contains much more varied and sensational adventures. Mill-worker, soldier in the Great War, sailor, teacher of English in Spain and Germany, Communist, novelist, political prisoner, correspondent in the Spanish War—that is part of the story. He visited the U.S.S.R. as a trade-union delegate in 1930 and came away hopeful rather than disillusioned, but afterwards parted company with the Communist Party for one of the usual reasons—unwillingness to tell lies. The most extraordinary episode of all is the history of his first book, *Under a Japanese Parasol*. He had it printed at his own expense, hawked it from door to door and made a handsome profit on it. The final chapter finds him back in the cotton-mill but with a feeling that fresh adventures are coming to him—and, judging from the rest of the book, he is probably not far wrong.

575. Correspondence with Ethel Mannin
October 1939

Two letters from Ethel Edith Mannin (1900–1984), prolific writer of novels, short stories, and books on travel and social, political, and religious topics survive; they are dated 20 September and 30 October 1939. In the first she expressed, among other things, her enthusiasm for *Coming Up for Air*. She was particularly impressed by Orwell's 'insistence on the thing I feel so strongly myself—that we've got to the end of a phase, as surely as they had in Aug. 1914, and that whatever the world is like when all this present insanity is over it won't be the world as we knew it before Sept. 1939.'

Orwell replied, in a letter now lost, sometime between Mannin's two letters, probably closer to 30 October. After what he had written in *Coming Up for Air*, Mannin said she was 'bitched buggered and bewildered' by the last paragraph of Orwell's letter. He had evidently written that he wanted to join the army. 'I can't think,' she wrote, 'of any reason why you should want to fight unless to get into the army and do anti-war propaganda there—but you don't indicate that. I thought you "went off the boil in 1916," I thought you thought it all crazy, this smashing in of Nazi faces. For the luv of Mike write a few lines to lighten our darkness. Even a p.c. if you don't feel like another letter.' The quotation about going off the boil refers to Orwell's disillusionment with military force after the carnage of the Battle of the Somme. George Bowling was wounded in 1916, in *Coming Up for Air*, see *CW*, VII, 83, 113.

Orwell's friend Reg Reynolds married Ethel Mannin in 1938. Interested in his writing, they visited Orwell when he was in the hospital at Aylesford. Like Reynolds, a Quaker, Mannin was a committed pacifist throughout her life. She was also the treasurer of Solidaridad Internacional Antifascista, an organisation of which Orwell was a sponsor; see *434*.

576. To Cyril Connolly
Sunday, [12 November 1939?[1]]   Typewritten

The Stores   Wallington   Nr. Baldock   HERTS

Dear Cyril,

In case this reaches you in time and you haven't already made all kinds of arrangements—I asked you to come down here next weekend, ie, the 18th. But I now find my wife can only come down here alternate weekends at present as she works on a late shift one week and an early one the next. So could you perhaps make it the next weekend, ie. the 25th? I'd like you to meet her. I gave you information about how to get here in my other letter I think.

Yours
Eric

1. Weekends at this time began on Saturdays about mid-day, and the only Saturdays dated the 18th, as mentioned in this letter, in 1939 and 1940 were in February, March, and November 1939 and May 1940. In February and March 1939 Orwell and his wife were in Morocco, and it was probably about the middle of May 1940 that Orwell left Wallington and moved to London. November 1939 seems most likely, and the meeting may have been connected with the inclusion of an essay from *Inside the Whale* in *Horizon*, which Connolly and Stephen Spender were then about to launch; the first issue appeared in January 1940.

577. Review of *Teamsman* by Crichton Porteous

The Listener, 23 November 1939

To anyone who fears that we are moving into a mechanised age in which human beings will lose all desire for contact with the soil, this book ought to be reassuring. The author, brought up in Manchester, with good prospects in the cotton trade, fled from his desk in order to learn farming from the bottom upwards. He stayed at it for several years on several farms, and when he finally left to take up a post on a newspaper, it was only with the intention of earning enough money to come back to the land as 'his own master'.

His book has the fascination nearly always belonging to books which really describe *work*. The whole year-long battle of life on a farm, the hunts for strayed cows and struggles with tricky horses, the back-breaking labour of hoisting bales of straw, the prickle of chaff under your shirt, the 'feel' (quite different in every case) of the plough, the drill-plough, the harrow and the disc cultivator, the icy misery of ploughing in a side wind, the pleasant smell of manure on sunny March days, the frosty mornings when the horses' shoes skid on the road and the waggon starts backwards downhill—these and a thousand other details are described with a minuteness that never becomes tedious, if only because the author's own enthusiasm is infectious. Even such a seemingly dull job as levering a stone gatepost out of the ground becomes interesting when Mr. Porteous tells you about it.

Two farmers figure in the book, one of them old fashioned, self-reliant, conscientious, a real artist, the other more up-to-date and more commercially minded. In the end Mr. Porteous came to understand and admire both types. What his book brings out very forcibly, however, is the enormous gulf that lies between any kind of independent farmer and a hired labourer. The truth is that the natural human love of the soil raises a very difficult problem—not completely solved even in Soviet Russia—because no merely economic improvement does away with the difference between owning one's own land and cultivating someone else's. There is a rather pathetic picture of the middle-aged Abel, Mr. Porteous' fellow-labourer on Mr. Basil's farm, who was a Socialist and denounced the 'idle rich', including Mr.

Basil, but yearned for a holding of his own—a thing he was about as likely to get as a Rolls-Royce car.

The wood engravings by Kingsley Cook are most of them rather too 'country'. But they include a couple of excellent plans of the two farms, the kind of illustrations that really illustrate and which every book of this sort ought to have.

578. Review of *Hotel in Flight* by Nancy Johnstone

The Adelphi, December 1939

How many millions of people in Spain and elsewhere are now looking back on the Spanish war and asking themselves what the devil it was all about? The thing had begun to seem meaningless even before the European kaleidoscope had twisted itself into its new pattern, and practically every foreigner who was involved seems to have brought away the impression of having been mixed up in a nightmare. Some months ago I was talking to a British soldier who was coming home from Gibraltar on a Japanese liner. A year earlier he had deserted from the Gibraltar garrison and with great difficulty made his way round to Valencia to join the Spanish Government forces. He had no sooner got there than he was arrested as a spy, flung into prison and forgotten about for six months. Then the British consul managed to extricate him and ship him back to Gibraltar, where he received another six months for desertion. This might almost be an allegorical history of the Spanish war.

Mrs. Johnstone's book, sequel to an earlier one, deals with the last eighteen months of the war, the period during which the Spanish Government's cause was becoming more and more obviously hopeless. She and her husband kept a hotel at Tossa on the Catalan coast, which became a rendezvous for journalists and visiting literary men, besides insufferable "politicals" of all colours. Starting off with the comic-opera conditions which still prevailed in 1937, the book becomes increasingly a story of food-shortage and tobacco-shortage, air-raids, spy-mania and refugee children, and ends with the terrible retreat into France and the stench and misery of the concentration camps round Perpignan. Much of the atmosphere will be horribly familiar to anyone who was in Spain at any period of the war. The sense of never having quite enough to eat, the muddle, the inefficiency, the inability to understand what is happening, the feeling that everything is fading away into a sort of mist of fear, suspicion, red tape and obscure political jealousies—it is all there, with plenty of crude physical adventure into the bargain. Mrs. Johnstone's picture of the concentration camps on the French-Spanish border is dreadful enough, but there is one observation that she makes and which ought to be underlined, and that is that the French Government is the only one that has actually done anything appreciable for the refugees from Fascist countries. Whereas the British Government made a grant of £12,000 for the Spanish refugees, their keep at the beginning was costing the French Government £17,000 *a day*, and presumably is not costing much less even now. It is worth remembering that at any time during the past ten years close on 10 per cent. of the population of France has consisted of foreigners, quite largely political refugees. After all, there is something to be said for "bourgeois" democracy.

This book gives a valuable picture of the retreat and will no doubt help to stop up some historical gaps, but it does not seem to me a very good book, *as a book.* Why is it that auto-biographical journalism of this type always has to be so chirpily facetious? As soon as I glanced into the book and saw the style in which it was written I began looking for the dog. Books of this kind almost always have a comic dog which is a great filler-up of paragraph-ends; however, the part is filled by Mrs. Johnstone's husband. The probability is that if a really good book is ever written about the Spanish war it will be by a Spaniard, and probably not a "politically conscious" one. Good war books are nearly always written from the angle of a *victim,* which is just what the average man is in relation to war. What vitiated the outlook of most of the foreigners in Spain, and especially the English and Americans, was the knowledge at the back of their minds that they would probably succeed in escaping from Spain in the end. Moreover, if they had gone there deliberately to take part, they knew what the war was about, or thought they did. But what did it mean to the great mass of the Spanish people? We simply do not know as yet. Looking back on casual contacts with peasants, shopkeepers, street-hawkers, even militiamen, I now suspect that great numbers of these people had no feelings about the war whatever, except a wish that it were over. Mrs. Johnstone's picture of the stolid inhabitants of the little seaport town of Tossa half-consciously confirms this. One question that is still not satisfactorily answered is why the war went on so long. After the beginning of 1938 it was obvious to anyone with any military knowledge that the Government could not win, and even by the summer of 1937 the odds were in Franco's favour. Did the mass of the Spanish people really feel that even the atrocious sufferings of the later part of the war were preferable to surrender— or did they continue to fight at least partly because the whole of left-wing opinion from Moscow to New York was driving them on? Perhaps we shall know the answer when we begin to hear what the war looked like to Spanish conscripts and non-combatants, and not merely to foreign volunteers.

579. 'Marrakech'

New Writing, New Series No. 3, Christmas 1939[1]

As the corpse went past the flies left the restaurant table in a cloud and rushed after it, but they came back a few minutes later.

The little crowd of mourners—all men and boys, no women—threaded their way across the market-place between the piles of pomegranates and the taxis and the camels, wailing a short chant over and over again. What really appeals to the flies is that the corpses here are never put into coffins, they are merely wrapped in a piece of rag and carried on a rough wooden bier on the shoulders of four friends. When the friends get to the burying-ground they hack an oblong hole a foot or two deep, dump the body in it and fling over it a little of the dried-up, lumpy earth, which is like broken brick. No gravestone, no name, no identifying mark of any kind. The burying-ground is merely a huge waste of hummocky earth, like a derelict building-lot. After a month or two no one can even be certain where his own relatives are buried.

When you walk through a town like this—two hundred thousand inhabitants, of whom at least twenty thousand own literally nothing except the rags they stand up in—when you see how the people live, and still more how easily they die, it is always difficult to believe that you are walking among human beings. All colonial empires are in reality founded upon that fact. The people have brown faces—besides, there are so many of them! Are they really the same flesh as yourself? Do they even have names? Or are they merely a kind of undifferentiated brown stuff, about as individual as bees or coral insects? They rise out of the earth, they sweat and starve for a few years, and then they sink back into the nameless mounds of the graveyard and nobody notices that they are gone. And even the graves themselves soon fade back into the soil. Sometimes, out for a walk, as you break your way through the prickly pear, you notice that it is rather bumpy underfoot, and only a certain regularity in the bumps tells you that you are walking over skeletons.

I was feeding one of the gazelles in the public gardens.

Gazelles are almost the only animals that look good to eat when they are still alive, in fact, one can hardly look at their hindquarters without thinking of mint sauce. The gazelle I was feeding seemed to know that this thought was in my mind, for though it took the piece of bread I was holding out it obviously did not like me. It nibbled rapidly at the bread, then lowered its head and tried to butt me, then took another nibble and then butted again. Probably its idea was that if it could drive me away the bread would somehow remain hanging in mid-air.

An Arab navvy working on the path nearby lowered his heavy hoe and sidled slowly towards us. He looked from the gazelle to the bread and from the bread to the gazelle, with a sort of quiet amazement, as though he had never seen anything quite like this before. Finally he said shyly in French:

'*I* could eat some of that bread.'

I tore off a piece and he stowed it gratefully in some secret place under his rags. This man is an employee of the Municipality.

When you go through the Jewish quarters you gather some idea of what the medieval ghettoes were probably like. Under their Moorish rulers the Jews were only allowed to own land in certain restricted areas, and after centuries of this kind of treatment they have ceased to bother about overcrowding. Many of the streets are a good deal less than six feet wide, the houses are completely windowless, and sore-eyed children cluster everywhere in unbelievable numbers, like clouds of flies. Down the centre of the street there is generally running a little river of urine.

In the bazaar huge families of Jews, all dressed in the long black robe and little black skull-cap, are working in dark fly-infested booths that look like caves. A carpenter sits cross-legged at a prehistoric lathe, turning chair-legs at lightning speed. He works the lathe with a bow in his right hand and guides the chisel with his left foot, and thanks to a lifetime of sitting in this position his left leg is warped out of shape. At his side his grandson, aged six, is already starting on the simpler parts of the job.

I was just passing the coppermiths' booths when somebody noticed that I was lighting a cigarette. Instantly, from the dark holes all round, there was a frenzied rush of Jews, many of them old grandfathers with flowing grey beards, all clamouring for a cigarette. Even a blind man somewhere at the back of one of the booths heard a rumour of cigarettes and came crawling out, groping in the air with his hand. In about a minute I had used up the whole packet. None of these people, I suppose, works less than twelve hours a day, and every one of them looks on a cigarette as a more or less impossible luxury.

As the Jews live in self-contained communities they follow the same trades as the Arabs, except for agriculture. Fruit-sellers, potters, silversmiths, blacksmiths, butchers, leatherworkers, tailors, water-carriers, beggars, porters—whichever way you look you see nothing but Jews. As a matter of fact there are thirteen thousand of them, all living in the space of a few acres. A good job Hitler isn't here. Perhaps he is on his way, however. You hear the usual dark rumours about the Jews, not only from the Arabs but from the poorer Europeans.

'Yes, *mon vieux*, they took my job away from me and gave it to a Jew. The Jews! They're the real rulers of this country, you know. They've got all the money. They control the banks, finance—everything.'

'But,' I said, 'isn't it a fact that the average Jew is a labourer working for about a penny an hour?'

'Ah, that's only for show! They're all moneylenders really. They're cunning, the Jews.'

In just the same way, a couple of hundred years ago, poor old women used to be burned for witchcraft when they could not even work enough magic to get themselves a square meal.

All people who work with their hands are partly invisible, and the more important the work they do, the less visible they are. Still, a white skin is always fairly conspicuous. In northern Europe, when you see a labourer ploughing a field, you probably give him a second glance. In a hot country, anywhere south of Gibraltar or east of Suez, the chances are that you don't even see him. I have noticed this again and again. In a tropical landscape one's eye takes in everything except the human-beings. It takes in the dried-up soil, the prickly pear, the palm-tree and the distant mountain, but it always misses the peasant hoeing at his patch. He is the same colour as the earth, and a great deal less interesting to look at.

It is only because of this that the starved countries of Asia and Africa are accepted as tourist resorts. No one would think of running cheap trips to the Distressed Areas. But where the human-beings have brown skins their poverty is simply not noticed. What does Morocco mean to a Frenchman? An orange-grove or a job in Government service. Or to an Englishman? Camels, castles, palm-trees, Foreign Legionaires, brass trays and bandits. One could probably live here for years without noticing that for nine-tenths of the people the reality of life is an endless, back-breaking struggle to wring a little food out of an eroded soil.

Most of Morocco is so desolate that no wild animal bigger than a hare can live on it. Huge areas which were once covered with forest have turned into a treeless waste where the soil is exactly like broken-up brick. Nevertheless a good deal of it is cultivated, with frightful labour. Everything is done by hand. Long lines of women, bent double like inverted capital L's, work their way slowly across the fields, tearing up the prickly weeds with their hands, and the peasant gathering lucerne for fodder pulls it up stalk by stalk instead of reaping it, thus saving an inch or two on each stalk. The plough is a wretched wooden thing, so frail that one can easily carry it on one's shoulder, and fitted underneath with a rough iron spike which stirs the soil to a depth of about four inches. This is as much as the strength of the animals is equal to. It is usual to plough with a cow and a donkey yoked together. Two donkeys would not be quite strong enough, but on the other hand two cows would cost a little more to feed. The peasants possess no harrows, they merely plough the soil several times over in different directions, finally leaving it in rough furrows, after which the whole field has to be shaped with hoes into small oblong patches, to conserve water. Except for a day or two after the rare rainstorms there is never enough water. Along the edges of the fields channels are hacked out to a depth of thirty or forty feet to get at the tiny trickles which run through the subsoil.

Every afternoon a file of very old women passes down the road outside my house, each carrying a load of firewood. All of them are mummified with age and the sun, and all of them are tiny. It seems to be generally the case in primitive communities that the women, when they get beyond a certain age, shrink to the size of children. One day a poor old creature who could not have been more than four feet tall crept past me under a vast load of wood. I stopped her and put a five-sou piece (a little more than a farthing) into her hand. She answered with a shrill wail, almost a scream, which was partly gratitude but mainly surprise. I suppose that from her point of view, by taking any notice of her, I seemed almost to be violating a law of nature. She accepted her status as an old woman, that is to say as a beast of burden. When a family is travelling it is quite usual to see a father and a grown-up son riding ahead on donkeys, and an old woman following on foot, carrying the baggage.

But what is strange about these people is their invisibility. For several weeks, always at about the same time of day, the file of old women had hobbled past the house with their firewood, and though they had registered themselves on my eyeballs I cannot truly say that I had seen them. Firewood was passing—that was how I saw it. It was only that one day I happened to be walking behind them, and the curious up-and-down motion of a load of wood drew my attention to the human being underneath it. Then for the first time I noticed the poor old earth-coloured bodies, bodies reduced to bones and leathery skin, bent double under the crushing weight. Yet I suppose I had not been five minutes on Moroccan soil before I noticed the overloading of the donkeys and was infuriated by it. There is no question that the donkeys are damnably treated. The Moroccan donkey is hardly bigger than a St. Bernard dog, it carries a load which in the British Army would be considered too much for a fifteen-hands mule, and very often its pack-saddle is not taken off its back for weeks together. But what is peculiarly pitiful is that it is the most willing creature on earth, it follows its master like a dog and does not need either bridle or halter. After a dozen years of devoted work it suddenly drops dead, whereupon its master tips it into the ditch and the village dogs have torn its guts out before it is cold.

This kind of thing makes one's blood boil, whereas—on the whole—the plight of the human beings does not. I am not commenting, merely pointing to a fact. People with brown skins are next door to invisible. Anyone can be sorry for the donkey with its galled back, but it is generally owing to some kind of accident if one even notices the old woman under her load of sticks.

As the storks flew northward the negroes were marching southward—a long, dusty column, infantry, screw-gun batteries and then more infantry, four or five thousand men in all, winding up the road with a clumping of boots and a clatter of iron wheels.

They were Senegalese, the blackest negroes in Africa, so black that sometimes it is difficult to see whereabouts on their necks the hair begins. Their splendid bodies were hidden in reach-me-down khaki uniforms, their feet squashed into boots that looked like blocks of wood, and every tin hat seemed to be a couple of sizes too small. It was very hot and the men had marched a long way. They slumped under the weight of their packs and the curiously sensitive black faces were glistening with sweat.

As they went past a tall, very young negro turned and caught my eye. But the look he gave me was not in the least the kind of look you might expect. Not hostile, not contemptuous, not sullen, not even inquisitive. It was the shy, wide-eyed negro look, which actually is a look of profound respect. I saw how it was. This wretched boy, who is a French citizen and has therefore been dragged from the forest to scrub floors and catch syphilis in garrison towns, actually has feelings of reverence before a white skin. He has been taught that the white race are his masters, and he still believes it.

But there is one thought which every white man (and in this connection it doesn't matter twopence if he calls himself a Socialist) thinks when he sees a black army marching past. 'How much longer can we go on kidding these people? How long before they turn their guns in the other direction?'

It was curious, really. Every white man there had this thought stowed somewhere or other in his mind. I had it, so had the other onlookers, so had the officers on their sweating chargers and the white N.C.O.'s marching in the ranks. It was a kind of secret which we all knew and were too clever to tell; only the negroes didn't know it. And really it was almost like watching a flock of cattle to see the long column, a mile or two miles of armed men, flowing peacefully up the road, while the great white birds drifted over them in the opposite direction, glittering like scraps of paper.

1. John Lehmann, (see *312, n. 1*), editor of *New Writing*, wrote to Orwell on 12 April 1939 accepting this essay, which he liked very much indeed.

580. Review of *Baltic Roundabout* by Bernard Newman; *I Gathered No Moss* by John Gibbons; *A Man in the East* by Max Relton

Time and Tide, 2 December 1939

In a narrowing world the professional travellers are still slinking to and fro, rather like the foxes and badgers which exist here and there in the woods of outer London. If you are willing to cut out three-quarters of Asia, parts of Africa and South America, any country bordering on the inland seas and any country which is or recently has been at war, a certain amount of movement is still permitted—always provided, of course, that you have plenty of money, no camera and a passport with no incriminating marks on it. But every year another portion of the earth is fenced off. Mr Bernard Newman, for instance, author of *Baltic Roundabout*, must be looking at a good many names on the map and wondering whether he will ever see their originals again. He was in Albania in 1935, in Spain in 1936, in Czechoslovakia in 1937, and, as he says, trouble always followed soon afterwards. In 1938 it was the Baltic countries. He bicycled right round the Baltic, two thousand nine hundred and ninety-five kilometres, with living expenses of five shillings a day and total travelling expenses of two shillings—bicycle repairs in Latvia.

And what paradises they all sound, those small Baltic countries! They seem to possess everything except the power to defend themselves. The gem of the lot, at any rate in Mr Newman's estimation, is evidently Finland. Naturally the name of Finland calls up a sort of composite picture of birch forests, snow, Lapps, reindeer and even—if one's geography is a little hazy—Eskimos. But as a matter of fact, in spite of its small population, it is a thriving and progressive country, with enlightened laws and little inequality or real poverty. Everyone owns a bit of land, even lawyers and doctors go home periodically to work on the family farm, there is no illiteracy, the consumption of books is the highest per head of any population in Europe, and both men and women can walk about naked without attracting attention. The Finns, who produced Nurmi,[1] are very proud of their athletic record, and, Mr Newman remarks hopefully, "Helsinki has the honour of housing the Olympic Games of 1940". He does not say whether the competitors will wear gas-masks.

It is a far cry from the Baltic to the rainy village in Portugal where Mr Gibbons spent a winter. Everything is more primitive, of course, less sanitary, but perhaps more colourful. The food (every travel-book that is any good tells you about the food) sounds delicious, though it is rather disconcerting to learn that if you drink too much cheap wine you are liable to have a wine-fungus—one of those enormous things that sometimes sprout on barrels—growing inside you. Mr Gibbons belongs to the Belloc school of travellers, the enthusiasts of Latin Europe, large families, the Catholic Church, ox-carts and traditional dances. His book is rather breathlessly written, a day-to-day record of the happenings in the little mountain village, the bullocks marching round the olive-press and the pig being killed outside the window, but most of it is very readable. He is a keen admirer of Dr Salazar, who has performed the miracle of balancing the national budget and is determined to keep Portugal an unindustrialized peasant republic. Perhaps he is right—at any rate the peasants in Tras-Os-Montes sound as though they were happy, which is more than can be said for the people in Sheffield and Manchester.

A Man in the East is good material spoiled by a rather heavy, tiresome-style of writing. It is a record of a journey through parts of western China and Indo-China, and it contains some interesting information about the Sino-Japanese war and French colonial methods in the Far East. But it is all rather too "literary" and heavy-handed, with too many humorous asides about red light quarters and cosmopolitan fellow-travellers speaking broken English, etc., etc. There is the usual photograph of Mr Relton sitting rifle in hand on a dead tiger. I never see one of these without wanting to see a photo of a tiger sitting on a big-game hunter. All these three books are illustrated, but except for one or two in *Baltic Roundabout*, it cannot be said that their photographs have much pictorial value.

1. Paavo Nurmi (1897–1973), the 'Flying Finn,' won nine gold medals at the Olympic Games of 1920, 1924, and 1928, and set twenty-two world records.

581. To Leonard Moore

Friday [8 December 1939]   Typewritten

The Stores   Wallington   Nr. Baldock   HERTS.

Dear Mr Moore,

I have finished my book (the book of essays—the title is INSIDE THE WHALE) and have typed most of it but my wife is typing another portion in London. Meanwhile Cyril Connolly and Stephen Spender, who as perhaps you know are starting a new monthly called HORIZON, want to see the MS. in case they would like to print one of the essays in their paper.[1] I don't know if any of them are really suitable for this, but if they do wish to use one of them, would that be all right with the publisher? Could one arrange things? As you may remember Gollancz wanted to see the book but whether he'll publish it I don't know, as there is at any rate one passage which politically won't appeal to him.[2] If Gollancz refuses it, what about trying Warburg again? I met him a little while back and he was very anxious to have my next non-fiction book, so perhaps we might get a good offer out of him for this, though no doubt it would be better to get the money in advance if possible. I am arranging with Connolly to keep the MS. only a few days. I should think it would be best not to say anything to any publisher about this beforehand, because if Connolly and Co. don't want any of it, which they well may not, it might prejudice him against the book.

Do you know what has happened to the Albatross people?[3] You may remember we signed up a contract with them for COMING UP FOR AIR just before war broke out. Have they gone west, I wonder?

Yours sincerely
Eric Blair

1. *Inside the Whale* consisted of the essay with that title, 'Charles Dickens,' and 'Boys' Weeklies.' An abridged version of the last was published in *Horizon* the same month as book publication, March 1940; see *596*.
2. In fact, *Inside the Whale* appealed greatly to Victor Gollancz, who did publish it. He wrote to Orwell on 1 January 1940 (misdated 1939) to express his delight: 'It is, if I may say so, first rate.' He was in complete sympathy with Orwell's general political point of view, 'though I fight against pessimism.' He suggested that the only thing worth doing was 'to try to find some way of reconciling the inevitable totalitarian economics with individual freedom.' Finally, he asked Orwell whether he could lend him a copy of Henry Miller's *Tropic of Cancer*, of which he had not heard. Exactly four weeks after Gollancz wrote, Orwell returned to him the page proofs of *Inside the Whale*.
3. Although Albatross and Tauchnitz were German firms, the contract Orwell signed was from their Paris office. See *561, n. 1*. William B. Todd and Ann Bowden in their *Tauchnitz International Editions in English* record a document in the Albatross archive that notes that the publisher still hoped in 1940 to publish *Coming Up for Air*. This states that it was one of the books that should have been exploited in 1940. After Paris was occupied by the Germans, 14 June 1940, a decree was issued forbidding the sale of British books first published after 1870 (Todd and Bowden, item 5365), and that finally ended Orwell's hopes for an Albatross edition.

APPENDIX 4

582. Domestic Diary

This Domestic Diary continues from 518.

<u>1.1.39</u>:   *Three eggs.*
The cock pigeon, which at first was rather sorry for himself, no doubt owing to having been confined in a cage & having had his wings bound, is better & trying to fly a little. The female at first courting him, walking round him & bowing.
Another dead donkey, with two dogs tearing its entrails out. The third I have seen. They never seem to bury them when they die.
The pepper trees, whose peppercorns were ripening about September, have now got a fresh crop on them. The nasturtiums which were nipped by the frost are mostly dead. Ditto the vegetable marrows, & the foliage of the brinjals is all withered off.
Clear & fine, not particularly cold, nice sun & no wind.
E. saw four more storks.
The oranges etc., & even apparently the lemon blossom, not in the least damaged by the frost.
<u>2.1.39</u>:   *Two eggs.*
<u>3.1.39</u>:   *Three eggs.*
<u>4.1.39</u>:   *Three eggs.*
Clear, fine & generally rather cold (wearing light undervest, cotton shirt, pullover, coat, light pants & grey flannel bags), & do not find this too much.
Night before last the cock pigeon, which was only just regaining its power of flight, disappeared, evidently destroyed by one of the Arabs' dogs. Bought another yesterday (Frs. 6.). This one's wings are all right. Put him for the night in the cage, in the morning found the hen outside. Opened the door & they flew off together.
<u>5.1.39</u>:   *Two eggs.*
<u>6.1.39</u>:   *Three eggs.*
<u>7.1.39</u>:   *Three eggs. There are now 3 hens broody. The pigeons are all right.*
Yesterday saw some men fishing in the Oued Tensift. Miserable little fish about the size of sardines. The bait is a kind of small earthworm which is found in the mud beside the river.
Day before yesterday came on some men waiting with a she-camel which had fallen in the middle of the bridge over the Oued. It was apparently about to

have a calf. Belly greatly swollen up, sexual organs bleeding slightly. The creature lay on its side, its head in the air, sniffing, with a kind of air of astonishment, but evidently not in pain. An hour or so later just the same. Today passed that way. Big pool of blood on the ground, & the marks of something bloody being dragged away. Calf probably born dead.

Clear, very fine, cold in the shade, warm in the sun. We now have a hot water bottle every night, & 3 blankets & a rug on the bed.

<u>8.1.39</u>: *Three eggs.*

<u>9.1.39</u>: *Two eggs. Saw large flock of green plover, apparently the same as in England. Clear & fine, afternoons fairly warm.*

<u>10.1.39</u>: *Three eggs.*

<u>11.1.39</u>: *One egg.*

<u>12.1.39</u>: *Three eggs.*

<u>13.1.39</u>: *Two eggs. (135 since 26.10.38.)*

In the cleft of the rock on the N. side of one of the little hills near hear° are growing a plant like angelica, a fleshy plant with round leaves & quantities of moss. Evidently these can only grow in places where the sun does not reach them at any time.

<u>14.1.39</u>:
to   } *Four eggs (about 4 of the hens now broody.)*
<u>17.1.39</u>[1]:

Saw a stork standing among the ibises the other day. It is enormous—English heron would look small beside it.

Greenfinch evidently exists here as well as the goldfinch, both as in Europe. Broad beans grown round here are very good, no black fly at all. It seems tangerines are damaged by frost though ordinary oranges are not.

1. Orwell mistakenly gave the year as '37' for 14.1.39 and 17.1.39.

<u>18.2.39</u>: *Spent a week at Taddert, 1650 m. up in the Atlas, about 95 km. from Marrakech, & since then have been ill for nearly 3 weeks (about 10 days in bed.)*

Most essential points about Taddert are noted in the other diary.[1] Birds seen there are as follow: raven (I rather suspect that the so-called crows down here are ravens too), partridge (fairly common), hawk, some other much larger predatory bird, possibly eagle (only seen in the distance), rock dove & wood-pigeon, blue tit, other birds much as down here, but no storks or ibises. No animals. Found in the snow on a peak tracks conceivably of mouflon, but probably goat. There was some reference to some animal called blet or bilet (presumably Arab word) which was liable to come & kill chickens etc. Tame peacocks kept at the hotel seemed to do well. Breeds of domestic animals much as here, except the sheep, which are quite different with very silky wool. Camels are used, but not taken off the main roads. Donkeys seem able to ascend almost all hills.

Trees etc.: oak (smallish), very tiny dwarf oak, wild broom, kind of heather stuff, as in Spain, blackberry, wild daffodil (or some kind of wild tulip—not in flower now), species of ash, small fir tree, various plants of sedum &

saxifrage type at tops of peaks, a few with very beautiful flowers daisy.[2] Walnuts grow profusely, but not wild. Almonds are grown & appear to do well. Fig tree will just grow at about 5000 feet, but does not do well. The spring crop is barley, which is cut in June & followed by maize. Grass in places very good, almost like England. This is only in vicinity of streams, & evidently it has to be cultivated. In the grass a kind of edible sorrel, used in salads.

The river again much swollen after the rain of two days ago. The other day the water very clear & could see the fish, small ones about 4" long, of barbel type (grubbing along the bottom). Shall try for them when the water subsides again. Weeds have grown tremendously & the fields are fairly green. One or two of our nasturtiums in bloom, & sweet peas etc. have grown fairly well, but I have quite neglected the garden.

Owing to illness lost count of the eggs. The hens laid 19 in the week we were away. At present only about 1 is laying.

For about 10 consecutive days the cream has tasted of garlic, some days enough to make it uneatable. Evidently the cows have got hold of some wild garlic. Williams[3] says he saw the killing of the last lion in Morocco, in 1924. Panthers & gazelles said to be still fairly common south of the Atlas.

20.2.39: Wallflowers (good specimans) are blooming at the café near here. Pomegranate trees just putting forth their buds, which are brilliant red. Weeds pretty thick everywhere. This is probably as green as the country ever gets, but there are still considerable dried-up patches. Yesterday saw some wheat green but in fairly good ear.

[On page opposite:]

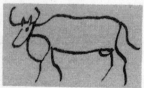

Local method of hobbling cow with grass rope (base of horn to below knee).

Saw two storks nesting today. The nest is enormous, about twice as wide as a heron's nest & also several feet deep, a huge mass of twigs filling a whole fork of a large tree. The hen was evidently in the act of laying an egg, the cock standing beside her; presently she got up & they stood side by side.

Our hen pigeon laid two more eggs & sat there for some days, then both she & the cock were mysteriously destroyed & disappeared—only a few feathers left. Said to be cats but suspect humans. That makes 4 we have lost &, of course, we shall not have any more. They evidently breed readily here. Three or four of those at the café now have eggs.

It is getting noticeably hotter & flies beginning to be a nuisance again.

Forgot to mention that at Taddert the people had camel's hair ropes, very pliable & seemed strong.

22.2.39: Heavy mist yesterday morning. In general distinctly hotter. A lot of wildflowers now, two of marigold type, a sort of daisy, & various others.

24.2.39: Pretty heavy rain last night & this morning.

Found sprays of fennel, which evidently grows here. Saw very large slow-

moving black & white birds, evidently of hawk tribe. Forgot to mention curious property of human shadows, noticed at Taddert. Sometimes one stands on a crag whose shadow is cast hundreds of feet below. If one stands right on the edge of it, naturally one's shadow is cast beyond that of the crag. But I notice that whereas the shadow of the rock is black & solid, that of the human body, at anything over about 50 feet, is faint & indistinct, like the shadow of a bush. At short distances this is not noticeable & the shadow seems solid, but at long distances, say 200 feet & over, one seems to have almost no shadow at all. At certain distances the body as a whole has a sort of shadow, but, eg., the arm by itself none. I do not know whether this is because, relative to rock, the human body is not opaque, or whether it is merely a question of size.

1. Orwell's Morocco Diary for 27 January 1939; see *530*.
2. 'daisy' is an interlinear insertion.
3. Presumably an American serving in the French Foreign Legion, described in Orwell's Morocco Diary, 12 March 1939; see *538*.

<u>4.3.39:</u> *A good deal hotter. Flies not so bad again, however, perhaps owing to rain.*
A boy offered me a quail which he had just caught the other day. Much the same as those in Spain.
Many wild flowers now, including some the same or almost the same as in England. Poppies, bacon & eggs,[1] a sort of small marguerite not unlike the English daisy, a very tiny flower of primula or polyanthus type, some small flowers resembling dandelions, & a purple flower with petals not unlike those of a foxglove, but smaller. Also anchusa, bird's eye.[2] Wild marigolds are much the commonest, growing in thick clumps everywhere.
Barley is now in good ear, though still green, in many fields. Where identifiable, nearly all the crops I have seen are barley. They vary, but on the whole seem good. Cherry trees everywhere in blossom. Apples coming into leaf. Pomegranate buds getting large—these evidently put forth leaves before flowers. Lemon trees have fruit at all stages from blossom to ripe fruit on them simultaneously. These apparently continue the year round. Fig buds just appearing. Broad beans about ready to pick (green), lettuces now very good, also peas, carrots & rather small turnips. Evidently some vegetables can be grown more or less continuously here. It is noticeable that there are extremely few insect pests on the vegetables. Men cutting some tall grass resembling wheat or barley, but presumably not that, used for fodder. People also everywhere cutting & carrying home donkey-loads of the weeds which have sprung up everywhere.
The other day caught a young water-tortoise about this size or perhaps a little smaller. Perfectly formed, but at this age the tail is relatively larger. Presumably it had not been long out of the egg, so this must be the breeding season. Have not seen any adult tortoises for some time past. Yesterday saw a centipede about 3-4" long—the first seen here.

9.3.39: *Quite hot, but today cloudy. Most of our nasturtiums in flower & everything else growing rapidly.*
Mosquitoes rather bad.
M. Simont uses blood, in considerable quantities (which he can get as he is a butcher) for manuring the orange trees.
11.3.39: *Yesterday found a dead snake, about 2' long, the first seen in Morocco.*
Very hot. It is said that this year there has been more rain than usual, so it should be a good year.
Another wildflower now common is pale yellow with deeper yellow centre, about 2" across, & resembles a small sunflower.
16.3.39: *Yesterday not quite so hot, overcast & clouds of dust. Ditto today, probably presaging rain.*
Other wildflowers here: a kind of small scabius,° several vetches, one of them very pretty, with a flower about the size of that of a garden pea, in two colours, pink & magenta. Several new ones in the last few days which I cannot identify. In many places the ground is now actually covered with them, predominantly the wild marigold, a pale yellow flower which is evidently mustard, & a smallish daisy not unlike the English one.
Yesterday three greenfinches, a cock & two hens, sitting on the telephone wires:

1st. greenfinch:	*"Little bit of bread."*
2nd. .. :	*"Little bit of bread."*
1st. .. :	*"Little bit of bread."*
2nd. .. :	*"Little bit of bread."*
3rd. (the cock):	*"Che-e-e-e-e-se!"*

Men still ploughing in places. Yesterday a man sowing, broadcast out of a bag. Flocks of domestic pigeons swooping down to try & steal the seed, & the men chasing them off.
Yesterday saw a very young camel cub, evidently only a few days born as it still had a bit of navel-string. Nevertheless its legs were almost as long as its mother's.
Cavalry passing yesterday. Note that all the horses seem to be stallions.
28.3.39: *On board ss. Yasukunimaru (N.Y.K) in bay° of Biscay. The following was written in Marrakech on 21.3.39 to be written into the diary when the latter was unpacked:—*
Until this afternoon, the last 3 or 4 days astonishingly cold. Two days ago in the midst of a rainstorm there was a few minutes' hail.
At the public gardens many of the animals mating. Tortoises copulating, the male standing almost upright & the female when she moved dragging him round, so that probably he has a long flexible penis which can go round the edge of the shell. Ostriches showing signs of mating, the male chasing the female into a corner & getting astride her (not treading as with flying birds), the female when frightened hiding her head in the corner as a captured hare will do, so perhaps there is some truth in the tales about ostriches hiding their heads in the sand. Presumably these two are of the same species, but male & female very different in appearance, the male's plumage being black & the

female's a kind of dirty grey. Male's neck is red, female's grey. Both have bare necks & thighs. Height of either bird something over 7'. They would not eat bread. Frogs making a great noise, though there were tadpoles about already. Male peacocks when displaying shiver their quills with a rustling sound, as though the wind were blowing through them. One monkey (tailless ground monkey of more or less baboon type) has a baby. Evidently about two days old, & making some attempts to move about on its own, which its mother does not allow. As she runs on all fours the baby clings to her under-side with its four legs, looking forward with its face upside down. Its hair is black, whereas that of its parents is yellowish-brown. Fingers, unlike those of its parents, are bare & much more manlike than those of adults. The monkey which is evidently the father, & another male, taking great interest in the baby, handling & examining it gently, & also gnashing their teeth at it as they do when angry with one another, but as the baby showed no fear it is presumably not a hostile gesture. The baby screamed with fright when it caught sight of E. & myself, on two occasions.
The tortoises have an egg. They have laid it inside their stone hutch, so it probably won't hatch.
The father monkey copulated with the mother, or began to do so, when she was carrying the baby in her arms.

We left Casablanca 4 pm on 26.3.39, passed Cape Finisterre 7 am on 28th & should pass Ushant 7 am on 29th. Run for the last 12 hours 378³ miles (notes on this ship are in the other diary.) Weather after leaving Casablanca somewhat choppy, now while crossing the bay very calm, ie. not rough enough to disturb a ship of this tonnage. Of 3 passages across the bay I have made, only one was rough. Have seen no life at all, except the gulls which have followed the ship from Casablanca, & some flights of ducks flying northward, some of them at least 50 miles from land. No seasickness, though the first 24 hours the ship rolled sufficiently to have made me sick if I had not taken Vasano.

The last few days in Casablanca beastly cold. Struck by the changed appearance of the country when coming from M. to C. by train, ie. the temporary greenness everywhere. Crops look pretty good, though great variation in different places. Wildflowers in huge patches, & the little compounds round the Arabs' huts so smothered in weeds that sometimes even the huts themselves were almost hidden. E. saw camels ploughing. I hadn't seen this before & thought it didn't happen, but evidently it is fairly usual as it was one of the things represented on the base of Lyautey's statue.[4] On this ship several kinds of plant, some of palm type, another of the laurel type, & some of the usual Japanese stunted fir trees, are successfully grown & look healthy.

---

1. Somerset name for water crowfoot (*Ranunculus fluitans*); Wiltshire name for toadflax (*Linaria vulgaris*); see Geoffrey Grigson, *The Englishman's Flora*, 41, 296. Or possibly the bulbous buttercup.

2. 'Also anchusa, bird's eye' is at the foot of the page, which ends with 'those of' in preceding sentence, Grigson gives bird's eye as the popular name of sixteen plants.
3. Orwell originally wrote the mileage as 347.
4. For Marshal Lyautey, see *511, n.1.*

<u>10.4.39.</u> Southwold: *Have been here since 1.4.39, but spent most of the last week in bed.*
A week ago, on arrival, weather mostly coldish, very still & rather misty. Thick sea mist on 2.4.39. Blackthorn flowering in places. Primroses abundant. Wild daffodils also plentiful, but for the most part not completely open. Fruit trees budding fairly strongly. Saw one of I do not know what kind (purplish flower) in blossom in a sheltered place two days ago. Roses, herbaceous plants etc. sprouting strongly. Starlings still in flocks on 2.4.39. Larks singing hard. Some asparagus heads a few inches above ground.
<u>12.4.39.</u> Wallington: *Yesterday[1] exceedingly warm & fine, said to have been the warmest day for that date for 70 years. Today even more so.*
We have now 26 hens, the youngest about 11 months. Yesterday 7 eggs (the hens have only recently started laying again.) Everything greatly neglected, full of weeds etc., ground very hard & dry, attributed to heavy falls of rain, then no rain at all for some weeks.
Although the hedges etc. are more forward when one gets away from the sea, the spring on the whole seems backward.
Flowers now in bloom in the garden: polyanthus, aubretia, scilla, grape hyacinth, oxalis, a few narcissi. Many daffodils in the field. These are very° double & evidently not real wild daffodil but bulbs dropped there by accident. Bullaces & plums coming into blossom. Apple trees budding but no blossom yet. Pears in full blossom. Roses sprouting fairly strongly. I note that one of the standards which died is sprouting from the root, so evidently the stock can live when the scion is dead. Peonies sprouting strongly. Crocuses are just over. A few tulips in bud. A few leeks & parsnips in the garden (the latter have survived the winter without covering up & tops are still green), otherwise no vegetables. It appears that owing to severe frosts there are no winter greens locally.
Bats out everywhere. Have not found any birds' nests yet.
Wildflowers out: violets, primroses, celandine, anemones.
A little rhubarb showing. Blackcurrant bushes etc. for the most part have grown very weedy, probably for lack of hoeing round etc. Strawberries have all run & are covered with weeds but look fairly strong.
Sowed cos lettuce.
Leaf mould (beech) put down at end of 1937 is now well rotted down.
Found two thrushe's°eggs under the hedge—no nest, somewhat mysterious, but perhaps left there by a child.
Today a stack being thrashed—oats, & seemingly no rats & few mice. Tried Marx[2] with a live baby mouse. He smelt & licked it but made no move to eat it.

Pigeons making their mating flight fly steeply up into the air then volplane down.

Four eggs.

<u>13.4.39</u>: *Not so warm. A very light shower in the evening. Very dark night.*

A few pansies & wallflowers starting to bloom. Pansies spread by self-sowing almost as much as marigolds. Red saxifrage coming into flower.

Ten eggs.

<u>14.4.39</u>: *Cloudy, & a few small showers. Cold after dark.*

Saw two swallows (not martins). This is rather early for this locality & a latish year. No one else has seen any.

All day cleaning out strawberries, which have not been touched since last year. It seems one plant will put out anything up to 12 or 15 runners. These seem to develop the best roots when they have rooted in very hard soil. Used some of them to fill up gaps & make another row. Doubtful whether they will take, but Titley[3] says it is not too late. Wallflowers in sheltered positions are full out. No apple blossom anywhere yet.

The 12 pullets which the Hollingsworths got from 24 of our eggs (White Leghorn x Buff Orpington—Sussex) have laid 1500 eggs since last autumn, or about 20 eggs per bird per month. They have been fed throughout on pig meal instead of ordinary laying mash. In the same period our own pullets of the same mating have not laid (ie. are only beginning now) owing to underfeeding.

Eight eggs.

For the first time M.[4] gave a quart today.

<u>15.4.39</u>: *Chilly, windy in the evening, & light showers. Began clearing out rhubarb patch, otherwise busy moving hen-houses. Evidently it helps a good deal if one can induce them to eat a meal in or very near the houses immediately after moving these, otherwise they always wander back to the original site.*

M. behaving as though on heat. Not certain, but shall note date (next should be 5–6 May.)

Saw another swallow. Thrush is sitting on eggs in our hedge. Dead nettle in flower. Sloe blossom quite pretty. The little tree I planted in the hedge 2 years [ago][5] & imagined to be a crab (because I found it under the apple tree & thought it was a sucker) turns out to be a bullace or wild plum.

Eight eggs.

<u>16.4.39</u>: *Rather chilly with sunny intervals, not much wind. A very light shower in the morning.*

Cowslips in flower here & there. This I think is rather early. Bluebells also beginning, a few in almost full bloom. This undoubtedly is unusually early. Wild cherries in full bloom. Sycamore leaves opening. Apple blossom almost about to open. Another thrush sitting [on] eggs in the hedge. Found a blackbird's nest with eggs. These are the only nests I have found hitherto.

The pond up by the church has become so stagnant that it no longer has duckweed, only the scummy green stuff. Nevertheless there are still a few newts in it.

Summer time began today, M's morning yield consequently small, but picked up in the evening.

Ten eggs. (Price of eggs sold yesterday 1/9 a score).

<u>17.4.39</u>: Rather chilly, some wind, occasional showers.

Buds of the walnut beginning to open. Lettuce seeds sown on 12.4.39 are germinating. A few tulips almost open.

Ten eggs. (57 this week.)

<u>18.4.39</u>: Fine but chilly.

Sowed broad beans. The ones sowed earlier are well up. Planted alyssum & antirhynums.°

Found a hatched thrush's egg—the first this year.

Five eggs.

Walnut buds opening.

<u>19.4.39</u>: Clear, sunny & rather warm.

Starlings have been courting for some days past, & flying about with straw in their beaks. One starling, presumably the male, sits on a bough erecting its neck feathers & making a rapid clicking noise with its beak, besides the usual crooning. A fair amount of swallows about. No martins yet.

Sowed peas (Notcutt's Lincoln, 1½ ft.) Sprayed about half the nettles under the walnut tree with sodium chlorate. Sitting-eggs came today but cannot obtain broody hens yet. M. restless & off her feed, possibly still on heat.

Very clear weather for the eclipse of the sun (anular,° starting at 6.28 pm, which was easily visible. At the time of the greatest eclipse, 7.15 pm when nearly half the sun was covered, it became somewhat dark & cold, but not enough so for any reactions to be noticeable in birds etc. The hens did not go into the houses.

Nine eggs. (Today's price 1/8d a score.)

<u>20.4.39</u>: Fine & very warm all day.

Bluebells everywhere. White starlike single flower with many petals (Star of Bethlehem?) now in bloom. In the garden, forget-me-nots, tulips & one or two anemones in bloom.

The thrush near the bullace tree has not deserted her nest, as I had imagined. It is evident therefore that they can be off the nest a considerable time without the eggs getting cold.

Apple blossom just about bursting.

Impossible to get broody hens anywhere. Nobody seems to have any.

Ten eggs (plus another 5 laid out, since about the 14th).

<u>21.4.39</u>: Fine & warm all day. Very dry.

Believe I saw the first shoot of bindweed today. Scythed down a patch of nettles to see the result. It is said one can eradicate them if they are scythed down 3 or 4 times in the year. Those treated with the sodium chlorate are dying.

Sowed broccoli, savoys, leeks, sprouts, cos lettuce.

Thirteen eggs.

<u>22.4.39</u>: Cold & windy, with some sunny intervals & a few spots of rain.

Flag irises budding. Some apple blossom full out.

Planted early potatoes (Eclipse, about 10 lb.)

Procured two broody hens, but not putting them on the eggs till tomorrow, to make certain.
Paid for hens 3/6 each.
Water hens on the pond evidently have nest.
Twelve[6] eggs.

[Newspaper cutting: 'Nettles have their Uses'—as a vegetable; to make beer]

<u>23.4.39</u>: *Raining, but not hard, almost all day.*
Lilacs almost out. Bindweed well up.
Great difficulties with so-called broody hens. One, after much reluctance, began to sit, but only took 8 eggs. The other evidently not broody at all, escaped & got among the other hens. This sitting of eggs probably wasted (2/ 6 the dozen.) Notice that when this hen went among the others they did not make hostile demonstration, as is usual. Probably owing to there being no cock. Tom Ridly[7] says that when keeping eggs awaiting a hen one should turn them daily, as in the incubator.
Put on a new cylinder of calor-gas.
Thirteen eggs. (It appears Titley is getting 2/–a score for his eggs.)
<u>24.4.39</u>: *Mostly fine, with rainy intervals, cold in the evening.*
Applied more sodium chlorate. Nettles treated previously have blackened. One hen refuses to sit. Took her home, as she may go broody again in familiar surroundings. The other sitting well on 11 eggs. She broke one in getting off to feed, so gave her one from the other sitting. Not certain of the effect of this—it will be 12–24 hours behind the others.
Preparing ground for turnips etc. Where the potatoes were last year there are practically no weeds.
A few strawberries beginning to blossom.
Fourteen eggs. (76 in this week–as from Sat. next shall begin ending week on Saturday.)

[From 25 April to 9 May Diary is written in Eileen's hand.]

<u>25.4.39</u>: *Raining most of the day, & cold. 14 eggs.*
<u>26.4.39</u>: *Sharp frost in the night. Raining. Short fall of snow in the morning. The doubtful hen sat the eggs during the night but was finally found not to be broody. Shall still put the eggs under a hen if obtainable, & watch results.*
Fifteen eggs (highest). 1/10 score.
<u>27.4.39</u>: *Sharp frost during night & hens' water frozen. Snow & sleet during most of the day. Short sunny intervals. Blossom seems undamaged.*
Perennial alyssum coming into flower. Scyllas & grape hyacinths coming to an end.
Starlings very busy obtaining straw for nests. Mrs. Anderson[8] heard cuckoo at 5.45. Caught a thrush in the kitchen, unhurt; a full-grown bird, very yellow inside beak.
Sixteen eggs (highest).
<u>28.4.39</u>: *9 eggs.*

29.4.39: *12 eggs*
30.4.39: *14 eggs. Came to Greenwich.*

1. '*Yesterday*'] '*Today,*' which is crossed out
2. Orwell and Eileen's dog.
3. A neighbour.
4. Muriel, Orwell's goat. Crick, plate 19, shows Orwell feeding her.
5. Orwell omitted 'ago' in starting a new page.
6. Orwell originally wrote 'eleven.'
7. A neighbour; correct spelling 'Ridley.'
8. A neighbour who 'did' for the Orwells, according to Monica Bald in *Remembering Orwell*, 115.

3.5.39: *Outside Miller Hospital,* [1] *starlings & sparrows stripping bark, apparently to make nests. Some small boughs completely stripped.*
8.5.39: *Visit to Wallington. Plum blossom over, apple full out (a great quantity). First peas ½"–1" tall. First beans 3". Second beans not showing. Rhubarb growing but not good (? protection necessary here for good crop; Mr. A.* [2] *has all his in tubs). Strawberries in flower. In last three days main crop potatoes, onions, carrots, turnips, second peas & radishes sown.*
Four nestlings in thrush's nest in hedge.
In flower: wallflowers, tulips, pansies, arabis (full out & decorative), yellow alyssum, aubretia, forgetmenots° & a few narcissi. Roses not in bud. Gooseberries mainly taken by frost or birds. Sowed grass seed in bare patches & scattered lawn sand.
Hens have laid 92 eggs in 8 days.
9.5.39: *Young pigeons in nest outside hospital window.*

[From 16 May the Diary is again written in Orwell's hand.]

16.5.39. London: *Weather for the most part showery, with fine intervals. In Greenwich Park, chestnuts, pink chestnuts (but not the Spanish ones) in flower, also lilac, hawthorn. Some of the wild ducks have ducklings. Some roses in bud. Tulips & wallflowers about at their best. Noted the following named tulips, all good kinds: Venus (cerise rose), Allard Pierson (light crimson), Miss Blanche (cream), William Pitt (bright crimson), Louis XIV (brownish mauve), Pride of Harlem (bright pink), Remembrance (pale mauve), Ambrosia (Daily Mail rose), Bartigon (sealing wax red), Nauticus (magenta), Rev. Ewbank (very pale mauve), Sultan (very dark brown, almost black).*

[Newspaper cuttings: Recipes using Sour Milk—'Like Christmas Cake'; 'A Danish Recipe'; 'Yoghourt as in Jugoslavia'; 'Swedish Filmjolk'; 'Salad Dressing'; 'Scaba Putra from Latvia'; these recipes, and other hints Orwell cut out, were contributed by readers to the newspapers.]

21.5.39: *Today & yesterday fine, but it is still not any too warm. Roses here are in full bud & almost out. Greenfly very bad. Lupins almost out. London Pride (kind of large saxifrage) is out. The gardener here* [3] *says that the number of varieties of roses is much exaggerated, as old varieties which have* dropped out of fashion & been almost forgotten are from time to time revived under a new name. Saw yesterday a swift & a turtle dove, the first I have seen this year, owing to illness. Hawthorn is well out, especially the pink. Hay looks pretty good.

At the Zoo[4] on 19.5.39. much interested in the manatee, which I had only vaguely heard of before. An animal about the size of a large seal, with broad tail behind & two flippers of some kind in front. The head is doglike, with small eyes, the surface of the body seems like that of an elephant, but is slimy from being in the water. Movements very sluggish. The peculiar feature is the mouth, which is fringed with large hairs & acts with a kind of sucking movement to draw food in. The creature is very tame & lets itself be touched. It appears that this is the only vegetarian water-mammal. Could not be sure whether it inhabits fresh or salt water, or both.

The elephant refuses radishes, which both deer & monkeys eat readily. Marmoset refuses spring onions, which most monkeys eat. Note that some S. American monkeys can almost hang by the tail alone, ie. by the tail & one hand or foot. Mouflon, the N. African kind, have bred very freely in the Zoo & look in better condition than those in Marrakech. Two families of lion cubs at present, & evidently attempts are being made to cross a lion & a tiger.[5]

25.5.39: Yesterday & the day before very warm. Today overcast, chilly enough to have a fire, & a few drops of rain.

Got back[6] yesterday after nearly 3 weeks' absence. Soil is very dry, weeds terrible except in kitchen garden. The field is now almost completely ruined with nettles & hemlock, but there is a small patch or two, about 200 sq. yards, which may yield a little hay. Grass everywhere is lush & very green. Plenty of fruit forming on the apples. Practically no currants or gooseberries in the kitchen garden, but plenty on the odd bushes in the flower garden. First (dwarf) peas about 4" high, the second (taller) about 2", first broad beans 6" or 8" high, a few early potatoes showing. Second potatoes, French beans, carrots, onions etc. not showing (all these planted very late). Radishes showing. A lot of blossom on the strawberries, even on some of the last year's runners. Tulips & wallflowers coming to an end. Flowers in full bloom: aubretia, yellow alyssum (very good), forget-me-nots, saxifrage, pansies. Budding: cheddar pinks, peonies, sweet williams, bush roses (not ramblers). Plenty of blossom on the loganberries.

From 9.5.39—23.5.39 inclusive there were 200 eggs. On 24.5.39 there were 14. Today 17. Shall start account afresh this Sunday, but I think there are none we have not recorded. Six chicks, now 10–12 days old, healthy but seem backward as to size. It appears the losses from this clutch (11 eggs) at the beginning were due to a mole which burrowed under the coop & buried some of the chicks. Eggs now are very good, much larger than a month back. Yesterday a tiny egg, about the size of a water-hen's (said locally, like a double egg, to be "always the first or the last" of a clutch). Three hens broody.

M. seems well, rather thin, appetite good. Still giving over 1½ pints (close on a year in milk now.)

Yesterday planted a dozen carnations.

435

26.5.39: *Warm. Ground is very dry. Fly is in the turnips. Many apples forming. Strawberries should be netted about a fortnight from now.*
Titly° has potatoes already earthed up. He says Catriona do not keep well for seed but store all right if gently treated. Blue flax in bloom. Some gooseberries almost ready to pick. Of the other batch of eggs 5 chicks have hatched; expected none, as the eggs had been about 3 weeks before a hen was found, & then the hen left them after a week & another had to be put on them. Planted antirhynums°
14 eggs.

N.B. 12.4.–26.5 (inc.) 550 eggs (26 hens.)

(Continued in Vol. II.) [Orwell's note]

VOL. II [Orwell's note]

27.5.39: *Overcast in the morning, fine & warm in the afternoon. Blue speedwell & bugle out everywhere. Buttercups about at their tallest. Dandelions seeding. Large toadstools in the fields.*
Strawed strawberries. Applied sodium chlorate to the remaining patch under the walnut tree.
Yesterday watched a thrush cracking a snail on a flat stone. Not, as I had thought, by pecking at it, but picking it up & knocking it on the stone.
15 eggs. Sold 50 eggs today, the largest batch sold hitherto. (1/10 a score). Eggs to date (see vol. I) 565.
Week starts tomorrow.

  [Newspaper cuttings: 'Gelatine Moulds'—for plaster casting; 'A Seed-Sowing Tip'—using an old cocoa tin; 'Capturing Queen Wasps']

28.5.39 *(Whit Sunday): Very chilly in early morning, the rest of the day fine & sunny. Some salvias were planted last night. Daily Mail rose now almost ready to open, buds on Dorothy Perkins & Albertine. Delphinium buds forming, peonies not far from opening.*
13 eggs (plus 7 laid out = 20). Today starts new egg week.
29.5.39: *Very fine & warm. Netted strawberries. Took M. to the billy but fear she is not on heat. Mr. N.[7] says they usually only are on autumn-spring. M. greatly afraid of a cow. The cow, on the other hand, frightened of a half-grown billy kid which was there.*
16 eggs.

  [Newspaper cuttings: 'Wet Mash for Laying Period'; 'Feeding Chicks'; 'Feeding Ducklings']

30.5.39: *Very fine & warm. Planted tomatoes (12), putting sacking over to protect them from the sun. One cheddar pink is out. A fine drizzle for a little while in the morning. Note that netting strawberries does not seem to inhibit the bees to any extent.*
14[8] eggs.

31.5.39: *Fine & warm, but strikes very chilly as soon as the sun begins to go in. Tomatoes (protected from the sun with sacking) are O.K. A few French & runner beans showing.*
M's mating no good. When bringing her back found she had not been milked since taking her there. (ie. 48 hours) & her udders were very distended. Milked her & obtained a quart, which seemed not soured or otherwise unsatisfactory. Do not know whether this will put her milk-yield back.
17 eggs. (sold 50 at 2/– a score).
Saw a white owl this evening.

1. The references to Miller Hospital, the visit to Greenwich, where Eileen's brother, Laurence O'Shaughnessy, lived, and Eileen's writing the diary may indicate that Orwell was undergoing tests under O'Shaughnessy's direction, possibly as an in-patient for a day or two.
2. Possibly Mr. Anderson, a Wallington neighbour.
3. Either the O'Shaughnessys' or at Greenwich Park.
4. Presumably London Zoo, in Regent's Park.
5. The result was the tigon, a zoo creation.
6. To The Stores, Wallington.
7. Probably Mr. Nicholls, a neighbour who kept goats, and who, according to Orwell, had a 'broken-down old wreck' not suitable for mating with Muriel, as he explained to Jack Common; see 516.
8. Orwell originally wrote '16.'

1.6.39: *Cold in the morning, warmed up later. Very windy. Began stick-ing° peas, put new perches in new henhouse. Uncovered tomatoes.*
11 eggs.
2.6.39: *Very hot, very dry, a good deal of wind. Young seedlings tending to droop. Titley has peonies, columbines full out. Honeysuckle also full out. A sweet william here & there beginning to open. Apples on the grenadier about the size of marbles. Ditto T's cherries.*
Stacked up some dried nettles etc. for litter. Set 10 duck eggs. Prepared ground for lettuces. Moved chicks.
M's milk has gone right back as a result of the upset. Less than a pint yesterday.
15 eggs. Weighed some eggs & found that only a very few are under 2 oz. M. gave about 1½ pts., so perhaps is going back to normal.
3.6.39: *Very hot & dry. Planted 1 score of T's lettuces & about a dozen (smaller) of our own. Protected with sacking, as with the tomatoes. E. planted 7 dahlias.*
The hen had pushed away 4 of the duck eggs, which had become quite cold. Put on another hen, removing one egg. Not certain whether this will have killed these eggs (which had been sat on 24 hours.)
12 eggs. Sold 40 at 2/– a score. Total this week 98 (+7=105).
4.6.39: *Extremely hot & dry. Made larger runs for chicks, putting sacking over as shade. Had to take the sacking from the lettuces, which had not wilted owing to being covered. A few sweet williams coming out. The other very small dianthus is coming out. These shut up at night, the cheddar pinks do not. Many greenfly on the roses. Squirted them with soap & water. M. gave 1¾ pts. today, so is about back to normal.*

437

14 eggs.
E. saw a white owl again last night.
<u>5.6.39</u>: *Unbearably hot. Everything is drying up. A sweet william out. Ragged robin out.*
Sowed peas (English wonder). Mulched tomatoes. French & runner beans have germinated very badly, so am sowing some in a box for fill-ups. New potatoes ready to be earthed up, a few of the maincrop showing.
5 eggs! (Presumably something to do with heat).
NB. that ½ pint of peas sows one of our rows (about 12 yards) thickly.
<u>6.6.39</u>: *Too hot to do much in the garden. Earthed up early potatoes.*
We are changing the hens on to Full-o-Pep, which is somewhat cheaper than Clarke's laying mash. Also getting corn etc. by the cwt., which effects a small saving. NB. that 1 cwt. each of Full-o-Pep & mixed corn begun today, & at 3 lb. a day of each should last till about July 12th. Great trouble with the broody hen, which at feeding time tries to rejoin the others. When caught & put into the coop, however, she goes back to her eggs.
Many turtle doves about.
11 eggs.
<u>7.6.39</u>: *Extremely dry & hot, but a little wind. There is fairly heavy dew at nights.*
Planted out 2 bush marrows, putting tins over them. E. cut the lawn with shears & then with the mower, which Albert H.[1] has sharpened (paid for sharpening 1/6). Continued sticking peas.
M. giving nearly a quart. Have sent for another goat, British-Alpine cross, kidded last month, £3.
9 eggs (plus 5 laid out = 14). Sold 1 score (2/–.)
<u>8.6.39</u>: *Very dry, not quite so hot.*
Prepared another marrow-bed, this time digging it less deeply & putting on 4-inch layer of lawn-clippings. Shall compare results of this style of bed with the other. Weeded & hoed the French & runner beans. Not much more than half of them are germinating. Uncovered the lettuces. Thinned out apples on the grenadier. About 60 left, but presumably not more than a dozen will stay on.
D.M.[2] rose is full out, delphiniums almost out.
M. is hardly eating any hard food, but her milk is not down.
12 eggs (plus 7 laid out = 19).
Duck eggs said to take 28 days or a month, so these are due out about June 30–July 2.
<u>9.6.39</u>: *Very dry, less hot. No signs of rain.*
Planted two more marrows & removed the covers from the others. Did more weeding. The turnips have completely disappeared & very few onions are left, & some of those wilting. Shall re-sow & plant after it has rained. Except the lettuces very little has germinated in the seed-bed. Eg. only 11 broccoli out of a packet. Maincrop potatoes now mostly up & look pretty good.
E. put six broodies in a sort of cage of wire netting, which may perhaps cure them.
The new goat arrived. Evidently had not been milked, so milked her,

obtaining 1½ pints, & another ½ pint tonight. Supposed to give 3–4 pints, but this business will no doubt have put her off, as with M. a few days back. Am not stripping M. & shall gradually get her down to one milking a day, also reducing her feed. M. very jealous, butting the other goat, stealing her food etc., the other goat (name Kate) not resisting.
10 eggs.

<u>10.6.39:</u> Extremely dry & pretty hot. Began hoeing maincrop potatoes, which are mostly through. Lettuces & marrows seem O.K. Many flowers in the garden drooping. The rainwater tank is now almost empty (the first time this has happened, but E. was here alone last summer).
K. wound herself up to her stake, then caught her hind leg & wound this so that it was twisted behind her neck & held there so tightly that I could only extricate her by undoing her collar. Very lame in consequence & ankle-joint swollen, but evidently nothing broken. Her yield today between 2 & 2½ pts. M. (not stripped) about 1½ pts.
8 eggs (plus 9 laid out = 17). Sold 2 score @ 2/–.
No. this week: 90.

<u>11.6.39:</u> Last night fairly heavy rain for 4–6 hours, which has freshened things up greatly. Today overcast & cooler.
Wildflowers now out: dogrose, poppies, campion, knapweed (a few), eggs & bacon,[3] scabious (a few), elder, sanfoin.[4] A few fruits on the wild plum tree.
K.'s leg better but her yield only about 2¼ pints, so am increasing her feed.
15 eggs.

<u>12.6.39:</u> There was evidently some rain during last night. This morning overcast & rather chilly, then from 4–6 in the afternoon heavy rain.
Finished hoeing maincrop potatoes, which are now practically all up. (There are 4 rows Epicure, 10 of Red King & 2 of King Edward. Excluding the Epicures, this ought to give about 3 cwt. of potatoes).
The hen sitting the duck eggs has twice moved them across the coop, presumably because moles burrowing below trouble her, but she seems to be sitting them all right.
E. planted out lobelia.
12 eggs.

<u>13.6.39:</u> Overcast, sunny intervals, some rain.
Took up tulips & planted out to finish their growth, also narcissi. Began putting up new hen-house (a shop-soiled one, price 17/6, which arrived uncreosoted & without roofing felt. Would accomodate° 10–12 full-grown hens.) Old H.[5] planted out more lettuces. Began earthing up early potatoes for the second time. One gap in the 4 rows. Let out the broody hens, hoping that some at least will have gone off by this time. Had to throw away 1 duck egg (now only 8) as the hen had turned it out.
A jackdaw has twice been hanging round the chicken coops, obviously with designs on the chickens.
11 eggs.

<u>14.6.39:</u> Bought 8 new R.I.R.[6] pullets, 3 to 3½ months old, well forward, 4/6 each.
Finished putting up new house, which however is not creosoted or roof-

felted yet, also the door needs adjustments. The old hen guarding the first lot of chicks has some sort of infection in her eye & will probably have to be destroyed.

3rd lot of peas (dwarf, sown 5.6.39) just showing. Runner & dwarf beans sown in box (6.6.39) coming up.

The broodies E. put in the cage, released yesterday, have[7] all (seven) gone back to normal.

K. now having 11 handfuls of feed at a meal, & yield rising very slightly (nearly 2½ pts.)

12 eggs. Sold 30 @ 2/– score.

15.6.39: Windy, coldish & occasional drizzle. Put up stakes & wires upon which to stretch strings for runner beans. Fixed door of henhouse & supported it off the ground.

K.'s milk yield increasing slightly.

15 eggs.

(NB began new bottle of iron pills yesterday).

16.6.39: Heavy rain in the night, raining on & off most of the day, till about 5 pm when it cleared up. Too wet to do much out of doors. Placed strings for beans (much too low), began preparing a patch for turnips in place of those which failed in the drought.

Am giving the hens grit & shell—the first time they have had it, as I thought it was not necessary on a chalky soil. However, of late some of the eggshells, though not thin, have been of rather bad texture. Now that the new house is raised the pullets get out under the edges in the mornings, so it is nowhere near foxproof until floored.

A few strawberries now red. Canterbury bells well out but want sticking. Grass is a lot better after the rain. Seem to be no gaps in maincrop potatoes.

15 eggs.

[Newspaper cutting: 'Cream Cheese from Goat's Milk']

17.6.39: Fine, fairly warm.

Sowed carnations (mixed perennial). Put roofing felt on henhouse. Paid for felt 9d a yard.

Both goats' milk badly down, no doubt owing to being unable to graze yesterday. Being indoors also seems to affect their appetite for hard food.

14 eggs. Sold 30 @ 2/– score.

No. this week: 94.

[Newspaper cutting: making corner posts for gates and fences]

18.6.39: Fine in the morning, raining fairly heavily most of the afternoon. The first ripe strawberry today. In spite of the net the birds are already getting at the partially ripe ones.

K's milk still down, only about 1 quart today.

13 eggs.

19.6.39: Fine most of the morning, raining most of the afternoon. Not cold. Ground now too wet to do much in garden. Put out runner beans to fill up gaps in row, sowed sweet williams & wallflowers, mended frame,

substituting windolite for glass. Note that windolite tends to develop small holes & [I] do not know whether it is repairable. Began thinning carrots, which, however, are largely gaps already, thanks to drought.
K's milk going up again (about 47 oz.)
15 eggs.
20.6.39: Fine in the morning, thunderstorm & fairly heavy rain in the afternoon. Earth too wet to do much. Started preparing place for a row of broccoli. Peonies almost out. Rambler (yellow) well out.
16 eggs.

[On facing page, in Orwell's hand:]

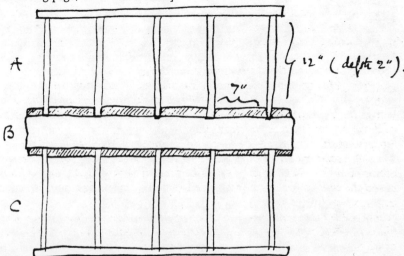

Mould° for concrete slabs. The shaded bits are nailed on (simpler than cutting tenons). A & C are each made in one piece, then jammed up against B, the ends of the sidepieces fitted into slots & weights placed against the ends. A & C can then be drawn away as the concrete begins to set. Except for B, the whole could be made of 2" by ½".

21.6.39: Cold, windy & some drizzle. Fire in the house all day. Did nothing out of doors. Did not put the goats out, owing to cold. Perennial Canterbury Bell (very poor flower) is well out.
11 eggs. Sold 40 @ 2/2 score.
22.6.39: Cold all day & very windy. Dense mist in the morning. Did nothing in garden.
14 eggs.
23.6.39: Overcast & drizzle but somewhat less cold. Did nothing in garden. Wallflowers sown 19.6.39 (in frame) beginning to show & carnations sown a day earlier also germinating. Thanks to the rain, a few carrots beginning to sprout in what were previously the gaps. Much of Innes's hay in & stacked. Peonies out. In Mrs B's garden mulleins out.
13 eggs.

[On 24 June Orwell went to Southwold to be with his father, who was very ill. Richard Blair died of cancer of the rectum on 28 June. Orwell was by his bedside. He returned to Wallington on 30 June. From 24–30 June the Diary is written in Eileen's hand.]

24.6.39: *Overcast & showery all the morning but sunny periods late & less cold. Goats out all day for the first time this week. A few very fine scabious out in the hedgerows but wild flowers much scarcer than a week or two ago. Albertine rose showing colour but not yet out; this & the bush roses have been in bud for a fortnight or more. Began earthing up maincrop potatoes. No gaps, though rather uneven growth.*

14 eggs. Total for week: 96[8]

25.vi°.39: *Fine all day & fairly warm until evening. Sweet williams, two red roses & one Albertine full out. A salvia & a marigold in bud. Some stonecrop in full flower. Stonecrop appears to flower erratically as one clump has been out for two or three weeks & others (all contemporary) are still in bud.*

15 eggs.

26.6.39: *Warm sunny morning. Threats of thunderstorms in afternoon but no thunder & little rain. Potatoes earthed up. Gaps filled in french bean rows with extras sown in a box in the frame when the original rows were found to have germinated badly—i.e. after an interval of ten days or so. There is very little difference in development. Blackfly have already settled on about a quarter of the broad beans, though not in great numbers; pinched out growing points. The strings for the runner beans were tangled & stretched by rain & wind. Apparently four or five stakes are necessary for one of our rows. Weeded & hoed onions which are now three or four inches tall but with many gaps in the rows. Beans & peas have grown very rapidly, some runner bean tendrils lengthening by a couple of inches since Saturday.*

12 eggs.

27.6.39: *Very hot & sunny. Thinned carrots & hoed peas etc. Planted out 48 larkspurs, removing some poor sweet williams. Apparently sweet williams sometimes 'shoot up' for several years but cannot be made to do so.*

15 eggs + 8 found in a nest.

28.6.39: *Much cooler & occasional showers. Mr H. finished cutting the hay & collected it today. Sowed turnips & planted out a row of mixed greens from the seed bed. Both broody hens with chickens laid today, & one (the youngest) had three other eggs hidden at the back of the coop.*

14 eggs + 3 in coop.

29.6.39: *Hot & sunny most of the day. One duck had hatched this morning. Later moved the hen to new coop & left the more backward eggs with another broody. By evening 7 ducks; the eightth° egg shows no sign of hatching but have put it under the hen for the night. The first ducks are fluffed up but show no disposition to walk about. Apparently ducklings are much slower to walk than chickens, being 'weak in the legs' (Mrs R.).*[9] *Made an awning with adjustable sacking cover & put flat dish of water in coop.*

Rehoed onions which are growing at last. Marrows also growing, one strongly. White rose out. 15 eggs.

<u>30.6.39</u>: *Ducklings still under hen this morning but in the afternoon came out to eat (brown bread crumbled with milk & dried a little with a sprinkling of chickmeal).*
Thundery weather with heavy showers.
14 eggs.

1. 'H' usually signifies 'Old Hatchett,' so Albert H. may be another neighbour at Wallington, perhaps Albert Hollingsworth; see *21.8.39*.
2. *Daily Mail*; see *16.5.39* and *28.5.39*.
3. See *4.3.39, n. 1*.
4. This is the spelling of sainfoin favoured by Orwell; see *Coming Up for Air* and *501, n. 2*.
5. Old Hatchett, a neighbour.
6. Rhode Island Red.
7. Orwell first wrote 'nearly all,' then crossed out 'nearly' and added 'seven' interlinearly.
8. Total was added later, in Orwell's hand.
9. Probably Mrs. Ridley, a neighbour.

<u>1.7.39</u>: *Fine most of morning, very heavy showers in afternoon.*
Garden mostly in good condition. Some strawberries ripe, a few broad beans fit to pick, onions improving, runner beans just starting to climb strings. Hay is cut & stacked in small stack about 6' by 5', but not certain yet whether we can preserve this. M.'s milk going off considerably. Ducklings all healthy & lively, young chicks making good growth. Such currants as there are are ripening.
Marigolds (a few) in flower. Wild scabius° appearing.
10 eggs (plus 14 laid out = 24).
Sold this week 72 @ 2/2d. Total this week = 120.
<u>2.7.39</u>: *Overcast most of day, a heavy shower in the afternoon, & cold enough to have a fire.*
Both the hens guarding chicks have begun laying eggs & the younger one showed a tendency to stray away. E. therefore put her with the other hens & put all chicks together with the other hen. This morning two of the youngest badly pecked, especially the one which for some reason is white. Have segregated these two, & we are going to wean the others at once. Three of the elder ones are already perching.
Picked about 1½ lb. of strawberries & had some broad beans (young, eaten pod & all). These are about the first produce of the garden. A few loganberries reddening. Apples on the grenadier as large as golf balls. Clarkia beginning to flower.
11 eggs.
Cylinder of Calor gas, started 8.6.39, gave out today.
Cwt. of Full-o-Pep, started 6.6.39, getting low in the bin. Should last till 12.7.39. Actually might last till about 8th or 10th, but some of it has been fed to the pullets occasionally.
<u>3.7.39</u>: *Warmer, sunny most of day.*
Planted pumpkin (somewhat too late, & in a too shady position). Earthed up north[1] side of maincrop potatoes. No gaps, but some very immature. Lifted tulip bulbs. One early potato withered up—trust not disease. Turnips (sown

28.6.39) are showing. One pullet limping.
15 eggs.

<u>4.7.39</u>: *Fine & hot. A few raspberries reddening. Phloxes in bud, also bergamot. Goats escaped this morning & ate a lot of fruit tree shoots, rose shoots & some tops of phloxes. Pullet still limping badly & fear some kind of paralysis, tho' she seems otherwise in good condition. Put gate on duck run & allowed the ducklings out of the coop. Today started new cwt. of Full-o-Pep & cwt. of corn. The pullets are also having from the latter, but of course not having laying mash. On the other hand 4 old fowls sold today. The mash therefore has to do for 24 hens, the corn for 32. Mash should therefore last about 35 days, corn about the same (allowing 1½ oz. per bird.) Shall try & reach the end before ordering new stuff next time, in order to see how it lasts out. This lot ought to give out about the 8th August, which is a Tuesday. Started the hens on a course of Karswood spice today.*
10 eggs.

<u>5.7.39</u>: *Hot. A short shower in the evening. Bergamot in bud. The white chick looks bad, & the pullet which is limping no better. A few loganberries ripe enough to pick. Started creosoting henhouse. Sowed radishes, cos lettuce, parsley. E. sowed F[rench] beans.*
10 eggs. Sold 2 score @ 2/6

<u>6.7.39</u>: *Very windy, & raining lightly most of the day. Too wet to do anything outside. Nasturtiums in flower. Roses now extremely good. Another 2 lb. strawberries. (3½ lb. to date—am noting amounts in order to see what weight of fruit that space produces).*
11 eggs.

<u>7.7.39</u>: *Some rain in the morning, hot in the afternoon. Transplanted onions as well as possible, but there are still some gaps. New cylinder of Calor gas begun today.*
9 eggs. Sold 8 @ 1½d.

<u>8.7.39</u>: *Raining much of the day, a fine interval in the evening, very windy. Picked some more loganberries. One hollyhock beginning to flower. A few runner beans show buds. Tomatoes flowering, also several marrows. One or two snapdragons beginning to flower. Have evidently been overfeeding the pullets, which are leaving some of their mash. The limping one no better, though otherwise seemingly all right in health, so shall segregate her tomorrow. A few self-sown potatoes uprooted today have potatoes only about the size of marbles on them. Putting the ducklings on mash from today.*
10 eggs. Sold 1/2 score @ 2/6. No. this week: 76

<u>9.7.39</u>: *Warm, no rain. The little apple tree (grenadier pippin)★ so weighted down with apples that we are obliged to support the branches. Kate[2] is unwell, refused food this evening & was sick, or threw up her cud. Muriel also somewhat off her feed. I suspect this is due to their being tethered in the hot sun without shade.*
Found wild canterbury bells. Wood pigeons still sitting on nests. No crab

★ *It seems the grenadier is a cooker, not an eater as I thought* [Orwell's note].

apples on the big tree this year, though the garden apples are everywhere good. Seemingly no wild cherries. The birds have had the few red currants there were in our garden. This evening caught & brought home some newt tadpoles in varying stages of development. They get the front legs first* (toads get hind legs—not certain about frogs) & have 4 fingers on each hand. Much more agile than toad tadpoles, diving into the mud when pursued. According to Edie W.,[3] adult newts if put into the aquarium with tadpoles will devour them. Found a water snail whose shell was as long as the top two joints of my forefinger; have never before seen one approaching this size.

Planted a slip of rambler rose, but believe this is too early.[†] Picked more loganberries.

12 eggs.

<u>10.7.39</u>: Overcast, warm & still. Some hollyhocks flowering. Madonna lilies & bergamot almost out. Did nothing in garden except weeding. K's appetite somewhat improved but bad drop in her milk today (only about 1¼ pt.) E. picked about 1½ lb. strawberries yesterday.

10 eggs.

<u>11.7.39</u>: Warm but not very sunny. Pricked out 90 wallflowers (flame). T.[5] thinks the lame pullet may have "the disease" (presumably coccidiosis) in which case it would be better to kill her. The infallible symptom is yellow dung, but apparently it usually starts with lameness in the left leg.

Started the goats on cotton cake to see whether they will eat it. K.'s milk normal again (2½ pts.) 2 lb. strawberries. Sussex hen is moulting.

12 eggs.

<u>12.7.39</u>: Hot. Madonna lilies out.
Bedstraw, mallows & knapweed in flower. Robin's pincushions on briars. Goats will not eat cake every time so shall give it them about once a week.

12 eggs. Sold 1½ score @ 2/8.

<u>13.7.39</u>: Hot. The lame hen segregated to watch developments.

14 eggs. Bergamot flowering.

<u>14.7.39</u>: Warm, but rainy. Took nets off strawberries & began weeding, which is almost impossible owing to the growth of the bindweed.
Phloxes (perennial) beginning to flower.

12 eggs.

<u>15.7.39</u>: Warm. A very short light shower in the evening. Weeded out the strawberries, as well as could be done, & picked off such as were ripe. More berries forming, but doubt if we shall get any now the nets are off.[‡] Yesterday found a late thrushe's° nest with one egg (bird on it). One white hen missing—possibly sitting somewhere on a nest, but afraid she is lost, as she has been gone since yesterday.

14 eggs. Sold 2 score @ 2/8. Total this week: 86.[§]

---

* Not quite certain about this. They seem to have all 4 legs when still only about ½–¾ inch long [Orwell's note].

† It took all right. But died in the frost Jan. 1940 [Orwell's note].

‡ Up to taking off nets, about 7½ lb @ 6d a lb = 3/9 [Orwell's note].

§ Improvement of 10 on last week. Hens have been on Karswood since 4.7.39 [Orwell's note].

Butcher says hens are laying better again, so eggs will go down [in price].
16.7.39: *Sharp shower in the morning, otherwise fairly warm. The white hen has turned up, evidently having slept out somewhere. Note that Innes has coppered over some of the chains, bolts etc. in his haymaking machinery in the same way as I did experimentally with the nails, so evidently it is not so impracticable after all. The copper where I attempted it crusted the threads of bolts so that they would not turn.*
All the small pools in the woods have dried up. Note that on one a waterhen had built a nest & then had to clear out when the pool dried up.
Seeds formed on bluebells, hips forming on briars.
12 eggs.

[On facing page, in Orwell's hand:]

To drill holes in Glass (according to "Smallholder"): Use small twist drill. Mark spot with glass-cutter, give a turn or two of the drill, then smear on grease, sprinkle with emery or carborundum powder & drill gently, not pressing.

17.7.39: *Warmish in morning, thunderstorms & heavy rain most of afternoon.*
Picked first peas, about 1 lb. Thinned out turnips, which are very good & untouched by the fly. Began digging patch for greens, but too wet to do much.
Hens which have made nests outside will apparently continue to sit there in the middle of pouring rain. Very small newt tadpoles put into aquarium seem to disappear. Fear the large ones may be eating them, but if so this must only occur at night. Note that the water-snail is able in some way to elevate himself to the top of the water & remain floating there—or possibly is naturally buoyant & only remains down when using suction.*
11 eggs. (1 double egg— the first for some time).
18.7.39: *Raining almost the whole day. Too wet to do much outside.*
Female flowers coming on first marrow.
11 eggs.
19.7.39: *Showers, but mostly fine. Everything now growing very fast. Many peas. A few tomatoes about the size of marbles. One or two marrows about size of peanuts.*
Not certain whether a pullet has begun laying prematurely or whether the mother hen which is still in the youngsters' run (& which lays a small egg) had laid out, but found an egg in that run today.
Sowed canterbury bells (prob. too late, but they do very well if treated as triennials.)
13 eggs (2 very small). Sold 35 for 4/3 (2/6 a score—should have been 4/4½).
20.7.39: *Some sun in the morning, otherwise almost continuous rain all day. Impossible to do anything outside. Notice that hens always eat less in*

---

* *Can also rise to surface when he wants to, or can remain on bottom without holding on* [Orwell's note].

this weather. Top of the hay under a few sacks is still dry in spite of the constant rain. Goats show slight tendency to diarrhea from eating wet grass. Stated today in letter in D. Tel. that for 1 person using electricity for all purposes, except a periodical coal fire for warming, 1800–2000 units is annual minimum consumption.
12 eggs (1 v. small—it is the mother hen that lays these).
21.7.39: *Fine part of the day, but overcast & damp in the morning, & a thunderstorm in the afternoon. Wheat yellowing. Planted out leeks (38 make a row.). Weeds very bad everywhere. This morning a female flower on a marrow opened; shut again this evening so presumably fertilised. Goats' yield down, owing to yesterday. Gooseberries almost ripe.*
13 eggs.
22.7.39: *Overcast & oppressive. A good deal of rain for about an hour in the evening. E. raised 3 roots of early potatoes (only 3 months sown). Few potatoes, about 1 lb. on the 3, but many young ones coming.*
12 eggs. Sold 1½ score @ 2/6. Total this week: 84.
23.7.39: *A little rain in the evening, otherwise dry, but overcast & not very warm. Many harebells. Found the first ripe dewberry. Oats almost ripe in some fields, wheat grains still milky. Seagulls about—one does not usually see them here. The Ridleys have a dahlia in bloom.*
12 eggs.
24.7.39: *Fine in morning, cold & miserable in afternoon. Wildflowers now in bloom: agrimony, perforated St. John's Wort, red dead nettle, wild mignonette, self-heal, woody nightshade, stitchwort. Found nest of wild bees in grass in churchyard. Nest of moss rather like that made by dormouse. Dahlias budding. Picked first of our own lettuces today, & first ripe gooseberries yesterday. Many peas.*
14 eggs (1 small). A little rain this evening.
25.7.39: *Fine & fairly hot. Endeavouring to stack the hay. 12 eggs (1 small).*

Probably about 26 July 1939 Orwell wrote to the Scientific Poultry Breeders' Association about the Food Purchase Scheme it ran for members. His letter has not survived, but one from S. R. Harvey, General Manager and Secretary of S.P.B.A. Supplies, Ltd., dated 28 July, gives details of discounts allowed on poultry feedstuffs, and also encloses details of association membership.

26.7.39: *Fine & warm. Finished thatching hay, as well as it can be done, which is not very well. However this is practice for another occasion when there is more hay. Stack is about 8' × 6' by 5' at highest point. Hoed out cabbages & turnips, both doing well.*
11 eggs (1 small). Sold 35 @ 2/6 score (4/3—ought to have been 4/4½).
27.7.39: *Hot. A very few drops of rain in the evening.*
Red mite is bad in the henhouses, partly no doubt owing to one or two hot days. Dealt with them with boiling water & sulphur afterwards, hoping this will be effective. NB. that plumber's blowlamp would be the best thing. Hen's appetite is off as usual in hot weather. Planted out a few cos lettuce, otherwise nothing except weeding. The pumpkin has now taken hold but is

still a small plant. The watersnail has laid some eggs. Don't [know] [6] *whether these creatures are bisexual or not.*

NB. that for storage purposes in tanks etc., 20 gallons *space will about hold 1 cwt. of meal, or more of grain (say 1¼ cwt.)*

14 eggs (2 small—believe 1 pullet is now laying).

<u>28.7.39</u>: *Some rain during last night. Hot. Nothing except weeding, mowing down thistles etc.*

9 eggs.

<u>29.7.39</u>: *Apparently a few spots of rain in the night. Hot today. Mowed nettles. 6 eggs! (possibly something to do with heat.) Sold 25 @ 2/6 score. Total this week: 78*

<u>30.7.39</u>: *A little rain during last night. Today hot. Canterbury bell seeds germinating. Pulled first carrots today. Earwigs now very troublesome.*

10 eggs (2 small).

<u>31.7.39</u>: *Most of day overcast, heavy showers & thunder about mid-day. Weeded onions. Pricked* [7] *out 35 carnations. The wallflowers planted on 11.7.39 about 3" to 4" high. One hollyhock which is coming into flower is white. There are therefore 4 colours (dark red, light red, pale pink, white) from the original dark seed. Peas are very good, much more than we can eat. Last cwt. of corn finished this morning. Begun on 4.7.39, should by calculation have lasted to about August 10th, but the 8 pullets have been fed on it for the last 3 weeks, also to some extent the 6 next chicks. Full-o-pep bought at same time only about 2/3 gone.*

11 eggs [8] *(3 pullets? Evidently at least 1 pullet is now laying.)*

1. Circled by Orwell; 'west' written by him on facing page.
2. Orwell originally wrote 'Kay.'
3. Edie W. was Mrs. Ridley's daughter; the W. stands for her husband Stanley's name.
4. Orwell originally wrote '9,' crossed it out, and substituted '7.' His letter to Leonard Moore of 11 June 1939 is also erroneously dated as 11.9.39; see *548, n. 1.*
5. Perhaps Mr. Titley.
6. Orwell omitted 'know' in starting a new page.
7. 'Planted' crossed out; 'Pricked' inserted.
8. *11 eggs]8 eggs*; presumably amended after the three pullets' eggs were found.

<u>1.8.39</u>: *Warm. A few drops of rain. Pricked* [1] *out wallflowers (yellow) & sweet williams. Calculate roughly that each row of peas (about 12 yards) will yield 15–20 lb. Started new cwt. of wheat & kibbled maize today. This has to do for 23 adult fowls & 8 pullets (almost full grown). At 1½ oz per bird per day should last till about September 8th.*

10 eggs (3 small – 3 pullets laying now.)

<u>2.8.39</u>: *Most of day overcast & rather chilly. Only weeding etc*

12 eggs. (2 pullets?). Sold 30 @ 2/6 score.

<u>3.8.39</u>: *Unbroken rain from early this morning till about 8 pm. One or two dahlias now in flower. Examining yesterday one of the large black slugs common at this time of year (about 4" long when extended) noticed that the curious hole they have a little way behind the head opens & shuts more or less*

* *NB. That apparently 20 galls. equals almost exactly 3 cubic ft.* [Orwell's note].

rhythmically, & has inside whitish tissue like sago pudding. Possibly this is their breathing hole?

Some oats cut, barley mostly ripe & looks very good, no wheat ripe. Toadflax in flower. Only one or two plums on the wild plum tree.

Gave M. her worm powder, with great difficulty, having kept her more or less without food all day.

12 eggs (1 small—1 pullet is now laying larger eggs.)

4.8.39: Raining most of day, with sunny intervals, windy. Ground now very sodden, everything growing very fast. Lifted some more early potatoes (about 3½ months). Not many on each root. Saw the lost hen again this morning. Mrs A. says she has seen her several mornings & thinks she is in the thick bushes up the west end of the field. She occasionally comes out to eat, usually in the very early morning. The trouble is that a fox or dog may get her before she has finished brooding.

13 eggs (3 small.)

5.8.39: Raining almost continuously until about 6.30 pm Parts of the day rain extremely heavy. Baldock high street said to have been flooded. Marrows swelling very rapidly. French & runner beans 3" or 4" long. Apples growing very fast.

Cylinder of calor gas, started 7.7.39, gave out yesterday (27 days). Started new cylinder today.

9 eggs (2 small). Sold 30 @ 2/6 score. Total this week: 77 of which 15 small.

6.8.39: No rain, fairly warm. The big crab tree in the lane has failed to produce any apples, but found others with fruit. Blackberries still only in flower. Hazel nuts still solid inside. Innes's cows due to calve shortly. Waterhens still have quite small chicks. Many young rabbits. Found dead cat in lane. Notice that hens will eat the large black slugs. Forgot to mention that on Thursday saw what I think must be a hawfinch. Greenfinches in the hen run from time to time, but goldfinches uncommon here.

11 eggs (3 small)

7.8.39: Finer. In the morning rather cold & a little rain, afternoon overcast & warm. Finished preparing ground for winter greens. Put slugs in prepared box to test what kinds of foodstuff they go after most. Yesterday found dead newt in the road, so they must be leaving the water now. A certain number of this year's frogs about, about the size of runner beans.

9 eggs (1 small).

8.8.39: Some rain & thunder, but most of day fairly fine though not hot. Goats' milk is badly off, less than a quart from the two, no doubt owing to the several days without grazing. Evenings now drawing in noticeably.

12 eggs (3 small).

9.8.39: Some rain² in the evening, otherwise warm, but overcast. Planted out 60 broccoli, rather late & all rather leggy & unpromising, but hope they may take. Impossible to get any kale etc., for which of course it is rather late.

10 eggs (2 small). Sold 30 @ 2/6 score.

10.8.39: Rain during much of the day. Cut side-shoots out of tomatoes (this should have been done much earlier), began preparing another patch for greens, put up another coop for the ducks, as the 7 of them can hardly crowd

into one coop now. Note that fresh goat manure when piled sets up a certain amount of heat, though seemingly not so much as horse manure.
10 eggs (2 small).

<u>11.8.39</u>: *Warm & fine. In the reservoir came upon waterhen with one very small chick. This was in close to the side & remained absolutely still, on my prodding it & turning it over with a stalk of hemlock it still made no move, so that I thought it was dead, then suddenly dived & remained under water for several minutes.*
The watersnail's eggs appear to have hatched & the creatures are moving about, but they are still jellified & in some kind of embryonic state, not, as I had thought, fully developed before they come out.
Cut first marrow today. Fair amount of beans now.
11 eggs (3 small).

<u>12.8.39</u>: *Warm & fine. Some carnations now well out.*
10 eggs (2 small). Sold 25 @ 2/6 score & 10 (pullets) @ 2/2 score.
Total this week: 73 (16 small).

<u>13.8.39</u>: *Warm & fine.*
10 eggs (2 small).

<u>14.8.39</u>: *Warm & fine. Damsons (such as there are) almost ripe. Finished getting ground ready for greens. At last found the lost hen, which was sitting on 13 eggs. She has been gone just a month. Altogether 6 broodies now (out of 23 hens). Put them all in E's cage this afternoon. Yesterday with great difficulty we weighed a duck, &, if we were not wrong, it was about 3¾ lb (6½ weeks). So we are going to send the 2 biggest to market tomorrow to see what they fetch.*
10 eggs (3 small).
Cwt. of Full-o-Pep gave out today. Started on 4.7.39—about 40 days. Should have been 35, so perhaps have been underfeeding them a bit. On the other hand in warm weather they often don't eat all they are given.
Saw a cuckoo this morning. They have been silent for some time & are about due to leave. Found a dead shrew mouse on the road. I do not know why, one always finds them dead about this time of year.

<u>15.8.39</u>: *Hot. Had some damsons stewed (rather sour.) Ground dries up very rapidly. A few larkspurs coming into flower, roses coming into second bloom (most of them not good owing to the species of blight they have this year). The pumpkin's largest shoot now about a yard long & 1 female flower. Not certain whether it can make its growth in time, ie. in the next 6–8 weeks. Found another dead shrew. Wasps beginning to be troublesome. The new snail has laid a lot of eggs. Now that the white broody is off her nest, something finds & eats the eggs. Suspect cat, but might be rats, jackdaws or other hens.*
Only 2/11 each (ie. 2/8 without commission) for 7-week ducklings weighing 4¼ lb. At this rate there is only a few pence profit on each bird, but we are buying mash in small quantities at which it costs 1½ lb.[3] At the price of Full-o-Pep (1¹⁄₁₀d per lb) there would be more.
11 eggs (2 small).

<u>16.8.39</u>: *Hot. Ground again very dried up. Hoed onions & flowers in nursery beds, watered pumpkin & tomatoes, cut down broad beans, which have*

got too big & are not worth leaving to ripen. Some turnips almost fit to pull. Cut second marrow. Grass which E. has cut is now quite good.
10 eggs (3 small). Sold 25 @ 2/6 score.
Ripe plums now only 2d lb.
17.8.39: Hot. Some blackberries reddening. Found a few mushrooms. Most of the corn now cut, & everyone working fast to get in the remainder while the good weather lasts. Coveys of partridges are mostly large (8–12 birds) but the young birds seem rather small. Saw bird which I cannot identify. In size colour & type by flight it resembled a waterhen, but apparently was not a waterhen, as it flew too well & took to the wing too readily, & also it was nowhere near water. It got up together with a hen pheasant, but was certainly not a pheasant at any stage of development. When Marx put up a covey of partridges the mother did the well known trick (it is sometimes denied that this really happens) of leading M. off by flying rather slowly & squawking, while the young ones flew away in a different direction. Saw what I believe was a fieldfare, though this seems very early. Cock goldfinch calling to mate makes sound rather like "chee-wa" (less like "cheese" than that of greenfinch).
8 eggs (3 small).
18.8.39: Hot. Refitted door to henhouse.
10 eggs (3 small).
19.8.39: Hot. Planted out 1 score each Brussels, savoys & purple sprouting broccoli. Paid 3d per score. Not very good plants & very dry, but fairly good roots, so they should take. Suspicion of club-root (which we have never had here) in one plant which I got rid of. Some white turnips (sown 28.6.39) ready to pull.
"Smallholder" claims wireworm in carrot beds etc. can be dealt with by 2 oz. per sq. yard of mixed napthaline & freshly slaked lime.
9 eggs (3 small). Sold 20 @ 2/6 score & 10 @ 2/– score
Total this week: 68 (19 small).
20.8.39: Hot in the morning. Then thunder & heavy showers. Raining hard tonight. Goats greatly terrified by the thunder, & M. managed to break loose from her chain.
Pinched out growing point of pumpkin. Gave onions their final thinning out. First peas about finished. Larkspurs flowering. Side shoots of tomatoes grow so fast that it is impossible to keep pace with them.
8 eggs (4 small—evidently another pullet laying.)
21.8.39: Hot till evening, then heavy thunder & rain. Cut side-shoots out of tomatoes, dug in a little ash from bonfire round their roots, cleared & burnt first lot of dwarf peas & began digging over this patch of ground, which will do for leeks. Planted some of those yellow flowers (sort of summer chrysanthemum) which Mrs Hollingworth gave us, though do not know whether they will take, as some are already in flower. Gave liquid manure to some of the larkspurs. A good many self-sown antirrhinums about.
Weighed the remaining 5 ducks, which go to market tomorrow. The 5 weigh just on 24 lb., the heaviest about 5¼ lb. They are just 7½ weeks old.
8 eggs (2 small).

<u>22.8.39</u>: *Drizzle in the morning, rest of day fine & hot. The mist is now very thick in the early mornings. Dug some more of the patch for the leeks, gave liquid manure to larkspurs etc. E. planted some more godetias. Only 11/– for 5 ducks weighing 24 lb. Complete account is in the egg book, but worth noting here that, putting aside the bread & milk of their first week, 91 lb. of mash (actually more—say 95 lb.—as they occasionally had some of the other birds' food) equals 32 lb. of meat, or about (allowing for everything) 3¼ lb. of feed for 1 lb of meat.*

One of the newts is now mature. Its gill formations are gone & it lies on top of the water with its head in the air much of the time. The watersnail was yesterday sucking at the piece of raw meat we put in for the newts.

Marx discovered to be very lousy, ears full of nits, no doubt partly owing to the hot weather. E. treating him with antiseptic soap, flea powder & also vinegar, which loosens the nits, allowing them to be combed out.

11 eggs (4 small). Cwt. of corn begun today.

<u>23.8.39</u>: *Hot. Dug some more of the patch for leeks, transferred the cockerels (5) to the small pen, deloused the hen-houses. Great trouble getting rid of the red mite, which multiplies very fast in this weather. They have to be burned out, but even so it is hard to make sure of them. A plumber's blowlamp is what one needs. When a house is infested badly the hens will not go into it. Found nest of 14 (Rhode) eggs laid out, evidently not very new, so shall not sell them or enter them in the account, though the one I tried was not bad.*

8 eggs (4 small). Sold 20 @ 2/6, & 10 @ 1/– score.

<u>24.8.39</u>: *Hot. Planted 2 rows leeks (about 75 plants). There are 5 different colours of larkspurs coming out.*

9 eggs (4 small).

<u>31.8.39</u>: *Ringwood[4] (Hants). 24–29.8.39 hot, yesterday & today fairly heavy rain. Blackberries are ripening in this district. Finches beginning to flock. Very heavy mists in the early mornings.*

1. Substituted for 'Planted,' which is crossed out.
2. Orwell first wrote 'A few spots of rain.'
3. One and a half pence per pound.
4. See *565, 28.8.39, n. 1.*

Orwell stayed with L. H. Myers at Ringwood from at least 24 to 31 August and, as his diary shows, was not back at Wallington until 5 September, two days after Britain's declaration of war following Germany's invasion of Poland on 1 September. He may have gone to Greenwich on 1 or 2 September, and was certainly there on 3 September; see *565, 28.8.39, n. 1.*

It was Myers who had provided the loan (intended as a gift) that enabled the Orwells to spend the winter of 1938–39 in French Morocco. Orwell did not know who his benefactor was until 1946, two years after Myers's death, when he made the first instalment on repaying what he took to be a debt. He sent this to Dorothy Plowman, who had acted as intermediary; see *2903.*

<u>5.9.39</u>: *Have not been able to keep up the diary owing to travelling to & fro, dislocation caused by the war etc. The weather has been mainly hot & still. On the night of 2.9.39 a tremendous thunderstorm which went on almost continuously all night.*

On returning to Wallington after 10 days absence find weeds are terrible. Turnips good & some carrots have now reached a very large size. Runner beans fairly good. The last lot of peas did not come to much. A number of marrows. One pumpkin about the size of a billiard ball. Apples on the grenadier almost ripe. Damsons & bullaces ripe. All the winter vegetables have taken all right. Early potatoes rather poor, only about 5–6 potatoes to a plant, but the later ones look as if they would be good. Onions fair. Lettuces have all gone to seed. Flowers in nursery beds (wallflowers 2 kinds, sweet williams & carnations) doing all right. Hollyhocks & marigolds almost over. Roses (not ramblers) blooming again. Larkspurs quite good. Bergamot over, & phloxes almost over. Dahlias full out. Some michaelmas daisies out. Grass has grown very tall in 10 days.

It seems that since 24.8.39 (ie. 12 days) the hens have laid only 85[1] eggs, mostly big ones. All the older hens are moulting. Goats have been a week on grass only owing to Clarke's failing to deliver grain last week but in good condition & still giving a reasonable amount of milk.

<u>6.9.39</u>: Very hot. Rooted up first lot of French beans & dug over that patch, which will do for spring cabbage. Cut side shoots out of tomatoes. These have not done at all well. All leaf & stalk, the plants growing so huge that it is almost impossible to get them to stand upright, & few & poor tomatoes (one or two now ripening.) Probable cause too much animal manure & not enough light.

10 eggs.

<u>7.9.39</u>: Very hot. Weeded out first lot of broccoli & dug between. Cut down nettles under the apple tree & applied 1 lb. sodium chlorate. A lot of apples but they are not very good or big, & many windfalls. Made 2–3 lb. apple jelly out of the windfalls.

8 eggs (1 small).

Forgot to mention that at Ringwood I several times saw large flocks of goldfinches, in one case over 30 in the flock.

NB. to count eggs for earlier days of this week at 7 a day, as during our absence they laid 85 in 12 days.

<u>8.9.39</u>: Hot. Blackberries not ripe yet. Have lifted the remainder of the early potatoes, which are very poor, only about 5 potatoes to a root.

8 eggs.

[Newspaper cuttings: 'Curing a Goat Skin';[2] 'For Gathering Out-of-Reach Fruit']

<u>9.9.39</u>: Very hot. Dug up 3rd batch of peas & dug over that piece of ground. Red mite again very bad. Most of the leghorns now moulting but not so many of the Rhodes. Notice that the birds' appetites always drop off in this weather, ditto the goats, though they don't drink much.

11 eggs. Sold 35 @ 3/- score. Total this week: 58

[Newspaper cutting: 'Feeding all Home-Grown Foods']

<u>10.9.39</u>: Warmish, but overcast. Dug the 2 rows of King Edward potatoes

(actually most of them are not K.E. but another larger kind, perhaps Great Scott). Again very poor though better than the earlies. The best had 16 sizeable potatoes to the root, average about 8. A great many I had to throw away as they were squashy. Everyone here is making the same complaint, so evidently we have some disease about. The first bush marrow has produced a great number of marrows. We had already cut 2 or 3 off it & now it has 4 more sizeable ones & others coming. The pumpkin has at last got hold & is swelling rapidly, so should have time to reach a fair size before the frosts.
8 eggs.
NB. that M. was showing signs of heat about 8th & 9th, so should come on again about the 30th.
11.9.39: Somewhat less warm, overcast, a very few drops of rain about dark. Last night's rain had made no difference to the soil.
Weeded out the onions. These will be ready to pick in 2–3 weeks, but are not good. Applied sodium chlorate to the nettles beyond the walnut tree. Picked 1 lb. of damsons & 3¼ of bullaces. The damsons made almost 2 lb. jam, so the bullaces should make 5 or 6. The 2 rows of potatoes made 3 small sacks, I should say 50 or at most 60 lb. so if the main crop are equally bad we shall have at most another 300 lb., which is not nearly enough.
Picked out 2 boiling fowls (the old light Sussex & the one which mothered the 2nd lot of chicks) to go to market tomorrow.
Swallows beginning to gather on the telegraph wires.
9 eggs.
12.9.39: Chilly (enough to have a fire), overcast & windy. Some light rain in the evening. Began cleaning out the maincrop potatoes & cutting the haulm preparatory to digging. They may as well however stay in the ground another fortnight to let the skins harden. Titley's spring cabbages are too young to plant out yet, but will be ready in a fortnight, so about 25.9.39³ will be the date for this. There should be room for 6 or 7 rows, ie. 100–150 plants. The bullaces only made 4 lb. of jam.
Sold the two old boiling fowls, 6/6 for the two, ie. about 7/6 but commission comes off this.
This morning saw what I am virtually certain was a flight of woodcock. Possibly they flock together for migration. About 8.30 a flight of about a dozen birds went over, & by their long beaks & general shape I thought for a moment they were curlews, which are never seen round here. However they were just a little too small for curlews & their flight a little too fast. At a little distance past me they made the characteristic sideways dip, & I realised they were woodcock. The thing that still makes me slightly uncertain is not there being a dozen of them together, but their being so early. Others I have seen just arriving on the Suffolk coast came in October.
NB. to save seed (about 28 lb.) when digging the maincrop potatoes.
9 eggs. (Not listing the pullets' eggs separately now as they are somewhat larger & sell for the same price. Titley says he is getting 3/4 a score from Moss's.)
13.9.39: Overcast in the morning, a sunny patch in the afternoon, then some drizzle. Finished cleaning out potato patch, began digging the bit next

to the tomatoes. One or two cockerels almost big enough for market.
7 eggs. Sold 30 @ 3/– score.

<u>14.9.39</u>: Overcast, a little drizzling rain, but fairly warm. Finished digging
the patch next the tomatoes. Lifted the first row of Red King as the whole of
that patch needs liming & it is simpler to lift the potatoes at once. They are
poor, but a little better than the K. Edwards, & only one or two rotten ones
among them. Am going to scrap the tomatoes as they will come to nothing.
Arranged to sell off all the fowls, as it is evident that we shall only be able to
come down here at weekends & it is impossible to continue with any
livestock. Shall probably make Mr N.[4] a present of the goats.
8 eggs.

<u>15.9.39</u>: Rainy, with sunny & windy intervals.
Lifted the remainder of the Red King. Very poor. As well as I can estimate, I
should say 300 lbs at most (10 rows—200 plants). Scrapped the tomatoes. Cut
down the nearer row of raspberries, which are perhaps worth keeping, very
drastically, & shall manure them heavily later, as I think it possible that row
may do something. Shall probably scrap the other one. Began digging patch
next the raspberries. Made 2 lb. blackberry jelly out of about 2 lb.
blackberries (garden) bought from Mrs Hollingsworth for 6d. Forgot to
mention that I picked the apples off the grenadier, which is I think 5 years old.
22[5] apples, weighing 7½ lb. The apples on the big tree are mostly rotting but
some will be all right.
8 eggs.

<u>16.9.39</u>: Chilly & misty in the morning, sunny but not too warm in the
day, a shower in the afternoon.
    Took up & burnt the final lot of peas, & dug over that patch. Arranged to
sell off the 8 March pullets @ 5/6 a bird (paid 4/6 for them).
11 eggs. Sold 1 score @ 3/–. Total this week: 60.

<u>17.9.39</u>: Windy. Sacked the potatoes, evidently about 300 lb. Gave the
sprouting broccoli some wood ash. Arranged to dispose of the goats. Picked
about 2 lb. blackberries.
6 eggs.

<u>28.9.39</u>: Have not been able to keep up the diary, as I have been away.[6] The
eggs are, however, entered in the hen book, though I think a certain number
were not recorded.
Typical autumn weather, except that of late the mornings have not been
misty. Nights very clear, & the moon, which is a little past full, very fine. A
certain amount of leaves yellowing.
Today planted out 60 spring cabbage. Paid 2d score for plants. Continued
clearing front flower bed. The chief difficulty is the loganberry against the
fence, which is now presumably too old to move. Some of the stems have
grown to 15 or 20 feet. Michaelmas daisies in flower, chrysanthemums not
yet. The pumpkin is about the size of a football, but I am afraid is going to
ripen at that size, as the leaves are turning a little. Most of the young broccoli
etc. doing well. E. gave them superphosphate last week. Made another 3½lb.
apple jelly.
Decided after all not to get rid of the older hens. Shall reduce the size of the

run the young ones are in now & use it for a breeding pen (Leghorn x Rhode) in the spring if we are here. The other part can be dug over for potatoes. If actually here we might also go in for rabbits & bees. Rabbits are not to be rationed. The butcher says that people will not as a rule buy tame rabbits for eating but their ideas change when meat gets short. Titley says he made a lot of money out of rabbits at the end of the last war.

4 eggs! (To date this week, including today 36).

Field & others are still getting in hay which has only just been cut, & say it still has some nutritive value in it.

29.9.39:   Cloudy but not cold. The nights & early mornings are reasonably warm at present. Finished cleaning out main flower bed & cleaned out the one in front of the kitchen. "Smallholder" advises sowing broad beans now & planting shallots, so shall do so if I get time.

6 eggs.

Put apples to soak for apple wine.

30.9.39:   Fine, still & fairly warm. Continued clearing & got nearly to the trellis. Note that the white rambler rose has layered itself here & there. Gave all the broccoli nitrate of potash. Picked more apples. There is still 10–15 lb. on the tree, but how many will keep I do not know. I am only trying to keep the larger ones.

5 eggs. Sold 15 @ 3/– score. (Also sold 15 on Wed.) Total for week: 47. This must be low record for this year.

---

1. Orwell originally wrote '69.'
2. Orwell may have had particular interest in this subject, as shown by his account of Flory's disastrous attempt to have a leopard skin cured for Elizabeth in Burmese Days; see CW, II, 226–27. He was later to cure skins on Jura.
3. Presumably the date is underlined as a reminder. Orwell was away for the ten days before his diary entry for 28 September, when he records planting sixty spring cabbages.
4. Perhaps Mr. Nicholls, the owner of the 'broken-down old wreck' of a male goat referred to by Orwell in a letter to Jack Common; see 516.
5. Orwell originally wrote '23.'
6. It is not known where Orwell was, nor what he had been doing. However, in his letter to Leonard Moore of 6 October 1939, he writes that Eileen has found a job in a government office, but 'I have so far failed to do so'; see 572. On 9 September he had offered his services (see 571), so perhaps he was away seeking war work.

1.10.39:   Fine but rather chilly. Made another 2 lb. apple jelly. Picked a few blackberries but had not time to go to the good places. Picked some more apples. There are not many large ones left now. Have put about 10–15 lb. on shelf behind a sack to keep the light out, hoping they may keep at any rate for a month or two.

Five eggs.

2.10.39:   Fine, rather cold. Beech nuts are now ripe. Yesterday saw good number of young pheasants, fairly well grown.

Selected two cockerels for market tomorrow, about 10 lb. the two.

Continued clearing out beds & got as far as the shed. Can finish tomorrow, then shall spread manure & leave it for a few days before turning in.

4 eggs.

Made a pound or two of blackberry jam, but it has come rather thick.
3.10.39: *Fine & chilly. A very few drops of rain in the afternoon. Finished clearing out the garden & transplanted a few small plants which were in the way, so tomorrow the manure can be spread.*
5 eggs. Got 6/6 for the two cockerels (ie. 7/– less commission). This works out at about 8d lb.

[Newspaper cutting: 'Making Coal Briquettes'[1]]

4.10.39: *Rather cold, violent wind. Picked up the first ripe walnut today. There are very few, however. Spread the manure. Hoed leeks. Spring cabbages have not taken root very well, owing to the drought. Uprooted the onions, which are very poor.*
6 eggs. Sold 14 @ 3/– score.
Made about 3 lb. apple ginger, which I am afraid is a little too gingery.
5.10.39: *Some rain in the night, the day overcast & rather muggy. A light shower or two in the afternoon. The ground is still very dry a few inches under the surface. Dug over all the flower garden except the small beds. After the earth has settled the new flowers can go in.*
6 eggs.
6.10.39: *Some more rain in the night & a little this morning. Some sunny periods, & not cold.*
Finished the flower garden. Planted 2 rows cabbage (36 plants). Cleared the place where the gooseberries are to go (it is too early to move them yet). Made experimentally a few briquettes of coal dust & clay. If successful will make a mould & sieve for making them on a larger scale. Evidently it is important to use only fine dust, also one must have a large metal receptacle for mixing in.
Tonight found a kind of phosphorescent worm or millipede, a thing I have never seen or heard of before. Going out on the lawn I noticed some phosphorescence, & noticed that this made a streak which constantly grew larger. I thought it must be a glowworm, except that I had never seen a glowworm which left its phosphorescence behind. After searching with an electric torch found it was a long very slender wormlike creature with many thin legs down each side & two sort of antennae on the head. The whole length about 1¼". Managed to catch him in a test-tube & bring him in, but his phosphorescence soon faded.
5 eggs.

[On facing page:]

pale yellow, very wriggly.   (legs relatively thinner
                                                                    than this.)

7.10.39: *Misty & still. A very few drops of rain. Beech nuts now ripe. Skinned & took the pith out of a largish marrow (about 18" long), & note that after doing this there is only about 2½ lb. of flesh. Bought Adco, 2/3 for 7 lb, which is said to be enough to make 7 cwt. of compost. It appears however that you must not put woody material among the rubbish, nor very large roots. Began digging shallow pit for compost. The briquettes burn fairly well when used together with coal, so shall make arrangements for making some more. Evidently the method is to mix clay & water till it is sloppy, then mix in with your coal dust, using only so much clay as is needed to bind the dust to a very stiff paste. Moulds must be very strong, as the stuff has to be tamped down forcibly.*

7 eggs. Sold 15 @ 3/– score. Total this week 38. (NB. started cylinder of calor gas today).

8.10.39: Picked about 2½ lb. blackberries. Finished making the pit for rubbish & treated the first two layers with Adco. Weather misty, still & rather cold.

6 eggs.

9.10.39: Continuous & mostly heavy rain till about 4 pm Violent wind, strong enough to loosen some of the rose bushes & lift some broccoli plants almost out of the ground. Staked some of the latter, otherwise too wet to do anything out of doors.

5 eggs.

10.10.39: Very still, warm & fairly sunny. A very few spots of rain in the evening. Ground greatly sodden, & a lot of chrysanthemums loosened by the wind. Dug trench for broad beans but cannot yet get the ground into sowing condition. That piece (beyond the runner beans) is full of lumps of fine clay. Took out some of the worst & dug in some sand & wood ash. Changed the manure into a larger container as I want the other for leaf mould. Moved the henhouse. Brought in the onions, which are extremely poor, & hung them up to dry. Only 10 large bunches, of which only 3 or 4 will really keep. Picked up a few walnuts but there are very few this year.

Yesterday made 2 lb. blackberry jelly. Note that 2½ lb. blackberries = 2 pints juice = 2 lb. jelly (actually a little over).

5 eggs.

11.10.39: Still, sunny & fairly warm. Ground a good deal dryer. Planted out 10 Canterbury bells, about 20 sweet williams, 20 carnations, 25 wallflowers (flame). Continue tomorrow if not raining. Added some more to compost heap. Staked some of the crysanthemums° etc. T. has not got the stakes yet so cannot finish off hen-run. Yesterday snapped the handle of the spade, but it seems one can get a new handle without having to buy a whole spade. Made a little apple jam, experimentally, but does not seem great success. Have made about 25 lb. of jam altogether.

8 eggs. Sold 25 @ 3/– score.

12.10.39: Fine autumn weather, as yesterday. Planted out about 25 more wallflowers, a few hollyhock seedlings, 20 bought tulip bulbs (2 black) & about 15 of our own, & about 30 daffodils, some bought, some of our own. Cut leaves off marrows to let them ripen. I have left one on each plant, one of them a very large one.

8 eggs.

13.10.39: Misty but not cold. Some swallows still about, flying very high. Mowed the lawn. Could not make much impression on it, as it has got long

again, but this will probably have to be its last cut this year. Nothing more now to be done in the flower garden expect° the little patch up by the trellis & to trim off edges of the grass & make up paths, but I cannot do all this until the spade is mended. Cleared out the patch where the rhubarb is, preparatory to digging. Gave all the broccoli etc. superphosphate. This will be their last feed. Some savoys ready to cut & a few sprouts almost ready, but all that first lot are very poor. Planted 2 doz. snowdrop bulbs. Put some hen-manure in the shed to dry. Tried mixture of coal-dust & tealeaves° in a paper bag, which will burn more or less, so shall keep sugar cartons for this purpose.
5 eggs (1 double egg.)

<u>14.10.39</u>: *Extremely heavy rain all night & in the morning. Cleared up a little in the afternoon. Began digging patch by rhubarb, otherwise impossible to do much out of doors.*
5 eggs. Sold 15 @ 3/– score. Total this week 42

<u>15.10.39</u>: *Continuous & mostly heavy rain all day. Impossible to do anything out of doors.*
8 eggs.

<u>16.10.39</u>: *Sunny, very still, fairly warm. I believe there was a slight frost last night. Saw the white owl again yesterday evening. Limed part of the vacant patch, the part nearest the raspberries. That bit is not to be manured as I want it for root-crops. Dug a little more of the patch by the rhubarb. Soil here rather sour & must be limed when dug. Cut down the runner beans & added a layer to the compost heap. Made up a little more of the garden path. Sold 4 cockerels for 9/– —poor price but they were very small.*
3 eggs!

<u>17.10.39</u>: *Still, fairly fine, not cold. Went into Baldock & bought mattock, 6/–. Also a little napthaline, said to be good weed-killer when mixed in equal quantities with lime. Cleared out place where the blackberries are to go. Elm trees are all yellowing, beech trees not so much.*
6 eggs.

<u>18.10.39</u>: *Rather cold, with some sharp showers. Could not do much out of doors. Cleaned up some of the path, & put in some stakes for the blackberries. Two more stakes are needed.*
7 eggs. Sold 20 @ 3/– score.

<u>19.10.39</u>: *Raining almost continuously till late evening. Impossible to do much out of doors. Dug a very little more of the rhubarb bed, cleaned up the remaining bit of the path, which however cannot be re-gravelled till I have got some more cinders (no coal delivered for the past 10 days). Tried experimentally some of the lime & napthalene mixture,* also crushed rock salt, both said to be good weed-killers. Tits are common about the house now. In the elm trees in the field some kind of bird makes a sawing noise every night. Don't know whether this can be the owls.*

* *Makes no impression whatever. T. thinks it would actually encourage weeds in the long run. However this mixture is also said to be good for expelling wire-worms.* [Orwell's note].

If possible the following things have to be done before the end of November:[2]
Move wire of hen-run.
Clear all the grass off the new patch & the bit joining it to the old garden.
Heap turf so as to rot.
Rough-dig the new patch.
Transplant all the fruit bushes.
Clean out & dig the patch where the fruit bushes have been.
Lime the vacant piece, the empty part of the rhubarb bed, & the place where the fruit bushes have been.
Clear out the remaining patch under the hedge & prepare bed for rambler.
Remove most of the chrysanthemums when they have withered back.
Take up & store dahlia roots.
Plant shallots.
Sow broad beans.
Plant phloxes, michaelmas daisies (if not too early.)
Plant roses, rambler & polyantha. Transplant peonies.
Transplant apple tree.
Procure and plant blackberries.
Collect several sacks dead leaves.
Clean out strawberry bed.
Possibly also:[3]
Make up paths in kitchen garden.
Make new bed by gate.
5 eggs.
20.10.39: *Fine, still, sunny but not particularly warm. Finished digging the rhubarb bed, prepared the frame for dead leaves, made up a little more of the path, grubbed up the last lot of French beans. T.*[4] *cannot get any stakes so shall have to buy some iron ones.*
5 eggs.
21.10.39: *Very fine, clear, still autumn weather, with a touch of mist. Distinctly chilly morning & evening. E., Lydia*[5] *& self picked 4½ lb. blackberries. Nuts seem to be already ripened & fallen. Oak trees now mostly yellow, hawthorn & ash leaves falling.*
7 eggs. Sold 15 @ 3/– score. Total this week: 41
22.10.39: *Very misty, not cold, a short spell of sun in the afternoon. No wind. Turned out & examined some of the bags of potatoes. Found that some K. Edwards had gone bad, but no Red Kings, or very few. Threw away the bad ones, changed into fresh bags & scattered a little lime on the heap. Hope this will be enough to prevent serious damage. Planted out a few clumps of aubretia. Cut the pumpkin which was ripening. Only about 10 lb. T. is selling first-rate cooking apples (called locally Meetrop or some such name—have not seen this apple before) at 1d lb., eating apples (Blenheims) @ 1½ lb. Cut the first savoy today. Arranged to let the milkman have our eggs @ 3/6 score instead of the 3/– the butcher has been paying. T. says you can get 3/8 at the market, but in that case there are commissions to come off.*
6 eggs.
23.10.39: *Not cold & fairly fine, but a few drops of drizzling rain in the*

evening. *Cleaned out the piece between the rockery & the trellis, made a bed of sorts, planted 20 forget-me-nots in it, made a bed ready for the rambler. There is now nothing to be done in the flower garden except to plant the flowers (phlox etc.) when they are ready, make up paths & perhaps cut the grass once again. Made 2 lb. apple jelly yesterday. Found some eggs of either worm or snail, about the size of match-heads, whitish, translucent.*
6 eggs.
24.10.39: *Evidently a good deal of rain last night. Today overcast, not cold, a few spots of rain in the afternoon. Leaves coming down pretty fast now.*
Today went into Baldock. Bought small sieve (2/–). Impossible to get iron stakes for wire netting. Timber also almost unprocurable. Managed to get 2 very poor 6 ft. stakes for gate-posts of hen-run. Put them up this evening, & shall shift wire tomorrow if not raining. Tried to mow grass, but the machine in its present state makes no impression. Shall have to leave it till the spring, then get it scythed. Mr K.[6] *mended the spade by using the handle of the broken fork. Quite a good mend but leaves the spade a bit short. Paid 1/–. Impossible to sow broad beans yet as the ground will not get fine. Clarke's sent shallots today & shall plant them by way of experiment when I get time. NB. that 2 lb. shallots = about 60 bulbs (say 2 rows). There are now 2 barn owls which live in the stumpy elm tree, & evidently it is they that make the sawing noise. I suppose these are the ones that used to be called screech-owls, & the ordinary brown owl is the one that makes the to-whoo noise.*
6 eggs. Started hens on course of Karswood today.★ Also giving them more shell grit.
25.10.39: *Fine, sunny, cold wind. Began clearing the vacant ground between the old garden & the new patch. Burnt a little of the rubbish. Limed another strip, also the rhubarb patch, but have not turned the lime in here. Collected the first sack of dead leaves (beech). Had noticed for 2 days that a brown hen was sitting out somewhere. Tonight found her nest—10 eggs, 1 broken. Took the eggs, which may possibly be good, being unfertilised. Tonight she had gone back to the empty nest. Put her in the house, & hope she may be cured in a few days. This morning*[7] *shifted the wire of the run. Posts are not long enough for gate posts, but can have an extra piece fitted on if I can get hold of some timber. Yesterday when sinking holes for the posts found that the chalk is only about 6″ beneath the surface, but possibly it isn't so all over the patch.*
4 eggs. Sold 20 @ 3/6 (to milkman).
26.10.39: *A very sharp white frost last night, the first severe frost of the year. The day overcast with a short sunny interval, & rather cold. Water in the hens' basin frozen solid this morning. Turned it, & this evening there was still a little ice left. The dahlias blackened immediately, & I am afraid the marrows I had left to ripen are done for, as they had gone a funny colour. Brought them in & added the haulm to the compost-heap, which is now completed except for the old straw which is still in the flower garden.*

★ *Lasted till 14.11.39 (26 hens)* [Orwell's note].

Finished clearing the waste patch, piled the turf in a heap & marked out where the path is to go. This leaves another yard width of soil. Began digging this as it will do for the shallots. Collected another sack of dead leaves & sprinkled a little saltpetre (advised in Smallholder) among them. Shall try & note the number of sacks collected so as to see what amount of mould they make. The turves old H. stacked earlier in the year have rotted down into beautiful fine loam, but I think I had first killed the grass on these with sodium chlorate, so presumably what I am stacking now will not rot so rapidly or completely. Put some wood-ash on the place for the broad beans. If I can't get that bit fine I must try & find space elsewhere & simply give the bad clayey patch a good liming. The broody hen goes to her nest every night. Last night she would have frozen to death if I had not happened to find her. Considerable number of goldfinches in the garden today.
7 eggs.

<u>27.10.39</u>: *I think there must have been a slight frost again last night. Today about midday heavy rumbling sound which may have been either thunder or gunfire, & soon afterwards heavy sleety rain. More showers in the afternoon. Ground is very soggy again. Could not do much out of doors owing to the rain. Dug a little of the patch for the shallots.*
6 eggs.

<u>28.10.39</u>: *Frost again last night (not so hard as before). All today raining almost continuously. Impossible to do anything out of doors. One double egg today.*
6 eggs. Total this week 41

1. Orwell attempted to put this into practice; see *6.10.39* entry.
2. All items have been ticked except 'Clean out & dig the patch where the fruit bushes have been' and 'Sow broad beans,' which are marked with a cross, '& the place where the fruit bushes have been' and 'Plant phloxes . . .' which are not marked at all.
3. These two tasks are marked with neither tick nor cross.
4. Titley.
5. Lydia Jackson (1899–1983), a friend of Eileen's from the time they met at University College London in 1934, wrote under the pen-name Elisaveta Fen; see *534A*. After being bombed out of her flat in 1940, she and her flat-mate, Patricia Donahue, rented the Orwells' cottage at Wallington. The 21st was a Saturday, so Eileen could come down from London for the weekend.
6. Unidentified neighbour.
7. Orwell originally wrote 'Tonight,' presumably when he was writing up his diary.

<u>3.11.39</u>: *Have been away since last Sunday (28th), only returning this evening. Everything is extremely sodden. Planted a few more crocus bulbs & took up dahlia roots, which may be worth keeping. In this time the hens have apparently only laid 28 eggs, less than 5 a day. Had not noted that before leaving on Sunday sold 1 score @ 4/-.*
<u>4.11.39</u>: *Damp, but not raining to any great extent. Finished digging the ground for the shallots (still very sodden & will need several fine days to dry it), manured the rhubarb, began clearing the new patch of thistles etc. Saw the white owl in the daytime. Very beautiful toadstools in the field now, pale bluey-green, slender stalk of same colour, mauve gills, the whole toadstool*

coated with sort of slimy stuff. Added another ½ sack of dead leaves to heap. 5 eggs. Total this week 33 (Mrs A. has obviously underfed them).

5.11.39: Some wind in the morning, then nice sunny weather. Ground has dried up somewhat. In the evening violent wind & a few drops of rain. The wind actually blew the roof off the small henhouse. Enormous flocks of starlings, some tens of thousands at a time, going over with a noise that sounds like heavy rain. The leaves are mostly down now. Elder leaves just coming down. As I remember it, the elms are being stripped much earlier this year than most.

Transplanted the gooseberry bushes. Trust I haven't damaged them. One or two still had green or greenish leaves, & others were so deep in the ground I had to damage their roots considerably getting them up. The soil there (this end of garden) is in places pure clay at only 1 foot below the surface. Dug some of this out & lightened the ground as well as possible with sand & turf-mould. Then limed the ground between the bushes & dug in, also pruned the bushes a little. Hope this wind will not blow them all loose again. Added another sack of leaves. [Total on facing page: 3½.]

9 eggs (probably some of these laid yesterday). Sold 30 @ 4/– score.

6.11.39: Evidently it rained very heavily during last night. Today windy, a few showers but most of the day sunny. Transplanted the peonies. They are said not to stand this well, but they had withered back & I took a good ball of soil with each. Planted the little rambler cutting, the one that was in a pot. This has rooted well but is of course a very tiny plant. Dug & manured a trench to plant the first lot of currants, but don't like to plant them till the ground is a little less sodden. Limed another small patch of ground. Forgot to mention that one of the gooseberry bushes I moved yesterday had layered itself. Evidently they do this spontaneously sometimes.

5 eggs.

7.11.39: Rather wet, too much so to do much out of doors: Considerable rain this evening. Planted first row of currants (ie. 6 red, 5 black). Have started using chaff instead of straw for nesting-boxes. Do not know whether it will prove too expensive, but should be easier to clean out & to rot down.

6 eggs.

There was a nest of field mice at the roots of one of the currant bushes, & they came running out, 5 in all, as I levered the plant up. Fatter & lighter-coloured than the house-mouse, with a long tail (I had always had an idea they had short ones) & rather slow-moving, with a sort of hopping movement, though they all managed to get away from me.

8.11.39: Dry, windy, sunny, not cold. Many goldfinches about. Took the remaining nettles, or most of them, out of the new patch. Put in 2 more stakes for blackberries. Limed another patch. Added 1 sack dead leaves. [Total on facing page: 4½.]

6 eggs. Sold 20 @ 4/4.

9.11.39: Sunny & still. Everything still seems very wet, but evidently there was no rain last night. Made up some more of the path. Unable to do much else, as the wheelbarrow is about at its last & I was trying to repair it.

5 eggs.

10.11.39: *Very fine, sunny, still weather. Dug the first trench of the new patch, planted shallots (not quite enough to make up the 2 rows), transplanted 3 rambler rose cuttings, 1 albertine, one of the yellowy-white kind, the other I don't know what kind. Made up path as far as trellis. Titley says in storing dahlia bulbs the important thing is to suspend them for a while stalk downwards, as the reason they rot is that moisture runs down the hole in the stalk into the roots. Bought some more apples (Blenheims) still 1½. lb. T. says he is getting 4/6 score for eggs.*
9 eggs.

11.11.39: *Very fine weather, as yesterday. Birds all singing almost as though it were spring. Notice that horse dung of some mares & their foals out in the fields is extremely dark, almost black, presumably from being out at grass with no corn. Added another sackful of leaves.* [Total on facing page: 6.]
5 eggs. Sold 1 score @ 4/4. Total this week 45.

12.11.39: *Windless, misty, sun just visible, rather chilly. Many fungi in the woods, including one which at a certain stage gets a sort of white fluffy mildew on it & smells rather like bad meat. Immense quantities of wood pigeons & large flights of starlings. Came on a field of what appeared to be weeds but think it may possibly be buckwheat, which is sometimes grown about here for the sake of the partridges. Small black three-cornered seed like a miniature beech nut. Brought home a patch of a kind of rough moss & stuck it on the rockery, hoping it will grow. Today at 3 pm hung out a lump of fat for the tits. They had found it at before° 5 pm*
5 eggs.

13.11.39: *Beautiful still, sunny day. Last night not at all cold. Cannot make sure whether when shallots spring out of the ground it is of their own accord or partly done by the pigeons. Sometimes they are about 1' from where they were planted. Dug 2 rows of the new patch, turned the compost heap, limed another patch, added one more sackful dead leaves.* [Total on facing page: 7.]
One hen is definitely broody.
6 eggs.

14.11.39: *Rather windy, looked like rain in middle of day but actually did not rain. Dug 2 more trenches in new patch. Cannot get on faster than this owing to chalky stony streak in the middle which is hard to break into. Dug trench for remaining black currants.*
6 eggs.

15.11.39: *Last night a little rain, today fine, still & mild. Dug 2 more trenches. Cut down some of the herbaceous plants. Some of the phloxes will have to be split up. Another double egg. By the look of them all the double eggs I have had recently come from the same bird, tho' it is always said locally that a double egg means the beginning or ending of a clutch.*
9 eggs. Sold 1 score @ 4/4.

16.11.39: *Some rain last night & almost continuous light rain all today. Impossible to do much out of doors. Limed another strip (lime now running short), transplanted a couple of currant bushes. Most of the trees are now completely bare. A few leaves still on the elms. Of the deciduous trees the ashes seem the last to go.*

4 eggs.

<u>17.11.39</u>: *Still, overcast but not more than a few spots of rain. Transplanted the remaining currant bushes except 2, which still have their leaves rather green. One of the bushes had layered itself. Cut the layer off & planted it experimentally. Limed another strip. There will be just enough lime for the remainder of the vacant patch but not for where the bushes have been. To do the whole garden would need a cwt. or somewhat over. Collected another sack of dead leaves. [Total on facing page: 8.] Added a little to compost heap.*

7 eggs (actually 8 but one broken).

<u>18.11.39</u>: *Rather rainy. Went into Baldock but failed to get any rose bushes. Bought a peony root which perhaps I can plant at the corner instead of a rose. Clarke's[1] say the shortage of grains, or difficulty of sending them to & fro, is actually much greater than the papers make out. Saw a bird which I think must have been a golden plover, though so far as I know they are not found round here. Slightly larger than a snipe (it was certainly not a snipe), redshank type of flight, but its back was brownish. Too far away to see its beak. The only thing that makes me doubtful is that its belly was almost white.*

9 eggs. Sold 1 score @ 4/4. (According to Clarke's the Gov.t are controlling the price at 4/–). Total this week 46.

<u>19.11.39</u>: *Some rain last night. Today still, fairly fine. Winter[2] time (deferred 2 months owing to the war) starts today so have to give the hens their evening meal about 3 pm. Dug one trench, transplanted the little rose (the one that was overgrown by the lavender) & planted peony (price of root 6d). These don't generally bloom the following year. Afraid I may have put the 3 peonies too close together.*

5 eggs. (Notice nearly always a bad lay after a wet day, as yesterday).

<u>20.11.39</u>: *Fine, still, reasonably warm. Planted 6 lupins (paid 9d), said to be mixed colours. NB. that T. says that with lupins one should spread their roots out & not insert them too deep. Limed & began digging the final strip. This will need more doing than the rest as the ground is very sour & full of weeds. Cut down the remaining phloxes, tied up some of the chrysanthemums which had been blown over. Difficult to do much these afternoons now it is winter-time. The chrysanths now in full flower, mostly dark reddy-brown, & few ugly purple & white ones which I shan't keep. Roses still attempting to flower, otherwise no flowers in the garden now. Michaelmas daisies are over & I have cut some of them down. The 2nd lot of Brussels sprouts (planted as little plants 19.8.39) sprouting[3] up, also some of the savoys planted at the same time beginning to hearten up a little. All that lot are small kinds. None of my broccoli yet heading to any extent, though the plants have grown well. T. says oak leaves make the best mould, & then beech.*

8 eggs. Sold 8 @ 2d each (a mistake – price miscalculated).

<u>21.11.39</u>: *Still, overcast, rather chilly. Did nothing out of doors. New cwt. Full-o-Pep begun today. Clarke's say the grain-shortage, such as there is, is of maize & dari (weatings).[4] The former comes from the Argentine. The latter was usually imported ready ground, & at present the English mills are*

not turning it out fast enough, though there is no shortage of wheat.
8 eggs.

<u>22.11.39</u>: *Much as yesterday. Dug some more of the limed patch, planted out the remaining black currants. A double egg again & also an egg of the type the Smallholder describes as pimpled. Tom R. says he saw a rat come out of our garden yesterday.*
9 eggs.

<u>23.11.39</u>: *Rain last night, light rain all day. Cold. Impossible to do much out of doors. Dug some more of the limed patch.*
8 eggs.

<u>24.11.39</u>: *Fine, still, rather cold. Finished digging limed patch. Trans-planted apple tree. Had great difficulty uprooting it & fear I damaged its roots seriously. Cut down remaining michaelmas daisies & transplanted one clump. Found nest of 11 eggs, not sat on & seemingly O.K., so will do for the house, but shall not enter them in book.*
4 eggs.

<u>25.11.39</u>: *Hard frost last night, which started about 4 pm. Thawed this morning about 10 am, cold & miserable all day. Lumps of ice turned out of hens' basins were still frozen in the evening. Made bonfire, added some of the hay which had rotted to the compost-heap. This uses up the Adco, which will not have made the 7 cwt. of manure as specified, but perhaps I used it too liberally.*
7 eggs. Sold 20 @ 4/4. Total this week: 49. + 12 laid out = 60.

<u>26.11.39</u>: *Cold & windy, rain some of the day. Stuck a root of wild briar in, experimentally, but not certain whether it will take as it had not much root. Shall plant some more as I want to try budding next year.*
10 eggs. Sold 4 @ 2d each & 5 at 5 for 1/–.

<u>27.11.39</u>: *Heavy rain in the night & all this morning. Finer & windless this afternoon. Everything very sodden. Dug another trench. Have now almost finished the amount I intend doing of the new bit. Stuck in 2 more briar roots. Shall plant about 6 of different heights & see how they do. Collected another sack of dead leaves. This amount (about 10 sacks)[5] fills the frame. Covered over with fine soil & shall not disturb till next year.*
7 eggs.

<u>28.11.39</u>: *Still, not too warm. Some frost in the night. Finished the new patch. This will take 5 or 6 rows of potatoes. Showed the briar stocks to T., who explained that one must cut the side shoots off & bud onto those which appear in spring.*
7 eggs.

<u>29.11.39</u>: *Rained in the night, fine today & reasonably warm. Started dig-ging the patch where the bushes were. This is in a terrible state & will take a long time to do, also is poor chalky soil & needs a lot of enriching. Began making path for henhouses, as the mud is very bad.*
6 eggs. Sold 1 score @ 4/4.

<u>30.11.39</u>: *Very mild & still. A very few light spots of rain. Bats were out (noticed midges flying about the other day, in spite of the recent frosts). Dug a little more of the weedy patch. Made up the front part of the path. Pruned*

the white rambler, I hope correctly. Have not seen or heard the owls for some time past.
8⁶ eggs.

1. Produced food for fowls.
2. Orwell originally wrote 'summer.'
3. Orwell wrote 'sproutening.'
4. Dari, or durra, is Indian millet. 'Wheatings' is a proprietary name for the residue of milled wheat. *OED*, Revised edition, 1991, dates it from 1931.
5. Orwell noted collecting 8½ sackfuls.
6. 8 is written over 7.

<u>1.12.39</u>: *A little windier & colder than yesterday. Did some more weeding, turned the compost heap, planted another root of briar, this time a much older one.*
9 eggs.
<u>2.12.39</u>: *Fine, still, not very warm.*
9 eggs. Sold 20 @ 4/4. Total this week: 56.
<u>3.12.39</u>: *Frost last night. Today fine, windy, coldish. The common lane waterlogged almost knee-deep in parts. Planted another briar root. Note that on post hammered in on 18.10.39 fungi are growing (the horizontal hard kind that look like ears) about 1" broad, so evidently these things grow fairly rapidly.*
7 eggs.
<u>4.12.39</u>: *Heavy rain in the early part of last night, then frost. A little rain this morning. Windy & cold.*
10 eggs. Sold 1 score @ 4/4.
<u>5.12.39</u>: *Windy, overcast & decidedly cold. Some sloes still on the bushes. Plovers sitting on the ground & crying.*
10 eggs.
<u>6.12.39</u>: *Cold last night but no frost. Today fine & cold.*
5 eggs. Sold 1 score @ 4/2.
<u>7.12.39</u>: *Very hard frost last night, which did not begin to thaw till afternoon. Thick mist in the evening. Mr R. turns over the frosted ground, digging the frost in, which he says kills the wireworms etc.*
9 eggs.
<u>8.12.39</u>: *Raining all day.*
10 eggs.
<u>9.12.39</u>: *Fine & rather cold. A little rain in the evening.*
8 eggs. Total this week: 59.
<u>10.12.39</u>: *Sunny in the morning, overcast in the afternoon, not cold. Transplanted another root of wild rose. Transferred the 4 young pullets to the main houses.*
8 eggs.
<u>11.12.39</u>: *Raw, chilly, thick mist most of day.*
7 eggs.
<u>12.12.39</u>: *(In London) Cold & overcast.*
<u>13.12.39</u>: *Cold, overcast, not windy.*

28.12.39:   *Back at Wallington. Very cold, but no wind. In London there were a few frosts &, round about Xmas, extremely dense mists, making traffic almost impossible. Here freezing hard since yesterday, & snowing all today. Extremely light dry snow, which clings to everything, even wire netting. One of the plants that carries the snow most beautifully is lavender. Even corrugated iron looks attractive with snow on it. White Leghorn hens on the snow look quite[1] dark yellow.*
In the time we have been away, ie. since 12.12.39 there have apparently been 101 eggs—a falling off but not so bad as I expected. Shall have to make the weeks up by guesswork but can get the actual numbers right. Mice have been very bad in the house during my absence, tearing up newspaper etc., etc. Must try poisoning them.
4 eggs (no doubt owing to cold.)
[NB. As to egg account:—the total number of eggs, including those laid on the 2 (unentered) days before we went away, & today's, is 120. I have entered the last two weeks @ 45 a week, which leaves 30 to be added to those of Friday-Sat. of this week: ie. this week's eggs will equal Friday. Sat's eggs + 30. This will make the total right even if the weeks are incorrect.][2]
29.12.39:   *Freezing hard all day, but no fresh snow. Water pipes frozen this morning. Saw a rabbit run across a pool on the ice. Oat stack being thrashed at the farm.*
4 eggs.
30.12.39:   *No thaw. A few light spots of snow.*
5 eggs. Total this week (see above): 39. Yesterday sold 5 @ 1/–.
31.12.39:   *Considerably warmer, & thawing this afternoon, but appears to be freezing again tonight.*
5 eggs.

1. Preceded by 'as nearly,' which is crossed out.
2. Orwell's square brackets.

Domestic Diary continues in Volume XII at 729A.

INDEX

Volume XI

This is an index of names of people, places, and institutions, and of titles of books, periodicals, and articles; it is not a topical index. It indexes all titles of books and articles in the text, headnotes and afternotes; passing references to people are unindexed. Numbered footnotes are more selectively indexed; thus books listed by an author in a footnote are not indexed unless they are significant to Orwell. Orwell's book titles are printed in CAPITALS; his poems, essays, articles, broadcasts, etc., are printed in upper and lower case roman within single quotation marks. Book titles by authors other than Orwell are in italic; if Orwell reviewed the book (in this volume), this is noted by 'Rev:', followed by the pagination, which is placed first and followed by a semi-colon; other references follow. Both books and authors are individually listed. If Orwell does not give an author's name, when known this is added in parentheses after the title. Articles etc., by authors other than Orwell are placed within double quotation marks. Page references are in roman except for those to numbered footnotes, which are in italic. The order of roman and italic is related to the order of references on the page. Editorial notes are printed in roman upper and lower without quotation marks. If an editorial note follows a title it is abbreviated to 'ed. note:' and the pagination follows. First and last page numbers are given of articles and these are placed before general references and followed by a semi-colon; specific page references are given for reviews of books reviewed as a group. The initial page number is given for letters. Punctuation is placed outside quotation marks to help separate information. Items in two languages are indexed only in English.

Letters by Orwell are given under the addressee's name and the first letter is preceded by 'L:', which stands for letters, letter-cards, and postcards; telegrams are distinguished by 'T:' to draw attention to their urgency. Letters from someone to Orwell follow the name of the sender and are indicated by 'L. to O:'. References to letters are given before general references and are separated by a semi-colon. References to Orwell (for example, in Eileen's letters) are listed under 'Orwell, refs to:'. Letters from Eileen are listed under her name and that of the recipient. Letters or notes in response to Orwell's articles and reviews which are printed or summarised in afternotes and footnotes are indicated by (L) after the sender's name or the page number. Parties (e.g. POUM, Communist Party) are indexed but not references to 'Communists,' 'Anarchists' etc. Names of those signing manifestoes (e.g. *489A* and *490*) are only exceptionally indexed, and names, etc., in Orwell's 'Diary of Events Leading Up to the War' are more selectively indexed. 'Spain' is so frequently referred to in 1937 and 1938 that, to avoid cluttering the index pointlessly, it is not usually indexed. Similarly, in the 'Morocco Diary' the country is only indexed where it is necessary to distinguish French and Spanish Morocco. Farewell wishes in letters to wives, husbands, children, and friends are not usually indexed, except for initial identification.

Items are listed alphabetically by the word or words up to the first comma, except that Mc and M' are regarded as Mac and precede words starting with 'M'. St and Sainte are regarded as Saint.

Three cautions. First, many names are known only by a surname and occasionally it cannot be certain that surnames appearing at different locations, even with the same

Index

initials, refer to the same person. Secondly, the use of quotation marks in the index differs from that in the text in order to make Orwell's work listed here readily apparent. Thirdly, a few titles and names are silently corrected.   P. D.; S.D.

Index

Casablanca, 191, 195, 197, 198, 199, 200, 201, 209, 211, 219, 239, 271, 331, 337, 343, 345, 346, 347, 429
Casado López, Sigismundo, 367, *368*
Casanovas, Juan, 293, *304*
Case for Germany, The, 388
Castillejo, José, *Wars of Ideas in Spain*, Rev: 103
Casualties in Spain, 34, *37*
Catalan Directorate, 298
Catalan Government, 55, 294, 297
Catalonia, 61, 102, 114, 133, 134, 172, 234, 293, 295, 298, 300, 333, 343, 382, *382*
Catalonia General Hospital, 25, 26
Catalonia Infelix, Rev: 103
Cattell, David T., 32
Caudwell, Christopher, *305*
Challaye, Félicien, 117, *119*, 189
Chamberlain, Neville, 151, 179, 183, *184*, 200, 206, *207*, 210, 216, 218, 222, 227, 238, 239, 240, *240*, 242, 244, 340, 369, *369*, 370, 373, *376*, 384, *384*, 400, *403*
Chambers, Arthur, 63
Champion, 411
Changkufeng, 393, *393*
Chapel Ridding, *182*
Charlesworth, Amy, L: 61, 76; 34, *62*, 68
Chartist Movement, 99
Chartreuse de Parme, La, 379, 380
Cheka: see NKVD
Chesterton, G. K., 61, 162
C(h)leuh, 252, *253*, 320, 321, 325, 330
Christy & Moore, 7, 8, 358; see also Leonard Moore
Churchill, Winston, 358, 366, *367*, 368, 369, 372, 386, *403*, 409
Church in Spain, The, Rev: 233-5; 235-6
Ciano, Count Galeazzo, *382*
Civil Guards, 55, 57, *60*, 85, 87, 133
Civil War in Spain, The, Rev: 172-4, Rev: 179; 175, *176*
Clé, La, 314, *314*
Clinton, Arthur, 21, *22*
Clue of History, The, Rev: 327-9
CNT (Confederación Nacional de Trabajadores), 31, 32, 55-7, 63, 136, 137, 141, *144*, 145, 194, 295, 296, 297, 298, 299, 300, 301, *305*
Cockburn, Claud (= Frank Pitcairn, *q.v.*), *377*, *386*
Coles, Tom, 85
Collen, J., *362*
Collings, Dr., 248, 267
Collings, Mrs Dennis (Eleanor Jacques), 11
Collins, Norman, 37, 38
Collis, J. S., 152
Collis, Maurice, *Trials in Burma*, Rev: 125

COMING UP FOR AIR, pubn. ed. note: 356; *78*, 100, *127*, *130*, 164, 175, *176*, *214*, *258*, *286*, *312*, *321*, *332*, *336*, *339*, *345*, *348*, 350, *351*, *355*, *357*, 358, 365, *376*, *385*, *386*, *393*, 403, 413
Comintern, 33, 35, 124, 202-4, *304*
Commission of Inquiry into Alleged Breaches of the Non-Intervention Agreement, *304*
Common, Jack, L: 93, 115, 122, 129, 134, 149, 171, 177, 180, 191, 204, 210, 221, 230, 259, 317, 330, 337, 344, 349; *The Freedom of the Streets*, Rev: 162-3; 149, 150; *Seven Shifts*, 129, *130*, 134, 149; 128, *133*, 207, 217, 249
   L. from Eileen, 128, 181
Common, Mary, L. from Eileen, 248; 337, 350
Common, Peter, 249
Communism and Man, Rev: 322-4
Communist International (journal), 32
Communist International, The, Rev: 202-4
Communist Party/Parties, 28, 32, 35, 39, 44, 45, 51, 62, 63, 69, 72, 73, *73*, 76, 77, 87, 94, 114, 124, 132, 151, 152, 155, 163, 174, 175, 202, 225, 255, 256, 292, 299, 339, 373, 387, 394, 398, 399, 400, 403, 412
Companys, Luis, 225, 294, *304*
Confederación Nacional de Trabajadores: see CNT
Connolly, Cyril, L: 27, 88, 100, 127, 145, 175, 202, 253, 413; *Enemies of Promise*, 202, 254; 66, 88(L), 100, 128, 176, 414, 422.
Conscientious objectors, 381, *381*, 389
Conservative Party, 222, 238, *238*, 244
Continental Hotel, Marrakech, 199
Continental Hotel, Tangier, 198
Controversy, 55, *60*, 71, 74, 89, 96, 213-4, 227, 238
Cook, Kingsley, 415
Copeman, Fred, 35, *37*
Corkhill, David, 32-3
Cornwall, 216
Cortada, Roldán, *305*
Cottman, Stafford, 18, 30, *51*, 64, 65, 68, 85
Council of the Generalidad, 301
"Country of the Blind", 253
Craig (Foreign Legion), 342-3
Crawford, J. A., 190
Crichton-Stuart, Patrick, *39*
Crick, Bernard, *73*, *78*, 83, *100*, 122, 156, 167, *187*, 197, *371*; *et passim*
Cripps, Sir Stafford, 354, *355*, 364, *364*, 381
Croft, Andy, "The Awkward Squaddie", 66-8

472

Index

Index

Index

Mitchison, Naomi, L: 163; 66, 135, *164*
Mitrinović, Dimitrije, 123, *123*
Modern Boy, 411
Moka, Barcelona, 49
Molotov, Vyacheslav, 400, *401*
Monflorite, 13
Mongolia, 377, 381
Monte Oscuro, 357
Monte Trazo, 357
Montseny(s), Federica, 298, *305*
Monzón, 59
Moore, Leonard, L: 37, 41, 52, 70, 74, 78,
    100, 120, 169, 170, 201, 214, 221, 241,
    258, 342, 348, 349, 352, 355, 365, 374,
    384, 410, 411, 422; *6, 7, 14, 120, 291*;
    L. from Eileen: *8, 10, 17, 150, 154, 157,
    158*
Moore, Mrs Sturge, 157, *157*
Morocco: see French Morocco; Spanish
    Morocco
'Morocco Diary', 193–5, *195–8*, 200, *207–
    10, 219–20, 228–30, 232–3, 251–3, 258–
    9, 314–5, 324–7, 342–4, 345–7*
Mortimer, Raymond, L: 116; 66, 118, 119(L)
Moscow, 31, 33, 36, 381, 389, 394, 395, 397
Mosley, Sir Oswald, 98, 341, 387, 393, 402
Moyle, Douglas, *17, 18, 63, 85, 97, 97, 392,
    392*
Mufti of Jerusalem, 391
Muir, John Ramsay, 364, *364*
Munich (Pact), *207, 242, 319, 369, 386, 387,
    403*
Muriel (goat), *178, 191, 210, 231, 261, 318,
    330, 338, 345, 350, 431, 432, 435, 436,
    438, 439*
Murray, David, 50, *50*
Murry, John Middleton, 54, 66, 104, 261,
    262, 331, 332
Murry, Kathleen Middleton, 104
Mussolini, Benito, 42
Mussolini's Roman Empire, 184
Myers, L. H., *133, 156, 262, 362, 400, 401,
    452*
'Mysterious Cart, That', 82–5
Mysterious Mr Bull, The, Rev: 353–4

Namier, L. B., *Foreign Correspondent: Twelve
    British Journalists*, Rev: 391
Napoleon, 87, 391
National Church League: see NCL
National Council of Labour, 245, *364*, 371
National Government, 244, 374
National Liberal Party, *374*, 376, *376*
National Republican Guard, 301
National Unemployed Workers' Movement:
    see NUWM
Nazi Party, *223*

NCL (National Church League), 292, *304*
"N" Document, 173, *174*, 185, 186, 225
"Necessity of Fascism, The" (pseudo-title),
    261
Negrín, Juan, 166, 384, *384*, 394
NEP (New Economic Policy, USSR); 316;
    and see Nepmen
Nepmen (New Economic Policy
    marketeers), 160
Nevinson, H. W., 389, *390*
New Economic Policy: see NEP and
    Nepmen
New English Weekly, L: 92, 153, 235; *91, 92,
    127, 135, 149, 158, 158*, 253, 290, 355,
    381
New Hostel, Aylesford, *155;* and see
    Preston Hall Sanatorium
New Leader, The, 15, 16, 18, 27, 47, 62, 63,
    76, 83, 89, 96, 129, 134, 174, 212, 226,
    238, 250, 255, 302, 319, 362; financial
    contribution, ed. note: 250
Newman, Bernard, *Baltic Roundabout*, Rev:
    421
News Chronicle, reprint of section of *The
    Road to Wigan Pier*, ed. note: 28; 41, 46,
    60, 69, 77, 80, 112, 153, 184, 238, 242,
    256, 290, 293–6, 299, 353, 362
New Statesman, 27, 53, 65, 66, 69, 71, 88,
    116, 117, 118, 120, 127, 153, 158, 177,
    184, 227, 242, 256, 262, 359
New Writing, 40, *40*, 67, 241–2, 312, *312*
Nibb, John, *324(L)*
Nicholls (Wallington), 261, 436, 437, 455(?),
    456
Nicolson, Harold, 402, *402*
Nietzsche, Friedrich, 113
"Night Attack on the Aragon Front", 18–20
Nin, Anaïs, *91*
Nin, Andrés, 58, 59, *60*, 64, 68, 117, 173,
    174, 186, 296
NINETEEN EIGHTY-FOUR, *160, 312*
NKVD (GPU, Cheka), 32, 33, 34, 35, 160,
    261, 322, 338, 339
NKVD Archive, Moscow, *18*, 36
'Not Counting Niggers' (= Rev. of *Union
    Now*), 358–61; *361*
'Notes on the Spanish Militias', 135–45
Nouvelle Revue Française, La: see NRF
NRF, 148
Nurmi, Paavo, 421, *422*
NUWM (National Unemployed Workers'
    Movement); 98

Oak, Liston, 27, *28*
Obelisk Press, 393, *393*
Observer, The, 16, 135, 155, 158, 238, 256,
    362, *369*

Index

Index